4. 99

The Designer

FOR THE WOMAN OF FASHION

C/B   C/B

A' LA SPIRITE CORSETS

NEWEST CREATIONS FROM PARIS

GRAND PRIZE ST. LOUIS EXPOSITION

THE
DESIGNER

VOL. XXI. No. 5   MARCH. 1905

⬚ CONDUCTED BY ⬚
LILIAN DYNEVOR RICE

LADIES' JACKETS. DESCRIBED ON PAGE 496

(ETON JACKET 9213)   (BLOUSE JACKET 9207)

LADIES' BOX-COAT AND COAT TOILETTE. DESCRIBED ON PAGE 498

(COAT 9219)

(COAT 9236 AND SKIRT 9150)

LADIES' TOILETTE AND COAT COSTUME. DESCRIBED ON PAGE 496
(WAIST 9217 AND SKIRT 9189)   (COSTUME 9232)

491

March, 1905

LADIES' SHIRT-WAIST TOILETTE. DESCRIBED ON PAGE 496
(SHIRT-WAIST 9221 AND SKIRT 9228)

LADIES' TOILETTES. DESCRIBED ON PAGES 496 AND 497

(WAIST 9225 AND SKIRT 9083)   (SHIRT-WAIST 9220 AND SKIRT 9202)

March, 1905

LADIES' EVENING TOILETTE. DESCRIBED ON PAGE 497
(WAIST 9198 AND SKIRT 9127)

The Designer

LADIES' TOILETTES. DESCRIBED ON PAGE 497

(WAIST 9185 AND SKIRT 8788)   (SHIRRED DRESS 9224)

493

March, 1905

STYLES FOR THE MONTH

LADIES' BLOUSE REDINGOTE OR JACKET. ILLUSTRATED ON THE FRONT COVER PAGE.

Ladies' redingote or jacket 9201 is in six sizes, from thirty-two to forty-two inches bust measure, price 15 cents, and is shown again on page 498. As here pictured, it is made of a combination of crimson chiffon velvet and white broadcloth, and is trimmed with black braid.

LADIES' ETON JACKET WITH VEST. ILLUSTRATED ON PAGE 489.

Ladies' Eton jacket 9213 is in seven sizes, from thirty-two to forty-four inches bust measure, price 15 cents, a different view of the design appearing on page 497. The present development shows it made of black broadcloth, with facings and vest of white moiré braided in black.

LADIES' BLOUSE JACKET. ILLUSTRATED ON PAGE 489.

Ladies' jacket 9207 is in six sizes. from thirty-two to forty-two inches bust measure, price 15 cents. The garment is again pictured on page 498, and is here made of tan meltonette, ivory-white doeskin and brown peau de soie, decorated with gold appliqué.

LADIES' BOX-COAT. ILLUSTRATED ON PAGE 490.

Ladies' box-coat 9219 is in seven sizes, from thirty - two to forty-four inches bust measure, price 15 cents, and is again pictured on page 497. Light-gray and white cloth are here used, with silver appliqué for the trimming.

LADIES' COAT TOILETTE. ILLUSTRATED ON PAGE 490.

Ladies' jacket 9236 is in seven sizes, from thirty-two to forty-four inches bust measure, price 15 cents, and is again pictured on page 499. Ladies' skirt 9150 is in

LADIES' JACKET TOILETTE. DESCRIBED ON PAGE 497
(Jacket 9207 and Skirt 9210)

seven sizes, twenty to thirty-two inches waist measure, price 15 cents. This toilette is made of blue cheviot and blue velvet, and is trimmed with bands of gray silk.

LADIES' TOILETTE. ILLUSTRATED ON PAGE 491.

Ladies' tucked waist 9217 is in seven sizes, from thirty-two to forty-four inches bust measure, price 15 cents, and is again pictured, but in different development, on page 500. Ladies' skirt 9189 is in six sizes, from twenty to thirty inches waist measure, price 15 cents, and is shown again on page 509. The toilette is here made of brown tweed and tan taffeta embroidered with brown.

LADIES' COAT COSTUME. ILLUSTRATED ON PAGE 491.

Ladies costume 9232 is in seven sizes, from thirty-two to forty-four inches bust measure, price 15 cents, and is shown again on page 499. Blue cheviot is used for this costume, with white broadcloth decorated with black appliqué for the vest, and black velvet for the collar, cuffs, etc.

LADIES' SHIRT-WAIST TOILETTE. ILLUSTRATED ON PAGE 492.

Ladies' shirt-waist 9221 is in six sizes, from thirty-two to forty-two inches bust measure, price 15 cents, and is shown again on page 503. Ladies' skirt 9223 is in seven sizes, from twenty to thirty-two inches waist measure, price 15 cents, another development appearing on page 507. Black-and-white louisine is combined with white taffeta for this toilette, with black velvet ribbon to trim.

LADIES' TOILETTE. ILLUSTRATED ON PAGE 493.

Ladies' surplice waist 9225 is in seven sizes, from thirty-two to forty-four inches bust measure, price 15 cents. and is shown again on page 502. Ladies' skirt 9083 is in seven sizes, from twenty to thirty-two inches waist measure, price 15 cents.

This toilette is made of tan taffeta glacé and cream-white embroidered taffeta. Lace appliqué supplies the trimming.

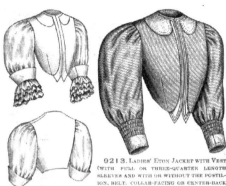

9213. LADIES' ETON JACKET WITH VEST (WITH FULL OR THREE-QUARTER LENGTH SLEEVES AND WITH OR WITHOUT THE POSTILION, BELT, COLLAR-FACING OR CENTER-BACK SEAM). Described on page 498.

LADIES' SHIRT-WAIST TOILETTE. ILLUSTRATED ON PAGE 493.

Ladies' shirt-waist 9220 is in seven sizes, from thirty-two to forty-four inches bust measure, price 15 cents, and is shown again on page 503. Ladies' skirt 9202 is in seven sizes, from twenty to thirty-two inches waist measure, price 15 cents, is shown again on page 506. Satin foulard is combined with Liberty satin for this toilette, with gray velvet ribbon and silver galloon to trim.

LADIES' EVENING TOILETTE. ILLUSTRATED ON PAGE 494.

Ladies' waist 9198 is in six sizes, from thirty-two to forty-two inches bust measure, price 15 cents, and is again shown on page 502. Ladies' skirt 9127 is in seven sizes, from twenty to thirty-two inches waist measure, price 15 cents. This handsome toilette is made of jet-spangled black tulle over light-blue silk.

LADIES' TOILETTE. ILLUSTRATED ON PAGE 495.

Ladies' waist 9185 is in five

sizes, from thirty-two to forty inches bust measure, price 15 cents, and is again pictured on page 502. Ladies' slightly gathered five-gored skirt 8788 is in seven sizes, from twenty to thirty-two inches waist measure, price 15 cents. Sea-green crêpe de Chine is used for both the garments, with white chiffon for the chemisette.

LADIES' SHIRRED DRESS. ILLUSTRATED ON PAGE 495.

Ladies' dress 9224 is in five sizes, from thirty-two to forty inches bust measure, price 15 cents. Another development of the design is presented on page 501, accompanied by a detailed description, and as here shown the dress is made of pale-pink silk mull, no trimming being employed.

LADIES' JACKET TOILETTE. ILLUSTRATED ON PAGE 496.

Ladies' blouse jacket 9207 is in six sizes, from thirty-two to forty-two inches bust measure, price 15 cents, and is shown again on pages 489 and 498. Ladies' skirt 9210 is in six sizes, from twenty to thirty inches waist measure, price 15 cents, and another development of the design is presented on page 507.

Brown brilliantine is used for the toilette, with écru taffeta for collar and cuffs and brown velvet for vest.

Long Hip Length   Three-Quarter Length

9219. LADIES' BOX-COAT IN THREE-QUARTER OR LONG HIP LENGTH (WITH COLLAR-FACING IN EITHER OF TWO OUTLINES, OR COLLARLESS, WITH BISHOP SLEEVES HAVING THE UNDER SIDES AND CUFFS IN ONE, OR COAT SLEEVES WITH OR WITHOUT THE CUFFS). Described on page 498.

9201. LADIES' BLOUSE REDINGOTE OR JACKET WITH VEST (WITH SLEEVES PLAITED OR GATHERED AT THE TOP AND WITH OR WITHOUT THE TURNED-UP CUFFS). Described on this page.

9213—LADIES' ETON JACKET WITH VEST. Illustrated on page 497.

The Eton jacket here pictured is developed in light-tan cloth combined with white cloth and trimmed with soutache braid. It is fitted by under-arm and shoulder seams, also single bust darts, and may have a seamed or whole back, whichever is preferred. The vest portions are attached to the fronts and the neck edge finished with a flat collar-facing. The lower edge of the jacket is completed with a belt, and postilion portions, which may be omitted, are attached to the back. Two styles of sleeve are provided: one is a full-length, one-seamed model, shirred to cuff depth and finished with a band. When the three-quarter length is preferred, the sleeve is cut away to the correct outline and finished with the flare turn-up cuff.

Serge, cheviot, tweed, cloth, velvet, velveteen, taffeta silk or peau de soie may be used to develop this design, with embroidery, braid or appliqué to trim. A figure view on page 489 shows a different development.

Ladies' jacket **9213** is in seven sizes, thirty-two to forty-four inches bust measure, price 15 cents. The thirty-six-inch bust size requires two and one-quarter yards of material forty-four inches wide or one and three-quarter yards fifty-four inches.

9219—LADIES' BOX-COAT IN THREE-QUARTER OR LONG HIP LENGTH. Illustrated on page 497.

This stylish coat is made of light-tan box-cloth and is fitted by under-arm and shoulder seams. The forward edges of the fronts are trimmed on the underside so that when they are opened they will produce the effect depicted in one small front view. Two styles of sleeve are provided: one is a

two-seamed coat sleeve finished with a one-piece cuff, and the other is in two pieces, the under-arm portion being cut with cuff extension which is attached to the gathered edge of the outside sleeve section. The neck edge of the coat may be finished with a collar-facing in either of two outlines, or may be left collarless.

Covert cloth, broadcloth, cheviot, tweed, box-cloth, taffeta silk, peau de soie, velour, velvet or satin rhadame may be used to develop this design.

A figure view on page 490 shows a different development.

Ladies' box-coat **9219** is in seven sizes, from thirty-two to forty-four inches bust measure, price 15 cents. The thirty-six-inch bust size requires for the coat, as shown in three-quarter length, three and five-eighth yards of material fifty-four inches wide.

9201—LADIES' BLOUSE REDINGOTE OR JACKET. Illustrated on this page.

Silver-gray kersey, gray silk and Russian appliqué gimp are the materials selected to make the handsome garment depicted in the accompanying illustration. The jacket portions are fitted by under-arm and shoulder seams, the forward part of the fronts being cut to form the revers which meet the two-piece rolling collar in notches. The vest portions are attached to the fronts and fasten down the center. The sleeve is a one-seamed model, gathered or plaited into the arm's-eye. The lower edge is gathered and completed by a one-piece deep cuff and a fancy turned-up flare portion, or the latter may be omitted. A shaped girdle is attached to the lower edge of the body portions with the long skirt or redingote portions; the latter, which are united by a center-back seam, may be omitted.

Kersey, covert cloth, broadcloth, velvet, panne, chiffon velvet, velveteen, taffeta, peau de soie or Venetian cloth may be used to develop this design.

9207, LADIES' BLOUSE JACKET WITH VEST (WITH SLEEVES PLAITED OR GATHERED AT THE TOP AND WITH OR WITHOUT THE PEPLUM OR CUFFS). Described on page 499.

ALL STANDARD PATTERNS 5, 10 AND 15 CENTS—NONE HIGHER.

Coat in Long Hip Length
Skirt in Instep Length *Coat in Redingote Length* *Coat in Long Hip Length*
Skirt in Short Round Length

9232. Ladies' Costume in Round, Short Round or Instep Length (consisting of a coat in redingote or long hip length with vest, leg-o'-mutton or bishop sleeves plaited or gathered at the top, and with or without the collar-facing; and a nine-gored umbrella or ripple skirt. with an inverted box plait or in habit style at the back). Described on this page.

A figure view is presented on the Front Cover Page. Ladies' blouse redingote or jacket 9201 is in six sizes, from thirty-two to forty-two inches bust measure, price 15 cents. The thirty-six-inch bust size requires four yards of material which measures fifty-four inches in width.

Coat in Redingote Length
Skirt in Round Length

9207—LADIES' BLOUSE JACKET WITH VEST. Illustrated on page 498.

Scotch cheviot and plain broadcloth are combined for this stylish jacket, which is trimmed with narrow soutache braid. The garment is fitted by under-arm and shoulder seams, the fronts and back are laid in tuck plaits which extend from the shoulder seams to the waistline, where the extra fulness is disposed in gathers. The forward edges of the fronts are laid back to form revers and the neck edge is finished with a flat collar-facing. Vest portions are attached beneath the forward edge of the fronts, and the one-seamed sleeve is gathered or plaited into the armhole. Its lower edge is gathered into a band, and a deep, one-piece turn-up cuff is provided. A belt is joined to the lower edge of the body portions, with the two-piece peplum.

Velvet, velveteen, velour, taffeta silk, peau de soie, cheviot, tweed, covert cloth or Venetian cloth may be used to develop this design.

Figure views on pages 489 and 496 show different developments.

Ladies' blouse jacket 9207 is in six sizes, from thirty-two to forty-two inches bust measure, price 15 cents. The thirty-six-inch bust size requires five and three-eighth yards of material measuring twenty-two inches in width or two and one-half yards fifty-four inches in width.

9236 — LADIES' TUCKED DOUBLE-BREASTED COAT OR JACKET IN LONG OR MEDIUM HIP LENGTH. Illustrated on this page.

This handsome coat is made of light-tan covert cloth and is fitted by side-back, under-arm and shoulder seams, also side-front seams. The backs and fronts of the coat are tucked and a belt confines the garment at the waistline. The sleeve is a two-seamed model, finished at the wrist by a one-piece turn-up cuff, which may be omitted. The neck edge of the garment may be completed with or without the fancy collar-facing.

A figure view on page 490 shows a different development.

Ladies coat 9236 is in seven sizes, from thirty-two to forty-four inches bust measure, price 15 cents. The thirty-six-inch bust size requires three and five-eighth yards of forty-four-inch material.

9232—LADIES' COSTUME IN ROUND, SHORT ROUND OR INSTEP LENGTH. Illustrated on this page.

This handsome costume is made of medium-light cloth with vest of white cloth and trimming of wide

Medium Hip Length   *Long Hip Length*

9236. Ladies' Tucked Double-Breasted Coat or Jacket in Long or Medium Hip Length (with or without the collar-facing or cuffs). Described on this page.

and narrow silk braid. The coat is fitted by center-back, side-back, under-arm and shoulder seams, also side-front seams. The side backs of the material are cut with extensions below the waistline, which are lapped as indicated. Two styles of sleeve are provided: one is a two-seamed leg-o'-mutton model, gathered into the arm's-eye and completed by an underfacing at the lower edge; the other is a one-seamed bishop sleeve finished with a straight cuff and turndown cuff piece. Either style sleeve may be gathered or plaited into the armhole. The neck edge may be finished with or without the flat collar-facing, and the coat closes down the center front, and

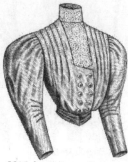

9217, LADIES' TUCKED WAIST (WITH CHEMISETTE). Described on page 501.

may be in redingote or long hip length. The nine-gored skirt fits the upper part of the figure smoothly, the fulness at the back being disposed in an inverted box plait, or the skirt may be finished in habit style.

Serge, tweed, camel's hair, cheviot, homespun, lightweight broadcloth, velvet, panne or taffeta may be used to develop this design, with braid, gimp, galloon, appliqué lace or Oriental trimming to decorate. A figure view on page 491 shows a different development.

Ladies' costume 9232 is in seven sizes, from thirty-two to forty-four inches bust measure, price 15 cents. Thirty-six-inch bust size requires, for round length with coat in redingote length, eight and seven-eighth yards of forty-four-inch material. The width of skirt at the lower edge in round length is four and three-quarter yards.

9242 — LADIES' PRINCESS DRESS IN LONG OR MEDIUM SWEEP OR ROUND LENGTH, CLOSED AT THE BACK OR LEFT SHOULDER AND SIDE. Illustrated on this page.

This handsome dress is made of pale-gray crêpe de satin, with bertha and sleeve frills

Long Sweep Length

Round Length

Medium Sweep Length   *Long Sweep Length*

9242, LADIES' PRINCESS DRESS IN LONG OR MEDIUM SWEEP OR ROUND LENGTH, CLOSED AT THE BACK OR LEFT SHOULDER AND SIDE (WITH HIGH, ROUND OR SQUARE NECK AND FULL-LENGTH LEG-O'-MUTTON OR PUFF SLEEVES OR ELBOW PUFF SLEEVES, AND WITH OR WITHOUT THE BERTHA; WITH AN INVERTED BOX PLAIT OR IN HABIT STYLE AT THE BACK; ALSO AVAILABLE AS A PRINCESS OR CORSAGE SKIRT IN EITHER OF TWO BODICE OUTLINES). Described on this page.

ALL STANDARD PATTERNS 5, 10 OR 15 CENTS -NONE HIGHER.

9196 — Ladies' Waist with Extra Under-Arm Gore: Suitable for Stout Figures (with or without the jabot revers, elbow cuffs or the tuxedo vest effect). Described on page 502.

lining, which may extend to the wrist or be cut away at the elbow. A one-piece fancy sleeve frill provided may be used. The bertha is in one piece and in fancy lower outline. When used it is attached to the waist portion of the dress at yoke depth.

Cashmere, lansdowne, drap d'été, taffeta, peau de soie, crêpe de Chine, satin crêpe, etamine, henrietta or novelty material may be used to effectively develop this handsome design.

Ladies' princess dress 9242 is in seven sizes, from thirty-two to forty-four inches bust measure, price 15 cents. The thirty-six-inch bust size requires, for medium sweep length with leg-o'-mutton sleeve, sixteen and three-eighth yards of material twenty-two inches wide. The width at the lower edge of the skirt in medium sweep length is five yards.

9217 — LADIES' TUCKED WAIST. Illustrated on page 500.

This attractive waist is made of light-écru taffeta combined with Arabian lace. It is mounted on a fitted body lining, the over-back is slightly shirred at the waistline and the upper portions of the lining fronts are concealed beneath the chemisette portion, the latter being attached to the right side and fastening on the left with hooks and eyes. The full fronts are tucked to yoke depth, and the fulness at the waistline is confined by shirring. A folded girdle completes the lower part of the waist and the sleeve is a one-seamed model mounted on a two-seamed lining. The outside sleeve is gathered into the arm's-eye. The fulness at the bend of the arm is disposed in tuck plaits. A back closing standing collar completes the neck edge of the garment, and taffeta silk, peau de soie, cashmere, nun's-veiling, crêpe de Chine, lawn, madras, chambray, linen or novelty material may be appropriately used to develop this design.

A figure view on page 491 shows a different development of the model.

of point de Venise lace. The garment is fitted by center-back, side-back, under-arm and shoulder seams, also side-front seams. The center-back portions are cut with extensions at the seam edges below the waistline, these being laid in an inverted box plait, or if preferred, the back may be finished in habit style. The dress may be made high necked as shown in the large front view, or when the round or square neck is desired the upper part of the garment may be cut away to the correct outline. Two styles of sleeve are provided: one is a full-length model, consisting of a one-seamed outside portion mounted on a two-seamed lining, and the other consists of a one-seamed puff mounted on a two-seamed, close-fitting

9224, Ladies' Shirred Dress Closed at the Back and in Medium Sweep (with high or low neck and full-length, elbow or single puff or frill sleeves; and a princess foundation). Described on page 502.

ALL STANDARD PATTERNS 5, 10 OR 15 CENTS—NONE HIGHER.

9185. LADIES', WAIST (EASED OR
DRAWN DOWN AT THE BACK, WITH FULL
LENGTH OR LONG ELBOW SLEEVES AND
WITH OR WITHOUT THE BERTHA FRILLS).
Described on page 503.

Ladies' tucked waist
9217 is in seven sizes, from
thirty-two to forty-four
inches bust measure, price
15 cents. The thir-
ty-six-inch bust size
requires four and five-
eighth yards of mate-
rial measuring twenty-
two inches in width.

9196—LADIES'
WAIST WITH EXTRA
UNDER-ARM GORE; SUITABLE FOR STOUT FIG-
URES. Illustrated on page 501.

This handsome waist is made of changeable violet
taffeta combined with violet panne, and is decorated
with fancy buttons. It is mounted on a fitted lining, the outer back is slightly shirred at the waistline and the fronts are shirred at the lower edges,
under-arm gores being inserted, as indicated. The
vest front is attached to the right side and fastens
on the left. Jabot revers are provided, but may
be omitted. The sleeve consists of a two-seamed,
close-fitting lining and a one-seamed outside portion; the latter is gathered to the undersleeve just
below the elbow, and finished
with a one-piece elbow cuff.
A standing collar completes
the neck of this garment and
a girdle completes the lower
edge of the body portions.

Taffeta silk, panne, velvet, chiffon velvet, peau
de soie, cashmere, drap d'été, lansdowne, voile,
etamine, serge or brilliantine may be used to develop
this design.

Ladies' waist 9196 is in eight sizes, from thirty-
four to forty-eight inches bust measure, price 15 cents.
The thirty-eight-inch bust size requires four and
one-half yards of material twenty-two inches wide.

9224—LADIES' SHIRRED DRESS, CLOSED AT
THE BACK AND IN MEDIUM SWEEP. Illustrated on
page 501.

This dainty dress is made of light-blue crêpe
de satin. The princess foundation is fitted by
center-front, side-front, under-arm, side-back and
shoulder seams. When the high-neck style is desired, the drop-shoulder yoke-facings, fitted by
shoulder seams, are used, and a standing collar
completes the neck edge. When the low neck is
preferred, the yoke-facings are omitted and the
upper part of the foundation is cut away. The full
front and back portions of the waist at the upper
and lower edges are shirred. The full-length sleeve
consists of a two-seamed, close-fitting lining on
which is mounted the one-
seamed outside sleeve, shirred
to cap depth at the shoulder
and divided into two puffs by

9225. LADIES' SURPLICE WAIST (WITH FULL OR THREE-QUARTER
LENGTH SLEEVES AND SURPLICE OR PLAIN BACK). Described on page 504.

a row of shirring. The lower edge of this portion is gathered to the lining below the elbow. When the elbow
sleeve is desired, the lower part of the lining is cut away;
and when the short puff is preferred, the lower part of
the lining and lower puff may be omitted. The full circular skirt is decorated with four nun tucks and a deep
hem. It is
shirred to shal-
low yoke depth
and attached to
the foundation
at the waistline,
where it is met
by the lower
edge of the
shirred waist
portions.

Crêpe de
Chine, peau de
cygne, nun's-
veiling, alba-
tross, lawn,
organdy, grena-
dine, net,

9198. LADIES' WAIST (EASED OR DRAWN DOWN AT THE BACK, WITH HIGH OR LOW NECK AND FULL-LENGTH SLEEVES
WITH MOUSQUETAIRE OR PLAIN LOWER PART OR WITH SHORT PUFF SLEEVES; WITH OR WITHOUT THE BERTHA).
Described on page 503.

ALL STANDARD PATTERNS 5, 10 OR 15 CENTS—NONE HIGHER.

chiffon or silk mull may be used to develop this design, with lace, embroidery, spangled passementerie or ribbon to trim. A figure view on page 495 shows a different development.

Ladies' shirred dress 9224 is in five sizes, from thirty-two to forty inches bust measure, price 15 cents. The thirty-six-inch bust size requires, as represented in large front view, fourteen and three-eighth yards of material which measures twenty-two inches in width. The width at the lower edge of the outside skirt is five and five-eighth yards.

*

9185—LADIES' WAIST. Illustrated on page 502.

This effective waist is charmingly developed in sea-green satin crêpe combined with white chiffon. The girdle is of green chiffon velvet. The garment is mounted on a fitted lining. The back and fronts of the material are gathered at the upper and lower edges, and completed by a folded two-piece girdle. The gathered chemisette portion is finished at the neck edge by a standing collar and may be outlined by bertha frills. The attractive sleeve consists of a two-seamed, close-fitting lining on which is mounted the one-seamed full outside portion. The lower part of the lining is overlaid with material from wrist to elbow, and the out-

9220. LADIES' TUCKED SHIRT-WAIST (WITH FULL VEST AND WITH OR WITHOUT THE VESTEES, REVERS OR CUFFS). Described on page 504.

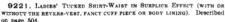

9221. LADIES' TUCKED SHIRT-WAIST IN SURPLICE EFFECT (WITH OR WITHOUT THE REVERS-VEST, FANCY CUFF PIECE OR BODY LINING). Described on page 504.

side sleeve is gathered at the upper and lower edges and shirred through the middle of the upper part to produce a butterfly effect. When the elbow sleeve is desired, the lower part of the lining is cut away.

Satin crêpe, chiffon velvet, panne, taffeta silk, peau de soie, voile, cashmere, net, grenadine, all-over lace or nun's-veiling may be used to develop this design.

A figure view on page 495 shows a different development.

Ladies' waist 9185 is in five sizes, from thirty-two to forty inches bust measure, price 15 cents. The thirty-six-inch bust size requires six yards of material which measures twenty-two inches in width.

*

9198—LADIES' WAIST. Illustrated on page 502.

Light-mauve peau de soie is used to make this charming waist. The yoke portions are of all-over lace and the bertha of lace flouncing. Frills of the peau de soie are used to trim the sleeves and fronts. The garment is mounted on a fitted lining and, when the high-

neck style is desired, the upper part of the foundation is overlaid to yoke depth back and front, otherwise the yoke-facings may be omitted and the lining cut away to the desired outline. The full back and fronts are gathered at the upper and lower edges, and the latter is completed by a two-piece folded girdle. The forward edge of the right front is finished with a shirred trimming band and the pattern provides a shirred bertha. The sleeves may be in either of three styles: the first is a full-length model consisting of a two-seamed, close-fitting undersleeve overlaid with plain or mousquetaire portion, and a one-seamed outside sleeve gathered at the upper edge and with the lower edge finished with a frilled band. The second is an elbow sleeve completed at the lower edge by frills, and the third is a short puffed sleeve.

Taffeta silk, peau de soie, peau de cygne, drap d'été, nun's-veiling, albatross, grenadine, satin striped gauze or flowered net may be used to develop this design.

A figure view on page 494 shows an entirely different development of this attractive model.

Ladies' waist 9198 is in six sizes, from thirty-two to forty-two inches bust measure, price 15 cents. The thirty-six-inch bust size requires

9234. LADIES' BOX-PLAITED SHIRT-WAIST CLOSED AT THE FRONT (WITH OR WITHOUT BODY LINING). Described on page 505.

ALL STANDARD PATTERNS 5, 10 OR 15 CENTS—NONE HIGHER.

9204, LADIES' BOX-PLAITED SHIRT-
WAIST (WITH LEG-O'-MUTTON SHIRT OR
TWO-SEAMED BOX-PLAITED BISHOP
SLEEVES, WITH OR WITHOUT THE BODY
LINING). Described on page 505.

for whole garment, seven and one-half yards of twenty-
two-inch material, or five and one-quarter yards thirty-six
inch, or four and one-half yards forty-four inches wide.

9225—LADIES' SURPLICE WAIST. Illustrated on page 502.

This graceful waist is made of figured foulard combined
with all-over lace. It is mounted on a fitted lining, the
upper portions of the back and front of the lining being
faced. The facing of the front is attached to the right
side and fastens on the left by means of hooks and
eyes. The surplice backs are shirred at the shoulder
seams and the slight fulness at the waistline is laid in
small plaits. The full surplice fronts are shirred at the
shoulder seams and gathered at the edges of the arm's-
eye, this arrangement producing the drooped effect.
A plain back, which may be used in preference to the
surplice backs, is supplied, and the sleeve, which may
be made in full or three-quarter length, consists of a
two-seamed lining and
a one-seamed outside
portion. The latter
is gathered at the up-
per edge, and the ful-
ness at the lower part
is disposed in a num-
ber of shirred length-
wise tucks. The
lower part of the lin-
ing is overlaid with
material. When the
three - quarter - length
sleeve is desired, the
lower part of the
full-length sleeve is
cut away. A stand-
ing collar completes
the neck edge of the
garment.

Foulard, nun's-
veiling, cashmere,
albatross, taffeta silk,
crêpe de Chine, satin
crêpe, grenadine, voile
or washable materials
may be used to de-
velop this design.

A figure view on
page 493 shows a dif-
ferent development.

Ladies' surplice waist 9225 is in seven sizes, from
thirty-two to forty-four inches bust measure, price 15
cents. The thirty-six-inch bust size requires five yards
of material which measures twenty-two inches in width.

9221—LADIES' TUCKED SHIRT-WAIST IN SUR-PLICE EFFECT. Illustrated on page 503.

Figured silk is used for this attractive shirt-waist;
the revers, cuffs and collar are made of plain silk and
trimmed with soutache braid.

The garment is mounted on a body lining. The
outer back is tucked from the neck edge to the waistline, where the slight fulness is disposed in shirring.
The fronts are tucked to yoke depth and confined by
shirring at the waistline, revers being attached to the
forward edges, as indicated. The shield portion is
attached to the right front and fastens on the left.
The sleeve is a one-seamed model completed by a
straight cuff, to which
is attached the fancy
turn-up cuff piece,
which may be omitted.
A standing collar com-
pletes the neck edge
and the fronts of the
material overlap grace-
fully in surplice fashion.

Taffeta silk, peau de
soie, satin rhadame, pop-
lin, pongee, foulard, cashmere, lansdowne, drap
d'été, flannel, linen, piqué,
duck or madras may be
used to develop this design.

Short Round Length

Instep Length   Round Length

9197. LADIES' SHIRT-WAIST COSTUME IN ROUND, SHORT ROUND OR INSTEP LENGTH (CONSISTING OF A
SHIRT-WAIST WITH LEG-O'-MUTTON OR REGULATION SHIRT SLEEVES AND WITH OR WITHOUT BODY LINING; AND
A SEVEN-GORED SKIRT WITH AN INVERTED BOX PLAIT OR GATHERS AT THE BACK, WITH OR WITHOUT A PLAIT
AT THE LOWER PART OF EACH SIDE SEAM; DESIRABLE FOR A WORK OR UNIFORM DRESS). Described on page 506.

ALL STANDARD PATTERNS 5, 10 OR 15 CENTS—NONE HIGHER.

A figure view on page 492 shows an entirely different development of this very attractive model.

Ladies' tucked shirt-waist 9221 is in six sizes, from thirty-two to forty-two inches bust measure, price 15 cents. The thirty-six-inch waist size requires four and five-eighth yards of material twenty-two inches wide.

9220—LADIES' TUCKED SHIRT-WAIST. Illustrated on page 503.

This attractive shirt-waist is made of Dutch-blue silk poplin combined with white silk, and is trimmed with velvet ribbon and silk gimp. The garment is mounted on a body lining. The outer back is laid in clusters of tucks stitched in box-plait effect and tapering gracefully to the waistline, where the slight extra fulness is disposed in shirring. The upper portions of the fronts are tucked to yoke depth and are shirred at the waistline. The forward

9212, LADIES' SHIRT-WAIST Closed at the Back (WITH TUCKED FRONT AND WITH OR WITHOUT THE FRONT YOKE OR BODY LINING), Described on page 507.

completed by a cuff which may be omitted. A narrow neckband finishes the neck edge, and the collar is a back-closing, standing model. A fancy girdle completes the lower part of the garment.

Taffeta silk, peau de soie, poplin, pongee, foulard, satin crêpe, lawn, madras, dimity, chambray, linen or novelty material may be used to develop this design.

A figure view on page 493 shows a different development.

Ladies' tucked shirt-waist 9220 is in seven sizes, from thirty-two to forty-four inches bust measure, price 15 cents. The thirty-six-inch bust size requires two and three-quarter yards of material forty-four inches wide.

9234—LADIES' BOX-PLAITED SHIRT-WAIST, CLOSED AT THE FRONT. Illustrated on page 503.

Light-toned chiffon taffeta is selected to make the pretty shirt-waist depicted in the accompanying illustration. It is mounted on a body lining, which may be omitted, and the outer back of the material is laid in five lengthwise box plaits, the slight fulness at the waistline being disposed in shirring. The full fronts are arranged in a wide cluster of lengthwise box plaits through the center, and box plaits extending to yoke depth on each side, shirring confining the fulness at the waistline. The sleeve is a one-seamed model with the fulness at the lower edge arranged in box plaits, and completed by a band cuff opening on the inside of the arm. A narrow neckband concealed beneath the back-closing standing collar finishes the neck edge.

Taffeta silk, pongee, peau de soie, voile, nun's-veiling, cashmere, lansdowne, China silk, linen, madras, lawn, swiss, dimity or piqué may be used to develop this design.

Ladies' box-plaited shirt-waist 9234 is in seven sizes, from thirty-two to forty-four inches bust measure, price 15 cents. The thirty-six-inch bust size requires four and one-quarter yards of material which measures twenty-two inches in width.

9204—LADIES' BOX-PLAITED SHIRT-WAIST. Illustrated on page 504.

This attractive waist is made of gray flannel and ornamented with velvet buttons. It is mounted on a body lining, which may be omitted. The outer fronts and back are slightly shirred at the waistline and the fronts are box-plaited to yoke depth; the forward edge of the right front is finished with a box plait, and the neck edge is completed by a narrow band. Two styles of sleeve are provided: one is a leg-o'-mutton shirt sleeve gathered at the upper and lower edge and

9183, LADIES' TUCKED SHIRT-WAIST (CLOSED IN FRONT AND WITH SAILOR OR BISHOP SLEEVES; WITH OR WITHOUT THE BODY LINING). Described on page 506.

edges may be finished with revers and vestee pieces, or both of these may be omitted. The full vest front is attached to the right side of the lining front and fastens on the left. The sleeve is an exceptionally pretty model fitted by inside and outside arm seams; it is gathered into the arm's-eye, and the fulness at the lower part is arranged in tuck plaits and

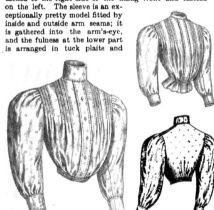

9226, LADIES' TUCKED SHIRT-WAIST (WITH BISHOP OR SHIRT SLEEVES, AND WITH OR WITHOUT THE BODY LINING). Described on page 507.

ALL STANDARD PATTERNS 5, 10 OR 15 CENTS—NONE HIGHER.

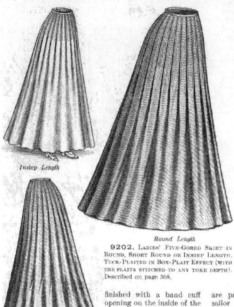

Instep Length

Round Length

9202. Ladies' Five-Gored Skirt in Round, Short Round or Instep Length, Tuck-Plaited in Box-Plait Effect (with the plaits stitched to any yoke depth). Described on page 508.

Short Round Length

finished with a band cuff opening on the inside of the arm, and having an overlapping end. The other is a one-seamed bishop model box-plaited nearly to the elbow, and completed by a band cuff. A back-closing standing collar finishes the neck edge and the garment fastens down the center front.

Taffeta silk, peau de soie, China silk, pongee, flannel, cashmere, albatross, nun's-veiling, linen, piqué, chambray or lawn may be used to develop this design.

Ladies' box-plaited shirt-waist **9204** is in seven sizes, from thirty-two to forty-four inches bust measure, price 15 cents. The thirty-six-inch bust size requires two and one-half yards of material which measures forty-four inches in width.

9197—LADIES' SHIRT-WAIST COS-TUME IN ROUND, SHORT ROUND OR INSTEP LENGTH. Illustrated on page 504.

This comfortable costume is made of white butchers' linen. The shirtwaist is mounted on a body lining, which may be omitted. The outer back and fronts are shirred at the waistline, and the fronts are gathered at the neck edge, the forward edge of the right front being completed with a box plait. Two styles of sleeve are provided; one is a one-seamed leg-o'-mutton model completed by a straight cuff and the other is a regulation one-seamed shirt sleeve, finished with a straight cuff, which opens with the sleeve on the

outside of the arm, the sleeve opening being faced. A standing collar finishes the neck edge, and the shirt-waist closes down the center front. The skirt is a seven-gored model and may be made with or without a plait at the lower part of each seam; the fulness at the back may be disposed in an inverted box plait or gathers.

Linen, madras, duck, percale, piqué, pongee, chambray, brilliantine, taffeta silk, flannel or sailcloth may be used to develop this design, and braid, gimp, galloon, embroidery, insertion or ribbon may be used to trim.

Ladies' shirt-waist costume **9197** is in eight sizes, from thirty-two to forty-six inches bust measure, price 15 cents. The thirty-six-inch bust size requires for round length, seven and seven-eighth yards of material which measures thirty-six inches in width. The width of the skirt at the lower edge in round length is four and one-half yards.

9183—LADIES' TUCKED SHIRT-WAIST. Illustrated on page 505.

This neat and pretty waist is made of light-blue Irish linen. It is mounted on a body lining which may be omitted. The back of the material is arranged in lengthwise tucks and is shirred at the waistline. The fronts are tucked to yoke depth at the upper part and confined by shirring at the waistline, the forward edge of the right front being finished with several lengthwise tucks. Two styles of sleeve are provided: one is a sailor model consisting of a two-seamed lining and an outside portion, the latter being tucked to yoke depth; the other is a one-seamed bishop model completed with a band cuff having an

Short Sweep Length

Short Sweep Length

Round Length

9241. Ladies' Skirt in Short Sweep or Round Length (consisting of a five-gored upper part tucked or gathered at the top and lengthened by a tucked or gathered circular flounce). Described on page 508.

ALL STANDARD PATTERNS 5, 10 OR 15 CENTS—NONE HIGHER.

overlapping end. A narrow neckband finishes the neck edge and the collar is a back-closing standing model.

Taffeta silk, peau de soie, peau de cygne, cashmere, nun's-veiling, madras, linen, piqué, duck, lawn or dimity may be used to develop this design.

Ladies' tucked shirt-waist 9183 is in seven sizes, from thirty-two to forty-four inches bust measure, price 15 cents. The thirty-six-inch bust size requires three and one-eighth yards of material measuring thirty-six inches in width.

9226—LADIES' TUCKED SHIRT-WAIST. Illustrated on page 505.

The shirt-waist here shown is made of white dotted swiss. It is mounted on a body lining, which may be omitted. The outer back is shirred at the waistline and the full fronts are tucked to yoke depth, the fulness at the waistline being confined by shirring. The forward edge of the right front is completed by a box plait. Two styles of sleeve are provided: one is a one-seamed bishop model completed by a straight cuff; the other is a one-seamed shirt sleeve, finished with a straight cuff which may open on the inside or the outside of the arm. A narrow neckband finishes the neck edge, and the standing collar is a back-closing model.

Linen, madras, chambray, taffeta silk, peau de soie, peau de cygne, lawn, dotted swiss or dimity may be used to develop this design.

Ladies' tucked shirt-waist 9226 is in seven sizes, from thirty-two to forty-four inches bust measure, and the price is 15 cents. The thirty-six-inch bust size requires two and seven-eighth yards of material which measures thirty-six inches in width.

9212—LADIES' SHIRT-WAIST CLOSED AT THE BACK. Illustrated on page 505.

This attractive shirt-waist is made of linen damask and is trimmed with lace insertion. It is mounted on a fitted body lining, which may be omitted. The outer front and backs are shirred at the waistline, and the front is tucked to bust depth. A yoke front is provided, but may be omitted. The one-seamed sleeve is completed by a deep cuff and the neck edge with a narrow neckband. The collar is a back-closing standing model.

Taffeta silk, peau de soie, Liberty silk, satin crêpe, crêpe de Chine, lawn, linen, dimity, batiste, chambray or madras may be used to develop this design, with braid, insertion, lace, ribbon, Persian band trimming or galloon to decorate.

Ladies' shirt-waist 9212 is in six sizes, from thirty-two to forty-two inches bust measure, price 15 cents. The thirty-six-inch bust size requires two and five-eighth yards of material which measures thirty-six inches in width or two and three-eighth yards of material forty-four inches in width.

Medium Sweep Length

9210, LADIES' SKIRT IN MEDIUM SWEEP OR ROUND LENGTH (CONSISTING OF A PANEL FRONT GORE TUCKED AT THE SIDE EDGES AND THREE SLIGHTLY GATHERED CIRCULAR SECTIONS FORMING THE SIDES AND BACK AND JOINED UNDER TUCKS). Described on page 509.

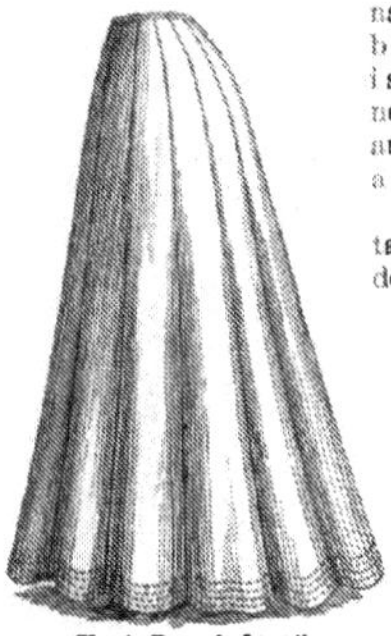

Round Length

Medium Sweep Length

Short Round Length

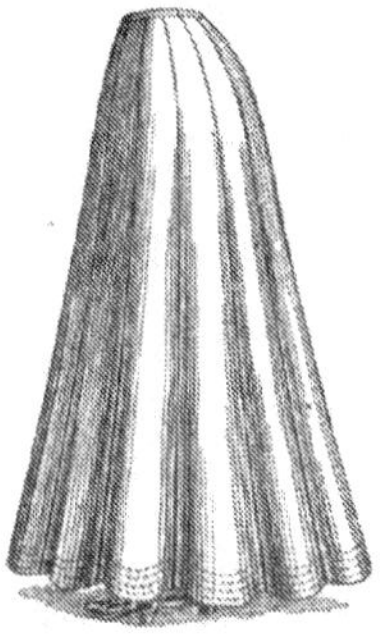

Instep Length

Round Length

9228, LADIES' ELEVEN-GORED SKIRT IN ROUND, SHORT ROUND OR INSTEP LENGTH (WITHOUT FULNESS TO DEEP YOKE DEPTH, WITH AN INVERTED BOX PLAIT OR IN HABIT STYLE AT THE BACK; SOMETIMES CALLED THE UMBRELLA OR RIPPLE SKIRT). Described on page 508.

ALL STANDARD PATTERNS 5, 10 OR 15 CENTS—NONE HIGHER.

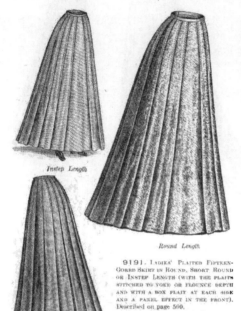

Instep Length

Round Length

Short Round Length

9191. LADIES' PLAITED FIFTEEN-GORED SKIRT IN ROUND, SHORT ROUND OR INSTEP LENGTH (WITH THE PLAITS STITCHED TO YOKE OR FLOUNCE DEPTH AND WITH A BOX PLAIT AT EACH SIDE AND A PANEL EFFECT IN THE FRONT). Described on page 509.

9202—LADIES' FIVE-GORED SKIRT IN ROUND, SHORT ROUND OR IN-STEP LENGTH, TUCK-PLAITED IN BOX-PLAIT EFFECT. Illustrated on page 506.

This attractive skirt is made of brown brilliantine, and represents one of the prettiest models designed this season. It consists of five gores, and the fulness at the upper part is disposed in tuck plaits, which may be stitched to any desired yoke depth in box-plait effect.

Serge, cheviot, tweed, lady's-cloth, etamine, voile, linen, piqué, chambray, madras or duck may be used to develop this design.

A figure view on page 493 shows an entirely different development of this model.

Ladies' five-gored skirt 9202 is in seven sizes, from twenty to thirty-two inches waist measure, corresponding to thirty-seven to fifty-four and one-half inches hip measure, price 15 cents. The twenty-four-inch waist size, corresponding to the forty-two-inch hip size, requires for round length, six and seven-eighth yards of material which is forty-four inches wide. Width at lower edge of skirt is four and one-half yards.

9241—LADIES' SKIRT IN SHORT SWEEP OR ROUND LENGTH. Illustrated on page 506.

This stylish skirt is made of flowered French lawn and is trimmed

with white embroidered appliqué. It consists of a five-gored upper part, which may be tucked or gathered at the top and finished with gathers or an inverted box plait at the back. The gored portions are lengthened by a circular flounce tucked or gathered at the upper edge.

Lawn, organdy, dimity, foulard, China silk, pongee, grenadine, voile, etamine, Brussels net, silk muslin, albatross or nun's-veiling may be used to develop this design, and lace, insertion, embroidery, ribbon, gimp or chiffon-and-silk passementerie may be used to trim.

Ladies' skirt 9241 is in seven sizes, from twenty to thirty-two inches waist measure, corresponding to thirty-seven to fifty-four and one-half inches hip measure, price 15 cents. The twenty-four-inch waist size, corresponding to the forty-two-inch hip size, requires five and seven-eighths yards of material which is thirty-six inches wide. The width of the skirt at the lower edge is five yards.

9228—LADIES' ELEVEN-GORED SKIRT IN ROUND, SHORT ROUND OR INSTEP LENGTH. Illustrated on page 507.

This handsome skirt is made of light-gray drap d'été with rows of stitching at shallow hem depth. It is an eleven-gored model with the back arranged in an inverted box plait, or, if preferred, the skirt may be finished in habit-back style. The upper portion of the garment fits the figure smoothly to deep yoke depth, thence the gores widen gradually, producing a ripple or umbrella effect at the lower part.

Serge, cheviot, tweed, drap d'été, etamine, taffeta silk, peau de soie, linen, piqué or duck may be used to develop this design, with braid, appliqué embroidery, ribbon, gimp, galloon or insertion to trim.

Round Length

Frou-Frou Length

Regulation Short Sweep Length

9238. LADIES' PLAITED SEVEN-GORED SKIRT IN FROU-FROU OR REGULATION SHORT SWEEP LENGTH OR IN ROUND LENGTH (SHIRRED IN CLUSTERS AT THE TOP). Described on page 509.

ALL STANDARD PATTERNS 5, 10 OR 15 CENTS—NONE HIGHER.

A figure view on page 492 shows a different development.

Ladies' skirt **9228** is in seven sizes, from twenty to thirty-two inches waist measure, corresponding to thirty-seven to fifty-four and one-half inches hip measure, price 15 cents. The twenty-four-inch waist size, corresponding to the forty-two-inch hip size, requires, for round length, four and one-quarter yards of material which is fifty-four inches in width. The width at the lower edge of the skirt is five and one-eighth yards.

9210—LADIES' SKIRT IN MEDIUM SWEEP OR ROUND LENGTH. Illustrated on page 507.

Ombré-tinted silk combined with light-tan cloth are the materials selected to make this graceful skirt. The panel or front gore is tucked at the side edges and attached to the three slightly gathered circular sections which form the sides and back of the skirt. The sections are tucked at the lower edges as indicated, and joined beneath the tucks. The upper edge of the garment is slightly gathered and is completed by a narrow belt, the placket closing occurring in the back.

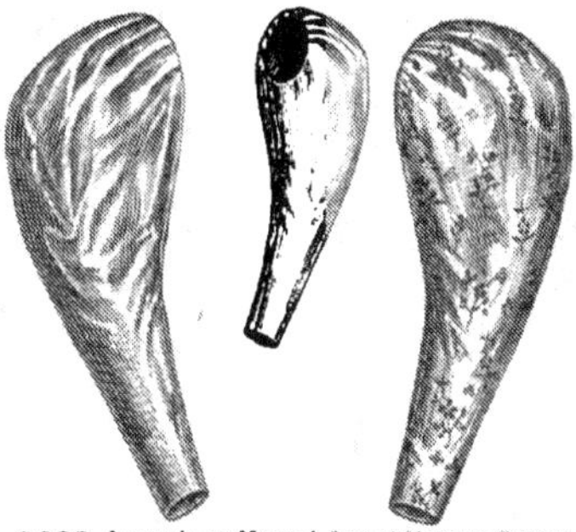

9230. LADIES' AND MISSES' LEG-O'-MUTTON SLEEVE (PLAITED OR GATHERED AT THE TOP, FOR WAISTS, DRESSES, ETC.). Described on page 510.

Taffeta, silk, velvet, panne, chiffon velvet, peau de soie, lansdowne, drap d'été, crêpe de Chine, lawn, dimity, sateen or linen may be used to develop this design, with lace, insertion, embroidery, ribbon, gimp or passementerie to decorate.

A figure view on page 496 shows a different development.

Ladies' skirt **9210** is in six sizes, from twenty to thirty inches waist measure, corresponding to thirty-seven to fifty-one inches hip measure, price 15 cents. The twenty-four-inch waist size, corresponding to the forty-two-inch hip size, requires nine and one-half yards of material which is twenty-two inches wide. The width of the skirt at the lower edge is four and three-quarter yards.

9191—LADIES' PLAITED FIFTEEN-GORED SKIRT IN ROUND, SHORT ROUND OR INSTEP LENGTH. Illustrated on page 508.

This stylish skirt is made of blue serge, and is a fifteen-gored model, each gore being cut with extensions at yoke depth, which are laid underneath to form the plaits and panel-front effect, box plaits being formed at each hip, while the fulness at the back of the garment is disposed in an inverted box plait. The plaits may be stitched down to yoke or flounce depth.

Brilliantine, serge, cheviot, tweed, lady's-cloth, Venetian cloth, taffeta silk, peau de soie, linen, chambray, piqué or duck may be used to develop this design, with braid, gimp, ribbon, appliqué or insertion to trim.

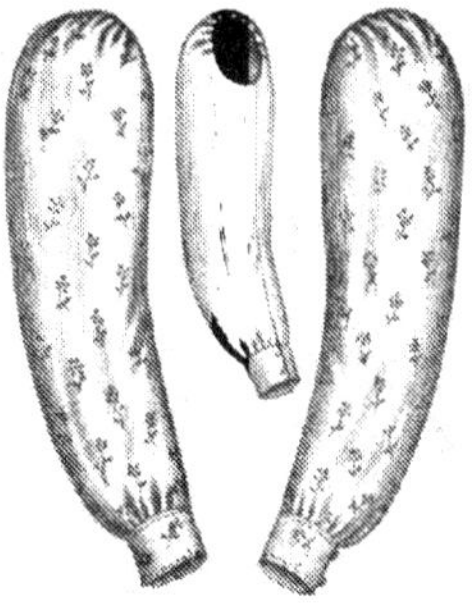

9184. LADIES' AND MISSES' SHIRT SLEEVE (CLOSED AT THE BACK OR FRONT AND WITH LINK OR BUTTONED CUFFS). Described on page 510.

Ladies' skirt **9191** is in seven sizes, from twenty to thirty-two inches waist measure, corresponding to thirty-seven to fifty-four and one-half inches hip measure, price 15 cents. The twenty-four-inch waist size, corresponding to the forty-two-inch hip size, requires for the skirt when in round length, six and three-eighth yards of material forty-four inches wide. The width of the skirt at the lower edge is five and three-quarter yards.

9238—LADIES' PLAITED SEVEN-GORED SKIRT IN FROU-FROU OR REGULATION SHORT SWEEP LENGTH OR ROUND LENGTH. Illustrated on page 508.

This handsome skirt is made of light-écru etamine, and is a seven-gored model disposed in side plaits and clusters of shirring at the top.

Ladies' skirt **9238** is in six sizes, from twenty to thirty inches waist measure, corresponding to thirty-seven to fifty-one inches hip measure, price 15 cents. The twenty-four-inch waist size, corresponding to the forty-two-inch hip size, requires for frou-frou length, eleven and five-eighth yards of material twenty-two inches wide or five and one-half yards fifty-four inches. The width at the lower edge of the skirt, five and seven-eighth yards.

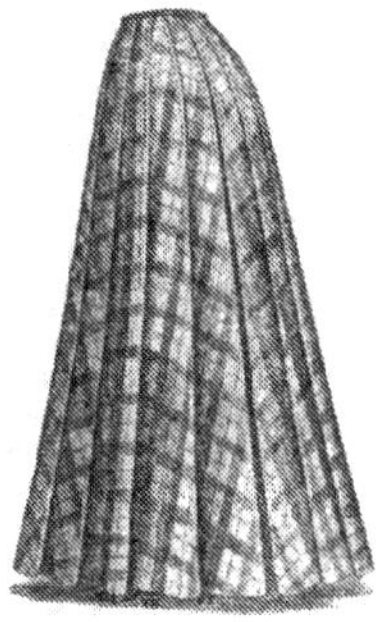

Short Round Length

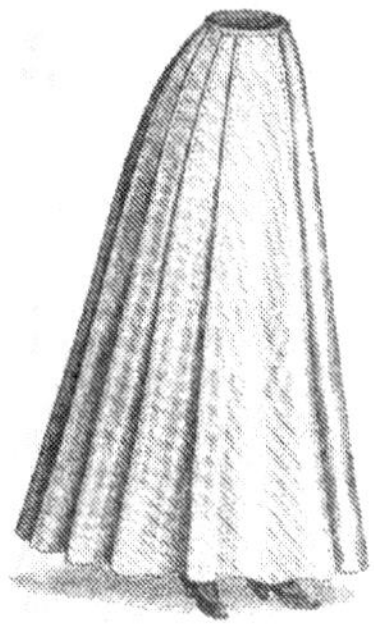

Instep Length

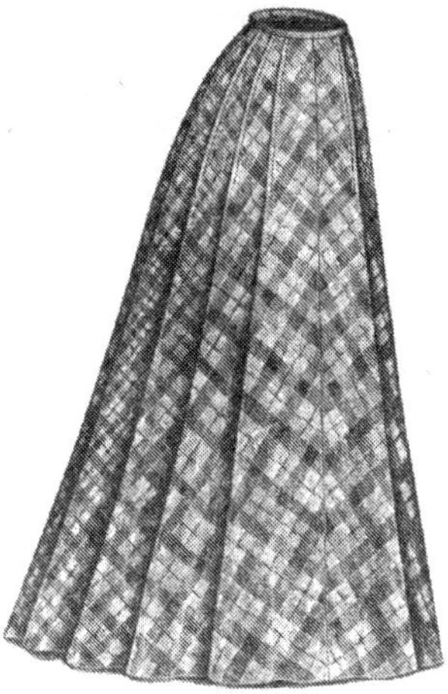

Round Length

9189. LADIES' PLAITED CIRCULAR SKIRT IN ROUND, SHORT ROUND OR INSTEP LENGTH (WITH OR WITHOUT THE CENTER-FRONT SEAM). Described on page 510.

9189—LADIES' PLAITED CIRCULAR SKIRT IN ROUND, SHORT ROUND OR INSTEP LENGTH. Illustrated on page 509.

Scotch plaid cheviot is the material selected to make this handsome skirt. When the center-front seam is used, it consists of two sections. When the plain, seamless front is preferred, it is in one circular piece. The fulness at the upper part of the garment is disposed in side plaits, which may be stitched to any desired depth, the back of skirt being finished with an inverted box plait.

Brilliantine, serge, cheviot, tweed, lady's-cloth, Venetian cloth, homespun, lansdowne, etamine, voile or linen may be used to develop this design, with braid, appliqué lace, insertion, embroidery or gimp to trim.

A figure view on page 491 shows a different development.

Ladies' skirt 9189 is in six sizes, from twenty to thirty inches waist measure, corresponding to thirty-seven to fifty-one inches hip measure, price 15 cents. The twenty-four-inch waist size, corresponding to the forty-two-inch hip size, requires for instep length without the center-front seam, four and three-quarter yards of material which measures forty-four inches in width. The width of the skirt at the lower edge is five yards.

9230—LADIES' AND MISSES' LEG-O'-MUTTON SLEEVE. Illustrated on page 509.

This stylish sleeve is made of light-gray flowered peau de soie, and is a two-seamed leg-o'-mutton model mounted on a two-seamed lining. The fulness at the upper edge may be disposed in gathers or plaits.

Ladies' and misses' sleeve 9230 is in seven sizes, from nine to fifteen inches arm measure, price 10 cents. The twelve-inch arm size requires one and three-quarter yards of material twenty-two inches wide or one yard forty-four inches in width.

9184—LADIES' AND MISSES' SHIRT SLEEVE. Illustrated on page 509.

This neat sleeve will be found suitable to use in shirtwaists or plain blouses. It is here made of figured madras

9246. LADIES' AND MISSES' CUFFS AND DOUBLE OR SINGLE-BREASTED NOTCHED AND SHAWL COLLARS WITH OR WITHOUT FACING OR VEST EXTENSIONS (FOR COATS, JACKETS, ETC.). Described on this page.

and is a one-seamed model with the fulness at the upper edge gathered. The lower edge is gathered into a straight cuff, which may be closed with links or buttons, or into a wristband. When the cuff is used, it opens with the sleeve on the outside of the arm, the sleeve opening being faced.

Ladies' and misses' shirt sleeve 9184 is in six sizes, from ten to fifteen inches arm measure, price 10 cents. The twelve-inch arm size requires one and five-eighth yards of material twenty-two inches wide; one and one-eighth yards thirty-six inches, or seven-eighth yard forty-four inches in width.

9246—LADIES' AND MISSES' CUFFS AND DOUBLE OR SINGLE-BREASTED NOTCHED OR SHAWL COLLARS WITH OR WITHOUT FACING OR VEST EXTENSIONS. Illustrated on this page.

The collars and cuffs depicted in this illustration are designed to be worn with jackets or short coats. The shawl-collar portions are united by a center-back seam and attached to the vest extensions, which are also joined by a center-back seam and close in a double or single-breasted fashion.

The notched collar is in two pieces and is attached to the upper edges of the vest portions. The latter are rolled back at the upper front edges to form lapels, which meet the rolling collar in notches. The vest extensions may be closed in single or double breasted style.

The cuff is a one-piece turn-up flare model finished with stitching or any preferred style of trimming.

Piqué, duck, linen, plain cloth, taffeta, peau de soie, satin, leather or suède kid may be used to develop this design, and braid, gimp, insertion, appliqué lace or embroidery may be used to trim.

Ladies' and misses' cuffs and double or single-breasted notched or shawl collars 9246 is in three sizes, from thirty-two to forty inches bust measure, price 10 cents. The thirty-six-inch bust size requires for either collar and the cuffs one and one-quarter yards of twenty-two-inch material, or for either vest, one and five-eighth yards of twenty-seven-inch material.

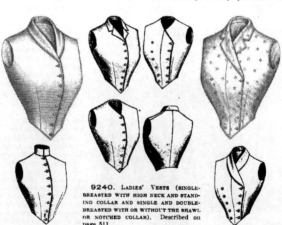

9240. LADIES' VESTS (SINGLE-BREASTED WITH HIGH NECK AND STANDING COLLAR AND SINGLE AND DOUBLE-BREASTED WITH OR WITHOUT THE SHAWL OR NOTCHED COLLAR). Described on page 511.

ALL STANDARD PATTERNS 5, 10 OR 15 CENTS—NONE HIGHER.

9240—LADIES' VESTS. Illustrated on page 510.

Fancy vesting and plain cloth were the materials selected to make the vests depicted in this illustration.

The double-breasted vest is fitted by center-front, center-back, under-arm and shoulder seams, also single bust darts, and the upper portions of the fronts are laid back to form the revers, which meet the rolling collar in notches; if preferred, the neck edge may be finished with the shawl collar or made collarless.

The single-breasted vest is fitted by center-back, under-arm and shoulder seams, also single bust darts; the upper portions of the vest fronts are laid back to form the small revers, which meet the rolling collar in notches; if preferred, the shawl collar may be used or the neck edge of the garment finished without a collar. A standing collar may finish the neck edge of the vest when it is made high.

Ladies' vests 9240 is in six sizes, from thirty-two to forty-two inches bust measure, price 10 cents. The thirty-six-inch bust size requires for either single-breasted vest one and three-quarter yards of twenty-seven-inch material, or for either double-breasted vest, one and three-quarter yards of material twenty-seven inches in width.

9229. SHIRRED HAT FOR LADIES, MISSES AND GIRLS. Described on this page.

9229 — SHIRRED HAT FOR LADIES, MISSES AND GIRLS. Illustrated on this page.

This pretty hat is made of white silk mull shirred on wires and decorated with a rosette of white Liberty satin. It consists of a full crown gathered to the wide brim, which consists of one shaped section folded in such a manner as to produce the lining as well as the outside portion. The brim is shirred to form the wire casings, and also the frill which gives the correct finish to the outer edge. A bias inside band conceals the joining of the crown and brim.

Ladies', misses' and girls' shirred hat 9229 is in three sizes, price 10 cents. The ladies' size requires three and one-quarter yards of twenty-two-inch material.

9194—LADIES' DRESSING-SACK WITH YOKE FRONT. Illustrated on this page.

The attractive dressing-sack here depicted is made of Japanese crêpe and plain light-blue silk.

It is fitted by center-back, side-back, under-arm and shoulder seams. The full fronts are gathered at the upper edges and attached to the lower edges of the yoke fronts. The pattern provides two styles of sleeve, either

of which may be used: one is a one-seamed bishop model, gathered into a band cuff, and the other is a one-seamed flowing model finished with a trimming band. The neck edge of the sack may be finished with a two-piece turn-down collar or with the continuation of the trimming band, which is also used to finish the forward edges of the fronts.

Kimono crêpe, cashmere, China silk, flannel, China crêpe, dimity, lawn or chambray may be used to develop this design.

Ladies' dressing-sack 9194 is in seven sizes, from thirty-two to forty-four inches bust measure, price 15

9194. LADIES' DRESSING-SACK WITH YOKE FRONT (WITH KIMONO BAND AND STANDING COLLAR IN ONE, OR WITH TURNOVER COLLAR, AND BELL OR BISHOP SLEEVES). Described on this page.

Ladies' corset-cover 9216 is in eight sizes, from thirty-two to forty-six inches bust measure, price 10 cents. The thirty-six-inch bust size requires for high neck and shield sleeves, one and three-eighth yards of material thirty-six inches wide, with two yards of edging, one and one-eighth yards of beading and two yards of ribbon to trim.

9216. LADIES' CORSET-COVER (WITH HIGH, SQUARE, ROUND OR V NECK, AND WITH OR WITHOUT THE FULL-LENGTH OR SHIELD SLEEVES). Described on this page.

cents. The thirty-six-inch bust size requires three and seven-eighth yards of material twenty-seven inches wide; two and seven-eighth yards thirty-six inches wide, or two and one-half yards forty-four inches, with two yards of twenty-two-inch material for the bands and three yards of ribbon for the ties.

9216 — LADIES' CORSET-COVER. Illustrated on this page.

The pretty corset-cover here shown is made of white nainsook and trimmed with lace edging. The small view depicts the garment with long sleeves and high neck. It is fitted by center-back, side-back, under-arm and shoulder seams, also single darts. Perforations are provided by which the neck may be cut in square, round or V-shaped outline, or, if preferred, the garment may be made with a high neck. Two styles of sleeve are provided: one is a shield sleeve and the other a two-seamed, full-length model, gathered into the arm's-eye.

MISSES' COSTUMES. DESCRIBED ON THIS PAGE
(Jacket Costume 9215)   (Sailor Costume 9195)

MISSES' JACKET COSTUME. ILLUSTRATED ON THIS PAGE.

Misses' costume 9215 is in four sizes, from fourteen to seventeen years, price 15 cents, and is again illustrated on page 518. As here shown it is made of gray frieze and is stylishly trimmed with black silk Hercules braid.

MISSES' SAILOR COSTUME. ILLUSTRATED ON THIS PAGE.

Misses' costume 9195 is in five sizes, from thirteen to seventeen years, price 15 cents. On page 519 is presented a different development of the design, which is here reproduced in blue serge and white linen, blue and white braid supplying the trimming.

GIRLS' DRESS. ILLUSTRATED ON PAGE 513.

Girls' dress 9199 is in nine sizes, from five to thirteen years, price 15 cents, and is shown in different development on page 520.

Pink Japanese silk is used for the frock in the present instance, with lace and insertion for decoration.

GIRLS' COSTUME. ILLUSTRATED ON PAGE 513.

Girls' costume 9188 is in ten sizes, from five to fourteen years, price 15 cents. The design appears again in different development on page 518, where it is accompanied by a detailed description. Gray French flannel

512

is here employed, the chemisette and the standing collar being made of tan táffeta overlaid with Irish crochet, and the trimming consists of white and tan braid.

Boys' Russian Suit. Illustrated on Page 513.

Boys' suit 9222 is in seven sizes, two to eight years, price 15 cents, and is shown again on page 525. It is here pictured in blue velvet combined with white cloth.

Boys' Suit and Children's Dress   described on this page
(Suit 9222)   (Dress 9182)

Misses' Tucked Costume. Illustrated on Page 513.

Misses' costume 9209 is in five sizes, from thirteen to seventeen years, price 15 cents. The design appears in different development on page 519.
Peacock-blue taffeta glacé and all-over lace are combined for this attractive costume as here shown, with darker-blue velvet ribbon and taffeta ruching to trim.

Misses' Tucked Long Coat. Illustrated on Page 514.

Misses' coat 9243 is in five sizes, from thirteen to seventeen years, price 15 cents. On page 516 appears another development of the design, which is here reproduced in black-and-white novelty cheviot, with braid to trim.

Little Girls' Shirred Long Coat. Illustrated on Page 514.

Little girls' coat 9218 is in nine sizes, from one to nine years, price 10 cents. Another view of the model is given on page 517, where it is accompanied by a detailed description. Rose-colored merino is employed for the coat in the present instance, with pink-and-black silk braid to trim.

Girls' Tucked Coat in Full or Three-Quarter Length. Illustrated on Page 514.

Girls' coat 9214 is in nine sizes, from five to thirteen years, price 15 cents. On page 516 is given another development of the model, which is here reproduced in black taffeta, and is trimmed with black and white braid.

Misses' Box-Plaited Costume. Illustrated on Page 514.

Misses' costume 9237 is in six sizes, from twelve to seventeen years, price 15 cents, and is shown again on page 518. The costume is here made of brown lady's-cloth.

Boys' Russian Suit. Illustrated on This Page.

Boys' suit 9222 is in seven sizes, from two to eight years, price 15 cents, and is again shown on pages 513 and 525. It is here reproduced in pink chambray and white linen, and the collar is trimmed with embroidered linen insertion.

Children's Shirred Dress. Illustrated on This Page.

Children's dress 9182 is in seven sizes, six months to six years, price 10 cents, and is shown again on page 521. It is here made of nainsook, Valenciennes lace and insertion.

Girls' Apron and Costume. described on this page
(Apron 9187)   (Costume 9186)

Girls' Apron. Illustrated on This Page.

Girls' apron 9187 is in five sizes, from four to twelve years, price 10 cents, and is presented in different development on page 523.
White lawn is used for the garment as here pictured, with embroidered swiss edging and insertion for trimming.

Girls' Box-Plaited Costume. Illustrated on This Page.

Girls' costume 9186 is in ten sizes, from five to fourteen years, price 15 cents, another view of the garment appearing on page 519. As here shown it is made of pale-blue cashmere, with trimming of narrow black velvet ribbon.

3

9200. CHILDREN'S PLAITED LONG COAT (WITH REMOVABLE SHIELD AND POINTED OR ROUND COLLAR, WITH OR WITHOUT THE CUFFS). Described on this page.

9200.—CHILDREN'S PLAITED LONG COAT. Illustrated on this page.

White piqué, linen embroidery and pearl buttons are used to make this coat, which is fitted by under-arm and shoulder seams. The fronts a r e laid in box plaits and the back is tuck-plaited from the shoulder seams to the waistline, where the fulness may be confined

Three-Quarter Length   Full Length

Full Length

9214. GIRLS' TUCKED COAT IN FULL OR THREE-QUARTER LENGTH (WITH BISHOP OR LEG-O'-MUTTON SLEEVES AND WITH OR WITHOUT THE COLLAR-FACING, CUFFS OR BELT). Described on this page.

by a belt. The one-seamed sleeve is completed by a band cuff, to which may be attached the one-piece turn-up cuff. The neck edge may be finished with a sailor collar in pointed or round outline, and a shield finished at the upper edge by a band collar is provided.

Children's coat 9200 is in eight sizes, from two to nine years, price 10 cents. The five-year size requires three yards of material forty-four inches wide.

9214—GIRLS' TUCKED COAT IN FULL OR THREE-QUARTER LENGTH. Illustrated on this page.

This stylish coat is developed in light-tan pongee and is fitted by under-arm and shoulder seams, the back and fronts being tucked to the waist-line, where they are confined by the plain belt. The neck edge may be finished with or without the flat fancy collar-facing, and two styles of sleeve are provided: one is a one-seamed bishop model completed by a band cuff, to which is attached the fancy one-piece turn-up cuff. The other is

9243. MISSES' TUCKED LONG COAT (WITH OR WITHOUT THE COLLAR-FACING OR CUFFS; SUITABLE FOR RAIN, AUTOMOBILING OR TRAVELING WEAR). Described on this page

a one-seamed leg-o'-mutton sleeve finished with a turn-up cuff. The collar-facing, cuffs and belt may all be omitted, and a figure view on page 514 shows a different development.

Girls' coat 9214 is in nine sizes, from five to thirteen years, price 15 cents. The nine-year size requires for full-length garment, three and one-quarter yards of material measuring fifty-four inches in width.

9243—MISSES' TUCKED LONG COAT. Illustrated on this page.

The pictured coat is made of light-tan English tweed. It is fitted by side-back, under-arm and shoulder seams, also side-front seams. The backs and fronts are laid in tuck-plaits and a belt confines the garment at the waistline. A fancy collar-facing is provided and the two-seamed sleeve may be completed by a turn-up cuff. Patch pockets having fancy lap piece may be attached to the coat fronts, if desired.

ALL STANDARD PATTERNS 5, 10 OR 15 CENTS—NONE HIGHER.

A figure view on page 514 shows a different development. Misses' tucked long coat 9243 is in five sizes, from thirteen to seventeen years, price 15 cents. The fifteen-year size requires four and one-quarter yards of material which measures fifty-four inches in width.

✦

9245—MISSES' BOX - PLAITED BLOUSE REDINGOTE OR JACKET WITH VESTEE. Illustrated on this page.

This handsome garment is made of tan Venetian cloth, with collar and cuffs of dark-brown stitched velvet. The jacket portions are mounted on a fitted lining. The outer back is tucked in box-plait effect, and the blouse fronts are tucked at the forward edges, the lower edges being gathered. A vestee-facing is supplied, but may be omitted, and the neck edge of the jacket may be finished with or without the flat fancy collar facing. The one - seamed sleeve is plaited into the one-piece turn-up cuff, and the lower edge of the jacket is finished

9245. MISSES' BOX-PLAITED BLOUSE REDINGOTE OR JACKET WITH VESTEE (WITH SLEEVES PLAITED OR GATHERED AT THE TOP AND TUCKED OR PLAITED AT THE BOTTOM). Described on this page.

with a belt, to which may be attached the redingote peplum.

Misses' jacket 9245 is in four sizes, from fourteen to seventeen years, price 15 cents. The fifteen-year size requires, with redingote peplum, three yards of material which measures fifty-four inches in width.

✦

9218 — LITTLE GIRLS' SHIRRED LONG COAT WITH YOKE. Illustrated on this page.

This pretty little coat is made of white silk and is trimmed with white silk braid. The yoke portions are fitted by shoulder seams, to which the back and fronts, which are shirred, are attached. The one-seamed sleeve is shirred to cuff depth and completed with a band. The cape portions, which may be cut with or without the stole extensions, are attached to the neck edge of the coat and a one-piece turn-down collar is provided. A figure view on page 514 shows a different development.

Little girls' coat 9218 is in nine sizes, from one to nine years, price 10 cents. The five-year size requires three and three-eighth yards of material thirty-six inches wide.

9218. LITTLE GIRLS' SHIRRED LONG COAT WITH YOKE (WITH THE CAPE HAVING STOLE EXTENSIONS, AND WITH OR WITHOUT THE COLLAR). Described on this page.

9244—MISSES' AND GIRLS DOUBLE-BREASTED BOX-COAT IN FULL OR THREE-QUARTER LENGTH. Illustrated on this page.

This stylish coat is made of brown covert cloth, and is fitted by under-arm and shoulder seams, also a center-back seam when the whole back is not desired. Two styles of sleeve are provided: one is a bishop model gathered or plaited

Three-Quarter Length   Full Length

Full Length   Three-Quarter Length

9244. MISSES' AND GIRLS' DOUBLE-BREASTED BOX-COAT IN FULL OR THREE-QUARTER LENGTH (WITH PLAITED OR GATHERED BISHOP OR LEG-O'-MUTTON SLEEVES, AND WITH OR WITHOUT THE COLLAR-FACING, CUFFS, BACK STRAP, POCKETS OR CENTER-BACK SEAM). Described on this page.

ALL STANDARD PATTERNS 5, 10 OR 15 CENTS—NONE HIGHER.

9215, MISSES' COSTUME (CONSIST-
ING OF A JACKET WITH VESTEE AND
PLAITED OR GATHERED SLEEVES WITH
OH WITHOUT THE SLIP CUFFS; AND A
SEVEN-GORED SKIRT WITH PLAITED EX-
TENSIONS AT GRADUATED FLOUNCE DEPTH
ON THE BACK EDGES OF THE FRONT AND
SIDE GORES AND AN INVERTED BOX PLAIT
AT THE BACK). Described on this page.

into the armhole and finished with fancy cuff, which may be omitted, and the other is a leg-o'-mutton sleeve. The neck edge of the coat may be finished with or without the collar-facing and the back of the garment is confined at the waistline by a belt. Pockets may be attached to the coat fronts.

Misses' and girls' double-breasted box-coat 9244 is in six sizes, from six to sixteen years, price 15 cents. The eight-year size requires, for full-length garment, two and three-eighth yards of material fifty-four inches in width.

9215—MISSES' COSTUME. Illustrated on this page.

This costume is made of dark-blue serge and trimmed with silk braid. The jacket is fitted by side-back, side-front, under-arm and shoulder seams. The vestee portions are

fitted by shoulder seams and attached to the forward and neck edges of the jacket fronts. The two-seamed sleeve may be gathered or plaited into the arm's-eye, and is completed by a slip cuff, which may be omitted. The seven-gored skirt has plaited extensions at flounce depth, which are lapped on the back edges of the front and side gores. The back is arranged in an inverted box plait, and the lower edge is faced or hemmed.

A figure view on page 512 shows a different development. Misses' costume 9215 is in four sizes, from fourteen to seventeen years, and the price is 15 cents. The fifteen-year size of garment requires three and five-eighth yards of material which measures fifty-four inches in width.

9188, GIRLS' COSTUME (CONSISTING OF A TUCKED BLOUSE WAIST WITH SHIELD; AND A PLAITED ONE-PIECE SKIRT ATTACHED TO THE UNDERBODY OR A BELT). Described on page 519.

9237 — MISSES' BOX - PLAITED COSTUME. Illustrated on this page.

This attractive dress is made of gray flannel, and with it is worn a white linen collar and cuffs and a red silk cravat.

The waist is provided with a body lining, which may be omitted. The outer back and fronts are box-plaited, and the fulness at the waistline is disposed in shirring. The one-seamed sleeve is completed by a band to which a turn-up cuff is attached. The neck edge is finished with a narrow band and a turn-down or standing collar may be used or,

9237, MISSES' BOX-PLAITED COSTUME (CONSISTING OF A BLOUSE WITH A TURN-DOWN OR STANDING COLLAR OR NECKBAND FOR ETON OR OTHER LINEN COLLAR AND WITH OR WITHOUT THE CUFFS, SKIRT PART OR BODY LINING; AND A SEVEN-GORED SKIRT; SOMETIMES CALLED THE "BUS-TER BROWN" COSTUME). Described on this page.

ALL STANDARD PATTERNS 5, 10 OR 15 CENTS—NONE HIGHER.

if preferred, Eton or other linen collars may be worn. The waist closes down the center front beneath the center box plait. The skirt is a seven-gored model with the fulness disposed in box plaits, which may be stitched down to deep yoke depth.

A figure view on page 514 shows a different development of the design.

Misses' costume **9237** is in six sizes, from twelve to seventeen years, price 15 cents. The fifteen-year size requires four and three-quarter yards of material fifty-four inches in width.

9188—GIRLS' COSTUME. Illustrated on page 518.

This pretty dress is here developed in light-tan lady's-cloth, the shield and collar being made of brown velvet.

9186, GIRLS' BOX-PLAITED COSTUME (CONSISTING OF A BLOUSE WITH TURN-DOWN COLLAR OR NECKBAND FOR ETON OR OTHER LINEN COLLAR; AND A FIVE-GORED SKIRT ATTACHED TO THE UNDERBODY OR A BELT). Described on this page.

The blouse waist is fitted by under-arm and shoulder seams, the fronts and back being tuck-plaited from the shoulder seams to the waistline, where the extra fulness is disposed in gathers and finished by a plain girdle. A trimming band finishes the neck edge and forward edges of the fronts. The one-seamed sleeve is completed by a band cuff. A shield finished at the upper edge by a standing collar is provided. The plaited skirt may be finished with a belt or attached to a fitted back-closing underwaist, and a figure view of the garment is shown on page 513.

Girls' costume 9188 is in ten sizes, from five to fourteen years, price 15 cents. The nine-year size requires five and three-eighth yards of material which is thirty-six inches wide.

9186 — GIRLS' BOX-PLAITED COSTUME. Illustrated on this page.

This costume is made of blue cashmere and trimmed with black braid. The blouse waist is box-plaited to yoke depth, and is fitted by under-arm and shoulder seams. Its lower edge is finished with a casing and draw-string. The forward edge of the right front is completed by a box plait. A narrow band and turn-down collar finish the neck edge. The one-seamed bishop sleeve is completed by a band cuff. The box-plaited, five-gored skirt is attached to the back-closing fitted underwaist. A figure view is shown on page 515.

Girls' box-plaited costume 9186 is in ten sizes, from five to fourteen years, price 15 cents. The nine-year size requires five and one-eighth yards of material which is twenty-seven inches wide.

9195, MISSES' COSTUME (CONSISTING OF A SAILOR BLOUSE WITH REMOVABLE SHIELD, SAILOR OR BISHOP SLEEVES, SQUARE OR ROUND SAILOR COLLAR AND WITH OR WITHOUT THE YOKE-FACINGS; AND A SIDE-PLAITED, FIVE-GORED SKIRT, WITH THE PLAITS STITCHED TO YOKE DEPTH). Described on page 520.

9209, MISSES' TUCKED COSTUME (CONSISTING OF A SURPLICE BLOUSE WAIST CLOSED AT THE BACK, WITH FULL-LENGTH OR ELBOW SLEEVES; AND A FIVE-GORED SKIRT WITH NUN TUCKS AT THE LOWER PART). Described on page 520.

ALL STANDARD PATTERNS 5, 10 OR 15 CENTS—NONE HIGHER.

9199, GIRLS' DRESS (IN HIGH NECK WITH ROUND YOKE OR IN LOW NECK WITHOUT THE YOKE; WITH BISHOP OR PUFF SLEEVES AND WITH OR WITHOUT THE BERTHA, AND WITH AN ATTACHED GATHERED FIVE-GORED SKIRT). Described on this page.

9195—MISSES' COSTUME. Illustrated on page 519.

This stylish costume is made of dark-blue serge. The blouse waist is fitted by under-arm and shoulder seams, and fancy yoke facings are provided. The lower edge of the blouse is finished with a casing and draw-string, and the upper front portions are cut away in a V, a shield finished with a standing collar being provided. Two styles of sleeve are provided: one is a one-seamed sailor sleeve with the fulness at the lower edge laid in tuck plaits and finished with or without a band cuff. The other is in bishop style and completed with a band cuff. A sailor collar in round or square outline may be used. The five-gored skirt is side-plaited and may be stitched to any desired yoke depth.

A figure view on page 512 shows a different development. Misses' costume 9195 is in five sizes, from thirteen to seventeen years, price 15 cents. The fifteen-year size requires seven and one-eighth yards of material thirty-six inches wide.

9209—MISSES' TUCKED COSTUME. Illustrated on page 519.

This attractive dress is made of

figured lawn and trimmed with lace insertion. The tucked waist portions, which are fitted by under-arm and shoulder seams, are mounted on a body lining, and shirred at the waistline. The fronts cross in surplice fashion, the lining front being faced in chemisette effect. A standing collar completes the neck edge save when the open neck is desired. The sleeve, which may be made in full or elbow length, consists of a two-seamed lining and a one-seamed puff portion, and is completed by a circular ruffle. The five-gored skirt is tucked to yoke depth and finished with nun tucks at the lower part.

A figure view on page 513 shows a different development.

Misses' costume 9209 is in five sizes, from thirteen to seventeen years, price 15 cents. The fifteen-year size requires seven and three-eighth yards of material thirty-six inches wide.

9199—GIRLS' DRESS. Illustrated on this page.

White nun's-veiling, lace, insertion and ribbon are used to make this pretty little dress, the waist of which is mounted on a fitted lining overlaid back and front to yoke depth. To the yoke the full front and backs are gathered and are shirred at the waistline. A bertha in fancy outline is provided. When the high-neck yoke is used it is finished with a standing collar. Two styles of sleeve are provided: one is a one-seamed bishop model finished with a band cuff, and the other is a short puff sleeve completed with a band. The five-gored skirt is gathered to the lower edge of the body portions.

A figure view on page 513 shows a different development.

Girls' dress 9199 is in nine sizes, from five to thirteen years, price 15 cents. The nine-year size requires two and three-quarter yards of material which measures forty-four inches in width.

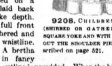

9208, CHILDREN'S DRESS (SHIRRED OR GATHERED TO A SQUARE YOKE AND WITH OR WITHOUT THE SHOULDER PIECES). Described on page 521.

9203, GIRLS' BOX-PLAITED COSTUME (CONSISTING OF A JACKET, CLOSED TO THE NECK WITH TURN-DOWN COLLAR, OR OPEN NECK AND FLAT FACING, AND WORN WITH OR WITHOUT A BLOUSE OR SHIRT-WAIST; AND A FIVE-GORED SKIRT ATTACHED TO THE UNDERBODY OR A BELT; FOR WEAR WITH PETTICOATS, BLOOMERS OR KNICKERBOCKERS; SOMETIMES CALLED THE "BUSTER BROWN" COSTUME). Described on this page.

9203—GIRLS' BOX-PLAITED COSTUME. Illustrated on this page.

Scotch cheviot is chosen to develop this stylish costume. The jacket is fitted by under-arm and shoulder seams, the fronts and back being box-plaited and confined at the waist by a belt. The neck edge is finished with a narrow band and turn-down collar, or the upper portions of the fronts may be cut away in a V and completed with a fancy collar-facing having extension front portions. The one-seamed sleeve is box-plaited at the wrist and finished with a band. The jacket closes in a double-breasted fashion. The skirt, which may be finished with a belt or attached to the underwaist, is a five-gored model with fulness disposed in box plaits. The underwaist is fitted by the usual seams and fastens down the back with buttons and buttonholes.

Flannel, serge, cheviot, tweed, covert cloth, brilliantine, homespun, duck, piqué or linen may be used to develop this design.

Girls' box-plaited costume 9203 is in nine sizes, from six to fourteen years, price 15 cents. The nine-year size requires six yards of material twenty-seven inches wide; four yards forty-four inches, or three yards fifty-four inches wide.

9208 — CHILDREN'S DRESS. Illustrated on page 520.

Sheer white lawn trimmed with lace edging and insertion is used for this dainty dress. The upper edges of the back and front of the material are shirred or gathered and attached to the lower edges of the yoke, the latter being fitted by shoulder seams. Fancy shoulder pieces are supplied, but may be omitted. The one-seamed bishop sleeve is completed by a band, and a standing collar finishes the neck edge.

Nainsook, chambray, lawn, China silk, madras and linen, flannel, cashmere, lansdowne, nun's-

9182, CHILDREN'S SHIRRED DRESS (WITH STRAIGHT LOWER EDGE AND INVERTED BOX-PLAITED FULNESS UNDER THE ARM; SOMETIMES CALLED THE BISHOP, VASSAR OR PEASANT DRESS). Described on this page.

veiling or challis may be used to develop this design, with lace, embroidery, ribbon or beading for decoration.

Children's dress 9208 is in seven sizes, from six months to six years, price 10 cents. The five-year size requires three and seven-eighth yards of material twenty-two inches wide; two and one-half yards of material thirty-six inches wide, or two yards of material which measures forty-four inches in width, with four and one-eighth yards of Valenciennes lace edging, two and seven-eighth yards of wide lace insertion for the collar, the wristband, etc., and two and three-eighth yards of narrow lace insertion to trim the free edges of the shoulder pieces.

9206. LITTLE GIRLS' DRESS (WITH OR WITHOUT THE POMPADOUR YOKE OR BERTHA AND WITH BISHOP OR FULL-LENGTH OR SHORT PUFF SLEEVES AND AN ATTACHED STRAIGHT SKIRT). Described on this page.

9182—CHILDREN'S SHIRRED DRESS. Illustrated on this page.

This dainty little dress is made of sheer white nainsook and is trimmed with lace edging. It is fitted by shoulder seams, the fulness under the arms being laid in inverted box plaits. The fulness at the neck edge of the dress is disposed in shirring, which is discontinued at yoke depth. A yoke-facing is attached to the underside of the garment. The sleeve is a one-seamed model shirred to cuff depth, and a stay is attached to the underside.

Nainsook, dimity, batiste, lawn, percale, chambray, linen, China silk, challis, lansdowne or nun's-veiling may be used to develop this design.

A figure view on page 515 shows a different development.

Children's dress 9182 is in seven sizes, from six months to six years, price 10 cents. The five-year size requires four and three-eighth yards of material twenty-two inches wide; two and five-eighth yards of thirty-six-inch material, or two and one-quarter yards forty-four inches wide. As represented, the dress will require two yards of embroidered flouncing, with one yard of thirty-six-inch plain lawn for the sleeves and the shirring stays.

9206—LITTLE GIRLS' DRESS. Illustrated on this page.

This pretty dress, as shown in the large front view, is made of figured lawn and trimmed with white swiss embroidery and insertion. The waist is mounted on a body lining, the latter being faced to form a Pompadour yoke, to which the full front and backs are gathered and the lower edges shirred. A bertha portion is provided, but may be omitted, and the neck edge is finished with

9235, GIRLS' DRESS (WITH HIGH OR ROUND NECK AND BISHOP OR PUFF SLEEVES, WITH OR WITHOUT THE BERTHA; AND AN ATTACHED THREE-PIECE SKIRT TUCKED AT THE LOWER PART). Described on page 522.

ALL STANDARD PATTERNS 5, 10 OR 15 CENTS—NONE HIGHER.

a standing collar unless the open neck be preferred. Two styles of sleeve are given: one is a one-seamed bishop model, and the other consists of a puffed section mounted on a two-seamed, close-fitting lining. When the short puffed sleeve is desired the lower part of the lining is cut away. The full straight skirt is gathered to the lower edge of the body portions.

Nainsook, dimity, lawn, swiss, China silk, challis, chambray or linen may be used to develop this design.

Little girls' dress 9206 is in eight sizes, from two to nine years, price 10 cents. The five-year size requires, as in high neck view, four and three-quarter yards of twenty-two-inch material, or three and one-quarter yards thirty-six inches wide, or two and five-eighth yards forty-four inches wide, with six and one-eighth yards of insertion to trim. As in the square-neck view, the dress will require four and one-eighth yards of material twenty-two inches wide, three yards thirty-six inches, or two and five-eighth yards forty-four inches wide, with four and one-half yards of insertion to trim the bertha, skirt, etc.

9235—GIRLS' DRESS. Illustrated on page 521.

The pictured dress is made of white organdy and trimmed with lace and insertion. The waist is mounted on a fitted lining, faced to yoke depth back and front when the high-neck style is desired, otherwise the yoke-facing is omitted and the upper part of the lining is cut away to the round neck outline. The full backs are gathered at the upper edge and shirred at the lower one. The front is laid in a center box plait and four side plaits at the upper edge, and is shirred at the waistline. A fancy bertha portion may outline the upper edge. Two styles of sleeve are provided: one is a bishop model finished by a band cuff, the other is a short puffed sleeve. The skirt is in three pieces, the front portion being plaited and attached to the full side portions. The latter are tucked at the lower part and are gathered to the lower edges of the body portions.

Cashmere, nun's-veiling, China silk, dimity, organdy, madras, linen, lawn or challis may be used to develop this design, with lace, embroidery, beading, ribbon or contrasting materials for trimming.

Girls' dress 9235 is in nine sizes, from five to thirteen years, price 15 cents. The nine-year size requires five and one-half yards of material twenty-seven inches wide, four and five-eighth yards thirty-six inches wide, or three and one-half yards of material forty-four inches wide. As represented in back view, it will require four and one-eighth yards of thirty-six inch lawn, with three and

one-quarter yards of lace edging and three and one-eighth yards of insertion to trim, or, four and three-quarter yards of lace insertion to trim, as in front view.

9193, MISSES' AND GIRLS' BLOUSE (WITH RUSSIAN CLOSING). Described on this page.

9239—MISSES' PLAITED SEVEN-GORED SKIRT. Illustrated on this page.

This stylish skirt is made of gray drap d'été. It is a seven-gored model, consisting of a front gore, two side-

9205, LITTLE GIRLS' OR BOYS' BOX-PLAITED DRESS WITH FRONT YOKE (WITH BODY AND SKIRT IN ONE AND WITH OR WITHOUT THE BELT; FOR WEAR WITH PETTICOATS, KNICKERBOCKERS OR BLOOMERS). Described on page 523.

front, two side and two back gores, the latter united by a center-back seam. The fulness of material at the upper part of skirt is disposed in plaits, which may be stitched down to any yoke depth. The lower edge of the garment is finished with a hem or facing, and a narrow belt completes the upper edge, the placket closing occurring in the back.

Serge, cheviot, tweed, brilliantine, lady's-cloth, taffeta, pongee, linen, duck or madras may be used to develop this design.

Misses' plaited seven-gored skirt 9239 is in five sizes, from thirteen to seventeen years, price 15 cents. The fifteen-year size requires seven yards of material which is twenty-two inches wide, six and three-quarter yards thirty-six inches wide, or four and three-eighth yards of material measuring forty-four inches in width.

9193—MISSES' AND GIRLS' BLOUSE. Illustrated on this page.

This stylish blouse is made of white linen and trimmed with blue linen braid. It is fitted by under-arm and shoulder seams, and the lower edge is finished with a casing and draw-string. The sleeve is a one-seamed model completed by a band cuff. The neck is finished with a standing

9239, MISSES' PLAITED SEVEN-GORED SKIRT (IN DOUBLE BOX-PLAIT EFFECT, WITH THE PLAITS STITCHED TO ANY YOKE DEPTH). Described on this page.

collar and the closing is effected along the left side with hooks and eyes or buttons and buttonholes.

Linen, pongee, duck, chambray, taffeta, serge, brilliantine, piqué or flannel may be used to develop this design.

9192, INFANTS' AND CHILDREN'S SACK (WITH BISHOP OR TWO-SEAMED SLEEVES, AND WITH OR WITHOUT THE BACK STRAP). Described on this page.

Misses' and girls' blouse **9193** is in seven sizes, from four to sixteen years, price 10 cents. The fourteen-year size requires two and five-eighths yards of material twenty-seven inches wide, one and three-quarter yards forty-

9233, LITTLE BOYS' APRON (WITH BOX-PLAITED FRONT). Described on this page.

four inches, or one and one-half yards of material which measures fifty-four inches in width, with one and one-half yards of wide braid and three yards of narrow braid to trim.

*

9205—LITTLE GIRLS' OR BOYS' BOX-PLAITED DRESS WITH FRONT YOKE. Illustrated on page 522.

This pretty little dress is made of blue linen and is fitted by under-arm and shoulder seams, the backs and front being box-plaited and the upper edge of the front attached to the lower edge of a yoke portion. A belt confines the dress at the waistline. The sleeve is a one-seamed bishop model gathered at the upper and lower edges and completed by a band cuff.

Linen, dimity, madras, chambray, China silk, flannel, cashmere or lansdowne may be used to develop this design.

Little girls' or boys' box-plaited dress **9205** is in nine sizes, from one to nine years, price 10 cents. The five-year size requires two and three-quarter yards of material measuring thirty-six inches in width.

*

9192—INFANTS' AND CHILDREN'S SACK. Illustrated on this page.

This dainty little sack is made of rose-pink French flannel and decorated with cat-stitching in floss silk.

The garment is fitted by under-arm and shoulder seams, and the back is laid in two box plaits, which may hang loose or be confined at the waistline by a strap portion. Two styles of sleeve are provided: a two-seamed coat sleeve, and a bishop model completed with a band cuff. A one-piece turn-down collar finishes the neck edge. A charming development of the little garment may be effected by using Japanese silk of a delicate light blue or rose color, and decorating the collar and small cuffs with a dainty design of rosebuds and leaves in hand embroidery.

Flannel, cashmere, bengaline silk, lady's-cloth, lansdowne, wadded China silk or flannelette may be used to effectively develop this design, with lace embroidery, insertion, ribbon or ruching for appropriate trimming.

Infants' and children's sack **9192** is in five sizes; infants, one, three, five and seven years, price 10 cents. The infants' size requires one and five-eighth yards of material twenty-seven inches wide, or seven-eighth yard forty-four inches.

*

9233—LITTLE BOYS' APRON. Illustrated on this page.

This neat little apron is made of checked gingham and trimmed with narrow embroidered edging. The garment is fitted by under-arm and shoulder seams. The front is laid in three box plaits and the sleeve is a bishop model completed by a band cuff. A two-piece turn-down collar finishes the neck edge, and the backs of the apron may be confined at the waistline by belt straps.

Gingham, brown holland, blue jean, madras, chambray or cambric may be used to develop this design.

Little boys' apron **9233** is in four sizes, from one to four years, price 10 cents. The three-year size requires two and one-half yards of material twenty-seven inches wide, or one and seven-eighths yards of material which is thirty-six inches wide, with one and one-quarter yards of narrow embroidered edging to trim the collar.

*

9187—GIRLS' APRON. Illustrated on this page.

This pretty apron is made of white cambric and trimmed with embroidered edging and insertion. The gabrielle front is united to the skirt portions, and the latter are gathered at the upper edges and finished with belt pieces. A band finishes the upper edge of the front and trimming bands are attached to the side edges of the front, passing over the shoulders and fastening to the belt in the back. Shoulder pieces are provided, and apron strings are attached to the ends of the belt.

Cambric, long-cloth, muslin, lawn, linen, dimity, batiste, chambray or percale may be used to develop this design.

9187, GIRLS' APRON (WITH GABRIELLE FRONT AND WITH OR WITHOUT THE SHOULDER PIECES). Described on this page.

A figure view on page 515 shows a different development. Girls' apron 9187 is in five sizes, from four to twelve years, price 10 cents. The eight-year size requires two and one-quarter yards of material thirty-six inches wide, with four and five-eighth yards of embroidered insertion and one and seven-eighth yards of embroidered edging.

9190 — MISSES' CORSET-COVER.
Illustrated on this page.

This pretty corset-cover is made of nainsook and trimmed with lace edging, beading and narrow washable satin ribbon. It is fitted by under-arm and tiny shoulder seams, the upper edges of the fronts being gathered and finished with a band of insertion or beading. The fulness at the waistline is regulated by a casing attached to the underside of the garment, and by draw-strings. Shield sleeves are provided, and the corset-cover closes down the center of the front.

Nainsook, dimity, batiste, lawn, long-cloth, linen, cambric or China silk may be used to develop this design.

9231. INFANTS' AND CHILDREN'S CAP (WITH OR WITHOUT THE TURN-BACK SECTION; SOMETIMES CALLED THE PEASANT BONNET). Described on this page.

9190. MISSES' CORSET-COVER (WITH OR WITHOUT THE SHIELD SLEEVES). Described on this page.

Misses' corset-cover 9190 is in five sizes, from thirteen to seventeen years, price 10 cents. The fifteen-year size requires one and one-eighth yards of material thirty-six inches wide, with three and three-eighth yards of lace edging, two and one-fourth yards of lace beading, and three and three-quarter yards of narrow satin ribbon to trim.

9231—INFANTS' AND CHILDREN'S CAP. Illustrated on this page.

This pretty little cap is made of white nainsook with frilling of Valenciennes lace edging. It consists of a round crown piece to which the gathered portion is attached. The turn-back section provided may be omitted. Strings are attached to the sides of the cap, which is sometimes called the peasant bonnet.

Taffeta silk, bengaline, peau de soie, nainsook, lawn, all-over lace or embroidery may be used to develop this design, with lace, embroidery, beading or ribbon to trim. The turn-back portion may be prettily decorated with hand-embroidery if desired, also the little round crown piece. Ribbons may be used for the tie strings, or strips of the bonnet material may be hemstitched for this purpose. An extremely pretty bonnet for a year-old baby is made by this model of handkerchief linen, the crown piece and turn-back portion being hand-worked in a design of tiny field daisies in eyelet embroidery. Pale-blue silk

forms the lining, which may be removed when it is necessary to launder the outer part of the cap.

Infants' and children's cap 9231 is in three sizes, for infants, one and three years, price 10 cents. The infants' size requires for cap with revers, one-half yard of material twenty-two to thirty-six inches wide, with one and three-quarter yards of lace edging; for cap without revers it requires one-half yard of material twenty-two to thirty-six inches wide. As represented in the first view the cap will require three-eighth yard of tucked lawn flouncing, with one-half yard of thirty-six-inch plain lawn for the strings and one and one-eighth yards of lace edging to trim.

9227—INFANTS' SHIRRED CLOAK WITH YOKE. Illustrated on this page.

This dainty little cloak for an infant as here pictured is made of cream-white bengaline and is trimmed with embroidery. To the lower edge of the yoke, that is fitted by shoulder seams, the back and fronts, which are united by under-arm seams and have the fulness at the upper edge being disposed in clusters of shirring, are attached. The sleeve is a one-seamed model completed by a fancy turn-up cuff. The neck edge may be finished with or without the fancy turn-down collar.

Cashmere, lansdowne, bengaline silk, peau de soie, lady's-cloth, drap d'été or pongee may be used to develop this design. Lace, insertion, embroidery, Tom Thumb fringe, ruching of ribbon or rows of narrow ribbon or braid may be used for the trimming of the garment. For the first warm days of spring this little coat would be very pretty made of white albatross, the collar and cuffs being of white taffeta edged with a frill of Valenciennes lace.

Infants' shirred cloak 9227 is in one size, price 10 cents. It requires four and three-quarter yards of material twenty-two inches wide; three and one-eighth yards thirty-six inches, or two and one-half yards forty-four inches wide.

9222—BOYS' RUSSIAN SUIT. Illustrated on page 525.

This stylish little suit as shown in one front view is made of white piqué and trimmed with embroidered edging and insertion. In the two other views it is made of dark-red linen, with a shield of white linen. The blouse is fitted by under-arm and shoulder seams; the sailor sleeve has the fulness at the wrist disposed in three box plaits and stitched to cuff depth. The upper portions of the fronts are cut away in a V, and a shield finished at the upper edge with a band collar is worn. The large sailor collar may be cut with round or square corners, and a belt confines the blouse at the waistline. The knickerbockers are fitted by center-front and back seams, also inside leg seams, and are finished at the lower edge of each leg with a casing run with elastic. The knickerbockers are made without a fly closing.

Serge, brilliantine, cheviot, flannel, piqué, duck or linen may be used to develop this design, with embroidery,

9227. INFANTS' SHIRRED CLOAK WITH YOKE (WITH OR WITHOUT THE COLLAR OR CUFFS). Described on this page.

heavy Irish or Arabian lace, braid or stitching to trim. This is a design which may be simply developed in wash materials for morning wear, or in velveteen, white corduroy, piqué, serge or bengaline for afternoon wear, and may then be handsomely trimmed. A handsome suit is made of light-blue lady's-cloth with a large collar of white linen and a shield of the same material. The collar is edged with deep Irish embroidery, and on the shield is worked the initials of the child, above an eight-pointed star, pale-blue silk being used. With the suit is worn a white leather belt held by an oval pearl buckle. In each of the corners of the white linen collar is worked a star to match that on the shield.

Figure views presented on pages 513 and 515 show different developments of this attractive model.

Boys' Russian suit **9222** is in seven sizes, from two to eight years, price 15 cents. The five-year size requires four and one-quarter yards of material twenty-seven inches wide; three and three-eighth yards thirty-six inches, or two and one-half yards forty-four inches, with, as in first front view, two and five-eighth yards of embroidered edging, and two and three-eighth yards of insertion to trim the large sailor collar and shield.

9223—BOYS' SUIT. Illustrated on this page.

Blue flannel is the material used to make this jaunty little suit as pictured in two of the views, while in the other one it is made of white linen, with an emblem worked in dark blue and red on the shield. Small pearl buttons close the front of the blouse. The sailor blouse is fitted by under-arm and shoulder seams; the neck may be made open, and the blouse worn with the shield, or the fronts may be made close to the throat and finished with a narrow neckband, for Eton or other linen collar. Either the box-plaited or sailor sleeve model may be used, and the lower edge of the blouse is finished with a casing and draw-string. The knickerbockers are fitted by center-front, center-back and inside leg seams, the lower edge of each leg being finished with a casing and elastic, and the garment may be made with or without a fly, according to the age of the boy for whom the suit is intended.

Flannel, serge, cheviot, tweed, piqué, duck or linen may be used to develop this design, with braid, stitching or embroidered emblems for the decoration of the suit.

Boys' suit **9223** is in eight sizes, from three to ten years, price 15 cents. The eight-year size requires four and one-quarter yards of material which is twenty-seven inches in width, or two and one-eighth yards fifty-four inches wide.

9211—MEN'S NEGLIGEE SHIRT. Illustrated on this page.

The shirt depicted in this illustration is made of striped black-and-white flannel and is fitted by under-arm and shoulder seams. The upper edge of the back is gathered

9222. BOYS' RUSSIAN SUIT (CONSISTING OF A BLOUSE WITH SHIELD AND A SAILOR COLLAR WITH ENDS EXTENDING TO THE LOWER EDGE OR JUST BELOW THE WAISTLINE; AND KNICKERBOCKERS WITHOUT A FLY). Described on page 524.

9223. BOYS' SUIT (CONSISTING OF A SAILOR BLOUSE WITH OPEN NECK, SAILOR COLLAR AND REMOVABLE SHIELD, OR WITH HIGH NECK AND BAND COLLAR OR NECKBAND FOR ETON OR OTHER LINEN COLLAR, AND WITH BOX-PLAITED OR SAILOR SLEEVES; AND KNICKERBOCKERS WITH OR WITHOUT A FLY). Described on this page.

to the lower edge of a square yoke. The sleeve is smoothly inserted in the armhole and may be finished with a permanent or detachable cuff. A narrow band finishes the neck edge and the collar provided is a one-piece turn-down model. A pocket with shaped lap may be attached to the left side of the shirt front, and the closing of the garment may be made in regulation or coat style.

Madras, chambray, flannel, pongee, Japanese silk, shirting muslin or linen may be used to develop this design.

Men's shirt **9211** is in eight sizes, from thirty-two to forty-six inches breast measure, price 15 cents. Each breast measure has two neck measures, varying one-half inch. The thirty-eight-inch breast size, corresponding to the fifteen and one-half, or sixteen-inch neck size, requires four and one-quarter yards of twenty-seven-inch material or three and three-eighth yards thirty-six inches, with three-eighth yard of thirty-six-inch linen for detachable cuffs.

9211. MEN'S NEGLIGEE SHIRT (WITH BOX-PLAIT OR LAP CLOSING IN REGULATION OR COAT STYLE AND WITH NECKBAND OR TURN-DOWN COLLAR AND WRISTBANDS OR PERMANENT OR DETACHABLE CUFFS). Described on this page.

POINTS ON DRESSMAKING

FINISHING THE FRONTS OF SHIRT-WAISTS

SHIRT-WAISTS have proven such useful garments that there seems little likelihood that they will ever be discarded. Designers find it necessary to exercise great ingenuity in order to create variations of style in a garment whose principal claim to favor is its simplicity. Wide plaits and narrow tucks and either real or simulated box plaits placed in various positions on the waist afford some variety, and different ways of arranging the front closing give further opportunity for originality. At illustrations I and II, the right and left sides of shirt-waist 8983 are shown. It will be found that the label on the pattern reads "cutting off the front edge of the left outside front at the double perforations top and bottom." This is because the closing is not made exactly at the center front, but the right side laps across and fastens to the left. Both sides of the front should be cut at the same time, doubling the material for this purpose, and the tucks or plaits should be arranged in place before the left front is trimmed away. In this model, as in most that have wide plaits, single-width material is not wide enough to cut the front without piecing, and when this is necessary, always make the joining where it may be concealed under a plait. In this instance the material was too narrow to cut the full width of the front, but the joining, if made according to the width of the material, allowing it to extend as far as it would reach, would make the seam come where it would show, so the cutting should be arranged that the joining may be concealed under a plait. In this case the plaits turn toward the back, so the material should be cut down straight, a seam beyond the last row of perforations that indicate the sewing line of the last plait. If the plaits turned toward the front, the seam should have been made at the next to the last row of perforations, bringing the seam at the front edge instead of the back edge of the sewing line of the plait. The remainder of the pattern of the front should be cut from the material, allowing a seam on the side that is to join the front; stitch this seam and press it to one side so it will be included *inside* the plait when that is stitched. This piecing as well as the way of cutting the

piece from the left side of the front may be seen at illustration I, where an inside view of this front portion is shown. The large simulated box plait at the center front is made on the right side and the closing is effected by a fly, in which buttonholes are worked, as seen at illustration II. The piece that is cut off the left front can be used to make this fly, which should be cut two and three-quarter inches wide. Turn in a seam at each side and double the strip lengthwise through the center. Baste the fold edge of the two turned-in edges together and then to the right front of the waist in such a position that the same row of stitching that forms the first plait will hold the fly as well. Buttonholes are to be worked in the fly and the left front is to be turned under for a hem, as directed in the pattern label, and buttons are to be sewed to it to correspond, in closing, with the buttonholes worked in the fly.

Shirt-waists are most frequently made unlined, though a lining is provided in most patterns. A silk waist would, perhaps, be better lined, especially if for wear in cool weather, both for warmth and because the lining will protect the silk from strain and make it wear longer. Illustration III shows the front of a lining in state of preparation. The lining should be basted and fitted, any necessary alterations made and the under-arm seams should be stitched. A seam three-eighths of an inch is allowed on each front edge. In fitting bring the fronts together and pin them three-eighths of an inch back of the raw edges, forming a seam toward the outside. Alteration may be made on this front seam also if necessary, and it should be marked to form a corrected front line and the edge trimmed to leave only a seam beyond this line. Cut a straight piece of the lining two inches wide and a trifle longer than the front edge of the lining, to serve as

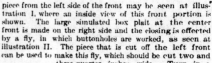

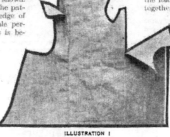

ILLUSTRATION I

ILLUSTRATION II

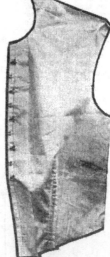

ILLUSTRATION III

8983

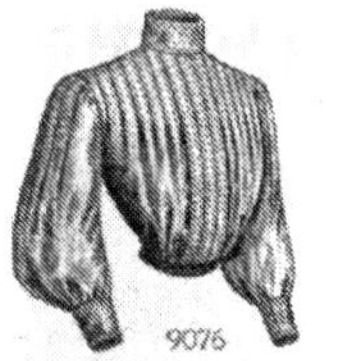

9076

9141

a facing for each side of the front. Place a piece on the outside of the lining with one edge even with the edge of the front, and stitch a seam three-eighths of an inch back from the edge; turn the facing over, making the fold come just at the seam, place a row of stitching one-eighth of an inch back of the edge and make a second row three-eighths of an inch back of the first. Make a second row of stitching three-eighths of an inch beyond the first row at each of the seams, notch the edges that extend beyond the stitching, and into each of the casings thus formed run a piece of whale or featherbone and tack it in place, as seen in the dart seam at illustration V. Place a bone in the casing made at each of the front edges, allowing it to reach to about the same height as the bone in the dart seam. Spread the back part of each hook and sew them on, alternating a hook and an eye, as seen in illustration III. Place the hooks well inside the edge and sew through the two rings at the back and also around the hook end, sewing this to the row of stitching near the edge. Sew completely through, allowing the stitches to show on the outside of the lining. Be sure to place the bone in the front before sewing the hooks and eyes on the lower part of the fronts. Observe care in sewing the hooks and eyes on the second side of the front that they shall be in exactly corresponding positions to those sewed to the first side. Turn under a seam at the edge of the facing piece and hem it over to the first row of stitching, covering the sewed parts of the hooks and eyes, as seen at illustration IV.

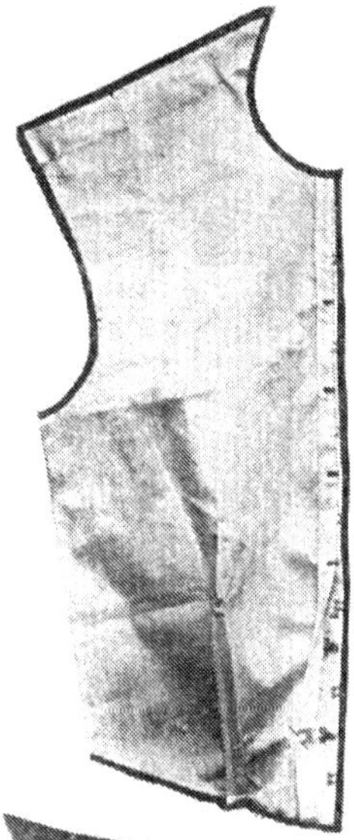

The underarm seam of the outside should be basted separately from the lining, but the shoulder seams are usually included in the same seam with those of the lining. If any alterations have been made at these seams in fitting the lining corresponding alterations must be made in the seams of the outer waist.

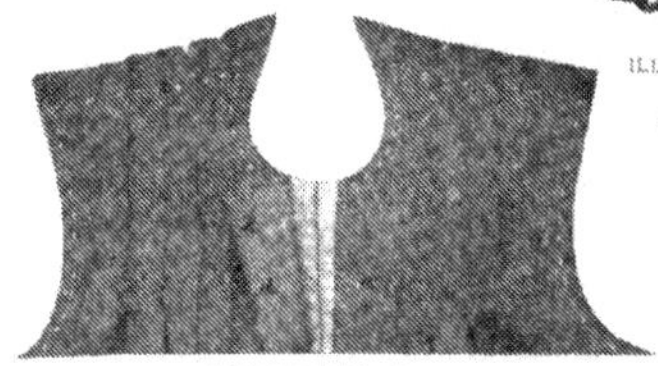

At illustration V is shown the way to close the outerwaist parts when the lining is used. Pattern 9076 was employed for the waist shown, but the method is always practically the same in waists of this description. The outside is placed on the lining with the center front of the outside (which in this case is the center of the middle box plait) at the edge of the lining. The outer waist is basted to the lining at the neck and the armholes only. The left outer front is placed on the left lining front in such a way that the tucks or plaits on both front portions shall correspond when the waist is fastened. This must be ascertained by hooking the lining at the front and bringing the lap on the right outside part over the left until the parts correspond; the left outer front is then pinned to the lining in this position and is basted to it at the neck and armholes, as was the right side. Small hooks should

be sewed to the right front and buttonholed loops to correspond worked on the left front; or a fly with buttonholes may be attached to the right front, as previously described, and buttons sewed to the left.

It is generally preferable to finish the neck of a shirt-waist with a neckband and make the collar detachable, that different collars and stocks may be worn with the same waist. The sleeves should be basted into the waist in an ordinary seam, and when they are stitched, a bias strip of lining about an inch and one-quarter wide should have one edge included in the seam, then be turned over and hemmed as a binding to cover the raw edges of the armhole seam.

A shirt-waist differing somewhat in style from either of these just described was used for illustration VI. The pattern is 9141 and the waist is intended to be worn with a chemisette and standing collar of either the same or a contrasting material and color; white piqué, tucked lawn and all-over embroideries are most used for this purpose. This waist, like either of the others, may be made with or without the lining. The fronts should be prepared as previously described, the only variation being the turned-over collar. For this it is necessary to cut two portions of the waist material and one of crinoline. Baste the crinoline and one section of the collar together, holding the crinoline uppermost. Baste these in a seam to the neck of the waist with the corresponding notches together. Turn over a seam all around the collar and turn under a seam around the remaining collar piece or facing and baste it to that already attached to the waist, easing it a little that it may not draw when the collar turns over. Hem it by hand to the neck of the waist and finish around the edges with one or more rows of stitching. The manner of attaching this collar and its facing is demonstrated at illustration VI.

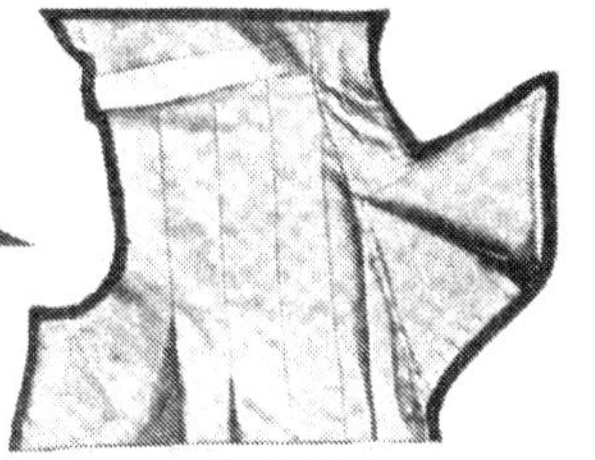

ILLUSTRATION IV

ILLUSTRATION V

ILLUSTRATION VI

In waists that have a number of plaits in the front, the fulness when drawn together at the waist is apt to be clumsy, and it is advisable to cut it off entirely below the desired waistline in the front and sew a tab-like piece of single material to it, or cut it away at the full part and finish with some of the cut-away portion as described in THE DESIGNER for March, 1904. The part that extends below the waistline does not usually have sufficient flare to fit smoothly over the hips, and it is necessary to slash it several times at the back and sides. The edges may be hemmed or, if the material is thick, they should be bound with seam-binding ribbon.

FOREWORDS REGARDING

By LAURA R. SEIPLE

TRULY this is an artistic age in the fashion line. When the woman of fashion spends as much time in selecting her footwear as she does her head-gear, then there is really nothing left to be said other than that her sense of sartorial-art must be expressed from the top of her pretty head to the sole of her dainty foot.

There are shoes with hose to match for every occasion. Perhaps the most noticeable change in street shoes is represented in the low-cut boot which is made precisely on the lines of a man's heavy shoe. The broad, flat extension sole, the low heel, the six big buttons and the leather employed in these mannish shoes show marked similarity to the stock in the men's department. For long walks, shopping and general utility there can be nothing more satisfactory than these soft calfskin boots; besides they are smart in general appearance on account of their broad, shapely last and low-cut top. Another smart new boot has a decidedly pointed toe, a Spanish heel, a plain patent-leather vamp and a glove-kid top, or it may be made to order with a suède top to match the gown. Sometimes the gown material is used instead of the suède. For general street wear a low shoe of calfskin with military heel and broad silk lace is quite the smartest sort. With the low-cuts sepa-

rate uppers or spats add chic appearance to any pair of feet. White broadcloth spats with large pearl buttons are among the newest styles. Shepherd's-plaid uppers are worn with a skirt of the same material.

There are many entirely new styles in ties. Black suède with cut-steel trimmings, brown suède with bronze nail-heads, pale-blue and pale-pink kid decorated with jet extending to the tip of the toe are shown among the representative styles. Slippers of two-tone kid are attracting much attention. White kid pumps with heel and top binding of tan, green, red, blue or black afford possibilities for handsome hose. These of course are for house wear.

Very novel are the patent-leather slippers having an etched design across the toe. These may be worn in the drawing-room or street, but on going out it is advisable to slip on a pair of uppers owing to the extremely low cut of the last. French heels have not the popularity to-day that they enjoyed a few months past. The Spanish heel, which is lower than the military but carries out the same shape, is the coming heel for both boots and ties.

Never was hosiery more tempting. Black grounds with dainty stripes or figures are displayed in great profusion. Not many drop-stitch effects are in evidence up

BLACK SUÈDE TIES WITH STEEL DECORATION; BRONZE KID SANDALS WITH GOLD BEADING; WHITE KID SLIPPERS WITH COLORED HEELS AND BINDING; PATENT-LEATHER DANCING-PUMPS, AND PATENT-LEATHER SLIPPERS WITH ETCHED TOES

FASHIONS AND FABRICS

to the present time, but there are some effective new thick-and-thin weaves in silk and silk-and-lisle simulating plaid. White and light-colored fishnet is a new weave that is bound to become a favorite. The mesh is very thin and open but made of heavy thread resembling twine, which fact insures it against tearing. Black-and-white embroidery in stripe effects and black with colored-silk feet may be counted among the staples of the year. Hosiery with black-lace medallions and insertion are recommended to go with dancing-pumps.

With all these attractive styles for milady dainty's pretty foot there are hosts of charming new fabrics for her new spring gowns as well. Crêpe soleil expresses a happy combination of crêpe de Chine and silk mousseline, bringing with it the soft, crêpy effect of the former and the width of the latter, making a practical combination which can be had at reasonable cost. Forty-four inches is the width generally shown in crêpe soleil, and the advantages it holds over crêpe de Chine are many. Another very beautiful new fabric is called chameleon crêpe. This also comes in wide measurements and is similar to soleil, the only difference being in the more pronounced crêpe effect. The colorings are exquisite, as the name implies. Under certain lights it sheds the softest rose-pink, then again a silvery green or lilac. However, there are always three or four distinct color combinations to the piece; different combinations of

course are worked in up each length. Chiffon is treated in the same manner, and when made over a foundation of deep-toned satin the effect is superb. Pompadour chiffon is clamoring for recognition in the world of fashion once more after a lapse of only a few months, and shows great roses in softest tints standing out against a pale foundation of a contrasting shade.

Vodka, that charming new amber tone, is shown in crêpes and silks and is almost certain to become the popular yellow of the season. Pastel shades have returned in all the new materials for both evening and street. Chiffon velvet in pastel blue, green and lilac is advanced as the choicest fabric for the first spring costume-suit.

Paris promises a revival of louisine to be followed by warp-printed taffetas and foulards in stripes and Jacquard effects. Just how true the prediction may be can only be judged by the number of exquisite models in these materials that have made their way here at this early day.

The most fashionable type of morning utility skirt is made to clear the ground by three inches, while dressy afternoon gowns intended for street wear may also escape the ground by at least one inch. For paying formal calls, or other formal daytime events, the long round skirt is the correct thing. For morning wear the tailor frock pure and simple has a greater vogue than for several seasons past, and the accepted model is the long coat with its severe lines.

MANNISH CALFSKIN SHOES; PATENT-LEATHER LOW SHOES; DRESS SHOES OF GLOVE KID AND PATENT-LEATHER; AND WHITE BROADCLOTH SPATS WORN WITH LOW SHOES HAVING ETCHED DESIGN ON TOE

BETWEEN-SEASONS MILLINERY

ON THE Front Cover Page of this number of THE DESIGNER appears an extremely stylish hat on the Louis shape, made of black-and-white French chip. It is simply trimmed with *choux* of black-and-white malines and with folds of black velvet.

The hat at the left of page 489 is made of light-blue panne velvet, the crown is concealed by a draping of black velvet, and a cluster of Parma violets with their foliage form a pompon at the right side.

The hat at the right is a "Corday" model of golden-brown taffeta, plaitings and folds of the taffeta being the only trimming.

At the left of page 490 is shown a wide-brimmed hat of black velvet. The brim is outlined by a silver cord and the crown encircled by a ruche of white-and-silver brocaded ribbon; an ostrich plume shading from white to deep gray trims the left side.

At the right of the same page is an effective hat of dark blue-and-white novelty straw, the decoration consisting of folds and drapery of blue malines and a long blue ostrich plume held by a cut-steel ornament.

The stylish hat at the left of page 491 is a brown-and-écru Japanese straw and is trimmed with brown ostrich tips. It has a "Tam" crown and a picturesquely curved brim, and is what might be termed a dressy "shirt-waist" hat.

The second hat on the same page is a handsome model of black French chip. White malines and glossy black plumes form the only trimming.

On page 496 appears a hat of écru Panama straw, the decoration of which consists of a wide band of brown velvet about the crown, and ostrich plumes shading from dark brown to orange at the tips.

At the head of this page are presented four practical, stylish and up-to-date models, which illustrate some of the shapes that will be in vogue with the coming of warm weather. The first, at the left, is a *chic* little toque of black straw, the brim being made of rows of the straw fluted and edged with a narrow rim of white straw, this giving an odd and attractive "magpie" effect, which is carried out by the blackbird which is placed a little to the left of the front, and which has a touch of white and orange in his plumage. The left side is further decorated with overlapping loops of deep orange-colored velvet ribbon.

The simple and girlish-looking hat next displayed is a wide-brimmed black leghorn, veiled with malines, and having the crown encircled with a full wreath of lavender orchids and pale-pink roses.

The third hat is a pearl-gray Tuscan straw, its only trimming being soft white ostrich plumes arranged in wreath fashion about the crown and curling over the brim at the back.

The last hat in the group is made of light-blue chiffon and black straw braid, and is of novel shaping. Small blue ostrich tips and jet ornaments supply the trimming.

The six hats shown in color on page 531 are all handsome for between-seasons wear. The first is made of pale-yellow straw and pale-pink Liberty satin, arranged in wheel-like pattern to form a turban, the only trimming being the drooping aigret at the left side.

The second hat is a picturesque little affair of hunter's-green chiffon velvet, a flight of yellow birds with a faint suggestion of lavender at the tips of their wings trimming the right side.

No. 3 is a stylish toque of dark-red feathers on a buckram foundation, and is simply trimmed with black-and-crimson made quills and a gilt ornament.

No. 4 is a handsome hat of dark-blue velvet, the underside being faced with lighter blue. A huge coq plume is attached to the crown and spreads out on the brim, and on the underside of the brim is shirred a bandeau of light-green velvet.

No. 5 is a charming little hat of violet-colored chip, trimmed with a windmill ruche of orchid-colored taffeta. A huge bow of the taffeta is placed under the brim on the left side toward the back.

No. 6 is a small hat of bronze felt, trimmed with a ruche of brown velvet and a bird and aigret shading from deep orange to light yellow.

No 7, on page 532, is made of finely plaited tan chiffon on a wire foundation, and is trimmed with folds of deeper tan Liberty satin and a single long brown quill.

No. 8 is another "Corday" model of corded white mousseline de soie, the underside of the brim being faced with white embroidered mull, a ruffle of the same outlining its edge.

The compact toque, No. 9, is made of shirred red velvet, and is trimmed with a flat bow of velvet ribbon.

No. 10 is a small hat of pale-yellow satin straw, beautiful plumes of white coq feathers supplying the trimming.

No. 11 is a turban of blue-and-white straw, and is trimmed with blue velvet and blue-and-white wings.

No. 12 is a handsome hat of white chiffon stretched on a wire foundation, the brim being bound with white velvet and appliquéd at intervals with motifs of Irish point. A long white plume is the only trimming employed.

No. 13 is a beautiful model of shirred tucks of pale-blue chiffon, a space in the center of the brim being left smooth and overlaid with black malines decorated with pale-yellow straw leaves. A pale-yellow ribbon rose and a jet butterfly trim the right side, and to the left side, under the brim toward the back, is caught a pale-blue ostrich plume by a jet buckle.

No. 14 is made of black and white paper straw and is trimmed with a cockade of the straw and a black quill.

BETWEEN-SEASONS MILLINERY. DESCRIBED ON PAGE 530

March, 1905

BETWEEN-SEASONS MILLINERY. DESCRIBED ON PAGE 530

A Between-Seasons Hat

By MARTHA KINSMAN

THE materials required for the pictured hat are seven yards of braid one and one-half inches wide, one yard of mousseline de soie, one and one-half yards of maline, seven and one-half yards of ribbon — four and one-half yards being of

COMPLETED HAT

a light shade and three yards of a darker shade—two fancy quills, one-eighth of a yard of velvet and one steel ornament. The braid used is of straw and maline plaited together.

The frame has the same measurements on both sides. To make it, commence with the head wire. Cut a piece twenty inches long, lap until it measures seventeen inches; fasten both ends securely with the tie wire. Measure and cut four pieces of wire about twenty-six inches in length, and measure and shape them to form the crown thus: about eight inches from one end of each wire make a decided bend-up; measure one inch for the height, then five and three-quarter inches across the top of the crown, then down one inch. The measurements are the same in all four wires. Fasten these wires to the head wire. The tip wire measures seventeen and one-quarter inches, and should next be fastened to the crown wires at equal spaces.

Tie all the intersecting wires together in the center of the crown. For the brim, bend all the outward wires out straight in front and sides and down in the back; then, beginning at the back and proceeding from the right around to the left side, measure the brim wires in the following order: One and one-half, one and one-half, one and three-quarter, two and one-quarter, two and one-half, two and one-quarter, two and three-quarter, and one and one-half inches. The brim wire measures twenty-eight inches. Beginning at the back and proceeding as before, fasten the brim wire to the outward wires to form the following spaces: Three and one-quarter, three and one-half, three and one-half, three and one-quarter, three and one-quarter, three and one-half, three and one-half, three and one-half, and three-quarter inches. Bend all the wires up to form the coronet. Next, beginning at the back, measure all the upward wires in the following order: Three, three, three and three-quarter, four and one-quarter, four and one-half, four and one-quarter, three and three-quarter, and three inches. The coronet wire measures thirty-two inches. Fasten the coronet wires to the upward wires to form the following spaces: Four and one-quarter, four, three and three-quarter, four, four, three and three-quarter, four, and four and one-quarter inches. The upward wires are fastened to the edge wire by giving them one twist around it, pinching firmly and cutting

FRAME

SIDE VIEW

BACK VIEW

off the superfluous wires. Bend the wires well forward and form a decided point in front. Add two extra wires between the brim and head wire, and two others between the brim and coronet wire. Also, add one extra brace wire between the front and side front wires and another between the side-front and side wires. Cut out the top of the crown and pinch down the wires.

The base and tip wires for the separate crown each measure nineteen inches. The height of the crown in front measures three inches; the side fronts, two and three-quarter inches; the side, side back and back, each two and one-half inches. The tip from front to back measures six and one-half inches; from side to side, four and one-half inches, and the diagonals each five and one-half inches. The frame is now ready for covering with chiffon or mousseline de soie, sewed on double to make a firm foundation.

For the facing cut the maline in lengthwise strips, four inches wide, fold in two folds, the second one one-quarter of an inch narrower than the first, and baste these folds in order to keep them even. Begin at brim and sew on folds, so that one overlaps the other; continue until the entire brim is covered. The sewing of the braid next claims our attention. For the crown, sew a plateau twelve inches in diameter; at the edge form a box plait two inches wide and sew it to the base of the crown in front. Allow the plateau to extend well out in a point in front, then pin it to the middle of the tip of the crown; form the extra fulness in two side plaits and sew to the crown, so they meet at the back as illustrated. Next sew one row of the braid to bind over the coronet wire; continue to sew the braid until the space between the coronet and crown is entirely covered. Do not sew the braid to the coronet, excepting the first row, but sew it free from the brim, then join it to the base of the crown.

The brim consists of shirred ribbon ornaments. The lightest shade of ribbon is divided into thirteen separate pieces, each twelve inches long. In each of these shirr two tucks one-quarter of an inch wide; the first one is made one inch from the edge and the second one inch from the first. Next cut lace wire in twenty-two pieces, each fourteen inches long. This allows two inches at each end. Run wire in outer tuck and draw it up to ten inches; join ends of wire by twisting; draw and tie sewing silk; the inside tuck should be allowed to puff out a little. Cut off corners of ribbon; gather and wind thread round wire. The thirteen light pieces finished, sew one of them to the coronet at the point directly in front and another one to the direct back. Five pieces are sewed to the right and six to the left side. The pieces should all incline toward front, as shown in illustration. The darker shade of ribbon is divided into nine pieces, which are made in the same way. These pieces are bent narrow, and are sewed on horizontally to cover the base of the light pieces.

The trimming is extremely simple. The fancy quills are sewed to the left side about five inches from the front. One quill is sewed outside and the other inside the coronet. A knot of velvet finishes the base of the quills and an ornament is sewed in position as illustrated. The lining is made and sewed in the usual way.

533

FASHIONABLE FRIVOLITIES

By LAURA R. SEIPLE

A FAR-SEEING designer has created and placed in the best shops many bewitching little frills and furbelows made of laces, chiffon and narrow ribbons wrought into daintiest jabot effects, cascades and plastrons. When the bodice to be made "like new" by these little accessories is to be worn for dressy afternoon functions as well as for evening, artificial flowers, mingled with filmy laces and soft chiffon plaitings, may be used to wonderful advantage.

A very fetching arrangement is made of one yard of eighteen-inch-wide English thread lace and four dozen button roses. Little festoon effects of roses fall over the arms and down one side of the front and a cluster of the same flowers finishes the draped front. The dainty affair has a ribbon foundation and may be transferred from one gown to another.

Great bunches of exquisite artificial flowers, roses, lilacs and wistaria with long stems and foliage are acknowledged par excellence for bodice garnishments. Ribbon and chiffon roses are also used for the same purpose, but not with the same result, for they crush easily and never look so natural as well-made muslin or velvet flowers.

The leg-o'-mutton sleeve of honorable lineage is

SHIELD BUCKLE

BODICE DECORATION

again the fashion—that is to say, for the upper portion of this particular part of the garment, let it be frock, bodice or coat; but for the lower treatment there are any number of fascinating modes to choose from. Perhaps the model extending just below the elbow and met by long mousquetaire gloves is enjoying the greatest favoritism. Many of the elbow sleeves might be termed fantastic, since they combine double and triple puffs held in place by rows of shirring or fine tucks, and are often finished with turned-back Louis cuffs disclosing a full frill of sheer lace. The elbow sleeve is really the picturesque novelty of the season and is sure of continued prosperity.

Morning frocks and waists have long sleeves, made attractive to the eye by separate cuffs which may be heavily embroidered and of odd shapes, turned back six and eight inches. Collars deep and collars narrow accompany such cuffs. Plain bands of heavy lace are made very charming by the addition of narrow mull plaitings edged with fine Valenciennes lace. English eyelet embroidery plays a stellar part in these accessories and is considered quite the smartest style among moderately priced combination sets. Real Irish point combined with heavy scrim comes more expensive, as do also wide Irish crochet sets.

Another late development in these separate collar-and-cuff sets is expressed in white kid and broadcloth. The

EMBROIDERED LINEN SET

FOR FEMININE FANCIES

edges are finished with hand-embroidery in silk or gold thread on a band of green or orange of the same material as the foundation. Other sets are of the same order, but the stock develops into a collar that extends below the neck in yoke effect. The scalloped edges are finished in buttonhole-stitch or with a fine soutache braid maneuvered in a fantastic scroll design. Such sets are worn with tailor or demi-tailor gowns with charming effect.

Following the deep girdle is the shield buckle, which is gem-like in perfection. For more than a decade have these monstrous buckles been reposing in the family safe of Fashion's elect; but now they are in vogue again and more pretentious than ever in designs carried out in gold or silver.

BEADED BAG

BAG OF ANTIQUE EMBROIDERY

Ceremonious bags of every description have crept into favor with all femininity. Fancy-colored leather, bead-work, art nouveau, antique embroidery, fine old brocades and modern hand-work make up

equally tempting to the artistic eye. Bags of huge proportions are made of strips of antique

COMBINED EMPIRE PURSE AND BAG

embroidery or of beaded canvas. From Paris comes the smart little Empire purse and bag combined. Its foundation is bronze leather and gold medallions and festoons in bold relief ornament one side, while on the opposite one a plain gold plate is provided for the owner's name and address.

All-kid corsets are the most recent fad, as it has been discovered that tight-fitting gowns and tiny waists require unusual care in producing the desired smooth effect; and the kid corsets fits like a glove. It is pliable and at the same time retains its shape to far greater extent than the finest coutil. It is soft and yielding and can be had in all colors, but fawn or beige seems to be the most satisfactory shade. This new corset consists of two pieces of kid faultlessly stretched over a whalebone foundation, so constructed that every movement of the body may be taken with ease and grace. Busts are higher and are constructed in such a manner that the wearer may fill out deficiencies with crinoline.

When We Go Automobiling

By ALINE DE CARDEVA

INCREAS-ING interest in the motor car brings us face to face with the ever-perplexing problem of "what to wear," for with utter disregard for the many serious accidents that occur from day to day, automobiling continues to be the favorite sport. To be an enthusiast over smart toggery for the amusement does not mean that one must be an owner of a car, for nowadays one is almost certain to have several intimate friends who are possessors of fine machines, and to go automobiling without a correct costume means not only a dissatisfied feeling but positive discomfort.

Unless one is going in for a steady diet of motoring it is not necessary to purchase a very elaborate automobile outfit, but an appropriate coat and head-gear are certainly essential. The coat may be of waterproof silk, mohair, cravenette, waterproof tweed or silk sacking of heavy weave. Silk rubber in a rich, warm blue or claret red makes a very attractive and serviceable motor coat. The motor coat last season was many-minded, expressing itself in tweeds, cloths, furs, leathers, silk and pongee, but since then it has been considerably enriched in its vocabulary of expressions, seeming to have discovered for its use new materials and new combinations; one might say new animals, for surely some of the furs employed on collars and cuffs are of strange, new names. Blue goat is one of the very smartest furs, while white curly dog, and astrakhan dyed to match the color of the automobile, are sold under a number of coined names. In Paris, furs are used all the year round. Dainty little cravats and big book muffs are not an unusual accompaniment on long automobile tours, when one is apt to be out at all hours and in all sorts of weather.

And then the motor coat has at its disposal all the wonderful imitation fur fabrics, including broadtail velvet and moleskin plush, the latter fabric, which is of silvery-gray hue, being in great favor this season.

A long coat is quite a necessary adjunct whether the season be warm or cold. One of the smartest long coats of the year is made of coarse silk sacking and lined with Siberian squirrel flanks; the deep turnover collar is of white curly dog. The full sleeves are finished at the wrists with heavy Chinese embroidery, similar to that seen on the bottom of mandarins' robes of the finer quality. Graduating silk frogs fasten the double-breasted fronts and plenty of commodious pockets are to be found inside. Dust color is the most popular in the handsomest motor coat, and the style is suited to all seasons.

Very swagger are the three-quarter coats of mixed tweed or homespun with loosely belted back and a touch of bright color at the wrists and throat. One of the most serviceable coats of double-texture silk rubber comes in dark blue, ruby, tan, brown or cream color, and reaches to the bottom of the skirt. It has a deep turnover collar fastening snugly at the throat. There is an inside attachment of silk which gathers upon an elastic around the waist and prevents the penetration of rain or dust. Another late addition to motor-car toggery is a thin dust coat made of waterproof silk. This is extremely loose and light in weight and is of such good cut that it will retain its style for many a day to come.

The only thing really required of an automobile coat is that it will shed rain and protect from dust. If additional warmth is required, one may wear one of the new sheepskin vests or a knitted sweater. These come in sizes for both men and women, and it is always the wise person who slips one in the bag before a journey is begun. Motor sweaters hanging straight from the shoulders and buttoning up the front or made in Norfolk jacket fashion with belt are among the new things for spring, and are liked better by the motor girl than the tight-fitting ones affected by the golf enthusiast.

The straight three-quarter coat, the three-quarter coat with full-belted back and the long blouse coat belted at the waist are all made in leather. Smart little leather coats reaching just below the hips often accompany a leather skirt of instep length. No trimming save a few rows of stitching is employed upon leather coats or dresses, as the cachet of such garments depends entirely upon their cut and severity of style. Leather coats are usually lined with heavy wool, although occasionally there may be a silk or satin lining with cotton interlining. Leather-covered buttons with metal rims are quite the nobbiest sort, although one frequently sees handsome gold, silver or gunmetal buttons.

For cold and inclement weather nothing looks so well as the entire leather costume. To be sure these are expensive, but so is everything that accompanies the auto. Leather sheds the dust, can be easily cleaned, always looks modish and wears forever. So the investment in a leather costume is not a bad one after all. The skirts are instep length, having many rows of stitching around the bottom, and the popular jacket is made on the order of a Norfolk. Stitched plaits and belt and leather-covered buttons furnish the trimmings on skirt and jacket.

The best-dressed women automobilists employ the lightest, most inconspicuous and plainest of styles for their auto costumes. Of course, when one is paying social calls or shopping, as much finery may be worn as though the family carriage and pair were in use, but for traveling through

A TRICORNE HAT AND AUTOMOBILE VEIL

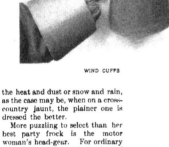

WIND CUFFS

the heat and dust or snow and rain, as the case may be, when on a cross-country jaunt, the plainer one is dressed the better.

More puzzling to select than her best party frock is the motor woman's head-gear. For ordinary use, very small, close-fitting hats of silk rubber or French kid are best. A small tricorne taffeta hat trimmed simply with a white cockade is a good motor hat. It is of becoming shape and is easily veiled. Silk rubber hoods may be permanently or otherwise attached to many of the new motor hats. A good style for dusty roads completely covers the back of the head and ends in a cape which protects the neck. The leather cap with straight visor is an excellent choice, but owing to its severe style few women take kindly to it.

Motor veils are legion. The smartest veil measures seven yards in length. It is shirred on a ring that rests on the crown of the hat, the ends are crossed in the back and tied in a huge bow at the side. Veils introduced from time to time having mica shields set in the front have never reached any degree of success. The shield continually blowing against the face is a great source of annoyance to the wearer. Quite the most satisfactory protec-

tion yet discovered seems to be the colored goggles inserted in a chiffon veil or in separate shields. The accompanying photograph represents green goggles mounted upon shields of baby calfskin.

Wind cuffs made of light-weight leather are in gauntlet effect and have a shirred piece at the wrist which fits closely. These are adaptable for any style sleeve or glove, and are worn by both sexes. Light lemon-colored buckskin gauntlet gloves with dark palms and wool jersey backs with chamois-skin palms are equally desirable and may be had at very reasonable cost. Another style buckles snugly around the wrist and is without cuff.

Leather garments for both chauffeur and owner are similar in style. When the owner himself drives his motor car he may wear a coat or the entire suit of black French kid. A trig little cap with visor or a small leather hat with stitched brim, which may be bent to suit the wearer's taste, are equally popular.

Goggles mounted in extension frames and having finest copper screens at the sides for ventilation are made comfortable to the face by bindings of fur, velvet or chenille. Jersey-back gauntlets are recommended for the driver. They allow more freedom than an all-leather glove.

Of more or less importance are

THE SHEEPSKIN VEST

KID SUIT, BUCKSKIN GLOVES AND GOGGLES

automobile robes, and every car, whether large or small, should be equipped with a dry and wet weather robe. Handsome fair-day squares are made of red leather and lined with bright plaid, stitched many times around the edge. Plainer ones are of leather lined with covert cloth.

Automobile toggery has reached a degree of perfection that it did not hold six months ago. Styles have been simplified, materials made lighter in weight without reducing their warmth and fewer garments are in evidence. Those that are, are so complete in themselves that many of the smaller details have been voted in the way and an aggravation to the wind, hence the substantial plainness of the present hat, coat and gown.

COSTUMES FOR CONFIRMATION WEAR

9100   8760   8855   9010

WAITING FOR THE CHURCH-BELLS

ARELY have the Christmas glories and the New Year display vanished from the shop-windows and counters when snowy fabrics and frost - like trimmings take their place, for confirmation is approaching with the drawing - near of Easter, and the fair little daughters must be made ready for this, the first great ceremony of the church in which they may take intelligent part. As young girls admitted to confirmation are usually between the ages of thirteen and seventeen, the costumes pictured on this and the two succeeding pages are designed for those of these ages, with the exception of the two toilettes on page 539, which are for young ladies from thirty-two to forty-two inches bust measure and twenty to thirty inches waist measure, and the Empire dress, 8915, on page 540, which is suitable for girls and misses from ten to seventeen years.

On this page the four costumes pictured combine attractively simplicity and effectiveness. The first, 9100, is made of white louisine and has a gathered yoke and full sleeves of white Liberty silk. It is trimmed with white satin ribbon arranged in fancy design and small Empire bows. If preferred, the skirt may be made without the tunic overskirt, and may have gathers or an inverted box plait at the back.

The second costume in the group is made by 8760 of white organdy and is trimmed with Valenciennes lace and insertion. The feature of this costume is the demure little fichu bertha. The gathered skirt may be made with or without the flounce. With the costume is worn a white moire sash, which is tied in a small bow at the back,

the long ends reaching nearly to the bottom of the skirt.

The shirred costume shown on the third figure is made of white albatross with a vest of white chiffon embroidery over white silk. Ruching of white satin ribbon is the simple trimming employed. The design is 8855, and it is one that will develop well in any soft material.

The last costume displayed is somewhat more elaborate than the other three. It is made by 9010, of white cashmere with fancy suspenders of white taffeta and a yoke of all-over lace. Wide and narrow lace edging supplies the trimming. The front straps are held by cut crystal buttons, but silver or mother-of-pearl buckles could be used for the same purpose.

The first figure on page 539 wears a costume of white nun's-veiling combined with tucked white chiffon, and trimmed with lace insertion and medallions. The design used is 8664, and it consists of a blouse waist opening at the back, which may be made with high or Dutch round neck and full-length or short puff sleeves, and a three-piece slightly gathered skirt. The bertha may be omitted and the yoke outlined with lace, ruching or insertion.

The seated figure at the left wears a costume of fine white nainsook made by 8807, and trimmed with flouncing of embroidered nainsook and lace appliqué. A white Liberty satin sash is worn about the waist, and the hair is tied with similar ribbon.

The tallest standing figure wears a toilette suitable for a young lady, and made of white silk mull and all-over lace. Lace edging supplies the trimming. The waist is made by 9128, which is a back-closing model, and the skirt by 9127. Both garments are prettily decorated with shirring, and are adaptable for development in soft materials such as Liberty silk, nun's-veiling, albatross, mull or

538

8664   9128 and 9127   8720

8807   8775   8979 and 8507

A GROUP OF LILY MAIDS
539

repoussé lace and insertion. The graceful draped waist is made by 8979 and the tucked circular flounce by 8507. Either of the toilettes for ladies pictured on this page would be perfectly suitable for an eighteen or nineteen-year-old girl, and are given because it frequently happens that the rite of confirmation is deferred until adult years.

Of the two figures shown at the head of this page the one at the left wears a pretty tucked costume of white taffeta with a yoke of all-over lace and trimming of white satin ribbon. It is made by 8827.

The figure at the right wears a costume of white wool crêpe. The yoke is made of lace insertion joined by narrow white moire ribbon, and lace appliqué trims the bertha. A sash of white moire ribbon is worn and a white rose made of satin ribbon is placed in the hair. The costume is made by 9115.

In the group at the lower part of the page the figure at the left wears a dress of white nun's-veiling with a yoke of white silk damassé trimmed with white brocaded ribbon and lace. The design is 8526.

On the center figure is shown an Empire dress made of white Japanese silk, made by 8915. The shirring and tucking of the garment form the only decoration.

The last dress is of white silk mull, narrow lace supplying the trimming for the many ruffles. The bretelles are held together at the front by straps of white ribbon, and the sleeves are trimmed to match. The design is 8601.

8827   9115
SIMPLE YET BECOMING DRESSES

chiffon, in combination with all-over lace or embroidery.

The next figure at the head of the page at the right wears a dress of white peau de soie with a yoke and undersleeves of white chiffon. White ribbon straps and buttons covered with white satin form the decoration. The design is 8720 and it consists of a blouse waist which may be made with or without the sleeve caps, and a skirt formed of a slightly gathered upper part tucked at the lower edge and lengthened by a tucked circular flounce.

The center figure at the lower part of the page wears a white crêpe de Chine dress trimmed with ruffles of embroidered chiffon, and it is made by 8775. The skirt may be made with or without the deep flounce or the ruffles which outline the drop-yoke. This model might be most attractively developed in white mull or organdy, with the yoke and lower sleeve portions made of all-over lace, fancy yoking or swiss embroidery, and the trimming consisting of embroidered ruffles.

The toilette for a young lady shown on the last figure in the group is made of fine white swiss, and is trimmed with

8526   8915   8601
ALL IN DOVE-LIKE WHITENESS

The Three Arts Club
By Lilian C. Paschal

"HOW AND where shall I live in New York while preparing for self-support?" This is an old riddle, anxiously propounded by every young woman who hesitates on the outer edge of the whirling currents of Manhattan life. She may feel a preparatory shiver of excitement, tinged with unconfessed dread, though not unmixed with the fearful joy of a venture; but when she finally holds her breath and takes the plunge, she is apt to find herself landed in the narrow confines of the proverbial fourth-floor back in the dreary barracks known as a middle-class boarding-house.

Recently, however, a far more agreeable solution to the vexatious problem has been evolved by the establishment of the Three Arts Club for students, modeled after the American Girls' Club in Paris. Here the diver, to resume the metaphor, must entertain sensations similar to those of the dreamer who jumps over a precipice and falls through space—to wake in the soft, warm embrace of a comfortable bed, with the morning sunlight slanting across the coverlet.

And sunshine, both literal and figurative, permeates the whole atmosphere of this unique home for young women students of the three arts—music, painting and the drama. Under its friendly roof may be had, for the merely nominal sum of from three to five dollars a week, all the advantages of the usual club life, together with the important addition of the comforts and privileges of home; for the new club-house, on the sunniest corner of Sixty-second Street and Lexington Avenue, combines both club and living-rooms within its four-story brownstone walls.

This combination is furnished by no other woman's organization in America. It accommodates at present about sixteen resident members, though the full membership of the club has almost reached the hundred mark—the enrollment numbering.

The need of such a student center was first recognized by its founder, Miss Jane Harriss Hall, specially detailed as diocesan deaconess for this work by Bishop Coadjutor Greer, who has lent his hearty interest, encouragement and support to the undertaking. Miss Hall has been greatly encouraged by the auspicious beginning and rapid growth of her pet project, the idea for which grew out of her connection with a club for students in the rear of old St. Mark's Church, away downtown in the old-fashioned section of New York, where young people of both sexes met for social evenings.

She saw then the urgent demand for some such club as her present institution. Many young women came to her to ask where they could find comfortable rooms, within the limited means of the student, in respectable, well-kept, well-lighted houses, and where they might receive their friends. So few lodging-houses have even a public parlor where the young women boarders may receive callers. Even in the places provided by societies there are so many rules and regulations and restrictions that the spirit of real home-life and freedom which the average girl needs, as a flower needs the sun, is utterly destroyed. Out of this need has arisen the Three Arts Club, which is in every sense a home.

And the Club is not lacking in that most vital of all home influences, the mother element. Deaconess Hall is one of those universal mothers whose capacity for home-making—that most rare and wonderful of the sciences—amounts to positive genius. She presides over the dainty tea-table in the big club-room every afternoon from four to six, where her sunny face, under the nun-like white cap in the soft light of the candles, makes a picture which is carried in the hearts of her girls long after they have passed from student-life into the wider currents of the world.

It is her exceptionally artistic taste, too, which is evidenced in the furnishings and hangings of the rooms. There are Liberty prints and draperies which she brought from her trip abroad a year or so ago for the purpose of studying the club's famous prototype in Paris. There are well-bound books and pictures, cozy corners and fern-filled window spaces, sofa-cushions and soft-shaded lights, arranged to delight the feminine eye which takes in comfort and encouragement from such subtle softnesses as these, as a general becomes more nearly invincible from a survey of his armies.

The house itself has been a roomy old mansion, and contains all the appointments that wealth commanded, high-arched, solid walnut doorways and cornices, great pier-glasses built above handsome marble mantels, wide windows on three sides of the house, and the many-branched candle-chandeliers that were all the delight of the builders of the generous yesterday when space was not at the premium it is nowadays.

Through the glass doors of the high-stooped entrance one enters a reception hall which is tiled in blue and white and spaciously mirrored on the left. To the right is the long drawing-room, done in terra-cotta, and also finding its own double repeated in the great glass on the south wall. There are always bowls of flowers about, showing personal pride and interest the girls feel in this congregating-place where they foregather daily to recount in cheerful chat many adventures, merry and otherwise, which they encounter in the highways and byways of their respective artistic pursuits.

In passing, it is a noticeable fact that there is in these gatherings of the clans a conspicuous lack of the petty gossip which too often prevails among the chattering groups in feminine gatherings, and which leaves its unpleasant stigma in the average person's idea of woman's

social life. These Club girls are one
and all far too busy and too sanely
wholesome in their aims and ambitions
to bother their level heads with each
other's trivial failings.

When the great folding-doors in the
rear of the long club-room are thrown
open, another pleasing and home-like
picture greets the eye. A spacious,
high-ceiled, bay-windowed room, done
in rich green, with a cozy open fire and a
handsome piano, is disclosed. This
apartment serves two purposes, that of
music-room and accommodation for the
transient visitors. The bagdad-covered
couches can be utilized as the most
comfortable of beds, and behind one
of the huge polished walnut doors is
a many-shelved lavatory with running
water. This is specially set apart for
the use of those whose stay is short,
particularly those of the dramatic students who are waiting for professional
engagements. So it happens that the
old room dispenses the dual hospitality
of welcoming the coming and speeding
the parting guest—who are glad of so

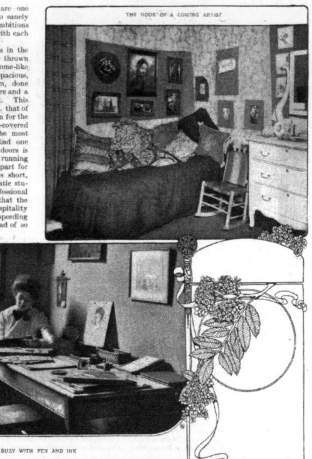

THE NOOK OF A COMING ARTIST

BUSY WITH PEN AND INK

pleasant a refuge in times of stress between seasons, but
who are also glad to go forth on new engagements.

This phase of the Three Arts Club is likewise peculiar to
itself, in offering shelter to the members of that increasing
army of climbers, known for some mysterious reason as
"the profession." Young women who are studying for
the stage, attending some one of the several excellent
dramatic schools established in New York City, find it a
most difficult matter to obtain decent quarters in the city,
owing to the narrow-minded old prejudice which exists
against all things and people Thespian. Many societies,
including the Women's Christian Union, refuse to take
them, in spite of the important new fact that the elevation
of the stage is a steady process, and that an actress may
be a refined, cultured, respectable member of the community. The presence together under one roof of a
deaconess with actresses affords much amusing curiosity
among the residents of the neighborhood, to most of
whom, by the way, the club is the object of lively interest.

In one respect only does the Three Arts Club differ
from its Paris model—it has no restaurant. The resident
members have the privileges afforded by the big kitchen
and dining-room in the basement where they get their
own cozy breakfasts and luncheons, all dinners being
taken outside. Each girl has her own particular cooking
utensils and her special shelf for keeping them in the wide
cupboards. The light housekeeping done here by pros-
pective authors, artists and actresses, clad in huge gingham aprons, amid much merry-making, plays no small
part in creating the delightful home atmosphere which
is the dominant and unique element of the club.

The front basement room, of generous size, used as a
dining-room, serves also as a sewing-room and is supplied
with an easy-running machine and cutting-table. Here
in the "den," as they term it, the girls who make their own
dresses—and there are several gifted in that line—may
be free from interruption when in the throes of "fitting on"
a half-finished garment.

ONE OF THE
COMFORTABLE
BEDROOMS

MISS HALL AND SOME OF HER GUESTS

simple cost of five cents each. Miss Hall, in her genial, delightful way, makes the scores who attend the pleasant function feel as though each has an equal right to the rooms and all that in them is, including herself, the best gift of all, as any of them would tell you.

The girls are all invited, nay, more than that, are expected, to receive and entertain their friends here whenever they wish, thus affording a pleasant opportunity to those unfortunates who belong to the "fourth-floor back" contingent. Needless to say, the Sunday suppers are the most popular features of the Club.

Thursday evening has been appointed as the special club evening for the receiving of outside friends, although these are welcome at all times. On these weekly occasions it is intended that something unusual in the way of amusement and recreation be provided, such as musical recitals, dramatic

There is the trimmest of little maids in snow-white cap and apron to "tend door" and help with the afternoon tea-things. The resident members make their own beds and keep their rooms in order, though a woman comes each Saturday to give the rooms a thorough cleaning and dusting. Several of the large square rooms on the upper stories have been partitioned off into two rooms, each one of a fair size and a pleasant outlook. A few of the bedrooms are large enough to accommodate two, though the single rooms are in far greater demand, the average girl much preferring to have a nook all her own, where she may be alone to rest when tired, and so be more ready for social cheer when she comes forth again.

The individual touches to the room furnishings bespeak the abode of art-lovers. The simple good taste which teaches that a few really good things are more to be desired than a large collection of inferior ones, is everywhere in strong evidence. Mrs. George C. Thomas gave a generous check toward the furniture, and Miss Hall has contributed many treasures of her own, which she has collected in her foreign travels.

The Sunday evening supper is the only meal served, and it is usually a very jolly affair. All the girls, those living outside as well as the resident guests, have the right to come to it and to bring their friends for the

readings, palm-reading and kindred features, giving the affair a little gala touch, which makes it something to be looked forward to with interested expectation.

During the last week of November a sale of art work was held for the benefit of the Club, which was largely patronized and served in lieu of the opening reception which heralded the advent of the Three Arts into clubdom only a little more than a year ago. The annual dues are only a dollar a year, so other methods of adding to the treasury are necessarily resorted to. The club has been the recipient of generous gifts of money and furniture from various wealthy persons interested in its welfare. Among these is Mrs. C. P. Hemenway, of Boston, who provided its first quarters in West Fifty-sixth Street, from which it removed to the new house at 803 Lexington Avenue

GETTING HER OWN BREAKFAST

THE COZY AFTERNOON TEA HOUR

last September. In its new quar ers the greater
part of the expense is met by the rental from the
living-rooms and studios, so it has become to a
great degree a self-supporting organization.

"I hope," says Miss Hall, "to see the Three
Arts Club the center of all the student-life in
New York. So far most of our members are art
students and we have a good many from the
dramatic schools. The students of music, both
vocal and instrumental, are harder to reach. They
are the most numerous of all, too. Not long ago I
procured a registry of all the students in New York,
and discovered that the women who were devoting
their time to music were nearly double in number to
those studying the other two arts. The trouble is that
in music the pupils study under many different teachers, and do not hear of the Club as do members of large
art and dramatic classes.

"The Club spent last June at the Holiday House, Lake
George, a beautiful place given by Spencer Trask and
Foster P. Peabody, of this city, to Miss M. W. Fuller, of
Troy, for a Girls' Friendly House and which she was good
enough to loan us for that month. There were thirty
girls and they formed a sketch class with Jerome Meyers
as instructor. Perhaps we may be equally fortunate next
summer.

"I have received many letters from all over the country
from mothers whose girls are coming to this big, roaring
city to study music, art or dramatics, and who are anxious
to place them under the protection of the Three Arts
Club. Its permanent success seems assured. In time,
it is my dream to have a house all our own, where, with
no rent to pay, and a club restaurant convenient—next
door—we may provide a club-home for fifty or a hundred
girls. I am sure I could fill such a house—so rapid and
spreading has been the growth of this newest of girls'
clubs."

In the wonderful increase in the army of brave women
who are self-supporting, there is a corresponding branch-
ing out to independence of the right kind, which the average boarding-house or the old-fashioned home for women

does not supply. This the club quarters, if its hopes of
augmentation in the future are realized, will give, and the
girl who resides under its roof will be as free to go and
come as would her brother in his masculine club, for it
will be understood, when she is admitted as a member,
that she has self-poise, and understands the laws of the
polite world too well to wilfully break them.

It is plainly evident in our great cities there are not
enough men escorts to go around, and it is not fair on
that account that the single woman be debarred from enjoyment of good dramatic entertainments, lectures, concerts,
and the like, to attend which she must necessarily be
out frequently until after ten o'clock at night, the hour
when the old-fashioned home for women and the average
boarding-house bar their doors. The latter may supply a
latch-key, but the former never does. This in itself is a
restriction unpleasant to an independent, honest, busy
woman, who after a day of hard work deserves her evening
of harmless amusement. Again, there are little rasping
rules where women have heretofore made their homes regarding the burning of gas, inviting friends to dinner
without permission, etc., etc., of all which the club girl
of the future will be blissfully free.

A GAME OF HIDE AND SEEK

By GERTRUDE NORTON

With Drawings by ELLIOT KEEN

AST summer I paid a visit to the family of Richard Sparks, a well-known rancher in Oklahoma. Mrs. Sparks is a woman of some forty odd years, and has spent nearly all her life on the frontier. One evening, at dusk, when the children were playing hide-and-seek in the back yard, she told me a story of an experience she had in the Indian Territory many years ago—a story that so thrilled me at the time that I have decided to try to repeat it.

"I have never watched the children playing hide-and-seek," she said, "without having brought to my mind one of the most memorable experiences of my life. It happened during the first year I lived in the Indian Territory, a good many years ago. I was a mere girl in years then, though I had been married half a year. Before my marriage I was telegraph operator at a little station on the old L. L. & G. Railroad (now the Lawrence and Southern) in Southern Kansas, and Richard Sparks—I always called him 'Dick' for short—was station agent at the next town south. We didn't see much of one another during the period of our engagement, and as time hung heavy on our hands I think we may be excused if we sometimes broke the monotony by using the company's wires in exchanging vows and carrying on our courtship. When we were married we resigned our positions and went on a ranch, leased from the Indians, in the Cherokee Nation, to engage in farming and stock-raising. We didn't have a great deal to begin with, and our house was a box structure of two rooms, a garret above for storing things, and a shed kitchen. Our ranch lay in a little valley twelve miles east of Russel Creek, near the line of the Shawnee reservation.

"There were not many whites in the locality, and most of our neighbors—if they could be called neighbors—were Shawnee Indians; but as they were partly civilized and quite friendly their presence did not trouble us. Unfortunately, there were some bad characters among them, and none worse than Yellow Dog, an almost full-blood Shawnee. His stealing, outlawry and deeds of violence made him feared and dreaded throughout the Territory. It happened soon after our arrival on the ranch, however, that he was caught and sent to prison. As Dick had been instrumental in capturing him, it was reported that he had declared his intention to revenge himself on my husband if he ever had the opportunity; and the opportunity came sooner than we expected, for he succeeded in making his escape and returned to his old haunts soon after his capture.

"If we had known this on that morning in June when Dick took his repeating rifle and rode down the trail toward Russel Creek, I should not have been left alone. But we knew nothing of it, and as Dick had promised to bring back a saddle of venison, I was in no wise reluctant to let him go, for, to tell the truth, our larder was in sad need of something of the kind.

"It was the first time he had left me alone, and he had no sooner vanished from sight than I regretted letting him go. He was sure to return before sunset, he said, and I think I never watched the sun so diligently before nor experienced a day that seemed so long.

"Between four and five o'clock in the evening I went out to the cattle-sheds to carry some water to a calf we kept tied in the shed. I was returning when I heard the sound of a horse's feet, and, looking up, I saw Kotchakoc, a friendly Shawnee, riding at a gallop along the trail. He glanced up as he saw me, and made a quick gesture with his hand toward the creek.

"'Yellow Dog,' him come back!' he said. 'Mebby come kill um *dagosha*' (white man).

"I listened to his words in a sort of stupefying fear, and for a moment I stood gazing helplessly about me, as if I expected to see the Indian desperado appear before me. Then, regaining my presence of mind, I would have signaled Kotchakoc to stop and explain more fully, but he had already galloped beyond hearing.

"I walked back to the house, a keen sense of impending danger assailing me. How I wished that I had detained Kotchakoc and asked him to remain with me till Dick's return—knowing he would gladly have obliged me—; but it was now too late to do so. Yellow Dog was at large again and might visit the ranch at any time to revenge himself for his capture.

"I tried to console myself with the thought that Dick might return at any moment, and as I moved about the house doing my work I kept a constant watch, now turning my eyes toward the trail leading to Russel Creek, now letting them wander to the blue line of brush that marked the course of Plum Creek. Once I thought I caught sight of an object moving close in the shadows of the plum bushes along the creek a half mile away. I was not mistaken, for a few minutes later I could see a dark figure approaching. It was moving along the course of a ra[illegible], and it was only at intervals that I could get a glimpse of it. I felt greatly alarmed, for the figure was that of an Indian, and in all probability Yellow Dog.

"I had put some wood in the stove preparatory to getting supper, but the sight of the Indian drove all thoughts of it from my mind. I closed the door and kept hidden from sight, and eagerly I looked down the trail leading to Russel Creek, hoping against hope that I might see Dick returning. But there was nothing but the long, winding trail to meet my gaze, and above it a half-dozen vultures circling darkly against the sky. With fear gripping at my heart, I began to consider what was best to do. Should I bar the door and try to defend myself against the Indian if he came, or would it be safer to hide myself somewhere about the premises? I chose the latter course.

"The Indian was still working his way cautiously through the ravine in the direction of the house, and as he dodged in and out of cover I was convinced that it was Yellow Dog. I had seen the Indian only once, and then when he was a prisoner, but I had not forgotten his face.

"There was no time to think. I must act at once. Hurriedly barring the door, I passed into the shed kitchen, slipped out at the door, locked it behind me and crept into a dense thicket of sumacs that grew a short distance from the house. All the time I had kept the shanty between the Indian and myself, and knew he had not seen me. Having gained the cover, I made my way to a point where I could command a view of the ravine. Peering out through an opening in the foliage, I could see the Indian approaching. He was keeping the cattle-shed between himself and the house, and in one hand carried a heavy pistol. As I looked into his evil face I recognized him at once as Yellow Dog. There was no mistaking his errand, and a sickening, dizzy sensation of fear came over me. I sank down weak and trembling, but still keeping my eyes upon him.

"On reaching the shed he came to a halt and stood peering in the direction of the house, keeping his body concealed behind the timbers. He stood thus for some time—a quarter of an hour, perhaps, but it seemed an age to me. Seeing no one, he left the shed and moved swiftly and noiselessly toward the house. Approaching the window, he peered in, holding his pistol in his hand. He next passed around to the front door, tried it softly, and, finding it fastened, stood glancing about the premises with crafty alertness.

"He was evidently becoming convinced that there was nobody about the place, for I heard him mutter, 'Tahlequah!' (all gone) under his breath. He kept running his eyes over the premises, evidently debating as to what he should do next. I had no doubt that he would plunder the place before quitting it, but this did not concern me much as I would willingly have surrendered our few valuables to have been rid of him.

"But he was in no hurry to act. With that peculiar cunning natural to the Indian, he was constantly alert. Of all things an Indian most dreads is to fall into a trap, not merely on account of the disaster it may bring, but the humiliation he feels at being outwitted.

"As he stood looking about him and listening, a most unfortunate thing happened. The fire I had kindled in the stove, which had been smoldering up to this time, suddenly burst into flame, and the smoke pouring from the chimney-top attracted his attention in an instant. To him this was an open book. It told him plainer than words that some one was about the place. Bestowing a hasty glance at the chimney, he slipped quickly away from the door, leaped into the sumac thicket and took refuge behind a little knoll not twenty yards from where I was concealed. I grew dizzy with fright, and the beating of my heart sounded like the roll of a drum in my ears. At first I was seized with an almost overpowering impulse to leap to my feet and take to flight—a mad and fatal impulse, had I carried it into effect—and it required all my power of self-possession to master it.

"Fortunately, the attention of the Indian was riveted on the house, and it was evident that he had no suspicion that anyone was concealed in the thicket. I soon realized

this and knew that my only hope of safety lay in remaining quiet. I sank lower and lower on the ground, till I lay flat in the grass, only elevating my head sufficiently to keep watch on the movements of the Shawnee. Presently the Indian arose and stood surveying the surroundings. It was evident that he was puzzled. Presently he seemed to grasp the situation—to have come to the conclusion that some one who was terrified at his presence was hiding about the place, for his low, muttered words indicated as much. He now walked boldly to the house and knocked on the door. Receiving no response, he walked around to the window, peered in, and taking a stick, broke it open. He stood there for a full minute watching and listening. Then he clambered in quickly.

"It now occurred to me that I might escape from the place, but I quickly realized that it would be impossible, for every few minutes he would thrust his head out at the window and glance in every direction, to make sure that he should not be taken by surprise.

"He did not stay in the house but a short time, and when he came out he began to go about the premises as if in search of some one who might be hiding there. He was evidently convinced that there were no men-folks about the place, and well knowing, as Indians do, the terror the average woman has for them, he went boldly about, searching every nook and corner. He forced his way into the small chicken-house, then went to some boxes piled against the shed and peered into them. He next explored the stable and passed through a patch of weeds growing near it. I watched his movements with a sinking heart. Any moment, I reflected, he might take it into his head to search the thicket in which I was concealed. So certain was I that he would do this that I began to form plans for changing my hiding-place. But how was I to leave the thicket without exposing myself to discovery? Just outside the patch of sumacs was a strip of high grass and sunflowers, and, worming myself along the ground, I managed to reach it. It extended to a little hollow some thirty yards away, and if I could only reach this—the approaching steps of Yellow Dog broke in upon me, and I saw him walking rapidly toward the patch of sumacs I had just left. I lay flat in the grass, not daring even to lift my head, and waited in that painful and breathless suspense that only one placed in my position can understand. I could hear the Shawnee beating through the brush and his grunts of dissatisfaction at the futility of his search. My face was down in the grass, and the hot, suffocating heat arising from the earth almost stifled me. Fortunately, I did not have to endure this for over a minute or two, for Yellow Dog passed quickly through the thicket and walked to the house again. I listened to his retreating footsteps, not venturing to lift my face from the ground. When I was sure that he had returned to the house I lifted my head and saw him entering the window again. As soon as he disappeared through the window I slipped back into the patch of sumacs again and sank down in its friendly cover. I breathed more easily now, for I hardly expected him to revisit the thicket.

"When he emerged from the house, which he did inside of five minutes, he carried a pair of blankets and some other articles, and a sudden hope that he would betake himself from the place came to me. But such was not his intention. He stopped for a moment as he came from the house and looked sharply in every direction. Then he muttered the words, 'Tahlequah! Dagosha phaywah lotseehee—dagusha nepwah!' (All gone. White man come soon—white man die!) I knew enough of the language to interpret the meaning of the words, and I was now beset with a new and not less terrible fear. Yellow Dog had now taken his position in the cattle-shed where he could command a view of the house, and standing there, with his body concealed, he waited and watched, pistol in hand, ready to ambush anyone who might approach the house. At any moment Dick might return and unconscious of the presence of the lurking foe, fall a victim to his deadly pistol. My situation was now doubly trying. I must manage in some way to watch for Dick's approach and warn him of the danger; this I could not do in my present position. As these thoughts passed through my mind I began to form a plan for outwitting the Shawnee. But first I must reach the house unobserved.

"Slowly and with infinite caution I crept to the left, worming myself along through the interlacing branches of the sumacs till I reached a point on the opposite side of the house from the shed; then with my heart in my mouth I crept to the back door of the house. My very flesh tingled with fear. So sharp was it that it was physical as well as mental pain. A single misstep, the slightest noise, would betray my presence, and this meant life or death, perhaps, to both my husband and myself. I did not dare let myself think of it. I slipped the key into the lock and turned it slowly and noiselessly. Then I withdrew the key, opened the door softly and entered, closing it behind me. I was not sure I had made no sound, but there was no time to be lost. In the center of the room stood a table, and directly over it was a large trap-door in the ceiling, which opened to the garret above. I clambered up-

" AGAIN I SENT THE LIGHT LEAPING ALONG THE TRAIL "

on the table, lifted the trap-door slowly and cautiously and drew myself up, closing the door behind me. I sat there panting with exertion, my heart beating tumultuously. A momentary weakness came over me, and I felt that I could not endure the strain much longer. A sickening fear lest I should faint seized me, and it required all my strength of mind to combat it.

"I did not venture to move for some moments. I breathed deeply, trying to overcome my weakness and calm my agitation. Gradually my strength came back, and, rising, I crept to the little window in the end of the attic and peered out. I could see the winding trail that led across the stretch of prairie in the direction of Russel Creek, but at first no sign of life was visible. I looked again, and then there emerged from a depression a horseman coming at a swift gallop. It needed not the second glance to tell me that it was Dick. The red sun, which was now nearing the horizon, hung in a yellow haze at his back, flooding the wide stretch of plain with its mellow light. How I thanked God that there was no cloud

in the sky. For with God's blessed sunlight I might transmit the message that would save our lives.

"There was a broken mirror among some pieces of furniture stored in the corner, and, bringing a large piece of this to the window, I sent a flash of light leaping across the stretch of plain to where Dick was galloping more than a mile away. How many times Dick and I had talked over the wires in the days of our courtship, and now under what different circumstances I began to speak to him through the flashes of light from the broken mirror. Using the flashes to represent the Morse alphabet, I kept repeating the word 'D-A-N-G-E-R— D-A-N-G-E-R— D-A-N-G-E-R!' I strained my eyes through the mellow light to watch the result. Would he see and understand? Yes. I saw him rise in his stirrups, and there was something white fluttering above his head, and I knew that he had seen and understood. How he urged his horse along the trail. I kissed the little piece of glass in my hand and wept hysterically. But my task was not yet done. I must warn him of the danger in more explicit words. Again I sent the light leaping along the trail with these words: 'Yellow Dog is hiding in shed with pistol.' I kept repeating this till his answering signal told me that he understood. I saw him take his rifle from his saddle and make a significant gesture, urging his horse forward with desperate energy. Then the whole plain became a blur before my eyes. I sank down in a dead faint.

"When I regained consciousness Dick was standing over me, tears of joy in his eyes. I was too happy just then to think of much else. We had both escaped death, and that was enough for me to know then. When he helped me down from the attic it was to find Yellow Dog lying in the shed securely bound, one of his legs broken by a bullet from Dick's rifle, and Kotchakoe, who had just arrived on the scene, standing guard over him.

"Dick had seen the Indian hiding in the shed and had opened fire on him at long range, breaking his leg. The authorities were very careful that he did not escape this time, and he was sent to Fort Smith and placed in the United States prison there. That was the last we ever saw of him, and it was the last time Dick ever left me alone while we remained in the Indian Territory."

FOUR LITTLE FABLES

THE SHEFFIELD PLATTER
By ROSE MILLS POWERS

IT WAS a Sheffield Platter,
   Shabby and worn of face,
That raised a fearful chatter
   'Mid the folk of Side-Board Place.

They snubbed the poor newcomer
   In a shameful way to see,
And raised the hateful rumor
   That he lacked pedigree.

The copper-luster Pitcher
   Turned up her pudgy nose,
And wished that he were richer,
   For she was scarce of beaus.

The willow-pattern Dishes,
   Of most patrician blue,
Declared him as officious—
   An upstart as they knew.

One night the Platter vanished,
   And none knew where he went;
But gossip whispered, "Banished,
   No doubt, for unpaid rent."

It was a fortnight later
   When he, whom all had spurned,
The shabby Sheffield Platter,
   To Side-Board Place returned.

But what a transformation!
   In a new suit of plate,
And with the reputation
   Of hall-mark, crest and date.

Because this swell of fashion
   Would never now propose,
The Pitcher, in a passion,
   Fell down and broke her nose.

And blue and ever bluer
   The dames of willow grew,
As few and ever fewer
   Declared him "Parvenu";

For pedigree and polish
   Soon found an easy way
The barriers to demolish
   That barred society.

So, for the Sheffield Platter
   Did better days befall—
By fashion, strange dictator,
   Made leader of them all.

THE POT AND THE KETTLE
By SARA C. HEINZERLING

THE dinner was over—the dishes were done—
   The pots and the pans put aside but the one
When the busy housewife was called for in haste,
And leaving the kitchen she hurriedly placed
This pot, which belonged on a low cupboard shelf,
And the kettle, which always had stood by itself
On the back of the range, side by side on the table,
And thereby arose the theme of this fable.

The kettle looked 'round with a frown and a hiss,
And scornfully murmured, "Dear me! How is this?
The madam for once clearly shows for a fact
That she is lamentably wanting in tact,
By thoughtlessly forcing one of my set
To equally mingle with vessels of jet—
This freak of hers surely is silly and strange—
She ought to have put me back on the range."

The pot, deeply wounded in spirit and pride,
Looked straight at the kettle and thus it replied:
"Pray, what is the difference, may I inquire,
To be on the range, o'er the very same fire,
Each boiling away as fast as we're able,
Or quietly sitting here on the table?
I confess I myself am too stupid to see
Just wherein the difference really may be."

Then, with much condescension and many a hiss,
The kettle replied, "Sir, the diff'rence is this—
Though we sit side by side, quite often 'tis true,
Just as different classes in churches oft do,
And frequently meet in a business relation,
We each occupy a different station—
For I, as you know, keep the clear water hot,
While you—well, you're only a black dinner-pot."

"Therefore, it's presumptuous for you to expect
To move as an equal among the select
Set of utensils to which I belong;
And believe me, dear sir, that I do you no wrong
When, like people of culture, I draw the line tight,
And decline to be more than just barely polite,
On occasions like this, when I find I am thrown
In your company, sir, by no wish of my own."

The pot, greatly angered, now stood on its mettle,
And boldly responded, "My dear Mistress Kettle,
Though you're far above me in beauty and station,
Your manners are bad and you lack penetration,
If you've lived to your age and have yet to find
That those truly great are both gentle and kind,
When and wherever they chance to be thrown
With people of different spheres from their own."

C L O T H E D   I N   R H Y M E

THE "TAIL" OF A FROG

By MARIE GROVE

OH, the elegant Mr. and Mrs. B. Frog,
　Well known in the Potter's Pond "swim,"
Dwelt in a locality very select,
　In apartments exceedingly trim
　And prim,
　In apartments exceedingly trim.

Both cultured and polished was Mr. B. Frog,
　And his wife was as cultured as he
('Twas known far and wide to the Potter's Pond folk
　How renowned was her family tree,
　Dear me!
　How renowned was her family tree).

Now, the Frogs had a son, Master Tadpole by name,
　The pride of his parents, but, oh,
So wayward they found it a difficult task
　To rear him the way he should go,
　Just so;
　To rear him the way he should go.

In the slimiest pools he could always be found,
　Where those rude little Crawfishes played,
A family shunned by all Potter's Pond folk,
　And of which even you are afraid,
　'Tis said;
　Of which even you are afraid.

It seemed that all pleadings and scoldings were vain,
　For company vile was his bent;
And mischief was brewing, twas safe to predict,
　Wherever the young scapegrace went;
　His bent,
　Was mischief wherever he went.

One day Master Tadpole was sent by Mama
　On an errand important to go,
All dressed in his prettiest suit, and his tail
　Adorned with a beautiful bow,
　Heigh ho!
　Adorned with a beautiful bow.

"Now, Taddy, please hurry," his good Mama plead
　"And don't tarry long by the way.
Be back in an hour—not later than that";
　And Tad promised sure to obey,
　That day;
　He promised her sure to obey.

But night was approaching ere Taddy appeared,
　And, oh, in the sorriest plight—
All covered with mud from his head to his toes,
　A truly most piteous sight,
　That's right;
　A truly most piteous sight.

His father grew stern as he viewed him all o'er.
　"Now, Tadpole," quoth he, "I must know
The reason of this, sir"; and poor Mama cried,
　"Oh, Tad! what's become of your bow?
　Oh! Oh!
　Pray what has become of your bow?"

And Tadpole, abashed, kept his eyes on the ground;
　To pity him you cannot fail;
For not only had vanished his beautiful bow,
　But he'd parted likewise with his tail,
　Vale, vale!
　And that is the last of the tale.

THE HAUGHTY FENCE-POST

By ELLEN MAY JONES

AN ARROGANT fence-post stood and said
　To some weeds that grew in a near-by place,
"I guard the domain of the garden-bed,
　While you do nothing but take up space.
"I should think you would know you are in the way,
　And that to exist you would be ashamed.
I'm carefully placed and hammered to stay,
　While you are not even so much as named."

The farmer came with his bright plowshare,
　Along where the weeds grew thick and tall—
'I'll plow them under," he said, "with care;
　They'll be good to fertilize the soil."
But the post, so proud of its high degree,
　Was soon divested of all its joys.
"You're rotten, and ready to drop," said he;
　"You'll make a good bonfire for the boys."

So the ground was plowed, and the wheat that grew
　From a soil enriched fed a king and queen;
But the post was burned; and a jolly crew
　Rejoiced in the merry bonfire's sheen.
There's a lesson in this for you and me:
　Don't boast of yourself and your friends underrate,
Lest good be disclosed which you cannot see,
　And your pride descends from its high estate.

5

THE LEAVES OF TREES

BY CRAIG S. THOMS

IT IS said that the most lonely place in the world is a crowded street where all faces are strange and you cannot call a soul by name. It is much the same in the crowds of trees that line streets, adorn parks, skirt streams and clothe mountains. To be able to call the trees by name is to number them among your friends, and to add to the interest of every vacation season, every romp in the woods and every walk out of doors.

The study of trees by their leaves is easier than that of birds or flowers. A few summers ago, while spending the month of August on one of the small islands in northern Lake Michigan, I was greatly

THE OAK LEAF

sun poured in its light to dapple the sod with pure gold and dark green! And what pleasing surprises came as, seated on some sun-lit stump, I examined with pocket-glass the handfuls of leaves that I had gathered, and compared them with the cuts of leaves in the tree manual that I carried under my arm!

Each day some new friendship was formed or some old acquaintance discovered; and the number of secrets revealed by the myriad tiny creatures to whom a tree or even a leaf is a world was an unfailing source of pleasure.

One who begins the study of leaves will shortly find the range of his interest broadening. Some are found partially eaten; others curled into homes; others stung into malformations; while still others bear tiny eggs. On the bark of dead trees and

THE WHITE ELM LEAF   THE HACKBERRY LEAF   THE BOX ELDER LEAF   THE GREEN ASH LEAF

disappointed that there were so few birds, and that flowers were so scarce; but in the trees I was abundantly satisfied, for of them there was a large variety, many of which were new to me. To study trees, one need not go at any particular time—only that he does not go in winter. He is never too early or too late, as so often happens with the birds or flowers. What nerve-resting rambles I had in the deep woods of the island, where tall elms and maples reared long aisles of shady arches! What exhilaration seized me as I emerged into some half-open grassy spot, where the

THE HAW LEAF   THE SILVER MAPLE LEAF

limbs are found numerous lichens and various fungi; in their wood, many grubs burrow, and woodpeckers chisel for them; in the interstices of bark insects lay their eggs, and larvæ pass the winter, and here the creepers and nuthatches gather them for food; about the sappy exudations, as also about tree-blossoms, bees buzz and insects congregate; flitting among upper branches are our smallest birds; in yon high swaying top a squirrel's nest of leaves is so solidly anchored in a crotch that the gusts of winter cannot dislodge it. One simply cannot stop when once the study of trees is begun.

It is one thing to recognize an oak or ash in the forest and quite another to recognize the wood of either when seen sawed and polished in interior finish or furnishings; but one will not long be interested in trees without becoming interested also in different kinds of wood.

It is one thing to recognize a tree as it stands in the timber and

THE BLACK WALNUT LEAF
THE COTTONWOOD LEAF

quite another—and I think a more difficult thing—to recognize its leaf when viewed singly. Indeed, a delightful way of entertaining a company of young people is to mount leaves on white cardboard and have them guess to what tree each belongs.

I know of no study that will so sharpen the powers of observation as the study of trees by their leaves. For example, it will be seen by the accompanying illustrations that the difference between the form of the elm and hackberry is very slight, but their veining and textures are different, while the trees are quite unlike. The box elder and ash are the same in general plan of leaflet grouping, but the individual leaflets are very dissimilar. The haw and the silver maple present certain similarities, though, of course, the trees are totally different. It certainly would require an expert to distinguish the leaves of poplar, aspen and cottonwood; and those of the various oaks are doubtless most perplexing of all.

The difficulty of identifying leaves arises in part from the fact that, while the general form of each kind is about the same, the particular outlines vary infinitely. Young ones are often quite different from old ones; and leaves may be picked from the same tree so different even in general outline that one might think them different species. Not infrequently very beautiful leaves, when viewed singly, are found on very homely trees. The haw is exquisite in form, proportions and beauty of outline, yet the tree is homely—gnarled, thorny, squatty, with crowded, elbowing branches. On the other hand, the oak-leaf is ragged and irregular; while the tree, wherever it has room, is well proportioned, and gives the impression both of beauty and strength.

It should be remembered, however, that Nature contemplates a tree as a whole, and not in parts. When cut from the tree, a branch loses much of its beauty, and cordwood does not approve itself to the artistic taste. The most exquisite charm of foliage is in the unity of style between tree-form and leaf-form. How strangely out of proportion would be the large, ragged oak-leaves upon the long, slender branches of the elm! The haw-leaf just mentioned, though beautiful in outline, has a squarish form and savage, deeply double-cut edges, in perfect keeping with the crowded, gnarled and thorny branches on which it grows. The oval, modestly serrated

elm-leaves and the slender, swaying elm branches are perfectly suited each to the other. What leaves could be placed upon the willows, other than their own, to give an equally pleasing effect? The narrow, tapering leaves and the long, wand-like stems or branches are one in style. How perfectly the leaf of the cottonwood atones for the shortcomings of the tree! The tree is straight and stiff, its branches almost at right angles to the trunk, and so brittle that they cannot bend far without breaking; but the roundish leaves are quite independent of yielding or swaying branches. On their long, flat stems they turn every whither, and give to the stiff, brittle tree an appearance of business-like activity which few others possess. Walnut, ash and hickory trees do not have the graceful twigs which maples and elms possess. Their symmetry is completed each season by putting out the long leaf-stalks on which their compound leaves are formed.

Some trees, like some flowers, put forth their blossoms before their leaves. The catkins of the cottonwood hang long and drooping before the bursting of a single leaf-bud. The seeds of the white elm have matured and given to the tree the appearance of being clothed with foliage, while as yet the leaves have scarcely shaken from their tiny tips their winter encasements. When the plum and cherry are robed in stainless white blossoms, their green leaves venture out very timidly, lest they seem to stain the spotless garments. Other trees, such as the box elders, walnuts, lindens and catalpas, put forth their leaves first, the blossoms following shortly afterward.

One need but walk over a mountain-side that has been swept by flame, and where trees are dead, to realize what a different world foliage makes both for man and beast. How bare everything is! What weariness in the unrelenting sunlight! What lack of interest in the far reaches of unprotected open! How far from him all wild creatures keep! And how unfriendly everything seems to be! Clothe the trees with foliage and all is changed. The whole world becomes more friendly.

And then, what is more than all, the leaves are lungs, breathing out oxygen and taking in carbonic-acid gas; while all creatures of the animal world breathe out carbonic-acid gas and take in oxygen. Somewhere I have seen it estimated that the leaves of a certain stately elm had a surface of several acres. Acres of lungs! pouring into our atmosphere the element that is essential to animal life, and taking up and utilizing a poison. Such, though with a hundred related uses, is doubtless the main function of foliage, each leaf of which possesses a beauty all its own, for no two are just alike.

HOUSEKEEPING all over the WORLD

By Laura B. Starr

II. EGYPTIAN   HOME LIFE

IN SOME parts of Egypt, and particularly among the poorer classes, life in general, and housekeeping in particular, are conducted on exceedingly simple lines. Many of the customs of Father Abraham's time,

master of the house, if she be a widow and live with him, or the first wife, attends to what ordering is not done by the master himself. As a rule he is verily master of the house, and not in name only.

WASHING VEGETABLES IN EGYPT   A TURKISH BRIDE

the most primitive possible, obtain in a large number of Egyptian families. For instance, the morning grinding of the corn at the entrance to the tent is still seen, and what is worse, heard, by many tourists. Two women sit by a large stone, each with a hand on a crank, while they chant in high, broken voices, and slowly grind the meal or flour for the day's necessities.

The markets of Egypt offer a great variety of vegetables, and the housekeeper there has little trouble in selecting her daily ménu. The cooks are for the most part men, though native women sometimes hold the position. The mother of the

Each Moslem is allowed four wives, but at the present time few avail themselves of this privilege; in fact none except the older and more conservative ones, who having them will not abandon them. In case there is more than one wife, each one lives with her children and servants separately from the others. Meals are served to each family in its own apartment—all of which are in the harem, i. e., that portion of the house set apart for the use of the women and children.

The master and grown sons are served in the selamlik, the living-room of the men's quarters. This room, like all others, is set about with low couches piled with cushions. A tabouret, or a folding stool, is used for holding the great brass tray on which the food is served. They eat without knives or forks. Flat cakes of unleavened bread are placed at each plate, and the diner breaks off a piece, folds and dips it into any dish he likes, carries it to his mouth, and eats bread and all. The principal dish of the meal is a stew or roast of lamb; this is placed in the center of the tray and each one helps himself, but as he always takes a fresh piece of bread before dipping in, all eating out of one dish is not so bad as at first it seems.

The absence of knives and forks makes it necessary to provide some means of cleaning the hands. At intervals a slave or servant comes with a jug and ewer and pours scented water over the extended fingers, and another follows with a handsome towel.

Every third course is a sweetmeat, which accounts for the inordinately stout women of the Orient, this and the sedentary lives they lead. A thin, slender, graceful woman is an unpleasant sight in Oriental eyes. Young girls who have not yet acquired the desired quantity of adipose tissue are put through a regular course of feeding when they are preparing for marriage. A thin woman has not the ghost of a chance of securing a husband; beauty is measured by avoirdupois.

As a rule, the kitchen is built quite separate from the house proper, and in every case the clay bakeoven is isolated. The bread is mixed in a basket, patted into thin round

INNER COURT OF
EGYPTIAN HOME

ROOM IN A CAIRO HAREM

cakes, and laid upon a piece of she[et] iron, then thrust into the oven, [if] there be one. Frequently an o[ut] door oven is improvised by setti[ng] up on edge three stones to form [a] square. A fire is built within a[nd] another thin stone is placed on t[op] and the large thin cakes of bre[ad] that look like giant pancakes, a[re] baked on this.

Pistachio nuts and rice are large[ly] used in the preparation of food, a[nd] there are many varieties of siru[p] and sweet drinks used by all class[es] Wine is never drunk by the faithf[ul] Mohammedan; water is served fr[om] a porous red clay bottle, called goulat.

All houses of any pretension a[re] built around a court with a founta[in] in the center; this is not for sho[w] but is a necessity, for every devo[ut] Mohammedan must perform his abl[u]tions before the five daily praye[rs] If prayer time overtakes the devot[ee] in the desert or away from water, he is allowed to use sand in its stead.

The Egyptian is very superstitious; so much so that he writes or carves a lucky sentence over his door to keep away the evil eye, which he fancies pervades all space and is ever ready to work mischief. The lintel and doorposts of palaces are often covered with a string of hieroglyphics which reveal to the initiated the title and offices of the owner. Occasionally one sees a stuffed crocodile over a door; this is supposed to bring great good luck.

The harem of a wealthy pasha with a quartet of wives is like a small hotel. There is a large drawing-room where all the ladies may receive visitors who are not intimate enough to be received in the private apartment. In most cases this room is furnished with chairs and tables, and occasionally there are other concessions to European taste. The little smoker's stands with cigarettes and matches are always present, for the Oriental ladies are much given to smoking, and consider a visitor very rude who refuses to smoke with them.

Familiar quotations from the Koran, the Moslem Bible, are cut, carved and embroidered everywhere; sometimes one sees an entire frieze consisting of these quotations. A decoration which the natives use for lining the tents which they erect for weddings and other festivals is frequently used by the artistic European for hangings in a room. The foundation is awning cloth and the design sewn on. The boy who does it works with the point of the needle from him, not running from right to left as we do. The designs are very conventional and practically all over. For instance, the center may be of compass pattern with shapes of turkey red appliquéd on, this circled with leaves of green or red, and an outside border of yellow. But whatever the design or shape of the piece, there will always be found a quotation from the Koran at top or bottom.

In the harem as in the selamlik, on luxurious divans the women sit surrounded by their servants, and smoke the great Turkish water-pipe or the omnipresent cigarette.

AN EGYPTIAN MOTHER
AND CHILD

Servants are so numerous that they are in each other's way, eunuchs are expensive luxuries, and only the very rich and conservative men keep them. They do the buying and daily catering and ordering for the entire family. A eunuch takes the place of a footman and rides on the box with the coachman. When ladies visit the house he meets them and conducts them through the narrow, winding stairways that lead to the harem; here he turns them over to a female servant, who falls upon her knees, kisses the hem of the visitor's skirts and gives the Arabic salutation, viz., she touches her forehead and breast, symbolic actions signifying that in thought, word and heart she is the slave of her superior.

Although husband and wife seem to live very much apart, it really is not the case, for the husband often seeks consolation, coffee and cigarettes with his family. While he is in the harem no one is allowed to disturb him or to call him, even upon important business. He may not visit the harem at all times. A white veil hanging on the door lintel warns him that strange ladies are within, and that he must not intrude. This signal the Moslem respects most religiously. Among the poorer people, the husband in mounting the harem stairs gives a peculiar warning cry, thus admonishing visitors to cover their faces.

The Egyptian women spend a great deal of time in the bath, parties of friends often spending the whole day there. Coffee is offered to visitors at all times, and is the last course of each meal. It is Turkish coffee, and is always half full of grounds, but it has a delicious taste and a fragrance not found in any other country. The thimble-like porcelain cups are set into a silver filigree holder delicate as gossamer.

The poor people live in mud huts, with roofs of palm branches or millet stalks. Nearly everyone has a pigeon house on the flat roof and goats and other domestic animals run about with the children. The women work in the fields, and they buy their food largely from the perambulating restaurants, and the corner shops.

The children of rich and poor are carried about astride the shoulder of nurse or mother, as the case may be. They are dear little brown things and seem to enjoy their high perch.

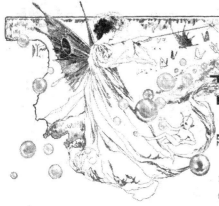

THE LEGEND OF THE SNOWDROP

BY ADDIE M. BASS

A FANTASY FOR LITTLE FOLKS

SCENE.—*Woods with Fairy's throne in center. The throne is effective if made to represent a moss bank or bower of ferns, but no flowers must be used in its construction.*

TIME.—*Midnight. Represent moonlight if possible by using a blue calcium light.*

CAST.—FAIRY QUEEN *and as many* FAIRIES *as can be on stage. Some of these* FAIRIES *to be* FLOWERS *afterward.* FLIES, MOTHS, BUTTERFLIES, GLOWWORMS.

COSTUMES.—FAIRIES *in conventional fairy costume; let it be as airy as possible. The spangles that are used to throw over Christmas trees can be very effectively employed. Have the* QUEEN *more elaborate than the other* FAIRIES. *Butterflies can be represented by little boys, if desired; have blue and yellow suits with large wings. The* MOTHS *should be in cotton, flannel or outing in gray or cream, with wings which fasten to the feet, if boys; to the bottom of the skirts, if girls.* GLOWWORMS *in flowing black robes, and concealed in the robe small lanterns which they show alternately by opening and closing the robe over it. The* FLOWERS *can be represented in two ways, by using the flowers (artificial will do) in wreaths or garlands, and trimmings on white dresses, but they will be more effective as follows:* ROSE: *Skirt of rose-colored near-silk cut in pieces similar to rose petals, the first row the length of a short skirt, the second shorter, the third still shorter, the bodice of the same color, with light-green laps, two in front, one on each shoulder and one in the back. There can be a hat of one large paper rose or a mass of roses.* LILY: *White near-silk, five petals wired so as to curl backward at bottom. This must be worn over a simple white skirt, the bodice of light green, and hat to represent a lily turned upside down.* VIOLET: *Same material in violet color, five petals, but not curled back, cap of flower.* MORNING-GLORY: *Light pink or blue tight skirt flared at the bottom, green cape and hat.* SUNFLOWER: *Yellow skirt, many petals same length, black bodice, yellow cap.* PASSION FLOWER: *Lavender skirt, white waist, green cape, yellow bow as nearly like the petals of a passion flower as possible.* PANSY: *Purple skirt, five large petals, waist to form one large pansy.* DAFFODIL: *Yellow plain skirt with five short panels of same, green bodice, yellow cap.* THISTLEDOWN *(who is afterward* SNOWDROP*): White dress with rows of white silk fringe, or white tissue-paper fringed out to look light and fluffy. In the second scene have the same or similar, much soiled and torn, utterly ruined. For* SNOWDROP *have a long, soft circular cloak, with five points tipped with green, and green hood. This double character should be taken by a very small child.*

SCENE I.—*The curtain rises on woodland scene with* GLOWWORMS *lying around, lights shining occasionally.*

FIRST GLOWWORM: 'Tis the hour of midnight and the Fairy train will soon be here.

SECOND GLOWWORM: The sounds of their light steps I hear on the lea.

THIRD GLOWWORM: My light shall brighten the plain for their dance.

ALL: And mine, and mine.

(*Enter the* FAIRIES, *skipping to music, from sides and back of stage, some driving* BUTTERFLIES *and* MOTHS, *which as soon as they are released go to trees and rest both hands on it as if posing, others come on by twos and threes; let there be no regular form as a march. The music must be light and airy, and the* FAIRIES *should never walk but trip in graceful dance steps.*)

FIRST FAIRY: The charmed hour has almost come when our gracious Queen will be here and we may know the fate that waits us.

SECOND FAIRY: Let us form the fairy circle and dance while we wait.

FIRST FIGURE: *All form circle and go half round, then back again.*

SECOND FIGURE: *Every second fairy drops inside of ring and others pass round, then back again.*

THIRD FIGURE: *Those inside ring join hands and form second ring. First ring raise hands, still holding, and second ring stoop and pass under, still holding hands. This makes a double ring; pass round and back.*

FOURTH FIGURE: *First ring loose hands and step inside center of ring, as in figure two. Second ring passes round and back.*

FIFTH FIGURE: *Repeat figure three with second ring on outside.*

SIXTH FIGURE: *Loose hands and round in single ring and back.* QUEEN *enters from right, driving two* BUTTER-FLIES.

Two FAIRIES *assist her to the throne.* BUTTERFLIES *go to trees and* FAIRIES *drop on knees.*

ALL: Welcome most gracious sovereign, to the bowers that Nature has prepared for thee. We humbly kneel to wait our Queen's behest.

QUEEN: Most loyal subjects arise and trip the fairy ring.

SEVENTH FIGURE: *Fairies rise and form two lines with hands up and* QUEEN *passes under arch; the rings then form circle. Ring around* QUEEN *and back again, holding hands up.*

EIGHTH FIGURE: *Two* FAIRIES *join* QUEEN *in ring, kneel on either side, forming pose, while ring goes round.* FAIRIES *back to place,* QUEEN *back on throne.*

FAIRIES *sing (see music on page 556):*

"Oh, where do fairies hide their heads,
When snow lies on the hill,
And frost does cover their mossy bed,
And crystal lies the rill,
And crystal lies the rill?
Beneath the moon they cannot skip
In circles o'er the plain,
And from the stream they cannot sip
Till green leaves come again.

"When they return there will be mirth
  And music in the air,
  And fairy voices in the earth,
  And mischief everywhere,
  And mischief everywhere.
The maids to keep the elves aloof
  Will bar their doors in vain;
No keyhole will be fairy-proof
  When green leaves come again,
No keyhole will be fairy-proof
  When green leaves come again."

"OH, WHERE DO FAIRIES HIDE THEIR HEADS ?"

(QUEEN *waves her hand, the* FAIRIES *fall in to attentive attitudes.*)

QUEEN (*rising*): My loyal subjects of the fairy realm, we have met this night not on pleasure bound, but to decide a most important question. We have in our band many willing subjects who have no work to do, and as we are a busy people there must be something found for them. We will now hear any suggestions that thoughtful fairies have to make.

FIRST FAIRY (*kneels to* QUEEN *and at a nod from her rises*): Most royal Queen, I suggest that a band of fairies go to the deep blue sea and in its caves hide, there to sing most beautiful songs and teach the fishes to make sweet music.

SECOND FAIRY (*salutes the* QUEEN): Gracious Queen of the Fairies, that idea is preposterous. The fishes can never learn to sing, and if they did, of what use would it be? The waves rush over them with such a mighty noise that they could never hear their own music. I have a plan which is much more plausible. Let the unemployed fairies go to the deep green woods and teach the songbirds new strains; many there are who warble only one note.

THIRD FAIRY (*salutes*): Happy Queen of the Fairies, what a monotonous world this would be if every bird should sing the same song, nor would we know which bird was singing if all sang just alike. Let the unemployed fairies go to the moon to find employment there in keeping its silver face bright.

ALL: No, no.

FOURTH FAIRY: Wise and youthful Queen, I am old, I have had much experience, and one thing I have noticed is lacking to make this great world perfect—let those who need employment from the ranks of the fairies form an order that shall be called the Flowers, and let each one belonging to the order assume some virtue or quality, the exercise of which shall be of benefit to the human race; and let her choose such a dress as shall be in keeping with the quality she has taken upon herself.

ALL: Good.

QUEEN: You have spoken most wisely, and it shall be as you have said; all of those who are to be found the new order shall have one month in which to select the

flower she will represent and the dress she will wear; let us have one round and disperse.

(FAIRIES *form ring round* QUEEN, *pass round, then back, then join hands and in twos dance off the stage as curtain falls.*)

SCENE II.—GLOWWORMS *Dance: Slow music. The* GLOWWORMS *pass slowly around the half-darkened stage, showing lights occasionally. Form two lines and come from right and left back, of stage, crossing in the center back to right and left, and cross in center. As they cross, each passes half around the other.*

SONG (*see music below*):
  "Glow, glow, bright the show,
    How the night we lighten
  Slow, slow make the glow,
    That the woods may brighten.

  "Glowworms, show your little light,
    Men and fairies leading,
  Through the darkness of the night
    All our glows are needing.

  "Glow, glow, bright the show,
    How the night we lighten,
  Slow, slow, make the glow,
    That the woods may brighten."

(GLOWWORMS *take same positions as in first scene. Enter* FAIRIES *as before and* QUEEN *driving Butterflies.* QUEEN *takes seat on throne. Fancy dances may be introduced here, if desired; if not, all form ring as in first scene.*)

BUTTERFLY (*enters, kneels to* QUEEN): Gracious Queen of the Fairies, the members of the new order are without.

QUEEN: Admit them, Butterfly.

(BUTTERFLY *leads in* FLOWERS, *who stand with hands clasped and head bowed.*)

QUEEN: My subjects, do you fully understand the nature of the work that is before you? (FLOWERS *bow their heads.*) And are you prepared to fulfil this work as becomes loyal subjects of our kingdom? (FLOWERS *bow.*) It is well. May you brighten the world, lighten the hearts of men, and give comfort to the sorrowful.

QUEEN (*waves her wand to the first*): What color and quality do you choose?

FIRST FLOWER: I choose the color of the sky at dawning, because then the world awakes to life and hope. I should

"GLOWWORM SONG"

like to be a token to all who see me of the love, the sweetness and the light that are in the world.

QUEEN: You have chosen both well and wisely. You shall be called the Rose, and shall represent both hope and happiness.

(*A robe of pink is brought by a* BUTTERFLY *and put on the* ROSE.)

QUEEN (*to* SECOND FLOWER): What is your choice?

SECOND FLOWER: I choose the color of the purple clouds at sunset, for the sun has departed and the world is in shadow. But as the light will surely come to us again,

I would that I might recall to memory the absent, and so give rise to thoughts of the joys of reunion.

QUEEN: Your choice is also wisely made. (BUTTER-FLIES *at a sign from* QUEEN *bring purple dress. As each other Fairy ceases speaking,* BUTTERFLIES *clothe them in appropriate robes.*) Take this robe of softest purple and become a Pansy, for the thoughts of friends. (*Turns to* THIRD Fairy): And what will this little Fairy take?

THIRD Fairy: I will choose the color of the deep blue sea. The world is full of trouble, and some there are who find it deep as is the sea, yet comfort may be found for all. Let my mission be to comfort those who sorrow.

QUEEN: You shall be called the Violet; your breath shall be so sweet and pure that when you speak to those in grief they shall indeed be comforted. (*To* FOURTH Fairy): And yours?

FOURTH Fairy: I wish to be of the pure gold of the sun, for I wish to rejoice the hearts of men as does the coming of the day.

QUEEN: You shall be called the Daffodil, and shall welcome in the spring each year; and all shall rejoice when you appear. (*To* FIFTH Fairy): And your choice?

FIFTH Fairy: I would be as white as the snows of winter, and like them inspire men to purity of life and thought. I want to make all better by my example in spotlessness.

QUEEN: You shall be called the Lily. By your example of purity all shall be taught that it is possible to also be pure. (*Turns to next.*) What is your wish?

SIXTH Fairy: I also would be of golden hue and teach adoration to all who know me. I would rise above the ground and look to heaven to offer up my constant prayer.

QUEEN: You may be the Sunflower, and as the glorious orb passes in his daily round you may follow his course and show to men it is right to keep the great example always before them. (*To* SEVENTH Fairy): What is your choice?

SEVENTH Fairy: I wish to be the color of the summer sky, so bright and blue, and of the rosy clouds about it, that I may speak of love and happiness to all.

QUEEN: And you shall be called the Morning-Glory, and shall be the first to open your eyes on the light of day, teaching men to be always watchful. And now, little one, you have seen how wisely all have chosen. I trust your choice has been as wisely made.

EIGHTH Fairy: I would be like the dark-purple storm clouds, but have a silver lining, that all men may know that there is hope.

QUEEN: Wise little Fairy! You shall be the Passion Flower. And now, the last—what do you wish that you may make all happy?

NINTH FAIRY: I only want to enjoy myself, so I will choose to be the Thistledown. Then I can skip about and dance in the golden sunlight.

QUEEN: Think, little fairy! you are so young and tiny you do not know what you are asking. Take time and reconsider, for what you have said is very weak and foolish, little one. There are many more flowers to choose.

(*All the* FAIRIES *look shocked and* NINTH *Fairy hangs her head, but does not answer.*)

QUEEN (*after a pause*): Are you still desirous of having your wish?

(FAIRY *bows her head.*)

QUEEN (*sadly*): Foolish child, I will give you what you ask, but, remember, your choice is ill-made and will not prosper you; your thoughts are only for yourself. The dress of Thistledown, though it may be beautiful at first, will not suffice to shield you from the cold; yet, as I have promised to give to each one what she should ask, you, shall have your wish.

QUEEN: Go, now, Flowers, and may you each fulfil your destiny as you have chosen.

(*The* FLOWERS *skip off the stage to bright music; the* FAIRIES *form ring and dance as the curtain falls.*)

SCENE III.—*Curtain rises on same scene with* FLOWERS *grouped about;* QUEEN *enters with her train; when she is seated the* FAIRIES *form ring and sing.*

SONG (*see music this page*): "Hark to the fairies' lively strain, While o'er the ground the steps resound, And hearts are glad, While all are mad To hear the joyous sound. Floating on some beam of light, Springing are these spirits bright, Now through the mazes hieing, then flying away.

"Hark to the fairies' lively strain, While o'er the ground the steps resound, And hearts are glad, While all are mad To hear the joyous sound. Sweet the linnet's strain, While o'er the ground the songs **resound**, And hearts are glad, While all are mad To hear the joyous sound."

[*Repeat "Hark to Fairies."*]

" HARK TO THE FAIRIES' LIVELY STRAIN "

QUEEN: Let us hear the report of the flowers. What has our Rose to report?

ROSE (*saluting*): Oh, Queen, I am happy in the labor assigned me. I have given hope to the broken-hearted. The blush that plays on the face of health and hope is called by my name. Nor have I let the wicked go unpunished. With the prick of my thorns have I stung those who intrude upon my privileges. For me the world is brighter.

QUEEN: Well done! Go, my Rose, and continue the work you have so well begun. What has the Pansy to say of her work?

PANSY (*saluting*): Oh, Queen, my mission has been a beautiful one. I have given thoughts to the lonely that have brought to them the memory of absent friends and they have blessed me.

QUEEN: You, too, have done your duty well. May you always be so blessed. And now, little Violet, what have you to say?

VIOLET (*saluting*): Mighty Queen, I have given comfort to the sorrowing and oppressed. My message has been a sweet one, and all who know me call me the modest Violet.

QUEEN: Modesty is a great virtue; you have done well. And now Daffodil—what have you done?

DAFFODIL (*saluting*): Most happy Queen, I am much beloved in my bright work. When I raise my head above the earth all rejoice that spring is here.

QUEEN: It is good to bring joy to the heart, Daffodil. Lily, how has your work succeeded?

LILY (*saluting*): Love, ambition, and purity have sought me and have loved my snowy robe and simple grace.

QUEEN: Purity is ever rewarded. Sunflower, how is it with you?

SUNFLOWER (*saluting*): Mighty Queen, I followed the great sun in his course and taught men to worship always and to never lose sight of the Father of all. They call me the example of men.

QUEEN: A wise choice. Now, Morning-glory?

MORNING-GLORY (*saluting*): Oh, Queen, I did your bidding and welcomed in the glorious morn, and delighted all by my grace and beauty.

QUEEN: That is well. Passion Flower?

PASSION FLOWER (*saluting*): Sorrow took courage at my presence.

(*At the end of the line the* THISTLEDOWN *stands all soiled and torn, with her head hung down. The* QUEEN *looks stern when she sees her.*)

QUEEN: You have also done well. Well, Thistledown, what have you done with your year?

THISTLEDOWN: Nothing.

QUEEN: Nothing! And have you been satisfied?

THISTLEDOWN (*weeping*): Oh, no, no, no!

QUEEN: You feel that you made an unwise choice when you wished only to be beautiful and amuse yourself?

THISTLEDOWN: Yes, oh, yes!

QUEEN: Then, that is one point in your favor. You at least realize your fault, but of course you have no report to make, so you may go as we have matters of importance to attend to.

THISTLEDOWN (*falling upon her knees*): Oh, Queen, give me some work to do like my sisters.

QUEEN: It is too late; you have made your choice, now you must abide by it; you have worn out your dress and a new one cannot be made for you; you are a useless subject; we cannot let you take up our time.

THISTLEDOWN: Gracious Queen, give me one more trial; anything, no matter how hard it may be, or how lowly, so that I may not feel that my life has been thrown away.

(*The* QUEEN *whispers with some of the* FAIRIES.)

QUEEN: You do not deserve clemency, but as you repent of your fault and wish to lead a different life we will see what can be done for you. There is but one vacancy, and that has been left because the duties attached to it are so difficult to perform and the privations so great that no fairy has felt that she could undertake them. But, if, as you say, you have truly repented of your folly, and wish to lead an honored and useful life, you must become a snowdrop, and early in the year, before the winter is done, you must push your way up through the cold, frozen earth and snow, and stand as a messenger to tell that spring is coming. It will be very hard, for flowers suffer in the freezing snow; the cold will be bitter and the winds will bite, but you will have your reward when men shall see you and rejoice that you herald the time of flowers. Have you courage to undertake all this?

THISTLEDOWN: Dear Queen, I will undertake it.

QUEEN (*to* FAIRIES): Combine these colors into pure white and lead her back. (THISTLEDOWN *is lead away to return in the garb of a Snowdrop.*) Now, my little Snowdrop, you are the herald of all flowers, may you have courage to faithfully perform your duties.

(FLOWERS *form arch and the* QUEEN *followed by her* FAIRIES, BUTTERFLIES, MOTHS, GLOWWORMS, *etc.*, *march under it and pass off the stage. Curtain falls.*)

GOD'S GIFTS

By GERTRUDE BRYANT JUBB

HE gave to the eye of the sculptor
   A vision of line and grace ;
And a hand that was true, to chisel
   The beauty of form and face.

He gave to the soul of the painter
   An ideal, wondrous fair ;
And out from its lights and shadows
   He fashioned a picture rare.

He gave to the great musician
   A voice that was sweet and clear—
And full of the softest cadence,
   That thousands rejoiced to hear.

He gave to the brave young lover
   A rosebud—all wet with dew ;
And he from its snowy petals
   Deciphered his answer true.

He gave to the lover of Nature
   The birds, and trees, and flowers ;
The brooks, with their babbling music,
   The shadowy, fragrant bowers.

But the "one gift" that is priceless,
   As pearls from the ocean wild,
He gave to the heart of woman—
   The love of a little child.

IN THE INTEREST
of BEAUTY

By
BERTHA HASBROOK

IV.—EXTRAVAGANT ECONOMIES

THE other day an eminent nerve specialist said to me with particularly earnest emphasis: "Women, almost without exception, are absolutely wasteful in their ways of saving money. They are recklessly extravagant of their health in order to save a few dollars. When the woman of business and the over-thrifty home-maker learn to afford summer vacations, golf clubs and riding-habits, they will save double the cost of all these—it now goes into our pockets."

It was very reckless of him, to be sure, to make such a statement, for nerve specialists will be obliged to rent smaller houses and do without automobiles when women learn the true way to economize. But it is his own fault if woman profits and he loses by this frankness. He gave it freely; it was not wrung from him, and he knew it was for publication. Perhaps he also knew, smiling in his well-tailored sleeve, that woman would continue to wreck herself, body and nerves, to the end of the chapter.

One type of woman does this in the social whirl; she belongs to another story. It is the woman who does it through her mistaken idea of economy that the doctor was talking about. She is the stenographer on a small salary; the artist or writer trying to establish herself in a great city; the mother of too many; the young wife trying to help her husband piece out a slender income by making a domestic drudge of herself. Each and every one of these is wilfully throwing away her health, her youth and her beauty.

Now, money is always to be had for the effort, but health, youth and beauty are not; therefore, they are the things to be treasured, even at the expense of some dollars. If you believe that you are a very thrifty young woman, if you are secretly

ARRAYED CORRECTLY FOR STORMY WEATHER

or boastfully priding yourself upon living upon nine or ten dollars a week, less maybe, and banking money, stop to look over the matter in a sensible manner. Are you sure, although you think you are being so economical, you are not being wantonly extravagant of your charms?

I knew two girls, plucky as girls are made, who came to New York to make a way for themselves. They rented a tiny room and determined to economize in every way possible until they could get a start in business. The first thing that occurred to them was to save money on their laundry.

Seventy-five cents a dozen, the regulation price in New York, looked an appalling price to them, for they had lived in a small town where the weekly family wash was put out at a very low price. They were dainty in their love of cleanliness, too, and felt they must have plenty of fresh linen if life was to be endurable.

"Let's see what we can accomplish with the tin basin and a bar of soap," one of them proposed.

Now, the couple had enough money to pay for the laundry, but they were a bit timid about spending it, so they set to work in their own room. Thus they washed piece after piece, one at a time, in the humble tin basin their landlady furnished them, and they tied a cord from the closet door to the chiffonier for a clothes-line, and thereupon they hung their clammy washing. Night after night these damp pieces hung there and the girls slept under them, and in the end one of them faced a doctor's bill for attendance upon her severe case of pneumonia, not to speak of her druggist's bill, which was far from small, either of which would have paid for many, many dozens of clean linen.

Economy in the matter of warm clothing seems to be a passion with the woman of small means.

" THE WORN-OUT GIRL WHO DARNS AFTER MIDNIGHT "

Perhaps she saves on her woolen underwear for the sake of a lace hat; perhaps she does it in order to lay away money in bank. Whether vanity or prudence be her motive, she is all wrong. Without health a woman cannot be beautiful, and she positively cannot have health unless she gives health a fair chance. Some women may be so rugged that they can stand the changes of our variable climate without making a difference in their underclothing, but they are the rarest exceptions to the rule, and the girl who boasts, "I never wear flannel," is usually the one who suffers from perpetual colds, neuralgia or backache. Yet it is almost impossible to make her believe her own false economy is the cause of her ills. She will blame the draughts about her, the weather, anything but herself.

Dress yourself properly for all weathers. All-wool underwear is somewhat expensive, but it is a winter necessity in any ordinarily cold climate, and you can not afford to economize on it. Moreover, you must have union suits. Physicians say that the weight of the woolen is not as important as the fact that the body be covered everywhere with equal warmth. A sleeveless shirt, no matter how warm, does not accomplish the purpose for which underwear is made.

Buy a good raincoat that will cover your dress well. Have sound overshoes of some kind: storm rubbers are excellent, in spite of all that has been said against them. There are high and high-priced waterproof boots that are extremely smart and useful, but you may really be unable to afford these, and the rubbers keep your feet equally dry. If you are taking country tramps, swallow your vanity and don rubber boots. If you are a business woman, keep a second supply of storm accessories on hand, so that you are never caught unprotected. Two dollars spent in extra rubbers and umbrella to be held in reserve at the office will save their value many times over in a single season, not only for the shoes and hat they will shelter from damage, but for fines for loss of time from business

and the doctor's bills which are apt to result from wet feet and shoulders.

Be lavish with yourself in the matter of heat. Don't try to convince yourself that you are plenty warm enough on a rainy spring night without turning on the gas stove. Suppose your gas bill should mount up a dollar or so higher in the course of the month, what of it? It is infinitely better to pay that extra dollar or so than to be attacked by unbecoming sniffles and, perhaps, a cough, which always lurks in the background when sniffles are about.

The worn-out girl who sits up after midnight to darn a pair of stockings that could be replaced for thirty-five cents, ought to be sent to bed with a sound spanking. Darning, especially by lamp or gas light, is racking to the nerves. Plenty of it is inflicted upon us anyway; for mercy's sake, let's not seek it. Stockings can often be bought for a quarter, very durable ones, and excellent ones are in every store for half a dollar the pair. Throw the holey pairs into the rag-bag and start afresh. Those late hours that you have been devoting to their repairing should bring you beauty sleep. Go to bed and wake to see what nature has been doing for you. She is the first and foremost beauty doctor of the world, despite what all the advertisements claim for Madame Adeline Arabelle and Madame Elise Fifine. She will smooth the wrinkles out of that very much puckered young brow and bring a pinkness to the cheeks and a sparkle to the eyes. Give her a fair chance before you are compelled to try the others.

Besides mending, you are very likely extravagant in making your own clothes. Don't, if you are a business woman. Buy your clothes ready-made, if you must, which is probably cheaper than going to a dressmaker. Save your nerves and save your eyes. A girl who has been giving proper attention to her business all day is not in a condition of mind or body to take up the profession of modiste after she

A POOR WAY TO SAVE MONEY

comes home, even if she herself is to be the beneficiary of her labors. Remember, too, that glasses are dreadfully unbecoming to a girlish face. Your eyes may be laying up a tremendous revenge for abuses heaped upon them.

It is pitiable to hear some tired women talk about the way they save nickels, always concluding with the observation, "Nickels count up." They forget that the tiny self-denials count up, too, sometimes very much to one's disadvantage. A woman will walk a mile in the heat to save one five-cent piece, which a street-car ride would cost. She will struggle with an overpacked suit case to save the second five-cent piece, for which a boy would gladly have carried it. Weary and warm, she will look longingly at a lemonade, but that would cost a third five-cent piece. She has now saved three of them and she arrives at home heated, dusty, and with a headache that puts her to bed for an afternoon. But she has the satisfying conviction that she has economized.

"SHE WILL STRUGGLE WITH A SUIT CASE TO SAVE FIVE CENTS."

The woman who works is usually stingy with herself in the matter of amusement. If she has generous friends who take her to theaters, concerts and lectures, this is not important, but if she is lonely and a stranger she must provide herself with an occasional treat. A rut is the thing to be most sedulously avoided. It is the getting into a rut which ages women faster than anything else. Take some of your own hard-earned money and invest it in a ticket to the first good concert or dramatic performance that comes your way. Go to the affair and forget the cost as much as if it concerned some other pocket than yours. Simply enjoy yourself. Induce another girl to go with you if possible, for companionship is a tonic, but go alone if you must rather than not go at all. If you are married, do this for the sake of your husband, whether he accompanies you or not. You must keep yourself cheery if you want to keep him devoted. No need for you to neglect your home duties for the little pleasure-taking. On the contrary, you will discover they are apt to prove much lighter for your occasional diversion.

Never economize in the matter of small toilet accessories—cold cream, good soap, manicure implements and the like—all of which serve to keep you dainty, sweet and altogether charming. You cannot afford such economy.

Indulge, by all means, in some form of physical culture. Choose whatever form seems best for you. It may be a gymnasium club, it may be a dancing class, it may be some game, such as bowling, tennis or golf—whatever it is, you cannot afford to do without some beautifier of this kind.

Beware of cheap fineries. Don't, I beg of you, purchase a ready-made coat or costume whose price betokens its worthlessness. In the beginning it will look smart, and you will congratulate yourself on having secured a bargain—hateful word! But wait until you are caught in an unexpected shower, or have given it strenuous service in crowded cars or on dusty avenues, and see how the skirt will shrink into unsightly ripples, how the coat will crease and wrinkle, how the sleeves will twist ungracefully, and how the entire suit will proclaim itself what it is—cheap. Better to have one suit made by a good tailor, of first-class sponged material, fitted as only an artist in the sartorial line can fit, than two from the bargain counter which will never look exactly right and that will require a dozen little additions which in the end will bring their cost nearly to that of the really good costume.

It is the same with millinery. The showy hat, put together of cotton-backed velvets, half-linen satin, paper-muslin flowers and feathers which in their present coloring and shaping never came from any bird known to the naturalist, looks all right in the window and, for the first week or so, on the head, then the colors fade, the velvet becomes hopelessly dusty, and the feathers begin to fly as the glue which held them together is dissolved in the sun or dampness. You have paid five or six dollars for the hat, maybe, and thought how economical you have been in comparison with some young woman who has spent ten dollars on a plain little velvet toque with a pheasant's plume at the side, yet that young woman is certain of getting two winters' good wear out of her toque, and even then the velvet and feathers are certainly good enough to use again, while your materials will not even be serviceable for a self-respecting pincushion.

Cheap gloves will split, and never fit the hand properly. Two-dollar gloves will wear twice as well, clean beautifully, make your hand look more shapely, and generally the manufacturer from whom you purchase them will keep them in perfect repair for you, not including the cleaning, of course.

Cheap shoes will hurt your feet, possibly produce corns and bunions, and will basely abuse your confidence by springing unexpected cracks when most inconvenient. Two pair of good shoes made to order will carry you through two years at least; what's more, will keep their shape.

These little extravagances pay. The woman who is healthy and fresh and attractive stands a better chance at every turn in the business world. A married woman's happiness hangs upon her ability to keep those qualities. Beware of extravagant economies. And remember: One dollar well spent for present needs is worth ten in the bank laid up for possible emergencies which may never arise.

HINTS FOR FURNISHING SMALL HOMES
BY MARY KILSYTH

THE common mistake in fitting up a small home is to overfill it with furniture. The superabundance of furnishings may not be a matter of direct outlay, but the accumulation of many years of housekeeping, the selections made for more spacious quarters or the generous gifts of friends.

From whatever source the contracted spaces have become overburdened, it is wise, in the home of small size, to do away with every article of furniture that is not absolutely essential for comfortable living. Decoration, also, may be restricted, with the exception of pictures, to such things as contribute use in combination with beauty. This double purpose of utility and ornament gives not only economy of space but saves in a pecuniary way, and, instead of investing in many

A SEAT ON THE STAIR LANDING

objects that are poor in quality, better prices can be paid for higher class articles.

In rooms of no very capacious extent the seating problem is often a difficult one. Enough chairs for the family may be provided, but great inconvenience is often caused by introducing extra seats for visitors. A window bench is, in such cases, a good substitute for a sofa. Or, an angle of the wall may be fitted with a seat of wood that is covered with a thin hair cushion. A built-in seat is also an advantage in a narrow hall, or on the stair landing, as a reading or sewing nook.

In one tiny home a low screen which formed part of a bedroom equipment was also a complete little sewing and work table, with pockets and shelves for holding thread, buttons, tape, needles and patterns. The screen was light enough to be easily handled,

A SCREEN FOR SEWING WORK

and so compact as to take a minimum amount of space when unfolded. Another space-saving device was originated in a sitting-room with an unused fireplace, as pictured on this page. Without the application of hammer or nails a book shelf was laid between the columns that supported the mantel.

One way to give the appearance of space to small dwellings is to lay the floors of connecting rooms and passageways with a plain or small-patterned carpet, and to cover all the walls alike in a plain paper or one that is printed in two tones of the same color. In either one of these arrangements there will be the question of harmonizing the different colors in the rooms with the one large amount of color introduced on walls or floor.

Color has so important a share in increasing or decreasing the apparent size of a room that it should be selected with infinite care. Red seems to contract the walls and give a feeling of density; light yellow or buff has an opposite effect. Low ceilings do not seem as prominent if colored a cream white as they do when tinted in a stronger color.

The height of a ceiling may be seemingly increased by using a striped paper with well-defined lines. Narrow hallways look wider when the walls are plain or covered with a paper of unobtrusive design. In all wall decoration in small houses or apartments the papers to avoid are those that proclaim themselves as "the latest thing," and in which prominent pattern and aggressive color force themselves disagreeably on the attention. Borders and friezes need not be considered for the walls of the small home, as windows and doorways cut into the spaces too much to make an upper-wall decoration desirable.

A SPACE-SAVING DEVICE

The furniture need not be on a miniature scale to suit the dimensions of a small house, but it should be in proportion to the lines of the room and suit the spaces in which it stands. Sometimes conventional appointments may be set aside for others that better suit certain conditions.

In a hallway where an oak hat-rack had for many years been in the way of everyone entering by the front door, a season of housecleaning fortunately found this piece of furniture too disabled to be put to further use. While looking about for another to take its place, some brass hat-hooks were fastened to the casing of the doorway and a narrow wooden settle was placed in a niche in the wall. The temporary arrangement proved to be so much more suitable that it was retained permanently.

Window treatment is another opportunity for making the interior of small houses seem less confined. Casement windows do not need more than a single curtain hung to the sill ready to be drawn at night. This plan was adopted in a summer home in the woods, selecting cotton material to match the color of the walls. Thin net or lace hung a little below the window-sill with not very much fullness does away with the stuffy feeling that long, heavy draperies give to contracted quarters.

The owner of a seashore cottage discovered a way to economize floor space and save an outlay of money for three articles of furniture by utilizing some unused doorways. In one, some shelves were fastened between the casing and filled with books and magazines; in another, a china closet was made by adding small doors with diamond panes of glass; in a third, some hooks for wraps, etc., were screwed under an upper shelf for a hat rest, and a lower shelf put in for holding shoes.

A WINDOW-BENCH TAKES THE PLACE OF A SOFA

THROUGH THE THICK OF THE STORM
BY HARRIET CARYL COX

DRAWING BY HORACE TAYLOR

IT CERTAINLY WAS a terrible storm.

For twenty-four .hours it had been snowing heavily, and the wind had gradually risen from a gentle blow to a fierce hurricane. With the increased cold the snow had grown finer, and now its keen particles beat and cut into the faces of unprotected travelers. Telegraph wires broke under its weight. Trains were belated. The evening papers had big scare-heads of the damage done in the harbor and along the coast, and there were sad tales of those who had died from cold and exposure.

The newsboys cried their headings for a moment, then retreated to a neighboring doorway to regain breath and warm chilled hands. Men shivered and the few women and children who chanced by ill luck to be abroad gasped for breath as they struggled to shelter.

Out in the bay the captain of the tug "Spitfire" beat a hasty retreat into his cabin. He was covered with ice, and his long beard was a mass of tiny icicles.

"I shall be most mightily glad to get in," he said to the second mate, as he unbuttoned his rubber jacket and sent bits of ice hissing against the hot stove. "I haven't seen anything like it in a dozen years, and I hope I sha'n't in another. The weather is so thick you can't see a thing. Just now we scraped the side of a schooner so that we must have left a mark on her. We're likely to run down or be run down, and I wish we were in."

He went to the window and tried to look out. A gust of snow beat against it like a handful of pebbles, and a fog-horn sounded with startling distinctness.

The captain opened the door with a bang and was out again in the storm. Behind the tug, in tow, was a small schooner. Her masts were stripped, and all save the lookout were below, safely sheltered from the storm. Suddenly there was a shout, and feet hurried over the deck.

"Boat adrift, and some one in it," was the lookout's reply, as his practised arm threw a life-belt toward the dark object below.

The line tightened.

"We've got 'em," said the mate as he made fast the rope, "but I'm thinking no boat won't live long in a sea like that," and he gazed anxiously down at the speck that rose and fell.

"We can't draw her up, and there's no way to signal the tug," he muttered, as he walked back to where the lookout stood, and peered forward into the blinding storm. The tug was steaming steadily ahead, and the rope was taut.

He raised his trumpet, and gave a loud "Tug ahoy!" but the words were caught by the wind, tossed to leeward and lost in the roar of the storm.

"They'll have to chance it, poor devils," and he gave the boat a parting glance as he went below.

The wind had subsided a little, and the flakes were softer and less biting. Morning was dawning, and one of the "Spitfire's" crew stood looking back at the looming figure of the schooner.

His keen eyes traveled along the hawser that held her in tow. There was something black on it. ' "Caught some wreckage, I reckon," he thought half-aloud, as he went for the glass.

The spot seemed to come nearer. "It's a dog," the watcher cried, and then beckoned to one of the crew. "No, it's a man."

Slowly along the hawser, hand over hand, the figure moved. A ladder was run over the side, and a sailor swiftly slid to the end and stood, hook in hand.

The figure stopped. One arm loosened. The body swayed.

The men ground their teeth. "Hold on—once more—there!" as the hand again clasped the rope. One clutch and the figure was within reach of the hook.

Arms were outstretched, and rough hands grasped the dripping body as the sailor sprang up the ladder with his burden. It was a boy. They took him into the cabin and applied restoratives. "He'll come out of it," the captain said, as he felt the heart beating stronger and more regularly.

"But now we'll see what it means," and he drew from between the lad's teeth a bit of oilskin.

Inside was a paper:

"Stop the tug. Small boat in tow lost. Woman inside. Almost swamped. Will put back for her. Hold till we signal to start up.   REDDING."

A hurried order, the sound of escaping steam, a swash of water against her sides, and the tug ceased to move save for a gentle drifting.

"And you came all the way over the hawser, through that ice-cold water, to tell us to stop?" the captain of the

564

"Spitfire" was saying an hour after, as the boy, clothed in a misfit suit made up from among the crew, leaned wearily against the side of the cabin, pressing now and then his purple, aching hands.

"Yes," answered the boy slowly and a bit impatiently. "There wa'n't anything else to do, was there? We couldn't make you hear no way. Tried hard enough. Tooted that horn till we were 'most dead, all of us, and the wind tore the noise all to nothing. Got desperate you see." He was started now. It had taken a long time for him to gain full consciousness, but now his tongue was fairly loosened.

The men drew nearer.

"The boat had got loose, you see," he continued, looking up wistfully into their faces. "After they pulled me up, somehow the rope got loose and off she shot, and I couldn't rest nohow, no more'n you could.

"There was a woman in that boat, you see. Couldn't leave her to get run down or froze to death, could I? She was most covered up with snow, any way, only I knew she was alive, 'cause she kept moaning like.

' No, 'twa'n't any great fun.

"Guess I ain't telling my story very straight, am I? Well, I reckon not. Head feels kind o' funny and light somehow." He pressed his hand to his forehead. "Try, though. You see, I live down to Jerry's Cove. Ain't got no folks. Work summers farming and do chores for my keep winters.

"Well, yesterday morning before the storm grew dreadful bad, this woman come to the house and wanted to be took over to the Pier awful.

"Told her we couldn't no how, but she took on awful. Said how she'd just got a paper 'most a week old, and how she'd read 'bout a man who'd been took sick up to New York and gone to the hospital and nobody seemed to know who 'twas, and he was pretty dangerous sick. Well, 'twas that woman's husband, and she was most crazy. My, but how she did take on!

"Hunter, he's the man I stay with, he told her 'twa'n't no use. She couldn't go nohow. Boat couldn't live in such a storm, and there wa'n't nobody who'd be fool enough to try it.

"Then she went all to pieces—and, well—somehow I couldn't stand it. Seemed so kinder heartless-like, with her husband a-dying way off there.

"Perhaps you know how 'twas?" suddenly looking up into the faces around him. The mate nodded acquiescence. "Well, she seemed to feel so everlastin' bad, and it seemed so desperate, and Hunter was so pig-headed, I just got my dander up and said I'd row her over to the Pier myself.

"Boat stops there twice a day, and if it didn't she could telegraph up. Hunter he swore awful, but I got the boat out and we piled in.

"But I wa'n't reckoning on quite so much sea. Got 'most half way to the Pier when a big wave sent my oar flying and knocked me clean over into the boat. Couldn't do nothing but drift, after that, and the woman she felt so bad she didn't say nothing but just lay there in the bottom of the boat, kinder half crying and too discouraged to move. Didn't care much 'bout anything. 'Twas kind o' tough." He drew his hand across his eyes. "Ain't never seen such a storm anyway. Covered her all up with some oilskins and crawled under 'em too, only kept popping my head out to see what was up. Boat most full of snow, too, and we drifted most forever, and, well—I guess I'd got pretty well discouraged, too, expecting most any minute to go to smash or get swamped. Lots o' boats out, but wouldn't none of 'em look at us, 'cept by and by someone looked over the side o' one and sighted us. My! but wa'n't I scared fear they'd think we was just an empty boat drifting and pass by same's the others had done.

"I jumped up and waved one of the oilskins, and I could see that they'd seen me. Then they threw a line with a life-belt on it. I fastened it so the boat was in tow, and they kept jerking, thinking they'd pull me up, but I couldn't leave the woman alone, you see.

"Pretty soon they seemed to catch on and threw another line, and I made that fast, and was going to send the woman up, but couldn't do nothing with her, she was so limp, and wouldn't help herself none. So I just put the belt on myself and let 'em haul me up.

" 'Bout soon's I landed, the boat broke away. Guess I hadn't fastened it tight enough. Thought she was a goner then sure, 'cause they couldn't put back for her, and the only way was to stop you, and they couldn't make you hear, no way.

"So I just said I'd come over the hawser and tell you. 'N they said I couldn't. Thought I could. Tried it when I followed the circus once and they wanted to teach me the tight rope, and I'd practised lots on a line in the barn.

"Course that was easy side o' this, 'cause there wa'n't nothing more than the barn floor underneath, and a few bumps if I fell. 'Twa'n't just exactly the same thing a-coming over that hawser all froze solid and covered with ice, and the wind a-twisting and turning me all the time, and the sleet a-cutting my face, and I was most froze anyway.

"And the waves just kept jumping up at me same's a dog does when he's chased a cat up a tree. And my head was kind er queer and buzzing. Well, 'twa'n't no easy matter and that's a fact.

"Once or twice thought I couldn't get here possible, then I thought of the woman tossing in the boat and I clutched a little harder, and pretty soon you hauled me in all right.

"My! but didn't your voices sound encouraging like. Didn't know I'd got anywhere near, 'cause I couldn t see anything.

"I guess I was pretty glad to get here, that's all."

He smiled up into the face of the captain.

"Quite enough for one day's job," returned that individual, while the sailors nodded assent.

"Now to get into the city. I'd like to see this thing through," and the captain walked to the window and looked out thoughtfully into the subsiding storm.

It was long before the visitors' hour at the city hospital when a curious trio knocked for admission.

"Oh! but you must let us in," the boy had insisted when they had been denied admission. "You just must. She's most dead, wanting to see her husband."

"I really think you might stretch a point in this case," the captain said, glancing down at the pitiful figure of the woman beside him. "She's most done for, coming through the storm."

But the woman said nothing — she had fainted from sheer exhaustion.

"It's all right now, ain't it?" the boy was saying cheerily, as he and the captain trudged back to the wharves half an hour later.

"Did look kind o' discouraging at first, though, but then 'twas all right soon's you made 'em understand. It must be very nice to be a captain, and speak so folks will listen to you."

He glanced up admiringly at the thoughtful face beside him.

"I guess we couldn't have got in after all if it hadn't been for you. And my! wa'n't that man glad to see his wife. 'Twas worth while coming through the storm for, wa'n't it? Aren't you glad we did?"

"Yes," the captain replied slowly, his eyes on the purple, swollen hands of the boy and noting his painful limp. "Yes, I'm glad you did."

The boy nodded cheerfully, and not noting the change of pronoun repeated again, " 'Twas kinder hard, but then, I'm glad we did it —and Hunter said we couldn't, but we did!"

His weather-beaten face glowed with satisfaction, but the recognition of himself as a hero never occurred to him.

6

A St. Patrick's Day Luncheon

By ELEANOR MARCHANT

"My mother and father were Irish,
And I was Irish too;
I bought a tin kettle for sixpence,
Iteled, it was Irish too."

O SANG my maid from the Emerald Isle, as she sorted the clothes in the laundry one blustery March morning, and with the lines of the doggerel came my inspiration to return my social obligations, that had accumulated during the winter months and that I had vainly racked my brains to suitably accomplish and at the same time keep well within the limits of my slender pocketbook. My preliminary preparations for the festivities began well in advance, for I realized that my hospitality must proceed from my brains and hands rather than dependence on an expensive caterer, with extensive floral decorations and elaborate souvenirs, that I knew were utterly beyond my resources. Naturally the invitations were my first consideration; these consisted of square white cards adorned with genuine shamrock from the "ould counthree," and bearing the motto, "Erin-go-Bragh," which means "Ireland forever," the invitations themselves being written with green ink and sealed with a tiny green seal.

Fortunately I had no regrets, and I heard incidentally that each of my guests-to-be were on the *qui vive* to attend my unique entertainment, so putting my faith in the adage, "that nothing succeeds like success," I made up my mind that they should not be disappointed, and went gaily to work. My menu was carefully planned with two objects in view, first that most of the viands should be of a nature to be suitably prepared the day before the luncheon, as my one maid would of necessity be both cook and waitress, and that as far as possible the edibles comprising the different courses should conform to the motif and green-and-white color-scheme selected for the luncheon. Finally the following was decided on:

"Leprechawn's" Broth
Murphy Puree   *Shamrock Crackers*
Celery   *Emerald Isles*   *Shillalah Rolls*
Creamed Halibut in Bells of Shandon Cases
Boned Chicken with Blarney Stone
Parnell Salad   *Erin-go-Bragh Pasties*
Potato Ice-Cream   *Pistachio Cake*
"St. Patrick's Tay"   *Deoch an Derais.*

The leprechawn's broth, named for the tiny mythical inhabitants of the fens of Ireland, was in reality the fruit course served in a novel manner, and as the day was cold and wintery, proved very acceptable. Select grape-fruit and after carefully cutting in halves and removing the pulp, stain the skins a vivid green with a vegetable dye (these may be purchased at any druggist's and are perfectly harmless). Shred the pulp into small particles with a silver fork, sprinkling with powdered cinnamon and grated nutmeg, and adding for each half of fruit one tablespoonful of powdered sugar, a teaspoonful of orange juice and sufficient mint cordial to color. At serving-time heat in a granite saucepan and fill into the skins, decorating with a few candied cherries; place in rather deep saucers, pouring in each a tablespoonful of brandy, that should be ignited just as luncheon is announced.

The Murphy puree was a cream-of-potato soup, with dainty green shamrocks floating in each portion. These were cut from a rich noodle paste colored green with a drop or two of the same coloring matter, and the shamrock crackers accompanying this course were shaped with a clover-shaped vegetable-cutter. My celery, with the aid of a sharp knife and scissors, I fashioned into tiny snakes, commemorating the banishment of reptiles from the Emerald Isle; while the Emerald Isles themselves consisted of large pitted olives served on a bed of cracked ice. The fish course owed its originality to the cases in which it was served; these were also of home manufacture, shaped in the form of miniature bells from white glazed paper, which in turn was covered with green paper crêpe and adorned with a tiny bell rope of baby ribbon, as shown in the illustration; they were then filled with the creamed fish, the clapper being realistically simulated with a small pitted olive.

The *pièce de resistance* of the luncheon, which consisted of boned chicken with blarney stones, was of course a "cold course"; the chicken was first carved in neat slices, and then cut with game shears into small harps, the strings and ornamentation being done with green mayonnaise pressed through a pastry tube; these were then arranged on individual plates, resting on a salpicon of vividly tinted green peas, that had been cooked with a few mint leaves. Of course this took time and patience to successfully carry out, but later on, when I heard the enthusiastic approval of my guests, I felt well repaid for my slight extra trouble. In planning for the salad, I felt instinctively that cabbage must form its basis, as a luncheon in honor of Ireland's patron saint without the national dish in some shape would prove very like Hamlet without the ghost. A handsome full head of cabbage was first secured, and with a very sharp knife the entire center was carefully removed, leaving the outer shell, which I utilized for the salad bowl; the vegetable was then finely shredded and placed in ice-water to crisp and harden; at serving-time equal quantities of cold cooked asparagus cut in small pieces, one chopped hard-boiled egg and half a cupful of hickory-nut meat were added, well moistened by the addition of a cupful of white mayonnaise; the salad was then placed in the unique receptacle, surmounted on top by a diminutive Irish flag, as shown in the illustration.

When it came to the dessert service I rightly felt if one was clever enough this might furnish the *chef d'œuvre* of the entertainment, and so it proved when I decided to give my guests "real potatoes"; these I made from chocolate ice-cream that had been frozen until very stiff, shaping each individual portion into a realistic "Murphy" by means of butter-paddles soaked in ice-water, and procuring the "eye effect" with bits of Jordan almonds inserted at irregular intervals; these I

border drooped tiny Irish flags
Four white candles in glass candlesticks were set at the four corners
of the table, with fluffy shades
of white crêpe paper, adorned by
rosettes of green baby ribbon,
and shamrocks cut from green tissue-paper, and small silver and
crystal compotiers holding olives,
salted nuts, cream peppermint and
crystallized mint leaves contributed
indirectly to the artistic effect.
At each individual cover, beside
the flat silver required for the menu,
was placed a service plate of green
china on which the fruit course
was served before luncheon was
announced, and resting against the

BELLS-OF-SHANDON CASES

POTATO ICE-CREAM

served on tiny paper napkins
printed in clover design, that closely
resembled the shamrock, accompanied by little cakes iced with
pistachio frosting and adorned with
the same emblem in darker green
fondant. Contrary to custom, "tay"
and not coffee completed the meal,
with *Deoch an Derais*—which
translated means the last cup at
the door—consisting of creme de
menthe cordial, served in tiny
green glasses, thus giving the tin-

crystal tumblers I arranged the place
cards, these consisting of tiny harps
cut from green cardboard, bearing
across the strings in gold paint the
guest's name and the date. The souvenirs, were candy-boxes in the shape of
small pigs each adorned with a necktie
of green ribbon and filled with old-fashioned peppermint lozenges. Fortunately
everything turned out exactly as I had
planned, and my St. Patrick Luncheon
was voted a signal success, while deep
within my own mind was the satisfactory thought that my twelve guests had
been entertained upon the five-dollar
limit I had set aside for that purpose.

SOUVENIR CANDY BOX

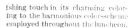

PARNELL SALAD

ishing touch in its charming coloring to the harmonious color-scheme
employed throughout the luncheon.

The table was simply arranged
by covering with a damask luncheon
cloth (woven in a conventional
clover design) laid over the asbestos pad; directly in the center resting on a silken Irish flag was placed
a wide-mouthed cut-glass vase filled
with feathery white carnations and
maiden-hair fern, while arranged
around the flowers to form a

507

INITIALING LINGERIE

By AMY S. MOERAN

IT IS usually customary to work letters or monograms on underwear in white thread, not only because it is more refined but because colors fade quickly when subjected to the constant washing which lingerie requires. Handkerchiefs, however, with colored borders or embroidery look extremely well if lettered to correspond.

One of the newest designs in handkerchiefs for men has a small oval of pink or blue linen appliquéd on one corner with a close buttonhole-stitch, and on this the initial letter is worked with white thread. For handkerchiefs intended for gifts, a novel idea is to obtain the signature of the person for whom they are intended. This is neatly traced across one corner, and worked in very fine thread. For gentlemen the full name should be used, as "A. F. Brown," but for a lady's handkerchief the proper name ("Helen" as in the illustration) will be more suitable. In letters or monograms for handkerchiefs the

very tiny ones are now more often seen than those of larger size, and the three neat little letters shown in the plate make a charming corner.

In marking a nightgown it is often difficult to select a desirable place, as the ruffles and embroidery yoke are apt to cover all the upper portion. When a deep ruffle is used the initials will look best if placed upon it near the lower edge, and three or four inches to the right of the center front of the garment. It is advisable to use single letters of a simple design for this purpose. The chemise nightgown lends itself readily to many pretty ways of marking. A perfectly plain one with the narrow embroidery beading edging the neck and sleeves can be marked in the center front with a very narrow graceful monogram, or the same style of monogram will look well placed at the top of the right sleeve. If a large single letter is desired, we would suggest using the Old English type and placing

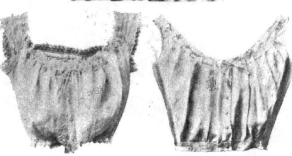

A GROUP OF INITIALED GARMENTS

it well up on the right side of the front near the shoulder. Two or three single letters, one beneath the other, will look well if placed on a line slanting in toward the neck.

In the January issue we referred to the ready-made letter medallions of fine white lawn that may be purchased at any of the large shops. The accompanying illustration shows one of these medallions neatly appliquéd on a chemise nightgown that is somewhat elaborately trimmed. For bridal sets or college girls' outfits, when a great many pieces are to be marked, these ready-made embroidered letters will be found a great saving of labor, as they come in varied sizes and are so well finished as to be easily mistaken for hand-embroidery. For a monogram in these medallions a special order must be given, as thus far the single letters only are kept in stock, though monograms may be obtained to order.

Drawers may be daintily worked with a monogram combined with a scalloped edge and a flower design in white hand-embroidery. When the ruffle is decorated with embroidery, lace insertion or tucks, the best place for the monogram will be in the center of the leg just above the ruffle. If floral or other decorations are not to be used, the monogram should be placed on the ruffle about an inch from the lower edge. We suggest two or three interlaced letters in preference to a monogram for this particular position. If only one large letter be desired, it could be worked on the ruffle above a one-inch hem finished with hemstitching. The letter could then be surrounded with three rows of French knots, which will give it a pretty medallion-like effect. When the drawers trimming is entirely composed of deep lace edging, a handsome letter or monogram could be embroidered on a piece of fine linen and appliquéd to the lace ruffle (about one inch from the lower edge) with a close buttonhole-stitch outlining a circle or oblong shape. The linen should then be trimmed off outside the

INITIALED HANDKERCHIEFS AND HAND-
EMBROIDERED LINEN HANDKERCHIEF-CASE

STYLES OF FANCY
INITIALS

buttonholing with scissors sufficiently sharp to leave no ragged edges.

Corset-covers may be marked in a variety of ways. When trimming of any sort runs up on the shoulder portion of a garment it will be found best to place the lettering on the right side of the buttonhole lap. If the entire front is covered with trimming, a single letter or small monogram can be worked on the buttonhole lap itself, b e t w e e n the first and second buttons or on the right side of the waistband about one and a half inches from the center front. If the front portion of a cover is decorated with tucks or lace insertions, it can be initialed high up on the right shoulder. When a peplum is used, the letters can be placed upon this near the lower edge. A chemise may be initialed in much the same manner as the corset-cover, except as there is usually no opening in the former it will lend itself to a more central form of decoration. It will therefore be best to put the marking directly in the front, even if a spray of flowers in embroidery is also desired, one illustration showing how nicely these may be combined. When a half-inch or broader ribbon is used to draw in the neck, the initial would probably be hidden by the bow if placed in the center front, in which case it would be well to use the shoulder effect. As a

general rule, a very large letter or monogram does not look well if placed anywhere but in the center front of a garment. The small letters are much more to be recommended for side or shoulder effects.

One of the newest monograms for underwear has a huge narrow Old English letter, which is shown in the illustration of the chemise. This can be used in various sizes on a set of underwear, being placed in the center front of the chemise and chemise nightgown, on the right side of the corset-cover and on the upper portion of the right leg of the drawers above the ruffle. An elaborate bridal set of fine linen lawn, heavily embroidered with tiny flowers, was shown at the St. Louis Exposition. A heart-shaped wreath of these flowers appeared on each garment with a small initial letter in the center. Another bridal set, which received a medal for originality of design, was made of dimity muslin. A flight of butterflies was embroidered on each piece, beginning at the right side with a large one, with broad, open wings and ending with a diminutive specimen in profile at the extreme left. In one of the wings of the largest butterflies two tiny script letters were worked in white marking cotton, these being the initials of the owner; all the other butterfly wings were filled in with tiny French knots.

Some Interesting Facts About Buttons

By ELEANOR COLBY

HAVE you ever thought what an unendurable place a buttonless world would be? If you have ever seen a poor, frenzied man searching for a lost collar-button, you know what pandemonium reigned, all because of the disappearance of one button. Multiply that one man by millions and the one button by quadrillions, and you can, in a faint measure, realize what the world would be if these indispensable little articles should suddenly vanish from its face.

In English law-making, the button has figured quite prominently. During the reign of Charles II., and even as late as that of George III., the button engrossed a great deal of the attention of the bewigged and bepowdered members of Parliament. Many were the acts and bills which were passed to regulate the kinds of buttons to be worn by certain people on certain occasions, and to control the manufacture and sale of these very necessary articles. The importation of buttons was forbidden, and a violater of this law was fined a hundred pounds.

In 1721 very stringent laws were passed against cloth buttons because they were displacing metal ones, much to the anxiety of the gold and silver smiths, as they bid fair to ruin their business. A tailor who used some cloth-covered buttons on a coat was not allowed to collect payment on the garment, and when the case was tried he was classed as a lawbreaker. Even a private person found wearing cloth buttons could be fined forty shillings, half of the money to go to the informer.

The expression, "I don't care a button about it," may still be used in utter disdain, but it might be well to mention whether you refer to the little bone buttons, that sell for two cents a dozen, or to the buttons that can be purchased in the New York dry-goods stores at five, eight and ten dollars apiece.

Very novel and clever button bags may be made and decorated with little figures whose heads and bodies are made of buttons. The illustrations show a few of these bags, though they are much more unique when seen in color. The center one is of scarlet broadcloth, the figures of black and scarlet buttons; the legs and arms being etched in color to match the buttons. Since broadcloth does not ravel, the ribbon drawing-string is run through slits in the bag.

The bag at the right is of white calico figured in blue. The border is plain blue to match the figure.

A pyrography outfit was used in making the bag at the left, though the same design might be very effectively developed in cloth. In the present instance tan leather was used, and the tree and trunk are burnt with a platinum point. The arms and legs of the children are etched so as to form a contrast with the burnt lines of the tree.

And Suggestions for a Button Party

ILLUSTRATIONS BY THE AUTHOR

 PROPOS of the clever uses to which buttons may be put, here is a hint as to a unique and inexpensive way of entertaining. It is called a "Button Bee," and may be an afternoon or evening affair, for the sterner sex will find as much amusement in the various diversions as will their weaker sisters. The invitations to this "Button Bee" should be decorated with a little button figure similar to those described on the previous page. The invitation may read like this:

> I am only a little button,
> But there are others besides me.
> Won't you come round on Friday night
> And join our "Button Bee"?
> Just bring ten buttons with you
> Of any shape or size,
> Of bone or cloth, of black or white,
> And try to win our prize.
> Some friends of yours are coming too—
> I know they've been invited—
> And if you'll only be our guest,
> We'll simply be delighted.

On entering the house each guest presents his ten admission buttons, receiving in return a ticket which reads: "This ticket is equivalent to ten buttons and each punch counts as a button." As his ticket is good for only ten punches, he will have to choose which attraction he will patronize. Across one corner of the hall a curtain or sheet is hung and a sign above it reads: "Palms Read Here, Price 3 Buttons." To make it still more effective, two pasteboard hands may be cut out, colored bright red and placed beneath the sign. Behind the curtain someone pretends to trace all sorts of strange things in the lines of the palm.

Then there is a "Bargain Sale" of rare curios. For two buttons one may purchase such things as "A Real Peace Pipe"—a piece of an old clay pipe—or a "Priceless Jewel of 1902"—a piece of coal. Any hostess can think of many such things for her bargain table.

Then there are contests which one may enter by paying an admission fee of one button, such as guessing the number of buttons in a bag or box, stringing buttons to see who can string the most in a given time, or seeing who can sew on the most buttons in ten minutes. Of course, strips of cloth and needles, thread and buttons must be provided for this. The thread must be fastened each time and each button must be sewed through four times.

Button bags such as those on page 572 make good prizes for the ladies, while a gold collar-button or a button-box would be suitable for a man.

The name card at each plate at supper may have a bachelor's button painted on it, or it may be a larger card having the first line of "Auld Lang Syne" on it, the notes being made of tiny black buttons as pictured below.

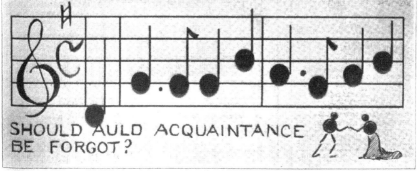

SHOULD AULD ACQUAINTANCE BE FORGOT?

Vol. XXI, No. 5.   The   MARCH, 1905

DESIGNER

CONDUCTED BY LILIAN DYNEVOR RICE

CONTENTS

Published monthly by the STANDARD FASHION COMPANY, 12-14-16 Vandam St. NEW YORK

Terms: Eighty Cents a Year in advance; Ten Cents a number

BRANCHES:
200-202 Monroe St., Chicago, Ill.
32 Richmond St., West, Toronto, Canada
1019 Market St., San Francisco, Cal.

Subscriptions are received by all Standard Fashion Agents, Newsdealers and Booksellers, or may be sent direct to the publishers.

Arnold Fabric Talks

FIL DE SOIE
Qual.
Col.
Yds.

Fil de Soie

The advance Spring model shown here is made from Arnold Fil de Soie, one of the most attractive new season's fabrics. Fil de Soie is a highly lustrous fabric having all the surface qualities of silk. The cloth is especially adapted in wearing to retain this silky lustre permanently. It is soft, smooth to the touch, falls naturally into beautiful folds, and is adaptable to all the desirable effects so much sought for in silks and more expensive fabrics. It is produced in all the newest silk effects in plaids, checks and pretty figures in beautiful color combinations, and is full of charming possibilities for making up the most attractive and inexpensive gowns for both street and home wear.

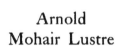

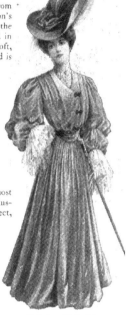

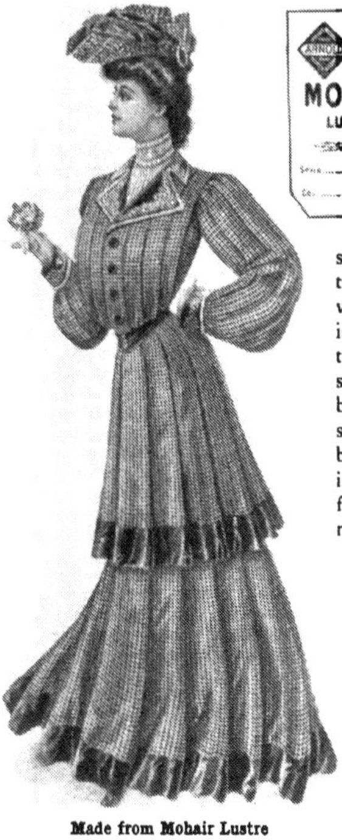

Made from Fil de Soie

MOHAIR
LUSTRE

Arnold Mohair Lustre

Arnold Mohair Lustre is a most stylish and serviceable fabric. Its wiry, lustrous crispness gives it a perfect Mohair effect, which is as lasting as the fabric itself. It is produced in all the foreign Mohair patterns, and also in a great variety of new suiting styles, from which selections can be made, not only for street wear, as shown in the accompanying illustration, but also for dress and morning wear. As it is unaffected by washing this entirely new fabric should appeal to every economical mother for misses' and children's dresses.

Made from Mohair Lustre

You should see the **Arnold Fil de Soie** and the **Arnold Mohair Lustre** before selecting wash fabrics for Spring and Summer use. They are for sale in all the better stores, and can always be recognized by our trade-mark on every ticket. Please look at our trade-mark carefully; it is a certificate of excellence—a token which gives every purchaser, from pieces bearing our trade-mark, the comfortable feeling that they have the very highest quality obtainable in its class, and our guarantee that the fabrics are printed or dyed in the newest designs and colors, and with the most expensive, permanent, sanitary colorings.

If your dealer cannot show you our new trade-marked wash goods, please give us his name and let us tell you of a reliable store that will gladly send you samples and deliver your goods satisfactorily.

Send Postal To-day for the Arnold Magazine of Fabrics and Fashions. It contains many superb plates of exclusive *advance* styles for Spring, in street costumes, house dresses and evening gowns, and tells, besides, of the great Arnold line of Spring fabrics.

This Trade-Mark
PRINT WORKS TRADE ARNOLD MARK NORTH ADAMS
Guarantees Satisfaction

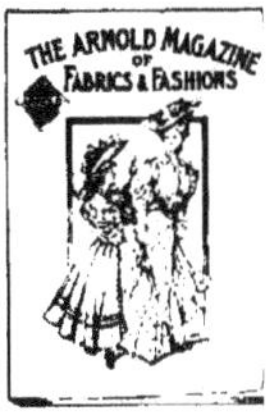

ARNOLD PRINT WORKS, Dept. B
40-42 Leonard St., New York

THE LION AND THE LAMB

A MARCH SERMON

By A. ALBION

HAVE you ever noticed the barking bravery with which a cur will chase a fleeing cat, and then, when the cat grows desperate and turns, how easily the cur is convinced that he has urgent business elsewhere? It is a funny sight; yet it is one that can be turned to account in giving courage to those of us who seem to be pursued by difficulties. When we run away from a difficulty the very timorousness of the heart makes the difficulty seem greater than it really is and convinces us that destruction pursues us. It is not for me to belittle difficulties and say that they are imaginary things, for each of us knows how real a thing it is that interferes with our hopes and our dreams; but certainly something can be said about the gain that comes from facing difficulties squarely. They shrink then to their natural size, and may quite often prove to have no terrifying existence at all. No shipwrecked sailor ever reaches his haven by fearing to strive through the long miles that separate him from safety; no minister ever takes his place in the pulpit and among the people as a teacher of good who fears to study or who fears to fight with those things that stand in the way of his high resolve; no business man succeeds who runs away from difficulties; no mother is in complete queenship over her home who goes in fear, all the days of her life, of some disaster that shall destroy that home or remove its support. In other words, it seems that we needs must face difficulties in order to be our best selves. What is the conclusion? Difficulties serve a magnificent purpose in the world, bringing out the refinement of courageous character; bringing forth the powers that would otherwise rest unknown and undeveloped beneath our calm exterior. Instead, therefore, of hiding our faces before difficulties we should welcome them as actual messengers to our best and most mighty selves. If we hear their message and try to turn away from it, we are ready to be overcome. If we hear their message and turn toward them a face glowing with courage and pure resolve, we cannot be overcome in the safest citadels of our nature.

You give praises unstintingly to the woman in your neighborhood who, left with encumbered property and many responsibilities, nevertheless made a brave struggle against adversity, held her belongings together and gave her children good preparation for life. You give praise to the man who lifts himself up practically by his own shoe-straps, having at the outset scarcely anything more to catch hold of; and you call him great if he wins for himself recognition and prosperity. Very well!

This praise you give is your own judge if you turn your face away from your own difficulties.

Rest assured of this—the strongest character that you know in your community must have fought with opposing forces in order to be strong. It is not necessary that you should know just what the soul-strife was about; it is not necessary that you should know the weakness that that strong character has triumphed over; but as sure as the character is strong and has the power to make you feel its strength, just so sure has there been a past time of mighty battle, sometimes condensed into one terrible occurrence in life and sometimes stretching over long years of opposition to adverse currents.

Then, too, the strife that may be needed to bring out the best in you is not at all the character of strife that may bring out the best in your neighbor. The temptations of the soul are different for every person, and, being different, can always be safely regarded as being overruled for good, for if each individual needs individual preparation to be his best in the world, then the trials of the individual surely may be regarded as at least under the direction of the Great Knower of All Things, giving to each tested one the power to get from his trials the strength to resist, and thus bringing good out of evil. All things, no matter how untoward they may seem, can work together for good in our lives, if our hearts are courageously ready to cooperate with the Almighty Power in bringing out the best that is in us.

We may take the wings of the morning and flee from the presence of testing, we may bury ourselves in the uttermost parts of the earth, and yet, as we can never get away from our own selves, neither can we get away from dread and fear if our hearts are lacking in courage. Each of us, right where we are placed, can imagine a more completely perfect condition, and the more fearful of us beg and beseech to be moved to a happier, easier state, but, as I have tried to show in this little sermon thus far, there is only one royal way to a happier state of mind and heart, and that is to meet with and down the conditions that are right before us, with our faces toward the foe. We must believe that the very disarming of our foe is most easily accomplished by facing it. Then, as we have already argued, trial and stress can have their perfect work in character, and thus seem at the end, when we look back, to have been good.

Answer me this: Is it not worth while to go through much if thereby we can attain strength? The principle that makes the boy glad to exercise and work until he finds a muscle bunching up on his arm, because he knows that with that muscle there is the possibility of prowess before him, is the same principle that should work in men and women, convincing them that it is worth while to strive in order that we may be strong. Strength acquired by striving forward and upward makes such resolves as "I will" and "I can" seem safe and sane.

Let us consider for a moment the infant that appeals to us so much by its helplessness. It is the sum of all the influences stretching back of it to the very beginning of life upon the earth. So are we! But a real man or a real woman is more than the mere embodiment of the past. There is something added — it is personal character, and that is acquired by the beating of circumstances upon the original being. Just as a stormy land grows trees of close fiber, just as the cold of winter brings forth the finer fur on the lower creatures, so the beating of life's tempests hardens our moral fiber and renders it able to withstand. Let us lift our voices in joy if out of our woes comes forth strength, and if out of our childishness there grows a fearless, purposeful, clear-visioned manhood and womanhood. We who know anything, know full well that "flowery beds of ease" are not what have made the world grow grand or us grow brave.

A strong character cannot fail to make itself felt, nor can it fail to give courage to others, therefore, as soon as we turn and face difficulties, we not only strengthen ourselves but we are preparing to be an influence of strength to those who come in contact with us. Is it possible to think of any higher grandeur in life than this—being good and brave and thus helping others to be good and brave?

This necessity for strife is shown to have within it nothing but blessing; for if its first result is to make us stronger and more truly what the possibilities of our nature have promised, then its later result is to make us more helpful to others, more inspiring, more inclined to lend of our own courage. These two attitudes of mind seem to be all that explains what the world has gained from the beginning until now—the possession of power within and the giving out of that power to others. Difficulties, therefore, instead of being personal affronts offered to us by the mismanagement of the world, prepare us to live and move and have our being in a world whose very knowledge of upward move has come from the sum of all the struggle of all its members.

Now we come to our text: It is the old proverb of March coming in like a lion and going out like a lamb. We can depend upon it that as long as life lasts the blustering approach of the Marches in our experience can be met and vanquished, until the roaring ceases, the blustering passes away, and the terrible object of our fears goes before us as meekly and as gently as a lamb.

JACQUELINE   FELICE   GRACIA

WHAT WOMEN ARE DOING

EDITED BY THE READERS OF THE DESIGNER

FIVE-DOLLAR PRIZE PARAGRAPH

A PRACTICAL SHOPPER

I know of a young lady in New York City who supports herself by doing practical shopping and by chaperoning young children at picnics and parties. She has regular customers for her shopping expeditions, who make out a list of articles required, and at stated times she calls for these lists and receives instructions regarding the articles to be purchased. The chaperoning usually occupies her evenings, and for each she charges at the rate of seventy-five cents an hour. Since she began this work there has scarcely a day passed in which she did not have one hour at least occupied and very often has the whole day, making thereby over ten dollars a day. As a result, she has saved a tidy little sum over and above her living expenses.   *H. C. S.*

THIS SMALL BEGINNING MADE A GOOD ENDING

One girl who had prepared for college, by the sudden death of her father was forced to give up this cherished plan and go to work instead. She had just graduated from high school and set out bravely to do the only thing she felt prepared to do well. For a year she taught an ungraded country school. The next year she worked in a lawyer's office in her own country town. From money thus earned she saved enough to go to a city and take a course in stenography. At the end of six months she obtained a position with one of the leading law firms in the city at ten dollars a week. She formed an evening class in stenography. She did extra typewriting between office hours. She did court reporting. She became agent for a certain typewriter. She next gave up her salaried position and opened a school in stenography in the center of the business section, at the same time doing all the outside work she could get. She bought land and put up several beautiful cottage houses at a nearby summer resort, made loans to real estate men, did a large amount of court reporting and conducted her large school of stenography, which is considered the best in this part of the country. She is still young, and a very remarkable woman, besides being worth several thousand dollars, all of which she has earned herself.   *E. C.*

A COOPERATIVE SCHEME

Two widows, Mrs. A., with one child, and Mrs. B., with two children, sought means for earning something toward their maintenance, and at the same time care for their babies—for such they are, their ages being, one, two and three years. Mrs. B. rents two rooms of her home to Mrs. A. for two dollars a month. Then Mrs. B. cares for Mrs. A.'s child with her own, during nine hours of the day, for twenty-five cents a day, while Mrs. A. clerks in a store. They procured the use of one window in the store where Mrs. A. clerks, where they displayed for sale fancy articles, such as collars, turnovers, handkerchiefs, sofa-pillows, Battenburg doilies, crocheted hoods, baby jackets, shoes, etc., which articles they make evenings and at odd times. Both do their own work and Mrs. B. does all her own and her children's sewing, and looks after her garden, yard and chickens. The scheme has proved profitable to them both.   *W. L. M.*

WHAT THE CHICKENS HAVE DONE

We lost our home and contents by fire five years ago, and were left without a dollar, a farm not wholly paid for, and no buildings on it. I have tried to help all I can, and now our farm is paid for and a five-room house built and a barn large enough for two horses. After my health gave out and I could not sit and sew, I took to poultry. We had some good white Wyandottes and brown Leghorns. I bought an incubator and brooder. I averaged seventy-five per cent. hatches and sold the little chicks at twelve cents each at a week old. I could not hatch them fast enough.

This year I will run two machines. I sold fifty dollars' worth of dressed poultry this last fall and my pullets hatched in April began laying when eggs were forty-eight cents a dozen, and are still filling the egg basket. I have forty hens and pullets and they buy their own feed and most of my groceries and meat for our family. I forgot to say, I kept all my March and April chicks myself, selling most of them for broilers at from twenty to thirty-eight cents a pound. I sell most of my eggs, etc., at my door. We live near two manufacturing villages. I never leave home for more than two hours at a time after I set my incubators in March, until I stop hatching in July. It is hard work, but it pays well in the end.

Molly

PROFITABLE MARKING ON LINEN

A bright young woman has actually earned about eight hundred dollars a year for the past three years by marking handkerchiefs with indelible ink. For practise she asked friends and relatives to let her mark their handkerchiefs. After she had marked a good many, she began to charge five cents a name or fifty cents a dozen. She left samples in store windows, designed capitals, copied monograms on table linen, etc. Sometimes a trousseau would bring her fifty dollars. The work was all done at home. She now has a very pleasant as well as profitable business, which enables her to be quite independent. *A. E. W.*

RAISING CATS

In this age of strenuous advancement, while we find so many fields open to women of a business turn, it is not surprising that one woman, right here in our midst, should find a good income in the raising of cats. The lady is a retired artist, and it was doubtless through the painting of the pretty creatures that she became so fond of them and interested in their care. Now in her declining years she finds in them a source of revenue. The breed most remunerative is the Angora. I chanced upon her and her pets one day not long ago, when she gave me many points on the history and care of the long-haired pussies. Hers are the pure-white variety. In answer to my several inquiries, she replied, readily, "Oh, no, they are not much trouble; a little more tender than the ordinary house cat, but they pay well for the care. Now, this one," calling a pure-white fluffy yearling, from among a dozen or more capering about her sitting-room, and taking him up tenderly in her arms, "will bring me twenty-five dollars." In answer to my gasp of astonishment, she went on: "Why, yesterday I filled an order from Milwaukee for a twelve-dollar pussy. But this one, you see, has the turquoise (the bright-blue) eyes; they bring more. He is sold.

One of these dainty, "ready-to-make" Corset Covers will be given away with each purchase of our Valenciennes Laces amounting to $1 or more.

COMPAGNIE DE VALENCE

NEW YORK, March 1st, 1905

To the Ladies of America:

This offer is made for a threefold purpose.

First, to introduce to you our line of Imported Valenciennes Laces, containing the largest assortment of designs ever brought to this country (at prices ranging from 1c. to $2 per yard) for Lingerie, Shirtwaists, Baby's Clothes, Handkerchiefs, Fancy Work, etc., at prices which mean a great money-saving, because our Laces go to all parts of the world direct from us to the users, without the many profits of importers, jobbers, commission houses and retail merchants.

Second, to introduce the superior merits of the Mousseline de Valence—the material from which these Corset Covers are made. We believe that it will outlaunder and outwear any material you have ever used for fine undermuslins, and we know that in appearance and "feel," it will compare favorably with goods sold in this country at a far higher price.

Third, to introduce the "ready-to-make" idea as applied to undermuslins. These Corset Covers are cut to your measure by experts and sent to you ready to put together.

Only one to a customer under the terms of the above offer; but where more than one are desired, we will supply them at 48c. each.

The "Ready-to-Make" idea is more fully described on page 575 of this magazine in the announcement of Spring and Summer Shirtwaists made by the Art Fabric Mills, who control the "Ready-to-Make" rights, and with whom we have made an arrangement by which these Corset Covers may be fashioned to your measure by their own skilled cutters.

At this season nearly every woman is interested in Lace Bargains. If you would buy at wholesale prices and from a stock that includes scores of exclusive designs, as well as all the staple patterns in all widths—Edgings, Insertions, Beadings, Allovers, etc.—write to us to send you our

Full Line of LACE SAMPLES—FREE!

Hundreds of Styles to Choose From at Bargain Prices

A postal card will bring you a full assortment.

We guarantee your perfect satisfaction with every purchase, or "your money back" without question and without delay.

HOW YOU ARE TO ORDER

If the lace patterns illustrated on this page do not cover your immediate needs, send first for our complete line of samples, which will be mailed you, free. From them choose the patterns you want and fill out the order blank we will send you, enclosing a proper remittance. Fill out, also, the self-measurement blank we send, that we may have accurate measurements for cutting and fitting the Corset Covers.

WHAT WE SEND

The day following receipt of your order (if same amounts to $1 or over) we will mail you the Laces and the "ready-to-make" Corset Cover, cut to your special measure, ready for you to put together and trim, in either of the designs shown above.

This method saves you all risk of loss from faulty cutting, saves cost of pattern, your time and your labor.

We sell direct to the consumer in every State in the Union now, and our designs are to be found in nearly every dry goods store of any size in this country.

We are making the above unusual offer because we want as quickly as possible to let every woman in America find out for herself that whenever she has a Lace need, we can fill it a little quicker, a little better and quite a little cheaper than any other establishment.

Remember, please, that we can sell only in lengths of three, six or twelve yards, as at our prices we cannot afford to have odd lengths remain.

We pay the postage on all orders and fill them the same day received.

Your obed't servants,

COMPAGNIE DE VALENCE

per LEON GIRARD

Sole Representative for the United States and Canada

96 Fifth Avenue, New York City

P. S.—I desire to appoint one woman in each neighborhood to receive orders for our laces. Would you like to?

What Women are Doing.—*Continued*

and goes East in a few days. And these little ones," turning to a couple of six-weeks-old white fuzzy balls gamboling at her feet, "with the turquoise eyes, bring five dollars each." Then, at my increased astonishment, she laughingly added, "Oh, yes, there's money even in raising cats."   *L. E.*

A TRAVELING MILLINER

A woman of my acquaintance who has a fair knowledge of millinery makes a comfortable living by going from house to house as a visiting hat trimmer. She takes the materials that accumulate from season to season and makes them into up-to-date head-gear. Her charge is twenty-five to fifty cents an hour. *S. S. H.*

A SELF-TAUGHT MACHINIST

Several years ago, my husband manufactured woodenware goods of all kinds, including butter-trays, or crates, as some people call them. The machines for making the trays, or rather for stitching the corners, were operated by women and girls. A woman, her two daughters and a small son applied for work and they were reluctantly accepted, for they were just from the country, and very ignorant. The woman and girls were given work at the butter-tray machines. These machines get out of order very easily and quite often, and a man had to be kept on that floor to look after these machines alone. My husband noticed that this country woman in a very short time made more trays than anybody in the room, and her machine was seldom out of repair. Upon closer examination he discovered she did her own repairing, and also kept her daughters' machines in splendid order. She gradually improved, until one day she was called into the office and offered the job of "boss" on that floor. She accepted and was given a much better salary than she had formerly received. She worked as mechanic there for years. I have known her to repair machinery in any and all parts of the building, and she was always consulted about changes to be made, and even in selecting new machinery. She was certainly a wonder. When my husband sold his business she was still at her post as head boss, and I am almost sure she is there to-day. She has educated her children, besides studying at night, and is a woman that I am proud to call my friend.   *X. X.*

A WOMAN SIGN PAINTER

A woman of my acquaintance has succeeded in establishing herself in an occupation not very often heard of as belonging to the female sex. Having the misfortune to lose her husband at an early age, she found the task of bread-earner forced upon her. She had a six-months'-old baby to support, and, never having had to earn her own living, was at a loss what to do, while her tender heart and love for her child would not allow her to be parted from it. So she wondered what she could do at home to earn a livelihood. She suddenly thought how successful she had been at school in drawing and painting, so having enough money to move and gain a little start, she moved to the suburbs, where no one knew her, and prepared a sign to put on the house to advertise her new venture. Her first work was for a neighbor near by, who wanted a "board and room" sign, and the fact of it being done so nicely was soon told from one to another. Then everyone endeavored to help her obtain work and urged her on. So, having a low rent, she was able to get along, slowly at first, but now she has succeeded in building up a nice little trade and can do her work at home, which is more to her than a larger income, on account of the comfort of the little one.   *F. C. G.*

A COUNTRY STEAM LAUNDRY

A useful enterprise, termed a "Steam Laundry," is conducted by four sisters in a New England village. On Mondays these sisters collect family washing from the near-by villages and surrounding country. The clothes are washed, ironed and delivered within three to five days. The charges are five cents per pound for washing and ironing, and an extra five cents for each starched garment; men's shirts, collars and cuffs at regular laundry prices. At the death of their parents these girls, living in the country, where it was hard to find remunerative work, and wishing to remain together and retain the old homestead, entered upon this work. At first they received few washings. In two years these few have increased to seventy-five. The work is very satisfactory, and the proprietors are always most courteous, the few articles which are lost being paid for by the laundry. As a financial business, one of the sisters said when questioned that they are doing so well their intention is to enlarge their accommodations.   *Mrs. J. L. S.*

THE MISTRESS OF THE SEWING-MACHINE

There is a young woman in our town who makes a splendid salary by her thorough knowledge of a certain sewing-machine. She arranged with a general agent to hold one opening every six months in each town in his territory, at which time she shows the machine he has to sell and all its attachments and the use of each. Aside from this, she has daily classes in her own town where she teaches embroidery, drawnwork and lace-making, all this being done by the machine.   *M. Z. H.*

THE KITCHEN KINGDOM

SOME SAVORY CODFISH RECIPES FOR LENTEN BREAKFASTS

By I. D. RICE

BAKED CODFISH.—Allow one quart of milk to come to a boil, then thicken with two tablespoonfuls of flour which have been moistened to a smooth paste with a little of the cold milk, and add two tablespoonfuls of finely chopped parsley, white pepper to taste, one well-beaten egg and half a cupful of butter. Stir until the sauce is thick. Freshen a large cupful of shredded codfish by putting it in a sieve, then letting cold water run over it, after which squeeze it perfectly dry in a clean cheesecloth. In the bottom of a baking-dish put a layer of bread-crums, then a layer of the fish, moistening both with a little of the white sauce; then sprinkle in another layer of crums and fish, and so on until the dish is full, making the last layer of the bread-crums. Bake until the top is a delicate brown.

Codfish Croquettes.—Freshen two cupfuls of shredded codfish as for the above recipe. Rub together three tablespoonfuls of flour with one of butter, and stir into half a pint of rich milk, adding a teaspoonful of finely chopped parsley and a quarter of a teaspoonful of onion juice. Boil the mixture until it thickens, then stir in the fish and boil up again. Season with pepper to taste and let it become cold; form into croquettes, dip in well-beaten egg, then in bread-crums and fry a light brown in very deep fat tried out from salt pork. Serve very hot.

Codfish Toast.—Heat a pint of new milk to the boiling point, and thicken with a teaspoonful of flour rubbed with one of butter, and stir in one cupful of freshened shredded cod. Season to taste with white pepper and boil for five minutes, beating constantly with a silver fork so that the mixture is perfectly smooth. Cut small squares of bread and toast to a delicate brown, butter lightly and pour over them the fish mixture. Cut four hard-boiled eggs into rings, removing the yolks and powdering the latter. Sprinkle the powdered yolks over the toast and decorate the platter with the rings of the white and with sprigs of parsley.

Codfish Timbales.—Beat six eggs, yolks and whites together, until very light then stir into them a cupful of freshened shredded codfish and a half pint of rich milk, adding a pinch of baking-soda and white pepper to taste. Pour the mixture into well-buttered muffin pans—not rings—set the pans in a baking-pan of boiling water and bake until the top is a light brown, then turn the timbales on a heated platter and serve with a decoration of parsley, and a cream sauce if desired, although the latter is not really necessary. When wanted, it should be made like the white sauce mentioned for the "Baked Codfish."

Ideal Codfish Cakes.—Boil sufficient white potatoes to make one cupful, and mash with a teaspoonful of butter until perfectly smooth, then add two cupfuls of freshened shredded codfish and one egg well beaten. Season with a teaspoonful of finely chopped chives if liked, and beat well, but do not form into balls. The mixture should be just thick enough to drop from the spoon. Fry in fat from salt pork until of a rich brown on both sides and serve at once.

DECORATIVE TIPS AND GASTRONOMIC CHIPS FOR MARCH

By M. PLETZ

There is a growing tendency to celebrate St. Patrick's Day in a social way, quite irrespective of nationality, and there is no end to the arrangement of decorations suited to the day. Invitations may be sent out on green paper encased in green envelopes.

A pretty fancy is to use enigmatic menu cards. The names of the dishes are written on big green cards. A luncheon menu might be as follows:

Shamrocks
Murphy Bisque
Fish Paddies   Olive Greens
Cork Croquettes with Emeralds
Hibernian Salad   Shillalahs
Spuds and Blarney Stones

The Shamrocks were dainty *hors d'œuvres*—thin slices of brown and white bread cut in the form of clover leaves, spread with caviar, and besprinkled with chopped olives, gherkins and parsley. Murphy Bisque is a creamy potato soup. Fish Paddies and Olive Greens are patties and olives. Cork Croquettes and Emeralds are chicken croquettes formed in cork shapes, and green peas. Hibernian Salad is sweetbreads diced, molded in green aspic, with a green mayonnaise and served on lettuce leaves; with this serve Shillelahs, puff paste in strips about the length of a finger, rolled to represent tiny cudgels, dipped in grated cheese and baked.

Spuds and Blarney Stones proved to be pistachio ice-cream in potato cases and sponge cakes cut in cubes, dipped in a fondant colored green, and decorated with bits of toasted almonds. A flat basket of oxalis, with its cloverlike leaves, would form a pretty centerpiece, and candy-boxes in the form of little black hats, with a green band, filled with green and white Jordan almonds, would be appropriate favors. White candles with green shades and green-and-white paper serviettes can help to carry the color-scheme along.

A willow luncheon is possible this month, with the silvery white catkins of the willow showing their sheen. A wreath of the catkins outlines the table mirror, and encircles small leaf-shaped dishes holding silver-covered bonbons. Silvery gray shades with green fringe crown the white candles, and egg-shell china is used. Cut glass and little willow baskets, heaped with sandwiches rolled into tiny cylinders, help out the idea. The menu must be in gray-and-white effects.

This is the orange season, and a delicious marmalade with a distinctive flavor is made with oranges and honey. Peel the oranges, removing every particle of white pith. Cut small; to one quart of this pulp and juice add one pound of honey and one-quarter pound of the thin yellow peel of the orange. Cut the peel into tiny bits, cover with half a pint of water and boil until tender; add to the pulp and honey, and cook together for half an hour, stirring frequently. Pour into small glasses and when perfectly cold, cover with paraffin. Oranges and rhubarb cooked together give an excellent imitation of the celebrated imported "Dundee Marmalade." To a quart of finely cut rhubarb add half a pint of water, simmer slowly for fifteen minutes, add a dozen oranges, peeled and divided, and the thin cut-up yellow rind of three; cook this together for half an hour and add to this amount one and a half pounds of sugar. Cook the whole half an hour, pour into small pots, and when cold, cover.

The peel of the oranges can be candied. It is delicious in ices and sherbets, and the strips when warm and pliable can be woven into little baskets in which bonbons or little mounds of ice-cream can be served. Let the peel of oranges, cut in halves, soak in a strong brine for three days. Drain, drop into cold water, let stand three days, changing the water twice daily.

It is the <u>cream</u> of the wheat that makes it so good to eat—for breakfast, luncheon and for dessert at dinner.

The Kitchen Kingdom.—Continued.

Cover with cold water, let come to a boil, then drain. Repeat if the peel tastes salty. Wipe free from moisture. Make a sirup of one pound of sugar and a pint of water to each pound of peel, cut into narrow strips. Boil slowly one hour, let cool partly, so it can be handled, then weave into little circular forms. Set in a dry, airy place to dry.

A thoughtless mistake is made in buying soup greens and using them as occasion demands. With flavorless greens and the best cut of beef, the soup will lack the fragrant aroma that the vegetables should supply. Delicious soup, at short notice, can be made from any good beef extract, provided the greens are perfectly fresh and capable of imparting their savory flavor to the soup.

Appreciation of nuts becomes more and more universal among housewives when the demand for new dishes comes up. Ice-cream croquettes are made of a yellow ice frozen very hard. At serving-time the ice is taken out with a scoop, which forms each portion into a pyramid. These are then rolled in almonds that have been blanched and browned in the oven, then crushed fine. Coat the little croquettes thoroughly with the powdered nuts and serve them with a sauce made with half a pint of cream whipped stiff, to which is added gradually half a cup of powdered sugar. Flavor with orange juice and maraschino. Make the sauce some time in advance of the time for serving and chill thoroughly.

An excellent ice is made by lining a mold with an orange sherbet. In the center put the following: Brown three ounces of blanched almonds in half an ounce of fresh butter, adding one ounce of sugar. When a deep brown, pound quickly until crushed fine. When cold, add to half a pint of cream which has been whipped stiff. Flavor with a teaspoonful of almond extract. Close the mold, bury it in ice and salt, and let it stand for at least three hours before serving.

Another delicious variation that is quickly made is to line a mold with the whipped cream and almond mixture, fill the center with peeled oranges cut very small, cover, bury in ice, and salt for three hours. Or line a mold with lady-fingers and fill the center with the cream and almond mixture, then freeze.

Try this novelty for luncheon some day in early spring when the appetite has become fickle: Whip half a pint of cream until stiff, add a ten-cent can of deviled ham, the juice and grated rind of a lemon, a teaspoonful of finely chopped parsley and a teaspoonful of onion juice. Press the compound into little paper cases and let it stand for an hour in a cool place. Unmold when serving, and place on crisp cress or mustard leaves and press with it a French dressing.

The Kitchen Kingdom.—*Continued.*

VARIOUS KINDS OF TOAST

By Frances E. Peck

On the breakfast tables of the Irish gentry one finds toast made as nowhere else—in fact, the Irish toast is the best in the world. Slightly dried (it is never left to chance, but closely watched), tinged a beautiful amber color, the edges powdered, dipped quicker than a flash into boiling water and then lavishly buttered on both sides, it is a dish which would appeal to and appease the heart of the Man of Wrath himself. English toast is also a commendable article, but the toast that appears on the table of the average American family is something too sad for tears. Cut in slices of varying thickness, these are placed on a wire toaster which is set on the stove. If the "cook lady" has plenty of leisure at her command the toaster is probably placed on the back of the range, where the bread dries— not toasts—to a teeth-breaking degree of hardness; but if pressed for time, the toaster is generally set over the direct fire while cooky hastens about her other duties, paying attention to the toast when she happens to think of it, which very often is not until her nostrils are assailed by the odor of burning bread. This variety of toast is generally scorched on the outside, while the interior is moist and clammy to a dyspepsia-producing extent.

Toast is preferably made from bread twenty-four hours old. It should be cut in slices not to exceed half an inch in thickness, placed in a dripping-pan and run into the oven until slightly dried through, then it should be toasted before, or over, a low, clear fire to a pale, even brown, buttered and sent to the table at once in a heated rack. Nothing cools more rapidly than toast, and when the slices touch each other they become moistened and tough; it should, therefore, never be served piled on a plate or in anything cold.

Subjoined are recipes for preparing appetizing "soft" toast dishes, suitable for the main dish for breakfast or for luncheon desserts:

Convent Toast.—Melt a piece of butter half the size of an egg, and when hot add a finely minced shallot and a teaspoonful of chives finely minced, dredge in a teaspoonful of flour, add a cupful of milk and a seasoning of salt and pepper; cook until smooth, add four hard-boiled eggs thinly sliced, and when thoroughly heated pour over rounds of hot buttered toast with pounded edges.

German Toast.—A delectable dish which the Hollanders—and I think the Germans—call "Poor Knights." Cut five or six slices of bread and place in a shallow pudding dish or pan. Beat three eggs, season with a pinch of salt and a trifle of sugar, add a cupful and a half of milk and pour over the bread. Let stand for two or three hours or until the bread has absorbed the custard.

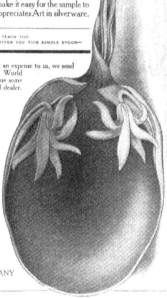

The Kitchen Kingdom.—*Concluded.*

Fry crisply brown in hot butter and serve dusted with cinnamon and sugar. This is not a dish to serve if the butter pot be low, for when frying, the "knights" absorb a great deal of butter, and must fairly swim in it.

Snow Cream Toast.—Blend smoothly together a tablespoonful each of flour and butter, dilute with a cupful of thin cream and add to a pint of cream which has reached the scalding point; cook until smooth, remove from the fire, season with salt and a tiny dusting of nutmeg and add the beaten white of an egg. Pour over rounds of crisp toast which have been rapidly dipped in boiling water. A delicious cheese cream toast is made by covering the slices with grated cheese before pouring over the cream. In this case do not dip the slices of toast into water.

Tomato Cream Toast.—To a cupful of stewed and strained tomatoes add a tablespoonful of butter and a seasoning of salt, and set on range to keep hot. In another vessel heat a cupful of milk, season with salt and thicken with a rounding teaspoonful of flour blended with a tablespoonful of butter. Toast rounds of bread to a delicate brown and lay on a shallow serving dish. Add half a saltspoonful of baking-soda to the tomato, and as soon as it ceases effervescing add very slowly to the cream, beating hard while so doing. Pour over the toast and serve immediately.

Apple Toast.—Peel, core and slice six apples. Melt a tablespoonful of butter in a granite or porcelain-lined frying-pan, turn in the apples and cook slowly until done, adding more butter at intervals if necessary, watching closely and stirring often to prevent burning. When cooked tender, add sugar to taste and turn over slices of hot buttered toast. Serve with cream as a luncheon sweet.

Celery Cream Toast.—An appetizing breakfast dish is this concoction, particularly if each round of bread is topped with a poached egg, delicately cooked, as a poached egg ought to be, in equal parts of milk and water slightly salted, the liquid spooned over the top of the egg until the yolk shows a golden heart through a filmy veil of white. But to return to our toast. When cooked celery has been served at dinner, reserve the water in which it has been boiled. At breakfast time take one cupful of this liquor, add one cupful of thin cream and place on the stove to heat. When at the boiling point thicken with one tablespoonful of flour rubbed smooth with a heaping tablespoonful of butter. Season with salt and white pepper and add two or three stalks of the cooked celery, if at hand, cut in small pieces. Turn over the toasted bread, trim each poached egg with a sharp knife, to a shapely form, or, better, cut with a biscuit cutter; lay gently on each round and serve on individual plates which have been well heated.

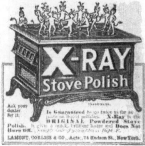

FLORICULTURE TALKS

By M. W. PARK

FICUS ELASTICA

THE India-Rubber plant, known as Ficus Elastica, is a grand and beautiful foliage plant, and deserves a place in every gardener's collection. Few, if any, can surpass it for beauty and elegance when well grown. It is a favorite with almost all cultivators of flowers, especially those who are fond of plants with luxuriant foliage. The leaves, which are oblong in shape, are of a thick, leathery texture and a dark, shining, green color. This plant is suitable for the decoration of halls, rooms and the windows of the dwelling-house, as well as for greenhouse and conservatory. It is a member of the Fig family, and one of the most ornamental of the species, and bears confinement in rooms better than most plants. It is, however, somewhat difficult if transplanted from a greenhouse to a dwelling-house to prevent the leaves from turning yellow and dropping off. The trouble is not always due to the manner in which it is treated or the soil it is given. A plant used to the high temperature of a greenhouse and highly fed is sometimes sensitive to the change, and cannot endure the cooler and drier air of a dwelling-house so well as one that has been hardened off by degrees before being transferred to a room or window.

When a Rubber plant has just been potted it should be kept in a shaded place for awhile and watered sparingly, until the roots are settled in the soil and new growth starts. It should then be given plenty of air, light and water during the growing season. Almost any amount of water can be given to the roots, and an occasional syringing or sponging is necessary to keep the leaves clean and bright. It is a plant that dislikes to have its leaves covered with dust, especially if the dust is allowed to remain any length of time and seems to enjoy being frequently washed or sponged.

Water should be given somewhat sparingly in winter. If watered too liberally at this season of the year the leaves are apt to turn yellow and drop off one by one. Almost all plants require a rest at some season of the year, and the Rubber plant is no exception. Although it remains green during winter, yet its growth is not so rapid as in summer, consequently a less amount of water is needed to keep it in a healthy condition. When growing in a room, an occasional supply of soot water is of great benefit to the plant. The soot causes the leaves to take on a richer, or deeper, green coloring, and the plant presents a healthier appearance.

It is not really necessary to always use a large pot for growing the Rubber plant. Some of the healthiest and most desirable specimens are grown in pots which are comparatively small in proportion to the size of the plant. In such cases, however, a stimulant in liquid form, such as the soot water, must be given quite frequently, especially during the summer months.

Propagation of the Rubber tree is easily effected by cuttings, which when inserted in sandy soil soon root, and can then be potted in three-inch pots. As soon as the pots fill with roots, shift into four-inch pots, then into larger pots as the plants continue to develop. They will grow most of the time if given a sunny position, but the sun should not be allowed to shine on the sides of the pot in which they are growing for the sun shining on the side of the pot causes it to become heated, and the roots coming in contact with the heated pot are injured. This affects the growth to a considerable extent, causing the leaves to turn yellow. To avoid this the pot containing the plant can be set in a larger vessel and the intervening space filled in with sphagnum moss.

Plants that are plunged in soil out of doors during summer need but little attention as they take care of themselves almost entirely.

The Ficus Elastica can be trained into almost any shape desired. If a bushy plant is wanted, cut the tops back and later pinch out the tips of the branches, cutting away all unruly ill-shaped side shoots, letting them grow only to the size and form you wish. A piece of raw potato slipped over the cut made when pruning will prevent the flow of sap, if it has a tendency to bleed. The potato can be left on until the cut heals or sap ceases to flow.

Small specimens of the Rubber plant are most attractive when they are restricted to a single stem and allowed to grow quite tall. These can be kept for awhile in the form suggested,

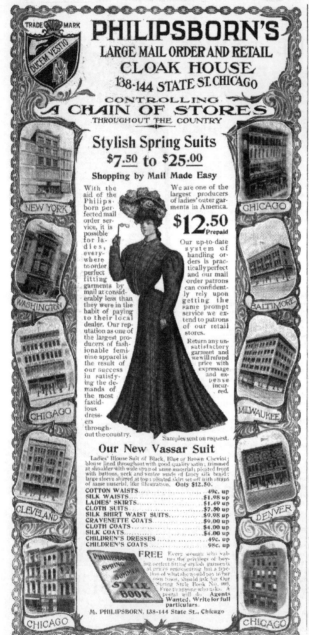
Floriculture.—Continued.

then by pinching out the terminals, may be grown into large-branched plants.

THE DAHLIA

The Dahlia is one of the showiest and most valuable plants for the summer garden. It is a native of Mexico and Central America, and may be grown in either a large or small garden. A large garden is best for growing the plants in groups, and when tastefully selected according to color, the effect is fine. Single specimens may be grown in small gardens with good effect. Few plants produce flowers that are more handsome for forming large bouquets than the Dahlia. The stems are long and admit of cutting to good advantage. A few blooms all of one color placed loosely in a high vase of water form a pleasing ornament for a stand or sideboard, and are exceedingly effective for decorating the dining-table.

The Dahlia is divided into several classes. The blooms of all are valuable for their rich, delicate texture, some appearing as soft and velvety as the richest velvet. The blooms are in many varieties of forms—some are single, some double and again there are others which are semi-double. Some are built like a honeycomb, others have flat petals, while those of the cactus class are curled or twisted.

Propagation of the Dahlia is effected by seeds, cuttings, division of the root and by grafting. The single varieties are produced freely from seeds. These, when sown in boxes early in spring and transplanted to the open ground as soon as danger of frost is past, will bloom freely throughout the late summer and fall months. The double Dahlia is also grown from seeds, but, although it will bloom the first season, it will not grow quite as freely as does the single variety.

Cuttings are easily started in the spring from the roots that have been kept over winter. About the beginning of February the roots should be covered with soil and given bottom heat. The sprouts will soon push up. These can be taken off and placed singly in pots of light leaf-mold and sand, and the pots set in a close frame and covered with glass. They will soon form roots. The cuttings root more readily when the young, tender shoots are taken, and as these are taken off other sprouts soon push up, so that quite a number of rooted plants can be had from a few clumps of tubers. The tops of the young shoots produced on plants growing in the garden start readily in summer, and will form tubers for the next summer's blooming. Plants that are syringed frequently during summer will form numerous tender shoots. These can be used for cuttings as soon as two or three joints are formed.

When dividing the tubers of the Dahlia for propagating, a portion of the stem must be left to each tuber or

Floriculture.—Concluded.

the latter will be of no value, as it will not sprout when completely detached from the parent stalk.

To get the best results with the Dahlia it is necessary to have a deep, rich, moist soil. The plant is a gross feeder and requires plenty of nourishment, in order that the blooms may come to full maturity and beauty. A good plan is to prepare the bed in the autumn for the next spring planting. The manure incorporated with the soil in autumn, and subject to the melting snow and rain of winter, will be thoroughly decayed when planting-time arrives. It is not advisable to apply fresh or strong manure in spring, as it causes the foliage to grow strong and luxuriant while the flowers will be sparingly produced.

A strong stake should be placed for the support of each Dahlia, when planting. These should be firmly set and extend several inches above ground. Each plant should be tied securely to the stake as soon as planted to prevent it from being broken off by strong winds. As growth advances, the plant should be kept tied to the stake, and the earlier tying should be carefully looked after to prevent the string from cutting into the soft growth of the stem or the branches.

Strong, tall-growing plants should be set three or four feet apart. Seedlings will not need quite so much space. When planting the Dahlia, a light, open position, free from the shade of trees, should be selected, but if this be somewhat protected from high winds by low-growing shrubs it will be all the better. It is not best to put Dahlia plants out much before the first of June, as even a very slight frost often injures them quite severely and stunts the growth, from which it takes them a long while to recover.

If the summer is dry the Dahlia will require frequent and copious waterings; an occasional supply of liquid manure after the buds are formed is also of great benefit. A mulch of some kind given after the last hoeing will prevent the soil from drying out too rapidly, and will aid in keeping the roots cool and moist. After the tops have been injured by frost in the fall, it is best to cut them down to within about six inches of the ground. If the weather is mild they need not be taken up till the latter part of November. If, however, sharp frosts and heavy rains are pretty certain to be prevalent in that particular locality the roots should be lifted at once. The soil that adheres to the tubers may be allowed to remain on them, and the tubers placed so the air will pass through and dry them. A clearly written label should be fastened to each stem to designate the color of that particular clump. When perfectly dry, the roots can be stored away in a cool, dry cellar or any other place which is frost-proof until time for spring planting.

THE DESIGNER

FOR LOVELY WOMAN

By JANE ELIOT

HINTS FOR MARCH

THIS is the month during which it is necessary to exercise more care than at any other time during the year. It is ever uncertain and deceptive and the warmer days tempt one to change the heavy, stuffy underwear for lighter weight, but do not yield to the temptation. Physicians all agree no change of this kind should be made, no matter how uncomfortable one may feel, until the first of May, and not then unless warm weather has set in. March is the month most dangerous for those afflicted with pulmonary trouble, probably because of the uncertainty of the weather as well as a peculiar atmospheric condition produced by the approach of spring. So beware.

Nothing is more ruinous to the delicacy of the complexion as well as the beauty of the eye than sharp winds, and the veil, which is a greater preserver of beauty than many are aware of, should be an important consideration; not too thick, as it strains the eye, but sufficiently so to act as a protection to the skin.

COSMETIC GLOVES

These gloves when designed to simply soften and whiten the hands are prepared by brushing the inside of a pair of stout kid or dogskin gloves with this mixture: Yolks of two fresh eggs; oil of sweet almonds, two tablespoonfuls; tincture of benzoin, a dessert-spoonful; rosewater a tablespoonful. Beat well together and keep in a closely corked bottle. The gloves should be freshly painted every night, and the same pair should not be used longer than two weeks.

Gloves made of india-rubber are preferred to those of kid for wearing at night. They confine the perspiration, keep the skin bathed in moist warmth, rendering it softer whiter and more delicate.

The ordinary rubber gloves so universally sold in the shops to-day are a great boon to the woman who has her own work to do. She is thereby enabled to wash her dishes without allowing the water to touch her hands, or to sweep without having them marred by dust or roughened by hard usage.

FOR THE COMPLEXION

A bottle of pure glycerin should form an indispensable adjunct to every woman's toilet-table. It is absolutely necessary that it should be *chemically pure*, otherwise it frequently contains salts of lime or lead, which will irritate and discolor the skin ; or, if applied to any part of the body where there is hair, the salts of lime will injure and finally destroy the hair bulbs, causing baldness and dropping out of the eyebrows or eyelashes. But the pure glycerin is effective, harmless, and enters into nearly every cosmetic receipt. A tablespoonful in a pint of water will soften the hands and protect them from the air. The following receipt will protect the face and hands from roughest weather: Mix one-fourth pure glycerin with three-fourths rosewater, and add a few drops of carbolic acid. Rub into the skin before going out. As a cosmetic preparation glycerin is also excellent, as it causes powder to adhere. After rubbing the glycerin mixture well in, wipe off thoroughly, then apply the powder.

No greasy preparation, creams or skin food should be allowed to touch the skin after it has become in the least rancid or altered, as the acrid substances then present are highly injurious to the complexion

For whitening and clearing the skin a London specialist constantly recommends in his practise citric acid, which is merely acid of lemons, and the following preparation: Fresh lemon juice, one wineglassful; rain-water, a pint; attar of roses, a few drops. Wash the face and hands with this several times a day, and let it remain on three or four minutes. A little piece of lemon will frequently remove any superficial stains not effaced by soap and water.

Peroxide of hydrogen will also remove yellowness from the face and neck, or the stains made by the collar-band.

Exposure to outdoor air immediately after washing the face or hands will inevitably make the skin look like parchment. Wait at least fifteen minutes after the face bath before going out.

Keep Your Youthful Figure

Fastidious women who find ordinary corsets unsatisfactory will find the

G-D Justrite Corset

a revelation in that it gives a youthful grace, comfort and ease to the wearer.
Price from $1.00 to $5.00 according to quality of material and trimming.

Have your new gown fitted over a G.-D. "Justrite" Corset.
Insist on seeing them at your dealer's or write us for free
"Corset Guide"—a help in choosing the right shape for you.

GAGE-DOWNS COMPANY   269 FIFTH AVENUE
                                     CHICAGO

KNITTING

KNITTING ABBREVIATIONS USED.—k—Knit plain, sl—Slip a stitch, p—Purl, n—Narrow, b—Bind, over th o—Thread over, o n—Over and narrow, k 2 tog—Knit 2 together. Make one—Make a stitch thus: Throw the thread in front of the needle and knit the next stitch, in the ordinary manner. (In the next row, or round, this throw-over is used as a stitch.) Or, knit one and purl one out of the same stitch. * Stars or asterisks or † daggers mean in either knitting, crochet or tatting that the details given between these signs are to be repeated as many times as directed before going on.

A DAINTY KNITTED SCARF

A VARIATION from the rather hackneyed garter stitch in which the shoulder scarf is usually fashioned will be welcomed by the woman who loves to wield the long wooden needles. A pair of these will be needed for the new stitch, a bone crochet hook and twelve skeins of Shetland floss.

Wind two skeins into separate balls, for two threads are used, and cast on 180 stitches. Knit across plain, always knitting the first stitch off the needle, as this is important.

Second row—Knit one; throw thread over twice; knit one; throw thread over twice, and repeat to end of row.

Third row—Knit one; drop one; knit two together; repeat to end of row.

Fourth row—Knit across plain.

Fifth row—Repeat from second row and continue until all but two skeins are knit, these having been reserved for the fringe.

In making the fringe use a piece of cardboard ten inches long on which to wind the floss. Cut across one end, separate seven strands, and tie into end of scarf. After the fringe is all tied over, tie two more rows, which gives a heavy three-knotted fringe. The scarf is two yards long and five-eighths wide without the fringe.

Infants' Booties

Materials: Two pair steel needles, one skein fine white Saxony. Cast

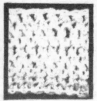

DETAIL SCARF STITCH

12 stitches on each of 3 needles, and knit around plain.

Knit 2, purl 2 for 4 rounds. Then purl 4 rounds, knit plain 4 rounds until

KNITTED SCARF

there are 3 purled bands. Then knit 10 plain rounds, making an eyelet by throwing the thread over and narrowing at each end of one needle. Continue to make the two eyelets 1 stitch further from the end every other round until 8 are made on one side, 7 on the other, the extra or eighth eyelet being the last one completing the point. In the meantime, when the 10 plain rows are knit, divide the stitches so the heel will be even with the front eyelets or laces. Knit the heel and foot as usual, and bind off the toe when narrowed down to 6 stitches. Lace up the front with cord and tassel or ribbon.

Ruffle Lace—Cast on 22 stitches. First row—S 1, k 2, o twice, p 2 tog., k 4, o twice, n., k 1, o twice, n., k 1, o twice, n., k. 5.

Second row—K 7, p 1, k 3, p 1, k 3, p 1, k 4, o twice, p 2 tog., k 3.

INFANTS' BOOTEE

Third row—S 1, k 2, o twice, p 2 tog., k 6, o twice, n., k 2, o twice, n., k 8.

Fourth row—K 10, p 1, k 4, p 1, k 6, o twice, p. 2 tog., k 3.

Fifth row—S 1, k 2, o twice, p 2 tog., k 8, o twice, n., k 3, o twice, n., k 7.

Sixth row—K 9, p 1, k 5, p 1, k 8, o twice, p 2 tog., k 3.

Seventh row—S 1, k 2, o twice, p 2 tog., k 1, o twice, n., k 7, o twice, n., k 4, o twice, n., k 6,

Eighth row—K 8, p 1, k 6, p 1, k 9, p 1, k 1, o twice, p 2 tog., k 3.

RUFFLE LACE

Ninth row—S 1, k 2, o twice, p 2 tog., k 27.

Tenth row—K 27, o twice, p 2 tog., k 3.

Eleventh row—S 1, k 2, o twice, p 2 tog., k 27.

Twelfth row—Bind off 10, k 16, o twice, p 2 tog., k 3.

Repeat from 1st row.

TO ENTERTAIN OUR FRIENDS

A LITERARY PARTY

By Marjorie March

AT A NOVEL literary party last March the invitations were sent out in the shape of little books. These were made of a few sheets of heavy paper, cut in small shape, folded, and sewed together with red silk. The invitations were written on the inner pages with red ink; the covers were made to represent a book cover by being stenciled in red. This work is very simple: cut a little square of thin cardboard for the stencil, and upon it with a sharp knife, cut any design or lettering wished. Then a little brush dipped in red stencil ink brushed over this surface will prepare all of the covers quickly.

The first game we played was a literary contest. As all of those bidden to the party were fond of "printer's ink" and matters pertaining thereto, some of us even scribbling a bit ourselves, this was merry fun. We were all supplied with a list of questions, numbered, a paper to put the answers upon, and a pencil. The questions were of this nature: The names of recent novels were given, the names of the author to be supplied; characters in modern fiction were named, the answer being to place them in the stories to which they belonged and also to give the author's name. We were asked to invent a good name for a novel; to write a rejection slip, taking the role of an editor (many of these were more funny and sarcastic than business-like), etc. Any hostess wishing to try this game will think of many other variations of the same idea. For the best paper handed in from this contest a year's subscription to a popular magazine was given.

The second game we played was more original. Each person was given a large piece of paper and told to drop a blot of ink near its top, fold it once and press with the fingers over the spot; then to open it and embellish the weird ink-like pictures suggested, enlarging upon them if we wished. This done, we were to write a nonsense story or verse about the astonishing ink-pictures thus produced.

We all exclaimed that it was the first time we had made ink-pictures since we were children in school, but as we are all "children of a larger growth" we were soon gathered around the tables with pen and ink, blotting our papers most admirably.

The reading of these stories and nonsense rhymes brought forth gay laughter. Two judges were appointed to decide upon the cleverest picture and story, the papers being unsigned. A prize of a generous box of note paper with envelopes was awarded the jolly girl who had made out of her "blot" two impossible ink animals which she

named the "Bumphantos" and the "Flyrocat." She rambled on in an amusing way about these two creatures, these being the first four lines of her story in verse:

"The Bumphantos and the Flyrocat
Lived in a pen and a well,
'Twas not a 'pig' but a fountain pen,
And an ink-well, I've heard tell,"
—etc., etc.

When the merriment of this contest had died away we were summoned to supper. This was served on the large round dining-room table left bare, doilies of pretty pink-and-blue paper being used instead of the cloth. The china was pink-and-white. In the center of the table a large round brass plate held a burden of moss, edged with sprays of pussy-willow. The same fluffy twigs were stuck in the moss, a few little paper butterflies alighting on their tips in graceful fluttering fashion. By fastening these on invisible wire a most natural effect can be obtained. About the base of the pussy-willows small hepatica plants were nestled in the moss. (These can easily be forced to bloom in the house in March.) Tiny pink pottery jars filled with sprays of pussy-willow were the place cards, and blue ribbon bows falling to the table, and tied about these little bouquets, bore our names written upon them in gold.

At each place, beside these were vases, were novel souvenirs in the shape of pretty glass ink-wells, filled with salted almonds!

The bonbon dishes were quaint little desks which can be found in toy stores among doll-house furnishings; and open books—these can always be obtained as candy boxes—filled with candied ginger. Four glass candlesticks of Colonial design held pink tapers, shielded by dainty pink and blue shades.

Our menu was as follows:

Sweetbread croquettes
Plain and jelly sandwiches.
Bird's-nest ices and "Dream of Spring" cake.
Apple jelly with whipped cream.
Bonbons.
Coffee.

The ices were in the shape of birds and were most ornamental. They were served in little nests made of macaroons, iced so that they would hold together. They were lined with tiny lace-paper doilies, upon which the birds rested. The "Dream of Spring" cake was indeed a novelty and very delicious. Squares of gingerbread, to represent Mother Earth, covered with pistache icing, pricked with a grater so that one might imagine it to be grass. Dashes of snow (whipped cream) were left in one corner, and imbedded in the realistic grass were candied violets. These squares of cake were served on individual plates, surrounded by whipped cream, and, as one of the guests remarked, were "surely a culinary 'poem' coming after the equally good 'prose' of the sandwiches and sweetbread croquettes."

A HAPPY HUNT

By N. H. FLANNER

HAVING invited six girl friends to tea, the thought occurred to me that I should like to make it an event somewhat unique or, at least, something a little out of the ordinary.

So after a proper adjustment of my "thinking cap" I decided that hunting their supper would be a new form of entertainment for my guests, and the experiment alone would prove it successful or otherwise. The success of my "hunt" is my reason for submitting it to THE DESIGNER readers. The supper having previously been prepared, except for a little "putting together" just before the time for the guests' arrival, I hid it in different places around the house—in the china closet, pantry, book-case, wood-box, dressers and on the mantel.

I had ready some slips of paper on which was written the part of the menu each one was to find, and which, when found, was to be taken to the kitchen to make ready for the table. One slip read, "Ham. Butter"; another, "Saratoga Chips. Bread"; still another, "Olives. Cake," etc. The ham was sliced and on the platter, the chips in a pasteboard box lined with oiled paper, the bread was in the loaf to be cut, also the cake, and the olives in the bottle to be opened. In addition to the above, I had fruit and potato salads.

For the potato salad I used cold boiled potatoes, and beets boiled and sliced, and had the mayonnaise dressing already prepared. On one slip I put "Potatoes. Beets," and on the other "Mayonnaise"; then the two guests who found these prepared the salad together.

My fruit salad contained oranges, bananas, pineapple and cocoanut, with a rich sirup to pour over. The oranges were peeled, but not shredded, the pineapple in can to be opened, and the bananas to be peeled and sliced, the sirup being ready to use. The butter, coffee and lemonade I placed on the table after everything else was ready.

Anyone finding a dish not belonging to her should keep very quiet, as the longer the hunt continues the merrier it will be. There was great sport finding the ingredients and more sport putting them together.

For the hunt to be a success the guests should be very congenial, and gentlemen may be asked, if the hostess thinks best. If invitations are issued, in addition to the hour, place, etc., call it a "Happy Hunt," and add the question, "What is it?"

My especial hunt, I am glad to say, was pronounced a great success.

HELLPS ALONG THE WAY

EDITED BY THE READERS OF THE DESIGNER

QUESTIONS

WHAT AILS THESE PIES?

Will some kind reader of THE DESIGNER, or contributor to "Helps Along the Way," please tell me how I can prevent my-lemon or custard pies from puffing up in the middle while baking, causing all the custard to go to the sides? I can make a very good pastry and filling, but it *will* puff up in spite of everything I do, and I have almost given up pie-baking in despair. I have often inquired among my friends about it. Some say they have the same trouble; others are unable to tell me the cause of it.   V. A. R.

WHAT WAS THE MATTER WITH THE CHICKENS?

In the fall I had forty-five little chickens, hatched out, which started off beautifully, but soon warts appeared about the eyes and mouth, which finally completely closed; of course, death resulted. Out of forty-five two are left. Will some one please give me the proper name for the disease and tell how to cope with it.   S. R.

TWO-DOLLAR PRIZE PARAGRAPH

MAKING OUR SLEEVES

I wish to tell THE DESIGNER readers how I changed some last year's shirt-waist sleeves to make them up to date. There was no up or down to the goods, so I ripped the sleeves apart and inverted them; for, as you all know, the newest sleeves are full at the shoulder instead of the wrist, and by so doing I have sleeves cut by the latest pattern. I used Standard Pattern No. 9090, and if you, dear readers, will do the same the result will be very satisfactory.

KATHERINE ERICSSON

REMEMBER THIS SHOULD YOU KNOCK OUT A TOOTH

I want to tell the readers of an experience my son has had. He was the proud possessor of an exceptionally fine set of well-cared-for teeth. One day, while at work, he had occasion to use a short step-ladder, the top of which just reached his mouth. No sooner had he placed his foot on the bottom step than the top flew over and struck his mouth with such force as to knock out one of his teeth and cut his lip quite badly. He placed the tooth in his pocket and called on the family physician, who sewed and plastered the lip, but our worry was all for the loss of the tooth. which we supposed must be replaced with a false one. Great was his surprise when on telling the dentist of his loss he was asked for the tooth that it might be replaced. It was a very, very painful operation, the most painful in dental surgery, the dentist told him, but it was entirely successful, although the tooth had been out two days.   MRS. S.

ANGEL FOOD IN A NEW FORM

Instead of using the common recipes for white cake, containing milk and butter, a very delicious cake may be made by baking angel food in layers and putting together with some favorite filling. Lemon jelly or fruit jelly seems to combine best with it. A jelly cake baked in this way took a prize at the fair over a great number of other excellent cakes, proving that in appearance and taste it was superior to those requiring much more time and more expensive ingredients.   T. A. S.

A GOOD ANTISEPTIC

Many persons do not know that a solution of salt and water is a useful antiseptic for ordinary cuts and skin wounds. Ever since a physician told me of its value I have used it with good effect. Dissolve the salt in the proportion of one tablespoonful to one pint of water. After the wound has been washed gently to remove any dirt that may be in it, bathe it with the salt water for several minutes, then put on plaster or a bandage. This treatment may cause the cut to smart a little at first, but will in the end relieve the pain, and prevent danger of blood-poisoning, which is sometimes caused by a slight wound if no antiseptic is applied.   F. B G.

SOAPSUDS AS A BLEACHER

Through the winter days the house-wife generally tries to make up her muslins for the next spring. What I mean are sheets, pillow-slips, under-wear, etc. When made of unbleached muslin, wet in strong soapsuds and put out of doors to freeze; continue this a few times and you will be sur-prised to find how white they will become. Now boil and iron them, and they are ready for use.

MRS. F. F. S.

A HELP TO STITCHES

I had often been annoyed when using sewing silk on the sewing-ma-chine by the silk slipping from the spool too rapidly and tangling around the spool spindle, thus bringing me to a halt, and causing sometimes a broken needle and vexed temper. One day I took a piece of beaver cloth, cut about the size of a quarter of a dollar, cut a hole in the center and placed it on the spindle, the spool silk on top. The result was splendidly satisfactory. I have had no trouble with my sewing silk since, and gladly pass my discov-ery on. N. P.

RED PEPPER FOR INDIGESTION

One of my neighbors was troubled very much with indigestion, and could get no relief until a friend ad-vised him to try eating red pepper. "Eat red pepper for indigestion?" exclaimed my neighbor. "Yes," said the friend, "just take the pepper and parch it carefully, without scorching, then pulverize it, and put it on everything you eat." "I followed his instructions and I am about well now," said my neighbor.

MARY S. GRAHAM

GIVE THE UNRULY MACHINE A BATH

I wish to tell my sewing sisters who get worried frequently over "that horrid old machine" a bit of useful experience. Now, when the tension has been turned both ways a dozen times, the oil-can turned up to allow the last drop to ooze out, the cloth run in and out to take off surplus oil, the thread changed, the needle replaced by a finer or coarser one, and in a fit of exasperation you cry out, "Oh, the contrary old thing!" just get 'up and leave it, and give your-self time to cool off a little. After an experience of this kind I grew des-perate. I declared, "I'll kill or cure!" So procuring a dishpan of warm water and a cake of soap, I deliberately unhitched the machinery from the table and bathed it. I washed in cracks and crevices, then rubbing it dry replaced it, and gave the lower part of the gearing the same treat-ment; since which time, with the delicate oiling occasionally that it needs, it is a "joy forever," and my oft-considered "trade" for a new one

Helps Along the Way.—*Continued.*

is called off, the strain from my tired feet is also gone, and, best of all, my nerves are settled, my machine runs light, and my work is satisfactory. Try giving your machine a bath, for the dirt gets into places too far for your oiling rag to reach. Hoping this will help some poor, distracted, worried worker, I am yours for service to others.   J. C. G.

A USEFUL LITTLE HELP

"There are better ways of doing things,
   If people did but know;
And so 'tis 'Little Helps' we need
   As through this world we go.

"Ofttimes 'tis but a little hint
   We need to lessen labor,
And if we pass it on, it may
   Be useful to a neighbor."

And right here let me thank "Betsy" for her little hint a short time ago. I often find it necessary to wash my hands while wearing "big sleeves," and her rubber band is just what was needed to keep them off the wet marble slab, and I could think of no way of meeting the difficulty until the November DESIGNER came, with its hint from a mere child which solved the problem. To many women, where and how to carry a watch is a question. It is readily and safely solved by making a little chamois pocket, with one side of the top about an inch longer than the other (much like a wall pocket). Pin the long top to the corset, underwaist or lining of the dress waist with a safety-pin, conveniently near the front opening. It takes but an instant to change this, and if made deep enough is perfectly safe.   CERESE

FEATHER COMFORTABLES

In England it is quite a fad to have feather comfortables. To make one, first take two pieces of sateen, silkoline or whatever material the comfortable is to be made of, have them the required size, lay one above the other and bind all around except one end. Next fill this covering with feathers until it is the required thickness. Bind the end. Put it in the quilting frame and quilt in the ordinary manner, spreading the feathers evenly as you quilt. This makes the nicest kind of quilt, being both light and warm, and is especially nice for covering for the children.
    ELIZABETH DEAN

A STORE-ROOM AID

To keep track of all the things in your store-room is not, as a rule, an easy matter, but I have hit upon a plan to know just what I have and just where to find it. When I fill a trunk I make a list of the things as I

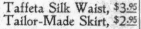

put them in. When the trunk is full I tack the complete list on the inside of the trunk lid; then when I need some erstwhile useless article that I remember having had, I consult my list to know if it is still in my possession. If it is in the trunk I can tell just how far down it is, for the contents have been listed from the bottom up. I label all packages and boxes, and thus save myself many a useless search. Indeed, I believe in labeling everything set aside for future use, and have known the practise to save much trouble, and sometimes life, as in the case of medicines, etc.   M. S. D.

KEEPING PARSLEY IN COLD WEATHER

We have all heard of various ways of keeping parsley over winter, such as packing it in salt, or in brine, or even, as one of your correspondents suggests, growing it in a pot in a window. In the first case it loses color, and when grown in a pot it is liable to get covered with tiny green insects. The idea of the latter is not appetizing. I find the best way is to gather it when fresh and green, chop fine as if I were going to use it, then spread it on wood and dry in a warm room (not in an oven, as this will turn it brown). When perfectly dry, put in a preserve-jar until wanted. It is of a beautiful green color, and when a little is sprinkled in soup or sauce you cannot tell it from fresh parsley. Other herbs are good treated the same way. And it is so convenient, too, being always ready for immediate use.   F. W. R.

OX GALL FOR CHILBLAINS

As this is the time of year when chilblains are troublesome, I wish to tell through "Helps" of an infallible remedy. Take say an eight - ounce bottle to your butcher and have him save you a beef's gall, fill the bottle two-thirds full, then ask him to fill up for you with alcohol. As it sours very quickly, the alcohol is just to preserve the gall. Apply this to the chilblains. One application will give relief and a few will cure. If this is used on the frosted parts just as soon as the frost is out, you will hardly know the parts have been frozen.   MADELINE

A LITTLE CULINARY TIP

Not long ago I saw a friend put some rice on to cook for supper and then sit down unconcernedly in another room to read a magazine. I asked her if she was not thinking about the rice boiling over. She replied that she never had any boil over. She then told me that she always put her lump of butter in the water instead of when she added the milk and salt. I have since tried it myself and the charm never fails. Try it and be convinced.   G.

598 . THE DESIGNER

MONEY FOR WOMEN

IN LACE MAKING

A Wonderful Little Machine for use in the home, on which any kind of Woven Lace can be made, yet it is so simple that a child can learn to operate it

A BOOK ON LACE MAKING FREE

A New Industry—Lace Making At Home

Do You Want To Make Money?

A sure income can be earned at home with this Little Loom

With it can be woven the most beautiful Cluny Lace, also other fine laces, such as Brussels, Smyrna, Guipure, Mechlin, Valenciennes, etc., something never done to any extent in America before. This little Loom is a recent invention. It is a beautiful little machine, an ornament to any lady's home. The operation of it is very simple and easily learned from the book of instructions which accompanies it. The work is very fascinating, much more so than

THE PRINCESS LACE LOOM

Embroidery, at which so many ladies devote the greater portion of their spare time. It affords a pleasant pastime for ladies of leisure, making beautiful laces for their own use, and for presents to relatives and friends. And to ladies living at home, who wish to earn money, it offers a golden opportunity with which to do so, as

WE GUARANTEE A MARKET FOR ALL LACE SENT US

by any one who purchases one of these Looms. The Laces made upon this Loom are real Lace. Equal to the finest imported hand-made Lace. With each Loom a Large assortment of beautiful Lace Patterns is furnished, also a set of bobbins, ready for work. Although these Looms have only been upon the market about two years, we have sold many thousands of them, and they have made friends wherever sold; we are daily receiving large numbers of complimentary letters praising them in the highest terms, saying how well pleased the writers are, and how easily they have learned to use them. It is our desire to place one of these Looms in every refined home in this country, and, judging from the large number already sold, and the satisfaction they are giving our customers, we feel that we shall accomplish this result, especially as

THE PRICE OF THE LOOM

is so low that every lady, even of the most moderate means, can afford to own one of them. Upon request we will send you free of charge our new book, "Practical Lace Making," which is handsomely illustrated with cuts of beautiful Laces, and contains a complete history of the Lace Making Art from its beginning down to the present day, together with a full description of this wonderful little Loom, the manner in which the Lace is woven, etc., in fact, everything you want to know. Write at once; do not delay. Address

TORCHON LACE CO., Book Dept. A. St. Louis, Mo.

Seven Novel Ideas for Napkin Rings

THE CHANGED CLOTHES-PIN

SUGGESTIONS for napkin rings, most of which may be made by the children as easily as by their elders, should be welcome indeed. Many people, who for one reason or another do not own silver rings, would appreciate one of these novelties as a gift, or they would make satisfactory substitutes for more elaborate rings, to use when camping out or roughing it in the country, where articles of value are, as a rule, only a burden and a care. As little trifles to be disposed of at fairs or bazaars they are always quick sellers, and as they cost so little to make can be priced very reasonably. The first illustration shows how even the common clothes-pin may be pressed into service. It is first sandpapered very smooth all over, then with the useful pyrographic needle or with oil paints is decorated with holly or any other small design, after which it is treated to a couple of coats of shellac. The initials or even the name of the one for whom it is intended may be burned or painted on one side. The napkin is slipped in between the prongs of the pin.

A strip of leather one inch and three-quarters wide is used for the next ring. This, as may be seen by referring to the illustration, has the edges finished with four rows of stitching, and is fastened into shape with leather thongs. A simple design is burned through the center, and this might be diversified by placing the owner's name in the center, letting the design run from it.

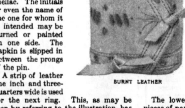

BURNT LEATHER

Instead of the thongs, small patent fasteners of nickel or brass might be used to hold the ring together.

The next illustration shows a group of three rings, one of which is crocheted and the other two made of raffia combined with sweet grass, reed and splint.

The lower left-hand ring is made of plain single-crochet stitches. A chain about six and three-quarter inches long is made, using coarse crochet cotton; join and work six rows of single crochet on this and then one row of double crochet, putting a stitch in every third hole. This makes a beading through which the ribbon is run. Then make six more rows of single crochet and finish the edge with a scallop made of five double-crochet stitches and fasten into previous row with a slip-stitch, five double-crochet, and fasten, etc. Make a row of scallops around the lower edge and starch stiff. When almost dry press into shape (the one illustrated is square) and then cover with a coat of shellac. When perfectly dry this ring is as firm and substantial as if made of metal. Of course the ribbon is not added until the shellac is dry. By putting the ring over a a ring or cylinder of wood while the shellac is drying, a perfectly round ring may be obtained. Any cotton of any preferred color or combinations of colors may be used, and when shellac-coated has all the brilliancy of glossy straw.

The lower raffia ring is made of two pieces of narrow splint and one of wide, all of which are seven inches long. The ends of these pieces are fastened together, making three rings, and these in turn are made into one by being woven with threads of sweet grass, under one, over one, under, over, until the splint is

A RING CROCHETED OF COTTON AND TWO RINGS WOVEN OF RAFFIA

irely covered. The wide center band
hen woven with raffia threads going
.he opposite direction, and the illus-
:ion clearly shows how the finished
ʒ should look.

'he third ring, which is placed on
of the two just described, is made

AN ODD BONE RING

RING OF LINEN EYELET EMBROIDERED

! reed, coiled and sewed with raffia,
ach stitch being taken into the previous
ɔw. The colored design is worked in
lter the ring is finished, and is simply
ɛwed over and over, a large-eyed blunt-
ɪded needle being employed.

The bone napkin ring is very simply
reated, but is none the less attractive.
imply have a smooth inch-wide section
awed from a large beef bone, and after
horoughly cleansing and drying it, and
moothing it both inside and out with
fine file or coarse sandpaper, burn a
ttle regular polka-dot pattern all over
he outside. Of course any preferred
attern may be burned in. A very hot
yrograph needle will be necessary, and
' a conventional design is used a little
oloring with oil paints thinned with
hellac will make it quite effective. The
olished bone looks like old ivory.

A piece of white linen eight by two
nd a quarter, with the edges turned
ack one-quarter of an inch and basted
ﬁ place and then buttonholed, makes
he next ring, and this has one great
dvantage over all the others, in that
vhen necessary it can be thoroughly
aundered with little trouble. The but-
onholing, as may be clearly seen, is
lone so as to make a sort of battlement
ﬀect on the inside edge, and three
yelet designs are worked through the
'enter. This ring fastens with a button
and buttonhole, which is unfastened
vhen the ring is laundered, but the
aapkin is rolled and slipped in in the
isual way. Tan or natural-colored
inen worked with dark-red or blue
:otton makes a ring that shows in pretty
:ontrast to the white napkin.

A CASE OF CONSCIENCE
A Sartorial Tragedy
By MARY WILHELMINA HASTINGS

"IF MADAME would wait one—two—minutes," said the attendant, and left me alone in the waiting-room. From the look of the place you would never dream what a love of a frock Gascoigne turned out, but anyone who had been to him once always went again—if she could afford it. It was a very simple gray voile that I was having made, plain of cut and absolutely untrimmed, for Gascoigne's trimmings were beyond the present ebb of my purse.

As I looked about my gaze was caught by a blue etamine upon a dress form. It was a stunning gown I could see at a glance, and its smartness was due to the unusual pattern in which the lace appliqué was put on. I was looking it over with that indefinable pang of non-possession when a startling succession of ideas presented itself. I had a retentive memory and deft New England fingers—moreover, similar appliqué was neither difficult nor expensive to procure—why could not I, myself, reproduce this charming pattern upon my too severe gray? At the time I was overcome with the brilliancy of the suggestion. I walked round and round the blue dress and embedded every detail of the outline within my mind.

I could hardly wait for my voile to be sent home, so anxious was I to begin work upon it.

Certainly I succeeded beyond my fondest hopes. The bold beauty of that design upon the soft gray filled me with elation, and in the righteous joy of accomplishment I donned it and went to read a paper upon Municipal Art at the Woman's Club. The paper was a success, and so, I may say, was the gray voile gown. Many an intimate friend patted me approvingly though secretly upon its well-fitting shoulder, and one woman, not even an intimate acquaintance, went so far as to ask me the name of its maker.

"Gascoigne," I answered, with conscious pride. She was a stout, overbearing woman, with a good many diamonds upon her fingers, and somehow Gascoigne's name gave me courage to meet her on common ground. I added casually that I would rather trust his workmanship than any other in the city.

"Ah, would you, indeed!" said the stout woman, non-commitally, and, still looking at my dream of a dress, she went away.

The next morning I received a visit from Gascoigne. The small Frenchman was roving excitedly up and down my diminutive drawing-room, and upon my appearance he thrust a paper in my hands, crying dramatically: "R–read,

Madame! There is a mistake, a confusion, a mystery! I do not understand!"

I unfolded the heavy, impressively coat-of-armed letter in vague trepidation, and read as my distracted visitor directed:

"MY DEAR GASCOIGNE:

"This afternoon I discovered a gown trimmed in exactly the same design as the one on my blue, which you claimed to have made exclusively for me. The wearer was Mrs. Prentice, of 247 Elm Street, and she gave your name as the maker. Needless to say, I countermand absolutely all my present orders in your establishment."

The signature was the signature of my interested acquaintance of the day before.

"There is some horrible misinformation," Gascoigne was declaring. "The gray gown was plain, comme ça, and the design for Madame Davis was out of my own head and was given to none other. And now Madame Davis is enraged and will withdraw her custom. Mon Dieu! Such a custom! It is all of a mystery. But perhaps Madame can explain?"

Well, Madame could and did explain. For over five minutes I explained steadily, with downcast eyes and burning cheeks, to an excitable little Frenchman, who greeted the painful revelation with cries of mingled amazement and horror.

"But I do not ondairstand," he repeated for the thousandth time, "what maker would dare to reproduce a Gascoigne pattern?"

"I made it myself," I confessed, miserably, stung with my own guilt. I was overcome with humiliation and a certain Puritanical conviction that I deserved it all. Where had been my New England conscience, where my honor, that without thought or care I had appropriated this man's work and unblushingly paraded it!

"Ah, I see," Gascoigne said softly. "Madame will write?"

"Write?"

"A letter—to Madame Davis."

"Indeed I will," I cried. "Oh. I am so sorry—you don't know how sorry I am. I never thought. It just struck me as a pretty pattern, and I copied it like any one in the stores. I am so sorry!"

That was not an easy letter to write. But I finally finished an explanation that I thought would satisfy any reasonable Christian soul and gave it to Gascoigne to mail.

The next day I spent a very low-spirited morning, with the memory of

Gascoigne's smile and a vision of the stout Mrs. Davis reading my humble epistle. In the midst of my reflections an imposing vehicle stopped before my door and Mrs. Davis herself descended.

If she had been a few moments earlier she would have caught me dusting the fragile glassware in my dining-room. As it was, I had time for a hasty scamper up-stairs and a few moments' panic-stricken reflection. I tried to assure myself that she had come in a spirit of kindliness to accept my explanation and laugh away the awkwardness, but I could not calm my flustered spirit. Then a most improper sense of the ridiculous urged me to receive her in the offending gown, but I conquered the prompting and descended soberly enough.

"I cannot tell you how glad I was to get this," she began at once, striking my letter, which she held in one hand, with the plump fingers of the other. She did not offer to shake hands, and I judged it inexpedient to ask her to be seated.

"I am extremely sorry," I began, but she paid not the slightest attention to me, and went on with her remarks.

"Gascoigne has always suited me remarkably well, and it is a great relief to discover *his* innocence and be able to resume his fittings."

"I am very sorry," I was beginning again, with less sorrow and more dignity than I had previously shown, but she waved me back with a majestic wave of her hand.

"It is very—unfortunate," she observed, with a manifest attempt to select a lenient expression. "You will, of course, oblige me by not wearing the dress again."

"I am afraid I can't do that," I answered. "But I can promise you never to wear it at the club again. That is, I believe, our only place of meeting."

"Quite so," said she, with obvious inflection. Then, after a pause, "I shall give mine to my maid."

"Mine is scarcely large enough for my servant," I observed, regretfully. There is no use in being slender if I can't derive a little benefit from it at times.

"I am sorry you cannot see your way clear to discarding the dress—inconvenient as it might be," snapped Mrs. Davis. "In *that* case I would have considered my lips sealed, but as it is now——" She shrugged her massive shoulders expressively and went forth to her carriage.

As it is now, I expect half the members of the club will know the story before the next meeting. She has given her gown to her maid, I know, for the girl wore it past the house twice to-day. On that account I shall wear my gray to the club, and I shall hold my head high, but never, no, never as long as I live, will I put plait or pattern upon dress of mine that does not come from a properly authorized design-book.

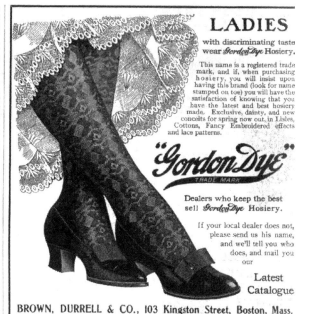

LADIES

with discriminating taste wear *Gordon Dye* Hosiery.

This name is a registered trade mark, and if, when purchasing hosiery, you will insist upon having this brand (look for name stamped on toe) you will have the satisfaction of knowing that you have the latest and best hosiery made. Exclusive, dainty, and new conceits for spring now out, in Lisles, Cottons, Fancy Embroidered effects and lace patterns.

"Gordon Dye"
TRADE MARK

Dealers who keep the best sell *Gordon Dye* Hosiery.

If your local dealer does not, please send us his name, and we'll tell you who does, and mail you our

Latest
Catalogue

BROWN, DURRELL & CO., 103 Kingston Street, Boston, Mass.

Canfield
Dress Shields

The Essentials of a perfect dress shield are:

Proof Against Moisture —Canfield Shields are guaranteed to protect your waists, and the guarantee is backed by an agreement to replace any waist injured when shield has been properly attached.

Washable —Canfield Shields may be renewed by washing over and over again, and keep as fresh as when new.

Durability—No other shield equals the Canfield Shield in long wearing qualities. Hence, Canfield Shields are most economical.

In use all over the world for over 25 years. Discriminating women insist on having CANFIELD DRESS SHIELDS. For sale everywhere.

CANFIELD RUBBER CO., 309 Mercer St., New York

Thirty years of experience enables us to give your storekeeper the BEST QUALITY and VALUE

ESTABLISHED 1874

THE CASTLE BRAID CO.

MANUFACTURERS OF THE
NEW MANHATTAN SKIRT BRAID
AND DIAMOND PULL-BRAIDS.

If your dealer does not have
SOLD BY THE BEST
CASTLE BRAID

Castle Trimmings, Castle Covered Buttons, Silk Corset and Shoe Laces, write to
The Castle Braid Co., 552 Broadway, New York.

THE MOTHERS' ADVISORY CLUB

EDITED BY THE READERS OF
THE DESIGNER

All letters, suggestions, etc., that we print in these columns, we will pay for at the rate of one dollar each, with a special price of five dollars each month for the one we consider the best. Fill out the certificate to be found at the head of this column, and pin, sew or paste it to the top of your letter. Write on one side of the paper only. Do not send in advice unless you have given it a personal test, and remember literary style is not necessary in this department, but good, sound maternal sense is what counts. One contributor may send in as many letters, questions or suggestions as she pleases at one time with one certificate, but a certificate will be required for each contributor.

Friendly discussion is what we want.

Sound, practical advice is what we want.

Interesting questions are what we want.

```
This is to certify

Name.............................

Street............................

Town.............................

State.............................

is a member of " THE MOTHERS'
        ADVISORY CLUB "
```

FIVE-DOLLAR PRIZE PARAGRAPH

Teach the Little Ones to Love One Another

TEACH the little ones to love one another when a new baby comes, instead of creating jealousy by reminding the first that his or her "nose is broken," and they are not baby any longer. It is hard enough as it is, for a little one who has been petted and fondled to see its place usurped by another. I have in my mind two little ones whose ages are three years and ten months respectively. The minute the little boy set eyes on his baby sister his little heart went out to her in love. Many times a day he has to put his arms around her, kiss her, and say, "oh, dear baby"; now she has a kiss and pat for "baba," as she calls him. When playing, if baby cries, the little boy will fly to her and try his best to amuse her. He esteems it a special privilege to carry her bottle to her. He never asks for pennies for himself, but if given one, will invariably ask for one for baby. Such love and devotion are seldom met with; it is my opinion much of it is due to having been taught to love instead of looking upon the new baby as a rival.   H. H.

Babies Should be Given Water

BABIES are often rendered restless and fretful by thirst, and should be given fresh, cold water (not ice-water) several times a day. A teaspoonful at a time is sufficient during the first six weeks. The little one's mouth and throat often become parched and dry, and milk will not satisfy it. Cold water given in this way will not give the baby colic, but will quiet it and will aid digestion. Thrush may be prevented, and sometimes very severe cases of it cured, by washing the baby's mouth after each feeding with a solution of boracic acid, in the proportion of one teaspoonful of the powder to a glass of water. The disease is attributable to improper food or neglect to wash the child's mouth after eating. Particles of milk should not be allowed to remain in the mouth, nor the tongue to become coated. Soft old linen, cut into pieces about an inch square, is nicest for washing the mouth, using a fresh piece each time.   L. L.

A Handy Baby-Basket

I WANT to tell THE DESIGNER readers about the pretty baby-basket which I made before baby came. I took two small wooden boxes thirteen inches long, nine inches wide, and five inches deep, and nailed them together sideways, then put a market-basket handle on where the two boxes came together. I then had a good-sized basket, divided in the middle. One side I lined inside with pale-blue sateen, with a little pin-cushion to match fastened to side. The other side I lined with white oilcloth, with pockets of the same. I then covered all around outside of basket with the blue sateen, with point d'esprit gathered over it, with a heading one-half inch wide at the top. I also covered handle with the same. In the oilcloth side I put soap, brushes, powder, sweet oil, olive oil, a small pair of blunt scissors, a twisted cotton cord, a small piece of old linen, and a wash-cloth and towels made of old table linen. On the other side I placed safety-pins of different sizes in cushion, and the whole suit of baby's first clothes. The cost of this basket was very small, and everyone who sees it admires it very much.   F. E. S.

and again, a story-telling contest, or a "spelling-bee." This light dissipation is followed by as much sleep as they choose to take—none of the children being "made" to rise on Saturday morning. This rests them and prepares them for the quiet of the Sabbath, and makes them ready for the activities of school-life again when Monday morning dawns.   ELLA HERMAN

Potato Poultice for Inflamed Eyes

A SHORT time ago our little boy was suffering with sore eyes caused by taking cold in them, after close application to his books. We tried several remedies to no good effect, then we applied scraped raw potato as a poultice. It proved very effective, by drawing out the inflammation, and he was able to return to his studies in a few days.
MRS. J. E. M.

That Jealous Little Fellow

ON READING Mrs. C. L. C's. article in October DESIGNER my heart went out to that poor little fellow who has been argued with and denied his dearest wishes for being jealous of his younger sister, and I wish to suggest a remedy which I am trying in a similar case. The secret is *love*. It is not enough that you know you love your boy, but let him know by your every word and action that both you and his sister love him. It is so natural for a child to form a dislike for one to whom he must "give up" and it would be so easy to favor a little girl with a sunny disposition that you will find it necessary to be ever on the alert lest his feeling of jealousy be well founded. Instead of denying his most cherished wishes for unkindness or selfishness toward his sister, try to overlook these in your constant watch for the least little word or action worthy of praise, and be ever ready with a reward when it is deserved rather than seeking some new punishment where it is merited. Let his every kind word or obliging act be met with a smile, a word of praise or a kiss of affection. Never argue with a boy—it does no good—for he cannot see the question from your view-point any more than you can from his, and constant nagging has a very demoralizing effect on health and happiness; rather cultivate a wholesome air of affection in the home. If your first efforts do not meet with success be patient, for he cannot resist continued kindness. Induce little sister to enter into your plan and she will enjoy it if you use tact. See that she always treats him with the kindness she herself desires, and in pleasantly sharing her goodies gives him the bigger portion. Last but not least, when a storm is brewing find something for both children to do. Idleness breeds mischief, and a quarrel is quickly forgotten in the pleasure of some little task or game. In fact, practise the Golden Rule, and remember that "Good is omnipotent in overcoming evil."   J. H.

KNOTS AND WHATNOTS

For the best-written letter of not over fifty words, accompanying the fullest list of answers to the puzzles on this page, we will pay a cash prize of two dollars ($2.00), and for the second, third, fourth and fifth best letters a cash prize of one dollar ($1.00) each. Write on one side of the paper only. No letters will be considered which are received after March 5th. Answers to March puzzles will appear in the April issue. January prize winners' names will be announced in the April number, and of February in the May number. Penmanship spelling and neatness will all be taken into consideration.

Address all communications to

THE EDITOR OF THE PUZZLE PAGE,
Standard Fashion Company,
12-16 Vandam Street, N. Y. City.

1.—METAGRAM

A word of six letters am I,
  I talk and I argue, and reason;
My first letter gone, I stretch out my hand
  To gather whatever's in season.

Behead me again, every one
  Is what I now mean, you may know;
But turn me around, and I'll make your heart bleed,
  Because I am suffering so.

Just one I shall be if the third
  From my other three letters is sundered;
Now ruthlessly cut off my head and my tail,
  I'll "bob up serenely"—a hundred!

2.—RIDDLE

Most everybody possesses me. Matters of etiquette concern me, and the seasons affect me noticeably. Sometimes I am tall and shiny. In hot weather I am often carried in the hand. I am sometimes very costly, but I am useful as well as ornamental. Sometimes the wind blows me away. I am different every season. Sometimes I am used to put money in. I am of many different shapes but always convex.

3.—MISSING NUMERALS

The words missing in the following paragraph can be expressed by Roman numerals. Supply the latter only.
Jennie was a good student and liked to— in her work, especially in drawing. One day she made a design of an — leaf, judging the proportions simply by her —. Another day she drew the picture of a — climbing upon the rocks. Happening to know an old sailor she showed the drawing to him. "Do you know what that is?" she asked. "— —," he replied; " it's just as natural as life. He's come up on the rocks to — in the sun. I've often seen 'em." "—!" exclaimed Jennie, "I wish I could go to —."

4.—DOUBLE DIAGONAL

1. Pleases.
2. A kind of silk.
3. Jail.
4. Fairy.
5. To pull apart.
6. Period of time.
7. The lines guiding a horse.
8. An ancient French law.
9. A city in the south of Italy.
10. A famous tree of the East.
11. A souvenir.
12. Relish.
Primals: a city in Europe.
Finals: a city in America.

5—PYRAMID

```
      . . . . .
    . . . . . . .
  . . . . . . . . .
. . . . . . . . . . .
```

Top of the upper stone: a signal fire.
Left-hand side of upper stone: a rod of iron or wood.
Right-hand side of upper stone: the fruit of certain trees.
Top of the second stone: a certain kind of earthenware.
Left-hand side of second stone: a number.
Right-hand side of second stone: a kind of beer.
Top of third stone: state of being monotonous.
Left-hand side of third stone: town north of Mecca.
Right-hand side of third stone: to notice.
Top of lower stone: state of being unintelligible.
Left-hand side of lower stone: a kind of sloth.
Right-hand side of lower stone: is seated.
Base of lower stone: not in a satisfactory state.

6.—BEHEADINGS

ehead an odd number and make
even.

ehead a building and get an article
f furniture.

ehead an animal and get his organ
f hearing.

ehead a vessel and get a grain.

ehead one who succeeds and get
ie inside.

ehead a fruit and get a kitchen
tove.

ehead below and get to possess.'

ehead a corridor and get every-
hing.

ehead need and get a busy insect.

ehead consented and get self-
shness.

ehead cold and get stiff.

ehead a mouth and get a curved
tructure.

-SENSE OUT OF NONSENSE

ac Sala sells 2 bags of 'corn to J.
p for $6.00. What I. Sala keeps
of in his day book is'the cash
—is that not clear?

the above statement in book-
ng lies hidden a question in geog-
y. What is the question?

SWERS TO FEBRUARY PUZZLES

PROBLEM—Minute hand pointing *South*.
ime; half-past one.

P1—Acacia, Isaac, Anna.

RHYMED ANIMALS—
l (peel); fox (rocks); lion (scion); hog
)g (fog); otter (cotter); beaver (lever);
d (shepherd); goat (boat); sheep (weep);
: (habit); weasels (measles).

A PROBLEM IN NAMES—
Jonathan (Jo Nathan).

AN ELIMINATED RHYME—
Old Mother Hubbard
Went to the cupboard
To get her poor dog a bone,
But when she got there
The cupboard was bare,
And so her poor dog got none.

A KITE—

```
            SOLUTION
                P
              A   A
          P   L   S
        E           T
    R   E   Q   U   I   R   E
        E           N
              N   G   I
            C   I   J
            E   N   O
              S   G   Y
                S
              T O O
              H A T
              E R E
              B I T
              O N E
                  G
```

SENSE OUT OF NONSENSE—Sugar is a noun.

BEHEADED RHYMES—
Swore, wore, ore.
Switch, witch, itch.
Skill, kill, ill.
Blend, lend, end.

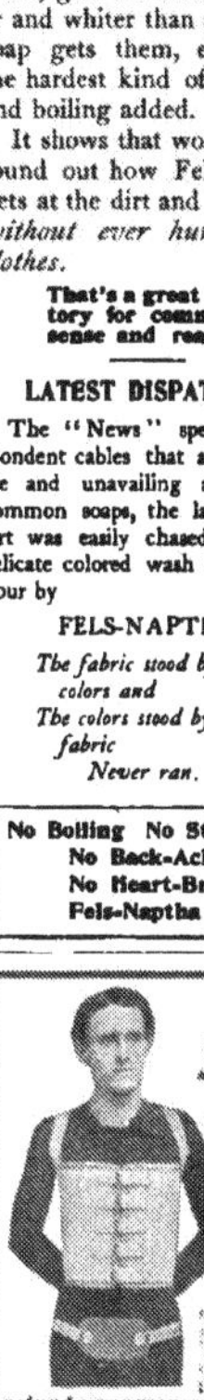

P1—
Yacht
Xebec
Zebra
Whelp.

CHARADE—
Met row poll l tan. Metropolitan.

'RIZE WINNERS FOR DECEMBER

to Katherine Haren, St. Louis, Mo., who
he only one who sent a correct list before
limit expired, $1 each to Kate Willis,
klyn, N. Y.; K. L. Holloway, Chesterfield,
; E. W. Depue, Kensington, Md.
NORABLE MENTION: Mrs. V. A. Gates.

Woman's Self-Control Her Nee

By A. S. ATKINSON, M.D.

IT HAS not always been admitted that woman had or needed self-control, which in an emergency would give her something of the courage of which heroes are made. Indeed, it was a matter of self-concept on the part of women of only a few generations ago that to be entirely and utterly feminine it was necessary to go into hysterics and show great fear and timidity on the slightest occasion. Fortunately, this belittling conception of woman is no longer popular; it is not admired by either sex. While the masculine woman is to be avoided, it is eminently fitting that the woman of the day should be something more than a bundle of uncontrolled nerves. She should be able to meet emergencies with a certain amount of self-possession and calmness that invariably makes her the master of the situation.

The modern woman has been benefited by the training and discipline of the outdoor life and recreation in more ways than one. In giving her better health it has banished many of the nervous disorders from her life; and with good health and strong nerves the matter of self-control has become a second nature to her. It is impossible to show perfect self-control and self-possession when the health is below the normal and nerves are half-starved. It is only by first attaining a perfectly normal condition that the nerves are held under subjection and made to perform the part of life's work designed for them. Feeding them with artificial foods and stimulating them with preparations from the chemist's laboratory do not strengthen and increase their powers of usefulness nearly so much and successfully as do good outdoor life and healthful exercise.

Bicycle riding, horseback riding, boating, and similar outdoor amusements perform more for woman than this; they give to her the health of mind and body she needs, and they also train the faculties in a way that adds greatly to the pleasure of existence. They discipline the mind and intellect so that self-control becomes a necessary sequence. No woman can ride a wheel, sail a boat or ride a horse without being prepared for emergencies and dangers of one kind or another. The woman who is a bundle of nerves can do none of these things successfully. The eye and faculties must be trained by the exercise for meeting constantly little dangers and mishaps which might cause an unsophisticated person to go into hysterics. The bicycle rider soon learns a nicety of decision in gauging distances that is remarkable, and at the same time a quickness in reaching a conclusion as to the best course of action to take in an emergency that is of great help. If it were not for this discipline

of eye and mind there would be inn erable collisions in the streets.

Likewise the modern woman who go for boating and yachting knows the danger on the water, and, that her and prompt action must avert it in course of a summer many times. But this reason she does not shrink from pleasure, but meets it with quiet. possessed courage that makes he heroine in the eyes of those who h never entered into outdoor sports.

This whole secondary effect of door games and recreation on woman's character and developm must in time develop her in ways seem unrelated at first thought. Pl ical self-control means in time men ethical, spiritual and esthetic self-cont No one can for long enjoy perfect mony of physical environments with being affected thereby mentally, spi ually, morally and intellectually. body is merely the house for the sp and soul, and it acts and reacts u what we call the mind and sp through subconscious processes that rarely consider.

It would be impossible to go i the psychology of the matter, there are sufficient every-day instan in every life to make the matter p to each one. When our health good and evenly balanced, all life se pleasant and roseate; we see beauties in nature and the works man, and there is sympathy betw us and our surroundings which add our enjoyment. In short, perfect he enables us to live as nature inte that we should, and in proportion t loss of normal health will be the crease in the power of our seeing brighter side of existence.

The habit of self-control exte beyond the nerves to the imaginati This most powerful factor in our li has mislead many in this world so t their perspective of existence has been wrong. There is nothing so gr and good in this world as imaginat —an imagination which will take out of self and project us into environments to enjoy something wh is little more substantial than a dre How many poor women, worked death and surrounded by poverty suffering, find, nevertheless, enjoym in life because they can release th minds from the toils of their lot enjoy the pleasures of the imaginati It is the cultivated imagination tl has given to us the great works of lite ture, art, music and science, and appreciate them to their utmost must have imagination to enter i sympathy with them. But the ins nation that is under no control, and n riot with one, is nothing less than curse; it may begin in a harmless w but it may bring us to the mad-hou

efore, self-control in this way is
ssential as that which brings our
ss under our command.

ntrol of the mind and soul will
us straight in those paths of duty
h we know to be true, and it is
of this which permits so many to
st all sorts of beliefs and ideas
h may be imposed upon a credulous
l. The healthy mind, like the
hy body, should halt well this
of the danger line. The woman
has become expert in yachting
not run into unnecessary risk and
er. It is her self-control which
ss her from any such folly. She
ss the difference between little
ers that can be easily met and
some by skill and those which
ing but fortunate accident could
l. There is the same distinction
ife between the small necessary
ers and pitfalls of conscience and
l, which all must face and over-
e, and those which are unnecessary,
are great stumbling-blocks, which
the mighty intellect or genius can
come.

st the imagination run riot, and it
soon destroy the mind for all good
lectual work; let the spirit of care-
ness and inconsistency control the
and one's beliefs and notions of
t and wrong in religion, morals, art
music may soon tumble to the
ind. There is indeed a danger of
soul and body beyond which we can-
afford to go, and it is well for us if
have both under such perfect con-
that there is never any danger of
er crossing it.

KNOWLEDGE

By M. E. S. HYMERS

S A GIRL she studied Latin,
Won a scholarship in Greek;
ry French and soft Italian
Like a native she could speak.
d I gloried in her knowledge,
Thought her wondrous wise and sweet.
ll at length her pretty German
Brought me suing at her feet.

sw we're married—mercy on us!
Stranger tongue she speaks to-day
san was ever writ in text-book
Or was wrought on ancient clay.
Muvver's pitty, itty Doodums—
Muvver's peshus manny-mies! "
s her tongue is rankest nonsense,
Rarest knowledge in her eyes.

ver language, dead or modern,
Had such wondrous charm as this,
here each answer is a gurgle,
And the pauses each a kiss.
ough I thought her wise in girlhood,
Seems she trebly so to me,
sw I hear her mother-prattle
To the baby on her knee.

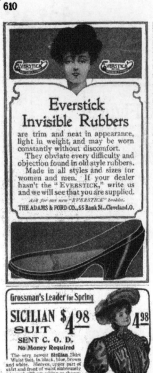

BUSINESS CARDS

The cards here pictured are reproduced in full size, and give suggestio of
the correct form for professional cards. White or gray tint egg-shell or li
finished cards are in the best taste.

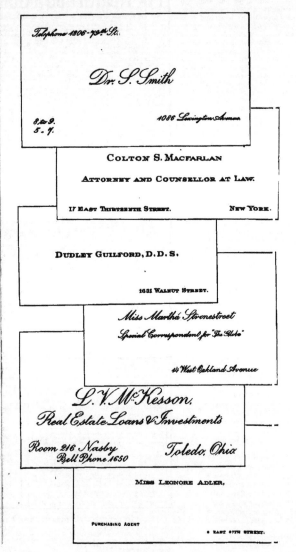

Telephone 1806-79th St.

Dr. S. Smith

8 to 9.   *1086 Lexington Avenue*
5 - 7.

COLTON S. MACFARLAN

ATTORNEY AND COUNSELLOR AT LAW.

17 EAST THIRTEENTH STREET.   NEW YORK.

DUDLEY GUILFORD, D. D. S.

1631 WALNUT STREET.

Miss Martha Stronestreet
Special Correspondent for "The Globe"

44 West Oakland Avenue

L. V. McKesson,
Real Estate Loans & Investments

Room 216 Nasby   *Toledo, Ohio*
Bell Phone 1650

MISS LEONORE ADLER,

PURCHASING AGENT   8 EAST 47TH STREET.

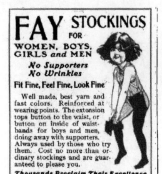

NOTES OF NEW BOOKS

By ALICE RANOUS CHUBB

"PAINTED SHADOWS," by Richard Le Gallienne. (Little, Brown & Company, Boston, Mass.) To the grown-up who is tired of strenuous romance, intricate detective mysteries, biographies that are microscopic in their close investigations of great lives, this book of short stories—essays, perhaps, it would be truer to call them—comes as pleasantly as does a volume of new fairy tales to the denizen of the nursery. In a way these are fairy tales for adults, for surely never were there such dainty, ethereal folk in the commonplace workaday world as Mr. Le Gallienne evokes by a wave of his magic pen. The masculine critics have been almost savagely severe in many instances with this, his most recent work, treating it far too seriously, when in point of fact it consists of butterfly fancies which are, we take it, only intended to please for the moment, and have no more reason for existing than the butterfly itself, yet nevertheless are things of beauty, therefore acceptable. "Poet, Take Thy Lute!" is, perhaps, the prettiest of the conceits, while "The Woman in Possession" contains a useful suggestion to wives young or old, albeit somewhat difficult to follow.

"THE MASQUERADERS," by Katherine Cecil Thurston. (Harper & Brothers, New York.) In "Doctor Jekyl and Mr. Hyde," the reading public were introduced to a man possessed of a dual nature, while in "The Masqueraders" we have two men, who in personal appearance are one, but there the likeness ends, for one is a hard-working, cynical, almost ascetic bachelor, while the other is a weak-natured, pleasure-loving Member of Parliament, who has become a victim to the morphine habit and who is a married man. The two change places, and forthwith begin a series of events which are of sufficiently interesting character to hold the reader's attention to the last page of the book. When that is read and one turns over in one's mind the entertainment afforded, one may be apt to pick flaws in the fabric, and to feel that the clever author has resorted to many little tricks of trade to win her points, sacrificing good taste in more than one instance, especially in the denouement. Even acknowledging the great gain to the world at large made by the change of positions of the two men, one cannot feel exactly enthusiastic toward a hero who, having "acquired" another man's position in society, his fortune and his wife, permits the author of his good luck—poor, worthless wretch though he was—to be hurried off to an unknown grave. However, the main object of modern fiction is to entertain, and in this "The Masqueraders" certainly scores a success.

"THE PRINCESS THORA," by Harris Burland. (Little, Brown & Company, Boston, Mass.) This is a romance of the "Prisoner of Zenda" type, and the scene of the marvelous adventures changes from present-day London to the Arctic regions, and ends in an island in the Polar sea, where habits and customs are the same as in the Middle Ages, where armor is still worn, and where tournaments and jousts are every-day occurrences. The *Princess*, who turns out to be no princess after all, is a golden-haired beauty who conquers the hearts of friends and foes, and yet who is won by a very commonplace Englishman. Some of the scenes are sufficiently realistic to cause the reader a thrill, notably the breaking up of the Paliocrystic sea, and again when the *Red King* dies fighting with his armor-clad, long-dead sons on either side of him.

"THE DAILY CHEER YEAR BOOK," by M. Allette Ayer. (Lee & Shepard. Boston, Mass.) This is a collection of cheerful verse and prose, culled from various sources and bound in a bright little blue-and-gold volume of just the right size for a tired hand to hold when its owner picks up the book in search of a little encouragement, which she will certainly find. Many of the verses are by anonymous authors, and again many of the names which appear are not notabilities in literary marts, but they are cheering for all that. The book would be a pleasant gift for a "shut-in" friend.

"THE THEATRICAL PRIMER," by H. A. Vivian (G. W. Dillingham Co.), is a mildly amusing little book which may serve to pass a weary hour on a railway journey, and it will undoubtedly elicit some hearty, appreciative laughter rom members of the profession. The ninitiated, however, will probably miss nany of the best points.

"MORNING THOUGHTS TO CHEER HE DAY," Selected and Arranged by Iaria H. Le Row (Little, Brown & Company, Boston). Hope and courage re united for the motto of this little ook, which comprises 840 well-chosen elections from many sources. Some f them are in verse, others in prose, and not one among them but is well vorth reading and thinking over, eing far removed from the almost rritatingly sentimental quotations which in so many cases form the principal part of books of this character. The following paragraph taken from its store seems to be the keynote of the entire volume, "Oh, friend, never strike sail to a fear! Come into port greatly, or sail with God the seas. . . . He has not learned the lesson of life who does not every day surmount a fear." —Emerson.

"THE ARK OF 1803," a Story of Louisiana Purchase Times, by C. A. Stephens (A. S. Barnes & Company, New York). This is a dramatic story of one of the greatest chapters of American history, and is written in a style which will appeal to the sturdy youth of the present day. The characters are fine, manly fellows, with nothing of the prig or the sneak about them, and their adventures while guiding the great ark laden with skins and pelts from Fish Creek, Ohio, to New Orleans, are thrilling enough to hold older readers' interest. Indians, river pirates, soldiers and trappers unite in giving stirring realism to the plot.

"THE MAKING OF MEENIE," by Edith L. Gilbert. (Lee & Shepard, Boston, Mass.) This is a continuation of "The Frolicsome Four," which the youngsters hailed with delight when it put in appearance last year. Miss Gilbert has a happy way of delineating childish characters which make young folks her friends and gives her books great popularity in the juvenile circles. Meenie is a rough but good-hearted little nurse to two lovable twins, Pearl and Joy, and although her name is given to the book the honors are shared by a great dog, the Frolicsome Four and Dorothy from Canada. The book is suitable for children from six to nine years of age.

"DOROTHY DAINTY AT SCHOOL," by Amy Brooks (Lee & Shepard, Boston). This is the third volume of "Dorothy Dainty Series." The little heroine is old enough for school in the present book, but her young friends will find her as entertaining a companion as ever, and will rejoice with her at the rescue of Nancy Ferris, who in the previous volume had been kidnapped and made into a little dancer much against her will.

"A LASS OF DORCHESTER," by Annie M. Barnes. (Lee & Shepard, Boston, Mass.) The place and time of this story are the Province of Carolina and the year 1702. The "Lass" is Miss Elizabeth Blew, the heroine of "Little Betty Blew," a popular book of last season. She is now grown up and just returned from Boston, where she has been to finish her education. Her father is Indian agent for the Government, and a man of thorough kindness and integrity. A rival tries desperately to supplant him in his position, stopping at nothing in the way of ruining business and alienating friends. Worst of all, the integrity of Betty's father is questioned. Stirring events, bringing in many quaint and peculiar customs, lead up to the climax, in which an attack is made upon the church by unfriendly Indians. Betty proves herself a heroine by her thrilling ride for timely help, and the finding of means whereby to prove her father's honor.

"AN HONOR GIRL," by Evelyn Raymond. (Lee & Shepard, Boston, Mass.) A bright story of a girl who, as the valedictorian and "honor girl" of her class at high school, wins a scholarship which would take her through Wellesley College. Family reverses bring it home to her that duty demands that she devote herself to helping her parents and wayward brother to face the future better than they seem likely to. She heroically surrenders her prize, with its glowing prospects, to a jealous rival, and with a brave humor says that she has matriculated in the College of Life, the hard features of which she happily styles the "Faculty," with "Professor Poverty" prominent among them. These prove excellent teachers, aided by "Professor Cheerfulness." Kind friends are won by her courage, her brother achieves manly character, and the family are finally reestablished on the road to prosperity—all better, happier, and more to each other than had selfishness not been so well met and overcome by "An Honor Girl."

"JASON'S QUEST," by D. O. S. Lowell, A.M., M.D., Master in Roxbury Latin School. (Lee & Shepard, Boston, Mass.) The story of the Golden Fleece will never lose its charm for young and old, and is not only excellent entertainment, but is a necessary part of the knowledge of every one who is to be considered as even ordinarily well educated. Professor Lowell has told the whole story of the renowned expedition of the Argonauts, together with the subsequent fortunes of Jason, in the happiest possible manner and with a most thorough scholarship, which, with great skill, he never allows to make his story "dry." Such books as this are exceptionally valuable to place in the hands of the young, and this handsome volume, with its many illustrations, both full-page and in the text, beautifully printed on fine paper, will make a choice gift.

FASHION NOTES FOR MEN

By ALINE DE CARDEVA

UNFINISHED worsted will be the prevailing material employed in dress coats. The collar and roll will be moderately wide and now and then a velvet collar will be noticed. Velvet cuffs will accompany the velvet collar in some instances, but this is largely a matter of choice. The skirts of the dress coat fall below the knees and the low waistline drops noticeably as it nears the front. The lapels will be finished either peaked and blunted and blind or prick-stitched. Although representative tailors advocate the peaked lapel, there is a strong tendency toward the rounded corners, while the shawl-roll is

DRESS COAT AND VEST

equally correct. The roll is long and the skirts decidedly tapered; blind-stitching is the generally popular finish for the edges. There is also a vogue for a little cord-bound finish. Sleeves may be completed by a stitched vent or a sewed-on cuff and the self-facing may extend to the buttonholes on both the peaked lapel and vent sleeve, but the shawl-roll will, of course, be faced to the extreme edge.

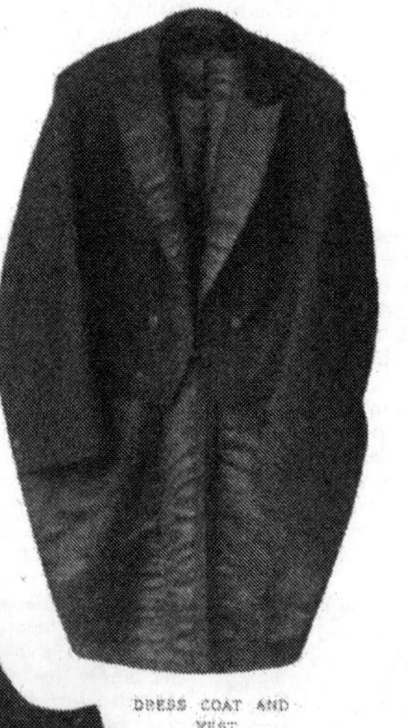

Waistcoats accompanying the evening coat may be of the same material or they may be of white moiré, figured silk or piqué. For evening weddings the smart waistcoat is made of white silk of a heavy quality. The opening is U shaped and the accepted style double breasted. Five fine pearl buttons arranged in V shape fasten the front. One of the smartest models of the season omits lapels. The edges are bound with a narrow white braid instead of stitching. Another style favored by many of the best tailors has wide shawl lapels finished on the edges with double rows of stitching. Buttons are employed upon fancy waistcoats more than ever. Mother-of-pearl, bullet and oval shape, and flat pearl with gold thread run through the eyelets are conspicuous among the novelties. The wedding vest of a member of New York's fashionables was made of heavy white moiré silk and lined with white satin. The buttons were solid pearl with the owner's monogram applied in gold. The buckle at the back was also of gold.

A great many men prefer a black waistcoat with the evening coat. In this instance the waistcoat is made of the same material as the coat, and may be either single or double breasted. The fashionable cut is low, having the shawl-roll lapels and four buttons. The edges are bound in narrow black

WHITE KID PIQUÉ STITCHED

tracing braid; either fancy or plain may be used. With the dress coat and white vest a white tie must always be worn. To be absolutely correct a white bow tie should also accompany the evening coat and black waistcoat. However, there are instances noted in the best society where middle-aged men invariably wear a black bow tie with full evening dress.

As to linen, there is little change to note. Dress shirts are made "coat" fashion—that is, they are open entirely down the front. Bosoms are very wide and plaited. Cuffs are attached and have round corners. The full-dress collar is high with slightly turned edges and fine white-mull string ties still hold in favor. With the Tuxedo or dinner coat a black string tie must be worn.

Dinner coats are now being made of dark-gray stuffs. Of course, the black garment will always hold first place, but, by way of change, Society has adopted to a great measure the dark-gray worsteds. The average length of the new dinner coat is thirty-one inches. The model is slightly shaped at the waistline, and, replacing the shawl collar faced all the way round the neck, that has been the general fashion for so long, the collar of the new spring style shows a notch where the lapels begin, and instead of the usual straight line they are cut with a curved inner edge, allowing more of the shirt front to be seen. The fronts do not narrow down in single-breasted effect, but overlap in a decidedly double-breasted fashion, and are worn buttoned or open.

One of the authoritative establishments of Fifth Avenue is showing a frock coat made of smoke-gray worsted cut very long, and having black satin lapels faced to the buttonholes only. The style is, of course, double-breasted, and fastens with six covered buttons. For daytime weddings the style is recommended by the best fashion critics. Light striped trousers and a fancy waistcoat must accompany the frock coat, and when worn at an afternoon wedding or formal function of any sort pearl-gray suède gloves should be used. A high collar and puff or Ascot tie in any pale shade is quite correct, although for weddings a white puff is the smartest.

Gloves at an evening wedding should always be white kid, piqué stitched, and two-button. The going-away gloves of the bridegroom may be of unfinished deerskin in a pale-yellow shade or they may be the same leather in dark-slate; heavy suède is also correct for afternoon and going-away dress, but light-weight inexpensive suèdes are not to be recommended.

UNFINISHED DEERSKIN

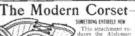

ANSWERS TO CORRESPONDENTS

RULES

IN ORDER to insure a reply under this heading it is necessary to give a pseudonym under which the querist may be answered. The full name and address of the writer must also be given. This will never, under any circumstances, be published. Questions which are to be answered in THE DESIGNER for April must reach the editor not later than February 12th.

No answers to correspondents will be sent by mail unless a two-cent stamp or stamped envelope is received at this office. Address all such letters to the EDITORIAL DEPARTMENT, STANDARD FASHION COMPANY, 12-16 Vandam St., New York City.

No contribution to "What Women Are Doing" or "Helps Along the Way" will be accepted unless accompanied by a duplicate of the certificate printed below, properly filled out. One certificate is necessary for each contributor. Two or more readers may not send in items or paragraphs on the same certificate, but one reader may send in as many items or paragraphs as he or she wishes in one letter, provided a filled-out certificate be enclosed in that letter. Certificate for "The Mothers' Club" will hereafter be given at the head of that department. When sending items or paragraphs, cut out the certificate, fill in name and address, and, pin, sew or paste the certificate to the letter which is sent with the items or paragraphs. The letter should also contain the address, plainly written.

CERTIFICATE OF MEMBERSHIP.

This is to certify I read THE DESIGNER, and wish to contribute to "What Women Are Doing," "Helps Along the Way."

Name ....

Address ....

A MOTHER—The glacial acetic acid would in all probability remove the roots of the hair as well as the mole, and in that case the hair would not grow again. If the hair grows over the mole we do not see how it is possible to remove the one without the other. Cannot the beard or mustache be cultivated so as to hide the mole? We know of many facial defects which are hidden in this way.

Answers to Correspondents.
Continued.

MISS EMMA C.—The face you so admire is that of Miss Ray Gilmore, a professional model, who at present is singing in "In Nordland," at the Lew Fields Theater, New York City.

M. G.—It is impossible for us to publish in these columns directions for massaging and shampooing so that you could undertake the work professionally. The best plan would be for you to take a course in such instruction from someone who thoroughly understands the business. Send us a stamped envelope directed to yourself and we will tell you the address of such a college in New York City, but as you live so far away perhaps this information will not be of service to you. Certainly in so large a city as yours there must be reliable teachers of such work.

NELLIE H.—The recipe referred to is a hair dye and is made as follows: One-quarter ounce of sax sulphur, one and one-half drams of sugar of lead, one ounce of best brandy, one-half ounce of glycerin, two ounces of rosewater, one pint of soft water. Mix well and add the water last of all. Let the compound stand a week before using, being careful to shake every day and before applying. Wet only the roots of the hair, and use as often as necessary, which will be about once in two weeks after the gray hairs have disappeared.

FLORENCE C. P.—We cannot make you a pattern such as you desire, but if you will send us a stamped envelope directed to yourself we will tell you where you can get stamped patterns of various kinds. Always remember to enclose a stamp or stamped envelope whenever you wish a reply by mail to a business letter.

DORETA.—Mourning is worn for either parent for two years, sometimes for three. Deep mourning, crape trimmed, with no white, is worn for three months. After that time the crape may be left off and narrow white frills or organdy bands worn at the neck and wrists. All black or all white is then worn for another year, and then lavender, gray and black-and-white for the remaining time. No lace, embroidery or jewelry should be worn with the all-black toilette.

A. A. G.—A man is always introduced to a woman, unless he is a notability. Do not rise when a man is introduced to you; merely bow politely and say, "I am happy to meet you." It is more graceful for you to rise when a woman is introduced, and you should certainly do so if she be an elderly woman. When introducing one woman to another, you can say, "Miss Brown, I want you to meet my friend, Miss Green." When introducing two men, simply say, "Mr. Brown, let me introduce Mr. Green."

Answers to Correspondents.
Continued.

MOTHER.—You can make the first cloak of merino, cashmere, bengaline, silk-finished henrietta or white silk, and silk embroidery, hand-embroidery, lace or ribbon would be appropriate for trimming. In this number of THE DESIGNER, among the fashion designs, you will find a pretty pattern for an infant's cloak, also one for the first bonnet, which may be of the same material as the cloak or of fine linen lawn, silk-lined.

DEBBIE.—It would be more conventional for your mother to issue the invitation for tea, but as it is perfectly informal, it would not be out of the way for you to ask the young man yourself when you meet him at church; and as he is a stranger, you say, to nearly everyone else in town except your family, it would be a graceful and kindly act to extend him the courtesy. It is unnecessary to make any extra preparations in his honor, as the Sunday evening meal in most families is always a little festival. Toast or hot biscuits, cold ham, tongue or chicken, lettuce or potato salad or radishes, preserves, cake, tea or chocolate would be ample.

MISS JESSIE O'NEIL.—In THE DESIGNER for November, 1904, you will find all the latest styles in wedding invitations reproduced in miniature size, and if you will send us a stamped envelope directed to yourself we will tell you where you may have work of this kind done in a satisfactory manner. The invitations should be issued at least two weeks before the ceremony.

HENRY.—If the ceremony takes place in the morning, noon or afternoon, the groom may wear a black cutaway or frock coat, gray trousers, enameled leather shoes, light or dark vest, pearl-gray or white silk Ascot tie, gray suède or tan kid gloves. If the wedding is in the evening, a dress suit will be necessary, with white lawn tie, white kid gloves, low-cut white or black vest, and enameled leather low shoes.

MARY H. S.—Serve the supper from a large table set in the dining-room and decorated with flowers. A pretty arrangement would be to place in the center of the table a large glass bowl filled with cut flowers and ferns and bank the outside of the bowl with flowers and evergreens. At two of the corners of the table place candelabra of glass, gilt or silver filled with white candles under pale-yellow shades. Small dishes filled with stuffed olives and salted nuts or bonbons may be arranged with the other viands on the table, and at one end coffee may be served, while at the other ice-cream or fruit punch may be dispensed. The bride should select two young ladies to preside. The menu may consist of chicken salad, dainty sandwiches of

RUBENS INFANT SHIRT

VOL. XXI

No. 6

THE
DESIGNER
for
April

10 CENTS A YEAR
POST-PAID

PUBLISHED MONTHLY BY THE
STANDARD FASHION COMPANY
12-15 VANDAM STREET, NEW YORK
33 RICHMOND STREET WEST, TORONTO, CANADA
ENTERED AT THE POST OFFICE, NEW YORK, AS SECOND-CLASS

10 CENTS A COPY

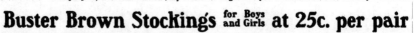

The CORSET MASTERPIECE

KABO in every way is a Corset Masterpiece.

In construction, materials and workmanship combined with the latest creations it stands above them all.

Every feature that pertains to comfort, such as gracefulness of figure and perfection of fit, is given special attention to assure absolute enjoyment when wearing a KABO Corset.

KABO Corsets on account of their great superiority received at St. Louis World's Fair,

GRAND PRIZE
HIGHEST AWARD

KABO Corsets have no brass eyelets. The KABO Corset is made in many styles, including an extensive assortment in newest ideas, such as Dip Hip, Straight Front and TAPERING WAIST Models.

Ask your dealer for KABO Corsets and if you do not receive them write to us and we will see that you are supplied.

Price $1.00 to $3.50

FREE To any lady who sends us the front of a corset box showing style of Kabo purchased, and 2 cents for postage, we will send free a set of Kabo Ribbon and Tape Needles, which are particularly desirable, as they enable a lady to pull the ribbon through the beading without crushing, instead of using a hairpin or fingers.

CATALOG SENT ON REQUEST

KABO CORSET CO.

CHICAGO
198 Monroe Street

NEW YORK
386 Broadway

KABO   KABO

Three Popular Styles of Kabo Corsets

Style No. 624 A low bust, tapering waist, dip hip corset for a medium figure, made in steeling cloth. Colors: White, Drab and Black. 11-inch 5-hook steel. 8½-inch waist. Lace trimmed on top. Front and side supporters. Sizes 18 to 30 . . . . **$1.00**

Style No. 711 A low bust, straight front, gored, dip hip corset, made for the average figure, of extra quality sterling jean. Colors White, Drab and Black. 11-inch 5-hook steel. 9-inch waist. Lace trimmed on top. Front and side supporters. Sizes 18 to 36 . . . . **$1.50**

Style No. 800 This garment produces slender effect in stout figures; especially designed with abdominal reenforcement to hold in abdomen firmly; substantial security button supporters on hip and front. Made of imported coutil. Colors White and Drab. Lace trimmed. Sizes 18 to 36, **$2.50**

ALL
STRAIGHT
FRONT
MODELS

C/B

A La Spirite
Corsets

FOR THE
WOMAN
OF FASHION

THE
DESIGNER

VOL. XXI. No. 6 APRIL, 1905

CONDUCTED BY
LILIAN DYNEVOR RICE

LADIES' JACKETS. DESCRIBED ON PAGE 628
(BLOUSE JACKET 9283) (ETON JACKET 9287)

621

LADIES' BLOUSE REDINGOTE AND JACKET TOILETTE. DESCRIBED ON PAGE 628
(REDINGOTE 9278)   (JACKET 9273 AND SKIRT 9269)

LADIES' BRIDAL DRESS AND BRIDESMAID'S TOILETTE. DESCRIBED ON PAGE 628

(PRINCESS DRESS 9242)   (WAIST 9279 AND SKIRT 9277)

623

LADIES' SHIRT-WAIST TOILETTES. DESCRIBED ON PAGES 628 AND 629

(SHIRT-WAIST 9262 AND SKIRT 9263)   (SHIRT-WAIST 9264 AND SKIRT 9112)

The Designer

LADIES' TOILETTE. DESCRIBED ON PAGE 829
(WAIST 9247 AND SKIRT 9241)

825

April, 1905

LADIES' SHIRT-WAIST TOILETTE.   DESCRIBED ON PAGE 629
(SHIRT-WAIST 9248 AND SKIRT 9135)

The Designer

LADIES' SHIRT-WAIST TOILETTE. ILLUSTRATED ON PAGE 624.

Ladies' surplice shirt-waist 9264 is in six sizes, from thirty-two to forty-two inches bust measure, price 15 cents, and appears in different development on page 635. Ladies' skirt 9112 is in eight sizes, from twenty to thirty-four inches waist measure, price 15 cents. Dark-blue burlingham and white linen lawn, hand-embroidered, are used for this toilette, narrow blue satin ribbon trimming the shirt-waist.

LADIES' TOILETTE. ILLUSTRATED ON PAGE 625.

Ladies' tucked waist 9247 is in six sizes, from thirty-two to forty-two inches bust measure, price 15 cents, and is presented in different development on page 635. Ladies' skirt 9241 is in seven sizes, from twenty to thirty-two inches waist measure, price 15 cents. Brown-and-white satin foulard and plain brown Liberty satin are combined for this pretty toilette, écru embroidered net being used for the full vest.

9266. LADIES' JACKET (WITH FULL LENGTH OR LONG ELBOW SLEEVES AND WITH OR WITHOUT THE VEST, GIRDLE ND LINING) Described on page 630.

LADIES' SHIRT-WAIST TOILETTE. ILLUSTRATED ON PAGE 626.

Ladies' tucked shirt-waist 9248 is in seven sizes, from thirty-two to forty-four inches bust measure, price 15 cents, another development of the design appearing on page 637, where it is accompanied by a detailed description, measurements for the quantity of material required for the making of the garment, etc. Ladies' tuck-plaited seven-gored skirt 9135 is in eight

LADIES' STREET TOILETTE. ILLUSTRATED ON PAGE 627.

Ladies' blouse redingote or jacket 9271 is in six sizes, from thirty-two to forty-two inches bust measure, price 15 cents, and is shown again, but in entirely different development, on page 631. Ladies' nine-gored skirt 9254 is in seven sizes, from twenty to thirty-two inches waist measure, price 15 cents, another view of the garment being given on page 640, where it is accompanied by a detailed description, measurements for the quantity of material required for making of the garment, also mention of some suitable fabrics for its reproduction. Deep rose-red henrietta is combined with still darker velvet for the toilette in the present instance.

LADIES' JACKET TOILETTE. ILLUSTRATED ON PAGE 627.

Ladies' jacket 9261 is in seven sizes, from thirty-two to forty-four inches bust measure, price 15 cents, another development of the design appearing on page 630. Ladies' fifteen-gored skirt 9249 is in seven sizes, from twenty to thirty-two inches waist measure, price 15 cents, another view of the garment being given on page 641, where it is accompanied by a detailed description, measurements for the quantity of material required, etc.

The jacket is here made of green broadcloth, the revers being faced with green peau de soie, and the vest made of novelty vesting. The skirt is made of camel's-hair cheviot.

LADIES' TOILETTE. ILLUSTRATED ON PAGE 628.

Ladies' waist 9253 is in six sizes, from thirty-two to forty-two inches bust meas-

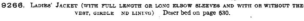

9287, LADIES' ETON JACKET (TUCKED IN INVERTED BOX - PLAIT EFFECT, WITH COLLAR - FACING IN EITHER OF TWO OUTLINES, FULL LENGTH OR LONG ELBOW SLEEVES AND WITH OR WITHOUT THE POSTILION OR BELT). Described on page 630.

sizes, from twenty to thirty-four inches waist measure, price 15 cents. The toilette as here pictured is made of gray cotton cheviot, the turn-down collar and the cuffs being made of white linen.

ure, price 15 cents, and is shown again on page 634. Ladies' skirt 9238 is in six sizes, twenty to thirty inches waist measure, price 15 cents. Tan taffeta and all-over lace are used for this toilette.

9266—LADIES' JACKET. Illustrated on page 629.

This effective jacket is made of dark-blue silk combined with light cloth and trimmed with fancy gimp. Lace ruffles may be worn in the sleeves if desired. The jacket portions are mounted on a body lining, the lining fronts being faced to form the vest. The back and fronts of the material are shirred on the shoulders, and the

9261, LADIES' JACKET WITH VEST (WITH PLAITED OR GATHERED SLEEVES AND WITH OR WITHOUT REVERS). Described on this page.

lower edges are gathered and completed by a trimming band. The neck edge is finished with a turn-down collar and the sleeve may be in either of two styles. One is a full-length, one-seamed bishop model gathered into the armhole. The lower edge is gathered into a band and completed by a one-piece turn-up cuff. The other sleeve is a full one-seamed elbow model with the lower edge gathered and finished with a deep frill of lace and band or with a turn-up cuff. A crush girdle may be attached to the lower part of the lining. The jacket fronts may be closed as shown in the large front view or rolled back to form revers, and the vest with the lining fronts fastens down the center with hooks and eyes.

Taffeta silk, peau de soie, satin rhadame, velvet, chiffon velvet, pongee or cloth may be used to develop this design. A figure view on the Front Cover Page shows a different development.

Ladies' jacket 9266 is in five sizes, from thirty-two to forty inches bust measure, price 15 cents. The thirty-six-inch bust size requires, as in upper large front view, five yards of material which is twenty-two inches wide.

9287—LADIES' ETON JACKET. Illustrated on page 629.

This attractive jacket is made of light-gray tweed with collar and cuffs of dark-green velvet outlined with white cloth, embroidered with dark-green French knots. It is fitted by side-back, side-front, under-arm and shoulder seams, the back and front portions being tucked in inverted box-plait effect. Two styles of sleeve are provided: one is a full-length, one-seamed model, gathered at the upper edge. Its lower edge is gathered into a band cuff. A turn-up cuff in fancy outline may be attached to the band, as indicated. The other sleeve is one-seamed and in elbow length. It is gathered at the upper and lower edges and completed by a sleeve band and a turn-up cuff. A deep flounce of lace may be attached to this sleeve, if desired. A fancy collar-facing is provided, but may be omitted, and the lower edge of the jacket

is finished with a belt, to which a postilion portion may be attached as shown in the upper back view.

Taffeta silk, satin rhadame, satin duchesse, pongee, tweed, covert cloth, cheviot, velvet or panne may be used to develop this design.

A figure view on page 621 shows a different development. Ladies' Eton jacket 9287 is in six sizes, from thirty-two to forty-two inches bust measure, price 15 cents. The thirty-six-inch bust size requires, for the garment when made with full-length sleeves, two and one-eighth yards of material which measures fifty-four inches in width.

9261 — LADIES' JACKET WITH VEST. Illustrated on this page.

This stylish jacket is made of light-tan covert cloth with vest of white cloth. It is fitted by center-back, side-back, under-arm and shoulder seams, also single bust darts. The center and side backs are cut with extensions which are lapped in plaits, as indicated. The upper portions of the fronts are laid back to form revers, or these may be omitted, and the neck edge may be finished with or without the flat collar-facing. The vest portions are attached to the fronts of the jacket and close down the center front

Seven-Eighths Length

Full Length   Seven-Eighths Length

9278. LADIES' BLOUSE REDINGOTE OR COAT IN FULL OR SEVEN-EIGHTHS LENGTH (WITH SLEEVES TUCKED OR SHIRRED AT THE WRIST AND WITH OR WITHOUT THE SHIRRINGS IN SKIRT; SUITABLE FOR RAIN, AUTOMOBILE OR TRAVELING WEAR). Described on page 631.

with buttons and buttonholes. The sleeve is a two-seamed model plaited or gathered into the armhole and finished with an underfacing.

Covert cloth, serge, cheviot, box-cloth, tweed, English flannel, taffeta silk, peau de soie, duck or piqué may be used to develop this design.

A figure view on page 627 shows a different development. Ladies' jacket 9261 is in seven sizes, from thirty-two to forty-four inches bust measure, price 15 cents. The thirty-six-inch bust size requires two and one-half yards of material forty-four inches wide or two yards fifty-four.

9278 — LADIES' BLOUSE REDINGOTE OR COAT IN FULL OR SEVEN-EIGHTHS LENGTH. Illustrated on page 630.

This trim and stylish coat is made of light-tan covert cloth. The waist portions are fitted by under-arm and shoulder seams, the lower edges of back and fronts being shirred, and finished with a shaped girdle having a dip front. The neck edge may be finished with or without the flat collar-facing. The sleeve is a one-seamed model, gathered into the armhole. The lower edge may be tucked or shirred, and is completed by a one-piece cuff. The skirt portions are united by a center-back seam, and are gathered or shirred to shallow yoke depth. They are attached to the belt and may be full or seven-eighths length.

Covert cloth, tweed, light-weight kersey, cravenette, serge, peau de soie or pongee may be used to develop this design, and a figure view is shown on page 622.

Ladies' blouse redingote or coat 9278 is in seven sizes, from thirty-two to forty-four inches bust measure, price 15 cents. The thirty-six-inch bust size requires, for full-length garment, four and seven-eighths yards

9273. LADIES' JACKET (WITH NOTCHED OR SHAWL COLLAR AND PLAITED OR GATHERED SLEEVES, AND WITH OR WITHOUT THE POCKET LAPS). Described on page 632.

of material forty-four inches wide or four and one-quarter yards of fifty-four-inch material.

9271 — LADIES' BLOUSE REDINGOTE OR JACKET. Illustrated on this page.

The full-length large front view depicts this handsome garment made of fawn-gray covert cloth, trimmed with Persian band embroidery and lined with light-gray peau de soie. The jacket portions are fitted by under-arm and shoulder seams, the fulness at the lower edges being disposed in dart-shaped tucks. The sleeve is a two-seamed model plaited or gathered into the armhole and finished with a turn-up cuff. A shaped girdle is attached to the lower edge of the jacket and a collar-facing, extending into a trimming band, is provided, but may be omitted. The skirt or redingote portions are in two pieces united by a center-back seam. The fulness in the back is disposed in plaits, and the extra fulness in the front and over the hips is arranged in dart-shaped tucks to yoke depth. If preferred the

9271. LADIES' BLOUSE REDINGOTE OR JACKET (WITH DART TUCKS OR GATHERS AT THE WAIST AND PLAITED OR GATHERED SLEEVES, AND WITH OR WITHOUT COLLAR-FACING OR CUFFS). Described on this page.

ALL STANDARD PATTERNS NOW 5, 10 OR 15 CENTS—NONE HIGHER

9283, LADIES' BLOUSE JACKET (WITH WIDE OR NARROW BELT, COLLAR IN EITHER OF TWO OUTLINES AND FULL-LENGTH OR LONG ELBOW SLEEVES PLAITED OR GATHERED AT THE TOP; WITH OR WITHOUT THE PEPLUM OR POSTILION). Described on page 633.

and braid, gimp, appliqué Russian or antique lace, galloon or Oriental trimming may be used effectively to decorate.

A figure view on page 627 shows a different development.

Ladies' blouse redingote or jacket 9271 is in six sizes, from thirty-two to forty-two inches bust measure, price 15 cents. The thirty-six-inch bust size requires for

upper edge of the skirt portions may be gathered and attached to the girdle. Short peplum portions may be used instead of the redingote skirt, if preferred. The fronts of the garment may be closed in double-breasted fashion, or rolled back, as indicated in one large front view of jacket.

Covert cloth, tweed, box-cloth, broadcloth, cheviot, velvet, velveteen, velour, panne, chiffon velvet, taffeta silk or peau de soie may be used to develop this design,

redingote, four and one-half yards of material forty-four inches wide or three and seven-eighth yards fifty-four inches.

9273—LADIES' JACKET. Illustrated on page 631.

This stylish jacket is made of tan covert cloth finished with machine-stitching.

It is fitted by center-back, side-back, under-arm and shoulder seams, also single bust darts. The center backs and side backs are cut with small extensions below the waistline, which are lapped in plaits, as indicated. The sleeve is a two-seamed model with fulness at the upper edge gathered or plaited, and the lower edge completed by an underfacing. The upper edges of the fronts are laid back to form lapels which meet the rolling collar in notches, or, if preferred, the small shawl collar may be used. The pattern provides pocket laps, which may, however, be omitted.

Covert cloth, melton, tweed, light-weight kersey, cheviot, serge, box-cloth or flannel may be used for this design.

Round Length

Round Length   *Short Sweep Length*

9280, LADIES' COSTUME IN SHORT SWEEP OR ROUND LENGTH (CONSISTING OF A WAIST CLOSED AT THE BACK, WITH HIGH OR DUTCH OR LOW ROUND NECK AND FULL-LENGTH OR LONG ELBOW SLEEVES, AND WITH OR WITHOUT THE BERTHA; AND A FIVE-GORED SKIRT SLIGHTLY GATHERED AT THE TOP AND WITH A CIRCULAR GATHERED FLOUNCE FROM BENEATH WHICH THE SKIRT MAY BE CUT AWAY). Described on page 633.

ALL STANDARD PATTERNS NOW 5, 10 OR 15 CENTS—NONE HIGHER

A figure view on page 622 shows a different development of the model.

Ladies' jacket 9273 is in eight sizes, from thirty-two to forty-six inches bust measure, price 15 cents. The thirty-six-inch bust size requires two and one-half yards of material forty-four inches wide or two yards of material fifty-four inches in width.

9283 — LADIES' BLOUSE JACKET. Illustrated on page 632.

Medium-weight light covert cloth and peau de soie are the materials chosen to develop this stylish jacket here depicted. It is fitted by under-arm and shoulder seams, the fronts being shirred at the lower edge and the forward edges faced so that they may be rolled back in revers effect. The rolling collar which finishes the neck edge may be cut in either of two outlines, and the one-seamed sleeve may be made in full or elbow length. When the full-length style is preferred, the lower edge of the sleeve is gathered and completed by a band and turn-up flare cuff. When the elbow sleeve is desired, the lower part of the full-length sleeve is cut away and the flare cuff attached. The shaped girdle is attached to the lower edge of the body portions, and a peplum, plaited in the back, may be attached to the lower edge of the girdle, or, if preferred, a postilion back may be used.

A figure view is shown on page 621.

Ladies' blouse jacket 9283 is in seven sizes, from thirty-two to forty-four inches bust measure, price 15 cents. The thirty-six-inch bust size requires two and one-eighth yards of material fifty-four inches wide.

Round Length

9267. LADIES' SHIRRED WAIST CLOSED AT THE BACK (WITH HIGH OR LOW OR DUTCH ROUND NECK AND FULL-LENGTH OR ELBOW SLEEVES IN EITHER OF TWO STYLES OR WITH SHORT PUFF SLEEVES). Described on page 634.

9280—LADIES' COSTUME IN SHORT SWEEP OR ROUND LENGTH. Illustrated on page 632.

This charming costume is made of figured lawn and is trimmed with insertion and lace. It is shown in the small front view developed in light-violet crêpe de Chine with bertha of point de Paris lace.

The waist of the costume is mounted on a fitted lining. The front and backs are gathered at the upper edge and shirred at the lower one. The yoke portions are fitted by shoulder seams, and when the high-neck style is preferred the neck edge is finished with a standing collar. If the Dutch or low round neck is desired, the upper part of the lining and yoke portions may be cut away. The bertha, which may be omitted, is in one piece with a fancy lower outline. Two styles of sleeve are provided: one is a full-length model consisting of a two-seamed, close-fitting lining and a one-seamed, full outside sleeve; the latter is gathered at the upper and lower edges. When the long elbow sleeve is used, the lower part of the lining sleeve is cut away and the outside sleeve is finished with a deep frill of lace. The waist fastens down the center of the back by

Short Sweep Length

9305. LADIES' TUCKED SHIRT-WAIST COSTUME IN SHORT SWEEP OR ROUND LENGTH (CONSISTING OF A SHIRT-WAIST WITH SURPLICE FRONTS, REMOVABLE CHEMISETTE AND FULL OR THREE-QUARTER LENGTH SLEEVES; AND A FIVE-GORED SKIRT WITH A CIRCULAR FLOUNCE FROM BENEATH WHICH THE SKIRT MAY BE CUT AWAY). Described on page 634.

means of hooks and eyes or buttons and buttonholes. The fulness at the upper edge of the five-gored skirt is gathered into a narrow belt, and a circular gathered flounce completed

9293. LADIES' WAIST CLOSED AT THE BACK (WITH FULL OR THREE-QUARTER LENGTH SLEEVES AND WITH OR WITHOUT THE BERTHA). Described on page 635.

by a hem is gathered to the lower part. The skirt may be cut away from beneath the flounce.

Lawn, dimity, organdy, foulard, crêpe de Chine, grenadine, satin-striped gauze, dotted swiss, nainsook or madras may be used to develop this design.

Ladies' costume 9280 is in six sizes, from thirty-two to forty-two inches bust measure, price 15 cents. The thirty-six-inch bust size requires, as in large view with skirt cut away beneath flounce, eight and three-quarter yards of material which is thirty-six inches wide. The width of the skirt at the lower edge is five yards.

9305—LADIES' TUCKED SHIRT-WAIST COSTUME IN SHORT SWEEP OR ROUND LENGTH. Illustrated on page 633.

This neat and stylish shirt-waist costume is made of flowered lawn and is trimmed with Valenciennes lace. A girdle of Liberty satin gives a pretty finish to the waist.

9253. LADIES' WAIST CLOSED AT THE LEFT SHOULDER AND SIDE (WITH HIGH OR DUTCH ROUND NECK AND FULL-LENGTH, SHORT THREE-QUARTER OR ELBOW SLEEVES). Described on page 635.

The waist is fitted by under-arm and shoulder seams, the back being arranged in clusters of lengthwise tucks which taper gracefully to the waistline, where the extra fulness is disposed in shirring. The surplice fronts are decorated with clusters of lengthwise tucks, also clusters of tucks extending to yoke depth only. The fulness at the waistline is disposed in shirring. The removable chemisette is tucked and finished at the upper edge by a standing collar. The one-seamed bishop sleeve is gathered into the armhole and the gathered lower edge is completed by a one-seamed deep cuff, which is omitted when the elbow sleeve is preferred. The skirt is a five-gored model with the fulness at the upper edge arranged in gathers. The circular flounce is disposed in clusters of short tucks and is attached to the lower part of the skirt; the latter may be cut away beneath it.

Foulard, pongee, crash, madras, sateen, taffeta, silk-and-linen material, linen, duck, lawn or organdy may be used to develop this costume, and lace, insertion, embroidery, ribbon, fancy braid or gimp may be used to decorate.

9279. LADIES' WAIST CLOSED AT THE BACK OR THE LEFT SHOULDER AND SIDE (TUCKED OR GATHERED TO A SCALLOPED YOKE AND WITH FULL-LENGTH OR ELBOW SLEEVES). Described on page 636.

Ladies' tucked shirt-waist costume 9305 is in seven sizes, from thirty-two to forty-four inches bust measure, price 15 cents. The thirty-six-inch bust size requires, with skirt cut away beneath flounce, eight and one-half yards of material which is thirty-six inches wide. The width at the lower edge of the skirt is five and three-eighth yards.

9267—LADIES' SHIRRED WAIST CLOSED AT THE BACK. Illustrated on page 633.

Figured lawn and Irish crochet lace are the materials selected to develop this attractive waist. It is mounted on a fitted lining, the front and backs of the material being shirred in round yoke effect. The fulness at the waistline is disposed in shirring, which is concealed beneath the girdle. The latter is in two pieces united by a center-front seam with the back edges gathered. When the high-neck style is used, the neck edge is completed by a standing collar; and when the low or Dutch round neck is preferred, the upper portions of the lining and material are cut away, as indicated. Three styles of sleeve are provided: one is a full-length model consisting of a two-seamed lining, and a one-seamed puffed outside sleeve. The lining is overlaid with material from the lower edge to the elbow, or, when the elbow sleeve is desired, the lining may be cut away and the full outside portion divided into two puffs by shirring. If the short puff sleeve be preferred, the lining and lower puff may be cut away.

Foulard, net, grenadine, China silk, crêpe de Chine, satin crêpe, lawn, dimity, dotted swiss, nainsook, batiste or organdy may be used to develop this design.

Ladies' shirred waist 9267 is in five sizes, from thirty-two to forty inches bust measure, price 15 cents. The thirty-six-inch bust size requires, as i large front view, two and seven-eighth yards of material which measures thirty-six inches wide.

9293—LADIES' WAIST CLOSED AT THE BACK.
Illustrated on page 634.

Silk-dotted batiste is the material selected to make this attractive waist, which is trimmed with lace insertion, beading and lace frilling. A girdle of rose-pink Liberty satin completes the lower edge of the garment. The

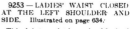

waist is mounted on a fitted lining, the full front and backs of the material being gathered at the upper edges and shirred at the waistline. The yoke portions are fitted by shoulder seams, and a fancy bertha in two pieces is provided but may be omitted. The sleeve, which may be made in full or three-quarter length, consists of a two-seamed, close-fitting lining and a one-seamed outside portion, the latter being gathered at the upper and lower edges. The lower part of the lining may be faced with material, or when the three-quarter length sleeve is preferred it may be cut away and the lower edge of the sleeve finished with a circular frill. The neck edge is completed by a standing collar. The girdle is in two pieces united by a center-front seam, the back edges being gathered as indicated.

Crêpe de Chine, mousseline de soie, chiffon, taffeta, peau de cygne, voile, satin crêpe, dotted swiss, Paris muslin, lawn or nainsook may be used to develop this design, and lace, insertion, embroidered chiffon, gimp or fancy braid may be used to trim.

Ladies' waist 9293 is in six sizes, from thirty-two to forty-two inches bust measure, price 15 cents. The thirty-six-inch bust size requires three and seven-eighth yards of material thirty-six inches in width.

9253 — LADIES' WAIST CLOSED AT THE LEFT SHOULDER AND SIDE. Illustrated on page 634.

This dainty waist is made of foulard combined with all-over lace. It is

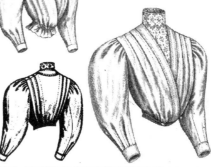

9264. LADIES' TUCKED SURPLICE SHIRT-WAIST (WITH OR WITHOUT THE BODY LINING). Described on page 636.

mounted on a fitted lining, the backs and front of the material being shirred at the lower edges. The fulness at the upper edge is disposed in clusters of shirrings and in lengthwise plaits. The yoke portions are cut with fancy lower outline and are included in the shoulder seams. A standing collar finishes the high neck, and when the Dutch round neck is preferred the upper portions of the lining and yoke are cut away as indicated in the small front view. The pattern provides three styles of sleeve, any one of which may be used. The full-length model consists of a two-seamed, close-fitting lining and a one-seamed outside portion, the latter divided into two puffs by a band of shirring. The three-quarter length style is produced by cutting away the lower part of the undersleeve and finishing the outside sleeve with a ruffle of lace. The short elbow sleeve is formed of the upper part of the lining and outside sleeve, the latter being finished at the lower edge by a band of shirring and a turn-up cuff.

A folded girdle completes the lower edge of the waist and the closing occurs down the center back.

Pongee, foulard, voile, taffeta, peau de cygne, poplin, crêpe de

9290. LADIES' TUCKED SHIRT-WAIST CLOSED AT THE BACK (WITH FULL-LENGTH OR LONG ELBOW SLEEVES AND WITH OR WITHOUT THE FANCY YOKE). Described on page 637.

9247. LADIES' TUCKED WAIST WITH VEST (EASED OR DRAWN DOWN AT THE BACK). Described on page 636.

Chine, Brussels net all-over lace, grenadine or washable materials may be used to develop this design, and lace, insertion, appliqué gimp, spangled passementerie, Oriental trimming or fancy braid may be used to decorate.

A figure view on page 628 shows a different development.

Ladies' waist 9253 is in six sizes, from thirty-two to forty-four inches bust measure, price 15 cents. The thirty-six-inch bust size requires four and seven-eighth yards of material twenty-two inches wide; three and one-eighth yards thirty-six inches, or two and three-quarter yards of material forty-four inches.

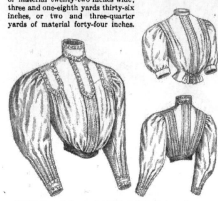

9295. LADIES' TUCKED SHIRT-WAIST CLOSED AT THE BACK (WITH FULL LENGTH OR ELBOW SLEEVES AND WITH OR WITHOUT THE STRAPS IN YOKE OUTLINE). Described on page 637.

9279—LADIES' WAIST CLOSED AT THE BACK OR THE LEFT SHOULDER AND SIDE. Illustrated on page 634.

This attractive waist is made of turquoise-blue crêpe de Chine, and is trimmed with lace insertion and silk gimp. It is mounted on a fitted lining, the outer front and backs being shirred at the lower edges. The upper part is disposed in small tucks to bust depth and attached to the scalloped yoke portions, the latter being fitted by shoulder seams. A folded girdle in two pieces united by a center-front seam conceals the shirring at the lower edges of the waist. The sleeve may be made in full length or long elbow style, and consists of a two-seamed, close-fitting lining and one-seamed outside portion. The latter is gathered at the upper edge, and the lower edge is gathered to the lining sleeve at the elbow, the lower portion of the lining being over-laid with material. When the long elbow sleeve is preferred the lining is cut away, as indicated, and the puff portion finished with a ruffle of lace or chiffon. A standing collar finishes the neck edge and the waist fastens down the center back or at the left shoulder and side.

Taffeta silk, peau de cygne, crêpe de Chine, satin crêpe, nun's-veiling, challis, organdy, lawn, dotted swiss, nainsook, dimity or madras may be used to develop this design, and lace, insertion, embroidery, ribbon, beading or gimp may be used to trim.

A figure view on page 623 shows an entirely different development of the model.

Ladies' waist 9279 is in six sizes, from thirty-two to forty-two inches bust measure, price 15 cents. The thirty-six-inch bust size requires four and three-eighth yards of material which is twenty-two inches in width.

9247—LADIES' TUCKED WAIST WITH VEST. Illustrated on page 635.

Russian-blue peau de cygne, white Brussels net, white cloth and appliqué are the materials chosen to develop this attractive waist. The fronts are decorated with loops of black velvet and small silver buttons.

The waist is mounted on a fitted lining, which is faced to form a small shallow yoke, and the vest portion is attached to the right side and fastens on the left by means of hooks and eyes. It is gathered at the upper edge and shirred at the lower one. The back and fronts are arranged in a number of narrow graduating tucks, the fulness at the waistline being disposed in shirring. The back may be eased or drawn down, whichever style is preferred. The forward edges of the fronts are finished with band facings, and a one-piece turn-down collar is attached to the upper edges of the back and fronts. A narrow band completes the neck edge, the collar being a standing model. The two-seamed sleeve is mounted on a two-seamed lining. It is gathered at the upper edge, and the lower edge is tucked on the outside of the arm and gathered on the under side. A fancy cuff completes the sleeve, and the lower edge of the body portions is finished by a folded girdle, which is in two pieces united by a center-back seam.

Taffeta silk, peau de soie, peau de cygne, pongee, crêpe de Chine, satin crêpe, lawn, dimity, organdy or madras may be used to develop this design, and lace, insertion, embroidered Persian trimming or gimp may be used to decorate.

A figure view on page 625 shows a different development of this model.

Ladies' tucked waist 9247 is in six sizes, from thirty-two to forty-two inches bust measure, price 15 cents. The thirty-six-inch bust size requires five yards of material which is twenty-two inches in width.

9264—LADIES' TUCKED SURPLICE SHIRT-WAIST. Illustrated on page 635.

This pretty shirt-waist is made of écru linen combined with all-over white embroidery. It is mounted on a body lining which may be omitted. The back of the material is arranged in clusters of wide tucks which taper slightly to the waistline, where the extra fulness is disposed in shirring. The surplice

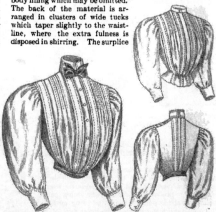

9303. LADIES' TUCKED SHIRT-WAIST (WITH COAT CLOSING AND TURN-DOWN OR STANDING COLLAR). Described on page 637.

fronts are tucked to yoke depth and confined by shirring at the waistline, a trimming band being used to finish the forward edges. The V-shaped chemisette is attached to the right front and fastens on the left side, the lining fronts closing down the center and the fronts of the material overlapping, as indicated. The sleeve is a two-seamed model, gathered into the armhole. The fulness at the lower edge is disposed in tucks and a band cuff which closes at the outside arm seam is attached. A standing collar finishes the neck edge.

Linen, crash, madras, chambray, lawn, dimity, pongee, taffeta, peau de soie, nun's-veiling or cashmere may be used to develop this design, and braid, gimp, ribbon, embroidered edging, Oriental trimming or appliqué lace may be used to trim.

A figure view on page 624 shows a different development.

Ladies' tucked surplice shirt-waist 9264 is in six sizes, from thirty-two to forty-two inches bust measure, price 15 cents. The thirty-six-inch bust size requires five and three-eighth yards of material twenty-two inches wide; three and seven-eighth yards thirty-six inches, or two and seven-eighth yards of material forty-four inches wide.

9290—LADIES' TUCKED SHIRT-WAIST CLOSED AT THE BACK. Illustrated on page 635.

This charming shirt-waist is made of light-green dotted lawn combined with all-over lace. It is fitted by under-arm and shoulder seams. The backs are arranged in five clusters of lengthwise tucks which taper to the waistline, where the extra fulness is disposed in shirring. The front is shirred at the waistline and the upper part is disposed in four clusters of tucks which are discontinued at yoke depth. The sleeve may be made in full length or elbow style, the full-length model consisting of a two-seamed, close-fitting lower part and a long one-seamed puff. The latter is gathered at the upper and lower edges, and when the elbow sleeve is preferred, the close-fitting lower portion of the sleeve is omitted. A narrow band completes the neck edge of the shirt-waist, and the collar is a back-closing standing model. A fancy yoke portion is provided, but may be omitted, and the garment fastens down the center back by means of buttons and buttonholes or hooks and eyes.

Taffeta silk, peau de cygne, mousseline de soie, net, grenadine, voile, dimity, nainsook, sateen, foulard, crêpe de Chine or novelty material may be used to develop this design, and lace, insertion, embroidery or ribbon may be used to trim.

Ladies' tucked shirt-waist 9290 is in six sizes, from thirty-two to

9248. LADIES' TUCKED SHIRT-WAIST (WITH STANDING OR "BUSTER BROWN" COLLAR). Described on page 638.

forty-two inches bust measure, price 15 cents. The thirty-six-inch bust size requires four and one-eighth yards of material which measures twenty-two inches in width.

9295—LADIES' TUCKED SHIRT-WAIST CLOSED AT THE BACK. Illustrated on page 636.

This stylish shirt-waist is made of tan pongee, and is trimmed with lace insertion. A belt of brown panne

gives a pretty finish to the lower edge of the garment. The shirt-waist is fitted by under-arm and shoulder seams. The front of the material is arranged in a cluster of lengthwise tucks through the center and in clusters of tucks extending to yoke depth on each side, the fulness at the waistline being confined by shirring. Three fancy strap portions are attached to the upper part of the front, as indicated. The backs are laid in clusters of lengthwise tucks, which taper gracefully to the waistline, where the extra fulness is disposed in shirrings. Two styles of sleeve are provided: one is a full length, two-seamed model, gathered

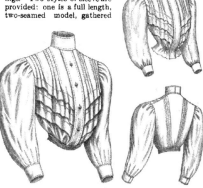

9262. LADIES' TUCKED SHIRT-WAIST (WITH SLEEVES DART-TUCKED OR GATHERED TO THE CUFFS). Described on page 638.

into the armhole and tucked from the wrist to the elbow. The lower edge is completed by a band cuff. The other is an elbow sleeve, gathered at the upper and lower edges and finished with a wide band. A narrow band completes the neck edge and the collar is a back-closing standing model. This shirt-waist fastens down the center of the back.

Pongee, China silk, poplin, peau de soie, taffeta, crash, linen, lawn, dimity or linen scrim may be used to develop this design, and lace appliqué, Oriental trimming or lace insertion may be used to decorate.

Ladies' tucked shirt-waist 9295 is in six sizes, from thirty-two to forty-two inches bust measure, price 15 cents. The thirty-six-inch bust size requires four and one-half yards of material twenty-two inches wide; two and seven-eighth yards thirty-six inches, or two and one-quarter yards of material forty-four inches in width, with, as represented, three and three-quarter yards of narrow lace insertion to trim.

9303—LADIES' TUCKED SHIRT-WAIST. Illustrated on page 636.

This attractive shirt-waist is made of pongee-colored cotton poplin with a collar of white linen, and tie and girdle of black satin. The back of the material is shirred at the waistline and arranged in lengthwise tucks in box-plait effect. The fronts are decorated with tucks extending to full length and yoke depth, and the fulness at the waistline is confined by shirring. The forward edges of the fronts are finished with hems and the neck edge is finished with a narrow band. Two styles of collar are provided: one is a back-closing standing model and the other consists of a band and turn-down collar piece. The sleeve is a one-seamed model, gathered into the armhole. The lower edge is also gathered and finished with a fancy cuff, the end of which is lapped at the back of the arm and closed with buttons and buttonholes. This shirt-waist fastens down the center of the front with buttons and buttonholes or hooks and eyes.

Pongee, taffeta, peau de soie, flannel, cashmere, lawn madras, dimity, batiste, linen, damask, cotton poplin, linen scrim, plain, embroidered or dotted swiss may be used to develop this design, and lace, insertion, embroidery, Persian trimming or ribbon may be used to decorate.

Ladies' tucked shirt-waist 9303 is in seven sizes, from thirty-two to forty-four inches bust measure, price 15 cents. The thirty-six-inch bust size requires four and one-half yards of material twenty-two inches wide; three and one-eighth yards, thirty-six inches, or two and three-eighth yards forty-four inches wide.

9248 — LADIES' TUCKED SHIRT-WAIST. Illustrated on page 637.

This pretty shirt-waist is made of Dutch-blue mercerized linen and has a collar and wristbands of white linen.

The garment is fitted by under-arm and shoulder seams, the back being arranged in lengthwise tucks which taper gracefully to the waistline, where the slight fulness is disposed in shirring. The fronts are tucked to deep yoke depth, the forward edge of the right front being tucked

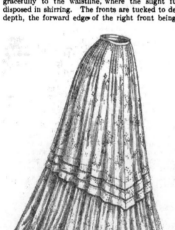

narrow band finishes the neck edge, and a standing or a "Buster Brown" collar may be used.

Linen, madras, chambray, crash, scrim, dimity, organdy, taffeta, Liberty satin, peau de soie, nun's-veiling, crêpe de Chine or albatross may be used to develop this design.

A figure view is shown on page 626.

Ladies' tucked shirt-waist 9248 is in seven sizes, from thirty-two to forty-four inches bust measure, price 15 cents. The thirty-six-inch bust size requires three and one-quarter yards of material thirty-six inches wide.

9262—LADIES' TUCKED SHIRT-WAIST. Illustrated on page 637.

This trim and stylish shirt-waist is made of self-colored linen. It is fitted by under-arm and shoulder seams. The back is arranged in two clusters of lengthwise tucks, the slight fulness at the waistline being shirred. The fronts are laid in clusters of graduated tucks to yoke depth, and in three downward-turning

9276. LADIES' SHIRT-WAIST WITH UNDER-ARM GORE (WITH PLAITS OR GATHERS AT THE NECK, TURN-DOWN OR STANDING COLLAR AND BISHOP OR SHIRT SLEEVES, AND WITH OR WITHOUT THE BACK-YOKE FACING OR BODY LINING; DESIRABLE FOR STOUT FIGURES). Described on page 639.

slanting tucks through the center, the fulness at the waistline being disposed in shirring. The forward edge of the right front is completed by a box plait. The sleeve is a one-seamed model gathered into the arm's-eye and dart-tucked or gathered to the straight cuff. The latter

Round Length

Short Sweep Length

Short Sweep Length

9263. LADIES' SKIRT IN SHORT SWEEP OR ROUND LENGTH (FORMED OF A TUCKED SIX-GORED UPPER PART LENGTHENED BY A GATHERED GRADUATED CIRCULAR FLOUNCE). Described on page 639.

opens with the sleeve on the outside of the arm. A narrow band finishes the neck edge and the collar is a back-closing standing model. The closing of the shirt-waist is effected down the center front.

Taffeta silk, peau de soie, peau de cygne, pongee, voile, linen, lawn, dimity, French cambric, madras or summer flannel may be used to develop this design, and appliqué lace, embroidery, braid, Persian trimming or insertion may be used to decorate.

to simulate a wide box plait. The fulness at the waistline is disposed in shirring. The one-seamed sleeve has the fulness on the outside of the arm disposed in two lengthwise tucks and is completed by a straight wristband. A

A figure view on page 624 shows a different development. Ladies' tucked shirt-waist 9262 is in six sizes, from thirty-two to forty-two inches bust measure, price 15 cents. The thirty-six-inch bust size requires two and seven-eighth yards of material thirty-six inches in width.

Taffeta silk, peau de soie, pongee, cotton poplin, linen, duck, piqué, lawn, nainsook or dimity may be used to develop this design.

Ladies' shirt-waist 9276 is in eight sizes, from thirty-four to forty-eight inches bust measure, price 15 cents.

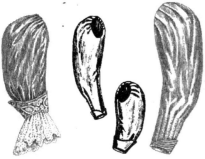

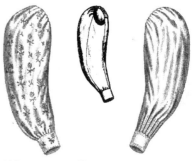

9296, LADIES' AND MISSES' ONE-SEAMED SLEEVE (PLAITED OR GATHERED AT THE TOP AND IN FULL OR ELBOW LENGTH; FOR COATS, JACKETS, ETC.). Described on page 640.

9257, LADIES' AND MISSES' TWO-SEAMED LEG-O'-MUTTON BISHOP SLEEVE (TUCKED OR GATHERED TO THE CUFF; FOR WAISTS, SHIRT-WAISTS, ETC.). Described on page 640.

9276—LADIES' SHIRT-WAIST WITH UNDER-ARM GORE. Illustrated on page 638.

This stylish shirt-waist is made of white linen, the cravat being of dark-blue silk. It is mounted on a body lining, which may be omitted, and an under-arm gore renders the garment desirable for stout figures. The outer back may be made with or without the back-yoke facing, and the slight fulness at the waistline is disposed in shirring. The fronts are shirred at the waistline and gathered at the neck edge. A box plait is used to finish the forward edge of the right front, and two styles of sleeve are provided: one is a one-seamed bishop model finished with a straight cuff, and the other is a plain shirt sleeve gathered

The thirty-eight-inch bust size requires two and three-quarter yards of material which is thirty-six inches wide.

9263—LADIES' SKIRT IN SHORT SWEEP OR ROUND LENGTH. Illustrated on page 638.

The graceful and stylish skirt depicted in this illustration is made of satin foulard and is without trimming. It has a six-gored upper part, with the fulness at the upper edge disposed in clusters of narrow tucks to yoke depth. The lower edges of the gored portion are finished with three downward-turning tucks and a gathered graduated circular flounce is attached beneath the lowest tuck as pictured.

Round Length.

Short Sweep Length

9251, LADIES' SKIRT IN SHORT SWEEP OR ROUND LENGTH (FORMED OF CIRCULAR SIDE SECTIONS SHIRRED OR GATHERED AT THE TOP, AND A CIRCULAR GATHERED FLOUNCE AND FRONT GORE IN ONE). Described on page 640.

Short Sweep Length

at the upper and lower edges and completed with a straight cuff. The neck edge of the garment is finished with a narrow band and either a back-closing standing collar or a turn-down collar.

Satin crêpe, peau de cygne, taffeta, voile, crêpe de Chine, cashmere, lansdowne, nun's-veiling, lawn, organdy, dimity, or satin foulard may be used to develop this design.

A figure view on page 624 shows a different development.

Ladies' skirt 9263 is in six sizes, from twenty to thirty inches waist measure, corresponding to thirty-seven to fifty-one inches hip measure, price 15 cents. The

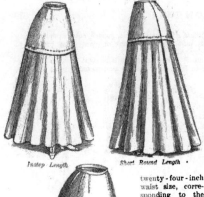

Instep Length   *Short Round Length*

Round Length

9288. LADIES' SKIRT IN ROUND, SHORT ROUND OR INSTEP LENGTH (WITH AN INVERTED BOX PLAIT AT THE BACK AND FORMED OF A DEEP YOKE PORTION WITH A TUCK AT LOWER EDGE AND LENGTHENED BY A SEVEN-GORED UMBRELLA OR RIPPLE FLOUNCE). Described on page 641.

twenty - four - inch waist size, corresponding to the forty-two-inch hip size, requires nine and five-eighth yards of material twenty-two inches wide. Width at lower edge of the skirt is five and three-eighth yards.

J&

9296—LA-DIES' AND MISSES' ONE-SEAMED SLEEVE. Illustrated on page 639.

This handsome sleeve, as shown in the elbow length, is made of peau de soie, and is trimmed with Persian embroidery and a deep frill of lace. The full-length sleeve is made of light-gray cloth having a cuff of white cloth braided with blue soutache. The elbow sleeve has the lower edge disposed in tucks and completed by a one-piece turn-up cuff. The full-length sleeve is tucked from the lower edge to just below the elbow and finished with a one-piece turned-up cuff. Either of the models may be plaited or gathered into the arm's-eye.

Ladies' and misses' one-seamed sleeve 9296 is in six sizes, from ten to fifteen inches arm measure, price 10 cents. The twelve-inch arm size requires, for full-length sleeve, two and one-eighth yards of twenty-two-inch material.

9257—LADIES' AND MISSES' TWO-SEAMED LEG-O'-MUTTON BISHOP SLEEVE. Illustrated on page 639.

The sleeve depicted in the accompanying illustration is made of figured lawn in one view and of pink chambray in the other. It is a design suitable for dress waists, shirt-waists or fancy blouses, and is a two-seamed model with the fulness at the upper edge disposed in gathers. The lower edge may be gathered or tucked, and completed by a straight cuff which opens on the outside of the arm.

Ladies' and misses' sleeve 9257 is in seven sizes, from nine to fifteen inches arm measure, price 10 cents. The twelve-inch arm size requires one and one-quarter yards of material which measures thirty-six inches in width.

J&

9251—LADIES' SKIRT IN SHORT SWEEP OR ROUND LENGTH. Illustrated on page 639.

This handsome skirt is made of ivory-white crêpe de Chine, and is trimmed with Russian lace appliqué. It is formed of circular side sections with the fulness at the upper edge disposed in gathers or shirred to yoke depth. Their lower edge is cut to form pointed tabs and a circular gathered flounce cut in one with the front gore is attached. A narrow belt completes the upper edge of the skirt, and the lower edge, which may be cut in short sweep or round length, is finished with a hem or facing.

Crêpe de Chine, lansdowne, cashmere, nun's-veiling, challis, taffeta, peau de soie, peau de cygne, organdy, lawn, dimity, foulard, sateen or Liberty satin may be used to develop this design, and appliqué lace, insertion, embroidery, ribbon, gimp, Oriental trimming or chiffon-and-silk passementerie may be used to decorate.

A figure view shown on the Front Cover Page presents the model in entirely different development.

Ladies' skirt 9251 is in five sizes, from twenty-two to thirty inches waist measure, corresponding to thirty-nine and one-half to fifty-one inches hip measure, price 15 cents. The twenty-four-inch waist size, corresponding to the forty-two-inch hip size, requires nine and seven-eighth yards of material twenty-two inches wide or six and one-half yards thirty-six inches. Width at lower edge of skirt is five and one-quarter yards.

Instep Length

Round Length   *Short Round Length*

9254. LADIES' NINE-GORED SKIRT IN ROUND, SHORT ROUND OR INSTEP LENGTH (WITH AN INVERTED BOX PLAIT OR IN HABIT STYLE AT THE BACK; SOMETIMES CALLED THE UMBRELLA OR RIPPLE SKIRT). Described on page 641.

ALL STANDARD PATTERNS NOW 5, 10 OR 15 CENTS—NONE HIGHER

9288—LADIES' SKIRT IN ROUND, SHORT ROUND OR INSTEP LENGTH. Illustrated on page 640.

This attractive skirt is made of light-blue mercerized linen, and consists of a deep circular-shaped yoke, which is fitted over the hips by dart-shaped tucks. It is finished at the lower edge by a tuck and lengthened by a seven-gored umbrella or ripple flounce.

Linen, duck, piqué, madras, pongee, foulard, serge, flannel, tweed, covert cloth or summer cheviot may be used to develop this design.

Ladies' skirt 9288 is in seven sizes, from twenty to thirty-two inches waist measure, corresponding to thirty-seven to fifty-four and one-half inches hip measure, price 15 cents. The twenty-four-inch waist size, corresponding to the forty-two-inch hip size, requires, for round length, three and five-eighth yards of fifty-four-inch material. Width at lower edge of skirt is four and one-half yards.

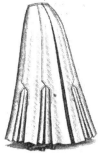

Instep Length

Short Round Length

9254—LADIES' NINE-GORED SKIRT, IN ROUND, SHORT ROUND OR INSTEP LENGTH. Illustrated on page 640.

This nine-gored stylish skirt is made of Holland-blue mercerized linen. It is sometimes called the "Umbrella" or "Ripple" skirt. The upper portion of the garment fits the figure smoothly, the back being finished in habit style or arranged in an inverted box plait. As the gores approach the lower part of the skirt they widen gradually, producing the graceful ripple effect.

Serge, cheviot, sailcloth, tweed, taffeta silk, peau de soie, linen, duck, piqué or madras may be used to develop this design, with braid, embroidery or stitching to trim.

A figure view on page 627 shows a different development.

Ladies' nine-gored skirt 9254 is in seven sizes, from twenty to thirty-two inches waist measure, corresponding to thirty-seven to fifty-four and one-half inches hip measure, price 15 cents. The twenty-four-inch waist size, corre-

sponding to the forty-two-inch hip size, requires for round length, four and one-half yards of material fifty-four inches wide. Width of skirt at lower edge is four and three-quarter yards.

9249—LADIES' FIFTEEN-GORED SKIRT IN ROUND, SHORT ROUND OR INSTEP LENGTH. Illustrated on this page.

This stylish skirt, which is sometimes known as the "Umbrella" or "Ripple" skirt, is made of black Panama cloth. The design is one that lends itself readily to a varied style of decoration, or may be developed without trimming. The skirt consists of fifteen gores, the upper portion of the garment being without fulness to deep yoke depth, thence the gores gradually widen to produce the graceful ripple effect. The back of the skirt may be finished in habit style or arranged in an inverted box plait.

Serge, etamine, taffeta silk, lady's-cloth, summer cheviot, tweed, piqué, duck, linen, gingham, chambray or foulard may be used to develop this design.

A figure view on page 627 shows a different development.

Ladies' fifteen-gored skirt 9249 is in seven sizes, from twenty to thirty-two inches waist measure, corresponding to thirty-seven to fifty-four and one-half inches hip measure, price 15 cents. The twenty-four-inch waist size, corresponding to the forty-two-inch hip size, requires for round length, four and five-eighth

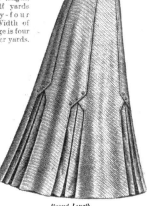

Round Length

9269, LADIES' SEVEN-GORED SKIRT, IN ROUND, SHORT ROUND OR INSTEP LENGTH (WITH PLAITED SECTIONS INSERTED AT THE LOWER PART). Described on page 642.

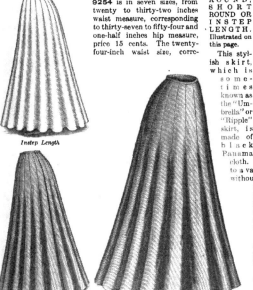

Instep Length

Short Round Length

Round Length.

9249, LADIES' FIFTEEN-GORED SKIRT IN ROUND, SHORT ROUND OR INSTEP LENGTH (WITHOUT FULNESS TO DEEP YOKE DEPTH AND WITH AN INVERTED BOX PLAIT OR IN HABIT STYLE AT THE BACK; SOMETIMES CALLED THE UMBRELLA OR RIPPLE SKIRT). Described on this page.

yards of material fifty-four inches wide. The width at the lower edge of the skirt is five and one-eighth yards.

9269—LADIES' SEVEN-GORED SKIRT IN ROUND, SHORT ROUND OR INSTEP LENGTH. Illustrated on page 641.

Light-brown etamine is used to develop this effective skirt. It is a seven-gored model, the gores being cut with shaped extensions at deep flounce depth, which are lapped as indicated, plaited sections being inserted at the lapped points.

Serge, cheviot, tweed, camel's hair, etamine, taffeta silk or peau de soie may be used to develop this design.

A figure view on page 622 shows a different development.

Ladies' seven-gored skirt 9269 is in seven sizes, from twenty to thirty-two inches waist measure, corresponding to thirty-seven to fifty-four and one-half inches hip measure, price 15 cents. The twenty-four-inch waist size, corresponding to the forty-two-inch hip size, requires for round length, five yards of material which measures forty-four inches in width. The width of the skirt at the lower edge is five and one-quarter yards.

9275—LADIES' DRESSING-SACK. Illustrated on this page.

Figured light-blue foulard is used to develop this pretty dressing-sack, which is trimmed with insertion and lace

9275. LADIES' DRESSING-SACK (WITH TWO STYLES OF COLLAR AND BELT OR BISHOP SLEEVES, AND WITH OR WITHOUT TIE-STRINGS). Described on this page.

ribbons. Two styles of sleeve are provided, and either may be used. One is a one-seamed flowing model gathered into the armhole and finished at the lower edge with a frill of lace, and the other is a one-seamed bishop sleeve gathered at the upper and lower edges and completed with a band cuff. The neck edge may be finished with a turn-down or fancy sailor collar, and ribbon tie-strings may be used. The sack fastens down the center front with buttons and buttonholes.

Foulard, China silk, cashmere, nun's-veiling, lansdowne, dimity, organdy, lawn or nainsook may be used to develop this design, and lace edging, insertion, ribbon, beading or embroidery may be used to trim.

Ladies' dressing-sack 9275 is in seven sizes, from thirty-two to forty-four inches bust measure, price 15 cents. The thirty-six-inch bust size requires four and one-half yards of material twenty-two inches wide; three yards thirty-six inches, or two and five-eighth yards of material forty-four inches wide.

9277—LADIES' SKIRT IN SHORT SWEEP OR ROUND LENGTH. Illustrated on this page.

This stylish skirt is made of pongee-colored foulard and trimmed with lace insertion. It is formed of a gored upper portion consisting of a front gore, two side gores and two back gores, the latter united by a center-back seam. The fulness at the upper edge is disposed in

Short Sweep Length

Round Length

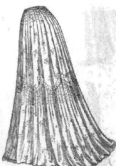

Short Sweep Length

9277. LADIES' SKIRT IN SHORT SWEEP OR ROUND LENGTH (FORMED OF A FIVE-GORED UPPER PART TUCKED OR GATHERED AT THE TOP AND SCALLOPED AT THE LOWER EDGE, AND LENGTHENED BY A TUCKED OR GATHERED CIRCULAR FLOUNCE). Described on this page.

edging. It is fitted by center-back, side-back, under-arm and shoulder seams. The fronts are tucked to yoke depth, and the fulness at the waistline may be confined by

gathers or in narrow tucks which extend to yoke depth. The lower edges of the gores are shaped in scallops, and a tucked or gathered circular flounce is attached. A narrow belt finishes the upper edge of the skirt and the lower edge may be completed with a hem or facing.

Pongee, foulard, crêpe de Chine, satin crêpe, nun's-veiling, cashmere, lansdowne, taffeta, peau de cygne, peau de soie, dimity, lawn, organdy, batiste, sateen or madras may be used to develop this design.

A figure view on page 623 shows a different development.

Ladies' skirt 9277 is in seven sizes, from twenty to thirty-two inches waist measure, corresponding to thirty-seven to fifty-four and one-half inches hip measure, price 15 cents. The twenty-four-inch waist size, corresponding to the forty-two-inch hip size, requires eight and seven-eighth yards of material twenty-two inches wide; six yards thirty-six inches, or five and three-eighth yards forty-four inches. Width of skirt at lower edge is five and one-quarter yards.

9299—LADIES' CORSET-COVER. Illustrated on this page.

This pretty corset-cover is made of sheer white nainsook, and is trimmed with beading, ribbon and lace edging. The garment may be made with a gathered or a fitted front, the latter being preferable for stout figures, as it may be boned with whalebone or featherbone if desired. The cover is fitted by under-arm, center-front and shoulder seams, also double bust darts. A circular basque piece is provided, but may be omitted. The backs of the garment are lapped, as indicated, and finished with strings or tapes which are brought around in front and tied. The arm's-eye may be finished with frills of lace or the shield sleeve, and the neck edge is completed by a frill of lace or embroidery.

Nainsook, dimity, batiste, cambric, French lawn, linen, China silk or long-cloth may be used to develop this design, and lace, insertion, beading, ribbon or embroidered edging may be used to trim the garment effectively.

Ladies' corset-cover 9299 is in seven sizes, from thirty-two to forty-four inches bust measure, price 10 cents. The thirty-six-inch bust size requires one and one-half yards of material thirty-six inches wide, with two and three-eighth yards of lace edging and two and one-quarter yards of narrow beading to trim,

9299. LADIES' CORSET-COVER (WITH FULL OR DART-FITTED FRONT AND BACKS CROSSED IN SUR-PLICE STYLE, AND WITH OR WITHOUT SHIELD SLEEVES). Described on this page.

and four yards of narrow satin ribbon to run through the beading.

9300—LADIES' SURPLICE WRAPPER. Illustrated on this page.

This attractive wrapper is made of turquoise-blue crêpe de satin, and trimmed with lace edging and insertion. The fulness of the fronts is confined by wide blue satin ribbons. The small view depicts the garment with flowing sleeves and without the fancy collar.

The wrapper is fitted by center-back, under-arm and shoulder seams, and is mounted on a fitted lining, which reaches to the hip line only. The backs of the wrapper are confined by shirring at the waistline and the loose fronts are tucked to yoke depth. Two styles of sleeve are provided: one is a one-seamed bishop model gathered at the upper and lower edges and completed by a band cuff, the other is in flowing style and finished with a trimming band or facing. The fronts of the wrapper overlap in surplice fashion, and a large fancy collar is provided. The chemisette consists of a V-shaped portion completed by a band collar.

Cashmere, nun's-veiling, challis, foulard, crêpe de Chine, China silk, lawn, dimity, chambray or cross-bar muslin may be used to develop this design, with lace, insertion, embroidery, ribbon or braid to trim. Ladies' surplice wrapper 9300 is in seven sizes, from thirty-two to forty-four inches bust measure, price 15 cents. The thirty-six-inch bust size requires twelve and three-eighth yards of material twenty-two inches wide; nine and three-eighth yards thirty-six inches, or seven and three-eighth yards forty-four inches; with five yards lace edging, one yard wide lace insertion, two and three-quarter yards narrow insertion, and three yards of ribbon for ties.

9300. LADIES' SURPLICE WRAPPER (WITH BISHOP OR BELL SLEEVES, FANCY COLLAR OR BAND FACING, AND WITH OR WITHOUT THE CHEMISETTE). Described on this page.

ALL STANDARD PATTERNS NOW 5, 10 OR 15 CENTS — NONE HIGHER

STANDARD FASHIONS FOR YOUNG PEOPLE

MISSES' JACKET COSTUME. ILLUSTRATED ON THIS PAGE.

Misses' costume 9297 is in four sizes, from fourteen to seventeen years, price 15 cents, another development of the design appearing on page 650, where it is accompanied by a detailed description, measurements for the quantity of material, etc.

As here pictured the costume is made of gray-and-blue novelty cheviot and dark-blue peau de soie, and is trimmed with silver gimp and white lace frills. The vest is made of novelty vesting, the ground of which is white and the figuring in blue and silver.

MISSES' SHIRRED COSTUME. ILLUSTRATED ON PAGE 645.

Misses' costume 9256 is in five sizes, from thirteen to seventeen years, price 15 cents, and is shown again on pages 646 and 651.

Light - blue mull and Valenciennes all-over are attractively combined for this very pretty costume in the present instance.

GIRLS' PLAITED DRESS. ILLUSTRATED ON PAGE 645.

Girls' dress 9259 is in eight sizes, from six to thirteen years, price 15 cents, and is again illustrated on page 654. It is here made of dark-red and white linen, and is trimmed with narrow red wash braid.

LITTLE GIRLS' PLAITED COAT. ILLUSTRATED ON PAGE 645.

Little girls' coat 9260 is in seven sizes, from two to eight years, price 10 cents. Another view of it is given on page 648. The present development shows the garment made of tan kersey, the collar, revers and cuffs being overlaid with Irish point.

MISSES' NORFOLK COSTUME. ILLUSTRATED ON PAGE 645.

Misses' costume 9272 is in four sizes, from fourteen to seventeen years, price 15 cents, and is shown in different development on page 650. Gray tweed is here used for the garment, with green velvet for the facings.

MISSES' JACKET COSTUME. DESCRIBED ON THIS PAGE
(Costume 9297)

GIRLS' DRESS. ILLUSTRATED ON PAGE 645.

Girls' dress 9255 is in eight sizes, from six to thirteen years, price 15 cents, and is shown again on page 653, where it is accompanied by a detailed description, measurements for the quantity of material required for the making of the garment, etc. It is here pictured as made of pale-green lawn polka-dotted with white, and is prettily trimmed with narrow white lace.

MISSES' TUCKED AND SHIRRED DRESS. ILLUSTRATED ON PAGE 646.

Misses' dress 9281 is in five sizes, from thirteen to seventeen years, price 15 cents, another view of it being presented on page 651, where it is accompanied by a detailed description, measurements for the quantity of material required, etc. The waist of the dress may be made with high or Dutch round neck, and full or three-quarter length sleeves. The skirt is five-gored.

White organdy is the material used for the pictured dress, the yoke being prettily decorated with white satin ribbon and lace appliqué and the three-quarter-length sleeves trimmed with lace frills.

GIRLS' DRESS. ILLUSTRATED ON PAGE 646.

Girls' dress 9294 is in seven sizes, from six to twelve years, price 15 cents, and is shown again on page 652. It is here made of blue-and-white louisine, the bands being of plain blue silk piped with blue velvet, and the guimpe of white organdy, which material is finely tucked for the front and the cuffs.

MISSES' SHIRRED COSTUME. ILLUSTRATED ON PAGE 646.

Misses' costume 9256 is in five sizes, from thirteen to seventeen years, price 15 cents, other views of the design appearing on pages 645 and 651. A detailed description of the garment is given on page 652, also measurements. It is here pictured in pale-pink flowered swiss, and is trimmed with lace insertion and edging.

The Designe

GIRLS' DRESS. ILLUSTRATED ON PAGE 646.

Girls' dress 9274 is in eight sizes, from five to twelve years, price 15 cents, and is again pictured on page 653, where it is accompanied by a detailed description, measurements for the quantity of material required for the making of the garment, also mention of some of the fabrics which will be found appropriate for the development of the model. The garment has a Pompadour yoke, which may be made high-necked and with standing collar

LITTLE GIRLS' DRESS AND GIRLS' APRON. DESCRIBED ON THIS PAGE
(Dress 9282)   (Apron 9265)

or with open neck. It may be made with or without sleeves or the suspender bertha, which may be in either of two styles.

Its present development shows the dress made of white albatross, the yoke being of all - over swiss embroidery. Narrow pipings of deep-red velvet form an effective contrast to the whiteness of the dress material, and bands of the swiss embroidery are used for the trimming of the pretty frock.

#

LITTLE GIRLS' DRESS. ILLUSTRATED ON THIS PAGE.

Little girls' dress 9282 is in six sizes, from two to seven years, price 10 cents, and is again pictured on page 655, where it is accompanied by a detailed description, measurements for the quantity of material required for the making of the garment, also mention of some of the fabrics and trimmings which will be found especially suitable for the reproduction of the model. The dress may be made with high or round neck and full-length, bishop or short puff sleeves, and may be made with or without the bertha.

In the present instance, the little dress is made of plain and dotted white swiss, and is trimmed with Valenciennes lace insertion and edging. A sash of white Liberty satin ribbon is worn about the waist.

#

GIRLS' APRON. ILLUSTRATED ON THIS PAGE.

Girls' apron 9265 is in five sizes, from two to ten years, price 10 cents, and is shown again on page 656.

Cross-bar cambric is used for the garment as here shown, narrow lace trimming the collar and wristbands.

#

LITTLE GIRLS' DRESS. ILLUSTRATED ON THIS PAGE.

Little girls' dress 9298 is in seven sizes, from two to eight years, price 10 cents, and is again presented on page 655, where it is accompanied by a detailed description, measurements for the quantity of material required for the making of the garment, also mention of some of the fabrics and trimmings which will be found especially appropriate for the effective reproduction of the model. The body and skirt are cut in one, and the skirt is straight at the lower edge; hence is especially suitable for development in flouncing, hemstitched or bordered materials. The garment is tucked or shirred at the waist and may have high or open neck, or be made with or without full-length or elbow sleeves.

This extremely pretty little frock as here shown is made of embroidered lawn flouncing, and the yoke and sleeves are trimmed with lace insertion.

#

CHILDREN'S COAT OR JACKET. ILLUSTRATED ON THIS PAGE.

Children's coat or jacket 9302 is in seven sizes, from one to seven years, price 10 cents, and is again pictured on page 649, where it is accompanied by a detailed description, measurements for the quantity of material required for the making of the garment, also mention of some of

LITTLE GIRLS' DRESS AND COAT OR JACKET. DESCRIBED ON THIS PAGE
(Dress 9298)   (Coat 9302)

the fabrics which will be found especially desirable for the reproduction of the model. The garment may be made in either of two lengths, and may have an open neck completed by a collar-facing or a high neck completed by a turnover collar. It may be made with or without the cape or cuffs.

The coat is here shown made of dark-blue taffeta glacé, with collar and cuff facings of white taffeta, and the fronts are closed with flat silver buttons.

9308. MISSES' TUCKED JACKET WITH VEST (WITH OR WITHOUT RE-VERS OR COLLAR-FACING). Described on this page.

9308—MISSES' TUCKED JACKET WITH VEST.
Illustrated on this page.

Russian-blue camel's-hair serge, blue velvet, white cloth and fancy braid were the materials chosen to construct this jaunty jacket, which is fitted by side-back, side-front, under-arm and shoulder seams. The backs and fronts of the material are tucked, and confined at the waistline by a half belt. The forward edges of the jacket fronts form revers and the vest portions are attached, as indicated. The revers may be

completed by a band cuff to which may be attached a one-piece turn-up cuff.

Taffeta silk, pongee, satin rhadame, peau de soie, poplin or brilliantine may be used to develop this design.

Girls' coat **9311** is in eight sizes, from five to twelve years, price 15 cents. The nine-year size requires five and five-eighth yards of twenty-two-inch material or three and one-eighth yards thirty-six inches.

9260—LITTLE GIRLS' PLAITED COAT IN FULL OR THREE-QUARTER LENGTH. Illustrated on this page.

This attractive little coat is made of light-tan covert cloth, with collar, revers and cuffs of Irish crochet lace. The coat is fitted by under-arm and shoulder seams; the fronts and back are arranged in inverted box plaits which are stitched down to yoke depth, thence they hang loose to the lower edge of the garment. The upper front portions are cut to form revers which meet the one-piece rolling collar in notches, and a circular cape portion is provided. The sleeve is a one-seamed bishop model which is gathered into the armhole. Its lower edge is also gathered and is completed by a band cuff to which a wide one-piece turn-up cuff may be attached.

Covert cloth, tweed, lady's-cloth, taffeta, peau de soie, pongee, linen or piqué may be used to develop this design, and lace appliqué, braid, embroidered silk, Oriental trimming or gimp may be used to decorate.

A figure view on page 645 shows a different development of the model.

Little girls' coat **9260** is in seven sizes, from two to eight years, price 10 cents. The five-year size requires for full-length garment, two and five-eighth yards of material which is fifty-four inches in width.

Full Length

Three-Quarter Length

9311. GIRLS' SHIRRED COAT IN FULL OR THREE-QUARTER LENGTH (WITH OR WITHOUT SHIRRINGS IN EMPIRE STYLE). Described on this page

9302—CHILDREN'S COAT OR JACKET IN EITHER OF TWO LENGTHS. Illustrated on page 649.

This stylish coat, as shown in the front view, is made of light-gray lady's-cloth and is trimmed with fancy galloon. It is fitted

omitted and the fronts of the jacket closed as shown in small front view. The neck edge may be finished with or without the flat collar-facing. The sleeve is a one-seamed model gathered or plaited into the armhole. Its lower edge is plaited and stitched to deep cuff depth, and may be completed by a turn-up cuff.

Serge, cheviot, tweed, camel's-hair, lady's-cloth, Venetian cloth, taffeta silk or velvet may be used to develop this design, and braid, gimp, galloon, appliqué lace or Persian trimming may be used to decorate.

Misses' jacket **9308** is in four sizes, from fourteen to seventeen years, price 15 cents. The fifteen-year size requires two and seven-eighth yards of material forty-four inches wide or two and three-eighth yards fifty-four inches.

9311—GIRLS' SHIRRED COAT IN FULL OR THREE-QUARTER LENGTH. Illustrated on this page.

Pongee and appliqué gimp were used to develop this stylish coat, which is fitted by under-arm and shoulder seams, and mounted on a short-waisted lining. The fulness of the back and fronts of the material is disposed in shirrings on the shoulders and at the short waistline in Empire style. A flat collar-facing in two pieces finishes the neck edge and the sleeve is a one-seamed model

Full Length

Short Three-Quarter Length

9260. LITTLE GIRLS' PLAITED COAT IN FULL OR SHORT THREE-QUARTER LENGTH (WITH OR WITHOUT THE CAPE OR CUFFS). Described on this page.

by under-arm and shoulder seams; the upper portions of the fronts may be made close to the throat and finished with a turn-down collar, or they may be cut away in a V-shaped opening and completed by a flat collar-facing. A circular cape portion is provided, but may be omitted. The sleeve is a one-seamed bishop model, gathered into a plain band, to which may be attached a turn-up cuff.

Lady's-cloth, Venetian cloth, cheviot, tweed, English flannel, velvet, pongee, taffeta, piqué or linen may be used to develop this design, and braid, appliqué lace, insertion or Oriental trimming may be used to ornament. A figure view on page 647 shows a different development. Children's coat 9302 is in seven sizes, from one to seven years, price 10 cents. Five-year size requires, as in large view, two and three-quarter yards of thirty-six-inch material or two and one-quarter yards forty-four inches.

9250—CHILDREN'S CAP. Illustrated on this page.

This dainty little cap is made of sheer white nainsook, and trimmed with embroidered edging and insertion. It is sometimes called the "Easy to Launder" bonnet, as the unfastening at the side and back portions permit the bonnet to be spread open and easily ironed. The cap consists of a plain front piece trimmed with narrow bands, and back and side portions cut in one and attached to the front piece. The lower edge of the back is laid in a scant box plait and finished with a narrow band. The sides are plaited at the lower edges and finished with bands. When the bonnet is arranged for wear, the back edges of the sides are joined by a small strap piece and buttons and buttonholes. The back portion is buttoned to the lower edges of the side portions, as indicated. Strings are attached to the forward edges.

Nainsook, dimity, lawn, linen, organdy, chambray, all-over lace, all-over embroidery or China silk may be used to develop this design, with lace insertion, embroidered edging or beading to trim.

Children's cap 9250 is in three sizes, from one to five years, price 10 cents. The five-year size requires three-quarters of a yard of material twenty-two inches wide or five-eighths of a yard thirty-six inches.

9310—GIRLS' COAT OR JACKET IN THREE-QUARTER OR REEFER LENGTH. Illustrated on this page.

This coat or jacket is made of brown camel's hair; trimmed with self-colored linen lace. It is fitted by under-arm and shoulder seams; the back of

the material is plaited, the plaits being stitched down to the waist-line, where a half belt confines the garment. The neck edge may be finished with or without the flat collar-facing, and the pattern provides pocket laps which may be attached to the fronts of the coat, and pockets may be inserted beneath them. The sleeve is a one-seamed model, gathered or plaited into the armhole

9250. CHILDREN'S CAP (SOMETIMES CALLED THE "EASY TO LAUNDER" BONNET). Described on this page.

Three-Quarter Length.   Reefer Length.

9310. GIRLS' COAT OR JACKET IN THREE-QUARTER OR REEFER LENGTH (WITH SACK FRONT AND TUCK-PLAITED BACK, PLAITED OR GATHERED SLEEVES AND WITH OR WITHOUT THE COLLAR-FACING, CUFFS OR BACK STRAP). Described on this page.

9302. CHILDREN'S COAT OR JACKET IN EITHER OF TWO LENGTHS (WITH COLLAR-FACING AND OPEN NECK, OR TURNOVER COLLAR AND CLOSED AT THE NECK, AND WITH OR WITHOUT THE CAPE). Described on page 648.

and finished with the band cuff, to which may be attached the turn-up cuff.

Serge, cheviot, tweed, camel's hair, taffeta, pongee or peau de soie may be used to develop this design, and braid, gimp, appliqué lace or Oriental trimming may be used to decorate.

Girls' coat 9310 is in nine sizes, from four to twelve years, price 10 cents. Nine-year size requires, for longer coat, four and five-eighth yards of twenty-two-inch material or two and three-eighth yards forty-four inches.

9272 — MISSES' NORFOLK COSTUME. Illustrated on page 650.

English tweed is the material used to make this stylish costume, the coat of which is fitted by center-back, side-back, under-arm and shoulder seams, also side-front seams. The center backs are cut with extensions below the waistline which are laid underneath in plaits. Applied box plaits conceal the side-back and side-front seams, and a belt

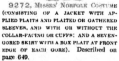

9272, MISSES' NORFOLK COSTUME (CONSISTING OF A JACKET WITH APPLIED PLAITS AND PLAITED OR GATHERED SLEEVES, AND WITH OR WITHOUT THE COLLAR-FACING OR CUFFS; AND A SEVEN-GORED SKIRT WITH A BOX PLAIT AT FRONT EDGE OF EACH GORE). Described on page 649.

slightly double-breasted fashion. The seven-gored skirt is box-plaited at the front edge of each gore, the plaits being stitched down to deep yoke depth. A narrow belt completes the upper edge of the garment and the fulness at the back is disposed in an inverted box plait.

Serge, summer cheviot, duck, piqué, linen, flannel, brilliantine or taffeta may be used to develop this design, and braid, galloon, appliqué embroidery or Persian trimming may be used to ornament. A figure view which is presented on page 645 shows a different development.

confines the garment at the waistline. The two-seamed sleeve may be plaited or gathered into the armhole, and may be finished with or without the one-piece turn-up cuff. The neck edge of the jacket may be finished with a fancy collar-facing, or may be made collarless. The garment fastens in a slightly double-breasted fashion. The seven-gored skirt is box-plaited at the front edge of each gore, the plaits being stitched down to deep yoke depth. A narrow belt completes the upper edge of the garment and the fulness at the back is disposed in an inverted box plait.

Misses' costume 9272 is in four sizes, from fourteen to seventeen years, price 15 cents. The fifteen-year size requires four and three-eighth yards of fifty-four-inch material.

9297 — MISSES' COSTUME. Illustrated on this page.

This attractive costume is made of tan Venetian cloth. The small back view shows the jacket trimmed with velvet and fancy galloon.

The jacket is fitted by under-arm and shoulder seams, also single bust darts. Vest portions are attached to the fronts, as indicated. The full-length sleeve is a one-seamed model, with the lower edge tucked, and finished with a fancy cuff. The elbow sleeve is also one-seamed and tucked at the lower edge, which is completed by a turn-up flare cuff and deep lace frill. A fancy collar-facing finishes the neck edge and the fastening of the garment is effected down the center front. The skirt is a nine-gored model with upper portion fitting the figure smoothly to deep yoke depth, and having an inverted box plait at the back. It is sometimes called the "Umbrella" or "Ripple" skirt.

Serge, cheviot, tweed, covert cloth, sailcloth, linen, pongee, taffeta silk, duck or piqué may

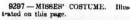

9304, MISSES' TUCKED SHIRT-WAIST CLOSED AT THE BACK (WITH FULL-LENGTH OR ELBOW SLEEVES, AND WITH OR WITHOUT THE FANCY YOKE-FACING). Described on this page.

be used to develop this design, and braid, appliqué lace, insertion, ribbon, gimp or embroidery may be used to trim. A figure view on page 644 shows a different development.

Misses' costume 9297 is in four sizes, from fourteen to seventeen years, price 15 cents. The fifteen-year size requires three and three-quarter yards of fifty-four-inch material.

9304 — MISSES' TUCKED SHIRT-WAIST CLOSED AT THE BACK. Illustrated on this page.

This shirt-waist is made of white lawn, and is trimmed with lace insertion. It is fitted by under-arm and shoulder seams. The backs are laid in clusters of lengthwise tucks and shirred at the waistline. The front is ornamented by clusters of tucks to yoke depth, and is shirred at the waistline. A fancy yoke-facing is provided, and the neck edge may be finished with or without the standing collar. The sleeve, which may be made in full or elbow length, consists of a one-seamed puff lengthened by a deep, one-seam cuff, which is omitted when the elbow sleeve

9297, MISSES' COSTUME (CONSISTING OF AN ETON JACKET WITH VEST AND FULL-LENGTH OR ELBOW SLEEVES, AND WITH OR WITHOUT THE FANCY COLLAR-FACING; AND A NINE-GORED SKIRT WITHOUT FULNESS TO DEEP YOKE DEPTH, AND WITH AN INVERTED BOX PLAIT AT THE BACK; SOMETIMES CALLED THE UMBRELLA OR RIPPLE SKIRT). Described on this page.

is preferred, the elbow sleeve being finished with a deep frill. The closing of the garment is effected down the center back.

Challis, nun's-veiling, taffeta, peau de cygne, crêpe de Chine, lawn, dimity, organdy, pongee or dotted swiss may be used to develop this design, and lace, insertion, embroidery, ribbon, beading or fancy braid may be used to trim.

Misses' shirt-waist 9304 is in five sizes, from thirteen to seventeen years, price 15 cents. The fifteen-year size requires two and three-eighth yards of thirty-six-inch material or two and one-quarter yards forty-four inches.

9268—GIRLS' AND MISSES' TUCKED GUIMPE OR BLOUSE. Illustrated on this page.

Dotted muslin is used to develop this pretty blouse, which is trimmed with lace insertion. It is fitted by under-arm and shoulder seams; the backs and front may be arranged in clusters of tucks to yoke or waistline depth, and the fulness at the waistline is disposed in shirrings for the blouse, or with a casing and drawing-string for the guimpe. A narrow band collar finishes the neck edge.

9281, MISSES' TUCKED AND SHIRRED DRESS (CONSISTING OF A WAIST WITH HIGH OR DUTCH ROUND NECK AND FULL OR THREE-QUARTER LENGTH SLEEVES; AND A FIVE-GORED SKIRT GATHERED AT THE TOP AND WITH OR WITHOUT THE SHIRRINGS). Described on this page.

The sleeve is a one-seamed bishop model finished with a band cuff. The garment fastens down the center back.

Muslin, lawn, organdy, China silk, dotted swiss, cambric or all-over embroidery may be used to develop this garment, and lace, insertion, beading or embroidery may be used to trim.

Girls' and misses' guimpe or blouse 9268 is in six sizes, from four to fourteen years, price 10 cents. The eight-year size requires one and five-eighth yards of material measuring thirty-six inches in width.

9281—MISSES' TUCKED AND SHIRRED DRESS. Illustrated on this page.

This pretty dress is made of figured lawn, and is trimmed with lace and insertion. The waist is mounted on a fitted lining, overlaid to yoke depth back and front. To the lower edge of the yoke the full backs and front are shirred, and the fulness through the center

disposed in three downward-turning tucks. The high neck is finished with a standing collar, or the neck edge may be cut in Dutch round style. Two styles of sleeve are provided: one is a full-length model consisting of a two-seamed lining and one-seamed tucked outside portion. The latter is gathered at the lower edge and attached to the under-sleeve at cuff depth. When the three-quarter sleeve is preferred, the lower portion of the lining is cut away and the outside sleeve finished with a circular frill. A gathered girdle completes the lower edge of the garment. The skirt is a five-gored model, with or without shirring at yoke depth. Its lower part is decorated with three downward-turning tucks and is finished with a hem.

Foulard, China silk, crêpe de Chine, cashmere, nun's-veiling, taffeta, net, mull, dimity, lawn, madras, organdy or dotted swiss may be used to develop this design, with lace, insertion or embroidery to trim.

9268, GIRLS' AND MISSES' TUCKED GUIMPE OR BLOUSE. Described on this page.

9256, MISSES' SHIRRED COSTUME (CONSISTING OF A WAIST WITH HIGH OR LOW OR DUTCH ROUND NECK AND FULL-LENGTH OR ELBOW SLEEVES, AND WITH OR WITHOUT THE BERTHA FRILLS; AND A SKIRT FORMED OF A GATHERED ONE-PIECE UPPER PART, WITH OR WITHOUT THE SHIRRINGS, AND LENGTHENED BY A SHIRRED CIRCULAR FLOUNCE). Described on page 652.

ALL STANDARD PATTERNS NOW 5, 10 OR 15 CENTS—NONE HIGHER

9270, GIRLS' COSTUME (CONSISTING OF AN ETON JACKET WITH ROUND OR SAILOR COLLAR AND BISHOP OR LEG-O'-MUTTON SLEEVES, TO BE WORN OVER A BLOUSE OR A SHIRT-WAIST, ETC., AND A FIVE-GORED KILT-PLAITED SKIRT). Described on this page.

9294, GIRLS' TUCKED DRESS (WITH GUIMPE). Described on page 653.

A figure view on page 646 shows a different development. Misses' dress 9281 is in five sizes, from thirteen to seventeen years, price 15 cents. The fifteen-year size requires seven and seven-eighth yards of thirty-six-inch material.

9256—MISSES' SHIRRED COSTUME. Illustrated on page 651.

This attractive costume is made of white dotted swiss combined with all-over lace and is trimmed with lace edging. The girdle is of rose-pink Liberty satin.

The waist of the costume is mounted on a fitted lining faced to yoke depth back and front for the high-neck style, or cut away to the correct outline when the low or Dutch round neck is desired. The full front and backs of the material are gathered at the upper edge and the fulness at the waistline is confined by shirring, which is concealed by a crush girdle gathered at the back edges. The sleeve, which may be made in full or elbow length, consists of a two-seamed, close-fitting undersleeve and a one-seamed full outside portion gathered at the upper edge. The lower edge is gathered to the undersleeve just below the elbow, the undersleeve being faced. When the elbow style is preferred the undersleeve may be cut

away and the puff portion finished with a circular, gathered frill. Graceful bertha frills may outline the upper edge of the front and backs, and a standing collar is provided for the high neck. The waist fastens down the center back with buttons and buttonholes or hooks and eyes. The skirt is formed of a gathered, one-piece upper part, which may be made with or without the shirrings, lengthened by a shirred circular flounce.

Dimity, foulard, China silk, batiste, nainsook, dotted swiss, organdy, lawn, chambray, mercerized madras or nun's-veiling may be used to develop this design, with lace, insertion, embroidery, ribbon or gimp to trim.

Figure views on pages 645 and 646 show different developments.

Misses' shirred costume 9256 is in five sizes, from thirteen to seventeen years, price 15 cents. The fifteen-year size requires seven and three-quarter yards of material which is thirty-six inches wide.

9270—GIRLS' COSTUME. Illustrated on this page.

This trim little costume is made of brown linen and is trimmed with écru linen lace and pearl buttons. The jacket is fitted by under-arm and shoulder seams. Two styles of sleeve are provided: one is a two-seamed leg-o'-mutton model, and the other is a one-seamed bishop model gathered at the upper and lower edges and completed by a band cuff. A round or sailor collar may be used to finish the neck edge, and the jacket fronts are closed by means of hooks and eyes. The five-gored skirt is kilt-plaited into a narrow belt and finished at the lower edge

9292, MISSES' COSTUME (CONSISTING OF A BLOUSE, TUCKED IN BOX-PLAIT EFFECT, TO BE SLIPPED OVER THE HEAD OR CLOSED IN FRONT WITH REMOVABLE SHIELD, AND WITH OR WITHOUT THE STAR SAILOR OR THE ROLLING COLLAR; AND A FIVE-GORED BOX-PLAITED SKIRT WITH THE PLAITS STITCHED TO ANY DESIRED YOKE DEPTH). Described on page 653.

ALL STANDARD PATTERNS NOW 5, 10 OR 15 CENTS—NONE HIGHER

Girls' costume **9270** is in eight sizes, from six to thirteen years, price 15 cents. The nine-year size requires five and one-eighth yards of material which measures thirty-six inches in width.

§

9294—GIRLS' TUCKED DRESS. Illustrated on page 652.

This pretty dress is made of buff chambray, and trimmed with embroidery. The guimpe is of white lawn and fancy tucking. The waist of the dress is mounted on a fitted lining, the outer fronts and backs being tucked to a short distance from the upper edge and are shirred at the waistline. A trimming band completes the forward and neck edge of the fronts and the neck edge of backs. The short, open sleeve is trimmed with a plain band and closing straps may decorate the fronts. The full straight skirt is gathered to the lower edge of the body portions, and is ornamented with three tucks. The guimpe is fitted by under-arm and shoulder seams, and the neck edge is finished with a standing collar. The one-seamed bishop sleeve is gathered into a band cuff and a casing with draw-strings is attached to the underside of the guimpe at the waistline. A figure view giving a different development is shown on page 641.

Girls' dress **9294** is in seven sizes, six to twelve years, price 15 cents. Nine-year size requires, for dress, three and three-eighth yards of thirty-six-inch material, with seven-eighth yard thirty-six-inch lawn and seven-eighth yard eighteen-inch yoking for guimpe.

§

9292—MISSES' COSTUME. Illustrated on page 652.

Gray mercerized linen, white linen and all-over embroidery are used to make this cos-

9274, GIRLS' DRESS (WITH POMPADOUR YOKE IN HIGH NECK OR WITH OPEN NECK, AND WITH OR WITHOUT THE SLEEVES OR THE SUSPENDER BERTHA IN EITHER OF TWO STYLES). Described on page 654

9255, GIRLS' DRESS (WITH HIGH OR ROUND NECK, BISHOP OR PUFF SLEEVES, AND AN ATTACHED SKIRT FORMED OF A STRAIGHT UPPER PART LENGTHENED BY A STRAIGHT FLOUNCE, AND WITH OR WITHOUT THE BERTHA). Described on page 654.

tume. The blouse is fitted by under-arm and shoulder seams, the back and fronts being tucked in box-plaited effect and shirred at the waistline. The neck edge of the blouse may be finished with or without the star sailor or rolling collar, and a removable shield finished at the upper edge with a standing collar is provided. The one-seamed sleeve is completed by a deep cuff. The skirt is a box-plaited, five-gored model.

Misses' costume **9292** is in five sizes, from thirteen to seventeen years, price 15 cents. Fifteen-year size requires eight and five-eighth yards of material twenty-seven inches wide or six yards forty-four inches.

§

9309—MISSES' TUCKED SHIRT-WAIST COSTUME. Illustrated on this page.

Light-green madras is used to make this costume, the collar and cuffs being of white linen. The waist is fitted by under-arm and shoulder seams; the back and fronts are tucked and the fulness in the waistline is disposed in shirring. The one-seamed sleeve is tucked at the lower part and finished with a plain cuff.

9309, MISSES' TUCKED SHIRT-WAIST COSTUME (CONSISTING OF A SHIRT-WAIST WITH TWO STYLES OF COLLAR, AND THE SLEEVES TUCKED OR GATHERED TO THE CUFFS; AND A SEVEN-GORED SKIRT WITH AN INVERTED BOX PLAIT AT THE BACK). Described on this page.

9258. MISSES' SEVEN-GORED SKIRT (WITHOUT FULNESS TO DEEP YOKE DEPTH AND WITH AN INVERTED BOX PLAIT OR IN HABIT STYLE AT THE BACK; SOMETIMES CALLED THE UMBRELLA OR RIPPLE SKIRT). Described on this page.

9307. GIRLS' DRESS (CONSISTING OF A BLOUSE WAIST WITH FANCY SAILOR COLLAR; AND A FIVE-PIECE UMBRELLA OR RIPPLE SKIRT ATTACHED TO AN UNDERWAIST WITH SHIELD FACING). Described on this page.

The neck edge is finished with a band, and a standing or turn-down collar. The seven-gored skirt has an inverted box plait at the back, and is disposed in tucks, which may be stitched down to deep yoke depth.

Misses' costume 9309 is in five sizes, from thirteen to seventeen years, price 15 cents. The fifteen-year size requires six and five-eighth yards of material which is thirty-six inches wide.

9274—GIRLS' DRESS. Illustrated on page 653.

Blue-and-white dotted lawn is used for this dress. It is trimmed with lace and insertion and the waist is mounted on a lining fitted by under-arm and shoulder seams, also single bust darts and faced to yoke depth back and front. The outer backs and front are shirred at the upper and lower edges and the high neck is finished with a standing collar, or when the Pompadour neck is preferred the lining is cut away as indicated. The sleeve, which may be omitted, is a one-seamed bishop model completed with a band cuff, and suspender and bretelle portions are provided. The full, straight skirt is gathered to the lower edge of the body portions.

A figure view on page 646 shows a different development. Girls' dress 9274 is in eight sizes, from five to twelve years, price 15 cents. The nine-year size requires three and one-half yards of material thirty-six inches in width.

9255—GIRLS' DRESS. Illustrated on page 653.

This dainty little dress is made of flowered organdy and trimmed with lace. The waist is mounted on a fitted lining, faced to yoke depth back and front. When the round-neck style is preferred, the upper portion of the foundation is cut away. The full front and backs of the material are gathered at the upper edges and shirred at the waistline, and a bertha in fancy outline may be attached. Two styles of sleeve are provided: one is a full-length bishop model completed by a band cuff, and the other is a short puff sleeve finished with a narrow band. The skirt consists of a straight upper portion lengthened by a straight flounce which is shirred at the upper edge.

Lawn, organdy, challis, dimity, China silk, madras, chambray or dotted swiss may be used to develop this design, with lace, insertion, embroidery or ribbon to trim.

A figure view on page 645 shows a different development.

Girls' dress 9255 is in eight sizes, from six to thirteen years, price 15 cents. Nine-year size requires six yards of twenty-two inch material or three and three-quarter yards of thirty-six-inch.

9258—MISSES' SEVEN-GORED SKIRT. Illustrated on this page.

Brown tweed is the material selected to make this seven-gored skirt, and the upper part fits the figure smoothly to deep yoke depth, thence the gores widen gradually in graceful ripple effect. The back may be finished in habit style or with an inverted box plait.

Misses' skirt 9258 is in five sizes, from thirteen to seventeen years, price 15 cents. The fifteen-year size requires three yards of material fifty-four inches wide.

9307—GIRLS' DRESS. Illustrated on this page.

This jaunty little dress is made of white duck combined with navy-blue linen. The blouse waist is fitted by under-arm and shoulder seams and is finished with a casing and draw-strings. The one-seamed sleeve is completed by a band cuff and a sailor collar is attached to the neck edge of the blouse. The skirt is a five-piece

9259. GIRLS' PLAITED DRESS (WITH HIGH OR POINTED NECK AND FULL LENGTH, LONG ELBOW OR SHORT PUFF SLEEVES, AND WITH OR WITHOUT THE BERTHA). Described on page 655.

umbrella or ripple model attached to the lower edge of an underwaist, which is fitted by under-arm and shoulder seams, also single bust darts, and is faced to simulate a shield. A standing collar completes its upper edge, and the fastening is effected down the center back.

Girls' dress 9307 is in eight sizes, from five to twelve years, price 15 cents. Nine-year size requires four yards of thirty-six-inch material or three yards forty-four.

9259—GIRLS' PLAITED DRESS. Illustrated on page 654.

This pretty dress is made of Russian-blue cashmere combined with silk of a lighter shade and is trimmed with gimp. The waist is mounted on a fitted lining faced to yoke depth back and front when the high-neck style is desired, or, when the pointed neck is preferred, the upper portions of the foundation are cut away. The outer front and backs are plaited, and the fulness at the lower edge is confined by shirring. A bertha in fancy outline is supplied, and the one-seamed sleeve, which is provided with a two-seamed lining, may be made in full length, elbow length or short puff style. The plaited skirt is attached to the lower edge of the body portions.

A figure view on page 645 shows a different development.

Girls' dress 9259 is in eight sizes, six to thirteen years, price 15 cents. Nine-year size requires four and three-quarter yards of thirty-six-inch goods or four and one-eighth yards forty-four inches.

9298—LITTLE GIRLS' DRESS. Illustrated on this page.

All-over lace, figured lawn and lace edging are the materials selected to make this dainty dress. The waist is mounted on a fitted lining, which may be overlaid to yoke depth back and front when the high-neck style is preferred, and cut away when the open-neck is used. The full backs and front of the material are cut in one with the skirt and are gathered at the upper edges, the fulness at the waistline being disposed in shirrings or tucks. The sleeve may be made in full or elbow length, and consists of a two-seamed lining and a one-seamed puff; the latter is gathered at the upper and lower edges and attached to the lining about an inch below the elbow.

9298, LITTLE GIRLS' DRESS (WITH BODY AND SKIRT IN ONE, STRAIGHT AT LOWER EDGE, TUCKED OR SHIRRED AT THE WAIST, AND WITH HIGH OR OPEN NECK, AND WITH OR WITHOUT FULL-LENGTH OR ELBOW SLEEVES; DESIRABLE FOR FLOUNCING, HEMSTITCHING, ETC.). Described on this page.

When the elbow sleeve is preferred, the lower part of the lining is cut away. Bretelle shoulder frills are provided.

9284, LITTLE GIRLS' DRESS (WITH OR WITHOUT THE GUIMPE OR BERTHA). Described on this page.

9282, LITTLE GIRLS' DRESS (WITH HIGH OR ROUND NECK AND FULL-LENGTH BISHOP OR SHORT PUFF SLEEVES, AND WITH OR WITHOUT THE BERTHA). Described on this page.

A figure view on page 647 shows a different development.

Little girls' dress 9298 is in seven sizes, from two to eight years, price 10 cents. The five-year size requires three and one-half yards of thirty-six inch material.

9284—LITTLE GIRLS' DRESS. Illustrated on this page.

This attractive little dress is made of flowered lawn, trimmed with lace edging. The guimpe is of white nainsook with yoke of all-over embroidery and trimming of insertion.

The waist of the dress is mounted on a fitted lining, and the full front and backs of the material are gathered at the upper edges and shirred at the lower ones. A bertha is provided and the sleeve is a one-seamed puff completed with a band. The full, straight skirt is gathered to the lower edge of the back-closing waist. The guimpe is fitted by under-arm and shoulder seams, and may be faced to yoke depth. The neck is finished with a standing collar, and the one-seamed bishop sleeve is completed by a band cuff. A casing with draw-strings is attached to the underside of the garment at the waistline.

Little girls' dress 9284 is in seven sizes, from two to eight years, price 10 cents. The five-year size requires for the dress, three yards of thirty-six-inch material; for the guimpe, one-half yard eighteen-inch embroidery with one-half yard of thirty-six-inch lawn is required.

9282—LITTLE GIRLS' DRESS. Illustrated on this page.

This charming little dress is made of pink-and-white dotted lawn, and is trimmed with insertion and lace

9306, CHILDREN'S SQUARE-YOKE DRESS (WITH OR WITHOUT THE BERTHA COLLAR). Described on this page.

edging. The long waist is mounted on a fitted lining, which may be overlaid to yoke depth back and front or may be cut away in round-neck outline. The full front and backs are gathered at the upper edges and shirred at the

9265, GIRLS' APRON (WITH BACK FRONT AND YOKE BACK AND HIGH OR ROUND NECK, AND WITH OR WITHOUT THE SLEEVES). Described on this page.

lower ones, and a fancy bertha may be attached to them. Two styles of sleeve are provided: one is a short puff gathered into the armhole and finished with a band, and the other is a full-length bishop sleeve gathered at the upper and lower edges and completed by a band cuff. A standing collar finishes the high neck. The full, straight skirt is gathered to the lower edge of the back-closing body portions. A figure view is shown on page 647.

Little girls' dress 9282 is in six sizes, from two to seven years, price 10 cents. The five-year size requires two and five-eighth yards of material thirty-six inches wide.

9306 — CHILDREN'S SQUARE-YOKE DRESS. Illustrated on this page.

This dainty little dress is made of sheer white lawn and trimmed

with lace edging and insertion. The skirt portions are fitted by under-arm seams and gathered to the lower edge of the yoke, which is fitted by shoulder seams. The sleeve is a one-seamed model completed by a band cuff. A fancy bertha is provided, also a standing collar, and the dress fastens down the center back.

Children's dress 9306 is in six sizes, from six months to five years, price 10 cents. The five-year size requires two and five-eighth yards of thirty-six-inch material.

9265 — GIRLS' APRON. Illustrated on this page.

The garment here pictured is fitted by under-arm and shoulder seams. The upper edge of the back is gathered to a straight yoke. When the high-neck style is desired, the neck edge of the apron is finished with a two-piece turn-down collar, and when the round neck is preferred, the upper portions of the garment are cut away to the correct outline and the upper edge completed by a bertha frill. The sleeve is a one-seamed bishop model gathered into a band, or the apron may be made without sleeves.

A figure view on page 647 shows a different development.

Girls' apron 9265 is in five sizes, from two to ten years, price 10 cents. The six-year size requires, as in large front view, three and one-half yards of material twenty-seven inches wide or three and one-eighth yards of material thirty-six inches in width.

9252, LITTLE GIRLS' APRON (WITH STRAIGHT LOWER EDGE AND AN INVERTED BOX PLAIT UNDER EACH ARM). Described on this page.

9301 — INFANTS' DRESS. Illustrated on this page.

This dainty little dress is fitted by under-arm and shoulder seams and is tucked to yoke depth. The one-seamed sleeve is gathered into the narrow wristband, and the neck edge is completed by a band.

Infants' dress 9301 is in one size, price 10 cents, and for it is required two and one-half yards of material thirty-six inches wide.

9252 — LITTLE GIRLS' APRON. Illustrated on this page.

The straight skirt of this pretty apron is gathered at the upper back and front edges and laid in an inverted box plait under each arm. Yoke bands finish the upper

9301, INFANTS' DRESS (WITH CLUSTER TUCKS TO YOKE DEPTH). Described on this page.

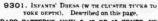
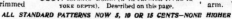

ALL STANDARD PATTERNS NOW 5, 10 OR 15 CENTS—NONE HIGHER

edge of the garment and the shoulder straps and bretelle ruffles may complete the arm's-eye.

Little girls' apron 9252 is in four sizes, from two to eight years, price 10 cents. The four-year size requires one and five-eighth yards of material which measures thirty-six-inches in width.

9291—LITTLE BOYS' TUCKED DRESS. Illustrated on this page.

This stylish little dress is made of white linen. It is fitted by under-arm and shoulder seams, with body and skirt in one; the back and fronts of the garment are tucked to the waistline, where they are confined by the belt. A removable shield finished at the upper edge by a band collar and closing at the back is provided, and the one-seamed sleeve is tucked to cuff depth.

Little boys' dress 9291 is in five sizes, from one to five years, price 10 cents. The five-year size requires two and one-half yards of material thirty-six inches wide.

9289—LITTLE BOYS' SUIT. Illustrated on this page.

White flannel and blue braid were used to construct this jaunty little suit, which consists of a blouse fitted by under-arm and shoulder seams, with either bishop or sailor sleeves and a sailor collar in either of two styles. The belt confines the garment at the waistline and the upper portions of the fronts are cut away in a V-shaped opening which discloses the shield; the latter is finished at the upper edge by a band collar. The knickerbockers are fitted by center front and back seams and inside leg seams; they are made without a fly, and the lower edge of the legs may be finished with casings and elastics.

Little boys' suit 9289 is in seven sizes, from two to eight years, price 15 cents. The four-year size requires two and one-eighth yards of forty-four-inch material.

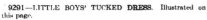

9291. LITTLE BOYS' TUCKED DRESS (WITH BODY AND SKIRT IN ONE AND WITH REMOVABLE SHIELD). Described on this page.

9286—BOYS' SHIRT-BLOUSE. Illustrated on this page.

This neat blouse as shown in the large front view is made of blue-and-white striped madras. In the other views it is made of gray flannel. It is fitted by under-arm and shoulder seams; the one-seamed sleeve is finished with a straight cuff which opens on the outside of the arm. The neck edge may be finished with an attached or detachable turnover or round collar or neckband for Eton or other linen collar. A back yoke-facing may be used and a patch pocket is attached to the left front of the blouse. The lower edge of the blouse is finished with a casing and draw-string, and the fastening of the garment is effected down the center front by means of buttons and buttonholes.

Percale, madras, gingham, linen, crash, pongee, serge, outing cloth or flannel may be used to appropriately develop this design.

Boys' shirt-blouse 9286 is in eleven sizes, from four to fourteen years, price 10 cents. The eight-year size requires two and one-eighth yards of material twenty-seven inches wide; one and three-quarter yards thirty-six inches, or one and three-eighth yards forty-four inches.

9286. BOYS' SHIRT-BLOUSE (WITH ATTACHED OR DETACHABLE TURNOVER OR ROUND COLLAR OR NECKBAND FOR ETON OR OTHER LINEN COLLAR AND WITH OR WITHOUT THE BACK YOKE-FACING). Described on this page.

9285. BOYS' SAILOR BLOUSE (WITH COLLAR IN EITHER OF TWO OUTLINES, SHIELD, AND SAILOR OR BOX-PLAITED SLEEVES). Described on this page.

9285—BOYS SAILOR BLOUSE. Illustrated on this page.

This stylish blouse as shown in two views is made of white linen and trimmed with dark-blue braid. One large front view shows it made of blue flannel. It is fitted by under-arm and shoulder seams, the upper portions of the fronts are cut away in a V-shaped opening, and the pattern provides a shield finished at the upper edge with a narrow band. The sailor collar may be finished in either of two outlines and is attached to the upper edges of the blouse. Two styles of sleeve are provided: one is a box-plaited model finished with a band cuff and the other is a sailor sleeve tuck-plaited to cuff depth. The lower edge of the blouse is finished with a casing and draw-string.

Flannel, brilliantine, linen, percale, madras or crash may be used to develop this design, and braid or ribbon may be used to trim.

Boys' sailor blouse 9285 is in ten sizes, from three to twelve years, price 10 cents. The eight-year size requires two and five-eighth yards of thirty-six-inch material.

9289. LITTLE BOYS' SUIT (CONSISTING OF A BLOUSE WITH SHIELD, EITHER OF TWO STYLES OF SAILOR COLLAR; SAILOR OR BISHOP SLEEVES; AND KNICKERBOCKERS WITHOUT A FLY). Described on this page.

ALL STANDARD PATTERNS NOW 5, 10 OR 15 CENTS—NONE HIGHER

POINTS ON DRESSMAKING

ONE-PIECE DRESSES FOR GIRLS AND BOYS

IT IS quite a usual thing for a garment, a hat or even some certain style of dressing the hair to be given the name of a character in popular fiction, but it seldom happens that a garment so named meets with the universal favor and retains its popularity so generally as have the little one-piece dresses named after Buster Brown, whose pranks, as depicted in one of the New York papers, have amused the grown folks and plunged many of the little ones into difficulties through trying to emulate him. These little dresses are on the Russian-blouse order, in that they hang from the shoulder, with waist and skirt in one. Their construction is not difficult, being, in fact, very much like that of a shirt-waist. Whether the suit be for a boy or girl, bloused knickerbockers are often worn underneath in lieu of petticoats; the construction of these is the same whether they are made of cloth or linen, and was fully described in THE DESIGNER for October, 1904. The two models illustrated are suitable for a little girl or a boy who has not yet been graduated into knickers.

Pattern 9171 is a box-plaited model closing in the front. In illustration I. is seen one side of the front with the plaits prepared. When the garment is being cut all the perforations must be plainly marked. When the material is linen, gingham, piqué or other goods of like character that will hold pin-marks, the perforations may be marked by running a carpet-needle through the material at each perforation before removing the pattern; but if woolen goods is used it will be necessary to mark each perforation with chalk, then trace through with tailor's tacks, as has been previously described in THE DESIGNER. The front edge is to be turned under at the large perforations to form a hem, but this hem is not stitched separately; it has its edge caught in the stitching of the first plait or tuck, as can be seen in the illustration. The perforations indicating the sewing-line of the box plait are brought together and stitched to form a wide plait, which is then shaped into a box plait by bringing its center line over the row of stitching and flattening it. It should be pressed, and may be stitched at each side three-eighths of an inch from the fold edge, the stitching answering the double purpose of being ornamental and of holding the box plait in shape. A crow toe may be worked at the

I.—HEM, TUCK AND PLAIT IN FRONT

II.— STITCHING ON BOX PLAIT FINISHED WITH CROW TOE

III.—FIRST STAGE OF MAKING CROW TOES

IV.—SECOND STAGE OF MAKING CROW TOES

end of each row of stitching, as seen in illustration II. The method of working was described in THE DESIGNER for February, or can be plainly understood by referring to illustrations III. and IV. The back is cut with the straight edge (which has a double perforation) on a fold of the material, and if this is single-width goods it is probable that it may be necessary to piece it at each side, concealing the seam under the box plait, as described last month in the instruction for cutting the fronts of shirt-waists. Bring the lines of perforations together and stitch the box plaits as for the fronts, then lap the line that marks the single row of perforations between the box plait and the center of the back till its edge is even with the center back and baste it there, but do not stitch it in a tuck as the front was stitched. Measure the width of the front tuck and at the same space from the center back make a row of stitching flat through the folded plait and the back portion underneath it. This will make the back correspond with the front, but the plaits at the center, being lapped much deeper than the front tucks, will give the necessary fulness in the skirt part below the stitching. The edges of the box plaits should be stitched to correspond with the front. The back with one side in state of preparation is shown in illustration V.

The sleeve may be finished by gathering into a wristband, but it will be more in keeping with the rest of the dress if the three little box plaits are laid in the wrist portion. Illustration VI. shows how to prepare them. Mark the large perforations with a continuous line and baste the fold edges indicated by the line of small perforations. Bring the fold edges at each side of each line of thread over even with it and baste the plait so formed; stitch through both plait and sleeve. After the plaits are stitched, stitch the seam of the sleeve and underface the wrist. Lay the box plait in the top of the sleeve by bringing each of the two center perforation-marks to the one just outside it. Gather the sleeve from each edge of the box plait to the notches but do not gather across the box plait.

Pattern 9205 closes in the back, and the front is finished at the top with a yoke. Illustration VII. shows the simplest way of attaching the yoke to the lower part. Cut the front, marking all the perforations carefully, and join the pieces necessary to complete the width where they may best be

V.—PLAITS LAID IN BACK

concealed. Form the plaits, stitch them and press them open, and stitch their fold edges if they are to have that finish. Cut the yoke and turn the lower edge under a seam, slashing the edge, where necessary, to make it lie flat. Baste the yoke to the top of the plaited portion and to the wrong side baste a piece of tape, seam-binding or a bias strip of the material with its edges turned under. Place two rows of stitching across the yoke, stitching from the outside. These will catch through the tape that is basted underneath and which covers the raw edges of the seam, making a neat finish on the inside.

The back is cut in two breadths with a hem at the straight edge of each. It is probable the back widths may not need piecing, but if they should require only a small corner it may be joined where

VI.—BOX-PLAITING SLEEVE AT WRIST

needed instead of cutting back to the sewing-line of a plait, but if the joining-line would run up the entire side it will be better to make the seam where it may be concealed. This seam may be bound below the plait with a bias strip of lining material. The way of arranging the hems and finishing the back is shown in illustration VIII. Small perforations in the pattern indicate where the left side of the back is to be trimmed away below the hemmed closing, but it is better not to cut this part off until after the seam has been sewed, though the perforations should be plainly marked on the breadth. After the box plaits have been stitched, turn under the extensions at the upper part of the back edges an inch and one-half, as directed, for hems, and crease or baste the fold edge, but before stitching the hems bring the edge of the right side (below the hems) on a line with the small single perforations in the left side and make a seam three-eighths of an inch back from the edge. The material of the left side beyond the seam may then be cut away and the raw edges of the seam bound with a strip of lining; or the extra material (after being cut across at the finish of the hem) may be turned over to form a binding, cutting away only about an inch of it, as shown in illustration VIII. The hems may be stitched and lapped, the right over the left, the fold edge of the right side reaching almost to the sewing-line of the first box plait on the left side. Turn under about one-quarter of an inch at the finish of the hems and stitch across with two rows of stitching to make the closing secure and neat. Close with buttons and buttonholes. Baste the under-arm and shoulder seams and try on, making any necessary alterations at these seams.

9205

When the dress is made of moderate-weight wash material, French seams should be used. To make these, the seams are basted along the perforations that mark

9171

the sewing-line, but with the raw edges toward the outside of the garment. After fitting, make any necessary alterations, then stitch the seams one-quarter of an inch outside of the bastings. After stitching, trim the extra seam width off, leaving one-eighth of an inch beyond the stitching; this applies to the wide or outlet seams only. On the ordinary seams, for which three-eighths of an inch allowance is made, no trimming away is necessary, as the one-quarter inch between the basting and the stitching will leave just one-eighth inch beyond the stitching. The bastings should now be removed and the seams reversed so they will come toward the inside of the garment; they are then basted again at the sewing-line and stitched, when it will be found that the raw edges are turned in and enclosed in the seam.

For heavier material, it will be better to make an ordinary seam toward the inside and press it open; the raw edges should then be bound separately, either with binding ribbon or with a narrow bias strip of lining. The bias strip should be stitched in a narrow seam to one raw edge of the seam; it should then be turned over and hemmed to the same seam edge, concealing the narrow seam just made, and forming a secure and neat binding. The seam may be given an outside finish and held open by a row of stitching, made from the outside, about one-eighth of an inch each side of the seam.

Lapped seams may be made down the sides if preferred. In this case both edges of the seam are turned to one side and a row of stitching is made, from the outside, about one-quarter of an inch from the seam, the stitching going through the three thicknesses — the outside and the two seam edges on the inside. When lapped seams are made, the hem and any other outside stitching should have two rows instead of one, with the same spacing as that at the seam, that all may correspond.

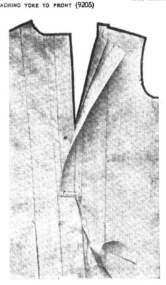

VII.—ATTACHING YOKE TO FRONT (9205)

VIII.—HEMMED CLOSING AT THE BACK

FASHIONABLE FRIVOLITIES

By LAURA R. SEIPLE

NEVER have fashion's fancies been so bewitching, and never have they been so multitudinous. There is a new whim on every side one turns, and, remarkable to state, most of them are practical as well as decorative. For instance, Miss America has managed to find a little vagary which is affording her the deepest satisfaction. And here it is. On the left sleeve of her linen shirtwaist she has her initials embroidered in characters resembling Chinese. The delusion is wrought with such perfection that John Chinaman himself glares at her with indignation, until he gains a better view and realizes that it is merely an imitation of his mother alphabet. In reality, the three initials are in plainest English when viewed from the proper distance and angle, only they are made to imitate Chinese characters as nearly as possible without losing all

YOKE OF FANCY FAGOTING, AND DOG COLLAR OF FRENCH JEWELS

significance. Heavy linen thread in deep Chinese colors is employed in making both the lettering and bracket. The embroidery is solid, combining several colors, and outlined with a brighter tone to bring them out.

Very lovely are the hand-embroidered shirt-waist patterns the best shops are showing. The front of a charming mull waist has a daisy pattern embroidered down the center, and separate pieces designed for collar and cuffs, all done in the daintiest shades of washable twist.

Handsome belts and ties made of soft silk have hideous dragons with flaming eyes deftly embroidered by American fingers, and resembling real Chinese work so perfectly that an expert might be puzzled as to its genuineness.

Another fad has the girl with nimble fingers. She is working night and day upon a white muslin gown which she is endeavoring to cover with dragons, butterflies and big Chinese roses, all done in coarse white cotton twist. Chinese

BOW TIE WITH REMOVABLE WASHABLE STOCK

660

SATIN STOCK WITH REMOVABLE WASHABLE COLLAR

FOR FEMININE FANCIES

blue embroidery with a dash of red here and there embellishes a striking costume, as does also Chinese blue and yellow; but all white seems to be favored, and after all is in far better taste, and one is not so apt to tire of it.

With her Chinese shirtwaist the smart girl will wear dragon cuff links or buttons made of Chinese coins. And her belt buckle will carry out the same idea.

Severe tailor-made stocks are again to be the smart neck dress. Two new models designed for a leading waist shop, whose reputation stands paramount, have detachable stocks made of white piqué and heavy linen. A pert taffeta bow finishes one stock and a tailored tie ending in diamond-shaped tabs buttons around the second stock. Other novelties in neckwear include collars of richly embroidered Oriental stuffs finished at the top with a bit of real lace and having extra pieces of silk laid in folds around the bottom. Sometimes an art *nouveau* buckle is used at the front, then again the silk folds may end in stitched squares, when a handsome button is employed to hold them in place.

Among the newest designs of collar and cuff sets broad effects are taking the lead. A Vandyke set made of mull bandings and linen stitches bears the hall-mark of individuality and exclusiveness. Deep collar and yoke combinations are shown in intricately wrought needlework and are designed to be worn with plain shirt-waists or blouses of linen.

Pretty little neck ruffles now so greatly in fashion can be economically made for oneself out of narrow wash laces. For a long and rather thin neck an

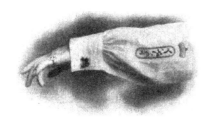

SLEEVE MARKED WITH OWNER'S INITIALS IN CHINESE EFFECT

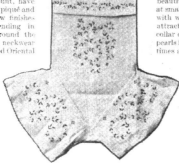

EMBROIDERED LINEN FOR SHIRT-WAIST

extremely becoming arrangement is fashioned of fine Valenciennes lace plaited on the edge of a strip of white swiss. The swiss is gathered on a collar-band and worn inside the dress collar. The ruffle stands up around the throat somewhat in Queen Anne style, and is strikingly becoming to certain types who can stand frills near the face. The same smart finish is used at the wrist of a severe sleeve.

With the collarless baby waist comes the revival of the imitation-jewel dog collar. Very beautiful are the designs one can purchase at small cost. Imitation pearls combined with white topaz and emeralds make an attractive neck ornament of the dog-collar order. Sometimes a single rope of pearls is twisted around the throat several times and held by an elaborate clasp.

A smart little fad is the chiffon scarf to match each frock. These scarfs are very long—four or five yards—and a yard wide. The ends are finished with a deep hem and sometimes a lace frill. Another scarf of rose-pink mousseline is covered with tiny ruffles of shaded gauze.

Many small bows are used in dressmaking and white afternoon toilettes are decorated with chiffon flowers, the rose being an especial favorite.

SATIN BELT EMBROIDERED IN CHINESE EFFECT

EARLY SPRING MILLINERY

THE picturesque broad-brimmed hat shown on the Front Cover Page of this issue of THE DESIGNER is well adapted to the early spring season, and is made of blue chiffon shirred on a wire foundation. It is trimmed with blue velvet and a plume shading from dark blue to almost white. The shape is particularly graceful.

On page 621 are shown two especially stylish hats. The one at the left is made of white horsehair braid, and is trimmed with a wreath-plume of white ostrich feathers and a stiff white aigret. The hat at the right of the same page is a handsome model made of alternate bands of black and white paper straw, and is trimmed with full drapery of white Liberty satin and ostrich plumes and aigret of mingled black and white.

The compact little turban pictured at the left of page 622 is made of écru rough straw, and is trimmed with cockade rosettes of brown Liberty satin ribbon. The hat at the right is a handsome white Panama straw, and is trimmed with soft white plumes and a huge rosette of white silk mull, which is placed at the turned-up part of the brim on the left side. A full drapery of the mull is carried around the crown toward the back, the ends being hidden under the plumes.

The pretty Charlotte Corday hat shown on the figure at the right of page 623 has a full crown of pale-pink mull, while the brim is made of white embroidered chiffon. Pink ostrich plumes and a twist of pink Liberty satin ribbon form the trimming, and strings of pink malines are knotted on the breast of the wearer.

The effective little Colonial hat pictured in color on page 627 is made of dark-red Tuscan straw, and is trimmed with folds of red malines and very full shaded red plumes. The second hat on the page is a spring-like model of soft-green rustic straw, and is trimmed with green Liberty silk and clusters of white lilacs.

At the head of this page are pictured four pretty hats for little girls. The first is a charming little gipsy shape of white rice straw and is trimmed with white moiré ribbon and clusters of field daisies. The second is somewhat on the sailor shape and is made of white Tuscan straw. It is simply and prettily trimmed with pale-pink ribbon and bunches of small pink roses without foliage. The third hat is made of white paper straw, very light in weight, and the underside of the wide brim is covered with ruffles of pale-blue chiffon. The crown is made of blue chiffon and is encircled by a wreath of blue forget-me-nots, and wide strings of blue Liberty satin tie it under the chin. The fourth hat is made of white chip, and is trimmed with huge many-looped rosettes of white satin ribbon, one of these being placed under the downward-turning brim at the left side toward the back.

The first hat shown in color on page 663 is a dainty little affair of green chip and the crown is encircled by a shirred band of green panne. Green ostrich plumes and a green aigret trim the left side, and under the upturned brim is placed a cluster of pale-pink roses which rest against the hair of the wearer.

Hat No. 2 is an odd and stylish model of light-brown paper straw and is of unusual shape. The crown is encircled by folds of amethyst velvet and roses and long quills of the same color supply the rest of the decoration.

No. 3 is a charming hat for spring wear, and is a pale mauve chip. Drapery of mauve chiffon taffeta conceals the crown and a rosette of the same material is placed under the brim at the back. Clusters of white violets with dull-green leaves and a mauve aigret are the only other trimmings used.

No. 4 is a wide-brimmed French chip, deep rose in color. The crown is of medium height and is almost concealed by a wreath-plume of a darker color than the hat. A bow of velvet and a half-wreath of field daisies trim the underside of the brim.

No. 5 is a pale-yellow leghorn with a stiffly wired brim. The crown is trimmed with black plumes and drapery of black malines and strings of the malines are knotted under the chin.

No. 6 is a picturesque Colonial shape of Russian-blue paper straw, and is trimmed with Liberty satin ribbon of still lighter shade.

The hats on page 664 are all practical models for traveling, shopping or general wear. No. 7 is a black fancy straw and is trimmed with folds of black velvet and pliable black quills.

No. 8 is made of a combination of black and white straw, and is trimmed with knots of black velvet and white quills. The shape is odd and stylish.

No. 9 has a crown of white Tuscan straw and a brim of wire covered with folds of white Liberty satin and black velvet. Rosettes of the two materials and a half-wreath of white roses placed about the crown are the decorations employed.

No. 10 is made of poppy-red rough straw, and is trimmed with folds of white Liberty satin and clusters of huge red and white poppies with golden hearts.

No. 11 is a pretty little toque of black-and-white horsehair braid, and is trimmed with flat white roses and buds made of silk velvet.

No. 12 is a fancy straw, light écru in color, and is trimmed with flat wings showing white, écru and brown shadings.

No. 13 is a dark-blue fancy straw. The right side is trimmed with shirred wheel ornaments, the making of which were described in THE DESIGNER for March. They are here made of dark-blue and white taffeta, and one larger than the rest holds at the back a wide blue quill which almost conceals the crown.

No. 14 is a Japanese straw with the underside of the brim covered with shirred mull. The crown is trimmed with a drapery and a huge bow of the mull held in front by a mother-of-pearl buckle.

EARLY SPRING MILLINERY. DESCRIBED ON PAGE 662

662

April, 1905

EARLY SPRING MILLINERY. DESCRIBED ON PAGE 662

Making an Envelope Hat

By MARTHA KINSMAN

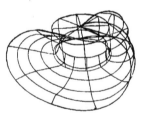

THE COMPLETED HAT

AS CAN be seen in the illustration of the frame the brim of the hat we take for the subject of our lesson this month rolls up very high and pointed at the left side, the point being fastened well over the crown. The style is decidedly becoming to many faces, and is one of the most popular of the early spring shapes.

The materials required to make the hat are one yard mousseline de soie for covering the frame, nine yards of maline, one and one-quarter yards fancy strip for facing, or six yards of hair braid one and one-half inches wide, three-quarters of a yard No. 12 black velvet ribbon, one bunch maiden-hair fern, six white roses, and one-quarter yard all-over lace.

The design would look well carried out in all black. A long snake plume could be substituted for the maline plaiting, in which case a slit should be cut in the brim at the left side, allowing the end of the feather to be passed through and fall on the hair.

To make the frame begin with the head-wire. For this cut a piece of wire twenty inches in length, lap until it measures seventeen and one-half inches, and fasten it with the tie-wire. Next, cut four pieces of wire twenty-six inches in length; about ten inches from one end of each of these wires make a decided bend up for the crown; measure one and one-half inches for the height, then six inches across the top of the crown, then down one and one-half inches. The measurements are the same in all four wires. First adjust the one which extends from front to back, next the wire which extends from side to side, and then the diagonal wires. These wires may be fastened to the head-wire by tying with tie-wire or by giving them one twist around the head-wire at the points indicated, which is the usual way. The tip-wire measures eighteen inches; tie this to the crown-wires, after which tie all the intersecting wires together in the center of the crown. Bend all the outward wires to conform to the shape of the brim, out straight in front, slightly curved upward at the right side, very high at the left side and down at the back, as shown in the second view; then, commencing at the back and proceeding from the right round to the left side, measure the brim-wires in the following order: Two and one-quarter, three, four and one-half, five and three-quarters, six and one-half, seven and one-half, eight and three-quarters, and three inches.

THE FRAME

READY FOR TRIMMING

The edge-wire measures forty-nine and one-half inches. Proceeding as before, from the right round to the left side, fasten the outward wires to the edge-wire to form the following spaces: Four and one-quarter, four and one-half, five and one-half, eight and one-quarter, five, nine and one-half, eight and one-half, and four inches. The brim-wires are fastened to the edge-wire by giving them one twist around it, then cutting off the superfluous wires. Add four extra wires between the head and edge wires; also add an extra brace-wire six and one-quarter inches long half way between the front and right side-front wires; add another one seven and one-half inches between the left side-front and the left side; then add a third brace-wire six and three-quarter inches long between the left side and left side-back. Cut out the tip of the crown and pinch down the wires. The tip and base of the separate crown measures twenty inches, the height three inches, and six and one-half inches across the top of the crown.

The frame finished, we now turn our attention to the making of the hat. Cover the brim smoothly outside and underneath with the mousseline de soie; also cover the crown. Take four yards in length; at about six inches from one edge shirr a group of eight tucks a little over one-quarter of an inch wide, allowing, after the first four which are closer, one-quarter of an inch space between the tucks. One and one-half inches from the last tuck shirr another one, in which run a wire. Arrange the tucks evenly by dividing in half and quarter spaces, then sew to the edge of the brim. Gather and sew to the inside of the crown. If hair braid is used, sew it on in rows, each overlapping the other. If the fancy strip is used, sew it to meet the tucks on the edge and sew the fulness inside the crown. Next cover the crown with the all-over lace and sew the crown to the brim. Make a band of white cape net one and one-half inches wide and twelve inches long, wire with lace wire, and cover with the mousseline de soie. Next, to make the ruching round the crown, take a piece of maline, on the double if very fine, five yards in length and six inches wide; plait in deep plaits as shown in the view of the completed hat; sew to the band for the ruche which encircles the brim; make a similar ruche to stand round the crown; between these twist the velvet ribbon. Sew the band to the brim, allowing the ruching to follow the outline of the hat; that is to say, it must be exactly the same distance all round from the edge of the hat. To fill in the space between the band and the crown, drape softly with the maline.

The hat is now ready for the trimming, which consists of a cluster of roses branched with maiden-hair fern. It is sewed firmly to the high point at the left side, as illustrated in the view of the completed hat. Let some of the flowers fall well down, to rest gracefully on the hair of the wearer.

The hat is ready for the lining of white Florentine silk which is made and sewed in in the usual way, very narrow white satin or lute string ribbon being used to draw in the fulness at the center.

FOREWORDS REGARDING

By LAURA R. SEIPLE

HERE is always something of unusual interest about the April bride's trousseau. It may be in the cut of her gown, the draping of her veil, or the arrangement of her bridal flowers. Then, again, it may be the individuality she expresses in the details of her outfit or all combined that makes the bride of early spring beautiful.

Perhaps the most noticeable change from regulation bridal effects this season is found in the adoption of lilies-of-the-valley as the favorite flower instead of time-honored orange-blossoms. There was a time when no other flower was ever heard of as being the correct accompaniment to the wedding gown, but now things have changed and the bride may choose her favorite blossom with which to adorn her fair self upon her wedding day. Lilies-of-the-valley, white orchids and gardenias or a combination of all three, with a spray of orange-blossoms besides, are frequently used in adorning a single bridal costume, while white lilacs, narcissus and white hyacinths are no less popular for the bride whose taste runs to simplicity rather than display. Of course, a wreath of orange-blossoms resting

A GRACEFUL VEIL ARRANGEMENT

FAN OF SILVER-SPANGLED WHITE GAUZE, LACE HANDKERCHIEF
AND LONG WHITE SUÈDE GLOVES

demurely around the crown of a pretty head is always appealing to the eye, and will, no doubt, be the accepted adornment of many spring brides who hold to old-fashioned fancies upon their wedding day.

To be truly fashionable one must be picturesque. One spring bride has chosen a novel way to wear her flowers which is sure to become a fad before the season is over. Her veil is made of plain white tulle, cut square and gathered straight across at the top. She will fasten it to her hair by means of large wire hair-pins and a bunch of lilies-of-the-valley at each side, meeting at the top. The effect will be jaunty and far more becoming than the usual flat arrangement universally adopted. There will be no jewels in her hair, which will be arranged in a simple knot on top of her head to serve as a foundation for the veil and flowers. Instead of the usual bride's bouquet she will carry a white ivory prayer-book having the pages marked by a slender shower of lilies-of-the-valley attached to narrow white ribbons.

Her only jewels will be the gift of the groom, which is a triple necklace of pearls fastened with a diamond clasp at the back. She will wear long white glacé kid gloves to meet the three-quarter sleeves of her wedding gown, and

FASHIONS AND FABRICS

instead of having the third finger cut to receive the wedding ring, she will slip the glove off her hand and tuck it in the opening at the wrist. Her handkerchief will be of finest Spanish lace with soft crêpe center, and her fan sheer gauze, spangled with silver disks and mounted upon mother-of-pearl sticks inlaid with silver.

This April bride's slippers are marvels of beauty. White satin is the foundation material, and over this Duchesse lace is drawn smoothly. Fluffy bows of tulle with a tiny spray of orange-blossoms, artificial, of course, nestling in the tulle loops ornament the toes. Her hose are to be of the finest white silk woven in a pretty fancy pattern.

And now comes the all-important feature— the gown and its material. First we must ask, where are the simple, artless frocks of the brides of old—the long, decorous sleeve, the high, severe collar, the plain, tight-fitting bodice and the stiff outline of the satin skirt? To tell the truth, they are carefully packed away in the chest with all the rest of the things dear to memory that are resting in the same cedar box. The bride of 1905 will adorn her fine athletic figure in just such lovely apparel as she fancies. It may be crêpe de Chine elaborately embroidered by hand or chiffon messaline or heavy satin veiled with plain chiffon, or if she prefers to lean toward

FLORAL PLACE-MARK FOR PRAYER-BOOK

applied flowers of the same material or white satin or silk veiled with web-like lace of wonderful design are all popular. Liberty gauze makes a charming bridal gown, and is not so expensive as to make it prohibitive to those in moderate circumstances.

For an inexpensive bridal frock white bobbinet will be found very desirable. A fluffy model may be chosen when this material is used, and quantities of Valenciennes lace with little stiff satin bows or bunches of small white flowers heading the flounce make a truly picturesque gown, and one that may be used for formal occasions after the wedding. On elaborate wedding gowns much hand-work is shown. The collar and bertha, cuffs and applied designs on the skirt are often pieces of gorgeous needlework.

English modes, she will choose heavy brocades, embossed silk or stiff satin; and her veil will be lace—costly lace—Brussels, rose point, point d'Alençon or Honiton.

At the French capital many brides choose more showy materials for their wedding gowns. Broché grenadine, sheer gauze embossed with scrolls or floral designs in high relief and outlined with silver and pearl ornaments, or chiffon with

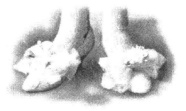

SATIN SLIPPERS COVERED WITH DUCHESSE LACE AND DECORATED WITH TULLE AND ORANGE-BLOSSOMS

667

"OVER THE SEA WITH THE SAILOR"

8561   8933   9077   4406

FOUR LITTLE TARS ON SHORE LEAVE

HE DATE when the first sailor costume came in vogue is one of the forgotten facts in history, but it was long before any reader of this article can remember, and from its first appearance it was made welcome and has survived, although undergoing many variations, to the present day, when, if possible, it is more fashionable than ever. Next to the "Buster Brown" dress, it is the most comfortable garb that a boy or girl, or even Madame herself, can assume, and the style lends itself to particularly effective development in summer fabrics.

For instance, what could be prettier or jauntier than the little suits and frocks shown at the head of this page? Boy and girl alike look happy and attractive in them. The first dress, 8561, a box-plaited model, is made of white linen and is trimmed with red washable braid. A scarlet silk tie and scarlet stockings and low shoes are worn with the little dress, as is also a wide sailor hat of white straw with a scarlet band and bow. A shield fills in the neck of the blouse, and this model is suitable for girls from four to thirteen years.

The suit next pictured is made by 8933, of a combination of brown flannel and écru linen, the linen portion being trimmed with brown braid. The sailor hat is of écru straw and has a band of brown ribbon. Brown shoes and stockings complete the outfit, which may be worn by boys from three to ten years. Another style of large collar is supplied with the suit, or the blouse may be made without the sailor collar and an Eton or other linen collar worn with it.

The dress on the third figure is made by 9077 of dark-blue-and-white French percale, the sailor collar being of dark-blue linen trimmed with bands of white linen, and the shield of white linen. The hat is a white sailor with a blue band, the stockings dark blue, and the shoes white kid with patent-leather foxings. The dress is suitable for girls from four to fourteen years.

The last child in the group wears a tar suit of blue duck, with a sailor collar and shield of white linen, the collar being widely bound with dark-blue linen and trimmed with blue braid. The tar cap is of white duck with a glazed-leather head-band. The shoes are white kid with enamel-leather foxing similar to those worn by the little girl next to him. The suit may be worn by boys from four to ten years and is made by 4406.

The jolly little group on page 669 shows many variations of the sailor dress. The first child wears a box-plaited dress of white piqué with a collar and shield of all-over embroidery, a tie of black grosgrain ribbon closing the ends of the sailor collar. The design is 8904, and it is suitable for girls from five to thirteen years. Black shoes and stockings are worn with the dress, as here pictured.

The jaunty little frock on the next child is made of pink chambray and white linen. The sailor collar is widely bound with the chambray and is trimmed with pink washable braid. A tie of black ribbon matches effectively in line with the black stockings and patent-leather low shoes worn with the dress, the design for which is 8725, suitable for girls from five to thirteen years.

The adult figure wears a sailor costume for ladies from thirty-two to forty-two inches bust measure, and the design is 8726. As here pictured, it is made of silver-green linen, the sailor collar and shield being of white linen, and the former trimmed with dark-green washable braid and tied with a ribbon of black Liberty satin.

The little lass standing at the top of the stairs wears a dainty sailor frock of pink-and-white zephyr combined with white lawn, a white leather belt and a tie of deep, rose-colored ribbon completing the effect. The hair is tied with ribbon to match. The design for the dress is 8812, and it is suitable for girls from four to thirteen years.

The lad who stands next to her wears an outfit composed of sailor blouse 8591 and knee trousers 8589, the blouse being suitable for boys from three to twelve years, and the trousers, which have a fly, for boys from five to sixteen years. The outfit is here made of blue-and-white

8904   8725   8726   8812   8773   8591 8589   9047

THE JOLLY CREW OF THE GOOD SHIP " HOME ".

669

Galatea, the sailor collar being of plain blue linen trimmed with white braid, and the shield of white linen with a blue emblem worked on the front.

The tiny boy holding by his big sister's hand wears a white linen suit made by 8773. The sailor collar is trimmed with dark-red braid and a belt of red enameled leather is worn about the waist. White socks and red morocco ankle-tie slippers are worn with the suit, which is appropriate for little boys from two to eight years.

The last child on the page wears a pretty little frock of pongee worked with light-blue polka dots. The sailor collar is made of plain light-blue Japanese silk and the shield of plain pongee. A big bow of blue ribbon is tied beneath the sailor collar, and brown stockings and shoes are worn with the dress, which is made by 9047, and is suitable for little girls from two to nine years.

The first dress shown on this page is made by 8912, of blue-and-white gingham combined with plain white linen, and is trimmed with blue braid. It may be worn by misses from thirteen to seventeen years. The little girl shown in the same group wears a sailor costume of red-and-white percale with a

plain white linen collar. The frock is made by 8626.

In the upper group the first child wears a dress, made by 8083, of white serge, with a shield of white piqué and a large collar of white piqué polka-dotted with blue. The dress is

8083   8732   8756   8955

WHEN THE BREEZES BLOW

8912   TWO SAILORS FROM THE SCHOOL-SHIP

designed for girls from four to twelve years. White socks, patent-leather ankle-ties and a big, dark-blue sailor hat complete the outfit.

The young girl wears a tucked costume, made by 8732, of blue flannel, with a large collar and shield of white flannel trimmed with blue braid. The design is appropriate for misses from thirteen to seventeen years.

The standing child wears a dress of scarlet-and-white Scotch zephyr in combination with white linen, made by 8756, and suitable for girls from six to thirteen years. The hat is a white straw sailor with a scarlet band; the stockings are scarlet, and the low shoes soft black kid with patent-leather tips.

The last dress pictured is made of blue serge, with a collar of blue taffeta trimmed with white braid and a shield of white linen. The design is 8955, and it is suitable for either little girls or little boys, from two to nine years.

Emblems, such as stars, anchors, flags or stripes, in red, white and blue silk, or of some color to match the trimming, are much in vogue for the sailor suits, and may be worked on one sleeve—never on both—or on the vest or sailor collar; sometimes on all three in the one suit. A variation from the emblem idea is to have the initials of the wearer worked on the left sleeve, either just above or just below the elbow. Wash silks are used for the embroidery.

THE ART OF PYRO-SCULPTURE

BY JESSIE GARWOOD FRITTS

THAT little firebrand of artistic endeavor—the platinum point—has been a medium for varied expression in the field of decorative art, not only for amateurs who merely dabble, but for those who are serious enough to attain to something of the professional's skill.

It would seem that pyrography has fairly run the gamut of ornamental possibilities; yet in pyro-sculpture, its latest development, it has achieved its greatest artistic success.

Pyro-sculpture decorations are plastically embossed, really carved out in relief, with a specially constructed and extra strong platinum knife-point. The finished article differs from the ordinary carved wood on the market for burning purposes in that the figures are modeled as carefully as with a sculptor's tool. It depends upon the taste of the amateur and the character of the decorations whether or not colors are used. At times only the natural color of the wood is left, and the varying brown shades of the more or less burned parts are rich and produce a most refined effect. The color treatment is, however, even more desirable for many articles. It is never allowed brilliant expression, but is confined to mezzo-tints which harmonize perfectly with the character of the work, suggesting, too, the mellowness of age. In many instances pyro-sculpture is more effective for decorations than wood-carving; for, with the rapid-working, white-hot point, after a little practise, an amateur can give the wood as finely modulated and plastic form as any skilled professional carver. Moreover, the burning gives to the wood an exquisite soft finish, altogether desirable, which result cannot possibly be obtained by mere carving.

Special articles are manufactured for the benefit of the pyro-sculptor, as the wood must be extra heavy and the pieces very strong in their construction. It is also possible to buy pieces roughly carved out so that the hardest work is done, and all that is left for the amateur to do is to put in the fine modulations with the point and finish the work.

A HALL CHAIR

For the benefit of those, however, who prefer to do it all themselves, from the very beginning, the few suggestions here given may not come amiss.

Aside from the point, a sharp chisel will facilitate the removal of the superfluous background, as it would be too tedious a matter to burn it all out.

To begin, the outline of the design is gone over carefully with the point, burning very deeply and evenly, otherwise when the background is cut away the relief figures may split.

Chisel out the background roughly, about an eighth of an inch below the design, and then burn the surface with long even strokes. The ornamentation, whatever it may be, is then modeled carefully with the platinum point, and when the scorching is finished the entire surface must be scrubbed vigorously with a dry, clean brush, having long, stiff bristles. Now it is ready for the tinting. Sometimes it is the design and sometimes the background which receives the color, but if no tinting is desired more care should be taken in toning with the point. A soft finish is given by polishing with wax. Under no circumstances should shellac or varnish be used.

In selecting a point for this work one must be sure that it is of the highest grade obtainable. The heaviness of the work is a thorough test of durability, and the platinum should be able to stand a very high temperature.

An ordinary point will do, however, if one is satisfied to buy the articles already carved. This is a great saving of time and labor, but the superficial skill required in finishing it takes away half the zest of the work for the truly ambitious artist.

If one is an adept with carving tools, the same effect may be obtained by a broad handling of them, and the detail worked out with the point.

It is a good plan to have two brushes at hand—one a good-sized fiber scrubbing brush, and a rather heavy bristle brush for polishing purposes. The wax used for finishing may be a regular pyrography

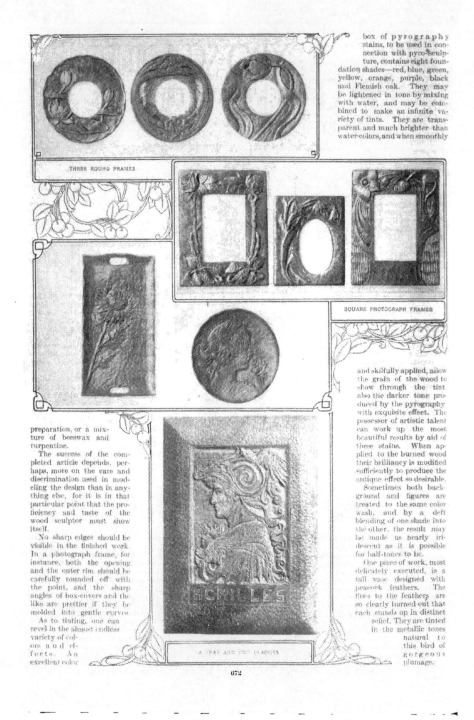

THREE ROUND FRAMES

SQUARE PHOTOGRAPH FRAMES

A TRAY AND TWO PLAQUES

box of pyrography stains, to be used in connection with pyro-sculpture, contains eight foundation shades—red, blue, green, yellow, orange, purple, black and Flemish oak. They may be lightened in tone by mixing with water, and may be combined to make an infinite variety of tints. They are transparent and much brighter than water-colors, and when smoothly and skilfully applied, allow the grain of the wood to show through the tint also the darker tone produced by the pyrography with exquisite effect. The possessor of artistic talent can work up the most beautiful results by aid of these stains. When applied to the burned wood their brilliancy is modified sufficiently to produce the antique effect so desirable.

Sometimes both background and figures are treated to the same color wash, and by a deft blending of one shade into the other, the result may be made as nearly iridescent as it is possible for half-tones to be.

One piece of work, most delicately executed, is a tall vase designed with peacock feathers. The fines to the feathers are so clearly burned out that each stands up in distinct relief. They are tinted in the metallic tones natural to this bird of gorgeous plumage.

preparation, or a mixture of beeswax and turpentine.

The success of the completed article depends, perhaps, more on the care and discrimination used in modeling the design than in anything else, for it is in that particular point that the proficiency and taste of the wood sculptor must show itself.

No sharp edges should be visible in the finished work. In a photograph frame, for instance, both the opening and the outer rim should be carefully rounded off with the point, and the sharp angles of box-covers and the like are prettier if they be molded into gentle curves.

As to tinting, one can revel in the almost endless variety of colors and effects. An excellent color

A charming example of back-ground coloring is a box done in verde green—this laid over the burned surface gives a striking resemblance to metal. A five-pointed leaf is embossed upon the cover. The leaf is exquisite in its formation, and is a delicate light brown, having been left untinted. Jardinières are especially pretty with this treatment.

Geranium branches are used to artistic advantage on a wall cabinet, the blossoms being tinted a dull red, and the leaves richly zoned in their natural colors. Nasturtium blossoms with their glowing yellow and orange tints and broad green leaves may be used very effectively, while the magnolia flower in white,

pleasing softness of old ivory.

Pyro-sculpture suggests many possibilities in furniture decoration to the really artistic craftsman who cares to exercise originality, and who welcomes a change from the straight lines of rigid simplicity to more graceful models, voluptuous in their curves and treatment. Buffet doors, low bookcases, hall chairs, frames for mirrors, tabourets, chests and the like are all obtainable in plain hard wood suitable for the work. Tinting is rarely employed for articles of furniture, and is only unobjectionable when used with a very discriminating taste. Picture-frames burned in this manner are works of art in them-

SCREEN

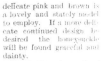

delicate pink and brown is a lovely and stately model to employ. If a more delicate continued design be desired the honeysuckle will be found graceful and dainty.

In an upward growth of narcissus on a frame, the blossoms retain much of their natural delicate beauty by having been burned very lightly before they were given a wash of white and the yellow centers put in. The effect is not startling as might be imagined, but the flowers have the

VASES, FRAMES AND A SEAT

selves, yet do not detract from the value of photograph, etching or print, as do the ordinary decorated frames. For smaller articles of ornament pyro-sculpture offers an endless variety of beautiful designs.

This latest development of modern pyrography might be called the Renaissance of an old Flemish art, and will serve to give a distinction never hoped for by "burnt wood" in its commonly accepted sense.

IN HOUSEKEEPING all over the WORLD
By Laura B. Starr

III. THE FRENCH HOUSEHOLD

THE French household begins the day with a breakfast that differs very materially from the American breakfast, or even the English morning meal, which is not so heavy as ours. This first meal may be early or late, according to the station and occupation of the members of the household, but it always consists of the same thing, viz., bread (butter is used occasionally) and coffee. It is a movable feast and eaten more often than not in one's chamber. There is no gathering around the family board at what is called *le petit déjeuner.*

The large breakfast, the first substantial meal of the day, is served at noon and consists of several courses, with one and often two of meat, and is always accompanied by wine, the *vin ordinaire* of the country, without which even the commonest peasant does not eat his crust.

The cook goes to market with a huge basket and brings home the food herself. There are two excellent reasons for allowing her to do the marketing: First, she knows exactly what she wants and selects meat, fruit and vegetables with great care. She will carefully examine every potato in a half-bushel to select the half-dozen she wishes to bake for the midday meal; she rejects every imperfect one and *will* have those she buys of the same size. Potatoes for boiling or frying are selected with the same care. Each vegetable is carefully inspected from various points of view until she is satisfied that she has a good specimen. This careful cook is more particular, if possible, with her fruit and her flowers, for the French are very fond of flowers and keep the table decorated with them as late in the season as possible. The second reason for the cook bringing home the food herself is that several sous are saved, as one must pay two sous to each person who brings anything to the house — from shop or market. Then, again, she receives a small commission on all she buys, but as she shows such care and discretion this small recompense is certainly earned.

Unsalted butter is used for bread and is bought fresh every day; salted butter is used for cooking, and the French cook makes away with great quantities of it. She puts large lumps of it in the dripping-pan with her roasting meat, which process certainly imparts the most delicious flavor, and she uses salt much more liberally then we do.

The seasoning of the food is a great art. With us, for instance, our cooking-teachers instruct us that to preserve the flavor and blood of a roast is the first consideration; not so with the French cook. She adds a few spoonfuls of madeira wine to the gravy of the roasting fillet and bastes it so constantly

Photographs by Nadar, Paris

ANTIQUE CARVED MANTEL

THE DESIGNER

with the tiniest bit of onion and lettuce, so carefully managed that few except the c could say what had been used.

The range in the ordinary kitchen is ra a crude affair compared to our modern but the cooks are good managers, and w cooking contrive to have their different cou finished in time to serve properly. To American housekeeper the want of hot w would be the greatest deprivation. Fuel i expensive that the utmost economy is e cised in managing the fire. As many th as possible are cooked at one time; someti the vegetables for dinner are cooked in morning and then heated fresh at dinner-ti The number and variety of kitchen ute

SOME OLD FRENCH HOUSES

TYPES OF FRENCH PEASANT WOMEN

are not great. The greater par the ordinary cooking is done

WHERE THE FRESH FISH COME FROM

while cooking that the meat as well as the sauce has a delicious nutty flavor. Her aim is to season her food so well that no one flavor predominates, and her pride is very much hurt if she sees anyone adding salt, pepper or butter to the viands she has prepared.

Cheese, also, is much more generally used than with us. For instance, when a cauliflower is boiled it is covered with a white sauce and this sprinkled with grated cheese and set in the oven to brown. Various other vegetables are treated in the same way. Peas and beans are flavored

AT A FRENCH MARKET

casseroles, which are jars or pots of a variety of sizes, with short handles, made of coarse, common red clay, glazed on the inside only. They are very cheap, being sold for one, two, three or more sous, according to the size. Better utensils are invariably of copper, and it is the cook's greatest pride to keep them so bright she can see her face in them.

The ordinary bed of the French supports a canopy and what we would consider stuffy side curtains, for the people are no more fond of the night air than they are of the continual bathing indulged in by the English and Americans.

desires. Lines for drying are stretched along the roof of the boat, for the use of which a few extra sous are paid. A small boat containing an ironing-stove and table is attached to each large one; extra is paid for the use of these, but the poorer women who go there to do their own washing, and many of the others too, for that matter, carry the clothes home rough-dried and do the ironing themselves. Sheets, common towels and other coarse pieces are carefully folded and not ironed at all.

The servants who are sent to *le plat,* as they say when they gó to the wash-boat, often take advantage of

PEASANT'S COTTAGE IN SOUTH OF FRANCE

The French housekeeper has an almost unlimited amount of napery. Until the past few years twelve dozen napkins, towels, tablecloths, etc., were considered only a very ordinary outfit for a bride. And how generous they are in their measures. The common serviette is a yard square, and all sheets, even those of the poorest people, measure three yards in length. Great care is taken in selecting the bride's household linen, and the best that can be afforded is bought, for she takes so great a quantity to her new home that it lasts through her lifetime and often that of her children.

There are no conveniences for washing in a French house, or rather in a French apartment, for the greater part of the population of a city or village live in apartments. Private houses are called hotels, and only the very rich can afford to live in them. Some families more fortunate than others send their clothes to a laundress in the country. The washing is not taken in the bulk at so much a week, as it often is with us, but each piece is paid for separately. The prices vary in different cities, but nowhere is so exorbitant a price charged as at some of our own American hotels. In all the large cities there are laundry boats on the river, where the poor people and the servants of the better class go to do their washing. At first glance these boats look like double-sized house-boats, but on inspection one discovers that they are divided in the middle by a lengthwise partition. Boilers and shelves for baskets are ranged in rows along the partition. Tubs with hot-water pipes are built along the outer edge of the boat, which is open. Here for a small sum per hour a laundress may secure a tub and boiler for whatever length of time she

their mistresses in this manner: They carry the clothes to the boat and hire one of the laundresses there to do their washing while they visit their friends or loiter about, of course taking good care that the extra money comes out of the mistresses' pockets. The French washboard is not corrugated, like ours, but quite smooth, and on the boats is stationary at the side of the tub. The washer holds the garment in her left hand on the board, then rubs with the other. The clothes are rinsed over the side of the boat in the river.

The French laundress is far more careful of buttons, tapes, etc., than either the English or American "wash-lady." In Brittany and other parts of rural France the people have only two or four wash-days in a year. Of course, this requires an immense store of linen, but it is the chief aim of every Breton woman to possess enough to postpone wash-day for six months if possible. At these open-air laundries the whole neighborhood gathers at the same time. The women kneel on flat flags or in wooden troughs around an open pool or by the riverside, and beat and bruise their linen on the stones with a wooden paddle. They use little or no soap, but manage to get their clothes a snowy white.

The French dinner-table is a pretty sight, with small vases of flowers at the four corners and a fruit or flower piece in the center. There is not the array of table cutlery that is thought to be necessary on an American table. At the right of each plate is a glass or silver rest, such as are used for carving knife and fork, and upon this rests the pointed steel knife, that is used for several courses. The dessert knives are silver, with round blades.

but the pointed steel ones, large or small and well sharpened, are used for all other courses.

Carving is never done at the table, and every dish is passed twice so that one may have a chance to taste and try any unfamiliar viand. Soup is eaten from the point of the spoon, and usually with a more or less disagreeable gurgle; and many otherwise very well-bred people do not hesitate to use a knife for lifting food to the mouth. Coffee is always served in the salon, and in many cases the hostess, if she chances not to be familiar with the habits of her guests, will ask each one privately if he takes a demi-tasse. Economy is the watchword of every Frenchman, and while a hostess in nowise begrudges a cup of coffee to anyone, she thinks it wild extravagance to make more than she is certain to use.

The French wife and mother can bring up her family on a small income and can make them comfortable on a very moderate one. She prides herself on her economy, and takes great delight in showing a well-dressed and well-fed family and then announcing the small sum with which she has done it.

Women have such a variety of occupations in France that we do not always find the wife even of a poor man doing her own cooking and housework. She often finds it more profitable to assist her husband in his business or to embark in business on her own account than to stop at home attending to domestic affairs.

Bread, pastry and everything else that can be had in the shops are bought, and one may buy many more kinds of cooked food in Paris or Lyons than in New York. This and having the washing done out of the house relieve the pressure of work, and not so many servants are needed as at home.

As a rule, the French mother in the city does not nurse and bring up her children. A few days after a child is born it is taken away from the mother and given to a wet-nurse in the country, where it remains until it is old enough to go to school. The government takes a hand in this as it does in most things, and it sends inspectors to investigate the condition of the children and nurses. Thus it will be seen that baby-farming in France is conducted on very different principles from the same business in America.

The decrease of the population in France has alarmed the authorities, and very stringent laws regarding both child and mother have been passed. The length of time a working-woman must rest after the birth of her child before returning to the factory or workshop is regulated by this very paternal government. That there is need of this care is shown by the following baby-law which forbids anyone to give solid food of any kind to infants under one year of age without the written authority of a qualified physician. It is also forbidden to use the long rubber tubes on nursing-bottles on account of the difficulty of keeping them sterilized.

Life in rural France is far more interesting than in the cities, where of necessity there must be a certain amount of sameness about it. The peasant of Brittany

lives in a cottage which the old shanties of Harlem or the shacks of the Western prairies would put to shame for comfort and cleanliness. Often the roofs are thatched, and usually there is but one room, seldom more than two, for one could hardly dignify the small space under the roof a chamber, yet here it is that some members of the family must sleep. The floor is of "puddled" or compressed clay, or perhaps only the beaten earth rush-strewn. There is as a rule no lath-and-plaster ceiling. A few strips of scantling or rails are bound together like a raft and suspended a few inches from the center of the roof, making the only storage place the house affords. Hooks and nails are arranged along the edges. The few pieces of furniture are of the simplest and most primitive description. There is always a *lit clos*, or shut-in bed, built in a convenient space in the wall. The doors of these beds, even in the houses of very poor peasants, are beautifully carved, for the men are skilled in the use of the knife. The cabinet bed, the linen press and the clock are the three things to which the most care is given. The people are proud of their carved furniture and rub it till it has a wonderful polish.

In Brittany the children sleep in the closed beds with the parents or in cribs near the fireplace. Very young children are lashed in their cradles, which are called *brancles*, and hung out of harm's way from the crosspiece overhead. In the most primitive cottages there is a stationary square table in the center of the room; bowls or basins are let into it along the sides, and at meal-time the pottage or lentil soup is poured into these and each person takes a large spoon from the rack hanging above the table, and, helping himself to the bread, eats his meal without more ado.

The loaves of bread are large, as if baked in a milk-pan, and there is a good-sized hole in the center through which the arm may be passed. It is no unusual sight to see a bread-seller going through the streets with half a dozen on each arm. In the house the loaf is laid on a wooden platter which has a wicker cover; when not in use it is kept on a shelf high up among the rafters.

Women work on the farm and fetch and carry loads that are back-breaking, and it is little wonder that they look twice their age. When too old to really labor they are set to mind the cattle, and this they do faithfully, standing for hours, unsheltered from the sun, patiently knitting the heavy woolen stockings worn by the peasantry.

The exteriors of the old houses in town and country are often picturesque. The façades of some are rich in carving, others have been disfigured by the use of modern stucco. Story projects beyond story, all covered with fantastic ornaments and surmounted by quaint weather-cocks, the nooks and corners formed by the angles of these old houses being very fascinating to the artistic eye.

Except in modern houses in large cities there are no perpendicular fires; this arises from the scarcity of fuel in France. The cooking is done on logs of wood or limbs of trees cut into short lengths and laid horizontally on the brick fireplace. Charcoal is used in stoves where there is any fire.

INTERIOR OF A BRETON KITCHEN

Speakin' of Cats and Erasmus

By C. D. RUGGERI

A Monologue

IF ANYBODY ever sez anythin' to me about a black cat bein' good luck, he'll meet with a sudden an' fearful end, that's all. Black cats may be lucky to some folks but they aint to me.

You know Erasmus Simpkins, don't you? Well, he's ben comin' to see me fer nigh on to two years, and he's a very nice young man, as men go, and makes a good livin' an' all that, an' I'm sorter fond o' him into the bargain, an' I'm shore he does set a heap by me. But he is *bashful*—he's awful bashful. He's the bashfullest man I ever saw. There's no bringing him to the point a-tall. Now some men can be brought to the top notch o' affection, an', incidental, proposin', by a supply o' good victuals, served regular every evenin' for a week or so, an' then jealousy works with some on em, and so forth.

I tried the first long ago. Ma an' I fed Erasmus everythin' as he ever sed he liked, but t'warn't no use. He'd just simply look at me sort o' admirin' while he wuz eatin', and when he wuz goin', along about nine o'clock, he'd sorter moisten his lips, an' look as if he were trying to pluck up courage, an' say, "Patience—Patience—" (an' goodness knows I've got a name thet suits me, fer if ever anybody wuz compelled to be patient I'm thet person) "Patience," he'd say, "I wanter tell ye somethin'." Then there'd be a long pause, and I'd think to myself, 'Well, this time it's comin', sure!' "I—I—Good-night, Patience," An' then he'd bolt out, too scairt to do anythin' else.

It wuz wearyin', there's no use denyin'. It wuz just downright discouragin'.

I see thet kind o' thing warn't no use, so I made a firm resolve. I'd make him jealous. I didn't see exactly how I wuz goin' to accomplish it, but, good land o' Goshen, I just naturally had to do somethin'. I'm not as young as I used ter be, though thet needn't go any further, an' while I ain't dyin' anxious to be married, still so long as there's a man thet likes me, an' thet I

" MA AND I FED ERASMUS EVERYTHING HE EVER SAID HE LIKED "

like, I don't see the use of spendin' any more time in delay an' foolishness.

An' I got my chance the other night.

Mrs. Jones wuz sick, an' she sent her brother over to ask me if I'd come an' read to her fer about an hour in the evenin'. So I put on my hat an' went with Hiram (that's Mrs. Jones' brother, who's an old bachelor), an' as I was goin' out I sez to Liza (that's the hired girl). "If Erasmus Simpkins calls this evenin'," I sez, "you tell him I'm not to home, an' you might mention thet I have gone out along o' Hiram Coles."

I knew well enough that'd make quite an impression on Erasmus, because ever sence Erasmus began to take me home from choir rehearsal, prayer meetin' an' like that, I haven't gone out anywhere along o' anybody else.

I'm afraid the readin' that night didn't do either Mrs. Jones or me much good. I wuz thet nervous an' wonderin' how Erasmus wuz takin' it all I didn't hardly know one word from the other. But, nex' night. I foun' it had worked all right. Erasmus came as usual an' looked kind o' sot, as if he'd sorter made up his mind to somethin' at last. His countenance wuz agitated, an' I kinder felt sorry for him, yet I knew now I'd got so far I mus' keep on doin' what I'd determined to do, an' I mistrusted if I could only get him a little more agitated, an' sorter get him to thinkin' he wuzn't the only man in Biggsville thet might take a fancy to me, I could then gently turn him roun' so as to set things all right for both of us.

"Oh," he sez, trying to speak quite calm and selected, "where did ye go las' evenin' I'd like to know?"

"Where do you suppose," I sez, kind o' offhand.

"I don't know," sez he, a trifle more excited, "an' thet's why I asked you. Now, I tell ye what it is, Patience," he sez, continuing quite fast, "I am just that fond o' ye——" an' just' then our black cat came in with the tag end of a ball of twine in her mouth, and made straight for Erasmus. She is uncommon fond of Erasmus an' frolics around him considerable, but

" I PUT ON MY HAT AND WENT WITH HIRAM "

that night he didn't pay no attention to her, an' so she kep' fussin' aroun' his feet, tryin' to attract his notice. But he kept right on, an' I wuz too flustered to pay much attention to the cat, either.

"I'm thet f o n d o' ye, Patience, t h a t it sorter riles me to hear o' ye goin' out along o' Hiram Coles, or any-body else," he sez, risin' up an' beginnin' to walk the floor quite excited.

"It's comin'," thinks I, but you see I had calc'lated without my host, as the sayin' is.

A l l unbeknown to Erasmus an' me, that cat had twisted his feet all up in that twine she wuz tuggin' aroun', and they wuz all sort o' tied up together, Erasmus an' the cat an' t h e big w o o d e n rockin' chair, an' fust thing I know there wuz Erasmus Simpkins full length on the floor, with that old black cat under him, an' him using language somethin' awful for a church member. Every time he tried to get up his feet got twisted worse, an' his hands wuz so bungly 'count o' his bein' so ragin' mad that they wuz no use to him a-tall to loosen the cord nor nuthin', and there wuz the poor fellow a-cussin' to beat the band an' that old black cat a-squallin' loud enough to raise the very roof off the house.

Well, after ten minutes or so, when ma, who had come rushin' in from the kitchen at the noise, an' I had discon-nected him from the cord, we found he had a black eye an' a bump on his forehead, where he'd struck the mahogany table when he fell, an' of course arter thet there wuz nuthin' to do but to fix up his eye the best way we could with raw beefsteak an' send him home.

I never knew of any man making love to advantage with a black eye, even if he wuz in the humor for it, which Erasmus certainly wasn't that awful night.

Now it will take another whole year at the very least before he is worked up to the proper state o' courage

" LIZA "

again, if he ever is, an' if I've lost him for good an' all it's the fault o' that old black cat.

Notwithstandin' all that there is folks who persist in tellin' you a black cat is good luck. *Good luck!* I giv' that cat away mighty quick the next mornin' I can tell you.

THEY HAD COMPANY

By CORA GLEASON

MA says to please fill up this dish
With 'taters that are done ;
You see the Jinkses all have come—
We'll have a heap of fun !

An' jest two loaves of white bread, please,
If you can't spare us three ;
An' two jars of them yeller plums,
From off that leanin' tree.

She'd like a roll of butter, too,
We used the last at noon.
Ma says that she will pay you back—
She 'spects to churn right soon.

Now fill this little tin can up
With that sweet-smellin' tea ;
Mis' Jinks thinks she must have a cup—
Ma's tellin' her, you see.

An' have you any meat that's cooked ?
Yes ? That will go real nice
With a dish of them spiced pickles, please,
The ones you didn't slice.

You say that I can't take 'em all ?
Pa said I had a head
When I said I would git our Frank
To bring his bob-tail sled.

The Blue Pigeon

By Winwood Waitt.

QUAINT, many-gabled nook was the Misses Dene's *atelier*, up two-pair back—a rambling attic chamber under high-pitched rafters, with the soft spring sunshine stealing in at unexpected gable windows, and the winds playing fitful tunes among the creaking chimney-pots. On the wide ledge of the sunniest window stood a great Japanese flower-pot, out of whose green-lacquered depths rose the tall stems and waxen leaves of a splendid African lily, crowned with clusters of snowy, cup-shaped blossoms. And Nora Dene, feasting her artist soul upon the rich beauty of the rare exotic, thought there were few treasures of this world she would willingly accept in exchange for this crown-jewel of the queen of flowers. It was the Easter offering of one passionately beloved—the pale young student whose failing health and hopeless poverty made of their dream of love a hollow mockery.

They made a pretty picture this bright spring morning—the two rosy-cheeked disciples of Art, the Dene sisters, who pursued their graceful vocation in this high nest among the chimney-pots and swallows of Croyden Court. The wide window-seats were strewn with the colors and brushes that in their skilled hands achieved dainty bits of scenic and floral loveliness, by which the sisters gained a modest competence. A small cabinet stand, with many convenient drawers and compartments, filled a sunny angle. On it was a jumbled litter of broken old china and costly bric-à-brac in various stages of restoration.

Near by, upon a shelf, stood a marvelous bit of medieval art—a mutilated vase, tall and slender and most exquisitely molded, and of a tint and texture so pure and fine that its pellucid luster could be likened only to the moonlight shining through sea-water. The vase was apparently without crack or flaw, save that from the obverse side a large circular piece had been removed, with a clean, sharp fracture that left a doubt whether the mutilation was the result of accident or design. Close scrutiny, however, revealed the fact that the vase had been shattered into several fragments, and so deftly and skilfully joined again as to almost defy detection. This lovely vase was Nora's special pride and property. To her trained hand and wonderful skill was due its restoration, from a mere jumble of unintelligible fragments rescued from the débris of some dingy junk shop, whither her assiduous search for the rare and curious among the discarded waifs and strays of art had led her. She was skilled in ceramics, and had served an apprenticeship at Rokewood.

"And there is no clew yet to the missing fragment of your beloved Giotto?" asked Rena, the elder of the sisters, as she diligently painted in the glowing yellow hearts of a cluster of pansies upon a disk of porcelain.

"Not the shadow of a clew, Rena," sighed Nora, regretfully, "I am beginning to fear I shall have to abandon the search, and with it the dreams of the better fortune that, I feel are somehow linked with that mysterious vase."

Rena smiled, painting on in silence.

"I am sure there is a fortune in that vase, Rena, for the one who knows how to extricate it," cried Nora, energetically, nettled by Rena's evident lukewarmness, "and that out of it many good things are yet destined to come to us, if only——"

"Like the purse of Fortunatus, with its inexhaustible wealth!" laughed Rena. "But Nora, that *if* seems inexorably in the way."

"Yes," sighed Nora, despondently, "it does. I seem to have exhausted every resource."

"And after all it might prove to be time and labor wasted, Nora. It might not be a genuine Giotto."

"Oh, but it is!" declared Nora, decidedly. "I am positive it is one of the three *amphorae* attributed to him, and known to have been in existence within the century. I have studied the drawings of the Florentine collection in the Dusseldorf Gallery, and I cannot be misled. There is a richness and purity of conception and outline that belong to Giotto alone. I am satisfied the missing fragment bears the signature of that great master, since I fail to find it upon the body of the vase."

"You are fretting yourself into a fever, Nora;" complained Rena, "your eyes have an expression of perpetually looking out for something—the unattainable, I presume; positively there is an embryo wrinkle across your nose! I have noticed several in your temper of late."

"The ravages of hope deferred, no doubt," assented Nora, good-humoredly. "Rena, dear, you do not guess the fairy fabric of bright dreams I have fashioned out of that patched-up bit of old pottery" (with an involuntary glance toward the lilies nodding in the sunshine). "To think how patiently I have toiled all these months to build up that lovely creation out of shattered ruin into almost perfect beauty; and now to be baffled, just as success seemed assured! Oh, Rena, I dreamed last night that I had finished it——"

"A bad omen, if dreams really do go by contraries," interrupted Rena, oracularly, adding a fleck of violet gold to the purple-velvet petal of her last pansy, and holding the plaque off at arm's length to note the effect. "I believe I almost hate the Giotto vase. You are making of it an uncanny sort of fetich; you think of it by day, and you dream of it by night—to the detriment of more wholesome thought, I fear."

Nora laid down the sea-green scarf upon which she was painting a bunch of creamy-leaved, scarlet-eyed Narcissus, and, turning to the window, buried her face in the cool cups of the great waxen lilies.

"It is because I know the value of the prize I strive for, Rena," she said, with a tremble in her voice. "Restored, the vase is worth hundreds, nay thousands, of dollars. Do you know what possibilities, golden and beautiful, may lie in that? Health and hope renewed for *him*, and life-long happiness for both of us! As the vase stands now it is comparatively worthless—save as a relic to be coveted by some antiquarian and curio-hunter. Rena, do you know that Mrs. Ponsonby Vansittart has offered a thousand dollars for the restored Giotto?"

"A thousand dollars!" gasped Rena, incredulously. "Is the woman quite sane, Nora?"

"She is an enthusiastic antiquarian, with the rarely fine judgment of a real virtuoso and the purse of a female Crœsus. She is crazy to possess the Giotto."

"A thousand dollars!" reiterated Rena, in a maze of bewilderment.

"And I had builded such high hopes upon the attainment of it! Not for myself alone, Rena. Little sister, you too would have shared in our good fortune." She kissed the topmost blossom of the great cluster of lilies and took up her unfinished task with a weary sigh.

Rena looked at her with soft gray eyes of compassion. "Dear little unselfish sister," she whispered, "I know of whom you are thinking. Edgar might yet be spared to us could he but seek a milder, more congenial climate."

"Evidently the lost fragment of the Giotto vase contained a fine drawing?" questioned Rena.

"Without doubt."

"And was most likely selected from the remaining fragments for that reason?"

"Assuredly it was."

"Nora, have you ever interviewed the Sieur U'Dessa, the picturesque old image vender, who inhabits some gloomy nook of Croyden Court?"

"The drunken old Greek who starves and beats poor little Toni? Certainly not. But why, pray?"

"I hardly know why, dear," returned Rena thoughtfully, "save that, in skurrying to and fro and skirmishing up and down the purlieus of the city, I did not know but that you might have carried the war into Asia Minor—made an incursion into Greece, as it were. Who knows what these prying, insatiate china and old-clo' scavengers may not pick up in the way of barter or thievery?"

"I must confess the idea had not occurred to me," said Nora. "Rena, someone is coming up the stair."

" DOWN FLASHED THE LOVELY WHITE LILY "

"Mrs. Ponsonby Vansittart!" whispered Rena, glancing hurriedly into the tiny oval mirror above the oak buffet; "I can distinguish the swish of her silk skirts a block away."

A knock sounded at the door of the *atelier*, and at Nora's bidding there entered a stout, middle-aged lady, in a sweeping robe of rustling black silk, that made a prodigious frou-frou as she moved. She was attended by an elderly gentleman, whose distinguished air and dignified bearing bore the unmistakable stamp of traveled culture.

"Good morning, young ladies," panted Mrs. Ponsonby Vansittart. sinking into the comfortable "sleepy hollow" Nora offered, and fanning herself vigorously. "A lovely morning! But, oh, those stairs! I have called to examine the Giotto vase, Miss Dene, and have taken the liberty to bring my agent, Mr. Ballentyne to pass judgment upon it. The Misses Dene, Professor Ballentyne."

Professor Urquhart Ballentyne, dilettante and virtuoso, bowed with old-world courtliness, his keen eyes, behind their gold-rimmed glasses, seeming to take in all things visible at one comprehensive glance. They alighted instantly upon the tall base, gleaming against its velvet background, and his thin face glowed as, with a hasty "Permit me," he stepped to the shelf that supported it.

"What do you say, Professor?" inquired Mrs. Ponsonby Vansittart, anxiously, "is it a genuine Giotto?"

"Unquestionably, Madam." returned the professor, taking the vase up carefully, and examining it with microscopic closeness. "This is undoubtedly the work of the great master. The missing vignette will be found to bear his unmistakable signature—an odd and beautiful conceit, madam: a bee *or* upon a grape leaf *argent*. This vase is presumably one of a trio executed by Giotto, and known as the 'Three Graces,' belonging originally to the Barberini collection. The vignette represents a segment of marsh, with a heron in flight against a luminous evening sky. Giotto was famed for his marvelous sky effects. Observe, here are yet discernible the tops of feathery reeds and grasses. Yes, this is undoubtedly the long-lost Heron Vase, that dates back to the fourteenth century. What a pity it should be thus mutilated! But even in its present condition it is worth its weight in gold, young ladies," added the professor, smiling benignly down upon Nora.

"Why, this is admirable work!" continued he, turning the vase about and scrutinizing it closely, "these joins are absolutely imperceptible, save under a strong glass. To whom are we indebted for this clever restoration?"

"To my sister, Nora," answered Rena. delightedly.

"And you have not found the missing piece, Miss Dene?" questioned Mrs. Ponsonby Vansittart, eagerly.

5

"No, Madam; I am sadly afraid I shall never find it. I have about abandoned all hope of its recovery."

"Find it, Miss Dene, and I will give you fifteen hundred dollars for the vase."

"Fifteen hundred dollars represents but a fraction of the value of the vase," interrupted the professor, coolly; "*I* will give you two thousand, Miss Dene."

"Twenty-five hundred!" bid Mrs. Ponsonby, with an angry spark beginning to kindle in her gray eyes. "I have set my heart upon its possession."

"In that case," said the professor, blandly, "I beg to withdraw my offer. Otherwise I should consider it a prize worth contending for."

Nora's eyes filled with tears.

"I will make one more effort, Madam, though I confess frankly the search seems preposterously absurd. It is like the hunt for the proverbial needle in the haystack—time and labor worse than wasted."

"Deliver the vase to me within sixty days and I will write you a check for twenty-five hundred dollars," said Madam, sententiously, making her adieus.

"Nora," said Rena, as the rustle of Mrs. Ponsonby's skirts faded in the distance, "it seems to me more than ever like a chapter out of a fairy tale—too good to be true. With that sum in hand you and Edgar might safely undertake a bridal tour of Southern Europe."

Just then a sharp cry of anger and distress sounded.

"What *is* the trouble?" ejaculated Nora, hastily thrusting her curly head out of the open window that overlooked the dismal 'court' below. Again the cry rose, mingled with shouts of derisive laughter.

"That wicked Irish Maggie is teasing poor Toni again, perhaps," she said, indignantly, craning her graceful neck to get a better view of the outbreak below.

Groups of noisy, children rioted around the open doors of the overcrowded tenements. In the midst of one of these swarms a tall, bare-legged, red-haired, but not uncomely, girl of twelve years was laughing at the futile efforts of an ill-clad and grotesquely deformed little child to reach and d:ag down the clenched hand she held high above her unkempt head. Tears were running down the pale, pinched face of the lad. His childish voice had an intonation of real grief and distress, as he tugged at the ragged sleeve.

"Maggie! Maggie!" called Nora's clear voice. "For shame! A great girl like you—to tease that poor baby. What have you taken from him, Maggie Riordon?"

"Shure, it's his blissid blue pigeon, Miss!" Maggie looked up, with eyes dancing with malicious mischief. "It's a bit av broken chany he kapes wid him, day an' night, loike it wor a rilic, miss. I axed him wud he let me see it—but sorra a bit wud he, in his own dirthy paw, avic. Now oi've a mind to smash it and fling it in the kennel."

She made a threatening demonstration that wrung a fresh wail from the little one, whose fluffy dark head barely reached her elbow. At the sound of Nora's voice the child had ceased his frantic screams but stood, sobbing softly, still clinging doggedly to the ragged sleeve.

"Give it to him this moment, Maggie—do, Maggie, like a good girl," coaxed Nora. "Give it to him and you shall have a big red apple." Miss Dene reached back and took from a basket on the window-shelf one of two rosy apples that served to eke out the sisters' frugal midday meal.

"See, Maggie! This shall be yours when you return Toni's plaything."

A cunning light flashed into Maggie's gray eyes as they wandered from the apple to the cluster of creamy, golden-dusted lilies nodding over Nora's shoulder.

"An' can Oi have wan av the pretty white posies beyant?" she questioned.

Nora hesitated, and drew back half angrily, her fair sensitive face flushing and paling. Part with even one of her treasured blooms? Fling it down to that audacious little savage, to be bandied about in unclean hands, and presently cast aside and trodden in the mire of the gutter! Her lover's gift—and each leaf and bud dearer to her than gold or gems bestowed by another! Toni was staring up at her, with big, imploring eyes, the beautiful dusky eyes of his dead Greek mother. Something in Maggie's hand glimmered with opalescent luster as she lifted it in the sunlight, with a feint of flinging it away.

"Gimme the posy, miss, or Oi'll smash the chany!" she cried. "Gimme the purty white posy an' Toni can have the apple along wid his ould blue pigeon," she repeated, in a sudden burst of generosity. "Gimme the posy afore Oi count tin or here goes! *Wan—two—tree——*"

With a deep sigh Nora turned hastily and plucked the radiant blossom.

"Put the plaything in Toni's hand first," she commanded. "and the flower is yours. So! Now, hold your apron, Maggie, and look out for your head."

Maggie caught the apple dexterously, and flung it after the retreating Toni, then stood on tip-toe with outstretched apron to receive the coveted flower. Down flashed the lovely white lily, scattering odor and gold dust as it fell. and with a shriek of rapture Maggie rushed away to exhibit her prize to her envious fellow-ragamuffins.

"Well, of all things, Nora Dene! How could you be so foolish? What would Edgar Wyand say?"

"Edgar would understand," said Nora simply. "Maggie would have kept her word, and destroyed the poor child's plaything—some toy picked up out of the gutter, no doubt, poor little beggar. If you could have but witnessed the look of adoring gratitude he flashed up at me as he ran away, hugging his recovered treasure."

The days had come and gone, and with them the breezy freshness of the springtime had departed. With early June had come the sultriness of the midsummer, and already in the over-built and densely populated portions of the city the heat had grown unendurable.

"We must get away by Saturday, at the very latest," said Rena, as the sisters lounged in their dismantled *atelier*, while the last red gleam of daylight faded, and the hot purple gloom of a breathless night came down upon the city. "Have you finished your packing, Nora? The prospect of another day like this one seems unbearable."

"Yes, I have finished—all save the yet unfinished Giotto vase. That I shall not entrust to the mercy of the baggage-smashers, but will carry it myself. And my precious lily—that is to be sent to the greenhouse early on Saturday morning."

"And so Edgar has abandoned the idea of a European tour and decided to stay in the office of Trickem & Pickem. Nora, it is sheer suicidal folly. If ever incipient consumption was written upon a human countenance it is upon Edgar Wyand's."

Nora dropped her face upon her hands with a low sob. "And he must stay on here, Rena, for the lack of a pitiful sum—pitiful, indeed, when weighed against a precious human life. Oh, my love, my love!"

She leaned her head upon the wide window-ledge with a heavy sigh, and stared up at the tremulous white stars beginning to glisten in the dark blue vault above. Rena fidgeted restlessly; the hard ticking of the little Swiss clock on the chimney-shelf seemed to set her nerves on edge.

"I have left out some odds and ends that are to be the perquisites of good-natured Mrs. Riordon," she said. "since she has kindly offered to look after our small possessions here during our stay at Ripple Brook Farm."

"And the jar of strawberry-jam for the sick child," interpolated Nora, lifting her head from the window-ledge. "Poor little Toni! It was angelically kind of the good soul to take that motherless mite and care for him so tenderly when his drunken old grandfather deserted him."

"Your friend, Mrs. Riordon, is an angel, Nora."

Nora smiled faintly. Her idea of an angel hardly accorded with the appearance presented by fat and frowsy. but warm-hearted, Mrs. Riordon.

"She is a born Irish woman, Rena. You could hardly expect her to be less than kind and generous."

A quick, light step, like the patter of bare feet, sounded without the chamber door; somebody knocked timidly

" BELIKES IT'S SOMETHIN' HE WUD BE AFTHER GIVIN' YE, MISS," WHISPERED MRS. RIORDON

on the lintel, and at Rena's startled "Who's there?" a ragged little apparition crept out of the gloom of the landing and stood on the threshold, twisting the corners of its tattered apron, its great eyes full of pleased wonder as they peered about the bare but potlessly tidy room.

"It's Miss Nora bees wanted, shure," said Maggie Riordon, awkwardly. "Little Toni, he bees very bad the night. He's out of his head, allanna, an' axes for Miss Nora continooal. Mither said wud ye be so kind as to come an spake till him. Mebbe it wud quiet him. He can't last till marnin, the docther says."

"I will go instantly," said Nora, rising hurriedly. "Run on, Maggie, and say that I am coming."

It was a miserable, mean and unwholesome place— the ill-kept, low-ceiled, and ill-ventilated room where the little hunchback lay, breathing his cramped and colorless young life out in labored gasps. The quick tears sprung to Nora's eyes, as, leaning above the sick child, and laying her cool hand upon his fevered forehead, she felt the small hot fingers close upon her own convulsively. He was coming up out of the depths of unconsciousness for a moment, and, like a drowning child, he caught and clung to the pitying hand of this good angel.

The dying child looked up at her with wide imploring eyes; looked up at her out of the shadow and mystery of Death. His pale lips moved, but the words he would have uttered reached her straining ears in broken accents only. With his disentangled hand he fumbled weakly about the pillow that supported his hot head. The great hollow dark eyes grew yet more passionately imploring in their yearning appeal—like the eyes of some stricken dumb creature in its death agony.

"What is it he wishes, Mrs. Riordon?" asked Nora, crying softly, and turning to that motherly soul, who sat at the head of the low couch, fanning the sick child assiduously.

"Belikes it's somethin' he wud be afther givin' ye, Miss," whispered Mrs. Riordon in return, as she moistened the white lips with a bit of cracked ice—a luxury provided by Nora's thoughtfulness. "He's hilt it in his hand iver since he was tuk down—a rubbishin' bit av chany wid a

picter on it; an' all last night an' to-day, aven in his slape, he kipt a mutterin' about Miss Norry an' the blue pigeon."

"It's under the piller now," volunteered Maggie, from the foot of the bed, where she sat huddled in a heap on the floor. "It's the bit av ould chrockery Oi sthole from him the day. He never lits go av it, an' he tould me if he died it was for Miss Norry."

"What is it, Toni?" asked Miss Dene, softly, bending close to the moving lips. "What can I do for you, poor little lad?"

The wasted hand crept gropingly under the pillow; the dying child, with a supreme effort, seemed to shake off the lethargy that bound him. He presently withdrew his hand and laid something in Nora's hand—something that glimmered in the faint light of the sick-room.

"I wanted to give it to you, my pretty lady," he said in liquid, broken English—"my lovely blue pigeon! You gave the beautiful white flower for it—the flower of our Blessed Lady—and now it is yours."

Nora had turned white as the dying child. She held the gleaming something up to the light with a shaking hand. Yes, there it was—the lustrous circle of pellucid tint and texture—the marvelous handiwork of the divine old master! And exquisitely limned upon the fragment was the bold free drawing of a stretch of marsh; and clear and sharp against the luminous background the silhouette of a crested heron with broad wings strained in flight.

"Where did you get this, Toni?—oh, Toni, you have indeed bequeathed to me a precious legacy!"

The dark eyes glowed as he gasped painfully, "I found it, a long time ago, among the broken pottery in an old cellar, where we once lived. It is beautiful—it is like the spring—and the sunshine—and the blue sky I see— just over there——" And, with a long-drawn sigh of infinite content, the fluffy head fell back, the dark eyes closed upon the troubles of this world, the small voice ceased forever.

And Nora, with eyes filled with tearful gratitude and rapture, in passionate wonder and amaze, clasped in her hand the long-sought fragment of her precious Giotto vase!

THE LARGEST MUSICAL CLUB OF AMERICAN WOMEN

By LIDA ROSE McCABE

HOW a handful of women sowed a seed a score of years ago, nurtured it through varying vicissitudes, and when about to despair of fruition suddenly wakened to fame, prosperity and public recognition as art educators, is the record of the Women's Musical Club of Ohio's Capital.

With the opening of the season of 1901-02, the club's associate membership had dwindled to ninety-seven, a lamentable falling off from the two hundred strong reached in former years. In the fall of 1904, however, more than 1,200 members enrolled, fifty applications were filed and hundreds turned from the doors of its first artist recital, while a goodly sum was in the treasury, and a concert grand Steinway piano added to its original possession—a Chickering which had been bought in tentative days.

How the miracle was wrought is not "another" story, but THE story, which it is our purpose to tell for the guidance and encouragement of organizations struggling along on the same or closely similar lines.

After the manner of the Great Middle West, it remains good form in Columbus to bewail the lack of musical culture and popular appreciation, while, the truth must be told, dwellers in the capital city in their own way have always been more or less a music-loving community. As a serious cult or esthetic indulgence music, until very recent years, has been, however, almost wholly confined to the foreign element.

In the reflected glory of a Maennerchor and Liederkranz of more than fifty years' standing, with prizes won in State and national Saengerfests, and a Welsh Choral with laurels wrested at home and abroad, the Capital in former years has been perfectly content to bask, bestirring itself at intervals to sustain a local orchestra of no mean merit.

That it fostered the early ambition of its famous townswoman, the lamented and widely known Lilian Bailey Henschel, wife of the still more widely known George Henschel, is to the music-lovers of that city no less a matter of pride than that from thence sprung to prominence the Al. G. Field's Minstrels.

MRS. ELLA MAY SMITH,
PRESIDENT WOMEN'S MUSICAL CLUB

Of national renown of long standing is its Republican Glee Club, which has sung five Presidents into the White House, and recently in a prize contest for original campaign music elicited meritorious compositions, not only from its own members but from some of the best talent of the country.

From the Americanized foreign element has sprung largely in recent years two men's singing clubs of more than local repute — the Orpheus and the Arion. Superior work and the introduction of Old World artists at public concerts have enabled these clubs to contribute not a little to the general musical culture. But most of this growth was in embryo, feeling its way as it were to popular favor; no attempt had been made by women, outside occasional mixed chorus, to band together in Apollo's name until 1884, when a few congenial souls under the inspiration of Miss Mary W. Failing resolved to "meet round" in the cause of good music.

There were no associate members, no critic, no public, only a dozen music-lovers interpreting for each other's pleasure the best musical thought according to their light.

The Club waxed until it outgrew the privacy and informality of its swaddling-clothes. With increased membership came a constitution, the hiring of a hall, and public recitals. In healthy sequence developed ambition to present great artists. Thither came in time, under the Club's auspices, Adele aus der Ohe, Edward McDowell, Mark Hambourg, Leonora Jackson and Louis Elson, the eminent musician pedagogue. These notable achievements were followed by what is known in the vulgar parlance of the market as a slump. In some unaccountable way interest and enthusiasm became laggards. Gradually associate membership fell, as has been said, from two hundred to ninety-seven. It looked for a time as if the labor of years was to be wiped out at one fell blow.

And the time?—never had it been riper for telling work. A generation had grown up since the Club's inception, grown up to profit by the musical instruction of the public schools (always of a high order in Columbus), while interurban railroads were daily bringing the city into closer personal touch with a score or more of

CLARA HERTENSTEIN, CELLO

progressive towns possessed of growing college-bred populace.

At this crisis rose a petticoated Orpheus, who unconsciously for years had been in training to lead just such a disheartened band into the Elysian Fields of the Heavenly Maid.

"A chiel amang them takin' notes" had been Mrs. Ella May Smith. Industrious student of the history and the literature of music, a composer of talent, a progressive teacher of the piano, Mrs. Smith had struggled for years to gain a foothold in the conservative community, meanwhile raising and educating a family of five children as few mothers of the old school could have done, all preaching to the contrary.

As a music critic on a local paper, Mrs. Smith had acquired something of the resourcefulness and dispatch of newspaper "go," and moreover had the courage of her convictions.

Fearful of the Club's dissolution, Mrs. Smith addressed for the first time an assembly of women. "Why not bring David Bispham to Columbus?" she suggested. The audacity of the proposition took away the members' breath. Had they not worked wearily and in vain to woo back renegade subscribers?

"There's some money in the treasury," continued Mrs. Smith. "If everyone will lend an energetic and helping hand it can be done. I am positive."

To the credit of the Club and backsliding members, all rallied heartily to the proposition, and, electing Mrs. Smith president, a new era set in.

Not only did Mr. David Bispham open the season of 1901-02, but Madame Schumann-Heink followed. Aside from these two artists' recitals there was a lecture by Arthur Farwell, and eight afternoon and two public Club recitals by the active members.

From ninety-seven the membership sprung to eight hundred. The force and influence of the Club as an art educator was publicly acknowledged. And how was the metamorphosis wrought?

When Bispham had been secured for the recital, printed circulars in the form of heart-to-heart talks were sent out by the Club, addressed to former patrons and members of the Club, asking for a renewal of their subscriptions.

Circulars were likewise mailed to all known or suspected music-lovers in neighboring towns. Not only was the coming of Bispham announced, but the possibility of Schumann-Heink intimated. The former price of season tickets, three dollars, was retained. It covered not only the Club's private and public recitals, but included the artists' recitals. In order to hear Bispham, however, season tickets must be purchased before the first artist recital.

The response was electric. The Bispham recital was the social affair of the season. It netted the Club more than two thousand dollars. On the occasion of the Schumann-Heink recital a veritable mob besieged the box-office. Lukewarm associates of former days, failing to secure seats upon the presentation of their tickets at the eleventh hour, threatened to sue the president. Overwhelmed by the unprecedented demand for seats, and powerless to increase the auditorium's capacity, Madame Schumann-Heink was telegraphed asking if fifty seats might be put upon the stage.

"Just leave me place to stand, that is all I ask," was the incomparable contralto's characteristically cheerful reply to the request. But even with this added space it was found necessary when the evening arrived to turn many people away.

MRS. TILLIE GEMUENDER LORD, ONE OF THE EARLIEST MEMBERS OF THE CLUB

MRS. CHRISTIAN C. BORD, VIOLA

In consequence of this courageous action of the members in engaging first-class talent for their recitals, the taking the bull by the horns at a propitious moment, so to speak, the Club opened the season of 1904–05 with more than twelve hundred associate members and a long list of applicants. The officers serve without salary. The active members pay one dollar annually for the privilege of playing before the associate members. The price of a single admission to a Club afternoon recital is twenty-five cents; to a public evening concert, fifty cents. All service is rendered cheerfully for the sole object of

with the artist recitals. The active members are thirty-eight, including a string quartet; the photographs of some of its members accompany this article. The Executive Board is ever on the alert to increase the active membership, but the standard of admission rises yearly.

Consider this season's artist recitals! In quality and variety what musical program of any prominent city of the East—certainly not Boston or New York—can match them?

Beginning with the "elect among women pianists," Fanny Bloomfield-Zeisler, followed by one

MISS MAUDE COCKINS, SECOND VIOLIN

MRS. CHARLES BRADFIELD MURREY,
VICE-PRESIDENT WOMEN'S MUSICAL CLUB

developing the musical talent of its members and to stimulate musical culture in Columbus.

A subject for sketch artists was the scene at the box-office preparatory to the coming of Fanny Bloomfield-Zeisler, who opened in October the first artist recital. As early as six o'clock in the morning ticket-holders or their representatives stood in line. When the hour for the opening of the recital arrived the city's cultured and fashionable people, together with large delegations from neighboring towns, filled every available space in the Board of Trade Auditorium, which has a seating capacity of some fourteen hundred.

"Can this be the 'struggling little club' I played before a few years ago?" asked America's foremost pianist. "Never have I played to a more prosperous organization than it has developed into."

In keeping with the scope of former years, the Club continues to study the composers by country. Last year was devoted to the little-known music of Russia. The Club recitals, six in number, alternate

of the five acknowledged American pianist-composers, Arthur Foote, comes Maude Powell, one of the world's best woman violinists; Allen Spencer and Pauline Woltmann, of Chicago, in program of ancient classics descending in chronological order to the modern romantic period; Madame Lilian Blauvelt in song recital; the season to close with the club's gifted vice-president, Mrs. Charles Bradfield Murrey as piano soloist with the Cincinnati Orchestra.

To stimulate interest in the Foote recital, the Club through its affiliations with organists and public choir singers had the musical programs of the leading churches on the Sunday preceding his coming made up wholly of the pianist-composer's compositions.

The Woman's Musical Club of Ohio's Capital is to-day the largest of its kind in the United States, if not in the world. What the organization has accomplished and what it will yet achieve are possible to every kindred organization with the courage to dare and to DO.

THE FLOWERS of TREES

By CRAIG S. THOMS

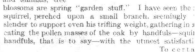

IT WOULD doubt-less be a surprise to many to be told that certain trees have flowers. The blossoms of apple, cherry and

before it, but by the time they pay their initial visit the blossoms of the silver maples have already opened, and I have seen half a dozen red-breasts feeding up-on them in a single high tree-top.

To certain birds and animals, tree

COTTONWOOD CATKINS

blossoms are spring "garden stuff." I have seen the squirrel, perched upon a small branch, seemingly slender to support even his trifling weight, gathering in cating the pollen masses of the oak by handfuls—squi handfuls, that is to say—with the utmost satisfacti

FLOWER CLUSTERS OF THE HAW

BLOOM OF THE MOUNTAIN-ASH

To certa birds the bl soms are hu ing preserv Many leaf b have not thrown off t winter jack when the ki lets come fr the South, numero

RED ELM BLOSSO

plum, of course, we have seen in orchards; and those of the wild crab, choke-cherry and haw we have gathered in the woods, but how many have observed the blossoms of the maples, elms and box-elders? The large white clusters of the mountain-ash we cannot pass with-out admiring, but the unobtrusive blossoms of oak, ash and hackberry are far more interesting. The glory of the catalpa clusters, each one of which is a bouquet, catches every eye, yet the waxy blossoms of the linden, hanging at the tips of their curiously crossing stems, and nearly hidden by the abundant blanket of leaves, will prove much more inviting to any flower lover who examines them closely.

In the very early spring some trees seem about to put forth their leaves, and then suddenly to change their minds. Such are the maples, elms, cottonwoods and ashes, but strange to say their blossoms appear before their leaves, and they are blooming. The white elms even mature their seeds, which literally clothe the tree with green before a leaf bud is open far enough to attract any notice.

Other trees put forth their leaves and flowers at one and the same time. Such are the box-elders, hackberries, walnuts and oaks, as may be seen from the accompanying illustrations if one has not the living subject to examine. Still others have abundant foliage before their blossoms appear. Such are the catalpas, mountain-ashes and lindens.

One often wonders where the first robins secure their food. They arrive with the first spring zephyr, and often

LINDEN OR BASSWOOD FLOWERS

flower buds are open, and their irresistible nectar has attracted new-born insects in abundance, which fact the kingly little hunt-ers are not long in finding, you may be sure.

Trees, like plants, present many

variations in the character of their blossoms. One group has the pistillate flowers on one tree and the staminate on another, the pollen being carried from stamen to pistil by the wind or by insects. Of these the box-elder, pictured on this page and again on page 689, is one of the best and most familiar examples. As nearly always in this group, the staminate flowers are the more conspicuous. The long, drooping clusters of stamen filaments seem to drape the box-elder branches with the most graceful and delicate lace-work. The tree never looks more beautiful than just before it begins to shed its pollen; at that time the leaves are young and hold all the charm of new-born life; their almost luminous green gives to the lighter yet duller tint of the "lace-work drapery" an exquisitely gauzy effect. When, however, the anthers are emptied of their pollen they turn dark, and until the filaments have dropped off or the rapidly growing leaves have covered them, the tree presents a somewhat forlorn and bedraggled appearance. As in all cases where fertilization depends upon the wind, the amount of pollen dust is almost beyond belief. Shake ever so slightly the limb of a staminate box-elder when the anthers are opening and a perfect rain of pollen will descend before your eyes.

A second group of trees has separate staminate and pistillate flowers, but both blooming on the same tree. Prominent in this group is the familiar black walnut, whose pollen masses may be plainly seen hanging in long green catkins from the bare portions of the branches, while the pistillate flowers are safely ensconced among the already well-developed leaf clusters at the twig-ends.

Of this group the oaks are also members, and the oak in blossom is a good example of the fact that many things in Nature are not beautiful until closely examined. Its bark is rough, its limbs are angular and jagged; viewed as a whole, it possesses little of beauty until

FLOWERS OF THE BOX-ELDER

HACKBERRY FLOWERS

your hand one of the daintiest sights in all the woodland. The beauty is largely in these new-born groups. Though so small, they are already perfect in outline, and

STAMINATED AND PISTILLATED SILVER MAPLE BLOSSOMS

PISTILLATED FLOWERS OF GREEN ASH

the delicate, velvety, baby leaves, which are of an exquisite pinkish-green, are a lovely sight, that fairly ravishes the heart of a tree lover.

To this group likewise belongs the honey locust, which has flowers that are exceedingly fragrant, so much so that a grove of, or even three or four, honey locusts in blossom will send their delightful odor for a long distance on the air, but which cannot be said to possess beauty. In the tree as a whole, however, there is beauty to be found in abundance. Notwithstanding its barricades of bristling thorns, wherever it has room it is peculiarly symmetrical, and in form and proportion is quite similar to the sugar maple. The flowers are not unlike the wistaria in shape and are of a beautiful creamy whiteness.

In this group, also, must be placed the green ash, whose pistillate flowers are as conspicuous as the staminate ones. The illustration shows them arranged in large masses, sometimes completely encircling the twigs, or grouped in club-like bunches at their ends.

A third group of trees have what are called "perfect flowers"—flowers combining both stamens and pistils. Here are found most trees with showy blossoms, such as our orchards boast—apple, cherry, plum, peach, etc. Yet, as is frequently the case, some blossoms of rarest beauty make little show. Those of the hackberry present even a disheveled appearance when viewed hanging upon the tree, as may be seen by the photograph on this page. A jumble of young leaves, bracts and scales are all massed and curled in seeming confusion, but when a single flower is closely inspected, it is seen to be a very delicate structure, and one looks up at the tall, stately tree in wonder that its beginning should be such a small, fragile thing.

I presume that all who know the trees have favorites among their flowers, just as people do among the flowers of plants, and my favorite is the linden. To be sure, the

gowned in its ample leaves of burnished green, but detach a twig when the long, slender strings of pollen masses are waving in the wind under the new-born leaf groups, and you hold in

choke-cherries put forth numerous white fragrant clusters, which attract all the nectar-sipping insects in the vicinity; and the haws fairly illumine their exquisite leaves with bunches of glowing white petals, until their stubborn thorns are quite forgotten. The common locusts hang out their heavy white clusters among a delicate drapery of drooping leaves, and one eagerly gathers the blooms for house decorations. Only the other day I saw a number of these trees so laden with masses of blossoms that the small twigs bent under their weight. Such a buzzing of bees was everywhere about them that one might have thought himself approaching a hive. The locust blossoms are beautiful, but they are so many and so crowded together that one is most charmed at the first look, and soon grows weary of them.

Just across the road from where the bees were gathering honey among the locusts stood a mountain-ash in half bloom. What is true of the wild rose is preeminently true of the mountain-ash—its flowers are most beautiful when half of them are in bud and half in bloom. When in full bloom, its flat clusters are too crowded for beauty at

PISTILLATED CATKIN OF WILLOW

close view, but when half the blossoms are in bud, and their folded petals look like so many snow-white pearls, the large cluster, which is always at the end of a branch and encircled by long, compound leaves, has a beauty that is unique among tree flowers. An artist once said to me that in a good painting, no matter where the eye fell upon the canvas it was led at once to the main object. This quality the mountainash flower-groups possess to a wonderful degree.

BLOSSOMS OF THE CHOKE-CHERRY

Each in itself is a complete bouquet, and wherever the eye may fall upon the radiating leaves, it is constantly led to the exquisite cluster of white at their center.

But I was saying that I loved the linden blossoms. There is something about a small flower that touches a responsive chord in me. I was descending the Bitter Root Mountains in Northern Idaho one day—following a ravine, in the bottom of which trickled a small mountain brook. The flowers I came upon were of many kinds, some as high as my head, but more than all of them, to me, was a dainty little pink-and-white blossom that nodded upon a stem only a few inches long, and nestled trustfully at the base of a great rock. And so, though I may be compelled to admit that the flowers of other trees are more beautiful, I love the linden most. It comes late in June, and is the companion of the matchless catalpa; it nestles modestly under the ample protection of broad leaves as they

STAMINATE FLOWERS OF BOX ELDER

flap, like great elephant ears, to warn intruders away. That the blossoms may have ample room to unfold their white waxen petals, they are attached to the ends of delicate, round stemlets, which hang at the end of the strong, winged stem in an orderly network of crosses. Here there is no crowding and no hurrying, for in the North the linden is among the last to bloom, and its flowers, when closely examined in blossom, in stem and in wing, have a charm of symmetry, order and beauty rarely surpassed.

Among other tree blossoms which are not here illustrated, but which are well known in almost all localities are the catalpa, mentioned above, which has a bell-shaped flower not unlike a tulip in coloring; the magnolia, that queen of trees, with its broad green leaves which are an adornment in themselves, and its great creamy blossoms of exquisite fragrance, and its cousin, the tulip tree, the leaf, blossom and fruit of which are all things of beauty. Then the chestnut tree must not be forgotten, for its flowers are dainty things, borne on a long stalk, the clusters resembling fringed tassels, and have a delicate fragrance which seems to possess a great attraction for the bees.

THE CALL OF SPRING
By BLANCHE ALLYN BANE

THIS is the song that I sing to you,
 This the boon from your hand, I pray
Come with me into the beckoning blue,
 " Over the hills and far away!"

Now is the time of the singing of birds,
 Now is the spring of souls to-day
Hark to the mystic, the luring words,
 " Over the hills and far away!"

Hand-maids meek of the virgin year;
 Violet nuns in their hoods of gray—
Show the path for our going, Dear,
 " Over the hills and far away!"

Now the winter is past and gone,
 " Spring!" is the word the breezes say,
And you will be glad as I lead you on,
 ' Over the hills and far away!"

DOORWAYS & ARCHES

THE architectural lines in the interior of a house are not often studied by the home-maker until some problem connected with its furnishing comes up. Yet these are intimately connected with the results that, as a whole, are striven for by everyone interested in home beautifying.

When a house is to be rented it is critically examined to see if the furniture on hand will suit the spaces. Up-stairs and down, parlor, dining-room and chambers, even the kitchen and bathroom, come into the careful survey in which, piece by piece, the articles on hand are, in imagination, put into possible positions.

"I have spent two weeks hunting for a house," says Mrs. Smith to her neighbor, Mrs. Brown, at their five - minute chat in market or at the grocer's counter, "and, do you know, I can't find one that I can put my sideboard in."

"When we moved last spring," responds Mrs. Brown, after a pause, in which her order for the day's supplies has been entered in the clerk's book, "I was in despair about my daughter's piano. It is one of those out-of-date, square old things that would not bring fifty dollars if it was sold, but perfectly good in tone, and as we can't afford a more expensive instrument merely for style, I have to plan for enough space to put it in. Finally, ridiculous as it may seem to one who has not had a similar experience, we had to move quite out of the neighborhood we preferred just to accommodate that stupid piano."

The furniture problem is of importance when changing an abode, yet consideration must also be paid at such times to the other furnishings for the house. The floor coverings, for instance, that in one home are exactly suited to their surroundings, are often quite useless when a change is made into another dwelling. To fit the window curtains from

COLUMNS IN A DRAWING-ROOM

690

one place to another is a further source of perplexity, and the adapting of old portières to doorways and arches is not at all a simple task for the housekeeper.

To the dweller in rented houses this fitting of furnishings for floors, doors and windows often brings into prominence an irritating restriction of interior lines, of spaces that no amount of ingenuity can harmonize, of walls that are impossible to bring into accord with furniture, coverings and draperies.

The builder of a house, on the other hand, has opportunities and advantages unknown to the tenant for suiting his furnishings already in possession to the new habitation, and no keener pleasure can be indulged in than the conjuring up of air-castles that, in the course of time, are realized in concrete form, in which the new (house) is incorporated with the old (furnishings).

In the treatment of archways and doors there is more of art and a greater utility than appears to the uninitiated. Within a few centuries there has come about a very marked difference in the interiors of houses, in the substitution of openings for doors. Formerly an entrance was made into a room only by a door that definitely closed away the rest of the house. The single door, however, was thought to be inadequate for entertainments, and a double door was invented, which in time was made to slide into the wall. This sliding-door has made the way for an opening in which no door whatever appears.

In vivid contrast to that olden time we now see one room thrown into another by the lowering of a beam from the ceiling, the forming of an arch or the introduction of pillars. A small flat or apartment divided in one of these ways gives the effect of more breathing space in a limited amount of room than when each portion is closed off by itself with a door. An equally good turn is done a room of imposing

screen is therefore desirable;
or the hanging may be
needed across the closed doors
to deaden the sound and prevent drafts. Besides these
utilitarian offices, a portière,
by its texture and color, con-
tributes to the decoration of
the room, and the addition
of sliding - doors should not
set aside the enjoyment of
this feature.

The student of interior
decoration knows that the
portière is not a modern discovery. Years and years ago
tapestries were hung against
walls and across doors to
keep out the cold currents of
air without thought to their
esthetic element. With the
coming of the sliding - door
(which was often too heavy to
be easily shifted) a hanging
again came into existence for
its earlier purpose, and its
adoption has become so general that it may be regarded as
a most convenient household
fixture that has come to stay.

A SQUARE OPENING INTO A DINING-ROOM

dimensions when it is partially broken
up with columns or arches, although
the aim is quite opposed to the first
proposition. But, like every device
that is originated in the attempt to
make the house beautiful, due restraint
in the introduction of an opening is
essential or the privacy of the home
will be done away with.

The sliding-door is a transition between the door on hinges and the
archway or opening, preceded by the
double door that folded back on
either side against the wall. The
sliding - door gives more wall space
than the folding-doors, and is generally adopted in the latest building.
In many instances, too, the sliding-
door may not need to be particularly
in evidence for the entire year, yet at
certain seasons be gladly welcomed.
The possibility of such a demand
makes the cautious builder provide,
along with the wide opening which is
popularly preferred, the sliding-door
that may be put aside until it is
wanted. Sometimes the question
comes up whether with sliding-doors
to hang a portière, and the answer
must depend upon the conditions of
each specific place. The doors may not always be in
use, or they may be too heavy to draw, and a partial

How often, however, do we see the idea of usefulness
for which the portière stands completely lost in an

591

excessive outward application of ornament. The material is "made up" with braid, fringe, appliqué, linings until the simplicity of its purpose disappears amid its ornate accessories. The proper placing of the portière is another part of the house furnishing which is very frequently misunderstood.

In none of the illustrations of doorways and arches is the portière adopted. In the drawing-room the columns are an architectural contribution to the room, and the open spaces at either side break up the space without shutting off the vista. The opening from the living-room into the dining-room would lose its dignity if a rod and curtains were admitted between the broad pillars. Instead, when the dining-room is being prepared for the meals a large screen is drawn before the opening.

The rounded archway between hall and library has no convenient position for the rod and sockets requisite for supporting a portière, and the throwing of the two parts of the house together gives a hospitable impression as soon as one enters the front door. A vestibule effect is attained in the Colonial hallway by the archway making the front hall a complete little entrance by itself, with the stairs in the background. The introduction of a portière would destroy the picture that the front door makes from the other end of the hall, and hide the landscape that is brought into the house when the upper portion of the Dutch door is ajar.

Where not to hang a portière is well suggested in the illustrations; yet, in places as unsuited as those pictured, one often finds a hanging filling neither practical nor artistic ends.

A portière in a doorway between a dining-room and kitchen is an evidence of the housekeeper's lack of good sense, for, in this position, a material of any kind would first absorb and then diffuse the odors of cooking. A bathroom portière, in something of the same way, would not be considered by the thoughtful very sanitary. When openings at these places need shelter an adjustable screen may take the place of a hanging. Another really dangerous position for a portière is at the head of a flight of stairs, or even before one or two steps. A back staircase may tempt the inexperienced to conceal its presence with a portière, but it is at too great a risk.

A VESTIBULE MADE   BY AN ARCH

If a good quality of material for the portière may be afforded, the question is still to be settled as to a single or double faced variety. Regular portières with two lengths to each pair are manufactured, and, pleasant to record, they are less showy in design and softer in coloring than they were a few years ago.

A material that is the same on both sides, or so nearly the same that it is not noticeable, needs only a hem at the top wide enough to carry the hook that is slipped into the ring, a wider hem at the bottom and narrow hems on each side. Sometimes the selvage takes the place of a hem at the sides. When two single-faced materials are to be used for a portière, the hems must be made before putting the two together; then the brass hooks are slipped between the top hems and sewed securely. Sometimes a lining of canton flannel is added to give thickness and warmth. The bottom hems are left each one by itself, and not fastened together, as one or the other will sag from time to time and require adjusting.

The portière should clear the floor without touching it. Loopings and drapings are not necessary, but a pulley attachment for heavy draperies is essential if they are to be kept in shape. Two pulley cords are threaded through rings and at either end they are drawn over traverse rings. The ends of the cord terminate in brass handles by which they are pulled, closing the portières without touching the material.

The brass hooks sewed to the portières' top hem are much neater than the safety-pin. In a single doorway one breadth of the usual fifty-inch goods is sufficient. In a double doorway six feet wide two breadths (each made into one curtain) are required. The extra width is put into box or side plaits at the top, or it may make its own natural folds if the hooks are sewed five inches apart on the top hem.

Two kinds of brass poles are sold for the doorway. One is of brass tubing and the other is a wooden pole covered with brass. The former is the more expensive, more durable and better in appearance than the latter. With a narrow opening and a light drapery, a wooden pole to match the woodwork may be used, but a wide span and a thick material require a metal support resting in sockets between the framework.

Dolly and the Easter Chickens

Dolly went to pay a call on her Easter
    chicks;
Thought they were a jolly crowd, full of
    funny tricks.

Tried to stroke their yellow down. "C
    ning fings!" said she:
"Does you miss your mama, dears? Co
    an' play wif me."

At her bidding thick they thronged, till she in
    dismay
Left her big straw hat behind, screamed and
    ran away.

"Little goose," the chickens said, "mak
    such a fuss!
All we wanted was to play. She invited u

IN THE INTEREST of BEAUTY

By
BERTHA HASBROOK

V.—A GYMNASIUM FOR A DOLLAR

OU can have it in your own home. You can fit it up without even a man to help. You can thrive upon it and grow lovely upon it, and meanwhile save all the fat fees which a glibly convincing gymnasium teacher wou'd otherwise be comfortably pocketing at your expense.

To be sure, there are certain kinds of apparatus which you cannot well imitate in your own home unless that home be of unusual size or possess an old-fashioned attic that spreads above the house from end to end. But you can have all that is necessary to an all-round physical training. The most up-to-date gymnasiums are doing away with elaborate apparatus, anyway, so you can boast of modernness. It is claimed by new thinkers that the gymnasium of the nineteenth century, during which physical training for women was a fad rather than a science, overworked women criminally and that much of the heavy apparatus used was responsible for this. If that apparatus were used discreetly it would be safe to keep it but teachers and girls are both alike ambitious and they are likely to overdo a good thing. Just because a girl's muscles are strong enough to lift a large iron dumb-bell, is no proof that she is physically able to endure the strain of doing so and preserving her health. The pulley weights were too often overloaded, the rowing machines were used too vigorously without long enough rests between.

Since the most approved methods order simple apparatus, then simple apparatus it must be. With four pieces, the sum total of which need not be over a dollar in cost, you can develop every part of your body and be prepared to enter into competition with a girl who has had gymnasium training.

The one drawback to such a system is that it will be hard to keep up the interest alone, so if there is a sister or a chum

THE BAR SUPPORTED
BY TWO CHAIRS

handy, put an arm around her and coax her to go into this home athletic work with you. Tell her that you can guarantee her a fuller throat, a prouder chest, a rounder arm and rosier cheeks.

The most expensive piece of appa'atus is the bar, and this cannot be set down at any absolute price. A bar sold in a sporting goods store is beautifully finished, supplied with elaborate fixtures, and offered at a good round sum. But, whether you live in a big town or a small one, you surely know of some job carpenter who has on hand a bit of lumber that he can finish off for you Ash, hickory or some similar wood must be used to insure strength. The bar must be smoothed so that your hands will not suffer; no further finish is needed. If you care to devote a room or an attic to the gymnasium, then you may go to the expense of having the bar supported by brackets of some kind; but I am considering the apparatus that can be introduced into any house and hidden in a closet overnight without upsetting a room for the sake of it. The bar supported by two chairs, two tables, or any articles that give a convenient height, will give work to your muscles. Let us allow seventy-five cents to the carpenter; the price he will charge will vary according to whether he does much work for you, whether he happens to have the proper piece of wood on hand, and, also, according to his disposition.

For ten cents you can buy a bit of rope, enough to skip with. Avoid manila, it twists. Hemp or cotton rope will serve excellently. A three-eighth-inch cotton rope is the best. Again you have the opportunity to spend more money if you like, for jumping-ropes with gaily decorated handles are to be had in the shops, but if you are going to keep within the original dollar, wrap the ends of the rope about your hands and be satisfied.

For another ten cents you can buy all the inch-wide cotton elastic that you need for a neck and wrist exerciser. One end of the strip must be fastened to the wall; the other should be made into a long loop to be slipped over the head.

For five cents your grocer will furnish you a barrel hoop, which you can wrap with a strip of cloth, and so avoid the risk of splinters.

Place the bar high enough to allow your legs to swing freely when you draw yourself up by your arms. Begin by merely raising yourself as high as you can while clasping the bar, and holding yourself quietly in this position for several counts. Increase the length of time day by day. The arms feel this effort all the way from wrists up, and the shoulder muscles work as well. Simple vaulting over the bar with the hand clasping it; a running jump over it, provided the room is long enough to allow this; or a standing jump will start the blood to tingling and the muscles will feel the wholesome tugging that they need to keep them sturdy.

The jumping-rope has long been famous as a flesh reducer. It is this because you can jump rapidly enough to burn away superfluous tissues. Hard exercise with it tears down flesh, a mild use of it will build up shapely legs in miraculous fashion. The more fancy steps you introduce into your jumping the better, if increasing the calf measurement is your end and aim. Any fancy dance steps aid this upbuilding. Alternate with left and right foot, and introduce double skips if you can. If you are trying to do away with avoirdupois, never mind the fancy steps. Go to work with a will to jump steadily until you are tired and perspiring. This does not mean that you are to overwork a weak heart; you must be your own judge of what is best for you. But pounds do not drop away before gentle gymnastics. You must

work hard if you are to accomplish anything perceptible in this line. Skip rapidly for awhile, one foot foremost, then jump with both feet until you are glad to drop into a chair.

Perhaps you wonder what is the use of a rope for all this. You could go through the motions of jumping without it. But recollect that all the time your arms and shoulders and chest are coming in for their share

THE JUMPING-ROPE AS A FLESH REDUCER

of the benefit. Throwing the rope brings all the muscles of the upper body into play, and they appreciate the fact and show their gratitude by giving you beautiful curves.

Hoop exercises are infinite in number, and may be specialized as you wish. For the chest, use the hoop in motions above the head and near the shoulders. For the hips, waist and abdomen, take the trunk twisting and bending exercises with it, and so on. Hold the hoop upright on the floor before you, clasp it with a hand on each side, raise it above the head and lower it until it is against your back, the hands grasping it a little above the shoulder level. This position forces the chest forward and the shoulders back. Hold it for a few seconds, then return to position and continue in two counts. Raise it above the head, inhaling; lower it, exhaling. Hold it before you in such a position that your face appears in the middle of it. Keeping it so, bend the trunk right and left. These are only a few of the possible movements. The hoop may be combined with mat work. Lying extended on a mattress on the floor, put the hoop over your ankles and draw them up and toward you until the legs are vertical. This is an excellent hip exercise.

The bit of elastic ribbon may look very insignificant, but upon it depends the shapeliness of your neck. With the elastic to offer resistance, you must bend the neck forward, backward, right and left, all the time discouraging the double chin and filling out the hollows. The same exercises either develop or reduce, according to how rapidly and violently you use them. Stand away from the elastic at such a distance that you can just reach it when both it and your arm are extended full length. Clasp it, stretch it toward you by force of wrist alone, relax and repeat. Go through the same motion, using the middle finger alone. Wrists and forearms will soon tell the tale of improvement.

Wrists, arms, shoulders, chest, hips, waist, abdomen, legs, neck —are you not well provided with gymnasium apparatus? Don't forget that it is all worthless unless your clothing is loose and your window is wide open.

THE NECK AND WRIST EXERCISE

VERSE FOR EASTERTIDE AND

EASTER

By BERTHA L. STINE

BENEATH her coverlid of snow
    The young Spring sleeps,
And dreaming, weeps
For all the treasures Winter seized
And hid from view.

But hark, the voice of Nature calls:
"Awake, sweet Spring!
    Arise and sing!
For Easter dawns, and what was dead
    Is born anew!"

EASTER DAWN

By HARRIET WHITNEY DURBIN

AWAKE, awake, oh, sleeping buds, in meadowland and
        mere,
In dale and swale and garden plot, for Easter Day is here!

In purple gloom the night has swept beyond the misty hill—
The April dawn, in silvery gown, is waiting at the sill.

From moor and marsh, from holm and croft, and brook-
        side far away
She calls her flower-children all to grace the Easter Day—

Majestic lilies, fair of breast as pigeon's milky wing;
And white and azure violets that breathe the soul of
        Spring;

Verbenas touched with rosy flame; the pansy's purple
        gem;
And in its regal purity, the Star of Bethlehem;

The lowly blood-root's bud of snow; the jonquil's disk
        of gold;
The flowers of the wind that spring so lightly from the
        mold.

Sweet April, snooded with the sun and zoned with tender
        light,
Is calling forth her blossom-babes from hollowland and
        height.

So come with nectaries of scent and aureoles of bloom—
'Tis Easter morn, and Christ the Lord is risen from
        the tomb.

A RAINY EASTER

By MINNA IRVING

IT RAINED so hard on Easter Day,
    A little girl I know
Found out she could not go to church;
    And did she cry? Oh, no.
She rummaged for a muslin frock
    Upon the nursery shelf,
And put it on, and straightway held
    An Easter by herself.

With sober face and silver voice
    She sang the carols through;
She couldn't find the book, but made
    Her "Cinderella" do;
The lilies in her childish arms
    (But don't you ever tell)
Were paper from the parlor vase—
    They pleased her quite as well.

She did not miss the organ's roll,
    Nor painted windows gay,
The graceful palms and banks of bloom,
    Nor sermon from her play,
Nor any of the holy things
    Of Easter Day a part—
Because, you see, she had the joy
    Of Easter in her heart.

POLLY'S APRIL FOOL

By KATHERINE DANIHER

SWEET POLLY was a winsome lass, with dimpled
    cheeks and round;
Her smiles were sought by love-sick swains in all the
    country round.
Who fell most willing captives to her beauty's magic
    spell,
And, with the wisdom of her sex, the lassie knew it
    well;
Was kindly gracious to them all, nor favor showed to one,
But many a time and oft her thoughts would dwell on
    honest John;
And lest, perchance, the tell-tale blush her feelings
    would betray,
Most wilful and perverse was she when John would come
    her way.

696

RHYMES FOR SPRING

Unlike the lovely heroines oft pictured in a book,
This charming maid could proudly boast that she knew
   how to cook.
So on the first of April she in dainty bib was found
Within the sunny kitchen, frying doughnuts crisp and
   round.
Such fresh and tempting goodies would an epicure
   beguile—
But why is Mistress Polly wearing such a roguish smile?
Beware! For every cruller has been filled with snowy wool,
All ready for some luckless wight to be an "April Fool."

A step upon the graveled path with inward glee she
   hears—
And lo! upon the vine-clad porch the sturdy John
   appears.
Full soon the winsome cook has gaily bade him eat his fill,
Attesting to the merits of the product of her skill.
All unsuspecting he of guile, nor thinks he of the day;
So, yielding to the maid's caprice, the poor youth
   chews away,
While thinking in his inmost heart, "My word! but
   these are tough,
Of Mistress Polly's cooking I have surely had enough.

"A maid who knows not how to cook, whate'er her
   charm may be,"
Quoth honest John unto himself, "would be no wife for
   me."
Now, judging by the standard of the heart's unfailing rule,
Was it John or was it Polly who became the "April
   Fool"?

THE HERALDRY OF SPRING

By ALOYSIUS COLL

A BASHFUL ring-dove yearned
   For his mate in the budding thorn,
And clouds of twittering swallows turned
   To the eaves in the old gray barn.

A robin high on the hill—
   Spring's smithy—forged a nest
With the anvil-patter of his bill,
   And the flame on his burning breast.

A lily stole to the bank
   Of the brook, and lifted up
Her chalice of sparkling dew, and drank
   A toast from the silver cup.

She made each genial guest
   At home in the house of Spring;
She roused the chipmunk to his jest,
   And mellowed the thrush to sing.

A poppy knelt in the pass,
   As the Sun went down the green—
He spied her, raised her from the grass,
   And made her his summer queen.

He lifted her lowly head;
   He made her the choice of a king;
He gave her a cloak of royal red,
   And a golden wedding-ring.

An ivy climbed the tower
   Of her castle in the rock;
The wild canary made his bower
   On an ancient hollyhock.

The ivy spread about
   Her rumor: "The Spring is near!"
The lookout bird above cried out:
   "She comes, she comes—she is here!"

The ring-doves bolder grew
   In the screen of the blackthorn leaves;
The mating swallows, two by two,
   Went up to the nesting eaves.

The poppy crowned a queen
   Looked up to the kingly Sun—
He kissed her there on her throne of green—
   I saw the magic done!

Then every mating bird,
   Sunbeam and opening flower
Looked up to me with a sudden word:
   "What of *your* heart this hour?"

The swallow and thrush and dove
   Pecked at a hidden door
And opened a way to the courts of love
   I never had known before!

I cried to the flowers: "Be still!"
   And "Silence!" to the thrush;
To the peeping Sun: "Go over the hill!"
   To the twittering swallows: "Hush!"

But Love stole out of the hours,
   And crowned me as her choice:
"I heard the call of the birds and flowers—
   I thought it was your voice!"

6

"OUR HEARTS BE PURE FROM EVIL"

AN EASTER STORY FOR YOUNG FOLKS

BY

GABRIELLE E. JACKSON.

"DID YOU SPEAK TO ME?"

"**Y**OU haven't average understanding. You are absolutely hopeless. You do not wish to study, so what can be expected? You will not work."

Each word fell with distinctness, precision, monotony, and was as uncompromising as the steady drip, drip of icy water during a February thaw.

"But, Miss Joy, I am not allowed to do any work at home. All——"

"That will do. This is neither the time nor place for explanations, and I do not care to hear them. I have no patience with people who say they *cannot* do this or that; it is, usually, *will not*. You should have done this supplementary work. I shall mark you very low for having failed to do it."

"Would that be fair to me, Miss Joy? I knew all of the regular lesson perfectly, but this work to be done at home was impossible for me——"

But again the girl's sweet voice was interrupted by the icy tones of the literature teacher, who uttered the one word: "Silence!" She had, however, the grace to drop her eyes before the big brown ones which looked into her own so steadily, and with such a rebuke in their clear, liquid depths that her own cold, steely ones were forced to shrink before that gaze.

The girl turned from the teacher's desk and, walking quietly to her own, sat down and began preparing a subject for the following day. Miss Joy opened her roll-book to mark the girls for the lesson just recited, while the class busied itself with some examination papers which had not been completed the previous day and were to be handed in that morning. A number of these papers lay upon the teacher's desk, and when she had finished her roll-book she began to examine them. It was close to the Easter holidays and all must be finished before Wednesday of the coming week. Miss Joy's left hand kept up a steady, nervous tattoo upon her desk as her right scored with a blue pencil one paper after another, and the silence of the room was broken only by the scratching of the girls' pens as they ran across their papers.

Miss Joy was a small, angular woman of forty or more years, rigidly erect and unbending both in figure and disposition. She ruled by "discipline" and "dignity," she said, and never did human being personify the former as did Miss Joy, although she frequently lost sight of the latter for lack of self-control. She had been teaching many years, and never yet had a word of affection been spoken in connection with her name. One generation of girls followed another through the school, but never was an "old girl" known to speak a kindly word of Miss

Joy or give the slightest indication of a warm sentiment for her. Her influence upon the girls in her classes varied with the temperaments of the individuals. Some feared; some hated; some despised her. Others lived in a constant state of rebellion, with a wild desire to "get even" at all hazards. The better bred, more self-possessed girls rigidly endured her. The sunny-souled, happy, sensitive, high-principled, delicately organized ones experienced a form of exquisite torture when brought in contact with a nature so diametrically opposed to their own.

Among the latter type was Lois Chilton. She had entered the school that year, coming from another distant town, and a greater contrast between her present unhappy surroundings and her former delightful ones it would be difficult to imagine. A few years before she had broken down from overstudy, and school had to be given up for eighteen months. Then came a year's work in Westleigh, where the raveled threads were so happily knitted together again, and now, at sixteen, she was a pupil in the Appleton School, where she was learning to understand a phase of life hitherto undreamed of. Sunny of soul, light-hearted, winning, quick to see the humorous side of everything, generous, affectionate, was Lois Chilton. She went through life finding it well worth living, and shedding sunshine for all who would take it. She had a fine mind, worked conscientiously and comprehendingly, concentrating all her efforts upon her subject and letting it sink in. She was truthful as truth itself, scorned subterfuge and meanness, and if in the wrong was always ready to admit it and "take her medicine," as she expressed it.

But "medicine," except in the form of a tonic, plenty of outdoor exercise and her gymnastic work, as well as a careful avoidance of overstudy, was never needed, and her intercourse with her other instructors, her parents and older people was that of the most delightful good-fellowship. They were, of course, her friends. She expected them to be so, why not? That an older person could entertain a grudging animosity toward a younger one was a condition of things quite beyond her grasp. But the year now drawing to its close had taught her much, and she was learning to distrust one of those "grown-ups" whom she had always been taught to trust and respect.

Why Miss Joy had signaled out Lois Chilton for the special object of her acrimony it would be hard to explain, unless it was the natural antagonism of such a nature as hers for its exact opposite. That she had made life a burden for the girl for seven months was past a

698

doubt, and unless some sort of halt was soon called the outcome was liable to prove serious for her pupil.

When she was placed in the school, Lois' physical condition had been made known to the principal, who, in turn, explained to her teachers that Lois would take only certain subjects, and limit the amount of work to that which could be prepared and recited during the five school hours, leaving her entirely free afterward for the outdoor exercise and physical training so essential. Miss Joy was fully aware of the conditions, but chose to discredit the need, and never for a single moment ceased to criticise the amount of work the girl did. She seemed to take a malicious delight in giving her just a little more than it was possible for her to do in the allotted time. Lessons long in themselves were made more taxing by supplementary reading, which could only be done after school hours. That she could not give the child a downright failure so long as the regular lessons were correctly recited she knew very well, but she could, and did, mark her disgracefully low, and taunt her with a lack of interest and inability; wound her by unjust accusations and irritate her almost beyond endurance. Day after day was this done, until poor Lois dreaded the literature class. More than once when on her way to school in the morning had she offered up a pathetic little prayer that "Miss Joy may be good-natured to-day," only to find Miss Joy more on edge than ever.

As Miss Joy worked upon the examination papers this morning her lips were compressed until only a thin line was visible to indicate them. Presently she glanced toward Lois' desk.

"Why are you not working upon your examination paper, Lois Chilton?" she demanded.

"I haven't——" began Lois.

"You haven't what?" broke in Miss Joy.

"You——"

"Never mind *me*. I wish to know why *you* are not working as the other girls are. Answer that question and say nothing else."

"I gave you——" when again that metallic voice interrupted.

But poor Lois Chilton had been goaded just a little too far that morning, and no amount of training can be counted upon to withstand the last straw. Looking Miss Joy squarely in the eyes, her own fairly blazing, but her mouth tightly closed, as though to repress words struggling to force themselves from her lips, she rose from her seat, shoulders squared and head erect, to walk straight up to Miss Joy's desk.

Like most cowardly, nagging natures, Miss Joy seemed actually to shrivel as the tall girl bore down upon her in her righteous wrath. For some time the teacher had striven by every artifice of her cold, vindictive nature to draw from Lois Chilton some word of impertinence or rebellious act; to provoke her into some discourtesy which would justify sending the girl to the principal's office. Yet never during all those miserable months had she succeeded in so doing. Even when Miss Joy was standing, Lois towered head and shoulders above her, and now as the small woman shrank into herself, the girl seemed a veritable personification of outraged justice coming to claim her rights.

She paused directly in front of Miss Joy, and said in a tone which her teacher had never before heard from those lips:

"Miss Joy, will you be good enough to open that drawer?" pointing to the upper drawer of the teacher's desk.

Without a word, but with a slightly trembling hand, Miss Joy complied. In the drawer lay a neatly written examination paper bearing Lois' name.

"Is not that the paper you wish, Miss Joy?"

"Certainly; certainly. How came it here? What do you mean by taking the liberty of placing it in my drawer?" Miss Joy was recovering herself, and had discovered a mare's nest.

"One moment, if you please, Miss Joy." The clear voice never faltered. "Do you recall that my paper was the only one completed when the period bell rang yesterday, and, at your own request, I handed it to you? You hastily opened that drawer and laid it there. And there is the period bell to end this recitation. I have the pleasure of wishing you good morning, Miss Joy."

She drew back from the desk, let fall the hand that had been pointing to her examination paper, and stepped into her place in the line which the girls had already formed at the ringing of the bell.

"You are insolent! Insolent!" cried Miss Joy, beside herself with passion. "I shall instantly report you. I shall make this examination so difficult for you that it will be impossible for you to pass! I shall be unsparing in my criticism of your paper! Do you hear me?"

But not another word did Lois Chilton utter as the class marched from the literature room; for the rules of the school brooked no delay once a period bell had rung.

An hour later she turned the corner of the street upon which her home stood. All the pretty color had vanished from her cheeks, her eyes looked heavy and dull, her lips had a sad little droop, and her step lacked its usual buoyancy. While still far down the block she saw her mother waiting for her upon their piazza, as she had never missed waiting since Lois began school at nine years of age. That little meeting each day had much to do with Lois' sunshine, and this year it had been a mighty safeguard against disaster, for Mrs. Chilton was by no means blind to the prevailing condition of affairs. She had watched with misgivings the effect it was having upon Lois, physically, mentally and morally, for this daughter was too precious to be marred by outer influences.

The hand which Lois placed in her mother's was icy cold, but the lips which rested against her cheek were hot and feverish. A shadow passed over Mrs. Chilton's face, to be instantly replaced by a bright smile, as she said:

"Come in to luncheon, Sweetheart; Katy has some delicious little rolls for us."

Instantly Lois' expression changed. Flinging her arms about her mother, she nestled her head in against her neck, and cried in a little, quivering voice, which told all too plainly of the nerve strain to which she had been submitted.

"What a precious, precious little mother you are! You always have something happy to say, and seem to know when I most need it. *You* couldn't roll me in a wet blanket, could you? And you whisk off those anyone else dares wrap me in, don't you? I couldn't live a single minute without you to brace me up!"

Mrs. Chilton laughed a happy little laugh as she replied:

"Isn't that what mothers were made for? Now sit down to your luncheon, and while you are enjoying your rolls I'll tell you some pleasant news. Papa is going to take us to Lakewood for Easter. We start on Monday."

Lois let fall the roll she held to clasp her hands in rapture, and cry:

"How perfectly splendid! A whole week outdoors and *no* Miss Joy! Oh, Mumsey, it has been an awful day, and I lost my temper, said dreadful things, and am going to lose my Lit. Exam., for Miss Joy said so. And I worked *so* hard," and the pretty head wagged despondently.

"No, dear, not your examination, because I have decided to withdraw you from the school. You will not return after Easter. I think the tax upon your strength has been a little too severe. I have written to Miss Appleton giving my reasons, and have requested her to send me all your papers, etc., by mail on Monday. After you have had a little holiday we will read and study together each morning, and you will lose very little. As for the outcome of the examination, you are not to worry over it. You have worked faithfully, and no one can do better than their best."

"I have, oh, Mumsey, I have!" cried Lois. "I don't feel a bit scared about anything but the Lit., and Miss Joy said to-day that she would make that impossible, so I dare say it isn't any use to hope for anything there."

Lois did not see the quick squaring of her mother's shoulders or the shutting together of the lips, so exactly as she herself had done not two hours before. Then Mrs. Chilton continued:

"I am delighted with the progress you have made this year, and I think you have earned your holiday. At any rate, I cannot spare my sunshiny daughter, to replace her with an overwrought, nervous one."

Just then the waitress went to answer the door-bell, and presently returned to say:

"Please, Mrs. Chilton, there's a man wishing to speak with you."

Mrs. Chilton rose from the table and went to the door. A trolley-car official raised his hat as he asked:

"Do you own a big red dog, lady?"

"Why, yes, we do. What is the matter? What has he done?"

"Well, I can't rightly say as he's done anythin'. It's more like what he won't do. He's squatted himself in the very middle of the track, and sits there like he owned it and all the earth, too, and unless I knock him into a cocked hat I don't see how I'm going to run my car. 'Course, it's only trial trips we're makin' yet, but in a few days we'll be a-runnin' reg'lar, and I don't want to start out by killin' no valuable dog, and gettin' run in for it. So I wisht you'd please call him home."

Mrs. Chilton collapsed upon the hall settee to laugh. Then she called to Lois: "Run out and persuade Don that the trolley company does own that property now, Lois, and that we have received full value for it. Assure him that the lot is now theirs, not ours, and he is under no obligation to mount guard over it."

The man smiled broadly, tipped his hat once more, and turned to follow Lois, who fled, laughing, down the steps to bring home the big Irish setter who could not be reconciled to the new order of things upon what he supposed was his mistress's property.

Don was a character. During the previous summer he had stood beside his mistress while a neighbor gathered for her a splendid bunch of scarlet geraniums and presented it with a graceful little speech. The next day, and the next, and the next, Don laid a fine geranium plant, roots and all, at Mrs. Chilton's feet, and looking into her face with as near an approach to their neighbor's smile as he could manage, asked in his dog language: "Wasn't that thoughtful of me?"

The neighbor did not agree. Neither did Mrs. Chilton feel especially gratified when Don undertook to keep the larder supplied with poultry after having observed the manner in which the gardener put an end to the life of a hapless chicken and then carried it to the house. Don could not talk, but he could and did think, as he proved later.

The following Monday, Lois' papers were sent home. She had passed in every subject excepting English literature. That paper was scored from end to end, every defect being magnified to the last degree. Her lips quivered as she looked at it over her mother's shoulder, for many of the points criticised were those upon which Miss Joy had insisted earlier in the year, but had afterward entirely forgotten. Under the circumstances it was impossible for her to pass.

A few hours later the family and Don were speeding toward Lakewood. Holy Week passed in all its hush of peace and rest. Many a weary heart and body had sought the soothing influence of Lakewood for moral and physical restoration. Many a tired brain was resting among the tall, whispering pines, whose beautiful, arching boughs had given the first hint of Gothic architecture long years before. Here in the silent wood, which were "God's first temples," restless spirits were calmed, fractious ones found peace and discouraged ones renewed hope.

Easter was very late that year, and in this sheltered inland region the foliage had already advanced more than elsewhere, and all the world was a tender green with pink and white hints of future blossoming.

Early Easter morning, Lois and Don stole away from the hotel and hurried off to a remote bit of woodland bordering a lake. From afar came the softened sound of church bells ringing for early service.

As she walked through the beautiful pine wood, filled with life-giving, aromatic odors and the glory of the early sunlight, Lois' thoughts were busy with recent happenings, and her heart filled with the spirit of the hour. Presently she spoke aloud, and Don paused to look up into her face as though to ask: "Did you speak to me?"

"No, it's all right, old fellow," she said. "I'm just having a little powwow with Lois Chilton, and trying to make her forget old scores to-day. It's hard work sometimes, Don, do you know that?" she asked, as she dropped upon a fallen pine log and took the dog's head in her hands. Don looked at her with almost human intelligence. "Yes," she continued, looking absently out over the crystal waters of the lake, now glowing in the sunlight, "dreadfully, dreadfully hard, for I never came so near hating anybody before, Don. I truly never, never did, and to-day I don't want to have a single unkind thought of anybody if I can help it; not even of Miss Joy. But she has hurt me cruelly so many times because she has been so unjust. Listen to the bells, Don. Do you know what they are saying?

"Our hearts be pure from evil,
That we may see aright,"

sang Lois, softly. "Listen, Don!"

As she spoke the last words, a piercing shriek came across the water from the further side of the lake, where two rowboats were moored to a stake close to the water's edge. The dog bounded to his feet as though it were the cry to which he was bidden harken. Lois glanced quickly in the direction as the cry was repeated, and saw a woman fall between the boats as she attempted to step from one to the other. Lois echoed the cry as she sprang to her feet and started to run around the border of the lake to the figure struggling in the water. As she sped along, she cried to Don:

"On, Don! On! Catch her! Catch her!"

By the way Lois was forced to go the distance was great, and had the rescue depended upon her the victim's chances would have been small. But Don could cut corners, and with a comprehending bark he plunged into the water and swam with all his might. Not a moment too soon did he reach the woman, who had now ceased to struggle, and, grasping her by her coat collar, he held on for dear life as he strove to swim with his burden. But the boats impeded him and he could only hold her head above the water until Lois arrived, breathless, for she was only a slender, little girl, and none too strong. As she hurried down the bank to the mooring, she gave a gasp of astonishment, and for a moment mistrusted her own sight, for the pallid, upturned face with its closed eyes and drenched locks was that of Miss Joy. Not one second did she wait to take breath, but bounded into one of the boats and, reaching down, drew the unconscious woman into it, then fell upon a thwart faint and exhausted. When aid, summoned by the intelligent Don's barks and whines, arrived from a near-by cottage, Lois sat holding her late enemy's head in her lap, and Miss Joy, once more conscious, was looking up into the girl's face with an expression in which gratitude, shame and a dawning wondering admiration were oddly mingled.

To help save a life—for Don was given his full meed of praise for his share in the matter—and to turn an enemy into a friend was Lois Chilton's pleasant record for that Easter. Nor did the good stop there, for the Appleton students were amazed to find a new Miss Joy when the Easter holidays ended—a Miss Joy who was actually human, almost gentle, in her changed personality, and who by degrees grew away from her old, hard self until it was evident that a miracle had been indeed wrought that wonderful Easter, and a nature had been made anew and for the better.

Dainty Things for the Bride's Boudoir

CANDLE SHADE

ALMOST every woman who is preparing a trousseau likes to plan for the pretty, dainty things she is going to have in her little "home of homes," and in no place is there as much opportunity for originality and the carrying out of schemes and ideas as in the furnishing of her guest chamber. Therefore a few suggestions may be of service to the bride-elect and prove a saving of precious time and energy.

One of the most effective styles of embroidery is the old-time ribbon work—slightly modified. It is especially well adapted for the dainty and ornamental little articles that make the boudoir so attractive, and the work is so fascinating and easily executed that it is not surprising that it is popular.

As in most fancywork, its chief aim is *effect* at the least expenditure of time and labor, and not only is this feature in its favor, but it also admits of the greatest scope for dainty and original motifs; in fact, the artistic effects that may be accomplished are quite *unlimited*, and may be most successfully applied as trimming for the reception gown or jacket, screens, sofa cushions, etc.

The color-scheme of this particular set is of a delicate pink shade, being a cheerful color and harmonizing admirably with almost every wood. The material used is silk moiré ribbon (about five inches in width), the "water" marks adding brightness, tone and finish to the article which is made of it; consequently it is more desirable than almost any other fabric for this kind of work, although satin or taffeta may also be used, often with excellent results.

The treatment is very simple, compared with the exhaustive methods of using filo. Forget-me-nots are particularly well suited for ribbon work and the amateur's fingers, and are suggestive of especially sweet and pretty sentiment for a bride; however, almost all small, dainty flowers may be used, such as daisies, buttercups, arbutis and lilies-of-

the-valley. With a ribbon slightly wider than the kind used for these articles, wistaria, fleur-de-lis, etc., may be made.

Draw the design in very lightly with a sharp-pointed lead pencil, or have it stamped on the material; or, better still, make a little sketch on paper and copy it. An ordinary long-eyed embroidery needle may be used, although for the heavier materials a blunt-pointed or tapestry needle would be preferable, avoiding puckering or splitting of the threads and preparing the fabric for the ribbon to be drawn through. For the set described, the regular embroidery needle was used, the size of the eye depending, naturally, upon the width of the ribbon, which sometimes varies slightly. The needle is threaded in the usual way for sewing, knotting the ribbon at the end. Begin with the flowers and draw the needle through from the outer edge of the petal to the center, or within two or three threads of the center, care being taken when using the ombré or shaded ribbons to draw it through so that the light side will come where the strongest light will fall on the flower — the dark side of the ribbon representing the shaded side or shadow of the petal. After the buds and flowers have been finished, begin on the leaves and treat in precisely the same way, using the lighter shadings of color for the top of the wreath and gradually coming to the darker tints at the bottom, where the bow-knot is supposed to hold the little stems together. Cut the ribbon when re-threading the needle about half an inch from the material (of course, on the underside), sewing the end down with cotton, thus preventing the ribbon from slipping through to the right side. Then outline the stems with a single strand of filo and put the centers in the flowers (which are made simply by taking a double thread of yellow filo, knotting at the end and making a French knot), twisting the silk over the needle but once for the small delicately colored flowers at the top of the wreath, and twice for the larger and deeper ones near the bow. The bow-knot is the finishing touch, and is practically laid on by holding the ribbon in place with the thumb of the left hand and sewing or tacking down with silk matching the ribbon in color, or number ninety white cotton may be used. If preferred, instead of having the ribbon lie flat where the loops of the bow converge, it may be drawn through the material and then tucked, thus giving the effect of a bow being actually tied. In sewing the bow-knot down at the edge, have as few stitches show as possible. Twist and turn the ribbon over as often as the design will allow. The more the ribbon is turned the more natural and artistic the bow-knot will be. After the loops of the bow are made, add a couple of ends and form the center of knot by drawing the ribbon through the material and back again to the underside.

Should it be impossible to

PHOTOGRAPH FRAME AND PINCUSHION

DUSTER-BAG   HANDKERCHIEF-BAG   SCARF-PIN HOLDER

CORSET-BAG

procure the ribbon in the pretty ombré effects, plain colors may be used in its place to advantage. In some instances the ordinary seam-binding may be substituted, which can be bought in a variety of shadings at almost any small dry goods store. Wild roses are especially pretty made of it. Should it be necessary to use the binding for the smaller flowers, forget-me-nots, etc., use it double.

CANDLESTICK SHADE.—Take a piece of five-inch ribbon of the length of the circumference of your mold, or holder; sew at lower edge the crystal fringe; at the top turn the edge toward the inside and form a narrow pocket for shirr-string; draw up tightly, using soft, narrow ribbon. and then add the plaited chiffon with the narrow ribbon at edge, and sew to the ribbon foundation; add a little spray of artificial forget-me-nots to carry out the idea of the set, also three little dainty bows.

PHOTO FRAME. — Cut a piece of cardboard heart-shaped, and pad slightly. Over this stretch the embroidered ribbon and slash the ribbon where the opening comes, then baste the edges back and forth, edge to edge, with strong cotton. Have a glass cut heart-shaped and *passé-partout* the edge with satin ribbon. Paste or sew on the back of pasteboard with a little arrangement for support, which may be procured at almost any embroidery store.

PINCUSHION.—Cut a piece of the five-inch moiré ribbon about an inch longer than the uncovered cushion, and work out the ribbon-work design. A pretty lace medallion may be added at either end. Stretch down the top piece tightly over the cushion, sticking pins all the way through into the cushion so that only the small head shows; then likewise

HANDKERCHIEF-CASE AND STOCK-HOLDER

a similar length of moiré for the underside; overhand the two edges firmly together; sew the ruffle of moiré ribbon (with shirred narrow satin ribbon on edge) onto the cushion, and then the accordion-plaited chiffon, to which may be added also the narrow satin ribbon shirred and Juby trimming of chiffon. Bows may be added at the ends if desired. A small cushion about ten inches in length, made to match the large one, is pretty for the dressing-table.

DUSTER BAG.—This is made exactly like the corset-bag, described on page 703, only the bag is made much shorter —about ten inches in length—or long enough so that the feather duster fits in it nicely and two-thirds of the handle is covered. Line with linen also.

HANDKERCHIEF BAG. — Draw a small circle on a piece of white cardboard, about the size of a tumbler opening, and cut out; then baste evenly on both sides some cotton-batting, after which lay the cardboard on a double piece of moiré and cut about half an inch from the cardboard. Baste the edges of one side over on the other side, turn the edges in and overhand together. Cut four lengths of moiré ribbon (about twelve or fourteen inches long) and whip together. Embroider the design and then shirr the ribbon about one-quarter inch from the bottom and overhand on to the covered cardboard disk; raw edge upward. Line with four pieces of ribbon made in similar manner, and sew to the disk, having the raw edges come together so that when the bag is finished no edges will appear either inside or outside. At the top of the bag fringe about one inch and form a

pocket for the draw-string by sewing the ribbon together. Shirr the accordion-plaited chiffon and add the little shirring of satin ribbon to edge of chiffon. Put in the drawing-string and make a full pretty bow for each string. A little sachet bag, made of the ribbon and ornamented, is tacked to the inside bag so that fresh sachet powder may be put in when necessary.

SCARF-PIN HOLDER.—This is also made of a piece of cardboard and, like the photograph frame, is padded, after

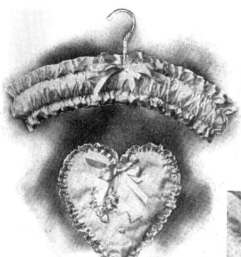

WAIST-HANGER AND SACHET

which it is lightly scented and covered with moiré ribbon, the edge of which is hidden by satin ribbon shirred in the middle and sewed to the disk. Attach ribbon loop and bow.

CORSET-BAG.—If the corset happens to be of the girdle or short-hipped type, the five-inch moiré ribbon may be used, otherwise a wider ribbon would be better. Embroider the wreath and sew the edges of two strips about twenty inches long together. Allow about four inches of the ribbon at the top for turning back; line with sheer linen and sew on a satin ribbon of pink of a width wider than the ribbon used for the drawing-strings. Chiffon may be added if desired.

HANDKERCHIEF-CASE.—A Duchesse lace handkerchief was used and a square pad about half an inch smaller than the handkerchief itself, made of scented cotton-batting covered with pink messaline (because of its soft texture), is tacked to the handkerchief at the corners, and ribbon drawn through the openings of the lace holds the case together.

STOCK-CASE.—Cut two pieces of white pasteboard sixteen inches long; lay on a thin layer of cotton-batting on each side and baste on the coverings of moiré ribbon; then whip the edges together; shirr narrow satin ribbon and overhand on to the edge of the case, on both parts of the case. The two finished parts are held together by ribbons sewed three inches from either end of the case and tied into bows. Ribbons are also attached to the inside of the case to hold the stocks in place, from bows diagonally to the center of the other edge. Ends are left for tying.

WAIST-HANGER.—Get a plain, wooden coat-hanger and wind some white muslin over and over until the frame is covered; then baste on some cotton-batting tightly but uniformly and use a small amount of sachet powder. Cover the handle of the hanger with narrow satin ribbon, and then take moiré ribbon twice the length of the hanger for each side and shirr so that a little ruffle is formed at either edge, leaving the opening through which to draw the coat-hanger at the center of one side, then pull your frame through and regulate the gatherings. Add bows where the handle is joined to the frame.

SACHET.—Cut the cotton-batting for this in a heart shape and cut the moiré about half an inch larger. Baste the cotton down to one side of the sachet and sprinkle sachet powder profusely between the layers of cotton. Turn the edge over and baste down. Shirr the narrow satin ribbon at the edge and at the other edge full on narrow Valenciennes lace; sew to edge of the sachet and then slip-stitch the upper part to the under part. Add bow. One of these sachets or smaller ones of similar shape may be made for each drawer of the dresser and chiffonier.

SOFA-CUSHION.—Cut three strips of five-inch moiré ribbon (or narrower if preferred) and two strips of lace insertion about two inches wide, the length of the pillow; over-hand the edges together firmly. Sketch your design on the ribbon and embroider. The lace

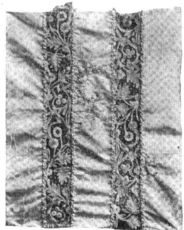

TOP FOR SOFA-CUSHION

employed in this particular case was one which had a suggestion of net in its design, thus forming a foundation for a few sprays of flowers to be carelessly scattered, care being taken to have the ends well concealed and firmly sewed down on the underside. The joining of the ribbon to the lace strips is covered by narrow pink satin ribbon, shirred in the middle. The pillow is lined with pink moiré and moiré ribbon ruffle added to edge, with the shirred narrow satin ribbon sewed to edge of that so that the ruffle will match the body part of the pillow, and accordion-plaited ruffle of chiffon laid on over it. Heavy cord may be substituted, knotted at the corners, in which case the narrow cord to match would be used at the edge of the ribbon where the lace joins, knotted an inch or two apart.

Lace Novelties Made with Bruges Braid

By SARA BLISS

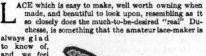

DEEP POINTED COLLAR

LACE which is easy to make, well worth owning when made, and beautiful to look upon, resembling as it so closely does the much-to-be-desired "real" Duchesse, is something that the amateur lace-maker is always glad to know of, and we feel sure that the illustrations of the articles made with Bruges braid will be more than welcome to the readers of The Designer. The extremely pretty handkerchief shown at the top of page 701 is quite simple, showing a combination of small flowers and leaves, the latter being massed at the corners and forming most of the edge. Except for a few spider-webs which fill the centers of the flowers, no lace stitches are used, for the background is simply made of bars of twisted thread. Even this piece of handwork could be dispensed with, or at least lessened, by using a fine picot or background braid such as is used in the collar illustrated on this page. This braid is so fine that it may be threaded through a needle and used like ordinary thread.

In setting the linen center in the lace border, care must be taken to have the work done neatly, and the most satisfactory results are obtained when the linen is put between two pieces of braid. This is done by cutting the piece of linen a seam larger than the center all around and basting it in place, being careful to keep the threads of the linen perfectly straight. Sew around the inside edge of the braid first, using very fine thread, then baste a second piece of braid on the other side of the linen and trim off the edges where they come beyond the braid. Sew on this second piece of braid at the inside edge and then overhand the outside edges of the two pieces of braid together. When a center is set in a lace border in this way, it should be almost impossible to tell which is the

particularly pleasing. The flowers are grouped together to form medallions, the centers of which are filled with a close single-mesh stitch. The three flowers which hang from the middle of the stock and make such a pleasing finish for the front have their centers filled with rings and tiny spiderwebs, which are placed around the edge.

In this day of lingerie waists, a handsome underwaist or corset-cover is almost a necessity and, although many pretty ones are made of fine nainsook trimmed with Valenciennes lace, it would be hard to find a more charming decoration than the yoke which forms the third illustration. Only a portion of it is shown, the right shoulder and front not being finished. The upper edge and the straps which go under the arm are made with a braid which is wide in places and then narrows in to almost a cord at regular intervals. Small buttonholed rings join these cord-like places together and three buttonholed bars fill in each of the intervening spaces. The centers of the large flowers are made with buttonholed rings and spiders, like those on the stock collar, and the background is filled with twisted bars and rings. Although one might hesitate and think it rather too much of an undertaking to make a yoke like this, a careful examination of the illustration will prove that the lace-work amounts to almost nothing, three-quarters of the design being made by merely basting

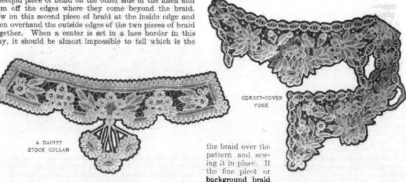

CORSET-COVER
YOKE

A DAINTY
STOCK COLLAR

right and which is the wrong side of the handkerchief, as no sewing stitches appear on either side.

Several varieties of braid are combined in the dainty stock collar shown in the above illustration. The design is very lacy and open, the irregular lower edge being

the braid over the pattern and sewing it in place. If the fine picot or background braid previously described was used for filling in the large spaces in place of the bars formed of twisted thread, the amount of the work would be still further reduced, and the general appearance of the yoke improved, if anything, by the change.

A deep-pointed collar, beautifully light and filmy in appearance, is shown in the first illustration. The main portion or body of the collar, which is also the most interesting feature, is formed entirely of buttonholed rings joined together with bars of twisted thread. The lace edge consists of a series of conventional crescent-shaped figures, with an inside irregular border of small roses and leaves that spring from quite a heavy cord which does duty for a stem. The stitchery in this collar, as indeed in all the articles that are shown, is very simple, for the greater portion of the lace made with the Bruges braid relies, for the most part, on the design, and a clever and judicious combination of the different varieties of braid, for its beauty, rather than on elaborate and sometimes difficult stitches. The latter

HANDKERCHIEF WITH BORDER OF BRUGES LACE

effect obtained, by simply omitting the last crescent-shaped figure on each side and pushing up the one that goes across the bottom. Another change would be to use a piece of tulle or fine Brussels net for the body of the collar instead of the rings and bars of twisted thread. This would do away with much of the work, and still the airy laciness would not be lost.

If this suggestion of using Brussels net is adopted, it would be advisable to break up the surface of the net and take away from the plain look and rather monotonous effect, by scattering small hand-worked dots or rings over the surface at regular intervals. These dots should be worked with fine lace thread, running or darning around a single hole of the net, twice—and it will be found that the use of these dots greatly

belong more generally to the laces made with Renaissance and the various novelty braids. The small roses are filled with a simple herring-bone or fagoting stitch, while the pointed figures, which outline the larger or outside curve of each crescent, have three or more lines of twisted thread in the open space, one in the exact center and the others springing from that, and by reason of these stitches the figures strongly resemble a series of small leaves. This collar is intended to fasten in the back and to be worn with a collarless, accordion-plaited or shirred waist of chiffon or mull. The shape of the collar could be changed if desired, and a round

A GRACEFUL BERTHA

improves the appearance of the net. Made of black silk braid, a collar like this would make a handsome decoration for a black net or chiffon waist.

In the last illustration a very lovely bertha is shown, and it would seem almost unnecessary to enter into a detailed description of it, all the stitches being so easily discernible. The little roses which are set at regular intervals just below the upper piece of braid and the large medallion effect at the center of the front all help to make a charming whole, and a dainty frock made of net, mull or organdy would need no other trimming.

HOOKS AND EYES

By MURIEL E. WINDRAM

"MAMA," queried Tommy, with a mischief-loving smile,
    "Did I hear you say you wanted hooks and eyes?"
His mother laid her sewing down and searched her basket through—
    "Why, yes," she said. "The very largest size."

"Well, then," replied gay Tommy, while his smile grew broader yet—
    "The very largest size, as you'll allow,
Is out there in the barnyard, all fastened hard and tight—
    The hooks and eyes that grow upon the cow!"

Vol. XXI, No. 6.   APRIL, 1905

The DESIGNER

CONDUCTED BY LILIAN DYNEVOR RICE

CONTENTS

Published monthly by the **STANDARD FASHION COMPANY**, 12-14-16 Vandam St. NEW YORK

Terms: Eighty Cents a Year in advance; Ten Cents a number

BRANCHES:
206-302 Monroe St., Chicago, Ill.
23 Richmond St., West, Toronto, Canada
1019 Market St., San Francisco, Cal.

Subscriptions are received by all Standard Fashion Agents, Newsdealers and Booksellers, or may be sent direct to the publishers.

Bakers' Marks

There is a story of an old lady who made up a batch of mince and apple pies.

Wishing to be able to distinguish one kind from the other she marked the mince pies **T M** for "tis mince" and the apple pies **T M** for "taint mince."

The baker's marks on the ordinary run of bakery products are of little more value for purposes of identification than the marks on the old lady's pies.

 *But HERE is a trade mark* that really identifies—that enables you to distinguish the world's best baking—the Biscuit, Crackers and Wafers made by the NATIONAL BISCUIT COMPANY. This trade mark appearing in red and white on each end of a package guarantees the contents to be of highest quality—pure, clean and fresh. To learn something of what this trade mark means try a package of either of the products mentioned below.

Lemon Snaps	**Butter Thin Biscuit**	**Graham Crackers**
An appetizing nibble with the flavor of the refreshing lemon. A revelation in modern baking.	Unique little biscuit, in much favor with those who want "something different."	Possessing the rich, nutty flavor of graham flour—unlike any graham crackers you ever tasted.

NATIONAL BISCUIT COMPANY

A Sermon on Fools in General and April Fools in Particular

By A. ALBION

HAVE you ever heard what Henry Ward Beecher said when, on the first of April, he received a letter and found inside the envelope merely a sheet of paper with the two words "April Fool" written on it? The great preacher looked at the inscription for a moment and then said: "Well, I have heard of absent-minded people who would write letters and then forget to sign their names, but here is one who has signed his name and forgotten to write the letter." Beecher thus cleverly turned the tables, making the sender appear to be a fool instead of the receiver. And really this will be true in many cases of the present day when the nonsense of April first is in full swing; for those who are sometimes quickest to regard others as fools, are, when you consider it carefully, themselves the greater fools.

How many times the tender, sweet imaginings of childhood, peopling the fields and the woods with fairies, are laughed at by old people, and teased or threatened or forced into what is called common sense. Yet in truth does not the child in its waking dreams get more from a flower and from a cloud than these who are so proud of their common sense; for to them flowers only clutter up the house, and clouds only mean rain or storm? The history of the human race shows that the child mind of the race in the past had its imaginings just as the little child of to-day has them, and out of the play of that imagination has come much that we prize in literature, in sculpture and in life. In fact the imaginings of the human mind have lifted us from an animal plane, from sordid every-day affairs to realize that there is a spirit in life visible to those who will keep their spirit-eyes open and undefiled as those of a child. The child is wise; the one who rebukes him is otherwise.

How many of you women yield the beautiful lines of your faces to scorn and contempt when you come across a dowdily dressed person trying, in a humble way, to do good and not in any-way seeking to attract attention to herself! You laugh at her, you make mock of her endeavor, you consider that she is a "nobody" just because she dresses plainly. You, in your short-sightedness, fail to see that in the moving forward of this great round world into moral realms, it is the character of the soul that counts and not the mere very trivial attributes of gloves and shoes, and hats and up-to-dateness. The things of the spirit are deeper than you are able to realize, and your shallowness makes their depths beyond your understanding, and therefore you fail to see in this servant of the good that which in the great scales of Everlasting Justice will outweigh your garb and your criticism and your narrow judgment and your ineffectiveness a thousandfold.

Some of you hard-headed men and some of you tight-fisted women name them fools who spend their time and their strength in doing things that make no money. Your summing up of common sense is that a man or a woman should rake and accumulate, as if raking and accumulating were the great chief end of life. Foolish though it may sound to some, the wise truth is that money-making is not at all a chief end; necessities we must have, else we could not live; but the gathering, just for the sake of gathering, or just for the sake of selfish indulgence or sloth, is foolish.

You may rake and scrape and save, you may make your life miserable with fears of monetary disaster, you may make those around you unhappy because you lay so much stress upon money, and you may at the last have an accumulation that shall assure you of bodily comfort the rest of your life. But what is all this? That which you have accumulated of material must drop at last from your hands, you cannot carry it with you any whither; but these who see in life, in the march of events or in the simple things like the woods and the fields something that speaks to their souls and prompts them from full hearts to try to make nature speak to others as it speaks to them—whether their interpretation be by books or by paintings or by speech, they leave something of lasting value behind them when they go. They go not empty away, for they leave the world better, higher, more clear-visioned, less material, less inclined to crib and to rake. Your wealth is of less worth than one true utterance given to the world, and your "good sense" of constant acquisition does less for the world than the feeble ones, no matter how poor or humble, who even only help forward a good thought in the world.

Some of you college girls yield at times to a silly narrowness which in all truth your college education should have saved you from. Some of you were put through higher institutions of learning by no merit of your own, but simply because a relative thought it "the proper thing" that you should be well educated. Because your opportunities came to you so easily and unsought, some of you are inclined to look down upon those who have to work their way through college by doing menial tasks, and you sometimes think that those without college education cannot amount to anything. Oh, children of

April first! You are blind. What does your veneer of education amount to compared with the facts and the thoughts and the purposes ground into the very being of those who have to work so hard for that which you receive so easily? One idea made part of their very selves puts them far ahead of you immediately, instead of their being hopelessly in the rear as you sometimes think.

It is not what we retain in our memories and can rattle off glibly with our tongues that makes us strong in this world of great thought. It is only what we actually absorb and make part of ourselves that really counts. The frost-like froth along the shores of the sea is of little moment; it is here one minute and then blown over the beach by the winds, and it is then no more! It is the great tides, the great currents that are part of the sea itself —these are the things that make the sea a benison to the world. Such influences live on forever. And thus it is also with those of this world who have taken to themselves any portion of the great tide of human purpose which must underlie all successful human education. They count: froth does not count, and when it is gone it is not missed.

And oh! what fools are those who think it necessary to ever remember and repeat the mistakes and the wrongs that others have done! They seem to think that a wrong once done can never be undone, that an evil habit once acquired can never be conquered, and that a false step once taken can never be rectified. Oh, slow of heart! believe it not. The power of good is greater than the power of evil. There is such a thing as sloughing off the dying and unworthy self, and thus entering again, as a little child, into the kingdom of the pure and the good. It must be so; for if one wrong fixed us forever in the wrong, where would there be any good? We have all done wrong, we have all fallen short of the immense dignity of ourselves; so, even as you who are now busy telling of the defects in others expect for yourselves charitable interpretation regarding your own errors— be they small or be they great—so in the same spirit must you deport yourself toward the rest of our struggling humanity.

All those who struggle upward are "wise in their generation" and unless you earnestly strive with and encourage those who are striving to be better, the judgment of the Ruler of this world, who has placed within us these upward impulses, must write across your own soul the word that alone fits, the word that sums up all the shortsightedness and defects of our natures, and that one word is *Fool*.

"With charity towards all and malice towards none" let us be wise in that wisdom which cometh down from above, always to the best of our ability —which is but work at the best—helping one another, encouraging one another, *for we are here a little while only!*

Arnold Fabric Talks

The unequalled facilities of the Arnold Print Works and Mills are skillfully employed in the production of wash fabrics that will merit the confidence and favor of American women.

The watch-word is not how cheap, but how good in quality, how beautiful in design, how perfect in finish the goods can be made.

With the advancing season new designs are constantly added to make the range of patterns in every line of Arnold goods thoroughly up-to-date in styles and colors, so as to satisfy the most exacting demand. These are shown by every dry goods dealer who cares to supply his customers with goods that may be depended upon for durability in wear and permanency of color, whether in printed patterns or plain shades.

Made from Mohair Lustre

¶ *You can identify our product by our trade-marked tickets on the outside wrapper. This trade-mark guarantees your entire satisfaction, and makes it worth your effort to give our goods a thorough trial.*

WHAT WOMEN ARE DOING

EDITED BY THE READERS OF THE DESIGNER

FIVE-DOLLAR PRIZE PARAGRAPH

RAISING FERRETS

Four years ago my husband, after much difficulty, succeeded in buying a ferret, paying five dollars for her; and the thought occurred to me, if these little animals bring such a price, why cannot I make money by raising them? I took a trip, combining business with pleasure, visited the ferret dealer, found out all I could about the breeding, caring for them, etc., purchased two females and a male, came home and went to work. The ferret is a small animal, white or brown, not unlike the mink or weasel, and is used in the winter to hunt rabbits, and at all times of the year in cities, to drive out and kill rats. They eat bread, milk, meat, and anything a cat or dog will; are playful as kittens and it is really a pleasure to take care of them. It costs less to feed them than it does to feed a hen or chicken. An old tool-house was repaired, boxes were made and placed in partitioned pens, and were filled with straw for beds. The ferrets must be separated after mating, for in six weeks the young will arrive, and the old males will destroy them if they are left with them. They breed twice in a season—April and September—and have from five to twelve in a litter. When they are born the little ones are blind and look like young mice, and obtain their food in the same way until about six weeks old, when their eyes open and they will eat bread and milk with their mothers. At three months old they are ready for market and will bring from three to five dollars apiece. Last year I shipped stock to twelve different States. The first year fifty dollars was realized, and last year, after all expenses were paid for advertising, shipping, boxes, etc., I found I had cleared twenty-five dollars for each month of the entire year, and had plenty of stock left to commence this year's work on a much larger scale. Don't think it's merely *play*, as it means steady, careful work for every day in the year; but what *I* have done other women certainly can do.   *Mrs. Robt. Smith*

SHE FOLLOWS TWO OCCUPATIONS SUC-
CESSFULLY

Two years ago a bright young book-keeper noticed a small candy store near a school-house in the residence district, which looked too shabby and ill-kept to pay its proprietor, and, recognizing an opportunity to make money, investigated. She found that the discouraged man inside was about to give up and shut up the shop. For a small sum down and the rest to be paid monthly she secured his little stock, arranged for a transfer of his lease, which called for only ten dollars a month, and took charge of the place. With the help of a younger sister who was not working she cleaned and brightened the store, trimmed the windows in an attractive way, and at once trade began to increase. Together the sisters made candies in the evening and put them fresh and tempting into the windows next day; also a card in the window saying that fresh tea-biscuit could be had every evening at 5:30. Orders came and profits increased. As soon as the original stock was paid for she went to a wholesale grocer and arranged for a small stock on thirty days' time. And whenever anyone asked for something she did not have in the grocery line she ordered a small quantity, and in that way simply supplied the demand. To-day the place is well stocked, bright and clean, and a great convenience in the neighborhood. The stock is paid for and she purchases for cash and in larger quantities, making greater profits; has one clerk, keeps the place open until nine o'clock —other groceries close at six—and is about to buy the building. All this without losing a day from her regular bookkeeping. At this rate, in five years she will be a fairly rich woman.   *X. Y. Z.*

PLEASANT WAY TO MAKE MONEY

A woman eager to help her husband pay for their home went into the floral business in this way. She obtained dealers' rates from several wholesale florists, then went among her friends taking orders for hyacinth bulbs at retail prices. When she had secured orders to the amount of ten dollars, she borrowed the money and bought ten dollars' worth of bulbs at wholesale, filled her orders, sold and potted the rest, growing them in her chamber window until in flower, when they brought fancy prices. In the spring she bought plants, taking a number of small orders, selling all she could from the box and potting the others. She also bought seed and propagated everything she could. By warm weather every window in the house was overflowing, and people who disliked the trouble of ordering for themselves were coming to her for plants. When it was safe to put the plants out of doors she increased her stock, both in variety and quantity, and found no trouble in disposing of all she did not wish to keep. In the fall she had a small green-house built, ordered wire designs and other floral supplies, and boldly announced herself a florist. Now she has orders for plants, cut flowers and funeral designs all the year round, and has the satisfaction of knowing that she added several hundred dollars to the family purse. *S. A. H.*

A PIANO-BOX FOR A HOME

My laundress is a white woman, whose checkered career of the past two years may prove as interesting to THE DESIGNER readers as it was to me. Left a widow with three children to support, she was forced to do whatever her hands found ready, and that quickly, in order to provide the daily necessities of life. She came to B——, a small western Texas town, and, in her own language, "landed with just two bits left, after buying a home." Her "home," as she naïvely expressed it, consisted of two piano-boxes, set in the middle of an unopened street and overstretched with canvas. "In those two piano-boxes we lived, cooked, ate and slept," she said, "for several months. I found plenty of work to do, at good prices. I washed, ironed, scrubbed and house-cleaned. My oldest boy has always been deranged from meningitis in infancy, but since coming here his mind has grown much clearer, and I am the happiest woman alive. Every-one has urged me to put him in an asylum, but I never would. I have stood by him when my own life and the other children's were in danger, for in his violent attacks he would try to kill us all." Mrs. B—— has now bought a lot, 100 by 50 feet, and is erecting a small but neat cottage upon it. She can truthfully say every nail and plank used has been earned to the

LC 1005
Pattern 4

LC 1005
Pattern 3

LC 1005
Pattern 2

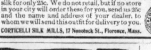

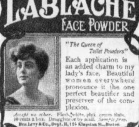

What Women are Doing.—*Continued.*

tune of the scrub-board, and while caring for an imbecile child. She holds the respect of all who know her and counts her friends by her patrons of whom there are a goodly number. She still keeps her piano-box house and proudly shows it when she relates her experience in utilizing it for a home for eight months.

Mrs. E. B. C.

SHE "SOLD THINGS"

A young woman, living in a small country town, began to look about her for some means of earning money. She had no special talents, but it occurred to her upon visiting the big market one Saturday, in the city ten miles from her home, that she might "sell things." She went home and thought the matter over. The following week she made six or eight pounds of delicious candy, for which she was famous, obtaining most of her recipes from old editions of THE DESIGNER. She also made several pounds of Saratoga chips or "potato roses," as she called them, cutting them with a slaw knife so that they curled up prettily when fried. Upon the payment of a small license fee, a friend procured a booth for her in the market, and the following Saturday she journeyed to the market with her wares. Friends, among the best people in the city, heard of her efforts and they readily patronized her. She got fifty cents a pound for her candy and thirty cents a pound for her "roses." The following week she enlarged her stock and added cream puffs to the list, which she sold for thirty cents a dozen. At the end of the first month, after deducting all expenses, including her railroad fare to the city, which was thirty-five cents the round trip, she found that she had cleared the neat sum of $32.64, spending three days each week at the market. It required work, but with some assistance it finally became a great pleasure to the young woman.

Nellie Morris Allen

RETOUCHING PHOTOGRAPHS

The thought has often occurred to me—why are there so few women retouchers on photographs? It takes only a few weeks to get an idea of what is to be done on a negative, and practise soon does wonders; besides it is a very pleasant occupation, and almost any photographer will be kind enough to teach a young woman who is worthy and really anxious to earn an honest living. After one has learned so her work is smooth she can command good wages, retouchers getting anywhere from five to twenty-five dollars a week. I know a young woman who retouches negatives for several studios, taking the work to her own home. When the season is dull in her immediate locality she solicits work from the towns near. The negatives are sent to her by paid express and she returns them promptly, making, some weeks, fifteen dollars. In all the articles I have read in these columns I have never seen this occupation advocated, and I sincerely hope this item may meet with the approval of many who are now in doubt, who will decide to become photographic retouchers. *F. H. M.*

ON A CAPITAL OF NINETY-SIX CENTS

It was some years ago. There were two little children needing support and education. What was to be done? The case was critical, but not hopeless. A healthy woman of twenty-nine years, with a trade, that of tailoress, thoroughly learned though never practised, did not despair, even though less than one dollar remained in the family treasury. In fact, to be exact, just ninety-six cents. Not a large capital, was it? Yet it brought success. Walking four miles into Boston, for the fare was high and not to be afforded, this money was invested at a tailor's shop. Several pieces of woolen cloth, half-a-dozen leather visors and some bits of lining and wadding were purchased. Six pretty caps for boys were made and placed for sale in the window of a tiny room—more entry than room—which overlooked the road. The price of each—fifty cents—was plainly marked upon the caps. Customers came. Before night the entire stock was sold—not to people desirous of helping a poor widow, but to parents glad of the opportunity to secure, at a fair price, strong and shapely headgear for their boisterous boys. Others saw the caps and orders came in for more. Larger pieces of cloth were bought and some small coats and trousers made. As every stitch was set on honor and the clothes never ripped, those who purchased once came again and again. To every caller the information was imparted that the tailoress was ready to make new suits or remodel old ones; to mend, re-line or cut down old garments. Work of this description came flowing in and help had to be hired. Ready-made and made-to-measure overalls for boys and men, warranted never to rip or lose a button, became a specialty, and soon the little shop had to be enlarged. Other articles were added, such as gloves, straw hats, mittens and other furnishing goods. For over twenty years the little shop was one of the local features of a town which has produced many enterprising men and women, though I doubt if many of these started in business and made a success of it on a capital of ninety-six cents. *E. F. W.*

PERSEVERANCE PAID IN THE END

My parents were plain farmer folks and thought that life fit for kings.

What Women are Doing.—Concluded

I did not; I was the restless bird in the nest. At seventeen I longed for a trade. I could not leave home for lack of funds and parents' consent But I kept teasing until I obtained consent, provided I earned the funds. Living in the pines of New Jersey, I thought of a plan to put those pine needles to good use. My consumptive aunt said their smell seemed to enable her to breathe more freely. My brother took me part way to Philadelphia, where among our city friends I obtained several orders for pine-needle pillows; then I went to the large stores and hospitals and explained my proposition, receiving encouraging orders. I raised lavender and made beautiful scent pads about the size of a large drawer and sold these also. I begged the proceeds of a row of strawberries, and the money for three baskets of every load of whatever vegetable went to market. I also picked peas and other things in season. In winter I gathered holly and other Christmas greens, and wove them into wreaths and garlands. My brother delivered those for me. I even husked corn, receiving the same pay as my brother. In fact, I did whatever my hands found to do. In one year I had money to enter a high-class tailoring establishment, where in two years I was earning twelve dollars per week. Since then I have married, met reverses, and at present am able to earn ten dollars per week for the support of my two children and myself, just through a little determination in the beginning. *E. R.*

HOW ONE GIRL HELPED

A young friend of mine, who lived alone with her widowed mother, wished to help eke out their small income, after leaving school. She could easily be spared from home duties from one till six afternoons, had had several terms of music lessons and could play fairly well. Why wouldn't some mother be glad to have her sit beside the little ones while they practised the tedious scales and runs; not to give lessons, but just to see that the practising was properly done. She secured a number of pupils at her first trial and eventually averaged five pupils an afternoon for five days, keeping Saturdays clear for herself, charged fifteen cents an hour, and her pupils showed a marked improvement in a short time. "You have no idea what a relief it is," said one lady to me; "she has such a nice way with Doris that the child absolutely looks forward to her practise hour now." In this way the young girl made at least fifteen dollars a month, enough to clothe herself nicely and occasionally treat "little mother" to a concert or the theater.

Orra Nelson

Crofts & Reed's
Soaps and Premiums

This Elegant Morris Chair GIVEN with only $15 worth of our goods. See catalogue for other styles with $10 worth and up.

Carpets GIVEN with $9 worth and up.

Couches. Extra well made. 14 styles. GIVEN with $10 worth and up.

This $10 Polished Oak Rocker GIVEN for using or selling $10 worth of our goods.

SHIPPED DIRECT from FACTORY TO HOME.

Washing Machine Hard to beat this one. GIVEN for using or selling $10 worth of our goods.

Chiffonier Quartered oak, golden oak finish, swell-front drawers. Easy to earn. Write for catalogue.

Teas and Coffees. Makers of Strictly High-Grade Laundry and Toilet Soaps, Flavoring Extracts, Baking Powder, Spices, Toilet Articles, Etc.

You get wholesale and retail dealers' profits and expenses in the form of some useful and valuable article as a premium, saving you about one-half the usual cost.

Write for large illustrated catalogue of nearly everything needed for the home and many other useful and valuable articles, including Parlor and Dining-Room Furniture, Refrigerators, Bookcases, Desks, Silverware, Rugs, Lace Curtains, Clocks, Watches, Jewelry, Ladies' Waists, Hats, Shoes, Boys' Suits, etc., *given with orders for your own use, or for selling $5 worth and up.*

YOU WILL FIND IT A GREAT SAVING to buy goods in this way.

30 Days' Free Trial
ON BOTH PREMIUM AND GOODS.

We make a specialty of giving the greatest possible values in

$10 Premiums with $10 Orders.

If No Premium is Desired, we will give you the goods at half price, in amounts of $2.50 and up. This means 2½c a bar for our best Laundry Soap, 12½c per one pound can pure Baking Powder, 12½c a box (3 cakes) for fine Toilet Soaps. Other goods in same proportion. *REMEMBER* you can make your own selection of Soaps, Perfumes, Extracts, Baking Powder, Spices, Teas, Coffees, etc., or you can have all Laundry or all Toilet Soap, or part of both.

Money Refunded if Everything is Not Entirely Satisfactory.

Our Goods and Premiums have been spoken of so highly so many times and by so many people, we know that our customers appreciate our efforts in trying to give them the *highest grade of goods* and the *most valuable premiums*, and we never stop trying to do better and better. We are constantly receiving letters similar to this:

Messrs. CROFTS & REED, Chicago, Ill.
Dear Sirs: I am sending you another club order. It gives me great pleasure to speak of the goods you manufacture; they are in every way first-class. Over ten years ago I began to introduce your goods in Bradford Co., Pa., and in less than two years had customers enough to take 1200 boxes of toilet soap and 200 bottles of extract. I am also secretary of soap clubs now, which brings a lovely premium once a month to the home of some member, all of which are more than satisfactory.
Yours truly,   MRS. I. C. ALDRICH, Towanda, Pa.

YOU CAN EASILY EARN

any article you wish by taking a few orders among your friends and neighbors, or by getting up a club order. Write for particulars. If you wish a cash commission and will devote all of your time to the business you can make

$20 TO $30 A WEEK

Handsome and Complete SAMPLE CASE FREE to Club Organizers and Solicitors. Illustrated Catalogue and Style Book sent FREE. Ask About Our Club Order Plan.

CROFTS & REED,
840-850 Austin Ave.,   Dept. 200,   CHICAGO, ILL.

Go-Carts and Sleeping Coaches GIVEN with small orders. See catalogue.

Two Smyrna Rugs 36x72 in., with $10 worth.

Ladies' Stylish Spring and Summer Suits, Skirts, Cravenettes and Jackets GIVEN with small assortment of soap, etc. Write for Fashion Book of latest styles.

100-Piece Dinner Set Beautiful three-color and gold decoration. Pleases everybody. Quality guaranteed. GIVEN with $14 assortment. Write for catalogue showing Dinner and Tea Sets. GIVEN for using or selling $9 worth and up.

Child's Storm Coat Made to order. GIVEN for using or selling $8 worth of our goods.

The Latest in Collars and Cuffs

THE use of separate collars and cuffs continues to grow in favor, and now that sleeves are increasing in size at the top and cuffs are reaching up to the elbow, the detachable cuffs are also growing deeper, some of them showing a gauntlet effect which is very pleasing.

The old-fashioned "Broderie Anglaise," or eyelet work, promises to be the most popular style of embroidery for the lingerie waists and accessory trimmings, which are now shown in such profusion in the shops, and embroidery of this kind is almost always combined with a little satin or French embroidery, which emphasizes and brings out, as

The sets are composed of narrow collars and deep cuffs; in the first set one a little of the eyelet-worked linen show and the points form deep Vandyke while in the second the edge of the collar shows shallow points and the cuff are square in effect. Small groups of eyelets are worked on the linen with several small leaves at both sides of the group done in satin-stitch. After the work on the linen is finished, the edge buttonhole

STOLE COLLAR

and cut out, the piece is basted on a cambric pattern similar to those used in lace work. The outline that is to be covered by the buttonholed bars and rings is stamped on this and the next step is to baste the rings in place

COLLAR AND CUFFS WITH VANDYKE POINTS

NARROW COLLAR AND DEEP, SQUARE CUFFS

it were, the more delicate beauty of the former work.

To combine the English and French embroidery with a kind of lace-stitch is a recent innovation, and that the result is all that could be asked for is shown in the two sets of collars and cuffs illustrated.

and also the piece of braid which finishes the edge. This braid is made of heavy linen and comes in two styles, with picots on both or on only one of its edges.

The work which joins the braid to the rings, and the latter to the linen, consists simply and solely of button-

ed bars of thread, with a picot
rked at varying intervals. These
's are known to embroiderers by the
ne of "Raleigh" bars and are worked
ording to the detail given in the
; illustration. As may be seen by
:rring to that, the pattern is first
:ered by a line of thread which is
sted closely at places, so as to shape
intervening spaces. After the pat-
1 has been entirely gone over with

DETAIL OF RALEIGH BARS

; thread, the latter is covered with
ttonhole stitches worked close togeth-
with a picot in the center of almost
ery bar.

Picots are made by placing the needle
.der the back of the stitch last made
d winding the needle with thread,
nding from left to right or away from
u. The more times the thread is
)und around the needle, the larger
ll the picot be. After the thread
s been wound the necessary number
times—ten times makes a fair-sized
:ot—place the thumb of the left hand
. top of the thread-covered needle,
lding it lightly yet firmly until the
:dle has been pulled all the way
rough. If this is not done, the
reads are apt to kink and knot and
e picot will not pull up smooth.
hen the picot is finished, continue
.king the buttonhole-stitches, pushing
e first one as close up to the one
.de previous to the picot as possible.
lese bars may also be made with a
ochet-needle, covering the lines of
read with single crochet-stitches,
.king the picots of three or four
.ain-stitches, worked very tight.
us way of working would, of course,
'ogress much more rapidly than the
Raleigh" bars, and the result would
'obably be equally satisfactory.

On page 716 is shown a stole collar
.ade of Teneriffe wheels and lace braid.
)llars like this look prettiest when
.orn with thin silk or lingerie waists,
.d surely nothing could be cooler or
.ore comfortable for a hot summer day.
The Teneriffe wheels may be bought
.ady made by the dozen at most of
.e large department stores and em-
·oidery shops; or, if one prefers, frames
· disks made of thin wood or celluloid
.ay be, bought, with the necessary
.aterials and directions, and the wheels
.ade at home.

One of these dainty"ready-to-make" Yokes or Corset Covers will be given away with each purchase of our Laces amounting to $2 or more

JEANNE   MARIE   CECILE   HORTENSE   LILLIAN

VALENCE PARIS   NEW YORK CALAIS

COMPAGNIE DE VALENCE

NEW YORK, March 1st, 1905.

To the Ladies of America: This offer is made for a threefold purpose.

First, to introduce to you our line of Imported Laces, containing the largest assortment of designs ever brought to this country (at prices ranging from 1c. to $3 per yard) for Lingerie, Shirtwaists, Baby's Clothes, Handkerchiefs or Fancy Work, in Imported Valenciennes, Mechlin, Torchon, etc., at prices which mean a great money-saving, because our Laces go to all parts of the world direct from us to the users, without the many profits of importers, jobbers, commission houses and retail merchants.

Second, to introduce the superior merits of two fabrics, the Mousseline de Valence—the material from which are made these Corset Covers—and the Linon de Valence, from which are made the Yokes. We believe that they will outlaunder and outwear any materials you have ever used, and we know that in appearance and "feel," they will compare favorably with goods sold in this country at far higher prices.

Third, to introduce the "ready-to-make" idea as applied to undermuslins and accessories. These Corset Covers and Yokes are cut to your measure by experts and sent to you ready to be put together.

Only one to a customer under the terms of the above offer; but where more than one are desired, we will supply them at 38c. each.

The "Ready-to-Make" idea is more fully described on page 721 of this magazine in the announcement of Summer Shirtwaists made by the "Ready-to-Make" Garment Co., who control the "Ready-to-Make" rights, and with whom we have made an arrangement by which these garments may be fashioned to your measure by their own skilled cutters. If you write to them direct at 346 Broadway, New York, they will send you free a handsomely illustrated catalogue of "Ready-to-Make" Undermuslins of all kinds, Infants' Layettes, etc., etc.

At this season nearly every woman is interested in Lace Bargains. If you would buy at wholesale prices and from a stock that includes scores of exclusive designs, as well as all the staple patterns, in all widths—Edgings, Insertions, Beadings, Allovers, etc.—write to us.

SEND FOR FULL LINE OF
LACE SAMPLES—FREE!
Hundreds of Styles to Choose From at Bargain Prices

A postal card will bring you a full assortment.
We guarantee your perfect satisfaction with every purchase, or "your money back" without question and without delay.

HOW YOU ARE TO ORDER

Send first for our complete line of samples, which will be mailed you, free. From them choose the designs you want and fill out the order blank we will send you, enclosing a proper remittance. Fill out, also, the self-measurement blank we send, that we may have accurate measurements for cutting and fitting the Corset Cover or the Yoke selected.

WHAT WE SEND

The day following receipt of your order (if same amounts to $2 or over) we will mail you the Laces and the "ready-to-make" Corset Cover or Yoke, cut to your special measure, ready for you to put together and trim, in either of the designs shown above.

This method saves you all risk of loss from faulty cutting, saves cost of pattern, your time and your labor.

We sell direct to the consumer in every State in the Union now, and our designs are to be found in nearly every dry goods store of any size in this country.

We are making the above unusual offer because we want as quickly as possible to let every woman in America find out for herself that whenever she has a Lace need, we can fill it a little quicker, a little better and quite a little cheaper than any other establishment.

Remember, please, that we can sell only in lengths of three, six or twelve yards, as at our prices we cannot afford to have odd lengths remain.

We pay the postage on all orders and fill them the same day received; but for your safety we recommend that all packages be sent by registered mail. If you desire this, add 8c. for registering—otherwise package will be mailed prepaid at your own risk.   Your obed't servants,

COMPAGNIE DE VALENCE
per LEON GIRARD
(Sole Representative for the United States and Canada)
96 Fifth Avenue, New York City.

P. S.—I desire to appoint one woman in each neighborhood to receive orders for our Laces. Would you like to?

FLORICULTURE TALKS

By M. W. PARK

PREPARING PLANTS IN SPRING FOR THE WINTER WINDOW

FOR winter blooming, carnations should be started, either from seeds or cuttings, in February or March, or early in April. The usual way is to set off the young seedlings when large enough in small pots, and shift as the plants grow till time to bed out. Then they should be given a sunny bed, and several times during the summer the tops should be pinched out to prevent blooming and cause the plants to grow strong and bushy. The florists usually have their plants in five-inch pots when time for bedding out arrives, and instead of turning the plants out of the pots they plunge them pots and all into the soil. In the autumn they are taken up, removed from the pots, and bedded in long beds on the greenhouse bench, where they usually bloom profusely during the winter months.

For window culture, when taken up in September the plants should be shifted or potted into six or seven inch pots and allowed to remain and bloom in these. Keep them in a rather cool place. See that the drainage is good, and supply water as the plants appear to require it. The soil should be composed of sifted loam with the addition of some leaf-mold, sand and manure which has been well rotted.

ABUTILONS, BEGONIAS AND OTHER PLANTS

Those pretty plants, Abutilons, may be treated in the same manner as carnations, propagating the plants early in spring, and keeping them growing throughout the summer, occasionally cutting back the tops to produce a shapely form. They can either be bedded out in the ground or plunged with their pots in the soil, then shifted or repotted in September. When bedded out, a portion of the tops should be removed at the time of repotting. This pruning will give more strength to the roots, and will enable them to sustain and push forward the new growth more vigorously.

With Begonias, however, the treatment is somewhat different. Young plants may be started from seeds, or cuttings in spring, and their growth encouraged by shifting from time to time, but they should not be bedded out. A shady place in the open air, where they will have the morning sun and be protected from high winds or storms, should be given them during summer, and sufficient water to keep them moist and growing, but not wet. Prune only enough to keep the plants in shape and encourage growth instead of bloom. If winter-blooming sorts are grown, as Begonia semperflorens, Meltoniensis, Rubros or Gracilis, but little difficulty will be experienced in getting the plants in flower during the winter season. The combination of loose, porous soil with good drainage will successfully produce healthy and well-developed plants.

Geraniums to bloom in winter should be started from seeds or cuttings early in spring and the young plants shifted as they develop until they occupy four-inch pots. They bloom best in small pots and the shifting should only be done when the roots have well covered the soil against the sides of the pot. At no time should the plant suffer for want of water, but on the other hand it should not be kept soaking wet at all times. When the plants are five or six inches high the points of shoots should be nipped back, and this process continued until a nice, bushy plant is obtained. During the summer all the buds that form should be promptly removed, and after the plants occupy four-inch pots water once or twice a week with weak soot water. Geraniums will flourish in any good soil, but must have proper drainage and plenty of sun. They enjoy the sunshine and should have the sunniest window convenient during the winter. The leaves are kept clean and the entire plant greatly benefited by frequent syringings.

Solanum Capsicastrum, commonly known as Jerusalem Cherry, makes a handsome plant for the winter window. This should also be started from seeds in early spring. The seeds germinate readily, and the young seedling plants should be potted in small pots at first and shifted from time to time, as they grow until autumn, when they should be encouraged to bloom and set their fruit. The flowers of the plant are insignificant, but the fruit or berries which follow are bright scarlet in color,

Floriculture.—*Continued.*

and when well set upon the plant make a handsome showing. Watered moderately during winter, the berries and clean, neatly cut foliage will remain on the plant throughout the winter, and if kept cool enough will often retain the berries from one season until the next crop is coming. The plant is not particular as to soil but will do well in any rich loam, and by pruning can be trained into any desired shape, and may be made to resemble miniature cherry trees. A cool window where it will get only the early morning sun will suit this plant quite well. Syringing thoroughly with fresh, clear water once a week will keep the leaves and the brilliant berries glossy and free from dust and insects.

There are many other plants that bloom well in the winter window, and that should be started from seeds planted in early spring and grown purposely for the window. By attending to this preparation at the proper time there need be no scarcity of blooms in the house during the winter season, especially if one has suitable windows and a little time to care for them. Plants of Impatiens Sultani Browallia Elata, Annual Chrysanthemum, Ten Weeks' Stock, Primroses, Chinese Forbesi and Obconica will all bloom well in the winter window when properly grown, and such plants are far hardier and healthier when started from seeds in spring.

ALONSOA

Alonsoa is a beautiful and charming little annual, growing fifteen or eighteen inches in height. It is evidently becoming one of the popular flowers of to-day. Not only can it be used as a summer bedding plant, for which it is very desirable on account of the brilliancy of its flowers, but it is also useful as a pot plant for the winter window. When bedded out, the plants may be massed together in plots by themselves or may be grown in connection with other plants contrasting in color of blooms.

The increase is readily effected by seeds or cuttings. Seeds should be sown as early in spring as possible, to make blooming plants throughout the summer.

One of the best species is Warscewiczii. It is somewhat perennial in habit, and has narrow, graceful foliage. The flowers are a bright crimson scarlet. Plants grown in a pot will bloom from June until late in autumn, if kept well fed with nourishing stimulants.

Alonsoa linifolia has foliage which is closely similar to that of Warscewiczii. It grows in neat and graceful formation, and bears clusters of rich scarlet flowers in profusion.

PARFUGIUM GRANDE

Farfugium Grande, or Leopard plant, as it is often called, is a handsome

Floriculture.—*Concluded.*

foliage plant. Its rich, glossy, dark-green leaves, irregularly spotted with white or cream color, make it an ornament to any plant collection. These leaves are somewhat heart-shaped, and vary greatly in size, according to treatment. On well-developed plants the leaves grow quite large, usually measuring from seven to eleven inches in breadth, and are borne on thick, fleshy stems. A soil composed of equal parts of leaf-mold, rich loam and sand suits it quite well. Plenty of water during the growing season, with a weekly dose of soot tea, and once in a great while a little liquid manure, will bring a plant pretty near to perfection, provided it has plenty of root room and good drainage. It does well in a window where it will have the morning sun but be shaded during the rest of the day. A period of rest of from five to six weeks is necessary for the development of a fine, healthy plant of Farfugium Grande. This is usually best given in winter, during which time it can be kept in a frost-proof cellar and watered sparingly, just enough to keep the soil slightly moist. When it has rested, or when you wish to start it into new growth, shift into a larger pot and cut away the old leaves. Bring the plant to stronger light and heat and gradually give more water. If a season of rest is neglected, the plant will become spindling, the leaves will loose their luster and finally drop off. If given too much water during the resting period the plant will be affected in the same manner. By cutting away the old leaves when repotting, the strength will go into the new growth and the plant will develop more rapidly. The Farfugium is said to be perfectly hardy in California, and even in southern Pennsylvania it is almost hardy. Roots of it have been known to endure quite severe winters, but it is not the wisest plan to leave the plants out of doors without protection.

The foliage should be washed or sponged carefully once or twice a week with clean water, to prevent dust from collecting on the leaves and to dislodge any insect that may happen to come in contact with the plant. If the pot in which the Farfugium is growing is well drained, water as hot as the hand will bear can be used when watering. Or boiling water can be poured in the saucer in which the pot is standing, allowing the plant to take up what it wants. After the plant is supplied the surplus water can be drained off. Cold water if allowed to remain in the saucer may cause decay at the roots, which will injure the plant seriously.

The Farfugium is principally grown for the beauty of its foliage; the flowers, being coarse and somewhat resembling a single dandelion, are not very attractive, and the foliage is finer when the plant is kept from blooming.

LAUNDERING A SHIRT-WAIST

By MARGARET PLETZ

IT IS very discouraging to have the erstwhile daintily colored shirt-waists return from the laundry ded and streaked, when, if intelligent .re had been given to the washing and ning, their ruin would have been .oided. The process of laundering ich garments is very simple, and with .reful attention to a few details the nists should emerge fresh and attractive om the tub.

If there are unwashable buttons, :move them, and if sure the colors o not fade, soak the garment for five .inutes in a suds made of white ap. This loosens the dirt so that hard .bbing is not necessary. In washing lored goods avoid ammonia, soda and ot water. Wash thoroughly, giving pecial attention to under parts of leeves, cuffs and front. Rinse in several waters, adding a little blue to the .st water. Lavender and green waists hould not be blued. The waist is now eady for starching. Mix three table-poonfuls of starch with half a cupful of old water, add one quart of boiling vater and cook twenty minutes. While :ooking, add a teaspoonful of borax; this .revents the starch from sticking to he iron. When the starch is luke-varm (it can be made of double strength nd cold water added to cool it), dip n the garment, wring and hang in the hade to dry. To hang once in the sun-hine will fade pink and blue sooner .han fifty washings. Wash white shirt-vaists in the same manner, but boil ten minutes, adding to each bucket of water .teaspoonful of borax. Rinse, blue, .tarch and hang in the sun to dry, as it nsures a snowy whiteness.

In using bluing, be very careful to have .ll the soap rinsed from the garments, .s bluing is usually a compound of ron salts, which is precipitated by the .lkali in the soap, hence the spots of ron rust found on clothing so often .fter laundering. If the spots do form through careless rinsing, wet them with .emon juice, cover with salt and put in the sun. This process can be em-ployed with white goods only.

When the waist is dry, sprinkle it with cold water until moderately damp. Have a bowl of cold starch ready, using one tablespoonful of starch to each pint of cold water. Dip the collar-band, cuffs and plait in front, one at a time, being careful that every part is saturated with starch. Squeeze as dry as possible. Fold the garment in a clean cloth for half an hour before ironing.

With waists of very delicate color, that may fade, use the following: To one gallon of lukewarm water add half a pint of gasoline. Put the waist in this, rub gently with the hands to remove

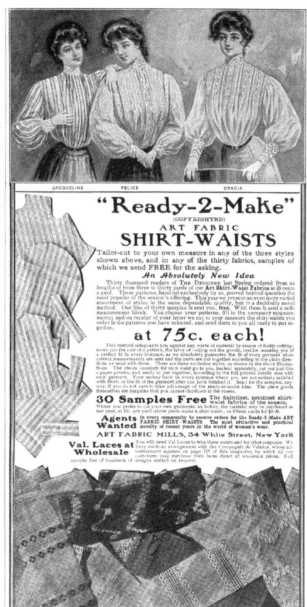

JACQUELINE   FELICE   GRACIA

"Ready-2-Make"
(COPYRIGHTED)

ART FABRIC
SHIRT-WAISTS

Tailor-cut to your own measure in any of the three styles shown above, and in any of the thirty fabrics, samples of which we send FREE for the asking.

An Absolutely New Idea

Thirty thousand readers of THE DESIGNER last Spring ordered from us lengths of from three to thirty yards of our Art Shirt-Waist Fabrics at 25 cents a yard. These patterns, handled exclusively by us, proved beyond question the most popular of the season's offering. This year we present an even more varied assortment of styles in the same dependable quality, but in a decidedly novel method. Our line of thirty samples is sent you, free. With them is sent a self-measurement blank. You choose your patterns, fill in the necessary measurements and on receipt of your letter we cut to your measure the shirt-waists you order in the patterns you have selected, and send them to you all ready to put together,

at 75c. each!

This method safeguards you against any waste of material by reason of faulty cutting; saves you the cost of a pattern, the labor of cutting and the goods, besides assuring you of a perfect fit in every instance, as we absolutely guarantee the fit of every garment when correct measurements are sent and the parts are put together according to the plain directions we send with them. There are three exclusive styles, as shown in the above illustration. The pieces complete for each waist go to you, packed separately, cut out just like a paper pattern, and ready to put together, according to the full printed details sent with each garment. Your money back in every instance where you are not entirely satisfied with fabric or the fit of the garment after you have finished it. Send for the samples, anyway, if you do not care to take advantage of the ready-to-make idea. The piece goods themselves are bargains that you cannot duplicate at the stores.

30 Samples Free The daintiest, prettiest shirt-waist fabrics of the season. Where you prefer to cut your own garments, as before, the material may be purchased as last year, at 25c. per yard (three yards make a shirt-waist), or fifteen yards for $3.00.

Agents Wanted in every community to receive orders for the Ready-2-Make ART FABRIC SHIRT-WAISTS. The most attractive and practical novelty of recent years in the world of woman's wear.

ART FABRIC MILLS, 34 White Street, New York

Val. Laces at Wholesale You will need Val Laces to trim these waists and for other purposes. We have made an arrangement with the Compagnie de Valence, whose advertisement appears on page 717 of this magazine, by which all our customers may purchase their laces direct at wholesale prices. Full sample line of hundreds of designs mailed on request.

Laundering a Shirt-Waist.—*Concluded.*

the dirt. Work as quickly as possible, squeezing and pressing the soiled parts until clean. Rinse in several waters and add bluing if necessary. Mix two tablespoonfuls of cold-water starch (this starch requires no boiling; several good brands are on the market) in one quart of lukewarm water. Dip the garment in this, press as dry as possible, roll up tightly in a clean white cloth and let lie one hour before ironing. Do not let the waist lie in the water and use no soap; the gasoline will dissolve the dirt.

Navy-blue or black lawns or sateens should never be washed in the same water in which white goods are washed. The bits of lint will cling to them and give a spotted appearance. Starch does the same thing very often. The best plan with such garments is to wash quickly in a warm lather of soap and water, dip in cold-water starch, roll in a cloth, and iron on the wrong side in two hours' time.

An infusion of bran is the best thing in which to wash buff or brown linen. Cover a pint of bran with a quart of hot water; let stand for an hour. Strain through cheesecloth. Divide in half, adding a gallon of water to each part. Wash the linen in one part, rinse in the other, wring dry, fold in a cloth, and iron in two hours. Iron the linen on the wrong side to avoid a shiny appearance. This process will render the linen like new. The cuffs and front plait may be dipped in cold starch, before ironing, if wanted a trifle stiffer.

Lawns, organdies and mulls appear as new, with that clear, fresh look so desirable in new goods, if rinsed in potato water. If the colors do not fade, wash in a lather of white soap and rinse in clean water; if the colors are liable to run, wash in gasoline and water, squeeze very dry and dip in the potato water. Squeeze as dry as possible and gently clap between the hands, until almost dry, roll in a clean cloth, and iron on wrong side in two hours' time. To prepare the potato water, wash and peel two potatoes, grate them into a quart of warm water. Let stand half an hour, strain through cheesecloth, and use. Starch will not be necessary, as the potatoes are starchy and give just the desirable crispness to the goods.

In ironing a shirt-waist, a sleeve-board and an iron with a long, slender point will facilitate matters. Cover the board with a heavy piece of old blanket and over this a clean white cloth.

When ironing a colored waist be careful not to use too hot an iron, yet it must be hot enough to smooth the fabric without blistering or sticking. An overheated iron will, however, ruin the colors as much as do hot sunshine, hot water and strong alkali. Stretch the front and back into shape, and if there are tucks smooth them out carefully with the hands before beginning operations. Begin ironing at the right side, iron around to the back and then the left side. The front plait must be stretched

and pulled perfectly straight before ironing; press it first on the wrong, then on the right, side of goods until perfectly dry. After this use the point of iron with heavy pressure along the stitching, always pressing one way; this brings the stitching into relief. In ironing the back and front, always run the iron up or down, never crosswise. Iron the cloth until dry, otherwise a mussed appearance will result. Next iron the collar-band and then the sleeves. If the sleeve is ironed without a sleeve-board, press it flat, with one fold on the seam, and iron on both sides of sleeve, then pull apart and press again. Finish the top of sleeve by putting the point of iron inside the sleeve and smoothing out the gathered top. Iron the cuffs last. Press the wrong side lightly, after pulling them out perfectly smooth and flat; turn and iron the right side until dry, then with the heel of the iron press very hard until a fine polish is produced. Now take hold of one end of the cuff, press the iron along to the other end, rolling the cuff over the iron as the pressing proceeds (this gives the cuff a rounded shape), fasten it with a stud, and the collar also, and hang up to dry. Iron embroidery on the wrong side over a well-padded board and pull out all scalloped edges as the iron is moved along. Piqué and heavy damask shirt-waists should be starched only on neckband, cuffs and front plait. Iron on the wrong side on a well-padded board, so as to bring the cords or figures into relief. White or colored silk waists, if the latter are of fast color, are washed in a suds of white soap and lukewarm water, rinsed and hung to dry. Before quite dry, iron either on the wrong side or by putting a piece of thin cloth between the silk and iron. Never use a very hot iron or hot water for white silk, as it yellows the silk, and putting a iron directly on silk takes out the sheen.

Wash a flannel waist in lukewarm suds, to which add a little borax to soften the water. Do not use a board, as the rubbing mats the flannel, but squeeze and press between the hands. Rinse in several waters of equal temperature, adding to the last water, to each gallon, a tablespoonful of glycerin. This renders the wool very soft. The secret of success in washing woolens is to have them dry as soon as possible after wetting. Never soak them or rub soap directly on the woolen, as both operations render the threads harsh. Run through the wringer, squeezing out as much moisture as you can, shake well and hang to dry. When nearly dry, iron as soon as possible. If not ready to iron at once let the garment become perfectly dry, as allowing it to lie in a half-dampened condition ruins woolen stuff. When ready, place a piece of slightly dampened cheesecloth over the flannel on the right side and press with a moderately hot iron. In removing the cloth the fibers of the flannel cling to it, giving the flannel a fluffy finish akin to new goods. Dampen the cheesecloth each time.

CLOAKS — SUITS — SKIRTS

It is easy to create a new style without regard to past or present vogue; *but* to make a style that is beautiful, in accord with the present tendencies, and, at the same time, entirely acceptable to the taste of practical American women—calls for the work of the most expert style artists.

In *Wooltex* garments our designers not only show the best and latest thoughts of the leading fashion centers, but they give expression to their own ideas for the fashionable and practical American women. *Wooltex* garments do not show a radical departure. They are in style—the newest style—but not obtrusively so. They retain their shape, too.

These two tan-colored covert jackets show what we mean. They are fully described in *Wooltex* Catalogue No. 52, which shows all the new styles in Jackets, Suits and Skirts.

Wooltex stands for more than style alone. It is a standard of good cloth, with perfect fit and tailoring and fine finish.

The *Wooltex* guarantee means if your *Wooltex* garment is not entirely satisfactory—in fabric, fit, finish and tailoring—your dealer will make it right with you. Whatever it costs, we pay him.

Ask your dealer for *Wooltex.*

Get the Wooltex Catalogue of SPRING STYLES No. 52

If your dealer hasn't it, write us.

H. BLACK & COMPANY, CLEVELAND AND NEW YORK

Crocheted Trimmings for Linen Dresses

ABBREVIATIONS USED IN CROCHETING: ch.—Chain. ch. st.—Chain stitch. s. c.—Single crochet. d. c.—Double crochet.—(Thread over once); tr. c.—Treble crochet.—(Thread over twice); d. tr. c.—Double treble crochet.—(Over three times); sl. st.—Slip stitch. st.—Stitch. o.—Over. p.—Picot. l.—Loop. k. st.—Knot stitch. Roll st.—Thread over the needle as many times as indicated. Repeat.—Work designated rows, rounds or portions of the work as many times as directed.

HEAVY linen thread and a steel hook are required.

Ivy-Leaf Design. — For first leaflet chain 20, turn, miss 2 ch and in the next 18 ch crochet as follows: 2 s c, 2 d c, 2 tr, 2 l tr (thread over 3 times), 2 (thread over 4 times), 2 l tr, 2 tr, 2 d c, 2 s c. 2d and 3d leaflets are made in similar fashion.

Stem: Chain 30, catch at point of first leaflet. This completes one ivy leaf. In making the succeeding leaves, crochet 2 leaflets in place of 3 before working the stem. After crocheting a piece of the length desired, break thread and finish the stems by working 35 s c under every 30 ch, and break thread. Begin at the 1st stem and work an edging around each similar to that around the leaves; turn and work back toward the beginning, an edging at the inside of each stem, which partly fills in the open spaces. In working this, draw the spool up through the open space first, then continue as usual.

The edging is worked as follows: 2 s c in 2 s c, 3 ch, catch in 2d s c and repeat around. The Irish picot edging is somewhat similar in appearance, but worked differently. Chain 5, catch back in 2d st from hook to form picot. Ch 1, miss 2 s c, catch with s c and repeat. Fasten and break thread.

Irish Crochet Lace. — Make 8 ch, join.

First row—1 ch, 20 s c under ring, sl st in 1st s c. Second row—6 ch, skip 1, 1 d c in next, * 3 ch, skip 1, 1 d c in next, repeat from * times. 3 ch, sl st in 3d of 6 ch. Third row—1 ch, 3 s c under 3 ch, 3 ch, 3 s c under same 3 ch, * 3 s c under next 3 ch, 3 ch, 3 s c under same 3 ch, repeat from * 4 times, * 7 s c

IVY LEAF DESIGN

under next 3 ch, repeat from * 3 times, sl st in 1st s c. To join wheels: join 2d of 3 ch on 1st point to 2d of 3 ch on 6th point on preceding wheel with s c.

For the top: 1 d c in 4th of first 7 s c. * 5 ch, 1 s c in 4th of next 7, 5 ch, 1 s c in 4th of next 7, 5 ch, 1 d c in next 7, 5 ch, 1 d c in 4th of 1st 7 s c on next wheel; repeat from * to end. Second row—7 s c under 5 ch, * 7 s c under

MEDALLION TRIMMING

next 5 ch, repeat from * to end. Third row—1 d c in 4th of 7 s c, * 4 ch, 1 d c in 4th of next 7, repeat from * to end. Fourth row—6 s c under 4 ch, * 6 s c under next 4 ch, repeat from *. Fifth row—1 d c in 3d and 4th of 6 s c, * 3 ch, 1 d c in 3d and 4th of next 6, repeat from *.

For the points: 1 s c in 3 ch on 2d point, * 5 ch, 1 s c in next point, 7 ch, 1 s c in next point, 5 ch, 1 s c in next point, 5 ch, 1 s c in 2d 3 ch on next wheel, repeat from *. Second row—2 s c under first 5 ch, * 3 ch, 6 s c under

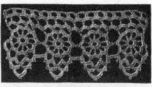

BUTTERFLY TRIMMING

same 5 ch, 5 s c under 7 ch, turn; 5 ch, sl st in 4th of preceding 6 s c, turn; 1 ch, 2 s c under 5 ch, 3 ch, 6 s c under same 5 ch, 5 s c under 7 ch, 4 s c under next 5, turn; 5 ch, sl st in 5th s c under 7 ch, turn; 1 ch, 4 s c under 5 ch, turn; 7 ch, sl st in 4th of preceding 6 s c, turn; 1 ch, 6 s c under 7 ch, 3 ch, 6 s c under same 7 ch, 2 s c under next 5, 3 ch, 2 s c under same 5, 7 s c under 5 ch between wheels, 2 s c under 1st 5 ch on next wheel; repeat from * for each point.

Butterfly Trimming. — Chain 25, catch and form ring. 40 s c under ring; 26 ch, catch in 2d st and form ring; 40 s c under ring; 26 ch, catch in 2d st and form ring; 40 s c under ring; 30 ch, catch with sl st in 23 s c of last ring; 50

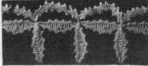

IRISH CROCHET LACE

ic under 30 ch, * 3 s c in 3 s c of 1st
ring, 3 ch, miss 1 s c, repeat from * within
1 s c of the end of the ring, then catch
in 5th s c of next ring; * 3 s c in 3 s c, 3 ch,

MEDALLION INSERTION

miss 1 s c, repeat from * all around to
within 4 s c of end of ring, catch in 5th
s c in next ring, * 3 s c in 3 s c, 3 ch,
miss 1 s c, repeat around ring to stem;
22 s c in 22 s c of stem. This completes
1 figure, except for filling in of centers,
which is done with needle and thread.
A spider is worked in each space.

Medallion Trimming.—Make 8 ch,
join. First row—1 ch, 20 s c under the
ring, sl st in 1st s c. Second row—6 ch,
skip 1, 1 d c in next, * 3 ch, skip 1, 1
d c in next, repeat from * 7 times, 3 ch,
sl st in 3d of 6 ch. Third row—1 ch, *
6 s c under 3 ch, repeat from * 9 times,
sl st in 1st and 2d s c. Fourth row—
1 ch, 1 s c in 3d and 4th s c, * 5 ch, 1 s c
in 3d and 4th of next 6 s c, repeat from
* 9 times, sl st in 1st and 2d s c. Fifth
row—1 ch, * 4 s c under 5 ch, 3 ch, 4 s c
under same 5 ch, repeat from * twice, 9
s c under next 5 ch, 4 s c under next 5
ch, 7 ch, turn, sl st in 5th of preceding 9
s c, turn, 2 s c under 7 ch, 3 ch, 3 s c
under same 7 ch, 3 ch, 1 s c under same
7, 3 ch, 3 s c under same, 3 ch, 2 s c
under same, 4 s c under 5 ch, * 4 s c,
3 ch, 4 s c under next 5 ch, repeat from
* twice; work next end same as 1st one,
sl st in 1st s c. The figures may be finished separately or joined by joining 2
picots on the end to 2 picots on end of
next figure with s c.

Medallion Insertion.—Make 8 ch,
join. First row—1 ch, 20 s c under the
ring, sl st in first s c. Second row—6
ch, skip 1, 1 d c in next, * 3 ch, skip
1, 1 d c in next; repeat from * 7
times, 3 ch, sl st in 3d of 6 ch.
Third row—1 ch, * 3 s c under 3 ch,
3 ch, 3 s c under same 3 ch, repeat from
* 9 times, sl st in 1st s c, join 1 loop
of 3 ch to loop of 3 ch on next wheel
with s c.

First row on side: 1 s c in 1st point, *
5 ch, 5 ch, 1 s c in next point, 6 ch, 1 s c
in next point, 5 ch, 1 s c in next point,
5 ch, 1 s c in 1st point on next wheel,
repeat from * to end. Second row—*
8 s c under 5 ch, 9 s c under 6 ch,
8 s c under next 5, 7 s c under 5 ch
between wheels, repeat from * to end.
Third row— * 1 s c in 2d, 3d and 4th
of 8 s c, 3 ch, 1 s c in 5th, 6th and 7th,
1 s c in 2d, 3d, 4th and 5th of 9 s c,
3 ch, 1 s c in 5th, 6th, 7th and 8th; 1 s c
in 2d, 3d and 4th of next 8 s c, 3 ch,
1 s c in 5th, 6th and 7th; 1 s c in 3d, 4th
and 5th of 7 s c between wheels; repeat
from * to end.

HELPS ALONG THE WAY

EDITED BY THE READERS
OF THE DESIGNER

QUESTION

OIL OF TAR AND TURPENTINE FOR DIPHTHERIA

Will someone please give the recipe in THE DESIGNER for burning oil of tar and turpentine together for diphtheria, and also recipe for making old-fashioned cough medicine from slippery-elm bark, flaxseed and lemons?

ANSWERS

No. 1

In reply to "What ails these pies?" in the March DESIGNER: In making custard or lemon pies, the secret of success lies in pressing the pastry on the tin so that not a bit of air can get under the crust to cause the puff; great care must be exercised, and if a little puff appears, puncture it with a fork and press the paste all over tight; then put in your filling and bake in a quick oven. MRS. C. F. G.

No. 2

The puffing-up of the crust is caused by heat expanding the bubbles of air left under the crust. If V. A. R. will begin in the middle and smooth the crust out toward the rim, lifting the edge a little as she smooths it, so as to get out all the air, and then take a small-tined fork and stick through the crust in several places over the bottom before putting in the filling, she will have no more trouble. Or, better still, purchase from the kitchen-furnishing department of some store perforated tins. These are full of tiny holes which prevent the trouble. F. H.

FOR THE CHICKENS OF S. R.

I think the chickens had the roup. What I have found to be good is: Grease their heads with lard and kerosene oil and give them chlorate of potash in their drinking water. Or, take a hot stove-lid, place it under the roost and pour carbolic acid on the lid. A person should try not to breathe while doing this and should get out as quickly as possible, closing

the hen-house up tight. I have found this to be good. Another remedy which I expect to try is six drops of aconite in a tablespoonful of water twice a day. This is a dose for grown chickens. Two doses is supposed to cure. Roup is very contagious, and the sick fowls should be kept away from the well ones. MRS. F. T. S.

TWO-DOLLAR PRIZE ITEM

HELP YOUR NEIGHBOR

Within a quiet country home,
Where goddess Fashion never comes.
A matron toiled from morn till night,
And still her children were a sight.

Their clothes were neat and clean
and good,
But naught of style she understood;
So after all her work and care
Those children made the people stare.

Then often clothes were laid aside
That others would have worn with
pride,
Because she did not understand
To utilize the things at hand.

Each month I sent (without my name)
The new DESIGNER when it came,
And watched the changes so complete
That marked those tots from head to
feet.

Twas mission work, the very best.
And naught that home has ever
blessed
More than the little unknown gift
That sent such dreadful styles adrift.
NONA

EASTER CHICKS

Last Easter a friend of mine made, without expense, fluffy little yellow chicks just coming out of the shell, which were the cutest and most natural things I have seen for a long time. First, she took egg-shells, saved for that purpose, which had been broken near the small end, and cut away irregularly. Next, she procured fine yellow cotton, such as jewelers use, and lightly shaped it into good representations of chickens; a few stitches concealed in the cotton aided in forming the head and slightly indicated wings. Two black beads formed the eyes, and for the beak, sunflower seeds! One end of the sunflower seed is pointed and one edge rounds more than the other, so that, placed right, they are just the shape of a bill. The cotton was wrapped around the bill, when the head was formed, and fastened with needle and thread. The chicks were then placed in the cut shells, leaving head and back exposed, and enough cotton in the shells to make them stay. When finished, they were placed in a low basket, lined with a white doily, and it didn't take a very lively imagination to make one think they were real. M. C. C.

GOLDEN EGGS FOR THE EASTER BREAK-FAST

I always have a nest of "golden eggs" for breakfast on Easter morning. My nest is a large round dish filled with green grass and leaves, and a few flowers if I have them. And this is the secret of my "golden eggs." I take a large handful of the dry skins of red onions, place them in an iron kettle and pour cold water over them. When they begin to boil I drop, carefully, into the pot one and one-half dozen fresh-laid eggs. I take up enought soft boiled for breakfast and leave the rest to boil hard. They will be a beautiful golden color. I wipe each egg with a slightly greased cloth and place in the nest in the center of the snowy table-cloth. The soft-boiled eggs can be easily distinguished, as they are a lighter color. The hard-boiled eggs are divided among the children after breakfast. They contrast beautifully with the bright-colored eggs in their baskets. E. R. E.

A NEW WAY TO CLEAN THE SCALP AND HAIR

If you have long, fine hair which tangles easily, if you take cold easily, or if you have very hard water to deal with, then my way of washing the hair and scalp will be worth your trying. The night before I clean my head I rub a very little vaseline on the scalp, using care not to get any of it on the hair. Then when I am ready to clean my head I get a little hot water, a cake of good toilet soap, a large, soft tooth-brush, a clean wash-cloth and two clean towels, crash if possible. I let my hair down and comb and brush it well. Then I part my hair and braid the front hair in three loose braids, and the back hair in two very loose braids. Next I dip the tooth-brush into the hot water, shake it gently to remove surplus water, rub it once on the cake of soap, and then I begin and scrub my scalp all over thoroughly, using care not to get much soap or water on the hair. The tooth-brush must be washed and re-soaped often during the job.

Helps Along the Way.—*Continued.*

After scrubbing the scalp in this way I dip the clean wash cloth in very hot, clear water and wring it dry as I can. Then I go all over the scalp with the cloth and remove the soap left by the brush. I fold the cloth over the first finger and go in among the roots of the hair without wetting the hair itself. As soon as all the soap has been removed, and the scalp is white and perfectly clean, I unbraid the hair, shake it out well, and then proceed to clean it in the following manner: I dip the wash rag in clear, hot water, wring it dry as possible, and fasten it over a stiff hair brush. Then I brush the hair with the cloth for at least five minutes. When I know the hair has been exposed to dust I take a clean towel and, after dipping it in hot water and wringing it quite dry, I place one thickness of it over my hand and then wipe the hair thoroughly. One is always surprised to see how black the towel is after the hair has been wiped in this way. I never put my hair up again until it is thoroughly dry, and I give it a sun bath if possible. I have cleaned my own hair in the way just described for a number of years and I am well satisfied with the results, as I have a fine head of hair. My sister, too, cleans her head in the same manner and finds it eminently satisfactory. People with dandruff or split hair will find this way of cleaning the hair very beneficial.

B. McE. KNIPE.

USEFUL TOYS

I wonder how many housekeepers know how greatly labor is lightened by the use of children's toys to aid in their work. I bought a child's broom and made an outing bag to fit loosely over it, drawing it up and tying it securely around the broom. This I always use to brush my walls and ceilings, the picture rail and pictures — it is so light in weight, and so much less cumbersome than the large broom or any long-handled brush — and the dust clings to the cover, which can be freed from it by shaking it out an open window. It does not send the dust about a room as a brush or feather duster does. I use the same little broom for brushing my bare floors and mattings, as it is more than convenient on account of its short handle to reach under all furniture. It goes where a dust brush or large broom cannot. I also purchased a toy carpet sweeper, that has also proved its value to lighten labor. I keep it in a closet in my sitting-room where I do my sewing, where it is always handy. Bits of thread and such will get on the floor and my little sweeper picks them up for me with almost no labor. Far easier than to tote a big sweeper from somewhere, or to pick them up "by hand," or even to brush them up. Two very inexpensive little helpers.

M. S. P.

FOR TENDER FEET

A German shoe merchant told me it was my feet and not the shoes, and advised me to try bathing my feet in cold water instead of warm. (I had always bathed them in very warm water.) He said it had cured him of tender feet. I took his advice and began that night, and bathed them in cold water every night, just before going to bed, for one year, and by that time I could wear any medium-weight shoe. I have kept it up ever since, two or three times each week, and rarely ever have a pain or ache in my feet now, and I attribute it all to the cold bath. This remedy has given so much help and comfort to me that I want others to try it.

MRS. J. L. M.

A NOVEL WASTE-PAPER BASKET

One of the old-fashioned splashers, made of round, wooden splints with roses painted on it, was converted into a pretty waste basket by fastening it securely around a round pasteboard box and then tying round it a band of ribbon at the top, finished with a bow, and another at the bottom.

E. A. C.

FINDING PLACE FOR THE BATHROOM

Our house was small and we could not afford to have a special room for a bathroom, so had a tub put into our own bedroom, and then had a frame made just large enough to cover it, with a cover to lift up and fasten to an eyelet screwed into the wall. When the frame was made I upholstered a mattress just that size with some nice tapestry and fastened it securely to the cover, and tacked on a valence, put a hook on the center of cover and arranged it so the folds would hide it when not in use. When the tub is in use the cover is lifted. It can be fastened to the eyelet screwed in the wall. Arranged nicely with couch pillows, it looks like a box couch and is ornamental as well as useful.

E. H.

FOR THE PIANO

During the last ten years I have been troubled more or less with moths in my piano. They would eat the felt off the hammers and injure the tone in general. When I bought a new piano last year I thought I would try some plan of ridding myself of the insects. During the summer time, when I left the city, and any other time when I was away and the piano was consequently closed, I put some pieces of camphor in both the upper and lower parts of the instrument. By wrapping the camphor in long strips of tissue paper, I was able to reach the hammers and the spaces far below them. I also opened the lower part of the piano, just above the pedals, and put two or three pieces there. I have not been troubled with moths since.

L. S.

When selecting table damask for every-day wear choose a pattern that nearly covers the ground. Such a table-cloth will wear better and look better than one of the same quality where there is a great deal of plain surface displayed. Before cutting linen or damask be sure to draw a thread, for otherwise, no matter how straight it may fold, it will probably only look so until it is washed. If cut by the thread, you may be sure of its washing straight. Don't throw away the trimmings from your new table-cloths. Those long linen threads you will need when your table-cloth begins to break a little; with them you can prolong its span of life many days. For removing fresh tea and coffee stains, place the stained linen over a large bowl and pour through it boiling water from the tea-kettle, held at a height to insure force. Old stains, which have become "set," should be soaked in cold water first, then in boiling water. Fruit stains will usually yield to boiling water, but if not, oxalic acid may be used, allowing three ounces of the crystal to one pint of water. Wet the stain with the solution and place over a kettle of hot water in the sunshine. The instant the stain disappears rinse well, wet the stain with ammonia to counteract the acid remaining, then rinse thoroughly again. If linen is allowed to fully dry, there will be difficulty in ironing the little fine wrinkles out, but if it is hung on the line and left until a little more than half dried, then brought in and subjected to the swift, even pressure of a hot iron, it will become beautifully glossy and smooth with comparatively little labor. Also try in ironing your table-cloths to have them folded in different ways, to vary the creases so that the wear will not come always in the same place.

LIZZIE MOWEN

BIT OF SPRING

Last winter, after there had been several hard frosts, I gathered branches from the lilac bushes and placed them in tall vases of water, changing the water every day. They were kept in the coolest room in the house. In a short time the buds began to swell, then tiny leaves appeared, and within six weeks lovely clusters of blossoms appeared, as fragrant as if grown out of doors in season. By bringing in a few branches every week I had flowers all winter.   MARY E. HARDING

O REMOVE A TIGHT FINGER RING

It is seldom necessary to file off a ring which is too tight to readily pass the joint of the finger. If the finger is swollen apply cold water, then wrap a small rag wet in hot water around the ring, to expand the metal, and soap the finger. A needle threaded with strong silk can then be passed

SKINNER'S SATIN

Guaranteed to Wear Two Seasons

Skinner's Guaranteed Satin (name woven in selvage) is the kind that you buy with pleasure and wear with pride; soft in sheen and fine in texture.

The reputation of fifty-seven years as silk manufacturers is behind our promise to replace the goods if they do not wear as guaranteed. Ours is a guarantee to be relied upon.

Skinner's Guaranteed Satins are extensively used; not only for linings, but for shirt-waists and garments.

If unable to obtain Skinner's Guaranteed Satins at your dry goods store, write to us for samples and send the name of your dealer. Don't accept a substitute—there is no other just as good.

WILLIAM SKINNER MFG. CO., 107-109 Bleecker Street, New York City

Helps Along the Way.—Concluded.

between the ring and finger, and a person holding the two ends and pulling the silk while slowly sliding it around the ring may readily remove the ring. Another way is to pass a piece of sewing silk under the ring and wind it snugly around the finger to the end. Then take the end below the ring and unwind, pulling on the ring at the same time.

E. B. POWELL

FOR SORE THROAT AND COLDS

My mother had chronic sore throat and catarrh. She had tried various remedies, with poor success, until someone told her of this remedy, which is cheap and one that anyone can use. Take cubeb berries (a dime's worth will last a long while), mash them and smoke them in a pipe, letting the smoke escape through the nose. It may seem difficult at first, but after a few trials will be easy. Nothing can surpass it for clearing the head, when the nose is stopped up and you feel as though you could not get another breath. If the throat is sore, or you are troubled with asthma or bronchitis, swallowing the smoke will give relief. It will also sweeten the breath, making it sweet and pure. A month's trial will cure the most stubborn case of ulcerated sore throat or catarrh. For those who cannot smoke, or for children, the uncrushed berries eaten are good for sore throat. My little daughter takes them to school and eats them to clear her head when she has a cold. Inhaling cologne is also good for colds, also snuffing a solution of salt in soft, warm water. When first taking cold use the following: 10 grams of choloroform, 8 centigrams of menthol. Five or six drops poured into the palm of the hand and inhaled into the nose and mouth will prevent taking further cold.

M. E. B.

KEEPING WATER HOT OVERNIGHT

Many a mother will be glad to know that a kitchen boiler will keep its water hot overnight if it is enwrapped from top to bottom with several folds of newspapers.

H. ROLKER

A CORN-HUSK PICTURE-FRAME

A pretty decoration for a country home is a corn-husk picture-frame. From a piece of pasteboard cut an oblong seven inches wide by nine inches long. Two inches from each side and two and one-half inches from top and bottom make points. Draw oval to points, and cut it out. Also cut out of a piece of pasteboard an oblong six and one-half inches wide and eight and one-half inches long; also a small oblong five inches by two and one-half inches, bend one and one-half inches down from top. When husking corn save husks and let dry in sun for one or two days; then take the piece of pasteboard with the oval cut out and wind husks around and sew together in the back. When all covered with husks, paste back on, putting paste on top and two sides, leaving bottom to slip picture in; then put paste on the small oblong down to bend and paste on back to stand picture up.

M. L. WATSON

RUBBER BOOTS FOR STRETCHING CARPET

A good carpet stretcher which I have found very helpful in house-cleaning is nothing but a pair of heavy rubber boots or shoes. Put on the boots after tacking down two sides of the carpet and commence at one of the sides, which has been tacked, and take long, hard, pushing steps until the other side is reached, then tack it and proceed until all has been stretched. This is one of the best carpet stretchers I ever knew of, and was the invention of an old grandma, so it is not common. BESS CLAPP.

DECORATIONS FOR THE HAIR

I originated some hair-bows for Christmas presents, which were exceedingly pretty and were very much liked by my friends. These friends wore them, and also showed them to others, and I soon had more orders than I could fill. I have been making them at odd times ever since, and selling them at a good profit. I used half a yard of white taffeta ribbon, nearly three inches wide, and made a bow as nearly the shape of a butterfly as possible, with the single ends much pointed for front wings, and loops overlapping them for the back wings. These were sewed to the upper side of a small piece of pasteboard, which was cut into the shape of a butterfly's body, the body was covered with a piece of ribbon, put crosswise, and fulled some. When completed, I decorated the butterflies with water-colors and touches of gold. I made the antennæ of fine white-silk hat-wire, curled over at the ends, and tinted or gilded to suit the requirements. The butterflies are very pretty made of ribbon in pale tints, and painted.

MABEL ROBINSON

A GINGER PLASTER

A plaster made of ground ginger mixed with boiling water is better than mustard, as it never blisters, and, therefore, is good to use on the face or neck in neuralgia or toothache. For hoarseness or croup burned alum pulverized and mixed with sugar will soon give relief. Powdered borax sprinkled in corners or behind sinks and cupboards is better to drive away roaches than anything I have tried.

E. H. B.

Lacqueret Will Beautify Your Home

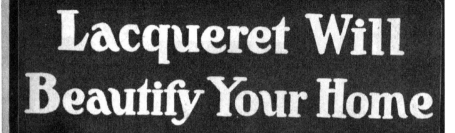

It will Quickly Give Old Furniture, Floors and Woodwork a Finish and Brilliancy Equal to New— Anyone Can Apply It.

You will be surprised to see how you can brighten up your old furniture, and make it look like new goods from the store. Lacqueret removes all scratches and other marks of age and wear and gives new life and lustre to everything made of wood.

Lacqueret will not settle and leave a thick, muddy deposit at the bottom of the can, consequently it does not show brush marks or laps, but gives a perfectly smooth and even finish.

It is positively the best floor finish made It dries in a night and wears like rawhide

Lacqueret is made only by Standard Varnish Works, the largest varnish makers in the world, and the *Original* manufacturers of lacquers in the United States. It is sold in convenient packages ready for use, in Light Oak, Dark Oak, Mahogany, Cherry, Walnut, Rosewood, Rich Red, Moss Green and "Clear."

Lacqueret is transparent, non-fading, brilliant and durable. It is superior to anything on the market for refinishing woodwork and giving it a brilliancy which is absolutely equal to new.

Lacqueret is being used in thousands of American homes and is giving universal satisfaction. If you want to brighten up your home at small expense, use Lacqueret.

Lacqueret is for sale by all dealers.

Quarts, pints and half pints put up in "Toy House "Cut Out" Cartons as above. Demand this package and accept no substitute. Larger packages put up in square sealed cans.

Ask your dealer or drop us a postal, for color card and instructive booklet, "THE DAINTY DECORATOR," which is full of useful hints for home decoration. Or, send 10 cents for sample can, stating color wanted, which will be forwarded at once, by mail, prepaid, Address,

STANDARD VARNISH WORKS
Lacqueret Dept. B-26

New York   Chicago   London, England

INTERNATIONAL VARNISH CO., Ltd.
Write Nearest Office   Lacqueret Dept. B-26   Toronto, Canada

THE KITCHEN KINGDOM

FLORAL DESSERTS FOR THE EASTER TABLE

By Eleanor Marchant

DAFFODIL BLANC-MANGE.—Soak one ounce of gelatin in a pint of rich milk for ten minutes, adding three tablespoonfuls of pineapple sirup, the grated rind of one lemon and a very little grated nutmeg; then place the ingredients over the fire and stir until the gelatin is entirely dissolved, adding the yolks of two well-beaten eggs just before removing from the fire; allow the mixture to cool but not harden, whipping with an egg-beater until light and creamy; then pour in a pint of sweetened whipped cream, flavored with a few drops of vanilla extract, and pour into a ring-mold, setting directly on the ice to become firm. The mold should be wrapped in paraffin paper, containing a few daffodil blossoms, and should be allowed to remain in this condition for at least twelve hours before serving, so that the fragrance of the flowers may be sufficiently absorbed by the dessert. At serving-time, unmold on an ornamental glass platter, surrounded with a border of whipped cream sprinkled with minced candied orange peel, and with a cluster of the bright yellow flowers inserted in the center.

Rose Mousse.—Boil two cupfuls of sugar and one of water to the soft-ball state; remove carefully from the fire and pour upon the stiffly beaten whites of four eggs, stirring constantly; then fold in one pint of cream whipped solid, coloring a delicate rose pink with a little strawberry juice and flavoring with a generous teaspoonful of rose extract. Turn immediately into a melon-mold and pack in ice and rock salt for at least four hours before serving. At serving-time turn out the mousse, ornamenting the frozen dainty with candied rose leaves arranged in the form of wild roses, with natural rose foliage.

Individual Violet Creams.—Prepare a rich, boiled custard by slowly heating a pint of milk in the double-boiler and when just at the boiling point, stir in the yolks of three eggs beaten with a heaping tablespoonful of sugar; continue the stirring until the custard is well thickened, when it should be immediately removed from the fire and allowed to cool; whip half a pint of cream solid, stirring in two tablespoonfuls of powdered sugar, and add to the custard, flavoring with a few drops of violet extract; turn the mixture at once into the freezer and when half frozen add a small tumblerful of grape jelly (this colors the cream an exquisite violet shade) and continue freezing in the usual manner; pack in small individual pasteboard boxes, ornamenting the upper surface of the cream with tiny candied violets and citron leaves.

Mint Frappé.—Steep a handful of chopped mint in a little hot water and, when the flavor is sufficiently extracted, strain into a pint of boiled frosting, to which has been added the juice of two oranges and a little lemon juice; beat with an egg-beater until light and creamy and then add a pint of whipped cream; freeze to the consistency of mush and serve in slender-stemmed crystal sherbet glasses, garnishing with tiny bunches of fresh mint and a few natural pansies.

Easter Pudding in Lily Blooms.—Soak one ounce of gelatin in a pint of cold water, then place over the fire and cook until the gelatin is dissolved; remove from the fire and, when almost cold, place the gelatin in a bowl set in a pan of ice-water and whip to a stiff froth, adding gradually during the process a pint of whipped cream, the stiffly beaten whites of two eggs, confectioner's sugar to suit the taste, and half a teaspoonful of almond flavoring; continue the beating until the mixture will almost resemble thick cake-batter, and then fill into large natural Easter lilies that have had the stamens removed and that have been washed in very cold water, or in lilies made of crêpe paper, inserting a stamen fashioned from candied orange peel in place of the natural one. Serve on a dessert plate resting on a dainty lace-paper doily.

Orange-Flower Savarins.—Line small timbale molds with split, blanched almonds, candied orange peel and angelica arranged to represent orange blossoms; then fill half full with brioche paste and allow them to raise to almost the top of the molds, baking in a hot oven for about twenty minutes; when cooked turn from the molds, cutting off the slightly rounded top of each, and moisten with a thick orange sirup to which has been added a few drops of orange flower extract. Serve, surrounded with sweetened whipped cream, sprinkled with chopped candied orange peel.

Brioche Paste for the above.—Dissolve half a yeast cake in a quarter of a cupful of tepid water, then add sufficient sifted flour to make a very soft ball of paste; drop this ball into a pan of warm water (being careful the water is not too hot to kill the yeast), cover and set in a warm place to rise, which takes about an hour, the ball of dough sinking to the bottom of the water at first, but later on rising to the top and being filled with bubbles. Meanwhile place three cupfuls of flour in a large mixing-bowl, making a small well in the center; into this put a scant half pound of softened butter, a saltspoonful of salt, one tablespoonful of sugar and two eggs broken in whole; work these ingredients together with the hand, gradually incorporating the flour, and adding one more egg in the process, beating with the hand until it loses its stickiness; then add the ball of dough and blend thoroughly; again place it to rise until double its size, which will take about four hours; then beat it down again and place over night in the ice-box. When ready to use it will still be quite soft, and should be handled quickly and delicately.

AN EASTER LUNCHEON

BY FRANCES E. PECK

At one of the prettiest Easter luncheons given last season the color-scheme was green and white and was carried out with rare effectiveness in the viands and the simple decorations.

The dining-room was not large, so the young hostess decided on two rather small round tables instead of one long one, the hostess presiding at one table and her guest of honor at the other until the fourth course was reached, when they changed places.

The tables were covered with creamy linen cloths, decorated with *entre-deux* of Brazilian point over pale-green silk. The table service was pure white as to china and pale green as to glass, the doilies having delicate traceries of green embroidery combined with Brazilian point medallions. In the center of each table stood a low, nest-shaped basket of wicker enameled pale green and filled with snow-white eggs. The baskets rested on circular mats of valley lilies with an outer fringe of asparagus fern. At each corner was a tiny wicker nest filled with egg-shaped bonbons. The egg-shaped, pale-green place-cards were lettered in silver, and with a tiny sheaf of lilies thrust through them. Each chairback was decorated with a large flat wreath of the asparagus hung by a pale-green ribbon, with a softly falling bunch of the lilies pendant from the ribbon, where it was fastened to the wreath.

The eggs in the basket were souvenirs of the occasion, and were distributed, accompanied by charming little filigree silver holders. The contents of the eggs

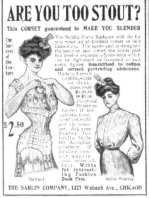

The Kitchen Kingdom.—*Continued.*

had been blown out, and the hostess, who was clever with her brush, had decorated one side of each with a pretty little water-color sketch.

The menu was as follows:

Salpicon of Fruit.
("*We are yours i' the garden.*")
Chicken Consommé Custard and Parsley Cubes.
("*Taste of it first.*")
Shad Vert Prè.
("*Eat of the fish.*")
Cucumbers.
("*Cowcumbers are cold in the third degree.*")
Bread-and-Butter Fingers.
("*I speak this in hunger for bread.*")
Creamed Sweetbreads in Timbale Cases.
("*A dish that I do love to feed upon.*")
Asparagus Tips with White Sauce in Green Peppers.
("*Have you this spring eaten any 'sparagus?*'")
Broiled Squabs on Hominy Squares. Cress Garnish, Bar le Duc Jelly.
("*An' lay it at its ease with gentle care.*")
Buttered String Beans.
("*How green you are and fresh.*")
Olives in White Aspic.
("*Tho' superfluous, a very necessary thing.*")
Blanched Lettuce and Almond Salad.
("*Here are lettuces for every man's lips.*")
Pistachio Ice-Cream in Ice Cups.
("*Blockhead! with a fork.*")
White Cake, Green Decorations.
("*Can one desire too much of a good thing?*")
Coffee.
("*Although the last, not least.*")

The salpicon of fruit, a mixture of seeded white grapes, bits of pineapple and grapefruit pulp sprinkled with sugar and dashed with wine, was served in short-stemmed, flat-bowled green champagne glasses. Shad *Vert Prè* was a Parisian dish with a fine and foreign flavor: Scale small, fine shad. Sprinkle with salt, pepper and chopped shallots. Place the fish in a deep buttered pan, dot with bits of butter, and pour over them white wine to half the depth of the fish, cover with buttered paper and cook for thirty minutes in a quick oven; when done, remove to a hot platter, and to the liquor in the pan add an equal measure of Allemande sauce, season with a pinch of chervil, and color a pale green with spinach coloring, reheat and pour a small quantity over the fish and serve the remainder in a bowl apart.

A fine recipe for Allemande sauce is as follows: Melt two tablespoonfuls of butter in a pan and gradually add three tablespoonfuls of flour. Cook slightly and then add two cupfuls of white broth; when boiling hot, pour slowly over the beaten whites of two eggs, stir constantly until the whites are thoroughly incorporated with the sauce, then finish with the juice of a lemon, taking care the sauce does not boil after adding the lemon juice.

To prepare the delectable creamed

sweetbreads, blanch in slightly acidulated water six heart sweetbreads, cut them in small pieces and put into a pan with a tablespoonful of butter, half a cupful of mushroom liquor and a cupful of cooking wine, and simmer for thirty minutes; then add six minced mushrooms, half a cupful of white sauce, a seasoning of salt and pepper, a dusting of nutmeg and, last of all, half a cupful of thick cream. Have at hand timbale cases, and before filling them brush the edges with white of egg and dip them in finely chopped parsley.

An appetizing little *hors d'œuvre* are olives in aspic: Take a pint of clear, strong chicken consommé highly seasoned with salt, white pepper and essence of mace, add a tablespoonful of gelatin softened in cold water, heat to the point of dissolving the gelatin; when cold, pour a little into egg-shaped molds, let become perfectly stiff, then add a layer of chopped olives; fill mold with the aspic and set to harden.

A green mayonnaise adds a touch of novelty to the salad, which is composed of two parts of shredded blanched lettuce and one part of sliced blanched almonds. To the mayonnaise made in the usual manner add finely chopped cress and spinach coloring.

THE NEGLECTED BIVALVE
By Eleanor Marchant

Clam Timbales.—Scald a pint of clams in their own liquor; drain and pass through a food-chopper, adding a cupful of grated bread-crumbs, four drops of Tabasco sauce, a saltspoonful of salt, a pinch of powdered mace and paprika, four tablespoonfuls of mushroom catsup and sufficient of the liquor to moisten thoroughly; pour into greased timbale molds that have been sprinkled with minced parsley, setting them in a pan filled with hot water, and bake twenty minutes in a moderate oven. Serve unmolded on rounds of hot graham toast, garnishing with bunches of crisp watercress.

Brown Fricassee of Clams in the Chafing-Dish.—Place in the chafing-dish two tablespoonfuls of butter, and when nicely browned add one tablespoonful of flour, stirring constantly until thoroughly blended, then add half a pint of the strained clam liquor, a teaspoonful of minced onion, a quarter of a teaspoonful of salt and a dash of white pepper; allow it to just reach the boiling point and place over the hot-water pan where it should gently simmer for about six minutes; meanwhile plump twenty-four clams of the little-neck variety, by pouring over them a quart of boiling water, drain carefully and add to the fricassee, together with a large tablespoonful of Madeira wine, re-cover and let stand four minutes longer; serving on hot pilot biscuit and sprinkling each portion with a little powdered cracker-crums.

Clam Soufflé.—Chop very finely a pint of "long" clams, that have been trained and dried (saving the liquor as the basis for broth for luncheon or supper). Place them in a mixing-bowl, adding a cupful of hot, boiled hominy, a teaspoonful of butter, the yolks of two eggs, three tablespoonfuls of rich cream, a saltspoonful of celery salt, a dash of cayenne, a pinch of salt and a dusting of powdered cinnamon; mix the ingredients together until smooth and creamy, allowing the mixture to cool but not harden; then fold in lightly the stiffly beaten whites of three eggs and turn into a soufflé dish, baking in a hot oven for about twenty-five minutes; serve immediately, accompanied by a melted butter sauce.

Clam Sausages.—For the occasional cold day that occurs even in spring, when something particularly tasty and savory is desired, these delicious little rolls will be found very acceptable. Cook two dozen large clams in their own liquor until the edges begin to curl, drain and chop very fine, adding one tablespoonful of chopped green peppers, two or three slices of minced Bologna sausage, a teaspoonful of tomato catsup, a saltspoonful of salt and a pinch of powdered allspice; shape with floured hands into diminutive little rolls and fry in hot fat to a golden brown; serve in a border around a mound of riced potatoes garnished with thinly sliced lemon and pitted olives.

Pickled Clams in Jelly.—Scald a pint of little-neck clams by covering with boiling white-wine vinegar, and adding to the vinegar six whole cloves, a piece of stick cinnamon, a bruised bay leaf, a saltspoonful of salt, a pinch of black pepper and a quarter of a teaspoonful of ground spices; allow the clams to stand in the spiced vinegar until it cools, when they should be drained and carefully dried. Prepare a rich aspic jelly, coloring it a delicate green with a few drops of spinach juice, and mold by its assistance in the bottom and around the sides of an ornamental mold feathery sprigs of parsley; when these are firmly in place, add a few clams and mold in the same manner, continuing the process until the mold is filled. Set directly on the ice to chill and harden, and at serving time unmold on a glass platter, garnishing with a border of heart lettuce leaves and accompanied by tiny anchovy sandwiches.

Clam Olives.—Parboil a dozen rashers of bacon, sliced very thin, for five minutes, drain, and when cold arrange on slices of buttered whole-wheat bread, also cut in thin slices; now place in the center of each piece of bacon three small clams, sprinkle with salt, pepper, a few drops of onion juice and Worcestershire sauce, and fold or roll over the bread into neat, compact rolls, fastening them in place by means of small wooden toothpicks; arrange them in a shallow pan, dot over with bits of butter and crisp in a hot oven; before sending to the table remove the tiny skewers and pile log-cabin fashion on a folded hem-stitched napkin, garnishing with watercress or other edible green.

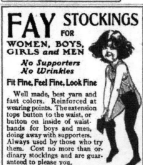

A DOMESTIC MASQUERADE

A STORY OF THE UNEXPECTED GUEST

By M. G. MORSE

LET me give you another cup of tea, Mrs. Wilson. And take one of the little cakes. Alys makes nice ones, doesn't she? She has developed quite a taste for cooking, lately. Did I tell you about the time she got the luncheon when I had unexpected company from New York? Oh, I had a dreadful time that day! And yet it was exceedingly funny, too. I can laugh about it now, but at the time I was almost too angry to live! Alys didn't feel that way, though; she laughed and laughed till I thought she'd certainly have hysterics, and she said it served her just right.

You see, it all happened because Martha, my servant girl, wanted to go to New York to do some shopping. She really had seemed to try to please me of late, and I thought I'd let her have a holiday. So we had an early breakfast, and Martha hustled the work out of the way and went off. She was to be back in time to get the late dinner, and Alys and I would get our own luncheon; just toast and eggs, with a bit of lemon jelly and some ginger cookies for dessert. The house was all in order, and Martha had swept off the sidewalk and let down the awnings and put out all the porch rugs and cushions, so that there wasn't much for us to do. I settled down in my room, in an easy-chair in the bay window, with the stockings to mend and the cat in my lap, and Alys said she thought she would make some fudge.

"It isn't often I can have the kitchen to myself," said she.

So she put on a big white housemaid's apron, with a bib and straps over the shoulders, and went down to the kitchen. I could hear her stirring around down there as she got together the materials for her candy, singing to herself as she worked. Then the doorbell rang. I knew Alys would go to the door, and I didn't want to disturb the cat, so I sat still. In a minute up came Alys with two cards on a tray.

"Mrs. George Henry Curtin, of Chicago, and Mrs. Alfred W. Hastings, of New York. Who in the world!" said I.

"Why, I believe it's *Frances* Curtin; of course it is, and I haven't seen her for fifteen years, at least; not since I was in Chicago. But who can Mrs. Hastings be?"

"Very likely a friend that she's visiting in New York, who has come out with her to see you," suggested Alys. "But do go along, Mummy; yes, your hair is all right, and so is your gown; you always look so nice in white piqué, you know."

With which flattering remark she skipped down the back stairs, to resume her candy-making—fortunately the fudge hadn't been on the fire when the doorbell rang—and left me to go to my callers.

I found Frances just the same dear soul as ever; but the woman she had with her was of a very different sort. She was what Alys calls "stunning"; very fashionably and elaborately dressed, with manners to match, and a most disagreeable way of putting up her gold-handled eyeglass and surveying you as if she weren't quite sure to what species you belonged. Good-hearted woman enough, I dare say, but with such a high-and-mighty, superior air, don't you know. I didn't see how Frances could enjoy staying at her house. And what do you think? I found out, presently, that they intended to spend the whole day with me, and there was I with no maid and nothing in the house for luncheon!

As soon as I could, I excused myself for a moment, and went to consult Alys. She was cutting up her fudge into delicious-looking squares. She gazed at me in dismay for a minute, then her face brightened and she executed a noiseless little dance of delight around the kitchen table.

"Never mind, Mummy!" she cried. "I'll get the luncheon, and I'll serve it, too, and it'll be perfectly all right, you'll see! Now, listen. They probably think I'm the maid already, for I looked just like one when I went to the door, and I took their cards in the most approved way. Don't mention your daughter at all, and then they won't know that you have one. Mrs. Curtin has never seen me, and if she has heard of me she has probably forgotten it. I'll bet you anything that they'll think I'm a first-class waitress."

"But there isn't anything in the house to eat," I remarked.

"Well, there's a telephone in the house, and a bicycle," she returned. "I'll telephone for some oysters, and we'll have creamed oysters on toast for the principal dish. Then I'll skip down to the delicatessen store and the Woman's Exchange, on my wheel, and get some more things. We'll have some sliced boiled ham and some Parker House rolls, and then potato salad for a separate course; and for dessert some of those lemon tarts from the exchange, that are always so good, and some hot chocolate. Won't that be a nice luncheon? And the range fire being out won't matter a bit, for I can do all the cooking that I need to on the gas-range. Now, go along and don't even think of luncheon again, and at precisely one o'clock it will be ready. And whatever you do, don't mention me. You must be sure not to be too nice to me at luncheon, either; this is to be a regular masquerade, and you mustn't spoil it!"

Well, I did as she said; I washed my hands of the whole matter, and went back to my guests. I knew Alys was perfectly capable of doing what she had undertaken, and I spent a pleasant enough morning, though I had to be on my guard every minute to avoid letting out the fact that I had a daughter.

The big clock in the hall was just striking one when a voice said, sweetly, "Luncheon is served, madam," and I looked up and saw Alys standing in the door. You would have laughed to see those two women look at her. Why, Mrs. Hastings put up her lorgnette and unmistakably stared. I didn't wonder, though, for Alys had turned herself into the dearest little maid you ever saw. She had bought a waitress's cap while she was out, and had pinned it on top of her fluffy pompadour, and it was too becoming for anything. Her dress was the black lawn slip that she wears under her new yellow-and-black silk muslin, and she had on a plain linen collar and cuffs, a black tie and the white bib-apron. She looked like the maid-servants you see on the stage, but not one bit like any that I ever saw at an employment office!

She waited at table with as much skill as if she had been trained in a school of domestic science, and she wasn't one bit awkward, but as graceful as if she were doing her Delsarte exercises. I saw Mrs. Hastings looking at her through her glass again and again. I was in a fidget the whole time for fear I'd give her away, and I know my conversation must have been very jerky and absent-minded. Alys, however, was cool enough, and enjoyed herself immensely. Her table was beautifully set with all the prettiest dishes, and in the center a lovely bowlful of pink roses and honeysuckle, with long sprays of the vine running to the corners of the table. The food was garnished with green, and looked wonderfully appetizing, and both the ladies did full justice to it.

After luncheon, Frances said to me:

"You certainly have a good cook, Laura. You keep two girls, I suppose?"

"No," said I, falteringly; "I only keep one."

"Why," exclaimed Frances, "does that young girl do all your work? She must be very clever."

I replied that she was a rather nice sort of girl; but my tone wasn't enthusiastic, for I was desperately afraid that I was getting into hot water.

"Have you had her long?" inquired Mrs. Hastings.

"No," I replied; "she isn't my regular girl, but is merely taking Martha's place while the latter has a little holiday."

I wondered what would come next, but Mrs. Hastings only said "Ah," and, to my supreme relief, dropped the subject.

But, oh, the worst of all was still to come. When my guests were preparing to go, Mrs. Hastings asked if I would let

POMPEIAI
MASSAGE CREA

The Simplicity of a Pompeian Massage

A few minutes, a few movements of the hands—the pleasurable duty is done.

Your mirror will tell the story in a day, so almost marvellous is the result of one application of **Pompeian Massage Cream**.

The reason is simple. The cream reaches the seat of a poor complexion—the pores of the skin—cleaning them instantly and thoroughly and permitting the rosy blood to flow through its natural channels, and to do its work in nourishing the skin and giving it the healthy glow desired by and admired in every woman. Its ingredients are entirely harmless, and it is food for the skin as meat is food for the body. It gives a charming contour to the face and form.

Contains positively no grease or oil, so does not (cannot) promote the growth of hair, which is naturally feared by all women, because of past unfortunate experiences with the customary greasy " cold creams " and cosmetics which flood the market.

It will not be necessary to apply powder, as **Pompeian Massage Cream** does not make the skin oily—it *removes all grease and skins* from a complexion that suffers from this offensive trouble. It imparts to the skin a healthy, natural glow, free from the artificial appearance given by powder.

Illustrated Book and a Sample

A liberal sample of Pompeian Massage Cream and one copy of our beautifully illustrated book on Facial Massage—a practical course which enables any woman to become expert in this most necessary of modern aids to beauty—will be sent FREE, if you will fill out the attached coupon or write us, giving the desired details.

We prefer you to buy of your dealer whenever possible. Do not accept a substitute for Pompeian under any circumstances. If your dealer does not keep it, send us his name, and we will send a 10c. or $1 jar of the Cream postpaid on receipt of price.

POMPEIAN MFG. CO.
87 Prospect St., Cleveland, Ohio

Name..........................
(Please say whether Mr., Mrs. or M

Address.........................

Dealer's Address................

Dealer's name...................

This dealer DOES NOT keep Pompeian Massage Cream

Do Your Own Knitting

Send for our new complete
"BEAR BRAND YARN Manual of Handiwork" (7th Edition) of what and how to knit and crochet. Easy to follow even by those with no experience. Contains more than 100 illustrations—with full directions. Be sure 10c. (stamps or silver). Bear Brand Yarns—soft, elastic and even of thread—insure beautiful and satisfactory results.

Bear Brand Yarn Manufacturers
Dept. A, New York City

The Eagle Mop
Wringer and Bucket
Combined

divests mopping and scrubbing o their most disagreeable feature. Wit the " Eagle," you wring mop or clot by foot pressure, the hands neve touching the water. Soapy, alkaline water discolors and roughens the skin.

Domestic Size

Grocery, Hardware, House Furnishing and Department Stores sell EAGLE MOP WRINGERS. If yours doesn't, we will kill order direct, express prepaid. *Write for handy booklet, and price.*

EAGLE COOPERAGE WORKS, Dept. A, Circleville, O.

ALL STANDARD PATTERNS
Are Now Reduced in Price to 5c., 10c. and 15c.

No matter how elaborate in design, no higher price will be charged for any patter
STANDARD FASHION COMPANY, New York

A Domestic Masquerade.—*Concluded.*

my maid get her a glass of water. I called Alys, but I was shaking in my shoes, for I knew she wasn't sent for for nothing. But what Mrs. Hastings actually did had never entered my head. When Alys brought the water, in a cut-glass tumbler on a silver tray, Mrs. Hastings beckoned her to one side.

"Mrs. Lancaster tells me," said she, "that you are only taking her regular servant's place for a short time. So I suppose that you will soon be out of a place. I am not very well satisfied with my own waitress, and I would be willing to give you a trial. Of course you would be glad of a chance to live in New York; all servant girls are. But before I could consent to take you on trial I should require your promise that you wouldn't have any relatives coming to see you, and that there should be no flirting nor nonsense of that sort with the tradesmen."

Of course she didn't intend me to hear what she said, but she had such a penetrating voice that I couldn't help it, and I was furious enough to kill her. The very idea of anyone talking like that to my daughter! But I kept a tight hold on myself and listened to hear what Alys would say. She is a dignified girl, you know, in spite of all her fun, and I expected that she would tell Mrs. Hastings who she really was, and overwhelm her with confusion. But that wasn't her idea at all; she had made up her mind to go on with the play to the very end. When she spoke to Mrs. Hastings, her voice was as sweet and as cool as ice-cream.

"Thank you, madam," said she; "I don't think I should care to live in New York. I shall not need to look for a place, either; there is a good home, and a permanent one, waiting for me just as soon as Mrs. Lancaster's maid comes back. But I thank you for your kind offer."

With that she made the stateliest kind of a bow, then took her tray and departed.

But as soon as Frances and Mrs. Hastings were fairly out of sight, she emerged from the kitchen, and I wish you could have seen her! She danced a two-step all around the hall; she pulled off her cap and tossed it into the air, then sat down on the floor and laughed. She laughed till the cat, curled up on the window-seat, sat up and looked at her in astonishment, and till the tears ran down her own cheeks. As for me, I couldn't help joining in at last; as I looked at her I could feel the wrinkles of vexation and disgust smoothing out of my face.

"Oh," gasped Alys, when she could speak, "it was so funny! I wouldn't have missed it for the world. Did you ever, oh, did you ever! But I was a success, wasn't I?"

"You certainly were, my dear," said I, "but you shall never do it again—never, even if we have the President's wife here to luncheon!"

HE MOTHERS' ADVISORY CLUB

EDITED BY THE READERS OF THE DESIGNER

This is to certify

Name..

Street...

Town...

State.......................

is a member of "THE MOTHERS' ADVISORY CLUB"

All letters, sugges ns, etc., that we int in these col ins, we will pay : at the rate of one llar each, with a ecial price of five llars each month r the one we con ler the best. Fill t the certificate to found at the head this column, and n, sew or paste it the top of your tter. Write on one de of the paper ily. Do not send advice unless you ive given it a per nal test, and re ember literary style is not necessary in this department, but good, sound maternal sense is what counts. One contributor may send in as many letters, questions or suggestions as she pleases at one time with one cer ificate, but a certificate will be required for each contributor.

Friendly discussion is what we want.

Sound, practical advice is what we want.

Interesting questions are what we want.

QUESTIONS

Quarrelsome Brothers

WILL some mother please advise ne how to make my two small boys be nore agreeable to each other. They ire very quarrelsome with each other; oth are sure to want the same thing it the same time, and they are always easing each other. Neither of them as a bad disposition, for they both get dong nicely with their other little playmates. I am sure they love each other, for when one is punished the ither is always sorry for him. I will be very thankful for an answer to this roblem and how to remedy the trouble.
ADA CHAPMAN

When the Bud Begins to Blossom

WILL other mothers please give their opinion. We live in a city of five housand, where it is customary for young ladies to attend places of amusenent, with their men friends as escorts, rithout a chaperon. My daughter only attends approved functions, and ve aim to number among our friends, or those who are allowed to be her scort at these places, only the best lass of men. She has no lover, being oo young, and in college yet. Now, hould she have only one man friend it a time, or is it best to have more. My idea is to have all the good men of ier "set" for friends, and thus not illow her name to be coupled with any one at her age, eighteen. I have a riend who does not approve of my nethod, saying it will make her appear lo be a flirt. This subject is certainly of great importance. Let us hear from others.
A. C. V.

Queer Playthings

WILL some mother give me some advice. My little boy is four years old, and I cannot break him of wanting to play with the chairs, always turned upside down on the floor. It is either street-car, wagon or train he wants to play all the time with the chairs. It is not because he hasn't plenty of toys, for he has no lack of things; in fact, I really think too many playthings. A long crying spell always follows when I insist on the chairs being put straight. I have tried everything I can think of to break him of such a habit, but without avail. Will some one kindly help me out.
MRS. H. B.

Weaning the Baby

I WOULD be glad to have the opinion of other mothers as to the proper age for weaning my baby boy. Physicians tell us when the child is from nine to eleven months old is the correct time, but the child is then too young for solid food, and has not cut more than eight teeth. How should he be nourished? If baby and mother are in good health, would it not be better to nurse him till he is fifteen or eighteen months old, supplementing other nourishment?
L. M. D.

Procrastination Is Her Fault

I HAVE a daughter of fifteen who is always willing to help me in any way she can. Still when I call on her, although she answers, "Yes, Mama," she seldom comes right away. Sometimes I call several times before she responds. Can some mother advise me in this matter? What can I do to break her of the habit?
J. A. M.

The Mothers' Advisory Club.—*Continued*

FIVE-DOLLAR PRIZE PARAGRAPH

Teaching Children the True Easter Spirit

HAS the increased celebration of Easter in recent years brought with it an increase of the true Easter spirit in all its participants? Our children can have no higher ideals of the day than those we give them. Let us mothers then, be careful when we plan the usual materialistic celebrations not to stop there, but in some way to lead our children to see the significance of all the little customs, and, one step farther, endeavor to so present the glorious Easter truth to them that their young hearts may thrill with real joy and gratitude to God. To gain the real attention of the child we must begin with the things in which he is already interested, linking our ideas to those things. Then there will be no chasm between the child's mind and ours, but a solid chain of thought by which it will come, link by link, to the thought in our mind. Applying these abstract principles to concrete things, I arranged a device last Easter which proved both interesting and helpful to my children, who range in age from ten to sixteen. For a centerpiece for the Easter morning breakfast-table I made a nest of eggs in a pretty, low round dish, I put straw (made of orange and lemon peel, cut in strips and candied). Upon this were placed large candy eggs, pretty enough to keep for souvenirs. There was one egg for each member of the family. The centerpiece was discussed and admired during the meal, but not until the dish was passed, at the end, did they discover the distinctive feature. A slip of paper was folded and fastened to each egg by a tiny pin thrust through both. These slips of paper each contained a question, and it was explained that after a minute or two for reflection each person would be asked to answer his or her question. Pleased with the surprise and taken by the resemblance to a game, the children did their best to give good answers to their questions which were afterward discussed by all. Any suitable questions could be given. Mine were: "What does the word 'Easter' mean?" "Why is it appropriate to decorate the church with Easter lilies and other flowers on Easter?" "Is there any connection between eggs and Easter?" "Why is music especially appropriate for Easter?" "Why should we rejoice on Easter Sunday?" The last question fell to the father. Very simply and tenderly he told the story of the first Easter, making clear to them just how what happened then made life different to all. "And so," he ended, "this should be the holiest, happiest day in all the year, because on this day Christ conquered sin and death. Because He died and rose again we need never fear death; because He lives we shall live also." As the children quietly left the room, we knew by the look on their sweet young faces that the true Easter spirit had found a place in their hearts.

ANABEL R. BARBER

Answer No. 1. For Mrs. H. A.—Supply the Deficiency Yourself

I WISH to tell Mrs. H. A. (who wrote in the February number) how we taught our little one politeness. She is a petted, spoiled child, having come to us fifteen years after the birth of our elder daughter. She exhibited much wilfulness, and oftentimes absolutely refused to say "please," or "thank you." She has a very bright little mind, so we explained to her that "please" and thank you" *must* be said. Therefore when she omitted the polite terms, we said them for her, and as in response to some wish of hers we said, "Thank you, sister" or "Please, dear mama," without seeming to notice 'her omission to do so, such an odd expression would come into her face. Fewer and fewer became the lapses of politeness, until now, at four and a half years of age, she is quite a polite little girl, and all this accomplished without punishment or unpleasant scenes.

MRS CHARLES AXLINE

Answer No. 2—Let Him Imbibe Politeness

MRS. H. A.: I have a little boy about the age of your own. I have never raised the question of politeness with him. Remember Miss Cary's lines:

'Politeness is to do and say
The kindest things in the kindest way,"

I have been telling myself that so long as he is good and kind he is well enough. Our little cousin, a child of the same age, is taught to be polite. This child is pliable and tractable. He readily says 'please" and "thank you," or whatever you ask him to say. He says things with an appearance of being pampered and tutored, and naturalness, the most charming quality a child can possess, is wanting. However, let us admit that the tot should be taught politeness. Yet, by all means, let him imbibe it. Do not give it to him in doses. If he *wants* to say the pretty little polite words he *will say them*. Make him *want* to say them. This can best be accomplished by saying them yourself, in his presence, as many times as you can, and without in the least referring him to it. If he does not soon pick it up, be patient. It will come. Above all things do not punish, for this course will make the polite words we so long to hear forever distasteful to him. Let your attitude toward him be one of persistent politeness and kindness, except at such times as he needs discipline, and insist that all with whom he is immediately associated do the same. With this rule in force in your home, your boy will be always in an atmosphere of gentleness, truth and kindness, which is politeness. He will soon become polite himself, and it will not be simply the addition of a few words or phrases, but for loyal principles you have grafted into his nature. B. B.

Comfort for Children

No binding armholes—slipping off shoulders—missing buttons nor torn buttonholes. Perfect ease and freedom of motion if your child wears a

WORTH WAIST

Supports all garments from shoulders. Child undressed by releasing three buttons. Splendidly made of the best, soft-finished jean. All buttons taped on. Wears and washes well. Only up-to-date waist of first-class quality offered at the price—25 cents.

Two styles: skeleton and closed waist. White and drab. Sizes 2 to 12 years.

WRITE FOR BOOKLET OF Worth Waists and other sensible specialties. FREE.

Sold by dealers. If yours hasn't them send 25 cents, state size and we will send post-paid.

The Worth Mfg. Co.
16-18-20-22 Boyden Place
Newark, N. J.

"A boon to Mothers"

writes C. M. Stevens, Meridian, Miss., of our Baby-jumper with Go-cart attachment. He further says: "My wife and baby Evelyn, as well as myself, are delighted with it."

Glascock's
Baby-jumper

Rocking Chair
Bed
High Chair
and
Go-cart
combined

Pleasure, comfort and safety for the baby all the time, for less money than a Go-cart alone of equally good workmanship. Well constructed on hygienic principles; easily changed to any position, thus preventing child growing tired and restless. Leading physicians urge "Glascock's"—the standard hygienic combinations—exclusive features.

Sold with or without Go-cart attachment.

30 days' trial FREE. Buy of your dealer, if possible, or write us. Write for "The Twentieth Century Baby" by Ellen D. Wade, this book M. D. An up-to-date manual for mothers. Sent to-day. free with a catalogue of Glascock's Baby-jumper.

GLASCOCK BROS. MFG. CO., Box 328, Muncie, Ind.

This Boy's Russian $1.35
Bloomer Suit, Prepaid

No. 30—Made of fine white duck or a dotted pique; plaited sleeve, white duck belt, full bloomer trousers. Sizes 2 to 6. Price, Prepaid........ $1.35

No. 68—Child's natural Irish Linen frock, made with round yoke and three box plaits down front and back, white piping and white duck metal finished belt. Excellent value. Sizes 2 to 8. Price, Prepaid....... $1.85

No. 9—as illustrated Girl's one-piece dress of pink or blue checked gingham. Yoke, belt, cuffs and double box plaits of white Pique. Plaited back; buttons invisibly in front. Sizes 3 to 10. Price, Prepaid $1.15

WE ORIGINATE STYLES

The cut and fit of our garments distinguish them from those of other makes. We use only such fabrics as will cause the of the looking and wearing as well as when new. Money refunded if not satisfactory. Write for our illustrated FREE catalogue of children's stylish garments in dress, French ginghams, piques and all seasonable novelties.

IDEAL SUIT COMPANY
85 to 87 Dearborn Street, CHICAGO, ILL.

GOLD MEDAL AT ST. LOUIS EXP.

Improved McDowell System

PROGRESSIVE DRESSMAKERS double their income using McDowell's perfect System of Dresscutting. You take measures, cut a perfect-size fit. Stays built for these and all the worry. Easy to Learn, Rapid to Use. Fits any Form. Follows every Fashion. Used by leading dress-makers. Thoroughly taught by mail. Send for circular M. DOWELL CO. Dept. A, 6 West 14th St., New York

The Mothers' Advisory Club.—*Continued.*

Answer No. 3—Close Your Ears Unless He is Polite

IN ANSWERING Mrs. H. A.'s question as to making her little boy more polite, I will tell her what I did. Something got the matter with my ears and I couldn't hear a question unless the "please" was used, and he thought it great fun when he would say "please" to see me give a little jump, and laugh and reply. Good nature is always contagious, a child welcomes anything that amuses him, and in a very short time the habit of "please" became fixed so it caused no notice. The "thank you" is harder to deal with, I've found. I think it is the self-conscious child who refuses to say it, because of drawing attention to himself. As he grows older and constantly hears others use it, he will also. Simply wait. Emphasize its necessity, but without punishment. Both my boys were obstinate in this respect. My eldest boy is now eleven and as polite as one could wish, and my boy of five more and more of his own accord uses "thanks" or "thank you." I know it is hard to wait, but one real boy's "thank you" from the heart is worth more than a dozen parrot-like repetitions. Children are all different, and we can't pour them all into the same mold of personality and politeness, while at three years old a boy is nothing but a baby with everything to learn. MRS. W. J. K.

Answer No. 4—This Mother Began Early

I SHOULD like to tell Mrs. H. A. what I have found to be a successful method of having my boy, aged two years, say "If you please," "thank you" and "you are welcome." From his earliest babyhood, as soon as he was large enough to reach his hand for his playthings, I always gave them to him with a "thank you." If I found any necessity for taking things from him, I invariably took them, even if necessary to use force, with "if you please," never under any circumstances omitting either. When he first began using a few words, though he got them sadly mixed he rarely omitted them, generally holding out his hand and saying "thank you" when he desired anything instead of "if you please." Now, at the age of two, he is learning to say "you're welcome" when one says to him "thank you." I never ask him to do anything without saying "please bring mama this," and then say "thank you" afterward; if he asks anything of me, merely saying "give me this or that," I ignore the request altogether. In a moment he knows what is wrong and asks properly, generally saying, "Now, mama, is that the way a little man talks?" I think if Mrs. H. A. will use unvarying politeness with her boy—and ignore all and every request not made politely, unless she is sure the child has forgotten how to make it properly, and then correct it pleasantly and grant it; otherwise,

Silk Warp
Lansdowne

Its beauty and adaptability are *a revelation,* to the woman of taste and discrimination.

Genuine perforated every 3 yards on the selvedge

W.M.F. READ

For sale at all good stores

---

99 Women out of 100

Should wear one of the seven sizes of the

SCOTT HIP FORM

It makes the figure symmetrical, causing the skirt to hang and drape gracefully. It overcomes that marked depression at the center of the back for stout women, or that flatness of the back and side hips for medium and slight women. The only hip form that can be worn comfortably with the corset for the long waist effect or over the corset for the short waist effect. Form-fitting, invisible, reversible, light in weight. Made in seven different sizes to meet the requirements of slight, medium and stout figures.

AVOID IMITATIONS—REFUSE ALL SUBSTITUTES!

and thoroughly ventilated.

All leading dry goods and corset dealers sell them. If you fail to find them, write for illustrated booklet to

CHARLES H. SCOTT & CO.
200-204 Centre St., New York 211-221 Madison St., Chicago

Manufacturers of The Scott Invisible Hip Forms, Bustles, Arm Scye Pads, Bust-forms, Blouses, Jewel Bags, and Double Safety Garter Pockets.

BICYCLES ON TRIAL

for 10 days. We ship on approval to anyone *without* a cent deposit.
Finest guaranteed
1905 Models.......... $10 to $24
with Coaster-Brakes and Puncture-Proof Tires
1903 and 1904 Models... $7 to $12
of Best Makes..........
500 SECOND-HAND WHEELS
All Makes and Models good as new.... $3 to $8
RIDER AGENTS WANTED in each town to ride and exhibit a sample bicycle. Write at once for Special Offer.
TIRES, SUNDRIES, AUTOMOBILES
MEAD CYCLE CO., Dept. F-21, Chicago

LEARN
TELEGRAPHY BOOKKEEPING or SHORTHAND

BY MAIL--AT YOUR OWN HOME

Anyone can learn it easily in a few weeks. We are unable to supply the demand for telegraph operators, bookkeepers and stenographers. No charge for tuition until position is secured. Write to-day for particulars.

MICHIGAN BUSINESS INSTITUTE
422 Institute Building, Kalamazoo, Mich.

The Mothers' Advisory Club.—*Concluded.*

pay no attention, even if it brings a howl to turn a deaf ear—she will be successful in the course of time. At least that has succeeded with one small and sometimes exceedingly contrary lad.　　　　　　　　Mrs. B.

Protect the Chest

THREE of my little ones have for the past three or four winters been troubled with bronchitis. On the slightest provocation they would take a severe cold, develop fever and cough incessantly. I was determined to prevent these recurring attacks, as nothing is quite such a drain on the system as bronchial trouble. I first assured myself that the cold was not due to improper hygiene, bathing, etc. I then went in search of a chest protector. I found that the chamois protector lined with flannel and interlined with cotton-batting was entirely too warm for our climate, besides being very expensive. So I bought a yard of chamois, took the pattern of a shield such as come with little boys' sailor blouse suits, and cut a half-dozen protectors by that pattern, fastening them at the neck with a button and buttonhole, and around the waist by means of tape. I did not line them, and found two for each child sufficient for several winters. Now, when the little folks come tearing home with their coats or jackets flying open I am not at all alarmed, knowing full well that the chamois shield next to the skin is an ample protector, while it is not so warm as to ever cause the child discomfort. It must be remembered, however, that it is not wise to ever leave off the chamois, even for a few hours, until the warm summer days have come.　　　　Mrs. C. B., Jr.

Look After the Children's Eyesight

IF YOUR child is backward in its lessons at school, don't think it is a dunce. Seek the cause; call on the teacher and try to find out the reason. My little girl seemed bright enough when I taught her at home, but the spelling lesson which she brought from school was so incorrect it made me wonder. I would say: "Why, Grace, what are these words?" "I don't know," she would answer. It seemed she could not even read her own writing. I would ask her if the words were called out to her; no, they were copied from the board. I found out later that she could not see, was too bashful to tell the teacher, and as the words were new to her she would put down anything she guessed. I saw the teacher, who then gave her more attention, and we found out that she really could not see the board. I then took her to an oculist who, after a thorough examination, said that she had a stigmatism of the eyes. Her eyes are so bright and clear that I never suspected anything wrong. She now wears glasses to correct that defect and is learning all right.　　　　　　　　C. H. W.

3,600 miles of Egg-O-See are manufactured and consumed annually, that is, over eight million packages are sold, and if these were laid touching each other end to would reach 3,600 miles, or from New York to San Francisco.

This is the largest showing ever made by any flaked wheat food factory in the w the use of Egg-O-See is steadily increasing. There must be a reason for this consumption.

It is simply a story of the very best flaked wheat food at the lowest possible p quality and price advertise it, one user brings another. Egg-O-See contains the muscle building, strength giving qualities of the whole wheat, the king of all cereals

It is thoroughly steam-cooked, and is made easily digestible by the addition diastase, the highest grade of malt. It is more nutritious than beef, and is infin healthful. It is wholesome and nourishing to people of all ages.

Egg-O-See is in no sense a medicated food, but its purity and strength giving make the use of medicine unnecessary.

A large package *AT ANY GROCERY FOR 10 CENTS.*

If you can find a grocer that does not sell Egg-O-See send us his name and 10 cents, mentioning this and we will send you a full sized package prepaid and a useful souvenir. Address the Egg- Quincy, Ill.

TO ENTERTAIN OUR FRIENDS

AN EASTER LILY PARTY

By MARY DAWSON

AN EXCEEDINGLY pretty little home entertainment is an Easter Lily affair. The plan is one that offers great chances of really delightful decorative effects, as well as for a series of fresh and original contests founded on the lovely bloom.

Crêpe-paper lilies and bands and rosettes of white-and-green crêpe paper make exquisite drapery for the drawing-room. Loop the bands of alternating green and white gracefully from point to point, fastening them here and there with bunches of paper lilies tied with paper ribbons.

Many girls enjoy a bit of dainty work without serious purpose for leisure hours, and any hostess having time for it can manufacture some very charming lily favors, for her masculine and feminine guests. For the girls, these take the form of lily wreaths to be worn during the evening and retained as souvenirs afterward. For the gentlemen, single blooms, real or artificial, are tied with narrow satin ribbons for dainty little boutonnieres.

Make the crowns by twisting pieces of very light wire to the required shape and covering them with green tissue paper. Cut the green paper into strips and cover the wire by rolling it over and under and drawing perfectly taut. To these frames the lilies are attached by wiring, sewing or tying.

The decorative effect of the party as a whole is greatly enhanced by having the girls wear white gowns.

The following games suggest a combination of mental and manual tests which the entertainer can either copy outright or vary to meet the particular requirements of her party:

GATHERING LILIES.—Secure a lily plant—not artificial this time—boasting at least half-a-dozen fine blooms. Blindfold each of the guests in turn, give him a pair of scissors and send him to clip a blossom. Of course, the majority of players will clip the empty air or will not clip at all, as each turn is limited to two minutes. All those clipping lilies retain the flowers clipped and draw for the prize. If but one person succeeds in reaching the lily plant, this person receives the prize. If none achieve the feat, no trophy is awarded.

LILY LETTERS.—This is a game of pure chance, but lacks any disturbing element which would render it inadvisable in a parlor. For it the hostess asks each guest to write his or her name on a sheet of paper, which is reproduced for the purpose. Some general rule should be agreed upon in the beginning as to whether or not middle names be included. The appellations are then carefully gone over and that which is found to contain the greatest number of letters that go to make up the word lily wins a

prize for the man or girl answering to it. A definite understanding should also be agreed on in advance as to whether a letter twice repeated in a name counts for two, etc.

CLIPPING LILIES.—A great deal of real skill is frequently manifested in what the children call "cutting out," and some very interesting work often results. Thus the clipping feature might be very cleverly introduced into a lily party by having the guests clip lilies. In order to give all clippers exactly equal chances the pieces of paper distributed for clipping should be of the same size. Half sheets of rather stiff note-paper are nice for the purpose. Unless it is possible to secure enough scissors to "go around," the players must cut in "turns," each turn lasting five minutes. Any disinterested person who does not witness the clipping may be appointed judge of the art work.

LILY BULBS.—Lily bulbs are welcome gifts at this season of the year, and the party-giver may offer hers in rather a novel fashion. For it will need a large wooden box filled with clean, dry earth, and a toy spade. The bulbs are wrapped in brown tissue-paper to make them the color of the soil. There should be several of these if the gathering is a large one. Bury the bulbs in the earth and have the guests draw numbered slips to decide the order of turns in digging. Each player is entitled to one dig. The bulb turned up by his spadeful of earth belongs to the successful digger. If the first round of digging fails to unearth all the bundles, players begin again in the same order as before.

A LILY DRAWING.—A simple game on the order of the ever-popular Donkey Contest could be arranged as follows: The hostess draws on the blackboard before the arrival of her invitees a lily plant with numerous branches but without blooms. Guests are blindfolded, one by one, and sent to draw a lily on one of the branches of the plant. Of course, the lilies fly wide of the mark of their proper sphere. If they do happen to reach the vicinity of the plant, they are apt to be provocative of much amusement as botanical specimens.

LILY QUOTATIONS. — The foregoing active, walk-about games should be varied from time to time with a test of mental agility. Such a competition might be arranged by having the players sit in a circle and by requesting each person to recall a quotation from some poet referring to the lily, or at least mentioning the name of the flower. All those who in the space of ten minutes can think of such a quotation draw for the prize.

LILY PUZZLES. — Another literary recreation can be built up on the various lilies made famous by history, song or story.

For this prepare a series of a dozen questions on the following plan:

THE DESIGNER

Just a Simple Twist

Test It Yourself

1. What are the "lilies" of France? Fleur-de-lis or iris blooms.

2. By what early monarch were they first adopted as the national insignia? Clovis.

3. Who was the "lily maid" of Tennyson's poems? Elaine.

4. What celebrated poem begins: " 'Twas in the time when lilies blow?'' Lady Clare.

5. Name an island-queen lily? Liliokaulani.

Any clever hostess can prepare as many more questions as she chooses.

Decorate with lilies a number of blank cards—half as many as there are to be guests present. Attach green ball pencils to the cards with narrow green satin ribbon. One lady and one gentleman become partners for the game and the card between them. Questions are answered on the reverse side of the card. The lady of the pair whose card at the expiration of half an hour shows the greatest number of correct answers receives a prize. If two or more cards are equally matched, the respective couples draw.

If the hostess thinks she cannot afford a substantial prize at the beginning of each contest, she can substitute two large prizes at the end of the evening's fun, giving points toward the award where individual prizes are mentioned here.

On the other hand, it is possible to secure a number of very inexpensive articles for what one would pay for two larger prizes. These trifles should all be suggestive of the blossom of the hour. A pretty blotting-pad, or book-mark, can be decorated in lily design, or a linen cover for a magazine may be so embroidered. Small quarter-pound boxes of candy may be decorated with pictures or sketches of lilies. A very attractive pen-wiper may be cut from white kid set off with green ribbons. The shading is put on with water-color. If one is clever at ribbon-work, a blossom may be evolved from a strip of white satin mounted on a wire covered with green silk and a wee yellow pincushion tucked away in the cup of the flower. Or a satin lily may be mounted on a stout hairpin and presented as a coiffure ornament.

Suggestions for these inexpensive prizes—which should cost less than a quarter apiece—are practically unlimited. The only requirement is a little ingenuity on the part of the fancy-worker.

If a supper follow upon the games, table trimmings and, so far as is tasty, the menu also, should be carried out in white and green.

For simple refreshments, the sandwiches are tied with green bébé ribbon, bonbons are white, the ice-cream is served in paper cases representing paper lilies, cakes have a white icing, while the coffee or chocolate is covered with whipped cream. Green-and-white china is employed, and candleshades, too, are white relieved with a lining of another color.

FOR LOVELY WOMAN

By JANE ELIOT

THE ART OF WALKING

WHAT woman exists who does not desire to appear as self-possessed and at ease in the drawing-room or in company as in the seclusion of her own boudoir? The secret lies in the carriage or walk, and the remedy for awkwardness and self-consciousness lies within oneself.

In this month of sunshine and flowers the art of walking may be practised to advantage. There can be no fad in walking. In the proper walk the head should be erect, the chest well thrown out, and by the muscles of the back the abdomen held up and inward. The figure will then represent perfect lines, and this position lifts the vital organs to their proper places, gives control over the muscles, and in strengthening the nervous system creates ease and self-possession. The most essential element in walking, standing or sitting is that the chest be thrown well forward; the rest of the body will then, if naturally relaxed, more readily assume the proper position.

The first principle in a correct carriage is that the body be erect and straight. It should never be held in the least rigid, but perfectly flexible and natural. No attempt should be made to throw back the shoulders, the advice so erroneously given to those inclined to stoop; when the chest is thrown forward the shoulders will assume their proper place.

Many diffident people when walking or standing do not know what to do with their hands. The hands and arms should hang easily, straight from the shoulder. As a test for correct attitude when standing, a string if hung from the tip of the nose should touch the chest and toes. The walk must be straight, as if following a perfectly straight line, not zigzag. Each step should be a foot apart, by one's own foot measurement. All jerky movements or bobbing up and down should be avoided. The bare foot is fashioned to grasp the ground, and when walking barefoot the ball should first touch the ground, but since fashion decrees a heel on the shoe the heel should touch the ground first.

To attain balance and smoothness in a beautiful carriage, practise, with a book resting on the head, walking straight on a chalked tape pinned in front of a long mirror; the marks should be two feet apart, measured by the length of one's own foot, and while walking one should breathe deeply. A beautiful carriage not only gives a distinguished bearing but affects the spirits. When the figure lines are out of proportion, the chest sunken, head forward and abdomen dragged down, no one can feel proud, happy or ambitious. But assume the correct position of the body, walk out into the pure air and breathe deeply, and it will create the inspiration to achieve wonders.

FOR A BEAUTIFUL FOOT

Above all things never wear a shoe that is too short. Compression will make the prettiest foot ugly and an ugly one unbearable. In the house, sandals or light gymnasium shoes should be worn; slippers and indolence create thick ankles. Walk in high, buttoned boots; the heel should be neither very high nor narrow, as this throws the body forward and predisposes the ankles to "turn" or give way, which is both painful and awkward. The center of the sole should rise above the heel and toe, to preserve the arch of the foot. Every woman who desires to have beautiful feet, and who walks a great deal, should have a pair of shoes for every day in the week, and the woman of leisure at least three or four pairs, and change them often. Old shoes are a menace to the feet; if worn until the heel is run down or one side of the shoe is worn thin, it causes calloused spots, which are most disfiguring and painful.

The feet should be bathed in tepid water every night before retiring. White castile soap is best for the purpose. If tender and sore, six or eight drops of carbolic acid in the water keeps them in perfect condition, otherwise a few drops of benzoin in the water is preferable.

Silk or lisle thread stockings have a softening effect on the skin, but no foot can be beautiful and have corns. The strong tincture of iodine applied daily is often an efficient remedy; another is to rub the disfiguring spots daily with pumice-stone. If the corns

well softened by soaking beforehand.
latter method, though tedious, is
factory, and particularly suited to
corns beween the toes. Callous
es may be cured by rubbing them
e daily with pumice-stone. Atten-
is as necessary for the toe-nails as
he finger-nails, and this care should
daily duty of the toilet. The nails
ld be kept clean with a soft brush;
a little shorter than the toe itself,
. a V-shaped nick in the center if
ned to grow in at the corners.

ROUGING

hile personally we do not approve
ouging and most certainly do not
mmend the use of such artifice, yet
many of our readers have written
concerning the matter that we
ctantly give the following short
cle on the subject:
luch of the rouge sold to-day is made
n an injurious article known as ver-
on, a form of mercury. Many of
so-called "theater rouges" are
rse, easily detected, and also injurious
the skin. The most natural and
ly harmless rouge is pure carmine,
ch can be bought in small quantity
iny drug store.
here are numerous forms in which
rouge may be used. One consists
merely the finest rice-meal tinged
h carmine and perfumed with attar
rose. Another, called enamel pow-
, is a mixture of equal parts of bis-
th and French chalk, colored and
ated in the same manner. These
perfectly harmless, but a pure car-
ie is in every way satisfactory. For
et use it should be kept in a box by
lf. The least particle should be
bed well into a soft cloth, which also
uld be kept in a separate box ready
use; dipping the cloth into the car-
ie and putting it on the face creates
unsightly, vulgar-looking daub.
Rouge applied in the fol owing man-
will defy detection: First with the
er-tips take a small particle of cold-
im, glycerin, or whichever prepara-
best suits the skin, and rub over
face. Then wipe off with a soft
dkerchief or piece of cheese-cloth.
v rub the prepared rouge-cloth lightly
r the cheeks, then with the finger-
extend or blend it almost to the
ples and down the side of the face
ost to the jaw-bone. In long, thin
s the rouge should not extend so
down.
lany make the mistake of applying
rouge in a round spot or of putting it
in patches of thick, bright color.
nust always be blended. The right
de should be a tone or two deeper
n one's own skin, not a bright hue.
here are several shades produced in
nine. The darkest is for brunette
is, but one should experiment until
suitable tint is secured, for rouging
in artifice which requires much to
ify it, and is only to be tolerated
n it assumes the tint of nature.
elessness in the application instils
nost unbecoming, unrefined effects.

This time
I want YOU
to write me

I am sending my
Kosmeo free to other
readers of this maga-
zine and, before this
offer is withdrawn, I
want to send it to you.

Don't put off again your accept-
ance of my offer. Don't give yourself another chance to forget it. Fill
out this coupon and mail it to me....
Will you do it *now*, please?

I ask only that you try my Kosmeo.
The trial shall cost you nothing.

I know what the trial will prove—or I would
not risk making this offer to You and to my
other readers.

Put on your face, neck, shoulders, and hands
some of the Kosmeo that I send you—let it stay
a few moments—rub it off—that is *positively* all
you need to do.

A clean, delicious freshness comes to
the skin that was hard and
dry, freckled, cloudy,
and chapped.

Kosmeo makes
and keeps the skin
clear, bright, soft,
velvety; looking
as fresh as a rose-
bud—feeling as
fresh as it looks.

THIS PORTRAIT of myself—made within the
year, by Tonnesen, Chicago—is shown as an example of what my KOSMEO will do—(I am a grandmother with grandchildren old enough to go to school).

Wind and Sun—
Worst Enemies of
a Good Complexion

Kosmeo is valuable not only for the good it does, but for the *harm* it forestalls.
Kosmeo prevents roughness and chapping, caused by harsh, cold, and dusty
winds. It prevents tan, freckles, and sunburn. It prevents wrinkles—which
always result from the dryness of the skin. Simply apply a little Kosmeo before
going out of doors. No veil can give such protection.
Men use Kosmeo after shaving to prevent the skin from becoming irritated and tender.
Kosmeo is different from any preparation you have used, or may be using.
Its reward is not a distant promise but is felt at once. You not only see the effect, you *feel* it—instantly.
The use of Kosmeo is not a task but a delight.
It needs no exhausting rubbing. Remember Kosmeo is unlike every
other preparation.
Kosmeo does not fill or enlarge the pores.
Kosmeo contains no mineral oils, and does not grow hair on
the face. It agrees with every skin—child's, woman's and man's.
Kosmeo is sold by the best druggists everywhere.
If your druggist does not sell Kosmeo, send me
his name and 50 cents, and I will send you a jar of
Kosmeo prepaid. (Be sure to send your druggist's
name.)

50¢

Mrs. *Gervaise Graham*

1305 Michigan Ave., Chicago.

The Kosmeo Sample that I want to send you is well worth writing
for. It is absolutely free to you. (The stamp on your letter is all
that you risk—and **I will repay even that,** if you ask it, after you
receive and try the Kosmeo that I send you.)
Here is the coupon that will bring you the free sample of my Kosmeo.
Cut out and sign it—**before you turn this page.**

MRS. GERVAISE GRAHAM, 1305 Michigan Ave., Chicago:

Please
send me, free, a   My druggist's name is...............   Does he sell Kosmeo?
sample of your
Kosmeo and   His address........................
your **Kosmeo**
booklet. I prom-   My name...........................
ise to read care-
fully the little   My address.........................
book you send
me and to try the
Kosmeo fairly.   *Fill out, and mail this Coupon at once.*

FASHION NOTES FOR MEN

By ALINE DE CARDEVA

NEVER since the days of powdered wigs and velvet knickerbockers has man plunged so deeply into frivolous fashions as he is now doing. Tie silks are no longer of sedate tones and simple textures. Brightest hues combined with novel weaves make up the assortment that meets the demands of the fashionable man. And not only gay colorings and fancy weaves suffice in these days, but he must have his crest deftly embroidered on the end of his Ascot or four-in-hand. Of course, the embroidered figure is not supposed to show; nevertheless, he knows it is there, tucked under his fancy waistcoat, and it is with a feeling of genuine satisfaction that he whips out the fancy end to exhibit it to a comrade whose tastes run in the same channel as his own.

Excellence in dress depends upon superiority in materials, correct style, correct cut and, last of all, good workmanship. Cheap silks are always flimsy no matter how carefully they may be worked up. Therefore it is advisable to pay a little more for ties and get something that holds its shape and style so long as there is a thread of the original material left.

The old-fashioned Ascot tie has returned after an absence of more than two years. It is altogether different from the English square, which is frequently taken for it and which has held the vogue for so long. The accompanying illustration reveals the difference, which lies in the wideness of the neckband and the manner in which the ends lap over, exposing the double-knot effect, which is not visible in the English square when correctly adjusted.

As to scarf-pins, there is little to mention. However, single stones plainly mounted seem to hold sway over fancy designs. One very noticeable feature is that almost invariably the pin harmonizes with the color of the tie. For instance, if the silk in the cravat is of dark red, a ruby or garnet cabochon is smartest. With any of the many shades of golden brown, so fashionable just now, a changeable cat's-eye is extremely attractive. With the new spring greens a malachite pin looks well,

as do also ... gets of green ... mounted in ... rough. Just ... there is a ... vailing mode ... fancy sapph ...

And sin... precious ... can be had ...number of fancy colors, borderi... blue, the admirer of unique jew... afforded ample opportunity to e... his fondness for a variety of sca... and cuff links, using these gem... complete set for evening wear, des... for a "gilded youth" consists of st... and cuff links made up ... choice sapphire caboch...

The shape of the w... linen collar shown in ... illustration is a good ... ample of the narrow-op... ing, rounded-corner st... recently introduced. Fr... now on the turnover... lar will be generally in ... throughout the spring... summer months. T... style is deep and cut... permit of greater freed... than last year's sha... When the very w... weather comes, narr... turnovers will be in e... dence, but will follow... same general style.

Some very handso... negligee shirts are m... with deep collars attach...

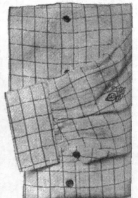

ASCOT TIE

NEGLIGEE SHIRT, SHOWING NARROW CUFF
MONOGRAM ON SLEEVE

is not a style to be adopted by the
with a slender bank account, nor for
man who indulges in long business
rs during the hot months, for once
collar becomes wilted it means a
nge of negligee and not the collar
e. Cuffs are also attached, and are
so wide as last year's models.
ere again appears the elaborate
kings. Just above the cuff on the
sleeve the crest or monogram is
ed. When the question arose as

COLLAR WITH NARROW OPENING AND
ROUNDED CORNERS

the advantage of expensive em-
dery upon shirt sleeves, the answer
that men when playing billiards
heir clubs frequently removed their
s, and to display the family coat
rms in this unassuming manner was
urce of gratification. One of the
rt shops makes a specialty of mono-
n and crest work, and their orders
so numerous for elaborate em-
dery on shirt sleeves and pajama
ets that they cannot begin to fill
n. Some of these designs cost
uch as five dollars for the work
e, so intricate are they in design
coloring. The same colors shown
he original crest must be employed,
when monograms alone are used
letters are done in different colors,
at they may be easily distinguished.
andkerchiefs and half-hose carry
the crest idea as well as ties, shirts
pajamas. Plain white linen hand-
hiefs of finest texture have heavy
nia embroidered in one corner.
n an extremist desires to intro-
the unusual he will have a pale
l border upon his handkerchiefs
the embroidery will repeat the
s contained in the plaid. Hose are
ted in the same manner at the top
always upon both.
ncy ribs in two tones with plain
are among the new styles in spring
ry. The darker color is intro-
d in the outer rib. Very few drop-
h weaves are shown as they are
altogether practical on account
eir frailty. After several seasons
ersistent wearing of drop-stitch
ts, men began to realize the cause
eir large hosiery bills, and now
weaves are altogether passé.
so many gaudy colors are displayed
former seasons, but the inevitable
l of brightness is frequently intro-
d in the way of a spray of hand-
oidery or in the clock.

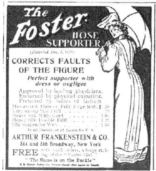

NOTES OF NEW BOOKS

"**T**HE MYSTERIOUS MR. SABIN,**" by E. Phillips Oppenheim. (Little, Brown & Company, Mass.) Mr. Oppenheim writes always an original book and seldom fails to hold the interest of his readers from start to finish, and this, his latest work, is no exception. Mysterious *Mr Sabin* is the principal character, and although our opinions of him are apt to be adverse while we read the first part of the book, in the end we are reluctantly obliged to give him admiration for his cool courage at least. A slender love story runs through the tale, but the main interest centers in the wonderful political intrigues of *Mr. Sabin*, which involve Germany, England, France and, to a small degree, America. *Sabin* is the only character which is made vivid with life, the others acting as foils to his maneuvers. His escape across the Atlantic is a well-written adventure, and is reserved till nearly the end of the book, thus maintaining the excitement to the very last, contrary to the planning of most story-tellers and playwrights, who seldom carry the promise of the opening chapters or scenes to a successful finish.

"THE APOLOGY OF AYLIFFE," by Ellen Olney Kirk. (Houghton, Mifflin & Company, New York.) This refined and charming love story, which appeared as a serial some time ago in THE DESIGNER, has at last been issued in book form, and will be hailed with delight by many of our readers who could not obtain complete files of our magazine containing the novel. *Ayliffe*, the sweetest of maidens, lives with her four delightful old aunts, each of whom is a character in her own particular way, and who possess two Persian cats and a droll dog that are forever at war, and of whose antics the dear ladies never grow weary. *Ayliffe* in the beginning of the book is merely a butterfly of fashion, a lovable butterfly, albeit, but later, when reverses come, she shows her sterling worth, and all who make her literary acquaintance will rejoice, we are sure, when true happiness is hers at last. Mrs. Kirk always writes delightfully and peacefully, and her gentle characters become to one as actual creatures of flesh and blood. "The Apology of Ayliffe" is the best

story she has produced for a long [...] and is the kind of romance which [...] safely be placed in the hands of y[...] girls, and which will be read with ple[...] by older women.

"THE MOST POPULAR COLL[...] SONGS." (Hinds, Noble & Eldredge, [...] York City.) So long as there are co[...] boys and girls so long will books of [...] kind have ready sale. All the old fa[...] ites and not a few new ones are [...] found in the present collection. Ea[...] Western, Northern and Souther[...] versities and colleges have each [...] tributed a share. The type, musical [...] otherwise, is large and clear, and [...] easily be read across shoulders of ro[...] ing young songsters crowding about [...] piano or the banjo.

"TALITHA CUMI," by Annie J. [...] land. (Lee & Shepard, Boston, Ma[...] This book is equally praisewor[...] whether viewed from the standpo[...] of the general reader, who loves an [...] teresting story with the genuin[...] human touch, or from that of the C[...] tian Scientist, whose ideas it embod[...] The story is of a family of five si[...] one of whom is regarded as hopele[...] deformed. The title will be recogni[...] as appropriately taken from the wo[...] of the Savior in healing the daug[...] of Jairus, Mark, v: 41, "And he [...] the damsel by the hand and said [...] her, 'Talitha Cumi,' which is, [...] interpreted, 'Damsel, I say unto [...] arise.'" The characters are so d[...] as to arouse a real and permanent [...] terest, whether or no the reader sh[...] in the belief of the author.

"THOUGHTS OF THE SPIRITUAL,[...] the Rev. Arthur Chambers. (Geor[...] Jacobs & Company, Philadel[...] Pa.) Mr. Chambers has given long [...] careful study to the subject of the fu[...] life and to the passages in Holy S[...] ture bearing thereon, and is pe[...] better qualified to write upon it tha[...] other man living. The immense s[...] of his two previous volumes ("[...] Life after Death" and "Man and [...] Spiritual World") and their num[...] translations attest the marked and [...] growing interest in this vital the[...] an interest which apparently s[...] with no people and in no country.

"THE SOLDIER OF THE VALLEY,[...] Nelson Lloyd. (Charles Scribner's [...]

Notes of New Books.—*Concluded.*

New York.) The spicy breath of the
mountains is in this book, and, sad as is
the termination of the little love story
which is its cause for being, we cannot
altogether pity the hero, who is destined
to live in the shadow of the great
blue hills. Nor, indeed, does he consider
himself in such doleful plight when their
majestic comfort and the company of
his dogs and pipe are left him. No, our
sympathy must go forth to the young
fellow who has turned his back on the
wide expanse of sky and land to take
up work in the crowded marts of men,
and all for naught, for even he does
not win the fickle lassie who came
to set the little village by the ears.
Most quaint and dryly witty are the
bits of homely wisdom scattered through
the chapters, and it is plainly evident
the author is fortunate enough to be on
close terms of friendship with some
highly intelligent canines. The true
lover of nature will surely love this book.

"CHILDREN IN LITERATURE," by
Mary H. Husted. (A. Flahagan Company, Chicago and New York.) The
writer has brought together in this little
volume the child characters which
Victor Hugo, Dickens and George
Eliot have made known to us, but she
had so great a store of little folks who
have grown famous through fiction to
draw from that we wonder at her re-
stricting herself to so small a company.
As far as it goes, the book will prove
interesting to most children, but it
would have been better to have left it
unillustrated than to warp the artistic
taste of Young America with such
dreadful pictures as accompany the
text. In these days, when illustration
can be made so good, and at so small
cost if need be, there is absolutely no
excuse for such crude cuts as are given.

"THE SENATOR," by Doctor Henry
Christopher McCook. (George W.
Jacobs & Company, Philadelphia,
Pa.) Perhaps nowhere else can be
found such picturesque descriptions of
village life in the early fifties as appear
in this volume, which is a tribute from
the author to the late Senator Hanna.
The homely scenes described are most
realistically pictured, impressing one
with its verity and nearness to life,
while at the same time they are charming in their simplicity. They are indeed
delightful word paintings of American
village life as it was to be found in many
parts of our country half a century or so
ago. While the book will be enjoyed by
all, it will be most appreciated by the
men and women past middle age who
have watched the old manner of life
gradually pass away, and cannot fail to
be of special interest to the many friends
of Senator Hanna. Indeed, the opening cantos, in connection with the full
"Biographical Notes" in prose, give
"The Senator" a distinct value as a
biography of Mr. Hanna, especially in
the opening and closing years of his life.

KNOTS AND WHATNOTS

For the best-written letter of not over fifty words, accompanying the fullest list of answers to the puzzles on this page, we will pay a cash prize of two dollars ($2.00), and for the second, third, fourth and fifth best letters a cash prize of one dollar ($1.00) each. Write on one side of the paper only. No letters will be considered which are received after April 30. Answers to April puzzles will appear in the May issue. February prize winners' names will be announced in the May number, and of March in the June number. Penmanship, spelling and neatness will all be taken into consideration.

Address all communications to
THE EDITOR OF THE PUZZLE PAGE,
Standard Fashion Company,
12-16 Vandam Street, N. Y. City.

1.—PROBLEM

Willie had as many dollars as Tommy had cents. Willie spent a fourth of his money and Tommy half of his. Willie now has one hundred and fifty times as much money as Tommy—how much had each in the first place?

2.—ELIMINATED POETRY

Ge m f yr brk—brch-tr
f yr yllw bk—brch-tr
Grwng by th rshng rvr
Tll nd sttly n th vlly.

3.—WORD SQUARE

To rub out
Competitions in speed.
Chemicals of a certain class—
A coarse marsh grass.
A town in Germany near the Rhine.

4.—CLOCK PROBLEM

A clock has four hands, one for the hours, one for the minutes, one for the seconds and one to indicate the month of the year. The second hand and the calendar hand are in a straight line, the former pointing to IX, the latter to III. The hour and minute hands are also in a straight line, at right angles to the former two (or so nearly so that the divergence cannot be noted.) What month and what time of day are indicated?

5.—SENSE OUT OF NONSENSE

In the sentence "Jack Fish is as good as his word," parse Jack. What is "as word"? Fish is what tense?

In the above paragraph ignore the grammar and look for a hidden question in natural history. What is that question?

6.—ENIGMA

I am a compound word and am always spelt the same way. Yet sometimes I contain no letters, sometimes contain but two or three and sometimes contain a hundred. The strangest thing is that you may add a letter to me but you must not take it away again, though equally queer is the fact that no matter how many you add I am always the same size.

7.—COMPOSITE WORD

```
. . . . . . .
. . . . . . .
. . . . . . .
. . . . . . .
```

H   *uprights*
    a writing material
    kinds
    across
    a fruit.

A   *uprights*
    a flower
    wideawake
    across
    a scarf.

T   *upright*
    a city in N. Y. State
    across
    a relish.

8.—ADDITIONS

Add a dark, resinous substance to yellowish, and get a colored Scotch cloth; to gain possession of, and get a mark to fire at; to itself, and get a drug.

Add a conveyance to leave, and get a ship's freight; to lad, and get a large dark-green bottle; to a place where minerals are found, and get a color; to at a distance, and get a plant famous for its seed.

Add a dog to eaten, and get a clergyman; to not many, and get an evening bell; to speak violently or rave, and get a small dried fruit; to the amount paid a landlord, and get swiftly flowing water; to part of an animal, and get to shorten; to a large fish, and get a celebrated Scotch game.

9.—PI

From the following thirty-three letters ake the names of three well-known merican songs:

a a a a, b, c, d d, e e e e e, g, h, i, l, m, p, n n n, r r r, s s, t t, x.

10.—RHYMED VESSELS

What kind of vessel rhymes with a rget ? with before the time? a bite? .e who screams? one who amuses? irchased ? to need? one who tugs? quarrel? a kind of cup? wha⁺ o yme with a kind of dance?

11.—REVERSIBLE WORD.

1. I do not —— the honor more than y ——.
2. He faced the clerk with a —— id demanded a —— of thread.
3. It was funny to watch the haughty)anish ——, —— in his easy-chair.
4. You can find the —— by observ- g the distant tree ——.
5. I like to take a —— on my bicycle, it Rover runs after and —— the tires.

ANSWERS TO MARCH PUZZLES

METAGRAM.— Preach, reach, each, ache, ace, c.

RIDDLE.—A Hat.

MISSING NUMERALS.—
Jennie was a good student and liked to XL her work, especially in drawing. One day ie made a design of an IV leaf, judging the "oportions entirely by her I. Another day she 'ew the picture of a CL climbing upon the icks. Happening to know an old sailor she iowed the drawing to him. "Do you know hat that is?" she asked. "II," he replied; t's just as natural as life. He's come up on ie rocks to LI in the sun. I've often seen m."
"MI" exclaimed Jennie; I wish I could go)C."

4. DOUBLE DIAGONALS.—

S U I T S	Suits.
T A F ZET A	Taffeta.
P R I S O N	Prison.
E L F	Elf.
T E A R	Tear.
E R A	Era.
R E I N	Rein.
S A L I C	Salic.
B R I N D I S I	Brindisi.
U P A S	Upas.
R E L I C	Relic.
G U S T O	Gusto.

5. PYRAMID.—
B E A C O N
A U
T E R R A C O T T A
E I
M O N O T O N O U S N E S .
O E
U N I N T E L L I G I B L E N E S S
N I
A T
U N S A T I S F A C T O R I N E S S

6. BEHEADINGS.—1. (s) even; 2. (s) table; . (h) ear; 4. (b) oat; 5. (w)inner; 6. (o)range; . (d)own; 8. (h)all; 9. (w)ant; 10. (a)greed; l. (f)rigid; 12. (m) arch.

7. SENSE OUT OF NONSENSE.—What is a ike?

PRIZE WINNERS FOR JANUARY.

$2 to Mrs. J. F. Snow, Wicomico Church, Va. il each to Margaret C. Boss, Athol, N. S.; Edith Wallace, Jamaica Plains, Mass.; E. W. Depue, Kensington, Md.; and Mrs. D. L. Jewett, Des loines, Ia.
HONORABLE MENTION: Katherine Hareu, Kate Willis, Bertha A. Cameron, Elizabeth B. Ballard, Elenor Hill, Mrs. E. L. Spooner, Jessie Howell Hull, Mrs H. P. McPherson, Charlie Lehmer, Vesta V. Ohlinger, Susie Green, How- ird Wright, B. Richards, Mrs. R. Eddy Chester Dorr, Elizabeth H. Browne.

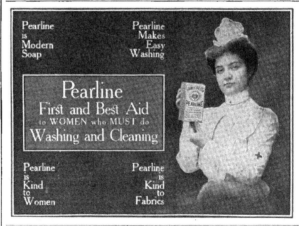

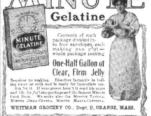

A PARLOR GARDEN PARTY
By MARJORIE MARCH

WHEN, in the early part of April,
Daphne sent me an invitation
to a "tea and garden party to
be given in her pretty parlor," my
curiosity was aroused.

She greeted us clad in a soft green
gown, some pussy willows caught by
a knot of velvet at her girdle. The
decorations of the parlor, that made
a fitting setting to her daintiness, called
forth our admiration.

"It is only because I have a cherry
tree that catches all of the morning sun
and so is the first to wear its spring
clothes," she said in explanation, for
here were blossoms, blossoms, everywhere. Great jars of mission pottery
were filled with their loveliness. Branches
were over the pictures and doorways,
and with green rugs on the floor and
little evergreen trees set in tubs about
the room it was hard to believe we were
not in the midst of a garden warm
with spring's presence.

Little tables, that were evidently to
be used in the playing of some game,
were placed around the room at intervals, while garden benches and rustic
chairs with red-and-green denim cushions invited us to comfort.

The novel call to supper was the winding of a horn, the manner in which
the harvesters are called to their meals
in some farming districts. The dining-
room was charming in its arrangement,
a veritable spring-bower. Wire netting
made a wainscoting around the room
and here were stacked evergreen
branches, making a background for
more sprays of the snowy cherry bloom.
Last year's bird's-nests filled with
pussy-willow sprays graced the side-
board. The chandelier had a Japanese
umbrella hanging from it, and blossoms were suspended by pink ribbons
from the tip of each rib, making a
dainty shower effect.

The table itself was a thing of beauty.
It was covered with a pale-green cloth,
over which a few smilax vines trailed
their way. The centerpiece was a
Dresden china Cupid with blossoms in
his hand, and with a few sprays upon
the cloth, as if he had just thrown them
there. The souvenirs were small water-
ing-pots filled with candy. The bonbon dishes were small fancy baskets
with a lining of pink crêpe paper. These
were filled with candied rose leaves and
pistache bonbons, and the combination
looked most tempting.

All the china used was pink and green,
and the silver was exceedingly plain, to
accord with rustic simplicity. Brass
candlesticks held white tapers, un-
shielded.

There were twelve of us besides our
host and hostess, for the large round
table held just fourteen, and Daphne
considers that a lucky number. Our

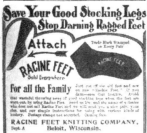
A Parlor Garden Party.—*Concluded.*

menu was as follows, and we found the old-fashioned high tea delicious.

Escalloped Oysters	Creamed Chicken
Tea Biscuit	*Sally Lunn*
Tea	*Chocolate*
Egg Salad with Mayonnaise	
Preserved Peaches and Pistache Ice-Cream	
Fancy Cakes	*Bonbons.*

After tea we went into the parlor to play the game of "Flowers." Each of the little tables before mentioned was provided with mucilage pots and brushes, and we seated ourselves, glancing at the implements inquiringly, it must be confessed.

Our host and hostess soon enlightened us as to the trial of skill, explaining that as they were the inventors of the game they would not play, but would be the judges and gather up the bouquets after their guests had finished arranging them.

Each of us was given a large piece of cardboard with a variety of leaves pasted upon it, and at the same time an envelope containing the missing blossoms. The cards were numbered and the envelopes bore corresponding numbers. Our work was to paste the flowers on to the stems and leaves belonging to them. Every card was different, so no neighborly intelligence could aid one, and the comparing and conjecture of botanical knowledge was funny in the extreme.

It was surprising to find how very little the most of us really knew about leaves. Pansy blooms were put on violet leaves and violets got mixed up with lilac leaves, and even worse mistakes than this were made by the bewildered botanists.

Daphne had made these cards by cutting apart many seed catalogues, and the novelty she displayed in her arrangement of them called forth the admiration of those who played the game. When the botanical test was over and all the cards finished, prizes were given to the man and to the girl whose cards showed the most perfect arrangement of blossoms. The man's prize was a silver pencil chased with a daisy design and the girl's prize was a real forget-me-not plant growing in an artistic little pot.

Then out came Daphne's guitar and a mandolin, which one of the musical guests had been asked to bring, and we sang songs to their accompaniment in our parlor-garden until the clock told us the "good-by" hour was at hand. Then we danced the old-time "up the middle and down again" as a finish to our spring festival, and with such surroundings never did the Virginia reel seem such a merry dance.

Daphne smiled on us happily when we gave her our thanks.

"As for a good time," one of the gayest of our party declared, "it grows with the flowers in a seed catalogue!" And we all agreed.

Etiquette Hints

IN THE MATTER OF EASTER GIFTS

INASMUCH as some of our readers appear to be a little perplexed as to the relationship of etiquette and the Easter gift, it may not be inappropriate to remark that, although the pretty custom of sending cards and gifts to one's relatives and friends in commemoration of Easter-tide still maintains its popularity, it is not in any sense a breach of etiquette to ignore it. The matter, indeed, is entirely subject to one's own discretion; and, although one's friends must certainly appreciate the courtesy should one choose to observe the time-honored custom, they should not, on the other hand, feel themselves slighted should one elect to do otherwise. Nor will they, in all probability; for under existing social conditions, it is so obviously impossible for any save the really wealthy to observe all the gift-making seasons with anything approaching universal satisfaction that a great many people boldly adopt the exactly opposite course of observing none of them except Christmas—and that only in so far as their own immediate kinsfolk and most intimate friends are concerned. As to the manner of sending Easter gifts, about which several correspondents have made anxious inquiries, that, too, is largely a personal affair, the acceptability of the offering depending in no small measure upon the spontaneity with which it is offered. Usually the donor's card is enclosed in the package, a brief Easter greeting being penciled upon it; but when the souvenir takes the form of an Easter-card the sender's visiting-card is generally considered superfluous. Gifts, whatever their nature, should be daintily wrapped up in white tissue-paper and tied with baby ribbon before being enclosed in their outer wrappings—which, of course, must be of stouter material in order to withstand the wear and tear of transportation—for it is one of the canons of good form that a gift must be presented in as neat and attractive a guise as possible. It should not be necessary—although, unfortunately, it is so—to say that all the expenses of transmission, whether of postage or express, must be scrupulously prepaid by the sender; for a present for which the recipient is required to pay, even in part, cannot conscientiously be called a present at all. Women, in sending Easter souvenirs to men who are not related to them, should select nothing more costly or imposing than pretty cards, the proprieties forbidding the presentation of gifts of any other type, save when the donor and the recipient are betrothed, in which case, of course the embargo is lifted. Similarly, men may present their women friends with the customary bouquet or basket of choice blossoms, a potted plant or a dainty box of bonbons; but only mothers, sisters or fiancées may receive gifts of greater value at their hands.

AS TO THE MAID OF HONOR

The approach of the season of weddings invariably brings an avalanche of queries upon the Etiquette Editor's desk, and the rule has held good in this as in previous years, although the subject of wedding etiquette has already been discussed to the point of barrenness in the columns of THE DESIGNER. In reply to a variety of questions it may be stated that the maid—or matron—of honor should, by preference, be a sister or other near relative of the bride, though, if the latter have no such near relative, a sister or relative of the bridegroom may officiate with equal propriety. It is quite customary nowadays for a married woman to assist at the ceremony as matron of honor in the place of the maid, though a few years since such a thing was utterly unheard of, the popular idea then being that the attendants of a young bride should all be young, unmarried women. The maid or matron of honor always takes precedence of the other bridesmaids, her duties during the ceremony consisting mainly of standing immediately behind the bride and taking charge of her gloves and bouquet. At the reception following the ceremony she relieves the bride as much as possible, receiving the guests as soon as the prescribed congratulations have been uttered and passing them on to others of the receiving party. Should the bride have no near male relative who can "give her away," that important office may very properly devolve upon the matron of honor, but never upon a maid of honor, custom demanding that the woman who discharges so onerous a duty be herself a personage of some importance and dignity. Usually it falls upon the mother of the bride when the latter possesses neither father nor brother. Under no circumstances can it, as one correspondent suggests, devolve upon the best man, whose sole duty it is to support and attend upon the bridegroom, and who could not consistently perform both offices at one time.

ANSWERS TO CORRESPONDENTS

RULES

IN ORDER to insure a reply under this heading it is necessary to give a pseudonym under which the querist may be answered. The full name and address of the writer must also be given. This will never, under any circumstances, be published. Questions which are to be answered in THE DESIGNER for May must reach the editor not later than March 12th.

No answers to correspondents will be sent by mail unless a two-cent stamp or stamped envelope is received at this office. Address all such letters to the EDITORIAL DEPARTMENT, STANDARD FASHION COMPANY, 12-16 Vandam St., New York City.

No contribution to "What Women Are Doing" or "Helps Along the Way" will be accepted unless accompanied by a duplicate of the certificate printed below, properly filled out. One certificate is necessary for each contributor. Two or more readers may not send in items or paragraphs on the same certificate, but one reader may send in as many items or paragraphs as he or she wishes in one letter, provided a filled-out certificate be enclosed in that letter. Certificate for "The Mothers' Club" will hereafter be given at the head of that department. When sending items or paragraphs, cut out the certificate, fill in name and address, and pin, sew or paste the certificate to the letter which is sent with the items or paragraphs. The letter should also contain the address, plainly written.

CERTIFICATE OF MEMBERSHIP.

This is to certify I read THE DESIGNER, and wish to contribute to "What Women Are Doing," "Helps Along the Way."

Name ....

Address ....

MILICENT R. S.—If you will look over pages 470 and 471 of THE DESIGNER for February, 1905, we think you will find under the title: "A Washington's Birthday Supper" just the style of entertainment you desire. If you do not possess a copy of the issue mentioned, we will send you one on receipt of ten cents in stamps or silver.

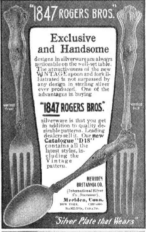

Answers to Correspondents.
Continued.

M. S. B. BALTIMORE.—If you attend the "At Home," you can leave your card. Almost always at an affair of the kind mentioned there is a maid or butler who opens the door and announces the guests by name as they enter the drawing-room, therefore all the guest has to do is to place her or his card in the card-receiver, which generally is placed on a hall-table within easy reach. If you do not attend the function you should enclose your visiting-card in a small card-envelope and mail it on the day of the reception, or so it will be received on that day. It is not necessary for a young woman to express her pleasure at meeting a young man who is an entire stranger to her, nor is it necessary for her to request him to call. She can simply bow gracefully when the time arrives for adieus to be made.

ROSE C. D.—The glacial acetic acid may be applied to the moles once or twice a day with a very finely pointed stick or match. Care should be taken not to touch the healthy skin surrounding the moles, and if the latter should become at all sore during the operation we would advise you to suspend treatment for forty-eight hours, or until the inflammation subsides. Very often the moles disappear in three or four days, according to their size, but the skin often remains red for a week or more after the moles have been removed.

ALICE REX.—We have a number of pretty and complete sets for infants, the price of each being fifteen cents. If you will send for our large illustrated catalogue, which will be mailed to you on receipt of twenty cents in stamps or silver, you will find we publish a number of attractive and practical garments for infants.

ADRIENNE.—The young girl's mother is the best judge of what is correct for her daughter to do, as she understands her disposition and temperament and also must know or should know all about her friends. Mannerisms differ widely in different localities. In the large Eastern cities it is not considered good form for a school-girl unattended to go anywhere with those of the opposite sex unless they are near relatives. Brown in almost any shade, dark blue, deep garnet, pale yellow, and certain shades of plum or lilac—those that have a pinkish tint—would be becoming to anyone with rather sallow complexion, blue eyes and brown hair. Clear white, that with a bluish tint, should also be very becoming to her.

A PATRON.—With a long crape mourning veil you will find a small bonnet that can be pinned close to the head far more comfortable for general wear than a hat which is apt to slip askew. As the long veil would prove very warm for summer,

Answers to Correspondents.

Continued.

vould advise you to get a small hat ecoming shape, trimmed with crape mourning silk, and wear a face of some thin stuff with a crape ler. As to the draping of the long we must refer you to some good ner, as the matter depends so h upon the shape of the bonnet. eems a strange thing to mention such subjects in connection, but ou will look at the picture of the al veil on page 666 you will see a e of draping the veil which would becoming to most faces, but with draping a small face veil would be necessary. We note what you for, and a soon as possible we will ish such an article in THE DE-ER.

iss R. S.—In the March DESIGNER, i, on page 618, under the answer to llie H.," you will find directions for ing a hair-dye which is said to be illent. If you do not possess this iber we will send it to you on the ipt of ten cents in stamps or silver.

osy O'GRADY.—All hair grows light-oward the ends. All you can do is ave the tips clipped every month, or, ou prefer, you can have them singed, th process is said to strengthen the rth of the hair.

liss ETHEL R.—We cannot give you address of the author of "Toilet le Chat," but we will be happy to rard to her any communication you / address to our care, if you will ember to enclose a stamp for the rarding of your letter, or to enclose n a stamped envelope.

), X.—We regret we cannot give you recipe for making Scotch scones n as were served at the St. Louis r, but if you will send us a stamped elope directed to yourself we will i you the address of an expert in the king line who we think can give you it you want. Lawrence Irwell, un-"The Kitchen Kingdom," in THE SIGNER for February, 1905, gives in otch Cookery" an excellent recipe making Scotch shortbread. I won-if this can be what you desire. If do not possess this number it will orwarded to you on the receipt of ten ts in stamps or silver.

Irs. A.—Send us a stamped envelope ited to yourself and we will give the addresses of several Women's changes where you may be able to your fancywork.

). D.—We think you will find the pe for "Berlin Crullers" very nice. cannot tell you what the chemical ion would be of using baking-powder I sour cream together, but are cer-l it would not be harmful.

RUBENS INFANT SHIRT

A Word to Mothers :

The Rubens Shirt is a veritable life-preserver. No child should be without it. It affords full protection to lungs and abdomen, thus preventing colds and coughs, so fatal to a great many children. Get the Rubens Shirt at once. Take no other, no matter what any unprogressive dealer may say. If he doesn't keep it write to us. The Rubens Shirt has gladdened the hearts of thousands of mothers. We want it accessible to all the world.

No Buttons   No Trouble

Patent Nos. 528,988—550,253.

BEWARE OF IMITATIONS!

The Genuine Rubens Shirt has this signature stamped on every garment—

Rubens

The Rubens Shirt is made in cotton, merino (half wool and half cotton), wool, silk and wool, and all silk to fit from birth to nine years. Sold at dry goods stores. Circulars, with price list, free. **Manufactured by**

RUBENS & MARBLE, 94 Market Street, CHICAGO

Be a Dressmaker

EARN $15 TO $50 A WEEK

We know a dressmaker—a woman—who receives $10,000.00 a year as designer of Marshall Field & Co.'s dressmaking department. Dressmakers are paid higher salaries than any other class of women. Some receive as high as $3,000 for making one gown. None of them receive less than the highest salaries usually paid women for other work.

You may not be able to earn $100 a week at the start, but we can teach you so that you will be one of the best paid women in your vicinity. If you are a stenographer, bookkeeper, housekeeper, or even a dressmaker, we will teach you so that you can soon double your income.

You Can Learn at Home by Mail

OLGA GOLDZIER WILL TEACH YOU

Olga Goldzier, one of the best known dressmakers in America, is Instructor-In-Chief, and personally prepares every lesson. She is a member of the faculty of Kossuth University and has first prizes, diplomas and gold medals awarded on gowns exhibited in Paris, Vienna and New York. Her system of teaching is simple and thorough. No patterns, charts or mechanical devices are used. Her instruction covers planning, designing, selection and care of materials, measure taking, pattern making, sewing, finishing and draping. The things so hard for most dressmakers are so simply explained that any one can do them. She teaches how to conduct a profitable dressmaking establishment. Her own establishment in Chicago is one of the largest and most exclusive in America. She teaches you how to successfully make your own and others' clothes. Any woman or girl who can read and write and who has a little taste can soon learn to make fine garments as well. It does not take long under Mrs. Goldzier's personal instruction. Write for handsome book, "How I Teach Dressmaking at Home." It is free.

WOMAN'S COLLEGE OF SCIENTIFIC DRESSMAKING

Dept. E, LA CROSSE, WISCONSIN

The **Velvet Grip**

Never Slips nor Tears   EVERY PAIR WARRANTED   FRONT PAD BELT

HOSE SUPPORTER

GIVING THE POPULAR STRAIGHT FRONT EFFECT

Correct Hygienic Comfortable

GEORGE FROST CO., Makers, Boston, Mass., U.S.A.

Sample sent, Cott., 25c. Mer., 50c. Silk, 75c.   Llc. under Pat. Dec. 5,'99

Answers to Correspondents.
Concluded.

KOSSUTH.—A widow and widow would not have as much ceremony a wedding as would those marrying the first time. There would be matron of honor nor bridesmaids, the bride would wear gray, lavender other light color rather than pure white. She can wear a bonnet or hat but no veil. The groom would be dressed in the usual way for either afternoon or evening, reception can follow the wedding.

BON VOYAGE.—You will be able to hire steamer chairs aboard ship, you will have to take your own steamer rug, air cushion or pillow and any comforts of that description that you may require. As a rule pets are allowed in the staterooms, but taken in charge by the steward.

DENTIST.—It is said that American dentists in the Philippine Islands are doing exceedingly well and are invariably liked and patronized by the natives who consider the gold crown and bridge work in advance of the workmanship of the Spanish or Filipino dentists. I cannot tell you the cost of the trip.

DRESSMAKER.—The canvas would have crumpled and rendered the jacket unsightly if you had first shrunk it. You should place the tailor's canvas in a pail of water and let it remain for at least ten minutes, then take it out and while still wet press it with very hot irons until it stiffens up again. This will enable you to stiffen the lower part of the skirt or the revers of the jacket, and at the same time the canvas will not break or shrink, as it would if the suggestion given be not followed.

GERTRUDE.—You must be very careful not to work in a dim light. It is needless to tell you that in doing the needlework or embroidery the light should always fall over your left shoulder, on account of the shadow which is otherwise cast by the hand. Any flickering light is bad for the eyes, but the soft light of a lamp shaded with green paper or porcelain shade will be found very comfortable to work by. We would advise you not to work too steadily, but to go out in the open as much as possible. Take long walks in the country when the weather is fine and as soon as warm weather arrives we would suggest that you take a sea trip.

Confidence of ... **Mother and Daughter**

Nothing
Better for
Aching
Feet

Makes
One Sweet
and
Clean

in SPIRO
BODY POWDER

We Guarantee Spiro Powder

to be the best toilet powder made. It is better than other toilet powders, because it not only does what they do, but it does something that they do not do, it

Destroys the Odor from Perspiration

Each box is insured, and if, after using, your judgment decides that it is not as represented, the dealer from whom you purchased will refund your money.

To Destroy the Odor from Perspiration—dust SPIRO under the arms, on the dress shields or other garments just as your case requires. Use it and be cool, sweet and clean.

To Relieve Burning, Aching Feet—dust SPIRO POWDER on the hose. It will also destroy that offensive odor from perspiring feet.

Chafing, Prickly Heat and Inflamed Parts can be instantly relieved by a dust of SPIRO.

Price 25c. per box, at all drug and department stores. What we have not room to say here we have said in our booklet, and if you will send to us the name of the druggist who doesn't keep SPIRO, we will mail to you immediately the following:

FREE { SAMPLE OF SPIRO POWDER
BOOKLET "HOW TO DESTROY THE ODOR FROM PERSPIRATION"
FREE PICTURE COUPON
MINIATURE COLORED VIEW OF NIAGARA FALLS

SAVE THIS SPIRO COUPON
SAVE THIS COUPON, IT IS A GIFT. Answer this advertisement, and you will receive another free Coupon. You will need only two more Coupons to get a beautiful large photographic reproduction of Niagara Falls, 18x16 inches, Summer or Winter view. The booklet tells you how.
SAVE THIS SPIRO COUPON

SPIRO POWDER COMPANY, No. 3 Spiro Block, Niagara Falls, N. Y.

We want to send to each reader of this ad. some of our beautiful pictures of Niagara Falls. Save the coupon in corner of ad., which is the starter. When you answer the ad. you receive another free coupon, then you have to get only two more from the 25c. boxes, and upon receipt of the four the picture will be mailed to you.

The only things that Buster Brown can't bust are the Buster Brown Stockings

COLGATE'S

TWO GREAT ANTISEPTIC POWDERS

VIOLET TALC ❀

DENTAL POWDER

THE SAFEST FOR YOU AND YOUR CHILDREN

COLGATE'S VIOLET TALC is unsurpassed for the toilet. The sensation of delightful freshness and softness imparted to the skin by this powder appeals to every dainty woman. After a bath, the powder proves cooling and refreshing; for swollen and tired feet it is a great relief.

THE NEW PATENTED SIFTER is a marvel of simplicity and perfection. It is a vast improvement over the old-fashioned kind which injured your finger nails when opening; it is always in place, and is the ideal sifter for a toilet or nursery powder. It is our patented invention of this past year, and is the first perfect sifter ever put on a Talc Powder Package. It is a complete package for home use and for traveling

COLGATE'S DENTAL POWDER because of its unusual smoothness, its dainty fragrance, its gentle abrasive properties, and its antiseptic qualities, is the ideal dentifrice. It is a refreshing stimulant for the gums, and an effective germicide for all decay-producing bacteria. Mothers should remember that constant care of the teeth in childhood means the saving of much dental trouble at maturity. The delightful flavor of this powder is so thoroughly enjoyed by children that you will find no difficulty in persuading them to clean their teeth regularly with it.

THE NEW STOPPER on both metal boxes and glass bottles, may have the opening regulated to suit the user, but the cap always remains attached. This feature is a saving to the user, and a boon to the traveler.

COLGATE & CO.

ESTABLISHED 1806   MAKERS OF FINE SOAPS AND PERFUMES   NEW YORK

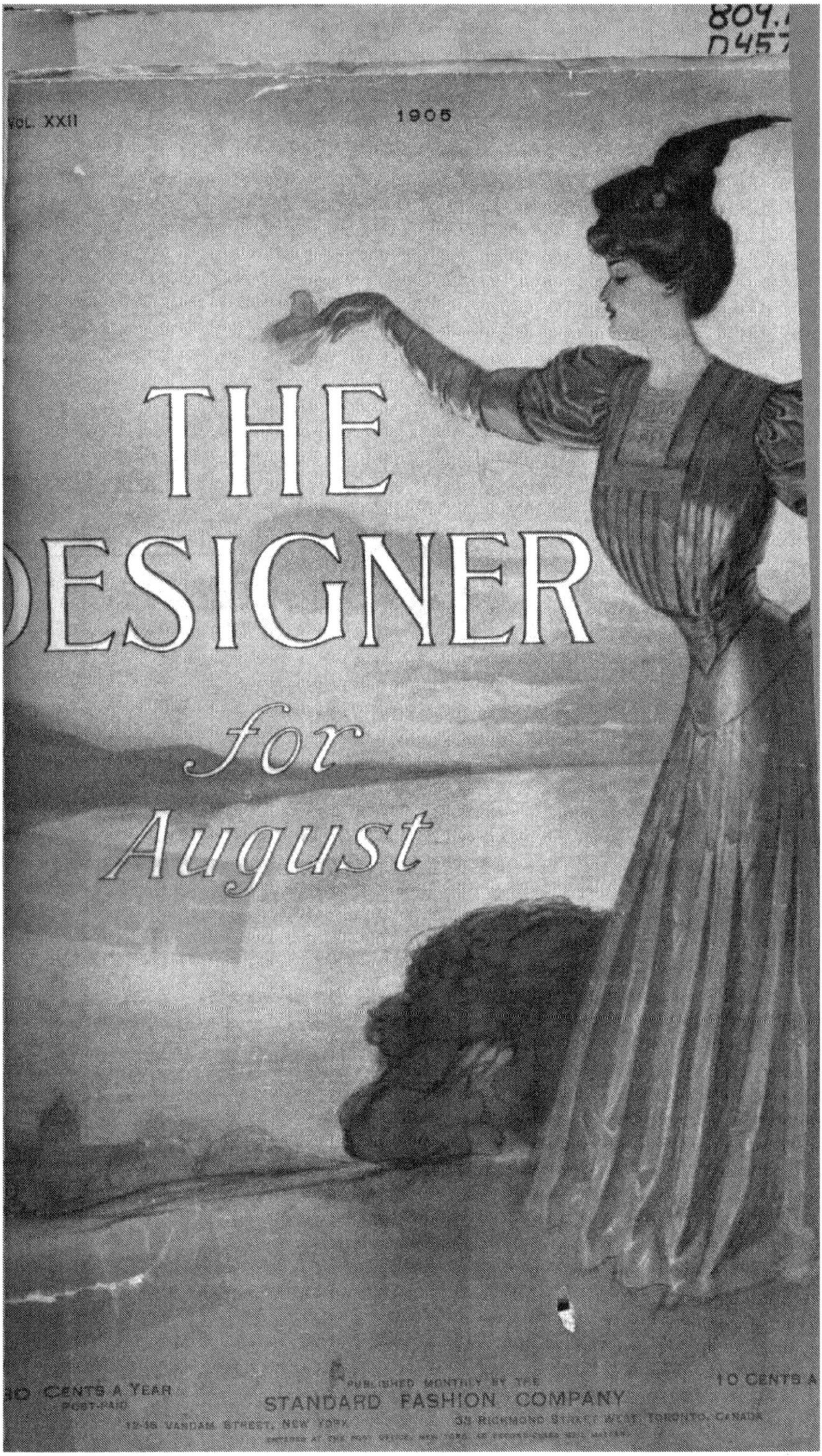

VOL. XXII   1905

THE
DESIGNER

for

August

PUBLISHED MONTHLY BY THE
STANDARD FASHION COMPANY
12-16 VANDAM STREET, NEW YORK   35 RICHMOND STREET WEST, TORONTO, CANADA
ENTERED AT THE POST OFFICE, NEW YORK, AS SECOND-CLASS MAIL MATTER

10 CENTS A YEAR
POST-PAID

10 CENTS A

BUSTER BROWN *Says—*

Say—if you ask your Ma to send me your dealer's name and 25 cents for a sample pair of my stockings—

Buster Brown Stockings for Boys and Girls
and Their Ma's

Fast Black or Money Back   **Will Wear—Won't Tear**

I'LL TELL YOU WHAT I'LL DO—

I'll send you free for three months my Magazine—a peculiar magazine—different from any other you ever saw. Lots of useful information—How to bring up a Father "by his Son"—"How to Make Baskets"— The Buster Brown Alphabet—"maybe you won't like this"—"A whole lot of new Stunts you never saw before"—and if you want to make money you can be Agent. Agents get a whole lot of good things—I got a lot of "Crex Rugs," with Tige and Me on 'em, to give to Agents—you can put these rugs alongside of your bed—and if you get mad at us you can turn the rug over and then you can't see us. If you don't laugh when you read this Magazine you are no friend of mine, 'cause you are a crank—'cause anybody that ain't got the toothache has got to laugh. I am laughing now at the big sign my Pa is putting up—

> **Over One Million pair of Buster Brown Stockings have been sold to satisfied customers—over One Hundred Thousand Dollars have been spent in advertising**

All this in one year—how about the next year? This is all true, too, 'cause we make stockings for healthy boys and girls who play—you can't keep quiet all the time unless you're sick—and if you're sick you won't need any stockings anyhow.

So many fellows have written me lists of Boys and Girls who wear my Stockings—so they can win the Acme Automobile—that I am nearly crazy writing to everybody to ask 'em if they wear 'em. Soon as I can count up I'll tell you who won—'cause this has got to be done right.

When you write be sure and tell your dealer's name—'cause Pa gets mad when you don't. Say—did you read about Pa and Me going to New Orleans? It's in the Magazine, and be sure and read about Bez and his Goat, it's the next story. Write me a letter.

Your friend, **BUSTER BROWN**, 346 Broadway, New Y...

If you live in Canada write me care of E. H. Walsh & Co., Toronto

P. S.— SAVE YOUR STOCKING COUPONS AND READ MY MAGAZINE WHAT THEY'RE GOOD FOR—B(

MENNEN'S
BORATED TALCUM
TOILET POWDER

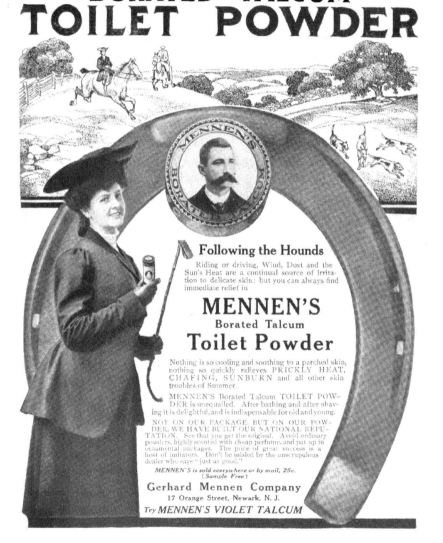

Following the Hounds

Riding or driving, Wind, Dust and the Sun's Heat are a continual source of irritation to delicate skin; but you can always find immediate relief in

MENNEN'S
Borated Talcum
Toilet Powder

Nothing is so cooling and soothing to a parched skin, nothing so quickly relieves PRICKLY HEAT, CHAFING, SUNBURN and all other skin troubles of Summer.

MENNEN'S Borated Talcum TOILET POWDER is unequalled. After bathing and after shaving it is delightful, and is indispensable for old and young.

NOT ON OUR PACKAGE, BUT ON OUR POWDER, WE HAVE BUILT OUR NATIONAL REPUTATION. See that you get the original. Avoid ordinary powders, highly scented with cheap perfume, and put up in ornamental packages. The price of great success is a host of imitators. Don't be misled by the unscrupulous dealer who says "just as good."

MENNEN'S is sold everywhere or by mail, 25c.
(Sample Free)

Gerhard Mennen Company
17 Orange Street, Newark, N. J.

Try MENNEN'S VIOLET TALCUM

Vol. XXII, No. 4. AUGUST, 1905

The DESIGNER

CONDUCTED BY LILIAN DYNEVOR RICE

Published monthly by the STANDARD FASHION COMPANY, 12-14-16 Vandam St.

NEW YORK

Terms: Eighty Cents a Year in advance; Ten Cents a number

CONTENTS

STYLES OF THE MONTH FOR LADIES (Illustrated)	381-403
STYLES OF THE MONTH FOR YOUNG PEOPLE (Illustrated)	404-415
SASHES AND BOWS (Illustrated)	416-417
FOREWORDS REGARDING FASHIONS AND FABRICS (Illustrated) *Laura R. Seiple*	418-419
FASHIONABLE FRIVOLITIES FOR FEMININE FANCIES (Illustrated) *Laura R. Seiple*	420-421
MILLINERY FOR LATE SUMMER (Illustrated)	422-424
MAKING A PLATEAU HAT (Illustrated) *Martha Kinsman*	425
FOR PRINCE AND PRINCESS BABIKINS (Illustrated) *Aline De Cardeva*	426-427
NEW DESIGNS IN UNDERWEAR (Illustrated)	428-430
A FLOATING HOTEL FOR WOMEN (Illustrated) *Jessie Garwood Fritz*	431-433
PA'S SPECS (Illustrated Short Story) *Harriet Whitney Durbin*	434-436
HOUSEKEEPING ALL OVER THE WORLD (Illustrated) Part VII —The Holland Housewife *Laura B. Starr*	437-440
THE TRANSFORMATION OF A FARM-HOUSE (Illustrated) *W. L. Bottomley*	441-443
HOW THE ICE HARVEST IS GATHERED, STORED AND DISTRIBUTED (Illustrated)	444-445
MISS GINTER OF GINTERVILLE (Illustrated Continued Story) Conclusion of Chapter IX—Chaps. X-XI *Nina Welles Tibbtt*	446-449
HOPE (Verses) *Katherine G. Terns*	449
IN THE INTEREST OF BREAD-WINNING (Illustrated) Part III —The Visiting Lady's Maid *Bertha Hasbrook*	450-451
THE TEMPTATION OF TOMMY (Illustrated Short Story for Children) *T. Jenkins Hains*	452-454
HOW ROSSITER SAW THE LADY MOON (Short Story for Children)	454
A VACATION EPISODE (Illustrated One-Act Farce) *L. O. Lennari*	455-457
JUST HOMELY VERSE FOR HOME FOLKS *Frank Farrington, Katherine L. Daniher, Alice May Douglas, Katherine March Chase, Josephine K. Teal*	458-459
SOME ORIGINAL IDEAS FOR THE HOME (Illustrated) *Mary Kilsyth*	460-461
A BABY IN CAMP *Harriet Caryl Cox*	462-463
NOVELTIES MADE FROM HANDKERCHIEFS (Illustrated)	464-465
CLUNY LACE FOR THE TABLE (Illustrated) *Grace Aline Luther*	466-467
AN AUGUST OUTING SONG (Verses) *Harvey Peake*	467
THE MOTHERS' ADVISORY CLUB *Edited by the Readers of* THE DESIGNER	468-470
FOR LOVELY WOMAN *Jane Eliot*	471
THE KITCHEN KINGDOM *Beatrice Sturgis, Eleanor Marchant, Agnes K. Shepard, E. M. Lucas*	472-474
A SEASIDE LUNCHEON (Illustrated) *Eleanor Marchant*	476-477
A SILK PATCHWORK QUILT WHICH IS SELF-LINED (Illustrated) *Maud Kedder*	478-479
HELPS ALONG THE WAY *Edited by the Readers of* THE DESIGNER	480-481
KNOTS AND WHATNOTS (Illustrated)	482-483
KNITTING (Illustrated)	484-485
FASHION NOTES FOR MEN (Illustrated) *Aline De Cardeva*	486-487
BOOK NOTES *Lilian Dynevor Rice*	488-489
WHAT WOMEN ARE DOING *Edited by the Readers of* THE DESIGNER	490-492
FLORICULTURAL TALKS *M. W. Park*	493-494
ANSWERS TO CORRESPONDENTS	495-496

BRANCHES:
300-302 Monroe St., Chicago, Ill.
43 Richmond St., West, Toronto, Canada
1019 Market St., San Francisco, Cal.

Subscriptions are received at all Standard Fashion Agents, Newsdealers and Booksellers, or may be sent direct to the publishers.

THE
DESIGNER

☙ CONDUCTED BY ☙
LILIAN DYNEVOR RICE

VOL. XXII. No. 4   AUGUST, 1905

LADIES' SHIRT-WAISTS. DESCRIBED ON PAGE 388
(SHIRT-WAIST 1123)   (SHIRT-WAIST 1127)

381

LADIES' SHIRT-WAIST COSTUME. DESCRIBED ON PAGE 388
(COSTUME 1168)

The Designer

LADIES' SHIRT-WAIST TOILETTES. DESCRIBED ON PAGE 388

(SHIRT-WAIST 1154 AND SKIRT 1157)   (SHIRT-WAIST 1137 AND SKIRT 9202)

283

August, 1905

LADIES' NEGLIGEE TOILETTE AND WRAPPER. Described on page 389
(Dressing-Sack 1128 and Petticoat 1160)   (Wrapper 1124)

LADIES' SHIRT-WAIST TOILETTE DESCRIBED ON PAGE 389
(SHIRT-WAIST 1158 AND SKIRT 1136)

August, 1905

LADIES' TOILETTES. DESCRIBED ON PAGE 389

(WAIST 1139 AND SKIRT 1114)   (SHIRT-WAIST 1149 AND SKIRT 1144)

The Designer

inches waist measure, price 15 cents. The garment, which is tuck-plaited in box-plait effect, the plaits being stitched to any yoke depth, may be in round, short round or instep length. In the present instance the toilette is made of golden-brown taffeta glacé, and with it are worn embroidered linen-lawn collar and cuffs.

*

Ladies' Negligee Toilette. Illustrated on Page 384.

Ladies' matinee or dressing-sack 1128 is in seven sizes, from thirty-two to forty-four inches bust measure, price 15 cents, and another view is given of it on page 396. It may have a circular or a gathered skirt portion, either of two styles of collar, and full-length or elbow sleeves. Ladies' five-gored petticoat 1160 is in eight sizes, from twenty-two to thirty-six inches waist measure, price 15 cents, and is shown again on page 402. The garment may be in round, short round or instep length, and is closed at the back or side. It has a slightly gathered circular flounce, may have an inverted box plait or drawing-string at the back, and is provided with a dust ruffle, which may be omitted. Both dressing-sack and petticoat are here made of dotted swiss, and are trimmed with swiss edging and wide ribbon-run beading.

*

Ladies' Wrapper. Illustrated on Page 384.

Ladies' wrapper 1124 is in seven sizes, from thirty-two to forty-four inches bust measure, price 15 cents, and is again pictured on page 395. The garment, which may be in short sweep or round length, may be made with turnover or standing collar, bishop or bell sleeves, and with or without the back yoke-facing, bertha or flounce. In the present development it is made of pale-blue lawn and all-over swiss embroidery, the bertha being prettily decorated with appliqué embroidery.

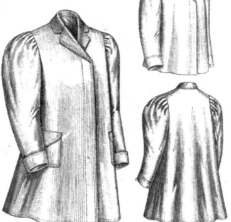

1165. Ladies' Box-Coat in Either of Two Lengths (with either of two styles of sleeve). Described on page 390.

Ladies' Shirt-Waist Toilette. Illustrated on Page 385.

Ladies' shirt-waist 1158 is in seven sizes, from thirty-two to forty-four inches bust measure, price 15 cents, another view of it appearing on page 392. It is closed at the side, and may have elbow sleeves or full-length sleeves tucked or gathered to the cuffs, and may be made with or without body lining. Ladies' seven-gored plaited skirt 1136 is in five sizes, from twenty-two to thirty inches waist measure, price 15 cents, and is again shown on page 398. Lavender linen is used for the toilette as here shown, with embroidered appliqué for the trimming.

*

Ladies' Shirred Toilette. Illustrated on Page 386.

Ladies' waist 1139 is in six sizes, from thirty-two to forty-two inches bust measure, price 15 cents, and is again pictured on page 391. Ladies' seven-gored skirt 1114 is in seven sizes, from twenty to thirty-two inches waist measure, price 15 cents. The garment may be tucked or shirred to deep yoke or flounce depth. It may

be in round or short sweep length. The toilette in the present instance is made of blue-and-white foulard.

*

Ladies' Shirt-Waist Toilette. Illustrated on Page 386.

Ladies' shirt-waist 1149 is in seven sizes, from thirty-two to forty-four inches bust measure, price 15 cents. On page 391 is shown another development of the design. Ladies' nine-gored skirt 1144 is in seven sizes, from twenty to thirty-two inches waist measure, price 15 cents. It may be made in round, short round or instep length, and has an inverted box plait at the back and one at each side seam below yoke depth. Strap decoration is provided, but may be omitted. The design is again presented on page 396.

The toilette is here pictured in green-and-blue plaid taffeta, with straps of plain-blue taffeta outlined with dark-green velvet. The collar and cuffs are of Irish crochet, and the girdle is made of green velvet.

*

Ladies' Toilette. Illustrated on Page 387.

Ladies' waist 1119 is in seven sizes, from thirty-two to forty-four inches bust measure, price 15 cents, another view of it appearing on page 390. Ladies' seven-gored skirt 1114 is in seven sizes, from twenty to thirty-two inches waist measure, price 15 cents. As here pictured, the toilette is developed in deep-red taffeta, with a chemisette of all-over Valenciennes lace.

*

Ladies' Toilette. Illustrated on Page 387.

Ladies' waist 1126 is in seven sizes, from thirty-two to forty-four inches bust measure, price 15 cents, another view of it being given on page 390. Ladies' seven-gored skirt 1132 is in eight sizes, from twenty to thirty-four inches waist measure, price 15 cents, and is shown again on page 397.

Heliotrope eolienne and all-over Chantilly lace are combined for this toilette, lace ruffles finishing the sleeves.

*

Ladies' Toilette. Illustrated on Page 388.

Ladies' waist 1012 is in seven sizes, from thirty-two to forty-four inches bust measure, price 15 cents. It may be closed at the back or the left shoulder and side, have a high or low or Dutch round or square neck, and full-length or elbow leg-o'-mutton or puff sleeves. Ladies' seven-gored skirt 9317 is in six sizes, from twenty to thirty inches waist measure, price 15 cents. The garment, which may be in short sweep or round length, may be gathered at the top or shirred or tucked in yoke outline, and may have three or fewer flounces.

As here shown, the toilette is made of white organdy, and is trimmed with ruffles and insertion of Oriental lace.

1165—LADIES' BOX-COAT IN EITHER OF TWO LENGTHS. Illustrated on page 389.

Gray-and-black striped English flannel is selected to make this stylish coat, which is lined with dark-gray satin and finished with stitching. It is fitted by underarm and shoulder seams; the upper portions of the fronts form lapels which meet the rolling collar in notches; the collar is a two-piece model covered with a one-piece facing. The sleeve may be in either of two styles: one is a two-seamed coat-sleeve model gathered into the armhole, and the other is a two-seamed sleeve plaited into the arm's-eye and completed by a one-piece turn-up cuff. Patch pockets are provided. The closing of the garment is effected down the front in fly fashion by means of buttons and buttonholes and the coat may be made in either of two lengths.

Covert cloth, tweed, camel's hair, cheviot, serge, box cloth or English flannel may be used to develop this design, and braid, velvet or galloon may be used to trim the garment in an effective manner.

Ladies' box-coat 1165 is in seven sizes, from thirty-two to forty-four inches bust measure, price 15 cents. The thirty-six-inch bust size requires four and one-eighth yards of material thirty-six inches wide; three and one-half yards forty-four inches, or two and three-quarter yards of material which is fifty-four inches in width.

*

1130—LADIES' BOX-PLAITED WAIST CLOSED AT THE SIDE. Illustrated on this page.

This attractive waist is made of Saxon-blue rajah and is trimmed with appliqué gimp, the yoke-facing being of finely tucked mousseline de soie. In the upper large front view, the waist is made of Liberty satin combined with all-over lace and trimmed with insertion and lace edging. It is mounted on a fitted lining, the over-back and fronts being arranged in a number of lengthwise box plaits. The fulness at the waistline is shirred, and the right front overlaps the left and fastens with hooks and eyes.

1130, LADIES' BOX-PLAITED WAIST CLOSED AT THE SIDE (WITH FULL-LENGTH OR ELBOW LEG-O'-MUTTON SLEEVES). Described on this page.

The Pompadour yoke is attached to the right side of the lining front and fastens on the left by means of hooks and eyes. A trimming band may be used to finish the upper portions of the fronts in the manner indicated,

1119, LADIES' WAIST (WITH OR WITHOUT THE UNDERSLEEVES OR SHIRRED VEST PORTION). Described on page 391.

or may be omitted. The sleeve, which may be developed in either of two styles, consists of a full-length, close-fitting, two-seamed undersleeve and a one-seamed outside portion. The latter is gathered into the armhole and

1126, LADIES' WAIST CLOSED AT THE SIDE (WITH FULL-LENGTH OR ELBOW SLEEVES). Described on page 391.

finished at the lower edge by a one-piece turn-up cuff. When the elbow-length sleeve is preferred, the undersleeve may be omitted or the lower part cut away. When the plain full-length sleeve is desired, the outside sleeve is omitted. A standing collar finishes the neck edge, and the gathered girdle completes the lower edge of the body portions.

Peau de soie, peau de cygne, pongee, voile, chiffon taffeta, grenadine, etamine, satin foulard or Liberty satin may be used to develop this design, and gimp, braid, insertion, embroidery, passementerie or ribbon may be used to trim.

A figure view is shown on the Front Cover Page.

Ladies' box-plaited waist 1130 is in six sizes, from thirty-two to forty-two inches bust measure, price 15 cents. The thirty-six-inch bust size requires four and three-quarter yards of material twenty-two inches wide; three yards thirty-six inches, or two and three-quarter yards forty-four inches. As represented in lower front view, two and three-quarter yards of forty-four-inch material were used, with three-eighths of a yard of eighteen-inch

1139. Ladies' Shirred Waist Closed at the Back (with high or Dutch square neck and full-length or elbow sleeves). Described on page 392.

tucked silk for collar, etc., and one and one-quarter yards of lace band trimming. As in the upper large front view, four and three-eighths yards of twenty-two-inch silk are used, with three-quarters of a yard of eighteen-inch all-over lace for yoke, standing collar and cuffs, one and three-eighth yards of lace edging for frills and one and one-quarter yards of insertion to trim.

1149. Ladies' Tucked Shirt-Waist (with the sleeves tucked or gathered to the cuffs and with or without the straps or body lining). Described on page 392.

1119—LADIES' WAIST. Illustrated on page 390.

This attractive waist is made of light-violet peau de cygne combined with all-over lace. It is mounted on a fitted lining. The outer back is arranged in two clusters of lengthwise tucks and the fulness at the waistline is shirred. The fronts are tucked to yoke depth and shirred at the waistline. The plain vest portion is attached to the right side of the lining and fastens on the left by means of hooks and eyes. A shorter shirred vest portion is provided, but may be omitted, as shown in the small view. The sleeve, which may be made in full or elbow length, consists of a two-seamed, close-fitting lining, and

one-seamed outside portion; the latter is gathered at the upper and lower edges and completed by a band and turn-up cuff. When the elbow sleeve is preferred, the lower portion of the undersleeve is cut away. The shirred girdle is in two pieces and is attached to the lower part of the body portions. A back-closing standing collar finishes the neck edge of the garment.

Peau de soie, peau de cygne, taffeta, satin crêpe, China crêpe, nun's-veiling, albatross, eolienne, grenadine or voile may be used to develop this design, and lace, insertion, embroidery, gimp, passementerie or appliqué lace may be used to decorate.

A figure view on page 387 shows a different development.

Ladies' waist 1119 is in seven sizes, from thirty-two to forty-four inches bust measure, price 15 cents. The thirty-six-inch bust size requires five and one-eighth yards of material twenty-two inches wide; two and seven-eighth yards forty-four inches, or two and three-eighth yards fifty-four inches. As represented in large view, four and five-eighth yards of twenty-two inch material were used, with one and one-eighth yards of eighteen-inch all-over lace for collar, etc. As represented in small front view, three and seven-eighth yards of material twenty-two inches wide are used, with one yard of eighteen-inch all-over lace.

1126—LADIES' WAIST CLOSED AT THE SIDE. Illustrated on page 390.

Ivory-white peau de soie, all-over point de Venise lace and white mousseline de soie are used to develop this handsome design, the mousseline being used to line the lace chemisette and lower sleeve portions. The waist is mounted on a fitted lining, the outer back and the front are tucked at the upper edge and shirred at the waistline, and the outer edge of the front is finished with a box plait, the fulness of the material near the right armhole being disposed in a box plait as illustrated. A trimming band finishes the upper edge of the front and

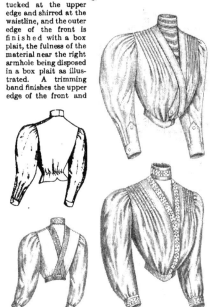

1123. Ladies' Surplice Shirt-Waist (with sleeves tucked or gathered into plain or fancy cuffs and with or without the suspender straps or body lining). Described on page 393.

the chemisette portion is attached to the right side of the lining and fastens on the left by means of hooks and eyes. A standing collar completes the neck edge. The sleeve consists of a two-seamed, close-fitting lining, which extends to the wrist and is overlaid with material, and a one-seamed outside portion. The latter portion is gathered into the armhole and the fulness at the lower part is disposed in a single box plait and two clusters of narrow lengthwise tucks, a band cuff having rounded ends being attached.

When the elbow sleeve is preferred, the lower part of the lining is cut away. A gathered girdle completes the lower part of the waist, and the closing of the right front is effected on the left side by means of hooks and eyes.

Taffeta, peau de soie, peau de cygne, foulard, pongee, voile, etamine, eolienne, grenadine or net may be used to develop this design, and lace, insertion, embroidery, passementerie, ribbon, braid or gimp may be used to ornament.

A figure view on page 387 shows a different development.

Ladies' waist 1126 is in seven sizes, from thirty-two to forty-four inches bust measure, price 15 cents. The thirty-six-inch bust size requires four and five-eighth yards of material twenty-two inches wide; two and three-eighth yards forty-four inches, or two yards fifty-four inches. As represented, four yards of twenty-two-inch material were used, with one yard of eighteen-inch all-over lace.

1139—LADIES' SHIRRED WAIST CLOSED AT THE BACK.
Illustrated on page 391.

Figured silk mull is combined with all-over Valenciennes lace for this effective waist. A crush girdle of rose-pink Liberty satin gives a pretty finish to the lower part of the garment. The waist is mounted on a fitted lining, the upper portions of the outer front and backs being shirred· to yoke depth, and also confined by shirrings at the waistline. The sleeve, which may be made in either of two styles, consists of a two-seamed, close-fitting undersleeve that extends to the wrist and may be overlaid with material to form a deep cuff, and a one-seamed puff attached to the undersleeve just below the elbow. When the elbow length is preferred, the lower portion of the close-fitting sleeve is cut away. The neck edge may be cut in Dutch square outline, or be made close to the throat and completed by a back-closing standing collar. The girdle is in one piece gathered at the back edges and attached to the lower part of the body portions. The garment closes down the center back by means of buttons and buttonholes.

Peau de soie, peau de cygne, taffeta silk, silk mull, lawn, organdy, dotted swiss, batiste, grenadine or dimity may be used to develop this design, and embroidered edging, insertion, beading, ribbon, gimp or passementerie may be used to decorate.

A figure view on page 386 shows a different development. Ladies' shirred waist 1139 is in six sizes, from thirty-two to forty-two inches bust measure, price 15 cents. The thirty-six-inch bust size requires four and three-eighth yards of material twenty-two inches wide; three yards thirty-six inches, or two and one-quarter yards forty-four inches. As represented in the back view, four yards of silk twenty-two inches in width were used, with seven-eighths of a yard of lace insertion for the neck trimming, and two and three-quarter yards of lace edging for the sleeve frills.

1149—LADIES' TUCKED SHIRT-WAIST.
Illustrated on page 391.

This pretty shirt-waist is made of light-gray rajah, .and is trimmed with dark-gray

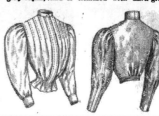

1127. LADIES' SHIRT-WAIST (WITH SLEEVES TUCKED IN DEEP CUFF OUTLINE OR TUCKED OR GATHERED TO A PLAIN CUFF AND WITH OR WITHOUT THE BODY LINING). Described on page 393.

velvet and silver buttons. The garment may be mounted on a body lining. The outer back is arranged in two lengthwise tucks, which extend down the center back, and is shirred at the waistline. The outer fronts are tucked to yoke depth, shirred at the waistline, and the forward edge of the right front is completed by a box plait stitched on the edges. Strap portions are provided, but may be omitted. The one-seamed sleeve is gathered or tucked at the lower edge, and completed by a cuff having fancy upper outline, and which opens on the outside of the arm. A narrow band finishes the neck edge and the collar is a back-closing standing model. The waist fastens down the center front underneath the box plait by means of hooks and eyes or buttons and buttonholes.

Taffeta, peau de soie, pongee, cotton poplin, cashmere, nun's-veiling, China silk, linen, crash, chambray or madras may be used to develop

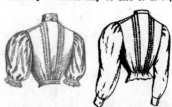

1158. LADIES' SHIRT-WAIST CLOSED AT THE SIDE (WITH FULL-LENGTH SLEEVES TUCKED OR GATHERED TO THE CUFFS OR ELBOW SLEEVES AND WITH OR WITHOUT BODY LINING). Described on page 393.

this design, and lace edging, insertion, embroidery, ribbon, appliqué or gimp may be used to trim the waist.

A figure view on page 386 shows a different development.

Ladies' tucked shirt-waist 1149 is in seven sizes, from thirty-two to forty-four inches bust measure, price 15 cents. The thirty-six-inch bust size requires four and one-eighth yards of material twenty-two inches wide; two and three-quarter yards thirty-six inches, or two and one-eighth yards forty-four inches. As represented, two yards of forty-four-inch material were used for the garment, with one and seven-eighth yards of twenty-two-inch velvet for the collar, the cuffs and the straps.

1123—LADIES' SURPLICE SHIRT-WAIST. Illustrated on page 391.

Light-blue cotton luster is used to make this pretty shirt-waist, which is trimmed with swiss insertion. It is mounted on a body lining, and the outer fronts and back are shirred at the waist-line, the surplice fronts being tucked to yoke depth, and may

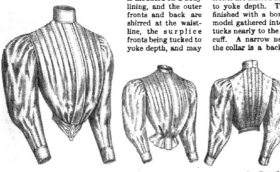

1137, LADIES' BOX-PLAITED SHIRT-WAIST (WITH OR WITHOUT THE BODY LINING). Described on page 394.

be decorated with a trimming band or suspender straps. The upper portions of the lining fronts are concealed beneath the chemisette portion, which is in one piece, finished at the upper edge by a back-closing standing collar. The sleeve is a one-seamed model, gathered into the armhole and having the fulness at the lower edge gathered or tucked and completed by a wristband or a fancy cuff. A narrow band girdle is provided for the garment.

Linen, crash, pongee, scrim, lavable taffeta, peau de soie, organdy, dimity, batiste, mull, chambray, madras or duck may be used to develop this design, with insertion, appliqué lace, embroidery, Persian band trimming, braid or galloon for trimming.

1154, LADIES' TUCKED SHIRT-WAIST (WITH YOKE FRONT AND WITH OR WITHOUT BODY LINING). Described on page 394.

A figure view on page 381 shows a different development.
Ladies' surplice shirt-waist 1123 is in seven sizes, from thirty-two to forty-four inches bust measure, price 15 cents. The thirty-six-inch bust size requires four and seven-eighth yards of material twenty-two inches wide; three and one-eighth yards thirty-six inches, or two and one-half yards forty-four inches, with one and seven-eighth yards of lace insertion to trim chemisette as in first front view, or with two and three-eighth yards of

embroidered insertion to trim, as in the lower front view. As represented in lower back view, two and one-half yards of thirty-six-inch light material, with one yard of thirty-six-inch dark material for suspender portion and belt.

1127—LADIES' SHIRT-WAIST. Illustrated on page 392.

Tan swiss is selected to develop this shirt-waist, which may be mounted on a body lining. The outer back and fronts are shirred at the waistline and the fronts are tucked to yoke depth. The forward edge of the right front is finished with a box plait and the sleeve is a one-seamed model gathered into a band cuff or disposed in lengthwise tucks nearly to the elbow and finished with or without the cuff. A narrow neckband completes the neck edge and the collar is a back-closing standing model. The closing of the garment is effected under the box plait by means of buttons and buttonholes, hooks and eyes or fancy shirt-waist pins.

Peau de soie, taffeta, pongee, linen, lawn, crash, scrim, cotton luster, madras or chambray may be used to develop this design, and lace, insertion, embroidery, braid, ribbon or gimp may be used to decorate.

A figure view on page 381 shows a different development.

Ladies' shirt-waist 1127 is in seven sizes, from thirty-two to forty-four inches bust measure, price 15 cents. The thirty-six-inch bust size requires four yards of material twenty-two inches wide and seven-eighth yards thirty-six inches, or two and one-eighth yards forty-four inches in width.

1158—LADIES' SHIRT-WAIST CLOSED AT THE SIDE. Illustrated on page 392.

White butchers' linen is the material used to make this stylish shirt-waist, which is decorated with fancy pearl buttons. A girdle of scarlet silk gives a pretty finish to the garment. The shirt-waist may be mounted on a body lining. The outer back is arranged in two clusters of lengthwise tucks and shirred at the waistline. The fronts are tucked to yoke depth and the vest front is finished with hem tucks on each edge and attached to the forward edge of the right front, the closing being on the left side. The fulness of the fronts at the waistline is disposed in shirrings, and two styles of sleeve are provided: one is a full-length, one-seamed model with the fulness at the lower edge gathered or disposed in narrow tucks and completed by a straight cuff which opens on the outside of the arm. The elbow sleeve is gathered at the upper and lower edges and finished with a narrow band and frill of lace. A narrow neckband completes the neck edge and the collar is a back-closing standing model.

Linen, crash, taffeta, peau de soie, linen duck, lawn, dimity, pongee or China silk may be used to develop this design, and insertion, hand-embroidery, Oriental trimming, ribbon or gimp may be used to trim.

A figure view on page 385 shows a different development.

Ladies' shirt-waist 1158 is in seven sizes, from thirty-two to forty-four inches bust measure, price 15 cents. The thirty-six-inch bust size requires four and one-eighth yards of material twenty-two inches wide; two and five-eighth yards thirty-six inches, or two yards of material which measures forty-four inches in width.

1137—LADIES' BOX-PLAITED SHIRT-WAIST. Illustrated on page 393.

White Irish linen is chosen to make this shirt-waist, which is fitted by under-arm and shoulder seams, and provided with a body lining, that may be omitted. The outer back is arranged in three box plaits stitched on the outer edges. The outer fronts are box-plaited and stitched to yoke depth and are shirred at the waistline. The forward edge of the right front is finished with a box plait. The sleeve is a one-seamed model with the fulness at the lower edge arranged in box plaits and completed by a straight cuff, which opens on the outside of the arm. A narrow band finishes the neck edge and the collar is a back-closing standing model. The closing of the garment is effected down the center front underneath the box plait with buttons and buttonholes or studs and eyelets.

Linen, crash, scrim, mercerized damask, taffeta, piqué, linen duck, lawn, dimity,

Round Length

1154—LADIES' TUCKED SHIRT-WAIST. Illustrated on page 393.

Light-tan linen is used to make this stylish shirt-waist. It is finished with stitching and provided with a body lining, that may be omitted. The outer back is arranged in lengthwise tucks which taper gracefully to the waistline, where the extra fulness is disposed in shirrings. The fronts are tucked to yoke depth and are attached to the lower edges of the fancy yoke, the tucked side extensions being laid over the yoke as indicated. The forward edge of the right front is finished with a box plait and the fulness of the fronts at the waistline is disposed in shirrings. The one-seamed sleeve has the lower edge gathered or tucked and finished by a one-piece fancy cuff. A narrow band completes the neck edge, and the collar is a back-closing standing model. The closing of the garment is effected down the center front by means of buttons and buttonholes.

Linen, crash, pongee, cotton poplin, chiffon taffeta, duck, piqué, cashmere, peau de soie or peau de cygne may be used to develop this design, and braid, gimp, appliqué lace, insertion, embroidery or Oriental trimming may be used to trim the garment.

A figure view on page 383 shows a different development.

Ladies' tucked shirt-waist 1154 is in six sizes, from thirty-two to forty-two inches bust measure, price 15 cents. The

Short Round Length

Instep Length

Round Length

1168. LADIES' SHIRT-WAIST COSTUME, IN ROUND, SHORT ROUND OR INSTEP LENGTH, WITH OR WITHOUT THE SUSPENDERS (CONSISTING OF A SHIRT-WAIST WITH OR WITHOUT BODY LINING; AND A NINE-GORED UMBRELLA OR RIPPLE SKIRT WITH AN INVERTED BOX PLAIT OR IN HABIT STYLE AT THE BACK). Described on this page.

French percale, peau de soie or madras may be used to develop this design successfully, and insertion, braid, appliqué lace, ribbon, Persian trimming or gimp may be used to ornament the garment in an effective manner.

A figure view on page 383 shows a different development.

Ladies' box-plaited shirt-waist 1137 is in seven sizes, from thirty-two to forty-four inches bust measure, price 15 cents. The thirty-six-inch bust size requires four and one-eighth yards of material twenty-two inches wide; three and one-eighth yards thirty-six inches, or two and one-half yards forty-four inches.

thirty-six-inch bust size requires four and three-eighth yards of material twenty-two inches wide; three yards thirty-six inches, or two and one-half yards forty-four inches.

1168—LADIES' SHIRT-WAIST COSTUME IN ROUND, SHORT ROUND OR INSTEP LENGTH WITH OR WITHOUT THE SUSPENDERS. Illustrated on this page.

This costume is made of blue mohair and white lawn. The shirt-waist is mounted on a body lining, which may be omitted. The outer back is shirred at the waistline, the fronts are tucked to yoke depth, and their fulness at the waistline is disposed in shirrings. The forward edge of the right front is completed by a box plait, and fancy suspender portions are provided. The sleeve is a one-seamed bishop model completed by a straight cuff, which opens on the outside of the arm. A narrow neckband finishes the neck edge and the collar is a back-closing standing model. The skirt is a nine-gored umbrella design, with the fulness at the back disposed in an inverted box plait or the back may be finished in habit style. A narrow belt finishes the upper edge of the skirt, and the lower edge is completed by a facing or hem. Strap portions are provided but may be omitted, as may also the bretelle suspenders.

Cotton poplin, linen duck, linon, crash, chambray, percale, pongee, foulard, China silk, sailcloth, mohair, serge or flannel may be used to develop this design, and braid, ribbon, appliqué gimp, Oriental trimming or insertion may be used to decorate.

A figure view on page 382 shows a different development.

inches, or six and five-eighth yards forty-four inches. The width of the skirt at the lower edge is five yards.

1124—LADIES' WRAPPER IN SHORT SWEEP OR ROUND LENGTH. Illustrated on this page.

This dainty wrapper is made of figured lawn and is trimmed with lace insertion and ribbon. It is fitted by center-back, side-back, under-arm and shoulder seams. The front lining portions are included in the under-arm and shoulder seams and are fitted by single bust darts. The circular-shaped yoke is included in the shoulder seams and the back yoke facing may be omitted. The full fronts are gathered to the lower edges of the yoke, and may be confined at the waist by ribbons or permitted to hang free, as preferred. The one-seamed sleeve may be made in flowing or bishop style, and is finished at the lower edge with a facing or gathered into a band cuff. A bertha is p ovided, and the neck edge may be finished with a standing or a turn-down collar. The gathered flounce, when used, is attached to the lower part of the wrapper, and the closing of the garment is effected down the center front by means of buttons and buttonholes or hooks and eyes.

Short Sweep Length

Round Length   *Short Sweep Length*   *Round Length*

1124. LADIES' WRAPPER IN SHORT SWEEP OR ROUND LENGTH (WITH TURNOVER OR STANDING COLLAR AND BISHOP OR BELL SLEEVES AND WITH OR WITHOUT THE BACK YOKE-FACING, BERTHA OR FLOUNCE). Described on this page.

Ladies' shirt-waist costume 1168 is in seven sizes, from thirty-two to forty-four inches bust measure, price 15 cents. The thirty-six-inch bust size requires with skirt in round length, twelve and five-eighth yards of material twenty-seven inches wide; nine yards thirty-six inches, or six and seven-eighth yards forty-four inches. As represented, five and five-eighth yards of forty-four-inch material were used, with two and five-eighth yards of thirty-six-inch material for waist. With skirt in instep length, are required eleven and three-eighth yards of material twenty-seven inches wide; eight and one-half yards thirty-six

Lawn, sateen, foulard, chambray, dotted swiss, dimity, flowered organdy, batiste, cashmere, nun's-veiling, albatross or flannel may be used to develop this design, and lace edging, braid, insertion, ribbon, gimp or embroidery may be used to trim.

A figure view on page 384 shows a different development.

Ladies' wrapper 1124 is in seven sizes, from thirty-two to forty-four inches bust measure, price 15 cents. The thirty-six-inch bust size requires sixteen and three-eighth yards of material twenty-two inches wide; ten and three-quarter yards thirty-six inches, or nine and one-eighth yards forty-four inches, with, as represented, six yards of lace insertion to trim the yoke, collar, cuffs and bertha, and three-and one-quarter yards of ribbon for ties.

1128 — LADIES' MATINEE OR DRESSING-SACK. Illustrated on this page.

This pretty dressing-sack is charmingly developed in pink-and-white Japanese silk, and is trimmed with lace edging, insertion, beading and ribbon. It is fitted by under-arm and shoulder seams, the back is confined by shirring at the waistline, and the fronts are tucked to yoke depth, and are shirred at the lower edge. The sleeve is a one-seamed model. For full length it may be gathered at the lower edge and finished with a band cuff, and for the elbow length the lower part of the sleeve is cut away and the lower edge completed by a band and frill of lace. Two styles of skirt are provided: one is circular, and the other is gathered at the upper edge. A ribbon belt or one of insertion may be used to conceal the joining of the skirt and body portions. The neck edge may be finished with a one-piece turn-down or a deep fancy collar. The sack closes down the center front with buttons and buttonholes or hooks and eyes.

China silk, kimono crêpe, China crêpe, lawn, organdy, batiste, dimity or swiss may be used to develop this design, and lace edging, insertion, embroidery, ribbon, appliqué, braid or beading may be used to decorate.

A figure view on page 384 shows a different development.

Ladies' matinee or dressing-sack 1128 is in seven sizes, from thirty-two to forty-four inches bust measure, price 15 cents. The thirty-six-inch bust size requires five yards of material twenty-two inches wide; three and three-quarter yards thirty-six inches, or three yards forty-four inches. As represented in large front view, three and three-eighth yards of thirty-six-inch material were used, with four and one-eighth yards of lace edging for ruffles, one

1128. LADIES' MATINEE OR DRESSING-SACK (WITH A CIRCULAR SKIRT PORTION, OR A GATHERED SKIRT PORTION HAVING STRAIGHT LOWER EDGE; EITHER OF TWO STYLES OF COLLAR AND FULL-LENGTH OR ELBOW SLEEVES). Described on this page.

and three-quarter yards of lace insertion, seven-eighths of a yard of lace beading for belt, and two and one-half yards of ribbon. As represented in small front view, two and one-half yards of thirty-six-inch material are required, with two and one-eighth yards of embroidered flouncing thirteen inches wide for the gathered skirt portion, one-half of a yard of all-over embroidery eighteen inches wide for collar and cuffs, two yards of embroidered insertion, and one and seven-eighth yards of narrow edging to trim.

1144—LADIES' NINE-GORED SKIRT, IN ROUND, SHORT ROUND OR INSTEP LENGTH. Illustrated on this page.

Gun-metal gray taffeta glacé is used to make this stylish skirt, which is a nine-gored model consisting of a front gore, two side-front, two side, two side-back and two back gores, the latter united by a center-back seam. The fulness at the back is disposed in an inverted box plait, and extensions, which are cut at the seam edges of each gore at yoke depth, are each arranged in an inverted box plait. Fancy strap portions are provided, and the skirt may be cut in round, short round or instep length. A narrow belt finishes the upper edge of the garment, and the lower edge is completed by a hem or underfacing.

Serge, tweed, lady's-cloth, cheviot, taffeta, peau de soie, linen, crash or cotton duck may be used to develop this design, and braid, gimp, ribbon, buttons or velvet piping may be used to trim.

A figure view on page 386 shows a different development.

Ladies' nine-gored skirt 1144 is in seven sizes, from twenty to thirty-two inches waist measure, corresponding to thirty-seven to fifty-four and one-half inches hip measure, price 15 cents. The twenty-four-inch waist size,

Round Length

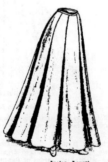

Instep Length   *Short Round Length*

1144. LADIES' NINE-GORED SKIRT, IN ROUND, SHORT ROUND OR INSTEP LENGTH (WITH AN INVERTED BOX PLAIT AT THE BACK AND ONE AT EACH SIDE SEAM BELOW YOKE DEPTH AND WITH OR WITHOUT THE STRAPS). Described on this page.

corresponding to the forty-two-inch hip size, requires for round length, eleven yards of material twenty-two inches wide; six yards forty-four inches, or four and three-quarter yards fifty-four inches, with seven yards of braid to trim as in back view. As represented for instep length, ten and five-eighth yards of twenty-two-inch material were used; five and three-quarter yards forty-four inches, or four and one-half yards fifty-four inches. The width of the skirt at the lower edge is five yards.

*

1132—LADIES' SEVEN-GORED SKIRT IN ROUND, SHORT ROUND OR INSTEP LENGTH. Illustrated on this page.

White linen is used to make this stylish skirt, which is a seven-gored model, consisting of a front, two side-front, two side and two back gores, the latter united by a center-back seam. The front, side-front and side gores are cut with extensions at deep yoke depth, the extensions being arranged in side plaits as indicated, and stitched to flounce depth or permitted to hang free as in large front view. The fulness of the skirt in the back is disposed in an inverted box plait. A narrow belt finishes the upper edge, and the lower edge is completed with a hem or facing.

Covert cloth, tweed, summer serge, mohair, canvas cloth, taffeta silk, peau de soie, linen, duck or piqué may be used to develop this design, and braid, insertion, embroidery, ribbon, gimp or Oriental trimming may be used to decorate.

A figure view on page 387 shows a different development.

Ladies' seven-gored skirt 1132 is in eight sizes, from twenty to thirty-four inches waist measure, corresponding to thirty-seven to fifty-seven and one-half inches hip measure, price 15 cents. The twenty-four-inch waist size, corresponding to the forty-two-

inch hip size, requires for round length, eight and three-quarter yards of material twenty-two inches wide; five and seven-eighth yards forty-four inches, or four and three-eighth yards fifty-four inches; or for instep length, eight and three-eighth yards twenty-two inches wide; five and five-eighth yards forty-four inches, or four and one-eighth yards fifty-four inches. The width of the skirt at lower edge is four and seven-eighth yards.

Round Length

Short Round Length *Instep Length*

1132, LADIES' SEVEN-GORED SKIRT IN ROUND, SHORT ROUND OR INSTEP LENGTH (HAVING TWO PLAITS AT EACH SIDE SEAM WITH OR WITHOUT THE STITCHING TO FLOUNCE DEPTH AND WITH AN INVERTED BOX PLAIT AT THE BACK). Described on this page.

1166, LADIES' DRESSING-SACK (WITH HIGH OR DUTCH ROUND NECK, STANDING OR TURNOVER COLLAR AND BISHOP OR FLOWING SLEEVES). Described on this page.

1166 — LADIES' DRESSING-SACK. Illustrated on this page.

This attractive dressing-sack as shown in the large front view is made of blue-and-white outing flannel and is trimmed with blue velvet ribbon. The front yoke is included in the shoulder seams, and the sack portions are fitted by center-back, side-back and under-arm seams; the loose fronts are gathered to the lower edges of the yoke and may be confined at the waistline by ribbons or permitted to hang free as shown in the small front view. The sleeve, which may be made in either of two styles, is a one-seamed model gathered into a band cuff, or permitted to hang loose in flowing style, and completed by a facing. The neck edge may be made in Dutch round outline and finished with a frill of lace, or a turn-down or standing collar may be used. The sack closes down the center front with buttons and buttonholes or hooks and eyes.

China silk, foulard, flannel, cashmere, nun's-veiling, albatross, outing flannel, lawn, batiste, swiss, organdy, kimono crêpe or dimity may be used to develop this design appropriately, and lace edging, insertion, embroidery, ribbon, fancy braid or appliqué gimp may be used to trim the garment in an effective manner.

Ladies' dressing-sack 1166 is in eight sizes, from thirty-two to forty-six inches bust measure, price 15 cents. The thirty-six-inch bust size requires three and one-half yards of material twenty-seven inches wide; two and three-quarter yards thirty-six inches, or two and one-half yards forty-four inches. As represented, four and one-eighth yards of braid to trim, and two yards of ribbon for ties. As represented in small front view, two and five-eighth yards of thirty-six-inch material were used, with one-half of a yard of eighteen-inch all-over embroidery, two and three-quarter yards of embroidered insertion to trim the sleeves and one yard of edging to trim the neck edge.

1136—LADIES' SEVEN-GORED PLAITED SKIRT IN ROUND, SHORT ROUND OR INSTEP LENGTH. Illustrated on this page.

This pretty skirt is made of light-gray etamine and consists of a front gore with yoke

A figure view on page 385 shows a different development. Ladies' seven-gored skirt 1136 is in five sizes, from twenty-two to thirty inches waist measure, corresponding to thirty-nine and one-half to fifty-one inches hip measure, price 15 cents. The twenty-four-inch waist size, corresponding to the forty-two-inch hip size, requires for round length, eight yards of material thirty-six inches wide; six and five-eighth yards forty-four inches, or five and one-quarter yards fifty-four inches; or for instep length, seven and five-eighth yards thirty-six inches wide or five yards fifty-four inches. The width of skirt at lower edge is five and one-quarter yards.

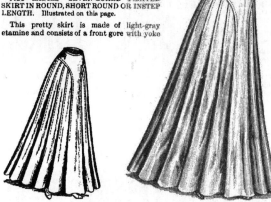
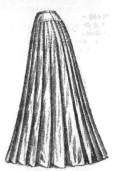

Instep Length   *Short Round Length*   *Round Length*

1136, LADIES' SEVEN-GORED PLAITED SKIRT IN ROUND, SHORT ROUND OR INSTEP LENGTH (WITH THE FRONT GORE EXTENDING INTO A YOKE AND WITH THE PLAITS STITCHED TO ANY DESIRED DEPTH; NOT DESIRABLE FOR STRIPED OR PLAID GOODS). Described on this page.

extensions and two side-front, two side and two back gores with the fulness laid in plaits which may be stitched to any desired depth. A narrow belt finishes the upper edge of the skirt and the fulness of the garment in the back is disposed in an inverted box plait. The lower edge may be completed with a facing or hem, and may be cut in round, short round or instep length. This skirt is not desirable for striped or plaid goods, but may be made of serge, cheviot, tweed, covert cloth, lady's-cloth, canvas, etamine, taffeta silk, peau de soie, linen, piqué, chambray or madras. Oriental embroidery, ribbon, gimp, insertion, appliqué lace or braid may be used to decorate.

1161—LADIES' SKIRT IN SHORT SWEEP, ROUND OR SHORT ROUND LENGTH. Illustrated on this page.

This handsome skirt is developed in blue Panama cloth, and is finished with silk stitching. It consists of a circular upper part, fitted over the hips by dart tucks and having the fulness in the back disposed in an inverted box plait, which is lengthened by a seven-gored box-plaited flounce portion that may be made with or without the plait stitchings. A narrow belt finishes the upper edge of

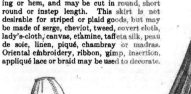

Short Round Length   *Round Length*   *Short Sweep Length*

1161, LADIES' SKIRT IN SHORT SWEEP, ROUND OR SHORT ROUND LENGTH (FORMED OF A CIRCULAR UPPER PART WITH DART TUCKS AT THE TOP AND LENGTHENED BY A SEVEN-GORED BOX-PLAITED FLOUNCE PORTION WITH OR WITHOUT THE PLAIT STITCHINGS). Described on this page.

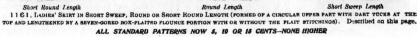

ALL STANDARD PATTERNS NOW 5, 10 OR 15 CENTS—NONE HIGHER

the garment, and the lower edge is completed by an underfacing or hem, and may be cut in short sweep, round or short round length.

Mohair, taffeta, peau de soie, cashmere, lady's-cloth, pongee, foulard, serge, cheviot, Panama cloth, etamine, voile, linen, chambray or crash may be used to develop this design, and braid, gimp, appliqué insertion, lace, Persian trimming or galloon may be used to decorate the garment in an effective manner.

Ladies' skirt 1161 is in six sizes, from twenty-two to thirty-two inches waist measure, corresponding to thirty-nine and one-half to fifty-four and one-half inches hip measure, price 15 cents. The twenty-four-inch waist size, corresponding to the forty-two-inch hip size, requires for short sweep length, seven and one-quarter yards of material twenty-seven inches wide; five and one-eighth yards forty-four inches, or four and one-half yards fifty-four inches, with two yards of trimming as in back view. For short round length are required six and three-quarter yards twenty-seven inches wide; four and seven-eighth yards forty-four inches, or four and one-eighth yards

may be used to develop this design, and braid, gimp, ribbon, galloon, appliqué embroidery, Oriental trimming or insertion may be used to decorate. The yoke may be made of all-over embroidery or heavy lace, and may be then lined with silk of a contrasting color. The pointed extensions may be held to the yoke by buttons, rosettes or small lace or embroidery medallions or braid ornaments.

A figure view on the Front Cover Page shows an entirely different development of this very stylish model.

Ladies' skirt 1129 is in seven sizes, from twenty to thirty-two inches waist measure, corresponding to thirty-seven to fifty-four and one-half inches hip measure, price 15 cents. The twenty-four-inch waist size, corresponding to the forty-two-inch hip size, requires for short sweep length, ten and three-quarter yards of material twenty-two inches wide; five and one-half yards forty-four inches, or four and five-eighth yards fifty-four inches; or for short round length, ten and one-eighth yards twenty-two inches wide; five yards forty-four inches, or four and three-eighth yards of material fifty-four inches in width. The width of the skirt at the lower edge is five yards.

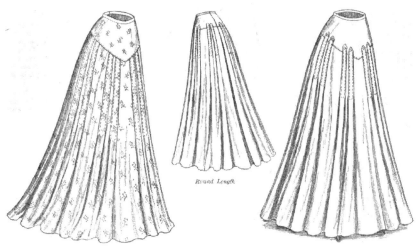

Round Length

Short Sweep Length   *Short Round Length*

1129. LADIES' SKIRT IN SHORT SWEEP, ROUND OR SHORT ROUND LENGTH (CONSISTING OF A YOKE AND A NINE-GORED BOX-PLAITED SKIRT PART WITH THE PLAITS STITCHED TO ANY DESIRED FLOUNCE DEPTH AND WITH OR WITHOUT THE POINTED EXTENSIONS). Described on this page.

of material fifty-four inches in width. The width of the skirt at the lower edge is five and one-quarter yards.

1129—LADIES' SKIRT IN SHORT SWEEP, ROUND OR SHORT ROUND LENGTH. Illustrated on this page.

This stylish skirt is made of figured linon and consists of a shaped yoke and a nine-gored skirt portion with fulness disposed in narrow box plaits, which may be stitched to any desired flounce depth. The upper portions of the plaits may be cut with pointed extensions, which, when desired, may overlap the yoke, and are stitched to it as indicated in strap effect. The fulness at the back is disposed in an inverted box plait. A narrow belt finishes the upper edge of the skirt and the lower edge is completed with a hem or an underfacing. The placket closing occurs in the back and is effected with hooks and eyes.

Linen, pongee, crash, mercerized cambric, duck, sail-cloth, piqué, foulard, taffeta, summer serge or mohair

1157—LADIES' SEVEN-GORED TUCK-PLAITED SKIRT IN ROUND, SHORT ROUND OR INSTEP LENGTH. Illustrated on page 400.

This attractive skirt is made of light tan covert cloth. It is a seven-gored model, consisting of a front, two side-front, two side and two back gores. The fulness at the front, sides and back of the garment is disposed in tuck plaits, which are stitched to yoke depth. Fancy strap portions are provided, but may be omitted. A narrow belt finishes the upper edge of the garment, and the lower edge may be completed with a hem or a facing. The placket closing occurs in the back.

Serge, cheviot, tweed, covert cloth, Venetian cloth, homespun, brilliantine, mohair, taffeta peau de soie or pongee may be used to develop this design, and braid, passementerie, gimp, ribbon, insertion or Oriental trimming may be used to ornament. A novel and handsome effect may be gained by making the straps of contrasting material to that employed for the remainder of the garment; for instance, for a cloth skirt, velvet or silk may be used for the straps, or for a linen or piqué skirt the straps may be made of embroidery or of heavy lace.

A figure view on page 383 shows an entirely different development of the design.

Ladies' seven-gored tuck-plaited skirt 1157 is in six sizes, from twenty-two to thirty-two inches waist measure, corresponding to thirty-nine and one-half to fifty-four and one-half inches hip measure, price 15 cents. The twenty-four-inch-waist size, corresponding to the forty-two-inch hip size, requires for round length, eleven and one-half yards of material twenty-two inches wide; seven yards forty-four inches, or five and five-eighths yards fifty-four inches. For instep length, are required ten and seven-eighth yards twenty-two inches wide; six and five-eighth yards forty-four inches, or five and one-quarter yards fifty-four inches. Width of skirt at lower edge is five and one-half yards.

1155—LADIES' WAIST OR BODY LINING CLOSED AT THE FRONT OR BACK AND WITH SEAMS RUNNING TO THE SHOULDER. Illustrated on page 401.

The garment depicted in the accompanying illustration is made of blue taffeta. It may be used for a waist or body lining and is fitted by center-front, side-back, under-arm and shoulder seams, also side-front and center-

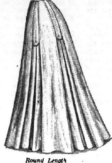

Round Length

Taffeta, linen-and-silk lining, percaline, silesia, sateen, satin or other desirable material may be used to construct this garment, and lace edging may be used to finish the low neck and elbow sleeves. This pattern may be used for a waist if desired, and can then be cut to the shallow pointed outline. The neck may be cut in the Dutch square, and a chemisette of lace, embroidery or lawn worn with the garment.

Ladies' waist or body lining 1155 is in nine sizes, from thirty-two to forty-eight inches bust measure, price 15 cents. The thirty-eight-inch bust size requires, as in high-necked view, four yards of material twenty-two inches wide or two and three-eighth yards thirty-six inches; or, as in low-necked view, two and one-quarter yards of material twenty-two inches wide or one and three-eighth yards thirty-six inches.

1147—LADIES' NINE-GORED FLARE SKIRT IN SHORT SWEEP, ROUND OR SHORT ROUND LENGTH. Illustrated on page 401.

This graceful skirt is made of brown cheviot. The design, which is one that lends itself readily to various styles of decoration, consisting of a front gore, two side-front, two side, two side-back and two back gores, the latter united by a center-back seam.

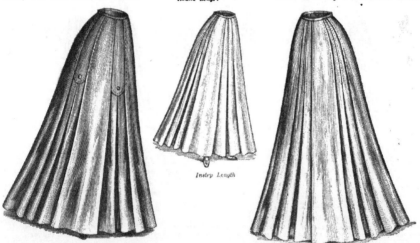

Short Round Length

Instep Length

Round Length

1157, LADIES' SEVEN-GORED TUCK-PLAITED SKIRT IN ROUND, SHORT ROUND OR INSTEP LENGTH (WITH OR WITHOUT THE STRAPS IN YOKE EFFECT). Described on page 399.

front seams when the garment is closed at the back, and a center-back seam when a front closing is preferred. The neck may be cut in high or Dutch or low round or square outline, and when made close to the throat is finished by a standing collar. The lower edge of the garment may be cut in deep or shallow round or pointed outline. The two-seamed sleeve may be made full or elbow length. When the elbow length is desired, the lower portion of the sleeve is cut away at the line of perforations provided. If preferred, the entire sleeve may be omitted and the armholes finished with ruffles of lace.

It fits the front and sides smoothly, and the fulness in the back is disposed in an inverted box plait, or, if preferred, the back may be finished in habit style, the latter arrangement making the garment absolutely close-fitting all around. A narrow belt completes the upper edge of the garment, and the lower edge, which may be in short sweep, round or short round length, is finished with a hem or an underfacing. The placket-closing occurs in the back, and may be effected with hooks and eyes or patent fasteners.

Serge, cheviot, tweed, camel's hair, peau de soie, taffeta, velvet, linen, duck or piqué may be used to develop this design, and braid, appliqué embroidery, insertion, gimp or Oriental trimming may be used to decorate. Each one of the seams may be outlined by either a narrow strapping of silk or the skirt material, or with piping of contrasting material. The piping is particularly pretty for linen, piqué, or duck skirts, and may then be made of linen of contrasting color. Insertion or lace may also be used over the seams.

flouncing, insertion and washable ribbon and are fitted by inside leg seams, the lower edge of the legs being shaped on the outside, as indicated. The fulness at the upper edge of the garment is disposed in scant plaits in the back and in darts at the front and sides. A facing is attached to the underside of the upper edge and the closing is effected in the back by means of buttons and buttonholes or tape tying-strings, as preferred. The umbrella flounces are slightly gathered at the upper edges and attached to the lower edge of the drawers legs.

Cambric, linen, nainsook, dimity, batiste, China silk or long-cloth may be used to develop this design, and lace edging, embroidered flouncing, insertion, beading or

1155. LADIES' WAIST OR BODY LINING, CLOSED AT THE FRONT OR BACK AND WITH SEAMS RUNNING TO THE SHOULDER (WITH LOWER EDGE IN DEEP OR SHALLOW ROUND OUTLINE OR IN POINTED OUTLINE AND WITH HIGH OR DUTCH OR LOW ROUND OR SQUARE NECK AND TWO-SEAMED FULL-LENGTH OR ELBOW SLEEVES). Described on page 400.

Ladies' nine-gored flare skirt 1147 is in eight sizes, from twenty-two to thirty-six inches waist measure, corresponding to thirty-nine and one-half to sixty and one-half inches hip measure, price 15 cents. The twenty-four-inch waist size, corresponding to the forty-two-inch hip size, requires for short sweep length, eleven and one-half yards of material twenty-two inches wide; five and five-eighth yards forty-four inches, or five yards fifty-four inches. For short round length are required ten and seven-eighth yards of material twenty-two inches wide; five yards forty-four inches, or three and three-quarter yards of material which measures fifty-four inches in width. Width of skirt at lower edge is five yards.

1142—LADIES' FRENCH OPEN DRAWERS.
Illustrated on page 402.

Nainsook is the material used to make the drawers depicted in the accompanying illustration. They are trimmed with embroidered

ribbon may be used to trim the garment. The umbrella flounces may be made of deep lace or embroidery or of fine cambric, which may be tucked before the ruffle is cut out. This design will be found especially suitable for stout figures as it fits with tailor closeness, causing no fulness about the hips.

Ladies' French open drawers 1142 is in six sizes, from twenty-two to thirty-two inches waist measure, corresponding to thirty-nine and one-half to fifty-four and one-half inches hip measure, price 10 cents. The twenty-four-inch waist size, corresponding to the forty-two-inch hip size, requires two and one-eighth yards of material thirty-six inches wide. As represented, one and one-quarter yards of thirty-six-inch material were used, with two and three-quarter yards of embroidery for flounce, one and seven-eighth yards of

Short Round Length   Round Length   Short Sweep Length

1147, LADIES' NINE-GORED FLARE SKIRT IN SHORT SWEEP, ROUND OR SHORT ROUND LENGTH (WITH AN INVERTED BOX PLAIT OR IN HABIT STYLE AT THE BACK). Described on page 400.

ALL STANDARD PATTERNS NOW 5, 10 OR 15 CENTS—NONE HIGHER

1142. LADIES' FRENCH OPEN DRAW-ERS. Described on page 401.

embroidered beading, and two and seven-eighth yards of ribbon to run in the beading.

1146 — LADIES' CORSET-COVER. Illustrated on this page.

This dainty corset-cover is made of white batiste and is trimmed with lace beading, ribbon and lace edging. The garment is fitted by under-arm and shoulder seams. The upper edge is finished with a band of ribbon-run beading. There is no front or back opening, the corset-cover being slipped over the head, and the fulness at the waistline is disposed in gathers by means of the band of ribbon-run beading. The armholes are finished with frills of lace and narrow bands of ribbon-run beading.

Dimity, nainsook, batiste, cambric, linen lawn, China silk or sheer long-cloth may be used to develop this design, and lace edging, embroidery, beading, ribbon or insertion may be used to trim. The particular desirability of this garment, aside from its graceful shaping, is that it can be made almost flat for laundering by drawing out the ribbon in the beading at the neck and waistline. Then, too, the garment can be worn under transparent waists having back or side closing, and there is no closing of the corset-cover itself to show through the material.

Ladies' corset-cover 1146 is in five sizes, from thirty-two to forty inches bust measure, price 10 cents. The thirty-six-inch bust size requires one and one-eighth yards of material thirty-six inches wide, with three and five-eighth yards of lace edging, three and three-quarter yards of

lace beading, and five and five-eighth yards of narrow ribbon to run in the beading and for the bows.

1160—LADIES' FIVE-GORED PETTICOAT IN ROUND, SHORT ROUND OR INSTEP LENGTH. Illustrated on this page.

This pretty petticoat, as shown in the large front view, is made of light-gray taffeta, and is trimmed with ruchings of the same material. It is a five-gored model, consisting of a front gore, two side and two back gores, the latter united by a center-back seam, and is fitted over the hips by darts. The fulness at the back may be arranged in an inverted box plait, or disposed by a casing and drawing-strings, as preferred. A slightly circular gathered flounce is attached to the lower portion of the petticoat, and the dust ruffle is provided, but may be omitted.

1146. LADIES' CORSET-COVER (TO BE SLIPPED OVER THE HEAD). Described on this page.

Taffeta, peau de soie, mohair, moreen, sateen, cotton moiré, cambric, long-cloth or nainsook may be used to develop this design, and lace edging, insertion, embroidery, ruching, braid or gimp may be used to trim. The gored portion of the skirt may be made of moreen or mohair, and the flounce of silk, or if a washable petticoat be desired, muslin or

Instep Length

Round Length

Short Round Length

Round Length

1160. LADIES' FIVE-GORED PETTICOAT IN ROUND, SHORT ROUND OR INSTEP LENGTH (CLOSED AT THE BACK OR SIDE, WITH A SLIGHTLY CIRCULAR GATHERED FLOUNCE AND AN INVERTED BOX PLAIT OR DRAWING-STRING AT THE BACK AND WITH OR WITHOUT THE DUST RUFFLE). Described on this page.

long-cloth may be used for the gored portion, and the flounce may be made of cambric and embroidery. A figure view is shown on page 384.

Ladies' petticoat 1160 is in eight sizes, twenty-two to thirty-six inches waist, corresponding to thirty-nine and one-half to sixty and one-half inches hip, price 15 cents. Twenty-four-inch waist size, corresponding to forty-two-inch hip size, requires twelve yards of material twenty-two inches wide; eight and one-eighth yards thirty-six inches, or seven and one-half yards forty-four inches, with eight and seven-eighth yards of ruching to trim as in front view. As represented in lower back view, seven and three-eighth yards of thirty-six-inch material were used, with two and one-half yards of insertion, four and one-quarter yards of embroidered beading and five and one-quarter yards of embroidered edging for ruffle which trims the flounce,

1140—LADIES' SACK APRON. Illustrated on this page.

Blue-and-white striped percale is used to make this apron, and the collar is trimmed with a frill of narrow Torchon lace. The garment is fitted by under-arm and shoulder seams. The sleeve is a full-length, one-seamed model completed by a band cuff. The neck edge may be cut in round or square outline, or may be made close to the throat and finished with a two-piece turn-down collar. Patch pockets are provided, and the lower edge of the garment is finished with a hem.

Gingham, chambray, percale, brown holland, blue jean, butchers' linen or denim may be used to develop this design, and the collar may be edged with embroidered edging or lace. This garment will be found useful not only while engaged in household duties, but while nursing, painting or modeling, as it completely protects the garment which may be worn underneath it. For any of these purposes the apron should be made of material of sufficient thickness so that water, grease or paint will not penetrate it.

Ladies' sack apron 1140 is in four sizes, from thirty-two to forty-four inches bust measure, price 15 cents. The thirty-six-inch bust size requires eight and one-half yards of material twenty-seven inches wide or six and three-eighth yards thirty-six inches, with one and three-eighth yards of edging to trim the collar.

1145—LADIES' CLOSED DRAWERS. Illustrated on this page.

White cambric, lace edging and insertion are the materials selected to make the

1145. LADIES' CLOSED DRAWERS (WITH OR WITHOUT THE UMBRELLA FLOUNCE). Described on this page.

drawers here pictured. The small view shows them made of linen and decorated with narrow tucks. The garment is fitted by center front and back seams, also inside leg seams, the fulness at the upper edge of the front and back of the garment being disposed in darts. The extra fulness at the back is disposed in two scant plaits on each side of the center-back seam. The lower edges of the drawers legs are finished with hems and an umbrella flounce is provided, but may be omitted as shown in the small front view, or a narrower ruffle may be used as pictured in the back view. The side closings are effected by buttons and buttonholes.

Cambric, linen, dimity, batiste, nainsook, long-cloth or China silk may be used to develop this design, and lace edging, insertion, beading, embroidery or tucking may be used to decorate. This is an excellent design for a woman of stout figure, as the dart-fitting does away with all fulness about the waist and hips, while the scant plaits at the back give sufficient width to the garment.

Ladies' closed drawers 1145 is in six sizes, from twenty-two to thirty-two inches waist measure, corresponding to thirty-nine and one-half to fifty-four and one-half inches hip measure, price 10 cents. The twenty-four-inch waist size, corresponding to the forty-two-inch hip size, requires two yards of material thirty-six inches wide. As represented, one and seven-eighth yards of material thirty-six inches wide are used, with three yards of edging for flounce or ruffle, two yards of insertion in front view or three and three-quarter yards of insertion as in back view.

1140. LADIES' SACK APRON (WITH HIGH OR ROUND OR SQUARE NECK). Described on this page.

ALL STANDARD PATTERNS NOW 5, 10 OR 15 CENTS—NONE HIGHER

MISSES' SHIRT-WAIST TOILETTE. ILLUSTRATED ON THIS PAGE.

Misses' and girls' tucked shirt-waist 1090 is in ten sizes, from eight to seventeen years, price 15 cents. The garment is closed at the back, and may have full or three-quarter length sleeves. Misses' seven-gored skirt 9258 is in five sizes, from thirteen to seventeen years, price 15 cents. It is without fulness to deep yoke depth, and may have an inverted box plait or be in habit style at the back, and is sometimes called the umbrella or ripple skirt. As here shown the shirt-waist is made of dotted swiss and the skirt of pink chambray.

GIRLS' GABRIELLE OR PRINCESS DRESS. ILLUSTRATED ON PAGE 405.

Girls' dress 1118 is in nine sizes, from four to twelve years, price 15 cents, and is shown again on page 410. The dress may be made with high or square neck, full-length or short puff sleeves, and with or without the bertha. It is made in the present instance of Saxon-blue chambray, and trimmed with embroidery and beading.

MISSES' SHIRT-WAIST COSTUME. ILLUSTRATED ON PAGE 405.

Misses' costume 1134 is in five sizes, from thirteen to seventeen years, price 15 cents. It consists of a tucked shirt-waist with removable chemisette and with the sleeves tucked or gathered to the cuffs; and a seven-gored umbrella or ripple skirt with an inverted box plait at the back and with or without tuck folds. Another view of the design is presented on page 410, where it is accompanied by a detailed description, measurements for the quantity of material required for the making of the garment, also mention of some of the fabrics which are suitable for its development. As here pictured it is made of tan linen, the chemisette and cuffs being embroidered.

MISSES' SHIRT-WAIST TOILETTE. DESCRIBED ON THIS PAGE
(Shirt-Waist 1090 and Skirt 9258)

CHILDREN'S DRESS. ILLUSTRATED ON PAGE 405.

Children's dress 1122 is in six sizes, from six months to five years, price 10 cents, and is presented in different development on page 413, where it is accompanied by a detailed description. The garment may have a high or square neck, bishop or short puff sleeves, and be made with or without the bertha. Nainsook is used for its development in the present instance, and the bertha is made of fine nainsook embroidery.

GIRLS' DRESS. ILLUSTRATED ON PAGE 405.

Girls' dress 1125 is in eight sizes, from five to twelve years, price 15 cents, and is again pictured on page 411. It may have full-length or elbow sleeves, and the body portions may be tucked or gathered to the scalloped yoke. The attached skirt may be tucked or gathered, as preferred. Flowered organdy is used for the dress, as here pictured.

MISSES' TUCKED COSTUME. ILLUSTRATED ON PAGE 406.

Misses' costume 1159 is in five sizes, from thirteen to seventeen years, price 15 cents. Another development of the design appears on page 409, and is accompanied by a detailed description, and measurements for the quantity of material required for the making of the garment, which consists of a blouse-waist with full-length or elbow sleeves, and with or without the bertha, and an attached or separate five-gored skirt with an inverted box plait at the back. The dress is here prettily made of flowered organdy and is trimmed with lace appliqué and edging.

LITTLE BOYS' DRESS. ILLUSTRATED ON PAGE 406.

Little boys' dress 1150 is in three sizes, from two to four years, price 10 cents, and is again pictured on page 414, where it is accompanied by a detailed description,

measurements, etc. The dress may have an attached or detachable turn-down collar or a collar band, and be made with or without detachable turned-up cuffs. It is here made of white linen.

GIRLS' DRESS. ILLUSTRATED ON PAGE 406.

Girls' dress 1152 is in eight sizes, from five to twelve years, price 15 cents, and is displayed in different development on page 411, where it is accompanied by a detailed description, measurements for the quantity of material required for the making of the garment, also mention of some of the fabrics which will be found appropriate for its reproduction. In the present instance the dress is made of blue-and-white plaid madras, with a bertha, yoke and wristbands of white lawn decorated with eyelet embroidery.

MISSES' TUCKED SHIRT-WAIST COSTUME. ILLUSTRATED ON PAGE 406.

Misses' costume 1141 is in five sizes, from thirteen to seventeen years, price 15 cents, and is again pictured on page 408. It consists of a shirt-waist closed at the side, with or without kimono sleeves or body lining; a yoke guimpe, and a five-gored skirt with tucks stitched to yoke or flounce depth, and having an inverted box plait at the back. The costume is here made of sage-green drap d'été with trimming bands of green-and-white novelty silk, and a yoke guimpe of sheer lawn and Valenciennes lace insertion.

CHILDREN'S DRESSES.   DESCRIBED ON THIS PAGE
(Dress 1121)   (Dress 1122)

GIRLS' DRESS. ILLUSTRATED ON THIS PAGE.

Girls' dress 1133 is in eight sizes, from five to twelve years, price 15 cents, and is again pictured on page 411. Blue chambray is used for its present development, the Pompadour yoke being made of swiss all-over embroidery.

GIRLS' DRESS. ILLUSTRATED ON THIS PAGE.

Girls' dress 1131 is in nine sizes, from four to twelve years, price 15 cents, another view of the garment being given on page 410. It is here made of dark-red linen with suspender straps, wristbands and belt of plaid gingham.

LITTLE GIRLS' OR BOYS' BOX-PLAITED DRESS. ILLUSTRATED ON THIS PAGE.

Little girls' or boys' dress 1121 is in six sizes, from two to seven years, price 10 cents, another view of it appearing on page 412. As here shown it is made of pink chambray with a Puritan collar and cuffs of white linen.

CHILDREN'S DRESS. ILLUSTRATED ON THIS PAGE.

Children's dress 1122 is in six sizes, from six months to five years, price 10 cents. Another view of the design appears on page 413. In the present instance it is made of pink-and-white lawn and the frill bertha is trimmed with Valenciennes edging and insertion.

GIRLS' DRESSES.   DESCRIBED ON THIS PAGE
(Dress 1133)   (Dress 1131)

1170, MISSES' BOX-COAT (WITH TWO-SEAMED L E G - O ' - M U T T O N SLEEVES, GATHERED OR PLAITED AT THE TOP OR WITH PLAIN COAT SLEEVES). Described on this page.

1170 — MISSES' BOX-COAT. Illustrated on this page.

Tan tweed is used to make this stylish coat, which is fitted by under-arm and shoulder seams, and for which two styles of sleeve are provided: one being a two-seamed coat sleeve finished with a hem at the lower edge, and the other a two-seamed leg-o'-mutton sleeve plaited into the armhole and completed by a one-piece turn-up cuff. Patch pockets with flaps may be attached to the coat fronts, and the neck edge is finished with a flat collar-facing, which may be omitted.

Misses' box-coat 1170 is in five sizes, thirteen to seventeen years, price 15 cents. The fifteen-year size requires two and one-half yards of fifty-four-inch material.

1141—MISSES' TUCKED SHIRT-WAIST COSTUME. Illustrated on this page.

This attractive costume is made of light-pink mercerized chambray and is trimmed with white linen bands. The yoke guimpe is of white lawn combined with all-over embroidery. The waist is mounted on a fitted lining, the outer back being arranged in lengthwise tucks and shirred

at the waistline. The tucked fronts blouse slightly and are shirred at the waistline. A trimming band may complete the upper edge of the back and fronts and forward edge of the right front. The kimono sleeve, which is in one piece, gathered into the armhole and opened on the outside of the arm, is finished with a trimming band. The back-closing yoke guimpe is fitted by under-arm and shoulder seams, and completed by a standing collar. The sleeve consists of a one-seamed full portion finished by a deep, one-seamed, close-fitting cuff. The five-gored skirt has an inverted box plait at the back and is tucked to yoke or flounce depth, and a side closing, matching the shirt-waist, may be simulated by a trimming band.

Madras, chambray, linen, crash, dimity, foulard, cashmere, flannel or mohair may be used to develop this design, and a figure v i e w is shown on page 406.

Misses' shirt-waist costume 1141 is in five sizes, thirteen to seventeen years,

1156, MISSES' COSTUME (CONSISTING OF A WAIST WITH VEST AND YOKE-FACING IN ONE AND AN ATTACHED OR SEPARATE SEVEN-GORED SKIRT WITH AN INVERTED BOX PLAIT AT THE BACK AND WITH OR WITHOUT THE TUCKS AT THE LOWER PART). Described on this page.

price 15 cents. The fifteen-year size requires seven and one-half yards of material thirty-six inches in width.

1156 — MISSES' COSTUME. Illustrated on this page.

This pretty costume is made of Saxon-blue rajah combined with all-over embroidery and fancy braid. The waist is mounted on a fitted lining, the front and upper portions of which are faced to form the yoke and vest. The box-plaited backs and full fronts are shirred at the waistline and may be decorated with a trimming band. The neck edge is finished with a standing collar, and the sleeve is a

1141, MISSES' TUCKED SHIRT-WAIST COSTUME (CONSISTING OF A YOKE GUIMPE, A SHIRT-WAIST CLOSED AT THE SIDE AND WITH OR WITHOUT THE KIMONO SLEEVES OR BODY LINING; AND A FIVE-GORED SKIRT WITH THE TUCKS STITCHED TO YOKE OR FLOUNCE DEPTH AND AN INVERTED BOX PLAIT AT THE BACK AND WITH OR WITHOUT THE TRIMMING BAND). Described on this page.

one-seamed model mounted on a two-seamed lining, trimmed with bands. The closing of the waist is effected down the center back. The attached or separate seven-gored skirt has an inverted box plait at the back, and the extra fulness is disposed in box plaits stitched to yoke depth. The skirt may be made with or without the tucks at the lower part.

Mohair, taffeta, cashmere, pongee, linen, chambray, foulard or voile may be used to develop this design.

Misses' costume 1156 is in five sizes, thirteen to seventeen years, price 15 cents. Fifteen-year size requires thirteen and one-quarter yards of twenty-two-inch material.

1172—MISSES' COSTUME. Illustrated on this page.

This handsome costume is made of dark-red pongee combined with all-over lace. The waist is mounted on a

1171. MISSES SEVEN-GORED FLARE SKIRT (WITH AN INVERTED BOX PLAIT AT THE BACK AND WITH OR WITHOUT THE GIRDLE, SUSPENDERS OR NUN TUCKS). Described on this page.

Misses' costume 1172 is in five sizes, thirteen to seventeen years, price 15 cents. Fifteen-year size requires ten and three-eighth yards of twenty-two-inch material.

1171—MISSES' SEVEN-GORED FLARE SKIRT. Illustrated on this page.

This pretty seven-gored flare skirt is made of myrtle-green serge. It fits the hips smoothly, the fulness at the

1172. MISSES' COSTUME (CONSISTING OF A WAIST WITH SQUARE YOKE, HIGH OR DUTCH NECK AND FULL - LENGTH OR ELBOW SLEEVES; AND AN ATTACHED OR SEPARATE FIVE-GORED SKIRT WITH AN INVERTED BOX PLAIT AT THE BACK AND A SLIGHTLY CIRCULAR FLOUNCE FROM BENEATH WHICH THE SKIRT MAY BE CUT AWAY, AND WITH OR WITHOUT THE SUSPENDERS). Described on this page.

fitted lining overlaid with a yoke, to which the tucked backs and front are attached, these portions being shirred at the waistline. The sleeve consists of a one-seamed full outside portion mounted on a two - seamed, close - fitting lining. When the elbow length is desired the under-sleeve is cut away. Suspenders are provided, and the neck edge is finished with a standing collar unless the Dutch round neck is preferred. The closing of the waist is effected down the center back by means of hooks and eyes. The five-gored skirt may be attached or made separate. The fulness over the hips is disposed in tucks and at the back is arranged in an inverted box plait. A slightly circular flounce, tucked at the upper edge is attached to the lower portion of the skirt.

Pongee, foulard, nun's - veiling, albatross, challis, lawn, dimity, madras or chambray may be used to develop this design, with lace, insertion, braid or ribbon to trim.

1159. MISSES' TUCKED COSTUME (CONSISTING OF A BLOUSE WAIST WITH FULL-LENGTH OR ELBOW SLEEVES AND WITH OR WITHOUT THE BERTHA; AND AN ATTACHED OR SEPARATE FIVE-GORED SKIRT WITH AN INVERTED BOX PLAIT AT THE BACK). Described on page 410.

back being disposed in an inverted box plait. The lower part flares gracefully and is trimmed with three nun tucks. A girdle with suspenders is provided, but may be omitted.

Serge, cheviot, tweed, mohair, homespun, taffeta, linen, duck or piqué may be used to develop this design, with lace, embroidery, insertion, braid or ribbon to trim.

Misses' skirt 1171 is in four sizes, from fourteen to seventeen years, price 15 cents. The fifteen-year size requires nine and five-eighth yards of material twenty-two inches wide; six and three-eighth yards thirty-six inches, or five yards forty-four inches.

1118, GIRLS' GABRIELLE OR PRINCESS DRESS (WITH HIGH OR SQUARE NECK AND FULL-LENGTH OR SHORT PUFF SLEEVES AND WITH OR WITHOUT THE BERTHA). Described on page 411.

1159—MISSES' TUCKED COSTUME.
Illustrated on page 409.

The dress here shown is made of pale-blue eolienne combined with all-over lace, fancy tucking and insertion. The back-closing waist is mounted on a fitted lining; the outer front and backs are arranged in cluster tucks to yoke depth and are shirred at the waistline. A bertha is provided, but may be omitted, and the neck edge is finished with a standing collar. The sleeve, which may be made in full or elbow length, consists of a two-seamed, close-fitting lining and a one-seamed puff, which is gathered into a narrow band and used alone when the elbow sleeve is preferred. The attached or separate five-gored skirt has the fulness disposed in cluster tucks and an inverted box plait at the back.

Foulard, cashmere, nun's-veiling, alba-

1131, GIRLS' DRESS (WITH SUSPENDER STRAPS). Described on page 411.

tross, challis, lawn, dotted swiss, dimity or linen may be used to develop this design, with lace, embroidery, ribbon or braid to trim.

A figure view on page 406 shows a different development.

Misses' costume 1159 is in five sizes, thirteen to seventeen years, price 15 cents. The fifteen-year size requires six and one-eighth yards of material thirty-six inches wide.

1134—MISSES' SHIRT-WAIST COSTUME. Illustrated on this page.

Blue-and-white figured crash is used for the stylish costume here depicted. The chemisette and cuffs are of white linen. The shirt-waist is mounted on a body lining. The back is arranged in lengthwise tucks and shirred at the waistline; the fronts are tucked to yoke depth and the fulness at the lower edge is disposed in shirring. The right front overlaps the left, and the removable chemisette is finished by a standing collar. The one-seamed sleeve has the fulness at the lower edge disposed in gathers or tucks and a fancy cuff is attached. The seven-gored umbrella skirt has an inverted box plait at the back and may be made with or without the tuck folds.

1134, MISSES' SHIRT-WAIST COSTUME (CONSISTING OF A TUCKED SHIRT-WAIST WITH RE-MOVABLE CHEMISETTE AND WITH THE SLEEVES TUCKED OR GATHERED TO THE CUFFS; AND A SEVEN-GORED UMBRELLA OR RIPPLE SKIRT WITH AN INVERTED BOX PLAIT AT THE BACK AND WITH OR WITHOUT THE TUCK FOLDS). Described on this page.

ALL STANDARD PATTERNS NOW 5, 10 OR 15 CENTS—NONE HIGHER

1125, GIRLS' DRESS (WITH FULL-LENGTH OR ELBOW SLEEVES AND THE BODY TUCKED OR GATHERED TO SCALLOPED YOKE, AND WITH OR WITHOUT THE TUCKS AT TOP OF SKIRT). Described on this page.

1152, GIRLS' DRESS. Described on page 412.

A figure view on page 405 shows a different development. Misses' costume 1134 is in five sizes, thirteen to seventeen years, price 15 cents. Fifteen-year size requires seven and five-eighth yards of thirty-six-inch material.

1118—GIRLS' GABRIELLE OR PRINCESS DRESS. Illustrated on page 410.

This dainty dress as in the front view is made of blue linen and trimmed with lace edging and insertion. It is fitted by side-front, side-back, under-arm and shoulder seams. The neck may be made high and finished with a standing collar, or cut in square outline. A shaped one-piece bertha is provided, and the sleeve is a one-seamed full-length model gathered into a band cuff, or when the short puff sleeve is preferred, the lower portion of the full-length sleeve is cut away, and a narrow band attached. The closing of the dress is made down the center back.

Taffeta, pongee, summer silk, linen, lawn, madras, chambray or percale. may be used to develop this design.

A figure view on page 405 shows a different development.

Girls' dress 1118 is in nine sizes, from four to twelve years, price 15 cents. The nine-year size requires three and one-quarter yards of material thirty-six inches wide.

1131—GIRLS' DRESS. Illustrated on page 410.

This pretty dress is made of gray serge and trimmed with dark-gray velvet piped with plaid silk. The back-closing waist portions are fitted by under-arm and shoulder seams, and are tucked to yoke depth, the fulness at the waistline being disposed in shirring. The one-seamed sleeve is completed by a band cuff, and a standing collar finishes the neck edge. Suspender portions are provided, and the plaited skirt is attached to the lower edges of the body portions, a belt concealing the joining.

Serge, cheviot, mohair, flannel, pongee, madras, linen or duck may be used to develop this design, with lace, embroidery, insertion or braid to trim the garment in an effective manner, and a figure view is shown on page 407.

Girls' dress 1131 is in nine sizes, from four to twelve years, price 15 cents. The nine-year size requires three yards of material forty-four inches in width.

1125—GIRLS' DRESS. Illustrated on this page.

Nile-green mercerized chambray is used for this attractive dress, the yoke and lower sleeve portions being of all-over embroidery. The back-closing waist is mounted on a fitted body lining overlaid with a scalloped yoke, to which the full front and backs are attached in gathers or tucks. They are shirred at the waistline. The sleeve, which may be made in full or elbow length, consists of a two-seamed lining extending to the wrist and overlaid with material, and a long one-seamed puff. When the elbow style is preferred the lower part of the lining is cut away. The one-piece skirt is tucked or gathered to the lower edge of the body portions, a ribbon belt or sash concealing the uniting, and is hemmed at the lower edge.

A figure view on page 405 shows a different development.

Girls' dress 1125 is in eight sizes, from five to twelve years, price 15 cents. The nine-year size requires three and one-half yards of material thirty-six inches wide.

1133, GIRLS' DRESS (WITH OR WITHOUT THE FRONT TRIMMING BANDS AND WITH AN ATTACHED STRAIGHT SKIRT PLAITED AT THE TOP). Described on page 412.

ALL STANDARD PATTERNS NOW 5, 10 OR 15 CENTS—NONE HIGHER

1152—GIRLS' DRESS. Illustrated on page 411.

White embroidered swiss is used to make this dainty dress and it is trimmed with embroidered insertion and edging. The yoke is made of all-over embroidery. The waist is mounted on a fitted lining overlaid to round-yoke depth. The gathered full backs and front are shirred at the waistline. The sleeve consists of a two-seamed, close-fitting lining, which extends to the wrist and is overlaid with material, and a long one-seamed puff. Bertha and suspender portions are provided, and the full straight skirt is tucked above the hem and attached to the lower edges of the back-closing body portions.

A figure view on page 406 shows a different development.

Girls' dress 1152 is in eight sizes, from five to twelve years, price 15 cents. The nine-year size requires five and one-quarter yards of material twenty-seven inches wide.

1133—GIRLS' DRESS. Illustrated on page 411.

This dress as depicted in the center view is made of blue cashmere combined with dark-blue velvet and blue-and-white plaided silk. The waist is mounted on a body lining faced in front to form the Pompadour yoke. The backs are arranged in lengthwise tucks and the fulness at the waistline is disposed in shirrings. The blouse front, which is tucked on each side to yoke depth and shirred at the lower edge, may be decorated with trimming bands, and a standing collar finishes the neck edge. The bishop sleeve is completed by a band cuff and the plaited attached straight skirt is finished by a hem at the lower edge. A belt conceals its joining to the waist.

Cashmere, foulard, flannel, linen, madras or chambray may be used to develop this design and a figure view is shown on page 407.

Girls' dress 1133 is in eight sizes, from five to twelve years, price 15 cents. The nine-year size requires three yards and three-quarter of material thirty-six inches wide.

1121—LITTLE GIRLS' OR BOYS' BOX-PLAITED DRESS. Illustrated on this page.

This stylish little dress in one view is made of light-tan linen, and in the other view of shepherd's plaid combined with white linen. It is fitted by under-arm and shoulder seams. The backs and front are box-plaited and extensions cut at the edges of the under-arm seams below the waistline are laid in inverted box plaits. A belt confines the garment at the waistline. The one-seamed sleeve is gathered into a band and a turn-up cuff is provided. A narrow band finishes the neck edge, and a Puritan or standing collar may be used. The closing of the dress is effected under the center-back box plait, and a figure view on page 407 shows a different development.

Little girls' or boys' dress 1121 is in six sizes, two to seven years, price 10 cents. The five-year size requires four and one-eighth yards of twenty-seven-inch material.

1163—GIRLS' BOX-PLAITED DRESS. Illustrated on this page.

This pretty dress is made of old-rose madras and trimmed with washable braid. The box-plaited waist and skirt portions are

cut in one and are confined at the waistline by a belt held in place by small straps attached to the under-arm seams at the waistline. The one-seamed bishop sleeve is gathered into the band cuff and a standing collar finishes

1121, LITTLE GIRLS' OR BOYS' BOX-PLAITED DRESS (WITH BODY AND SKIRT IN ONE AND DETACHABLE PURITAN COLLAR AND CUFFS OR ATTACHED BAND COLLAR). Described on this page.

the neck edge. The dress closing is effected down the center back, and the lower edge of the garment is hemmed.

Gingham, chambray, linen, duck, flannel, serge, galatea, crash or mohair may be used to develop this design.

1163, GIRLS' BOX-PLAITED DRESS (WITH BODY AND SKIRT IN ONE AND WITH SAILOR OR BISHOP SLEEVES). Described on this page.

A figure view on page 407 shows a different development.

Girls' dress 1163 is in eight sizes, five to twelve years, price 15 cents. The nine-year size requires five and one-eighth yards of material twenty-seven inches wide.

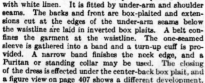

1162, LITTLE GIRLS' DRESS (WITH OR WITHOUT THE BERTHA). Described on page 413.

ALL STANDARD PATTERNS NOW 5, 10 OR 15 CENTS—NONE HIGHER

1162—LITTLE GIRLS' DRESS. Illustrated on page 412.

Pink chambray combined with all-over embroidery is used for this dress. The back-closing waist is mounted on a lining overlaid with a yoke which continues into a

1153. LITTLE GIRLS' BOX-PLAITED APRON (WITH HIGH OR ROUND NECK AND WITH OR WITHOUT THE SLEEVES OR POCKETS). Described on this page.

vest. The blouse front and backs are gathered at the upper edges and shirred at the waistline and the side edges of the fronts are attached to the vest extension. A gathered bertha is provided, and the one-seamed bishop sleeve is gathered into a band. The neck edge is finished

1122. CHILDREN'S DRESS (WITH HIGH OR SQUARE NECK AND BISHOP OR SHORT PUFF SLEEVES AND WITH OR WITHOUT THE BERTHA). Described on this page.

with a standing collar and the full straight skirt is gathered to the lower edge of the body portions.

Little girls' dress 1162 is in six sizes, from three to eight years, price 10 cents. The five-year size requires three yards of material which is thirty-six inches wide.

1116, LITTLE GIRLS' TUCKED DRESS (WITH OR WITHOUT THE BERTHA). Described on this page.

1153—LITTLE GIRLS' BOX-PLAITED APRON. Illustrated on this page.

The round yoke of this apron is fitted by shoulder seams, and to it are attached the box - plaited front and backs, which are fitted by under-arm seams. The one - seamed bishop sleeve is completed by a band cuff and the neck edge may be finished with a two-piece turn-down collar or may be cut in round outline. Patch pockets are provided.

Little girls' apron 1153 is in six sizes, two to twelve years, price 10 cents. Six-year size requires, with high neck and long sleeves, three and seven-eighth yards of material twenty-seven inches wide.

1122 — CHILDREN'S DRESS. Illustrated on this page.

White lawn and embroidery are used to make this dress. The square yoke is fitted by shoulder seams and to it the skirt portions, fitted by under-arm seams, are gathered. Two styles of sleeve are provided: one is a full-length, one-seamed model gathered into a band cuff, and the other is a short puff finished with a narrow band. The neck is completed by a band collar, and a bertha frill is provided, but may be omitted. When the square-neck style is preferred, the yoke is omitted. A figure view is shown on page 407.

Children's dress 1122 is in six sizes, six months to five years, price 10 cents. The five-year size requires three and five-eighth yards of material which measures twenty-seven inches in width.

1116 — LITTLE GIRLS' TUCKED DRESS. Illustrated on this page.

This pretty dress as shown in the first view is made of white lawn and trimmed with insertion. The back-closing waist is mounted on a fitted lining, the full front and backs being tucked to yoke depth, and the fulness at the waistline is disposed in shirring. The one-seamed bishop sleeve is finished with a band cuff. A standing collar completes the neck edge and a circular bertha is provided. The full straight skirt is tucked and is gathered to the lower edge of the body portions.

Little girls' dress 1116 is in seven sizes, two to eight years, price 10 cents. Five-year size requires, with bertha, three and three-quarter yards twenty-seven-inch material or two and one-quarter yards forty-four inches.

1143—MISSES' AND GIRLS' SACK APRON. Illustrated on page 414.

This neat dress protector is made of linen, and is fitted by under-arm and shoulder seams. The one-seamed sleeve is gathered into a wristband and the neck edge may be finished with a two-piece turn-down collar or cut out in round or square outline. Patch pockets are attached to the front.

Misses' and girls' sack apron 1143 is in four sizes, from eleven to seventeen years, price 10 cents. Fifteen-year size re- quires five and

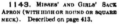

1143. Misses' and Girls' Sack Apron (with high or round or square neck). Described on page 413.

five - eighth yards of material which is twenty-seven inches wide.

1164—INFANTS' CLOAK. Illustrated on this page.

White lansdowne and silk braid are chosen for the cloak here depicted. It is fitted by under-arm and shoulder seams, and a circular cape may be attached to the neck edge underneath the one-piece turn-down collar, or the collar alone may be used. The one-seamed bishop sleeve is finished with a wristband.

Infants' cloak 1164 is in one size, price 10 cents. It requires three yards of material forty-four inches wide.

1120—MISSES' AND GIRLS' GUIMPE. Illustrated on this page.

Nainsook and insertion are used for this guimpe, which is fitted by under-arm and shoulder seams. The fulness at the neck edge of the front is disposed in gathers, and a casing and drawing-string at the waistline regulate the fulness. A standing collar finishes the neck edge and the

one-seamed bishop sleeve is gathered into a band. The guimpe closes down the back with buttons and buttonholes. Misses' and girls' guimpe 1120 is in eight sizes, from two to sixteen years, price 10 cents. The fourteen-year size requires two yards of material thirty-six inches wide.

1150—LITTLE BOYS' DRESS. Illustrated on this page.

Dark-red and white linen are used to make this dress. The box-plaited back and front are fitted by under-arm and shoulder seams, and are confined at the waistline by a belt. The one-seamed sleeve is gathered into a band cuff, and a turn-up detachable cuff is provided. The neck is completed by a band and a detachable or attached turn-down collar. A figure view is presented on page 406. .

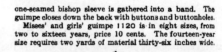

1120, Misses' and Girls' Guimpe. Described on this page.

Little boys' dress 1150 is in three sizes, from two to four years, price 10 cents. The three-year size requires two and five-eighth yards of material twenty-seven inches wide.

1150, Little Boys' Dress (with attached or detachable turn-down collar or with band collar and with or without the detachable turned-up cuffs). Described on this page. .

1138—INFANTS' AND CHILDREN'S SACK. Illustrated on page 415.

The square yoke of this sack is fitted by shoulder seams and to it the box-plaited back and fronts, joined by under-arm seams, are attached. Either a one-seamed flowing or a bishop sleeve may be used, and the latter is gathered into a band. A one-piece turn-down collar finishes the neck edge.

Infants' and children's sack 1138 is in four sizes, infants, one, three and five years, price 10 cents. The infants' size requires one and three-eighth yards of material twenty-seven inches in width.

1151 — LITTLE BOYS' SUIT. Illustrated on page 415.

White linen is used to make this stylish little suit, the blouse of which is fitted by under-arm and

1164, Infants' Cloak (with or without the cape or collar). Described on this page.

ALL STANDARD PATTERNS NOW 5, 10 OR 15 CENTS—NONE HIGHER

THE DESIGNER

shoulder seams, the left front being laid in a box plait through the center. The garment may be confined at the waistline by a belt, and the one-seamed sleeve is disposed in plaits to cuff depth. A band finishes the neck edge. The knickerbockers are made without a fly and are fitted by center-front, center-back and inside leg seams. Casings run with elastics finish the lower edge of each leg and the closing is effected on the sides with buttons and buttonholes.

Little boys' suit 1151 is in seven sizes, from two to eight years, price 15 cents. The five-year size requires three and one-eighth yards of material twenty-seven inches wide.

1135, LITTLE GIRLS' KIMONO WRAPPER OR SACK. Described on this page.

&

1135—LITTLE GIRLS' KIMONO WRAPPER OR SACK. Illustrated on this page.

This kimono is fitted by under-arm and shoulder seams. The fulness at the back is laid in an inverted box plait.

1138, INFANTS' AND CHILDREN'S SACK (WITH BISHOP OR BELL SLEEVES). Described on page 414.

The one-seamed flowing sleeve is completed by a trimming band and a band also finishes the neck edge and forward edges of the fronts. The garment may be made in sack length if preferred.

Little girls' wrapper or sack 1135 is in five sizes, one to nine years, price 10 cents. The five-year size requires for wrapper, three and one-eighth yards of thirty-six-inch material; or for sack, one and three-quarter yards of thirty-six-inch material.

1151, LITTLE BOYS' SUIT (CONSISTING OF A BLOUSE CLOSED AT THE SIDE AND KNICKERBOCKERS WITHOUT A FLY). Described on page 414.

&

1160—CHILDREN'S NIGHT-DRAWERS OR PAJAMAS. Illustrated on this page.

The garment here depicted is made of white drilling and trimmed with embroidered edging. It is fitted by center-front, under-arm and shoulder seams, also inside leg seams, and when the feet are preferred, soles are inserted. The upper back edge of the drawers portions is gathered into a belt. Two styles of sleeve are provided:

one a one-seamed model finished with row wristband, and t a two-seamed sleeve. finishes the neck edge.

Children's n i g h t - 1169 is in six sizes, twelve years, price 1 Four-year size requir and three-eighth yards rial twenty-seven inch

&

1117—MISSES' AND GIRLS' SQUARE-YOKE GOWN. Illustrated on this page.

The square yoke of this gown is fitted by seams and to it the full back and front, which ar by under-arm seams, are gathered. The full-length or elbow sleeve is a one-seamed model gathered into a narrow band. The neck edge of the gown may be finished with a turn-down collar or may be cut in Dutch square outline.

Misses' and girls' nightgown 1117 is in four sizes,

1169, CHILDREN'S NIGHT-DRAWERS MAS (WITH EITHER OF TWO STYLES OF SL WITH OR WITHOUT FEET). Described on

eleven to seventeen years, price 15 cents. Fift size requires, as in large front view, five and thre yards of thirty-six-inch material, or, as in back vi and seven-eighth yards of thirty-six-inch material

1117, MISSES' AND GIRLS' SQUARE-YOKE NIGHTGOW HIGH OR DUTCH SQUARE NECK AND FULL-LENGTH OR ELBOW Described on this page.

SASHES AND BOWS

I. A DRESDEN RIBBON SASH WITH ROSE GARNITURE

II. SASH WITH BUTTERFLY BOW

III. DETAIL OF BUTTERFLY BOW

SUGGESTIONS for tying sash ribbons are always in demand, though the kind of ribbon used whether plain or fancy often furnishes to a considerable degree ideas as to how it may best be arranged.

Handsome Dresden ribbon, eleven inches wide, was used for the sash shown in illustration I. The waist ribbon is crushed and tacked to featherbone four inches long to hold it to point shape in the front. A loop is formed at the top of one sash end, and in this four or five natural-looking roses with their foliage are sewed. The other and longer end is tied in a knot at two-thirds of its length and a smaller spray of the roses is thrust through the knot.

The sash shown in illustration II is suitable for a miss of twelve or fourteen. The waist ribbon is formed into a narrow girdle and the bow is shaped like a butterfly. Measure the size of the waist and cut a length of the ribbon five inches longer than this measure. At the center front make two one-quarter-inch shirr tucks with one-quarter-inch space between their sewing lines. Turn one of these tucks toward the right and the other toward the left. Make two more tucks at each side, at spaces of an inch and one-half. Draw the center tucks up to half the width of the ribbon (the ribbon illustrated was six and one-half inches wide) and sew a piece of featherbone, three and one-quarter inches long, underneath. Draw each of the two tucks at each side of the center to two and three-quarter and two inches respectively. Half-way between the center front and the back make one shirr tuck at each side and place a two-inch-long bone under it. There is no boning at the back, the ribbon ends are plaited together,

turned under and hemmed; a hook is sewed on one end and an eye on the other.

The butterfly bow, divided so its construction may be seen, is shown in illustration III. In making this bow it is not sewed, but coarse cotton is wound around each loop as it is formed. Begin with the right-hand loops and end, making first the upper half of the body of the butterfly. This measures six inches on the outer edge of the ribbon. Form this into an "ear" loop by holding the outside edge of the ribbon at three inches, in the left hand, and with the right gather closely together across the cut end and again at six inches, including, also, the inside edge of the ribbon between these two points. Make the wings of the butterfly in the same way, but make these loops measure eleven inches each. Wind each loop as it is made and tie the cotton to hold them securely. Leave a sash end nearly long enough to reach to the bottom of the skirt. Cut a piece of ribbon eight inches long. Cut the ends diagonally, lay the short piece evenly on the end of the sash and tie a knot at the center of the short piece, taking the two together as if they were one. The left-hand loops and end are made in the same way, except that the large "wings" are made first. Allow a short end of ribbon before beginning the loops, and use this to wrap across and join the two parts of the bow. Sew the bow to one end of the girdle.

The sash shown in illustration IV is a very simple one. The ribbon is brought around the waist and tied in a double knot at the back. A second piece of ribbon fourteen inches long has its ends trimmed diagonally and a knot tied near each end. The middle of this shorter ribbon is laid across the tied sash just below the knot and each end is passed first over, then under, the waist ribbon and pinned to the dress above the waist. The detail of the ribbon arrangement is shown in illustration V.

A suspender girdle, to wear with one of the long-waisted French dresses, is shown in illustration VI. Two widths of three-inch-wide Dresden ribbon, overhanded together, form the girdle, which has three clusters of shirr tucks at the front, each supported by featherbone. There are no sash-ends at the back; the girdle is finished by gathering the ribbon to form a heading at each end, concealing the hooks and eyes and bones. A length of

Dresden ribbon. The bones at the front and back are each six and three-quarter inches long, and the ribbon must be fitted to the figure, pinning it to the waist of the gown at the desired height and pinning it together at the front. Seams must be pinned in at the sides and at the back. Stitch these seams and cut the surplus ribbon away. Make two rows of gathers at the center front and at each seam and tack to featherbone. The bone at the side is

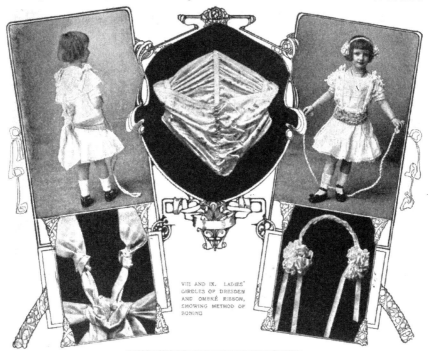

VIII AND IX. LADIES'
GIRDLES OF DRESDEN
AND OMBRÉ RIBBON,
SHOWING METHOD OF
BONING

IV AND V. SASH FOR SMALL CHILD, AND DETAIL SHOWING HOW TO AR- RANGE IT.

VI. SUSPENDER GIRDLE OF DRESDEN
RIBBON
VII. HAIR ORNAMENT

ribbon crosses each shoulder and knot-rosettes of baby rib-bon are sewed at front and back where the shoulder straps join the girdle; rosettes are placed at the shoulders also.

Knot-rosettes are used on the ribbon hair ornament, that is shown in detail in illus-tration VII. Three and one-half yards of ribbon are used for each rosette. It is tied in knots at intervals of three and one-half inches; the entire length is then folded evenly from knot to knot, forming a little bundle with knots at both ends. Tie the coarse cotton about the center, then tie a half-yard length of the ribbon around, letting the ends hang loose. These are to tie to a curl or a lock of the hair to hold the ornament in place. Three strands of the ribbon are braided together, a length of wire tape folded inside one of them, so that the band may be shaped to the head.

Two girdles suitable for ladies are shown on this page. The upper one is made of four lengths of three-inch-wide

three and one-half inches long. At the left side leave the rib-bon two inches beyond the cen-ter front, and do not join the rows here, but turn under and tack each end to form a point.

The girdle at the bottom of the page is made of two rows of shaded green ribbon, each six and one-half inches wide, and joined together with the darkest shade at the center. Three rows of shirr tucks are made at the back with three tucks in each row. The two outer clusters meet the center one at the bottom and slant an inch and one-half away from it at the top. The shaping at the waistline is managed in the girdle shown by making six shirr tucks at each side of the front closing. Each tuck is one-eighth of an inch deep and each successive tuck is shorter than the one before it. The tucks at both sides form a diamond-shaped shirring when the belt is finished, and draw it in snugly at the waist. Bones and hooks and eyes are placed at each end.

FOREWORDS REGARDING

By LAURA R. SEIPLE

THE fashionable sleeve is the elbow sleeve which is met by a long glove. When gloves are not worn, little lingerie sleeves are tacked in extending from the elbow to the hand. With these very often a lingerie chemisette to match is worn, especially when the waist is made in surplice effect. Sleeves show decided puffs at the top, expressing fulness rather than width.

We still see very full skirts and shall, in all probability, continue to do so during the early fall. Short bodices in contrasting colors have long postilion tabs and pointed revers, deep turned-back cuffs finishing the sleeves at the elbow. Much embroidery is employed upon tabs, revers and cuffs, and when vests are worn they also show quantities of elaborate hand-work. Linen gowns are made with tight-fitting vests, which must be closed at all times to give the desired effect.

Nothing heretofore woven can compare with the exquisite perfection of the silk-and-wool voiles of the present time. To be properly made a soft taffeta foundation should form the lining and the voile should be carefully draped over it so as not to lose any of its lightness and transparency. Of all summer materials for semi-dressy occasions voile is by far the most popular, and especially the pale shades of all-silk voile.

There are several decidedly new colors being introduced in Paris and Vienna, among them are *chair* (flesh color), tarnished copper, soleil-bronze (sun bronze), Parma violet, brick pink and mercury. All the pretty new fabrics of the year are being shown in these tones.

The redingote with tight-fitting bodice and long, loose skirt effect is smartened with a waistcoat of an-

tique floral cretonne, displaying lovely roses of soft pink and heliotrope shades tied with ribbons of gold thread deftly woven under the surface of the fabric. These materials may be obtained from first-class upholstering

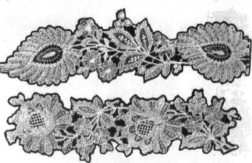

POINT DE GAUZE BANDING

establishments, and there are many very lovely patterns from which to choose. Light-weight tapestry is also a desirable material for vests, cuffs, collars and revers.

Straw flowers woven upon net and tiny colored beads outlining figures in laces and fabrics are making a rather sensational clamor for recognition among the novel trimmings. The work is difficult and, unless carefully executed, the result is not pleasing. However, every year must introduce its freaks of fashion.

Evening dresses and ball gowns are more bewitching than ever. There are some exquisite new crea-

POINT DE GAUZE FLOUNCE APPLIQUÉ

FASHIONS AND FABRICS

tions in lace, fine nets, white needlework and embroidered tissues for ball gowns. Pineapple gauze with appliqué designs in rose, lavender, yellow and blue are extremely

LINGERIE BANDING FOR WASH DRESSES

attractive and make up to advantage with little or no trimming whatever, being sufficiently lovely in themselves.

Chiffon voile is perhaps the most charming of the newer fabrics of the season. It comes in the finest and most sheer quality, patterned with tiny figures or floral designs in delicate hue, and of ten showered with elaborately embroidered scrolls in heavy work. Another exquisite pattern is colored in broché tones.

IMITATION IRISH CROCHET APPLIQUÉ

Of the heavier and more serviceable materials for street wear, there is a soft finished canvas which resembles crash but is very much finer in texture. This fabric made up with encrustations of heavy lace or heavy hand-embroidery upon colors is very effective and in excellent taste for all-day wear.

Heavy lace motifs, medallions, bands and all-overs in French and Irish crochet, point d'Alençon Escurials, silk Cluny and heavy Chantilly are reigning patterns for the moment. Irish crochet has been folded up and laid aside for three successive seasons only to be dragged out again before we have the opportunity to appreciate its loss. When Irish crochet was introduced four years ago, it was not thoroughly understood by many that it was to be the queen lace of the future, or for several years at least. Time has proven this, and now France is combining tape and Irish hand-work so cleverly that detection from the real is difficult unless closely examined.

Conspicuous among elegant lace for wraps is point Venise. This is not likely to become common until some manufacturer produces a good imitation. The few now on the market are so unlike the genuine that she who possesses a real point Venise garment may be assured of exclusiveness.

Very attractive lace coats are made of silk tape joined in Renaissance patterns. These garments come in cream color, white and deep écru, and all ready to mount on a silk lining.

FASHIONABLE FRIVOLITIES

By LAURA R. SEIPLE

A GREATER number of fancy shoes are being worn than ever before. A woman is not considered smartly gotten up if her shoes do not match in color the costume she wears. Since the coloring of leather has become a fine art it is possible to have shoes match almost any gown to-day, providing one cares to pay the price. Gray, tan, dark-blue, red and green shoes laced with wide ribbons of the same color are particularly stylish and set off a white costume wonderfully.

Marvels of beauty are the little gauze fans decorated by hand and mounted upon ivory sticks. Watteau scenes with every figure perfectly done have lace or spangled edges. Garlands of delicately painted flowers trail from one panel to the next in graceful sweeping clusters, and tiny jewels glisten here and there in the centers of little flowers filling and falling over the sides of long-handled baskets made of fine gold braid. All lace fans in black Chantilly or escurial are mounted upon ebony and teak wood, while white lace is invariably

In the centers are little sachets that waft sweetest whiffs of perfume. Among the novel fans there is one containing a tiny mirror in one side-stick and a powder puff no larger than the thumb nail in the other.

The party reticule is gaining in proportions. Quite the same shape is retained in handsome brocade and hand-painted bags, but more lavish are becoming the trimmings and fittings, for the smart opera bag comes fitted nowadays. There are bags containing separate compartments for cards, change, gloves, fan and powder puff; while more elaborate ones have beautifully mounted opera-glasses and a tiny gold drinking-cup which collapses and fits snugly in a little pocket made for it.

There is nothing more dainty to finish the filmy vest and half sleeves worn with simple gowns of taffeta and checked voile than this narrow lace of fine mesh and perfection in pattern. Another vogue for baby Valenciennes is noticed in its use on entire blouses where it is fulled and applied in wheel and scroll designs, sometimes alternating with

attached to mother-of-pearl sticks. Little flower fans close up to resemble a bouquet of freshly plucked blossoms.

pin-tucks, which, by the way, seem to run most conveniently as a guide for the sewing on of the lace.

FOR FEMININE FANCIES

Very elegant blouses are made of sheer handkerchiefs—a dozen of which can be had for three dollars; although only nine are required for a person of ordinary size. The model is first selected and the handkerchiefs laid on the pattern. The edges should be carefully fagoted together, or, when there is a lace edge, sew the two hems together, allowing the lace to stand out between the seams. The effect is very novel and dressy. Handkerchiefs with embroidered edges may be joined by a variety of fancy stitches, and very attractive are the blouses fashioned of them.

Exquisite little collar and cuff sets are found in numbers in the well-selected summer outfit. One of the most noticeable features of the new cuffs is the increased depth, due to the change of the modish sleeve. English eyelet, Irish crochet, Irish point and filet come in a variety of shapes and all so attractive that one scarcely knows which to choose when the number to be owned must be limited.

Stiff linen collars have taken on a new shape and style this summer. They are made to fit the neck snugly and button with two jeweled buttons at the back. To somewhat soften the severity dainty little

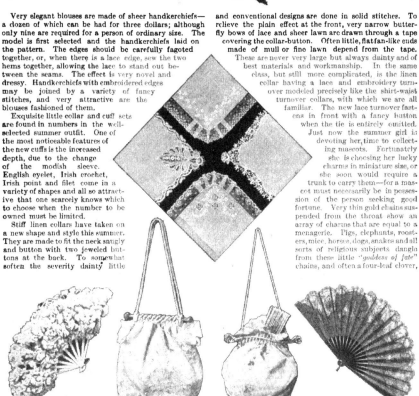

and conventional designs are done in solid stitches. To relieve the plain effect at the front, very narrow butterfly bows of lace and sheer lawn are drawn through a tape covering the collar-button. Often little, flat fan-like ends made of mull or fine lawn depend from the tape. These are never very large but always dainty and of best materials and workmanship. In the same class, but still more complicated, is the linen collar having a lace and embroidery turnover modeled precisely like the shirt-waist turnover collars, with which we are all familiar. The new lace turnover fastens in front with a fancy button when the tie is entirely omitted.

Just now the summer girl is devoting her time to collecting lucky mascots. Fortunately she is choosing her lucky charms in miniature size, or she soon would require a trunk to carry them—for a mascot must necessarily be in possession of the person seeking good fortune. Very thin gold chains suspended from the throat show an array of charms that are equal to a menagerie. Pigs, elephants, roosters, mice, horses, dogs, snakes and all sorts of religious subjects dangle from these little "goddess of fate" chains, and often a four-leaf clover,

turnover tops with pointed and scalloped edges are highly in favor. English eyelet embroidery and padded leaves   nearly three times the size of the pendants, is enclosed in a crystal disk and hangs from the center of the chain.

MILLINERY
FOR LATE SUMMER

ON THE Front Cover of this number of THE DESIGNER is shown a jaunty little polo turban, made of glossy black straw and trimmed with a single black wing. The polo turban has proved so convenient for all kind of wear that its popularity, contrary to general belief, has lasted throughout the summer.

The first hat shown on page 381 is a Continental shape of white Japanese straw. The crown is encircled with a band of black velvet, and white violets supply the trimming. The second hat on the same page is made of white horsehair, and is trimmed with white grosgrain ribbon.

On page 383 are shown two serviceable and stylish hats, the first of which is made of a black horsehair plateau, and is trimmed with pink and dark-red roses. The second is one of the new wide-brimmed sailors of brown straw, and is trimmed with brown grosgrain ribbon.

The hat on page 386 is a dark-blue straw, and is trimmed with blue taffeta and yellow and white roses.

A very pretty hat is pictured on page 387, and is made of Battenberg lace on a wire foundation. Ostrich-plumes of blended white and deep rose and deep-red roses supply the trimming. The second hat on the same page is a polo turban of lavender novelty straw, the crown being of white chip. A cluster of white roses is the only decoration.

At the head of this page are illustrated four handsome hats. The first at the left is of white chiffon, and is trimmed with a white aigret, white plumes and Irish crochet.

The second hat is made of black fiber. A wreath of large, loose-petaled white roses encircles the crown and a cluster of the flowers is placed at the back.

The third hat is made of black horsehair, and is trimmed with black plumes and black Liberty satin ribbon.

The last hat in the group is a plateau of white horsehair, and is trimmed with light-blue velvet ribbon, pale-pink and white roses and forget-me-nots.

The first hat shown in color on page 423 is a polo turban made entirely of small white flowers, and trimmed with two lavender ostrich-plumes.

Hat No. 2 is a picturesque model of green paper straw, trimmed with large pale-pink roses and their foliage. A half wreath of the roses is placed under the brim.

The stylish hat No. 3 is a horsehair plateau made of two shades of blue, and having the brim bound with black velvet. Blue plumes are the only decoration used.

No. 4 is one of the Dresden models, now in such vogue. It is made of Tuscan straw, and is trimmed with pale-green ribbon and pink roses.

No. 5 is a black straw plateau, and is trimmed with white owl heads and black-and-orange quills.

No. 6 is a wide-brimmed coral-red straw, trimmed with pink roses and coral-red ribbon, the combination being one of the popular oddities of the present season.

No. 7 is made of fancy heliotrope straw, the brim being outlined with a piping of heliotrope velvet. White roses trim the crown, and a cluster of the flowers with two long, shaded heliotrope ostrich-plumes is placed at the turned-up back of the hat, one of the plumes curling over the brim.

No. 8, on page 424, is a white chip bent into curves at the back, where a rosette of white satin ribbon and a cluster of white plumes are placed, and is trimmed with shorter plumes and white roses with dark-green foliage.

No. 9 is a charming model of white lace arranged transparently on a wire foundation. It is trimmed with clusters of lilacs, pink roses and forget-me-nots, a few loops of black velvet ribbon contrasting pleasingly with the lighter hues of the flowers and the white of the chiffon.

No. 10 is a black chip, trimmed with white plumes, small field-daisies, buttercups and corn-flowers.

No. 11 is made of a combination of white French chip and white Valenciennes lace. Clusters of small white roses and loops and bows of white satin ribbon supply the remainder of the trimming.

The medium-height crown of No. 12 is made entirely of forget-me-nots, while the brim is draped with pale-blue and white malines. Under the brim, *choux* of the malines rest against the hair of the wearer. Blue ostrich-plumes are attached at the right side, and are held by a filigree silver buckle.

Very quaint and reminiscent of 1860 is the bonnet-shaped hat, No. 13. It is made of white chip, and under the brim in front are massed pale-pink hyacinths. The low crown is trimmed with pale-pink Liberty satin ribbon and white lace, and strings of the ribbon are tied under the chin at the left side.

No. 14 is a handsome all-white hat, formed of a white horsehair plateau. The center of the plateau is cut out and a wire crown, covered first with chiffon, then with lace appliqué, is inserted. The appliqué extends upon the brim, and the right side is trimmed with white plumes.

No. 15 is a stylish polo turban made of pale-blue malines worked with small straw beads. Between the brim and the crown is a fold of straw-colored Liberty satin, and a twist of the satin at the left side holds a pale-blue wing.

422

MAKING A PLATEAU HAT

By MARTHA KINSMAN

O F T H E many varieties of materials used for making t h e head-gear for the spring and summer seasons not any have proved so successful as the plateau in its many combinations. The reason for its popularity is not difficult to find, as it can

THE COMPLETED HAT

be so easily draped into any shape to suit the wearer, the result giving the touch of individuality so much desired. The plateau can be draped to form the smallest bonnet or toque as well as the larger hat.

The hat used in the illustration is made of a Neapolitan plateau and is faced with embroidered hair braid. Any combination of shades or colors may be used. Saxon-blue, mulberry, heliotrope, white or Tuscan colors, in fact, any of the new shades, look well made up in this style.

The materials required to make the pictured hat are one plateau twenty inches in diameter, eight yards of hair braid one and one-half inches wide, four yards of maline, two yards of velvet ribbon No. 12, two bunches of foliage, three bunches of lilacs, one bunch of roses and two bunches of large rosebuds.

By referring to figure II it will be seen that the plateau is shaped on the high band which is such an important feature of the hats this season. To make this band, cut two pieces of wire twenty-two inches in length; lap until they measure nineteen inches. These wires are used for the top and bottom of the band which forms the crown of the hat. It is narrower in front and gradually widens to the back. The height of the band measures one and three-quarter inches in front, two inches at the side front, two and one-quarter inches at the side and two and one-half inches at the back and side back. One wire is added between the top and lower edge of the band. Cover the band smoothly with cape net, sew it to the wires, using a buttonhole-stitch. Next cover both sides with chiffon or taffeta silk and bind the lower edge with velvet.

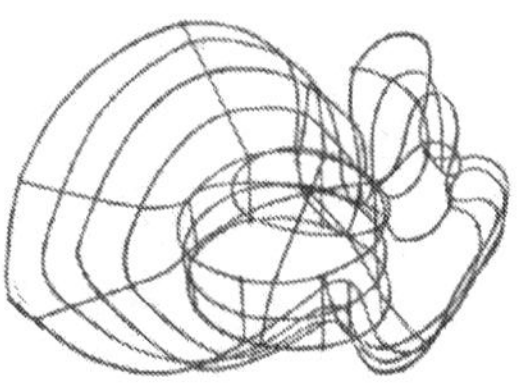

We next turn our attention to the plateau, which may be either wired and afterward draped on the high band, which is the usual way; or the wire frame may be made first, as shown in figure 1; in which case the plateau is pinned in the preferred position to the frame and then sewed to it, using a buttonhole-stitch. The frame is made

FIGURE I.—THE WIRE FRAME

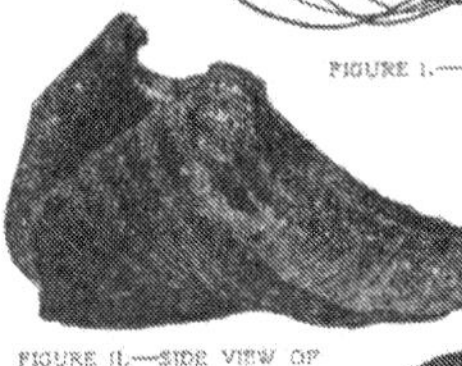

FIGURE II.—SIDE VIEW OF COVERED FRAME

FIGURE III.—FRONT VIEW OF COVERED FRAME

in the form of a plateau. It is nineteen inches in diameter; this allows the plateau, which measures twenty inches across, to extend one-half inch from the edge wire. One wire extends from the front to the back, one from side to side, and then there are two diagonal wires; all are of equal length and are fastened to the edge wire to form equal spaces. The edge wire measures fifty-seven inches.

Add three extra wires so as to form one-and-one-quarter-inch spaces between them. Add one other wire around the center of the crown. Next measure five and one-half inches for the width of the brim in front, at which point fasten the wire to the front of the band. Beginning at the front, measure twenty-four inches for the right side of the frame and fasten to the left side of the top of the crown. Curve up the wires high at the back. The left side is formed into curves, as clearly shown in figure III. Curve the back of the frame well forward over the crown. Place the plateau in position to the frame, and sew it to all the wires. Next point the frame in front and bend the hat down over the band at the back and otherwise shape it to suit the wearer. The hat is now ready for the facing, which is first covered with four thicknesses of maline and then with embroidered hair braid sewed on in rows.

We next turn our attention to the trimming. First branch the roses with foliage in a cluster and sew to the hat at the left side, then add a branch of lilac; near the front at the right side sew a cluster of buds with more lilacs, filling the entire front with the flowers and foliage, as shown in the picture of the completed hat at the head of this page. Drape the band with a full width of maline. A cluster of small lilacs fills in the space at the right side and a bunch of rosebuds with foliage at the left side. Make a large bow of the ribbon velvet and sew between the two clusters of flowers. Extend the foliage well up in the folds of the plateau at the back.

A novel way of trimming these hats is to use very small flowers, such as forget-me-nots, small buds or lilies-of-the-valley, or part of each. The flowers are branched in small wreaths about ten inches long, joined together with a button rose or buds. If the hat is trimmed in this way the crown should first be banked with plenty of maline, then lay the chain of wreaths across and use a few for trimming the band. Give the wreaths the appearance of extending through the hat.

For the lining, cut a piece of silk about five inches square, sew in the crown of the hat with a few long stitches. Take another piece of silk about five-eighths of a yard long and five inches wide, hem one side and run a shirring ribbon in the hem, using narrow taffeta ribbon for the purpose; fold over one end about an inch, and, working from right to left, sew in with a few long stitches. Join the ends at back and fasten ends of shirring ribbon. Cut a slit in hem directly in front; draw up shirring and tie ribbon in a small bow.

425

FOR PRINCE AND PRINCESS BABIKINS

By ALINE DE CARDEVA

MANY are the clever appointments modern ingenuity has devised for the health and comfort of the new baby. And never have these little accessories reached such a degree of perfection as now, each article seemingly more dainty than the last.

When the baby is only a few minutes old he is placed upon a tiny scale decorated with lace and ribbon, and made soft as a bird's nest with wadded satin. If the indicator stops at the figure seven, he is a normal child, although many infants weighing much less at birth are healthy babies. The nurse weighs her charge every third day until he is one month old, then once a week for six or eight weeks, after which time every three to four weeks during the year, or until the baby has outgrown the basket. The normal baby at birth should measure twenty inches in length, and at the end of the first year twenty-eight inches. The average length of the baby-basket is thirty-three inches without the padding and decoration. At the end of the fourteenth day of the wee member's life only one-half pound additional to his birth weight will register. But no alarm should be caused by this fact, for it is in accordance with nature's decree that weight is lost during the first three days of earthly existence. At the end of the third week another half-pound should have been gained, and so on until the eighth week, when one pound each month or an average weight of twenty pounds at the end of the first year should have been attained.

The fairy godmother could not have wielded her magic wand more effectively than when she caused the inspiration that produced the dainty crib displayed, which is all enamel and gold, and draped with costly lace over palest silk, pink or blue. The crib is made of willow and swings on a frame constructed of the same material. The whole is enameled white and decorated with gilding. On the bottom of the crib is a tiny mattress made of finest white hair and covered with silk rubber. The sides are tufted with the same white hair and covered with

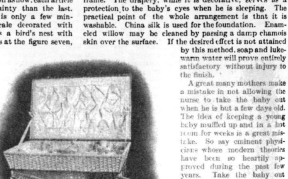

COMBINED HAMPER AND BABY-BASKET

fulled silk, finished at the top with a point d'esprit ruffle. The canopy is also of point d'esprit over silk, and the flounce is repeated around the edge. Puffs of net held in place by loops of wide ribbon ornament the top of the frame. The drapery, while it is decorative, serves as a protection to the baby's eyes when he is sleeping. The practical point of the whole arrangement is that it is washable. China silk is used for the foundation. Enameled willow may be cleaned by passing a damp chamois skin over the surface. If the desired effect is not attained by this method, soap and lukewarm water will prove entirely satisfactory without injury to the finish.

A great many mothers make a mistake in not allowing the nurse to take the baby out when he is but a few days old. The idea of keeping a young baby muffled up and in a hot room for weeks is a great mistake. So say eminent physicians whose modern theories have been so heartily approved during the past few years. Take the baby out

THE DRAPED CRADLE

for an airing at the end of the first week. Let him breathe plenty of fresh air to make his little lungs strong. Of course, this does not mean that the baby should be exposed to inclement weather. A safe rule is thus laid down by a famous physician: "In summer take the baby for his first ride when he is one week old, and send him out every day afterward when the weather is fine. In the fall and winter, when the temperature does not

COLLAPSIBLE BATHTUB

exceed sixty to sixty-five degrees Fahrenheit, he should be one month old before he is given his first open-air experience."

The newcomer who has an indulgent father rolls forth in an English carriage. The construction of this little palace on wheels reaches the nearest to perfection of anything in the coach line previously built. The springs are finest steel, and adjusted in such a manner that every motion of the wee vehicle produces a gentle sway. Like papa's big automobile, the wheels have rubber tires, and the cushions are upholstered in champagne-colored suède. The bed of the carriage is enameled maroon color with hair-lines of g o l d . Baby's monogram in contrasting shades sometimes adorns the sides. Enamel leather is employed for the covering of the hood-top and harmonizes with the tone of the body of the coach. The English carriage is becoming more and more popular in this country, and a close second is the well-made wicker go-cart with fine springs and rubber-tired wheels.

Along with all the rest of the modern nursery equipments, the wee one must own a bathtub. Not a metal or porcelain tub, but a collapsible rubber one. A bamboo frame, constructed of four poles crossed and pivoted, stands twenty-seven inches from the floor when in use. The basin,

THE FIRST SET OF TOILET ARTICLES

THE HYGIENIC GO-CART

THE ENGLISH COACH

or tub, is made of white pliable rubber, having an outlet for the water at one end. A miniature towel-rack and pockets for brushes, soap and sponge at either end of the frame complete the handy arrangement.

Baby must also have an individual washstand. Porcelain, highly glazed, furnishes an ideal composition for nursery furniture. Owing to its resistance to fire, water and all acids, as well as its sanitary properties, porcelain is generally considered preferable to wood employed in the s a m e capacity. T h e miniature washstand is equipped with a double basin, which fits in an opening in the top of the frame. A pitcher, puff-box and soap-dish are of the same material.

Of no small importance is the little one's toilet-set, which must be chosen with care to insure daintiness in both shape and decoration. The color-scheme of the layette should be carried out, and if there are forget-me-nots or roses embroidered on the linen, the same blossoms should be repeated in the decoration of the toilet articles as nearly as possible. A complete set includes tray, puff-box, soap-dish, camel's - hair brush and fine comb. A little rotary rattle having a teething ring attached to the handle is often counted as a necessary adjunct. For baby's first toilet-set, celluloid or ivory is far more desirable than china or crystal. Either is light of weight, easily handled and almost unbreakable.

As much latitude as one desires may be given the clothes-hamper. A very charming hamper is made of willow and contains two separate compartments, one for toilet articles and another for baby's tiny garments. The tray occupies the top of the hamper, while two little doors at the side disclose the space designed for the wardrobe. Soft silk over delicately perfumed cotton, and held down by tiny bows of baby-ribbon, finishes the bottom of both compartments and the lid. Both sides of the hamper-doors are decorated with ribbon bows, and the fittings of the toilet basket are replete with frills of dainty lace, beading and rosettes of narrow satin ribbon.

THE SCALE FOR WEIGHING THE BABY

(8090)   (9356 and 8949)   (9299 and 9062)   (7403)

NEW DESIGNS IN UNDERWEAR

With Illustrations from Drawings by LOUISE HUDSON

MONG the new designs for underwear the chemise in various styles appears prominently; not that this particular garment is new, by any means, but because every now and then it is banished from the up-to-date outfit, only to be restored to favor before many months pass. In the group of garments displayed at the head of this page two chemises are pictured. The first, at the left, is made by No. 8090, and can be made with or without a front closing. An inverted plait at the back below the waistline gives extra fulness to the skirt. As pictured the chemise is made of nainsook, and is trimmed with insertion. The chemise at the right has a shallow yoke. The design used is 7403, and it is here developed in nainsook and trimmed with German Val lace. The yoke is made of all-over embroidery.

The surplice corset-cover shown on the second figure from the left is suitable for development in flouncing. It is made by 9356, of fine nainsook flouncing. The petticoat worn with it is five gored and in round length, and is formed of three gathered, bias, overlapping sections which form a flounce that may be gathered to or buttoned on a five-gored upper part having an inverted box plait or gathers at the back, or which may be finished in habit style. The design is 8949, from twenty to thirty-four inches waist measure. It is here made of blue taffeta, lace trimmed.

On the next figure is shown a corset-cover made by 9299, which has a surplice back, and fronts that may be gathered or dart-fitted. It is here made of fine cambric and is trimmed with Valenciennes lace and edging. This garment, also the other corset-cover and the chemises shown on this page are from thirty-two to forty-four inches bust measure. With the corset-cover just described is worn a seven-gored petticoat made by 9062, from twenty to thirty-six inches waist measure, and is here made of white cambric trimmed with insertion and eyelet embroidery.

The first figure on page 429 wears a corset-cover made by 1044. The garment has a fitted back, and may be made with or without puff sleeves. It is here developed in nainsook and has simulated yoke pieces of tucking, eyelet embroidery and narrow Valenciennes lace. The five-gored petticoat is made by 8523, of English longcloth, and is trimmed with banding and edging of imitation English eyelet-work. It is suitable for women from twenty to thirty-four inches waist measure.

The second figure wears a corset-cover of fine cambric trimmed with Torchon insertion and edging, also beading run with satin ribbon. The garment, made by 1078, has shoulder seams only, and may have a square or round neck and box plait or hem closing. A basque skirt is provided for it, also puff sleeves. With it in the present instance is shown a pair of closed umbrella drawers, with a shaped belt, made by 1043, of cambric, and trimmed with insertion and edging. The drawers are made in sizes from twenty-two to thirty-four inches waist measure.

The center figure wears a corset-cover made by 9358, of nainsook, trimmed with tucking, swiss insertion and edging. The neck may be made square or round, and the back is fitted by a few gathers at the waistline. The open drawers worn with this corset-cover are made by 1017. They are here made of cambric, trimmed with insertion and edging, and are suitable for women from twenty-two to thirty-six inches waist measure.

The close-fitting bodice now in vogue has created a demand for tailor-fitting underwear, hence the corset-cover shown on the next figure is certain of popularity. It is made by 9216, and has a fitted back as well as front. The neck may be made high, low round or square, or in V shape, and the garment may be made with or without full-length or shield sleeves. It is suitable for women from thirty-two to forty-six inches bust measure, and is here made of cambric and trimmed with ribbon-run beading, insertion and

428

(1044 and 8523)   (1073 and 1043)   (9358 and 1017)   (9316 and 9123)   (1080 and 1073)

SOME NEW-STYLE TRIMMINGS AND PATTERNS FOR DAINTY LINGERIE

lace. The seven-gored petticoat is made by 9123, from twenty to thirty-four inches waist measure. The material employed is rose-colored taffeta glacé, trimmed with lace.

The last figure in the group wears a corset-cover suitable for development in flouncing. The design is 1080, and it is here made of embroidered flouncing with straps of white satin ribbon. The French open drawers worn with it are

quarter length bishop sleeves. The design is 8784, and it is here developed in nainsook with trimming of wide and narrow Valenciennes insertion and pale-blue satin ribbon. The third gown may be tucked or gathered at the neck edge, and may have a high or Dutch round or square neck and full or three-quarter length bishop sleeves. It is made by 8861, of English long-cloth, and is trimmed with insertion.

(8994)   (8784)   (8861)   (8927)   (8317)

NIGHTGOWNS WHICH ARE AS PRETTY AS THEY ARE COMFORTABLE

made by 1073, from twenty-two to thirty-six inches waist measure. The corset-covers on page 429 are made in sizes from thirty-two to forty-four inches bust measure.

The five nightgowns pictured on this page differ widely in design. The first, made by 8994, is made of cambric and has a round yoke of tucking. Insertion forms the trimming. The second gown is a picturesque garment with Pompadour neck, tucked or gathered fronts and full or three-

When made with high neck it is finished with a turn-down collar. The gown shown on the seated figure is made of cambric, and has a back yoke, extending over the shoulders, collar and cuffs of embroidery. It is made by 8927. The last gown is known as the Vassar, the Bishop or the Peasant gown, its sleeves continuing to the neck edge. It is made by 8317, of lawn, is trimmed with insertion and may have high or square neck and bishop or flowing sleeves.

A Floating Hotel for Women

By JESSIE GARWOOD FRITTS

THE "JACOB A. STAMLER"

FOR THREE brief, happy months a small fleet of gray-winged vessels snuggled close up to the pier at the foot of West Twenty-first Street, in New York harbor. Not one of the three boats made any outward pretense of being different from the other sea-craft whose placid sides are lapped by the water all day long. Yet, interested visitors—yes, and curiosity seekers, too—crowded the decks, and the fleet was pointed out to the casual observer as the unique exponent of the philanthropy of a rich man honestly trying to help his fellow-beings in general and the underpaid woman in particular.

When Mr. John Arbuckle opened his Deep Sea Hotel on February 7, 1905, over five hundred applicants for accommodations were turned away. One does not wonder that quarters so cheery and comfortable were eagerly sought, when they could be obtained for forty cents a day. The management, under the direction of Mr. Arbuckle, had carefully eliminated the bargain-counter features, by placing certain restrictions upon the would-be patrons so that the benefits of the establishment would be gained by the deserving rather than the grasping. Women who earned more than $8 a week were not eligible, and guests whose fortunes brightened while they were enjoying the hospitality of the floating inn were expected to give up their quarters to others who were still struggling to

get along on the tiniest of incomes.

Strange as it may seem, there were but a few cases of misrepresentation. Most of those who applied with the mistaken notion that cheap quarters were to be obtained with no restrictions save respectability, applauded the plan most heartily, and withdrew their applications with the best of grace as soon as the significance of the scheme was made known to them.

The *Jacob A. Stamler* was a large and handsome ship and the main deck was most inviting, with a music and reading room at one end, and the long dining-room at the other. The little office at the right of the center passageway was not the least important of the ship's appointments, and the man behind the counter was manager, captain and steward, all in one.

The big sitting-room served as common ground for the guests to meet socially, and was provided with a piano having a pianola attachment, while on a broad center-table were to be found the current magazines and newspapers. A cushion seat extended around three sides of the room, and between the square, white-curtained windows were hung good prints in neat, narrow frames. Plenty of rocking-chairs, and a bunch of bright flowers on the table, gave the room an inviting air of cozy comfort. The young women gathered there after dinner in the evenings, and were permitted

THE PLEASANT SITTING-ROOM

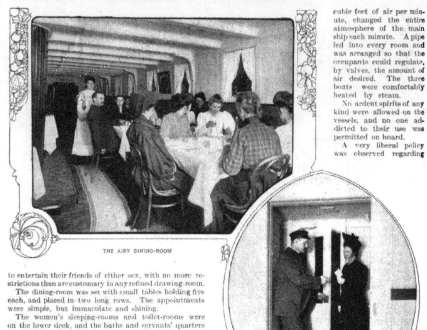

THE AIRY DINING-ROOM

PRESENTING HER
TICKET FOR SHORE
LEAVE

THE LITTLE WHITE CABIN

cubic feet of air per minute, changed the entire atmosphere of the main ship each minute. A pipe led into every room and was arranged so that the occupants could regulate, by valves, the amount of air desired. The three boats were comfortably heated by steam.

No ardent spirits of any kind were allowed on the vessels, and no one addicted to their use was permitted on board.

A very liberal policy was observed regarding to entertain their friends of either sex, with no more restrictions than are customary in any refined drawing-room.

The dining-room was set with small tables holding five each, and placed in two long rows. The appointments were simple, but immaculate and shining.

The women's sleeping-rooms and toilet-rooms were on the lower deck, and the baths and servants' quarters were below. Some of the sleeping-rooms were fitted with a bath, and no extra charge was made for these, but a slight discrimination was made by assigning them to women whose health was less vigorous, and who were most likely to be benefited by the additional comfort. In each room were two berths, and all were provided with simple toilet conveniences.

The floating hotel was, no doubt, far healthier than the ordinary city hotel or boarding-house, for sunshine, Nature's greatest purifier, shone all around the ships, which were moored in deep water, where neither sewer-gas nor the vitiated atmosphere of the crowded city could reach them.

A large fan, driving fifty thousand

amusements, and dancing and cards were both included in an evening's entertainment. Early hours were observed, however, and the electric lights were winked out promptly at ten o'clock. After this the passageways were lighted by long rows of lanterns, and a lantern in each stateroom served to light the way to bed for the belated night-owl. Permission to leave the ship in the evening was given by the manager, who wrote his name across the back of the guest's hotel ticket, and it was necessary to show this to the watchman, on returning, before one could gain admission. It was the watchman's duty to report the time of the guest's return, and the rules were rigid as to

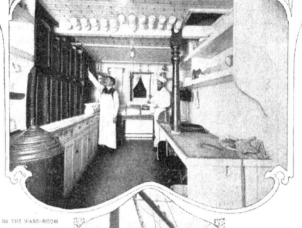

IN THE WARD-ROOM

reasonable hours being observed.

Among the anticipated summer pleasures of the Deep Sea Colony were moonlight voyages to Sandy Hook, leaving the city dock about nine o'clock P. M. and returning at five in the morning. A permanent provision for the summer was to be made on the upper deck, which had been specially fitted up for a promenade. Awnings were to be put up when desired to screen the deck from the too direct rays of the sun, and to serve as a protection from mist-laden air in the evenings.

Mr. Arbuckle took the keenest delight in the pleasure of these friends of his, and he frequently dined on the vessel and spent an evening there.

The cuisine provided good, substantial food and home-like cooking, and simply served by two neat waitresses. The breakfast menu always included a cereal, a meat course, and coffee, with muffins or toast. A luncheon menu taken at random from the week's bill of fare was fish balls, boiled potatoes, bread and butter, crullers and tea. Dinner was always in three courses, with soup, meat and two vegetables, dessert and coffee.

It would have been absurd to expect forty cents a day to cover the expense of such fare, together with the excellent accommodation for lodging. But because Mr. Arbuckle was willing to make up the deficit, more than two score and ten women, representing nearly all the

THE ORIGINATOR AND SOME OF HIS GUESTS

feminine trades and professions, were given a "lift" on the financial road, without injury to their self-respect. The women were in every case of the refined type, and their ages varied from twenty to thirty-five, with one guest sixteen, and one past fifty.

As may be imagined, the happy little community suffered keen disappointment when announcement was made about the middle of April that the floating hotel must go out of business because there was no place obtainable for docking the boat, the dock where it now lay being needed for other purposes. Great was the lamentation which went up, but of no avail, and each hard-working little woman had to pack her belongings and return to the old way of living in a stuffy hall bedroom up many stairs. That the plan was not abandoned because of lack of patronage—many of the guests would have been willing to pay twice the price asked if only the work might have gone on —is evidence that it was a feasible one, and as such is worthy of consideration not only by philanthropists who have the business woman's welfare at heart, but by others who desire to indorse the idea as a money maker. In cities adjacent to large bodies of water it would seem as if the plan might be made both pleasure-giving and profitable during the summer months. So as a valuable and novel suggestion, though its practical demonstration is no longer in existence, it is presented to DESIGNER readers.

PA'S SPECS

By HARRIET WHITNEY DURBIN

UESS you better take Henr'etty, Phœbe. Both girls are all of a squirm to go, but Henr'etty—Land o' parsnips, Pa, what in century are you a-trying to do?"

Mrs. Northup interrupted herself, irritably, as her eye alighted upon an ancient little man who was pawing wildly at a pile of mixed articles on the sewing-machine. He looked wrinkled and skimped up, like a dry old sponge. His head was almost bald, but for a lingering tuft which bristled up like a savage blue jay's crest.

"I'm a-tryin' to find them yanked specs o' mine," he snarled, his crest nodding and bobbing here and there as he dabbed into boxes and drawers.

"Well, you can't find 'em there"—his daughter's tone was positive—"leave them things alone. Look out, Pa, what you're a-doin'—there now, did anybody ever! There goes my basket an' all my buttons an' spools an' hooks an' eyes scattered all over creation. Look at 'em!"

"Yes, look at 'em—yank 'em!" The old man regarded the sewing materials he had precipitated upon the floor with a malevolent glare, and spitefully kicked a spool of blue silk under the machine. "Ef folks wasn't always possessed to hide my specs! Where's Henr'etty?"

"Henr'etty ain't come back from the store yet, an' nobody's hid your specs; you're always leavin' 'em around an' forgettin' where at—shoo, there, pa, look at you, windin' yourself up in my Hamburg! Ef you ain't enough to make a body turn yaller!"

"Here, I'll help hunt your specs, Pa." Mrs. Phœbe Clint attempted to withdraw herself from her rocking-chair, but found it difficult, as she was plump and fitted in very snugly.

"No," her father waved her back irascibly, "'tain't no use; takes you a hour to move. Nobody can't find 'em but Henr'etty." He bobbed out to the porch, muttering resentfully.

"Set still, Phœbe," counseled Mrs. Northup, "'s no use pesterin' about 'em; he'd lose 'em in a minute ef you did find 'em. We won't get half a chance to talk now you are here, an' you don't come more'n once in a century. About the girls—'course I couldn't spare both for the winter, so I reckoned you'd most likely want Henr'etty."

"Humph," Phœbe gave a little, half-doubtful grunt, "I got to get acquainted with 'em before I settle it. I haven't saw much of your girls since they've grown up. How'd you know but what I'd rather take Delia?"

"Well, I didn't," admitted Mrs. Northup, "not plumb. Of course, whichever goes'll have a mighty good start in the world, an' Henr'etty ain't as spry an' smart as Delia —ain't a patchin' to her about housekeepin'; Dely's smart as red peppers. But Henr'etty's a good little thing."

Mrs. Clint joggled comfortably back and forth in her rocker. "I'll let the whole thing wait awhile," she said, easily; "no use to settle it square off. I like a girl that's good at housekeepin'. Like as not I'll take Dely."

"Well, don't settle it till you get good an' ready," said Mrs. Northup, rising from her chair. "I got to go look after dinner. Keep an eye on Pa, Phœbe, till Henr'etty gets back; he does meddle so with everything, a body has to be at his heels every minute. Declare it's a hard job; the housework ain't a patchin' to it."

"Hurry up, Ma," hailed a brisk, blossom-cheeked maiden of eighteen, as Mrs. Northup arrived at the kitchen door, "my pies are all done, and your biscuits ain't in yet."

"Why didn't you put 'em in, then?" demanded her mother. "I couldn't hop out in a second when I was talkin' to your Aunt Phœbe."

"Had all I could 'tend to," returned the girl. "Henr'etty ought to've got here. 'S Aunt Phœbe going to take me?"

"Hope so. But I made out like I wanted her to take Henr'etty. Persuadin' Phœbe always was like trying to drive a pig. You got to make out like you want her to do just the opposite from what you do want, she's that contrary. Did you put the mushmelons in cold water?"

"No, I've got such a lot to do, and that's Hettie's job. She must be waiting for Connors to raise them nutmegs."

"Well, I wish she was here," Mrs. Northup breathed a tired sigh. "I do'no how we'd pull through a day without Henr'etty. Your gran'pa's a-stewing now about his specs; he's lost 'em again."

"He's forever-more losing 'em; he's worse than a two-year-old baby. He'd lose his head if it wasn't fast on-to him. I can't bother hunting specs; I want to run in and visit with Aunt Phœbe a bit and see if I can't wheedle her into taking me home with her."

The young lady carefully inspected her pompadour in the kitchen mirror, brushed a fluff of flour off her sleeve, and went into the sitting-room. It was not occupied. Mrs. Clint had gone out on the porch after her sister's departure, where she found her father sitting in an old armchair, looking forlorn and picking sulkily at the morning-glory leaves which danced in the glowing August sunlight.

"Aint you lonesome, Pa?" she asked cheerfully.

"'Tain't no matter ef I be." The little old man's face looked like a gnarly persimmon; his crest bristled defiantly.

"Let's you an' me go look at the flowers," his daughter suggested; "you used to be awful fond of flowers, Pa. Don't you remember the old garden at home, that you an' Ma raised, an' the phloxes an' basket flowers an' pinks an' love-in-a-puff, an' all of them?"

The old man looked up with a glimmer of brightness that clouded over again instantly. "Whut's the use?" he asked, dismally. "I couldn't see 'em good, I ain't got no specs. 'Sides, the' ain't no flowers here, only Dely's, an' she don't 'low me to tech 'em. Ef Henr'etty was here she'd git my specs."

"YES, LOOK AT 'EM—YANK 'EM!"

"Well, let's see," Phœbe looked about speculative-ly, "maybe we can find 'em; maybe they're in the parlor."

"Mebby they hain't," retorted the old man testily. "How'd they git there? Susan an' Dely raises the shingles clean off'n the roof 'f I go in there half a second, fear I'll spile the curtains, er smash their tidies an' brick-a-bats. They ain't nowhere where nobuddy but Henr'etty kin find 'em."

"Well, I reckon she'll hunt 'em when she comes," consoled Phœbe. "Her ma sent her to town to the grocery, an' she ain't back yet. Shan't we walk down the path an' set in the shade of that pretty tree a little, Pa?"

"Naw," grunted the difficult little man, "we'd tramp on some o' Dely's yanked ole vines ef we didn't p'int our toes jes' so. No-buddy can't walk on these premises. Flowers is nice ef you kin pick some, or even go smell 'em in the mornin', but Dely's so skeered o' me breakin' a leaf er something I das-sent look t'wards 'em but whut it's 'Grampa, don't you tetch them pinies,' 'Grampa, you keep away from my zeenies,' er what-somever. Henr'etty was goin' to raise me a bed of pretty-by-nights, so's I could pick 'em, but Dely she snapped up ever' eench o' ground an' wouldn't leave her hev a smidge. I ain't got nothin' I kin do, an' now I ain't got no specs to read with."

Mrs. Phœbe sat studying awhile.

"Wouldn't you like to have a little garden, Pa, to hoe an' dig in?" she asked at last. "You used to like gardening."

The old man looked up inquiringly, then shook his head.

"I reckon I'd like it all right, but I can't never. Susan she's got the back lot all laid off spang, an' raises truck, but she won't let me hoe none in it, fear I'll whack off a onion top er a eench o' sparrow-grass. I do'no weeds from mustard greens, she says, so I dassea't go a-nigh 'em. Yank everything—I wisht I's a turkle in a mud-hole, now my specs is gone."

"Pa," said Mrs. Clint, after a pause, "Susan wants me to take Henr'etty home with me—you know I'm a-goin' to take one of the girls for a great, long visit."

The little man gave his elbow a sudden angry jerk.

"Jest whut I knowed—I mout es well quit." His piping voice rose, feebly bitter. "I won't never hev no tea now, made fresh in the cup, ner no toast; Susan ain't got time to make 'em, an' Dely won't. An' they'll fry the bread all up crisp so's I can't bite it, an' not save me out a soft piece. My piller won't be warmed of cold nights; an' Dely'll run quick an' gether the aigs an' not let me git 'em. An' she won't cook me a batter cake an' let me eat it 'fore the others is baked of a mornin', when I'm holler an' empty. Henr'etty does. An' I won't *never* hev no specs an' can't read ner do nothin' but set an' set an' watch shadders an' wish I was a turkle —uh—h—h." A dismal, wailing groan ended the plaint. Mrs. Clint gazed thoughtfully at her father's fierce little topknot and weak, indignant blue eyes, and her plump brown face grew protectingly tender.

"Come 'long, Pa," said she gently, "let's us go down by the gate an' watch for Henr'etty, an' have a good talk."

Dinner was almost ready when Henrietta arrived, and Delia was making shrill lamentation concerning her sister's tardiness.

"Here's all the little dabs to do yet—melons to cut and tomatoes to slice, and the table to set, and saltcellars to fill, and the butter to be drawed out of the cistern, and fifty 'leven other things to do," she recited breathlessly, "and it's late now and not half time to do 'em all—well, Grampa can't have tea made in his cup; ain't time, and it's a messy way, anyhow; there's always half a peck of leaves in the cup to wash out. It's a nuisance, and so's Grampa. Hope *I'll* get away from the everlasting racket—that's all."

"I'll fix Grampa's tea in a minute, and help out with the other things," said Henrietta, as she hung her blue slat sunbonnet on a peg, "but I must run and look up his specs first. I had to wait so long for Joe Connors' customers, and then for him to pound up his sugar and find

his nutmegs I thought it would be sun-down time I'd get home, and I hustled till I'm all out o' breath."

The autumn day was warm; Henrietta's pink face was thickly beaded with perspiration, and her light, soft hair clung sleekly to her head with moisture; her mouth had the wide cheerfulness a naturally smiling mouth usually acquires, and her eyes held the tranquil blue gray of an evening sky. She went to her grandfather's armchair, where he always took his morning nap, slid her hand along a little ravine ,between the cushion and the chair-arm, and flourished aloft the missing spectacles.

" HERE YOU ARE, GRAMPA "

"Here you are, Grampa," she called to him, "they'd slipped down the little hollow they always do."

"Sure enough," shouted the little man, joyfully, "jest where I remember slipping 'em when I quit readin'. Thinks I, I'll jest slide 'em under there while I take a nap, an' I plumb forgot where in time I hed put the yanked things. Wull, ain't I glad—I knowed, though, Henr'etty 'd find 'em."

"Henr'etty's got a knack that beats all your 'faculty'," remarked Mrs. Clint. "Susan, I reckon I'll take your advice, after all, an' take Henr'etty home with me. I'm jest like Pa about forgettin' where I put things, an' Henr'etty'll fill a long-felt want, as the papers say."

Mrs. Northup looked suddenly dismayed.

"I honestly b'leeve I'll have to crawfish for once," said she, "an' back out o' my own advice. We'd turn plumb silly, I reckon, if Henr'etty wasn't here, 'specially when it comes to huntin' Pa's specs."

"Well, I want Henr'etty," insisted Mrs. Clint, "an' as for Pa's specs, I've fixed that. If you'd jest as soon, Susan, I'm a-going to take Pa, too."

"An' I'm a-goin', too," announced Pa, with an emphatic fling of his aggressive crest. "Phœbe's got a truck patch, an' says I kin dig in it all I'm a mind to, an' raise cucumbers, an' mebby a crook-neck squash vine, an' some pretty-by-nights in the side yard."

"Land of parsnips," ejaculated Mrs. Northup, whether in thankfulness or grief it was hard to say, "I never did!"

HOUSEKEEPING ALL OVER THE WORLD
BY LAURA B. STARR

PART VII
THE HOLLAND HOUSEWIFE

HOLLAND the land of dikes, wooden shoes and windmills, is the one in which the domestic arts flourish. Every woman of high or low degree is taught not only how to keep house, but how to do the actual work in case there is need of it. The Dutch lead simple lives and need no apostle to come out of France or any other country to teach them. The plane of living is low and very little satisfies them. The extremes of life are not so prominent as in most other countries.

The kitchen of a Dutch hausfrau is her pride and glory; the tables, walls and floors are scoured to snowy whiteness. Scrubbing seems to be a national pastime.

The copper saucepans, of which there are a great number, hang in regular order along the wall of the kitchen, reflecting objects like a mirror. Curiously enough these are for show and seldom used; the few with which the ordinary cooking is done are smaller and are kept near the fireplace, but are just as bright and shining as the others. The fireplace is tiled, and the mantel, often hung with chintz drapery, as clean and fresh as if there were no such thing as smoke or soot in the world. Shovel, tongs, poker and chains are polished to a degree of brightness; in fact, everything is as spick and span as if it had just come out of the shop.

One is soon convinced of the truth of the saying that, in the eyes of the Dutch, dirt is the worst form of sin. Laziness must come next in the category, for if indolence is allowed, dirt accumulates, and that is a condition of affairs not to be endured.

There are in every house two or three braziers of copper or brass for burning peat, which is the cheapest and principal fuel of Holland. Some of the braziers are very ornamental, particularly those that are brought into the sitting-room or the dining-room

A HOLLAND FIREPLACE

to boil water for tea or coffee, both of which are always made by the lady of the house.

As a tax must be paid for each servant over sixteen years of age, it goes without saying that the frugal Dutch manage with as few as possible; and servants must be first-class, for no one wishes to pay a tax on incapables. The man who cleans shoes, knives, lamps, etc., can be hired to come in for a certain number of hours each day; he has regular hours and customers, visiting, perhaps, four or six houses each day. Women who do heavy work and cleaning come, also, by the hour or day. Extra help for dinners and other entertainments are hired in the same way, and as they are members of the household there are no taxes to pay for them.

Many a lady of wealth and position keeps no maid, but has a woman or seamstress one or more days a week to repair her wardrobe and keep it fresh. Another woman comes once a month to do the family mending. This is, of course, when the washing is done once a month. In many households it is done only four times a year. This necessitates a very large amount of household and family linen, all of which is part of a bride's outfit. Lines are hung in the attic and the soiled linen is laid over them to prevent mildew or further soiling, as might be the case if it was packed in baskets. In all the cities and towns the washing is sent to laundries, but in the country, the peasant woman washes in the nearest stream, kneeling in a box or often on the cold stones, and dries her linen on the stones or bushes.

The Dutch love of home is proverbial; the long winters, the persistent rains, the dampness and variableness of the climate prevent the outdoor life common in countries where one may depend upon the weather with more certainty. These conditions have engendered a delightful domestic and strong

437

affection for one's own fireside. Given this state of things with the Dutch temperament and it naturally follows that the home will first of all be comfortable, and then as handsomely adorned as individual taste and means will permit. The women pride themselves upon the neatness of their homes and the beauty and elegance of their furniture to an extent not to be imagined by those who change and discard annually.

Cupboards and cabinets abound in Holland, for there must be some place to keep the great quantities of bric-à-brac, much of which is inherited. As no one seems ever to lose or get rid of an article, however insignificant, the accumulation in course of time becomes appalling. Racks for pipes, steins and plates are numerous; some are beautifully carved, others plain as to frame, but decorated more or less with paintings.

As some of the cupboards are hung high on the wall, and as the beds are far too high to step into, a short step-ladder is a necessary article of furniture, and it is amazing how decorative it becomes with carving and painting. In fact, even the commonest piece of furniture is treated in a decorative manner. Everything in a peasant's house is primitive, but it is also quaint. The seats of the rush-bottomed chairs are painted while the frame is decorated with vines and

BEDS BUILT IN THE WALL

QUAINT SILVER OF HOLLAND

A DUTCH INTERIOR OF THE BETTER CLASS

flowers in red, blue and green. Dower-chests, cabinets and other pieces are painted in rude fashion with flowers and figures. A three-legged folding table is painted brown and the whole top covered with scrolls, flowers and birds in the gaudiest coloring.

The Dutch woman, whatever her station, dearly loves a footstool, and no one ever sits down without having one offered as well as a chair. There are two kinds, with an infinite variety of each. The shape of the ordinary

housestool is familiar to us, but not the elaborate carving with which it is covered. Footstools of perforated metal and openwork carving have inside a tiny brazier to hold the smoldering peat.

The bed of the Dutch peasant is a curious one. It is often found by letting down a sort of trap-door in the wall, which discloses an opening like a cupboard without shelves. In here we find two great, soft, downy feather beds, one to sleep on and the other for covering. As they are four feet from the floor, the necessity for the small step-ladder will be seen; babies and small children are safely tucked away in a manger built across the foot.

In some of the old Dutch inns several beds of this description will be discovered let into the walls of one room, thus economizing space but at the same time doing away with any sort of privacy.

The Brittany peasant sleeps in a cupboard in the wall also; but it is a larger cupboard, and has, even in the houses of the very poor, elaborate and beautifully carved folding doors to shut it in.

In the houses of north Holland the walls are tiled from floor to ceiling with white tiles having a delicate blue figure in the center of the square; a blue-and-white border gives a fine finish to a charming effect. In one house the tiles

A DUTCH WOMAN IN COSTUME

SOME ODD ARTICLES OF FURNITURE

A YOUNG
DUTCH WOMAN

were all different, though all were of Biblical subjects. For instance, one gets the story of Samuel in a series of pictures; the Creation and the Expulsion from the Garden of Eden in another, while single tiles show Moses with the Tablet of Commandments, Jonah and the Whale, the Wicked Boys and the Bald-Headed Man, and the Feast of the Loaves and Fishes.

The broad, hospitable chimney has a huge hood extending well out into the room; this is tiled and finished with a band of wooden carving, dark with the smoke of two centuries. Four tiles on one side make the picture of a bird in a cage, and on the other side four others make a jolly old clock. A great portion of the wall opposite the door is taken up with small carved cupboards having small doors of panels and spindles.

The cradle in Friesland is a thing of joy, carved and painted, and rests upon a dais from which it is never moved. The mother rocks it as she moves about her work, by means of a stout cord attached to it and running through a pulley in the ceiling above, the cord being long enough to reach to the farthest corner of the room, so that the mother is literally always in touch with the child. In the illustration at the top of page 438 a cradle of this kind with the cord attached is shown, while at the head of the opposite page is pictured the quaintest of baby tenders, which seems to be a combination of go-cart and high chair, and which, like nearly all articles of Holland manufacture, is sufficiently substantial in construction to outlast several generations of infants.

In it the little one sits safe and contented, with his playthings ranged on a shelf in front of him, and his mother or attendant can wheel him from one room to another as her own change of occupation may require.

Some of the old houses in Amsterdam have wainscoted rooms with curiously carved woodwork, representing scenes in pastoral life and Bible stories. All the woodwork is dark, and were it not for the never-failing white curtains at the windows the rooms would be very somber. A winding staircase that shines like ebony leads to the upper rooms, the stairs, landing-places and floors being covered with rugs and handsome carpets. All the knobs, bolts and metal ornaments are polished until they look as if new from the shop.

The older women wear curious head-dresses with metal ornaments, gold or silver, according to their station. The cap varies in different parts of the country, and it is no uncommon thing to see a country-woman who wishes to make some concession to the fashions of to-day walking the streets of the city with a bonnet from Paris or Berlin perched on her head over the cap. To keep the head well covered indoors as well as out seems to be a peculiarity of the country, which is even sometimes seen in the men of the peasant class. The small cap, such as is shown in the illustrations of family life on page 439, is the universal head-covering for the male peasant. Sometimes it will have ear-lappets. Probably the origin of the custom of keeping

IN AN AMSTERDAM HOME

the head covered may be found in the fact that Holland being threaded by dikes is somewhat inclined to dampness, hence the caps for head protection and the thick wooden stockings and wooden shoes for foot-covering.

The Dutch cooks are famous. Most vegetables and some meats are stewed—i. e., cooked slowly on top of the stove so as to retain all the flavor. The Dutch insist upon having Java coffee, and they know how to make the most delicious amber-colored fluid ever placed before a coffee-drinker. Thick, rich cream is always served with it.

In dessert and cake making they excel, and, although the sweets have always lengthy

THE ODD HEAD-DRESS OF HOLLAND MATRONS

and—to foreigners—absolutely unpronounceable names, they are not nearly so productive of indigestion as some of our own dainties, which are compounded of far less rich ingredients.

The ordinary Dutch breakfast consists of tea, black and white bread, butter, cheese and possibly a pot of English jam. The white bread is cut into thick slices, spread

HOUSEHOLD TREASURES

with butter and overlaid with a very thin slice of black; some use cheese for the sandwich instead of butter. In addition, there is often a brown cake that looks like our hard gingerbread, and is very sweet and well spiced; honey is one of the principal ingredients. A thin slice of this particular cake is also eaten with a thick slice of white bread in sandwich fashion.

After breakfast, Madam brings a small wooden bowl and rack covered with fine linen towels and proceeds to wash the silver and china, using a small brush for the purpose. After one has seen the beautiful table appointments, one is not surprised that she prefers to see to their washing herself. Many of the articles have probably been in the family for a century or so, and to have a breakage occur would mean genuine heart sorrow. Table-cloths and napkins of exquisite linen are folded carefully in the creases and put into a press built on the same principle as a letter-press, which keeps them looking well much longer than when only folded.

Afternoon tea is an English importation in some Dutch households, but as a rule tea and biscuits are served at eight in the evening, and coffee, after the fashion of Germany, is taken in many households in the afternoon, with the accompaniment of cake or coffee bread. The Dutch are hearty eaters as a rule, and prefer good, solid meals to light luncheons.

The Dutch do not at all like our way of helping at table; they consider it very rude to serve anyone, as

CARVED FOOTSTOOLS

he is thereby deprived of choosing the kind and quantity he desires. As no one is served until the whole roast has been carved, and the plates are not warmed, it may be imagined that the food is somewhat cold by the time it is eaten. There is an old saying that there are two things that the Dutch girl chooses for herself, viz., her food and her husband.

The question of feeing servants is one of interest in Holland as elsewhere. One of the questions which a servant asks when taking a place is, "Do you have much company and what is the amount of fees?" If the amount stated is not large enough, the place is refused. The fees come from guests and from tradesmen who have bills over a specified sum.

It is the custom of guests dining at a house to give the maid a fee, which she in turn hands over to her mistress; it is put into the servants' box, which is opened four times a year and divided among the entire staff. Gentlemen give one guilder—forty cents—and ladies half that sum. The fees given by guests staying in a house are regulated by custom, according to the length of the visit—five guilders for a week's visit and longer stays accordingly.

When the trades-people collect their yearly bills, they give one per cent. to the servant; this is also put into the box. This extra amount is undoubtedly added to the bills, and is but a roundabout way of paying servants higher wages. This system has one advantage, if no other—it prevents bad temper and cross looks when company is expected, as is often the case among our servants. The expected fee makes each servant good-natured, and the hostess herself does not give new arrivals a warmer welcome than does the maid who opens the door. The fixed fee simplifies the matter for the guests, and after a stay in a Holland household one wishes the custom might be adopted in other countries.

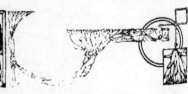

The Transformation of a Farmhouse

By W. L. BOTTOMLEY

FRONT VIEW OF TRANSFORMED HOUSE

THE ENTRANCE-HALL

TO THE average person the word "remodeling," when applied to an old building, calls up visions of inconvenience, discomfort, delay, expense and bad results. In nine cases out of ten these evils are the result of neglecting the possibilities in the old house and refusing to accept what cannot be avoided without changing the character of the whole. An old farmhouse may be easily changed without great expense into a summer cottage, meeting all the requirements of a modern family and losing nothing of the quaint charm of its age and associations. The usual fault is unnecessary destruction, tearing out and replacing, reconstruction and entire transformation, rather than modifying, adding to and adapting, as should be the case.

In New England, on Long Island, and in New York and New Jersey, along the seacoast and in the hills, stand numberless old farmhouses which, for no reason or another, can be bought for but little over their land value. Many an old farmhouse, neglected, but in fairly good repair, standing embowered in a grove of fine trees that have taken years to grow, is waiting for an appreciative eye to see, and someone willing and able to develop its possibilities, to change it almost beyond recognition and yet lose none of its charm. It needs perhaps only a judicious trimming of paint, the addition of a piazza, balcony or terrace, but still in character with the old building, and knocking down a few partitions so as to open up the interior, thereby gaining in comfort, dignity and space. It may even be necessary to move the house; a slight change of position will sometimes add greatly to the general effect.

This idea has lately been taken up in many parts of the East, notably in Massachusetts and on Long Island, where it amounts to a fashion—almost a rage.

In the heart of one of the oldest farming districts on Long Island, and situated near the ocean, is a house in which, in a simple and inexpensive manner, the change from the old to the new has been accomplished with most satisfactory results. Like all old farmhouses in the vicinity, it was built in a hollow as much sheltered from the wind and as close to the road as possible—just out of sight of a most attractive lake. The reverse of all this was essential for a summer cottage. At a cost of less than two hundred dollars, and by moving the house

about one hundred yards, the desired result was obtained. The house now commands views of the beautiful woods, the charming lake, and the broad sweep of the ocean beyond.

To overcome the unpleasing high and narrow effect of the original building, a dining-room was built out at one side, and a low, broad, hospitable piazza erected across the front. At one end the piazza widens into a porte-cochère, at the other end it forms a pretty and sheltered tea-room on which the French windows of the dining-room open. The flat roof of the piazza, covered with painted canvas, serves as a roomy, comfortable balcony for the bedrooms above.

The interior, with its tiny, cramped hall and numerous rooms, was unsuited to modern ideas, which require first a large entrance-hall, or living-room; second, that the rooms should open into each other by wide doorways; and third, a broad, easy stairway. In the front of the house, the six non-supporting partitions were torn down, leaving one large room. The door into the future library was enlarged, and a new doorway broken through the side-wall of the hall into the dining-room. The old stairs were widened and lengthened, as shown in the illustration on page 442; a light grille, separating the stairway from the hall, effectively and economically takes the place of balusters. The addition of a Dutch door and a window at the foot of the stairs completed the alterations of the hall.

The damaged walls could have been covered with matting, burlap or canvas—in this case canvas was employed—and, using various ancient Persian motifs, a rich design representing tiling was executed in oil paints, thinned with turpentine, giving a very solid mural effect.

A free and judicious use of color goes a long way toward furnishing a room. In this instance the color scheme employed in the middle wall varied from antique green and dull blues to peacock and emerald, heightened by warm ochers, clear touches of violet and a little brown. The frieze consists of a votive procession of Persian figures in a more brilliant key. Lounges covered with Indian draperies and heaped with pillows extend along the wall. These effective lounges consist merely of upholstered cotbeds, which cost three dollars and a half each, while the draperies of Indian print may be purchased at any department store for less than one dollar each. The floor is covered with manilla matting sewed together to form a

441

5

large rug, which is practically indestructible.

These strong decorations are accentuated by several bits of Russian and Oriental brass-work hung on the walls, which bring back pleasant remembrances of many a hunt in old Yiddish settlements. "But that is another story," as Kipling says.

The walls of the library opening from this cool, green room are a rich crimson relieved by the ivory-white enamel of the old woodwork. The floor is covered with pieces of rag carpet. The furniture here, which is all antique, came either from the garret of the old house or was the fruit of many an eager quest in the neighboring farmhouses. It consists of several fiddle-back chairs (picked up at one dollar each), now nicely scraped and polished, and a large, round, low table, with carved legs and green baize center. Where the best light can fall on its open lid stands a Hepplewhite mahogany desk. The walls of this room are treated with a red, transparent oil-stain applied directly to the plaster. Save for the coloring, this room is as it stood one hundred and fifty years ago.

The dining-room is entered directly from the hallway, and in pleasing contrast, instead of expensive lath and plaster and wall coverings, the treatment here is natural wood color. The constructive wall timbers and beams of the ceiling

THE STAIRWAY

SIDE VIEW OF HOUSE SHOWING PORTE-COCHÈRE

(stained weathered oak) remain exposed, and in the center of the room hangs a wrought-iron lamp. In place of the usual cornice, old blue-and-white Dutch tiles (twenty-five cents each) are arranged. The natural color of the walls has been preserved and enriched by the use of linseed oil, which is far cheaper, and in this case more effective, than varnish. Taking advantage of the spaces between the vertical uprights, pretty shelves filled with old-fashioned blue-and-white china, give the determining note of color.

At the sunset end of the room, a large bay with five windows overlooks the picturesque lake with its background of woods and rolling hills; beneath the windows a low, comfortable seat is built. The upholstery and cushions are in blue-and-white awning, and dainty fish-net curtains drape the window-panes without obscuring the view, and over these dark blue-jean curtains (which are practically unfading) are used instead of roller-shades. The various table-covers are of the same color, embroidered in heavy white cotton and trimmed with white cotton fringe. These are very decorative, and can be purchased for from twenty cents to seventy-five cents each. The furniture, in harmony with the rest of the woodwork, is stained weathered oak, and the sideboard, which in the city would have cost easily seventy-five dollars, was made by the country carpenter at the modest price of twenty-six dollars. It contains wine and silver closets and spacious shelves for decorative china. Its thin curtains are of dull-yellow silk.

In order to provide for a butler's pantry without the expense of an addition, a small bedroom which lay between the dining-room and kitchen was utilized; a doorway was opened at either end, a sink and drainer added, and a commodious china-closet built by the carpenter.

The kitchen was amply provided with shelves, and had a buttery and storeroom. Modern kitchen requirements were met by setting up a boiler, stove and sink, and a lean-to behind the house was changed into a most convenient and roomy laundry by the addition of a set of stone tubs.

When the house was moved, a windmill was built over the well and the water conveyed into a tank in the garret, thus securing an ample supply of water for all necessary plumbing.

Above the pantry and on the same plumbing stack, the corresponding room was made into a completely fitted bathroom with a wall covering of blue-and-white waterproof paper and a tile-patterned oilcloth on the floor.

THE BEDROOM

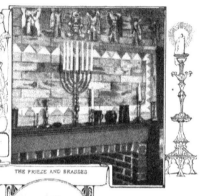

DUTCH WINDOW ON THE STAIRWAY

THE FRIEZE AND BRASSES

by light-yellow denim (twenty-five cents a yard). The frieze is formed of festoons of the yellow flowers and green leaves cut from the chintz and appliquéd on with book-binder's paste, and panels formed on the walls by means of these leaves disguise the joining of the denim. The effect is charming, and as the room faces north the yellow scheme is delightfully suggestive of perpetual sunshine. The employment of the chintz flowers and leaves is capable of being put into practical use in many ways in home beautifying, but its featuring in wall decoration as described, is certainly novel, and excellent results can be

Brown potato-sacking which had been washed is tacked on the walls of the second-story hall, and the lines of joining neatly concealed with a zigzag pattern formed of small pieces of split bamboo, which were obtained from an old bamboo-and-bead portière no longer in use. The panels thus formed an excellent background for a series of sketches and sporting pictures.

Throughout the bedrooms the woodwork is enameled ivory-white, and the tone of the decorations is, as it should be for sleeping rooms, light and cheerful. In the room illustrated, from the ceiling to the chair-rail light-blue denim covers the wall, with a darker shade below the chair-rail. The chairs are upholstered in blue-and-white figured chintz, and the window-curtains, tester, and valance of the four-post bed are made of the same quaint-looking material. The old mahogany furniture of this room is of most desirable pattern, and has been scraped and polished, while several undesirable articles of black walnut were wonderfully transformed by being first sandpapered, then given a few coats of white enamel paint. In the illustration is shown one of those convenient little chimney closets which were so indispensable to the early settlers as a place for their treasured books and gunpowder. The floor of this particular room is covered with white matting, on which lie rugs of rag carpet corresponding in tone with the walls and curtains; the rags for these, having been cut and sewed, were taken to the local weaver and woven into rugs for twenty-five cents a yard. This room after nightfall is lighted by the soft glow of candles, far preferable to lamplight, and excellent reproductions of Colonial glass candlesticks, costing twenty cents each, hold candles of a delicate sage green made from the wax berries gathered in the neighborhood.

In an adjoining bedroom, yellow is the predominating color. Here again harmony of tone is maintained between the wall and the upholstering. The cushions, wide curtains, bed draperies and chair-covers are all of light-yellow chintz, covered with garlands of green leaves and darker yellow flowers. Above the wainscoting the walls are covered

THE HOUSE IN ITS ORIGINAL STATE

obtained for comparatively small outlay. Flowers may also be cut from wall-paper and applied to plain papered surfaces in a similar manner.

No little ingenuity has been expended in these rooms in transforming every-day articles into things cozy and comfortably new. A discarded peach-basket covered with chintz makes a useful receptacle for waste paper. A close inspection of an attractive dressing-table reveals the familiar lines of a packing-box standing on castors, the interior being fitted with two roomy shelves. On the wall behind it hangs an oblong mirror; both are neatly and daintily covered with the chintz and finished with braid and brass-headed nails. Another box makes a broad, low window-seat, and the under part serves as a convenient receptacle for shoes. When one once becomes thoroughly imbued with the home-making spirit there seems to be no limit to the serviceable and pleasing articles one can develop from homely materials.

It will be seen that a very great improvement can be made both in the interior and exterior of an old house, if it is but thoughtfully and sympathetically studied. The work is fascinating if one really enters into it with zeal, and the given conditions and limitations imposed by the existing designs supply it with an added interest. If care and taste are exercised, the results artistically and practically are far more satisfying than in new houses.

443

How the Ice Harvest is Gathered.

MARKING OUT THE ICE SQUARES

SAWING THE ICE INTO BLOCKS OF
REGULAR SIZE

LIFTING OUT THE GREAT BLOCKS
OF FROZEN WATER AS FAST
AS THEY ARE SAWED

FILLING AN ICE-HOUSE: BLOCKS
OF ICE GOING UP ON THE
ENDLESS CHAIN

Photo by Brown Brothers, New York

STORED AND DISTRIBUTED

DOWN IN THE HOLD OF AN ICE BARGE
UNLOADING THE HUGE BLOCKS

A BARGE LYING AT DOCK WITH
A LOAD OF ICE

LOADING WAGONS FROM THE
BARGES AT THE DOCK

THE ICE MAN WEIGHING OUT THE SQUARES
OF COLD COMFORT FOR THE
HOME REFRIGERATOR

MISS GINTER OF GINTERVILLE
BY NINA WELLES TIBBOT

Illustrations by James Preston

(Commenced in May Number)

CONCLUSION OF CHAPTER IX

"If we should get all the things we want, what would we do with the time we spend regretting?"—Miss Ginter.

HILE Miss Ginter had been out with her guest, Ravish was in an agony of suspense. She stood behind the Virginia creeper and took notes.

"Land sakes," she began, probably addressing the beetles lurking under the creeper, "I never did see Miss Ginter act that way. She's perked up awful. Where in the world did she meet that fine-looking man? I 'spose she was rich and moved among city folks. She'll keep both of them young'uns now, because he's asked her to. She'd take a dozen, if he'd only look at her that way. They'll want some supper, and she's so nerved up, she couldn't get a meal in a week. I wonder if I'd better rig up any?"

A cry from the rear of the house brought Ravish to her senses with a start. At first she could not tell whether child or beast were in distress, but when she reached the scene the matter was soon explained.

"She was leanin' over the ash-barrel snoopin'," explained Dewey, "and she tumbled in." Ravish stood like one transfixed. Manila's long, slender legs were sticking up from the ash - barrel as straight as porcupine quills. Her head, with its mysterious-looking hat, was buried deep in wood-ashes. It took the combined efforts of Ravish and Dewey to get the young scavenger out of her element and on her feet. When the dust was brushed out of her eyes and her ill-fitting clothes were pulled into shape, it was discovered that she held something in her hand.

"What's that you've got?" demanded Ravish.

"It is a perfectly good cat. I saw it in the ash-barrel, and

when I reached in after it I leaned over too far and, of course, I toppled over. What made them throw that cat away?"

"It is one of Malty's dead kittens. Scrooges brought it over here and I threw it in there myself. What in the world do you want with a dead cat?"

Manila turned away in disgust. She had fingered over too many ash-barrels not to appreciate what it meant to find things in them that were whole and sound. "It's a perfectly good cat, all the same," she muttered defiantly to herself.

Ravish left Dewey and Manila to figure things out as best they could and went into the house to get supper.

"How lucky Miss Ginter made rolls! We'll have peach-butter and currant jell and——" She stopped short; her mind had wandered as far as the peacock cake and could go no further. Would it do to risk as valuable a life as the one with Miss Ginter, by feeding him anything of which one was not perfectly sure? "If I could only feed them scavengers something that would take them off," she said with a flourish of the bread-knife, "but a nice man like that—it would never do at all." Just then she looked up and saw Miss Ginter standing in the door.

"You may get supper, Ravish, as nice and as quick as you can. Get out the real damask and the solid silver, and you may set the table for two." Ravish eyed Miss Ginter with interest.

"I don't want to eat, so you two just set down and tea-tu-tea as long as you want to."

"That is very kind of you, Ravish." Miss Ginter smiled and went back to the parlor.

"This writing looks strangely familiar," Mr. MacIntosh was saying, as he held a letter he had picked up from the floor.

"I was looking them over and some fell out. I have given my escritoire away." He looked surprised and she explained. "They are making a Working Girls' Home and they asked me to give them something. And, well,

" DEWEY DROPPED HIS BREAD AND BUTTER AND SAT IN OPEN-MOUTHED CURIOSITY "

44

you understand there are so many calls, and unless one has a good deal, sometimes it is embarrassing. Any way, I have given this to them and I have been trying to clear out the rubbish."

He did not answer; he was looking at a youthful picture of himself. "Once, I was as young and boyish-looking as that," he was musing, and spoke softly, "and my head was full of dreams—*that never came true.*" He looked away from the photograph and toward the rose-bushes.

"You have probably realized far better ones, Mr. Mac-Intosh," Miss Ginter ventured to observe, also looking out at the roses.

"But they were not *those* dreams. Why must our first golden castles be tumbled to the ground? A world full of good things which come in after life cannot take the place of those first gilded palaces in those first rosy dreams."

"They were torn down because they were not real gold at all, but were only covered over with gilt that would rub right off. Besides, they hadn't any foundations—dream-castles never do have. The ones that came later were stronger, if they weren't so handsome. They were covered with paint that would stick even if it didn't glisten quite so brightly as the gilding."

"Perhaps you are right, you generally were in the old days, but I can never get over thinking that our first dreams are the best."

"The things we don't get, or can't get, are always bobbing up and making us think they are the best. The apple at the top of the tree is always the nicest until we get it down, and then it has a worm-hole in it, or has smut on it, or one side is withered. If we should get all the things we want what would we do with the time we spend regretting? You can pass more time regretting than any way I know of, unless you take to raising Angora kittens or training Irish setter pups." Miss Ginter spoke cheerfully and with positiveness, but there was a little quiver in her voice.

Her guest smiled, showing a row of very white teeth. "There never was but one Pauline." With which declaration he reached over and placed the picture in his lap. She raised her eyes and met those of Ravish, who was standing in the doorway. She had come to tell them that supper was waiting their appearance.

CHAPTER X

"Poverty may breed inventions, but it does have an awful smothering effect on virtues."—*Miss Ginter.*

For the first time in twenty years, Miss Ginter did not see the sun rise. She had retired late with her mind full to weariness of strange sensations. That Robert Mac-Intosh should cross her path again was hard to realize. Then came the other fact, that a couple of wharf-rats had been thrown upon her generosity. She dressed slowly with more than ordinary care. The bundle of old letters met her eyes, and she remembered that her escritoire was gone. She went down to the kitchen and found Ravish busy with the breakfast. Dewey and Manila were holding a heated discussion on the back porch.

"It's just ruinated," Manila was sobbing. Miss Ginter looked out of her window and saw Manila caressing her hat and lovingly fingering the purple aigret. "That was just the loveliest regret ever was. The hand-organ woman gived it to me fur mindin' her baby while she follered the circus off. Onct there was a green oyster feather with it, too."

" SHE DRESSED SLOWLY WITH MORE THAN ORDINARY CARE "

"An oyster feather, did you say?" Miss Ginter asked, joining the group.

"Yes; an oyster feather, and it sticked up and made the hat look lots beautifier. Oh, dear! I wish't I never'd seed that old ash-barrel." Manila stopped talking and labored more industriously with her hat.

"I think you mean an ostrich feather." Miss Ginter took the hat, repressing a smile. "I judge you are fond of trimmed hats."

"They are much prettier." Manila sighed.

Miss Ginter looked down at the bare, spindle legs and the comforter-cloth dress, and for the thousandth time wished she had money. "We will have to find you some clothes," she said, giving back the hat. "In the meantime take good care of what you have or they might fall off before I can sew some more together."

Ravish found a small table which she placed in the kitchen for Dewey and Manila. Here they ate after their own fashion and quarreled when they could not help it. This, their first breakfast, consisted of oatmeal, milk, toast and a cinnamon bun left over from the night before.

When they were quietly settled, Miss Ginter and Ravish betook themselves to the dining-room. Dewey listened until he heard the door close, then he pushed his glass of milk away from him and looked reproachfully at Manila.

"Such stuff as that to give a fellar to drink. I 'spose they think we don't know no better."

Manila edged a little closer, "What is it, Dewey?" she asked, peering into the glass.

"Why, it's all scum; can't you see it? The hand-organ woman feeds us better'n that. She gave us nice, clean, blue milk. This is filled up with buffy-looking chunks and the top is all yellow scum. I'll bet her cow is sick and she don't dare to drink the stuff herself, and so she peddles it off onto us. I'll show her she can't dope me; I ain't ready to have my ticket punched yet. Pass the water."

Manila passed the water, and, strangely enough, without comment, but a very weighty subject was absorbing her small mind. She watched Dewey until he was through drinking, then she edged a little nearer, her voice sinking to a whisper. "Do you know, there is something awful the matter with this house, and I think we'd better write Mr. MacIntosh right away."

Dewey dropped his bread and sat in open-mouthed curiosity. Manila proceeded. "That pie-face that gets the victuals was talkin' this mornin', and I heard her say there was a morkidge on this house. I wonder if that was what made the awful noise in the night? Somethin' scraped and scraped on the roof, till I was most afeerd to catch my breath. Did you ever see a morkidge, Dewey?"

Dewey shook his head solemnly.

"I never did neether, but by the way she talked it must be somethin' awful. I don't beleeve I ken ever sleep, till it's tuk off'n and throw'd away."

"Did it go round and round?" Dewey asked.

"It sounded that way and growed bigger all the time. It might scrape through and cum down an' kill us all. I most wish we hadn't cum."

Dewey sat very still and thought very hard, and at last he came to the conclusion that if there was something on the house that Miss Ginter and Ravish could not get off, it was no more than right for Mr. MacIntosh to come and get it off for them. "Like enough, it's too big fur 'em to lift," he explained to Manila. "I saw a ladder out by the shed most long enough; maybe he could splice it out 'n climb up to the chimbly in no time."

After breakfast was over, Dewey made a solemn request for paper and pencil. To write was a laborious process, and nothing but a sense of duty could have compelled him to make the effort. When he had finished, he took the letter to Manila for consultation. Together they went through the spelling and pronounced it correct. It read as follows:

"deir mister Mackuntuah.

"I wisht yu wud cum heir rit off az sumthin ails thu wummuns hous wheir we be. munila saz its a murkidge. whutever it is it scraps the ruf so we cant slep. ef yu kud cum rit off it mit sav us frum nervis proseeusion in the hed.
                                        "yus truly,
                                            "Dewey."

When he had finished, he asked the further favor of a stamp and "cover," which with much effort, he addressed. When he announced his intention of going to the post-office, Miss Ginter asked him to wait, as she was going to the store and might need him to carry home bundles.

"I wonder if Mr. Parsons would trust me for anything more?" Miss Ginter sat down and tapped her foot nervously. "I don't see any possible way of paying what I already owe, but here are those children, the two worst-looking objects I ever set my eyes on. I do wish Providence was a little more considerate and would give us things to do with as fast as we are given things to do. If I don't dress up those poor little unfortunates, people will talk about them; if I do dress them up, they will talk about me. What a time Mrs. Corbett would have singing my praises if I should fix these children up like other folks! Poverty may breed inventions, but it does have an awful smothering effect on virtues."

Miss Ginter sat silent for some time, then she stood up and pointed a small white finger at Ravish. "We must make up Percilla Perkins' shroud, which the Sewing Society left for me to work on," she announced with fervor.

"Miss Ginter!" Ravish exclaimed, but the words seemed to choke her and she turned her head the other way.

"Well, why not? She won't need a shroud for six months anyway, and by that time Muley will have another calf and I can sell it and buy her one."

"But s'posin' she should want one in a hurry?" Ravish held her hands locked in a rigid embrace.

"Well, the Lord knows I've got to use it up, and it does seem as though He'd be mindful enough of things not to send a corpse till He sends a shroud." Both women rocked in silence.

"I couldn't have picked out anything prettier," Miss Ginter observed cheerily. "It's a blue pin-stripe and plenty of it. She bought it when she was crazy, and it would be a real kindness to the public to take it and buy her something more appropriate when it is needed."

Now that the matter of dress was settled, Miss Ginter rose and made preparation to go. "You hunt up all the flour-sacks and press them out, and bring down all the stocking-legs from the garret chest, and when I get back we'll go to work in earnest." Ravish nodded and Miss Ginter led the way down the steps, followed by Dewey.

CHAPTER XI

"It's awful easy to trust Providence if you're squinting at a gold-mounted harness and holding both the lines, but you wait till the breeching is broke, and the tugs give out, and the tie-strap won't hold, and there's nothing left but a bridle buckle and a pair of whiffletrees, and you'll begin to think it's time to stop trusting and get out and do something yourself."—*Miss Ginter.*

"Manila, I wish you would stand still till I can get these gathers in straight. If you keep wiggling around that way, they'll be like a jug-handle—all on one side—and folks will think you've got a tumor. What does the paper say, Ravish?" Miss Ginter took her eyes from Manila long enough to give Ravish a look of deep concern.

"It's a column and a half, and it gives full-length pictures of both of them."

"What's his name?"

"He's got four of them, and each has all the letters of the alphabet, most. His last name is Smolinski, and he calls himself a prince."

"I don't mind so much his being Russian himself, if his feet are American. It's perfectly terrible when they aren't. We had a hired man once who was a Russian, feet and all, and we couldn't keep him in the house. We moved him to the barn, but father got it into his head it affected the milk, and we had to let him go. And her name, Ravish?"

"Marie Helen MacIntosh, only daughter of Mr. Robert MacIntosh."

"They don't say anything about her being the daughter of Mrs. MacIntosh. Won't Isabel be furious when she sees that? I suppose they're to have a grand wedding?"

"They are to be married at the Barrington-Browns' summer home."

"IT'S A COLUMN AND A HALF, AND IT GIVES FULL-LENGTH PICTURES OF BOTH OF THEM"

"That's at Newport. I wonder if Helen looks like her mother? She was real pretty, but she didn't have any more sense than a rag-doll. She had light, frizzy hair when she was young, and it always hung in her eyes. I expect she's poked it out by this time, but she used to look for all the world like a French poodle dog. The kind that have sore eyes unless you let their hair fall over and cover them up. She was very blond, very small, and wore spool-heel shoes. I often wondered what Robert found in her to admire. Perhaps, after all, it was what he didn't find that caught him. I have learned that the less a woman knows the better some men like them. They want the chance of telling what they know. I am sorry to say, the task has so overworked some that they have quit to let another fellow go on with their job."

"You are the meanest, meanest, meanest woman I ever seed!" Dewey brought his small fist down with a crash very close to Miss Ginter's face.

"What is the matter with you? You act like a bantam rooster."

"I don't care if I do. I'd be ashamed to talk like that about dead folks." There were tears in Dewey's eyes.

"Who in the world is dead?"

"Miss MacIntosh is. She was to our Christmas tree just before and gived every one of us an orange an' two candy canes."

"Do you mean to say that Robert MacIntosh hasn't any wife?"

"He hain't got none but the cemetary one."

Miss Ginter dropped her work and began rocking very hard. "And I sent her a bouquet of flowers and asked about her. I wonder what he will think of me?"

Relieved of her dress, Manila slipped out of the door. She pulled a stalk of pie-plant on the way and trailed it along in the dirt. Dewey ran back and filled his pockets with loaf sugar preparatory to enjoying a share in the pie-plant.

"You was awful sassy," Manila ventured. "Maybe she'll send us home."

"No she won't; my pants ain't done yet."

"She looked awful 'shamed when you'd done talkin'. I should think really, truly ladies wouldn't talk that way. It's most as bad as the hand-organ woman." They had eaten up the pie-plant and Dewey had gone to procure more. When he returned, the conversation was continued.

"I wonder why Mr. MacIntosh don't answer my letter?"

"Maybe it don't need no answer." Manila pushed some more pie-plant toward Dewey.

"For goodness sake, Manila, take that pie-plant away. I've eat so m ch it's set my insides to gnawin' till I feel as though they'd eat through and chew up my pants-buttons."

The children arose with one accord and returned to the house. They

" ' DID YOU SAY IT WAS PAID ? ' SHE ASKED, FIXING HER EYES ON HIS FURROWED FACE "

found the ladies in a state of great excitement. Miss Ginter was holding a paper in her hand and talking to Ravish.

"It's the mortgage, but what in the world have they sent it to me for?" She began spreading it out until half of her body was screened behind the great expanse of white paper. "And here is a *satisfaction!* What in the world is a *satisfaction?* I'll put my things on and go over and ask Deacon Hobbs what it means."

While Miss Ginter was pinning on her hat, Dewey was pulling Manila behind the kitchen door. "Now you see what you've done, don't you?" he said, giving her pigtail a twist. " Gee, but Mr. MacIntosh 'll be awful mad with you, workin' him all up like that about nothin'. Why a morkidge is only a paper. A paper couldn't hurt a house none, if it was on it. An' you said it scraped and kept you awake. There!" Dewey administered an extra twist to the pigtail and Manila screamed.

"You needn't holler; you'll feel worse'n that when Mr. MacIntosh goes back on you. Next time I come, I'll leave you to home."

"You won't neether, fur I'll leave myself first."

In another moment Dewey had repented of his cruelty, and the pair were sauntering together in the back yard.

Meanwhile Miss Ginter had reached Deacon Hobbs and was seated in his front room. "Did you say it was paid?" she asked, fixing her eyes on his furrowed face.

"Yes, Miss Ginter; it's fully paid, and there is the satisfaction."

"You don't know who paid it, do you?" There was the faintest tremor in her voice.

"Not for certain, I don't; but I have my suspicions."

"I suppose you might do a little guessing if you was a mind to set yourself about it."

Deacon Hobbs looked wise and t r i e d to smile. "The same Providence sent the mortgage that sent the satisfaction, only we can't see things that way when t h e y ' v e turned the shady side 'round."

"It was Aunt Betsy Selby that paid that mortgage," Miss Ginter said, bringing her h a n d s together with a gasp. "She said she'd never stop praying to have our place clear till that mortgage was taken up. She's worn herself out praying and has concluded to lift it herself. I told her to stop, that it wasn't any use, more than three years ago, but she wouldn't. You might as well try to move one of the Rocky Mountains as a Selby when once their mind is positively set."

"Strange, with your bringing up that you needed a reminder of the care of Providence." Deacon Hobbs leaned back and fumbled his watch-chain.

"It's awful easy to trust Providence if you're squinting at a gold-mounted harness and holding both the lines, but you wait till the breeching is broke, and the tugs give out, and the tie-strap won't hold, and there's nothing left but a bridle buckle and a pair of whiffletrees, and you'll think it's time to stop trusting and get out and do something yourself."

Miss Ginter rose to her feet as she spoke and prepared to take her departure. "Well, I am much obliged to you, Deacon Hobbs," she said, extending her hand cordially.

"Well, you needn't be," said the deacon; "it's a happy surprise to me, I tell you. I had given up ever getting anything out of that mortgage—except the premises."

(*To be Concluded*)

HOPE

By KATHARINE G. TERRY

OH, BARREN waste of fruitless days,
        And soul that thirsts, and thirsts in vain;
Gray skies that shut out sunny rays,
        And goals I never could attain;
Oh, trusted friends who have deceived,
        And tears too deep to overflow;
And things I craved, and half believed
        My hungry heart might sometime know;

Along the sinuous path of life
        I've met you all, and passed along;
Still catching in the din and strife
        The bars of some uplifting song;
Still dreaming of the flowery lanes
        That intersect life's darker ways,
The rainbows that succeed the rains,
        The golden light beyond the haze.

In the Interest of Bread-Winning

BY BERTHA HASBROOK

III—THE VISITING LADY'S MAID.

ONCE upon a time there was a Princess. Not a real Princess, because she lived in America where real ones don't grow; but she was just the same as one, because she had everything she wanted and more besides.

She had gowns and hats and carriages and caddies and an automobile. Moreover she was very beautiful, and her maid, a devoted servant, spent her entire time looking after the Princess' beauty. She massaged her and shampooed her and manicured her and kept her looking as fresh as a rosebud.

One day a dreadful thing happened. The gowns and the carriages and everything, even the maid, were swept away. It all had something to do with bulls and bears, which the Princess did not understand, but she did grasp the fact that she had to paddle her own canoe somehow. So just because she was an American girl instead of a real Princess, she went to work to do it in the most clever and practical way imaginable. This was what she did. She knew exactly how the once-faithful maid had attended to her grooming and kept her looking so lovely; and she decided that she could be a maid herself and take care of other people's beauty for them. Of course this was not what she would have called fun in the days of caddies and yachts; but there came a day when the contentment of duty done came over her as something happier than she had ever imagined it might be in those days when there was no such thing as duty ever mentioned.

The profession of visiting lady's maid is far pleasanter to most girls than the life of a maid employed in one home all the time. The latter position places her among the servants, while the former gives her entire independence. This was the work chosen by the once-wealthy girl mentioned above, and she has made a success of it far beyond her expectations, so that now she employs an assistant to take the easier work off her hands.

Few women of great wealth employ a visiting maid; these have maids of their own to serve them every day; but the prosperous members of what is financially considered the middle class supply her with all the work she can attend to. In most of our cities it is much harder for these people to find a first-class visiting maid than it is for her to find patrons. The profession is by no means overcrowded, and even when it does become so, there will be no need for you to step out, for you intend to live in that roomy place which always remains at the top.

Just as in the case of the house-to-house milliner, you can by means of this profession work up a clientage which may some day warrant your hanging out a shingle of your own and becoming the head of a "beauty parlor," which I trust you will never call it. If people know the worth of your work they will be willing to go to you when you cease to go to them. And if you never care to increase your business to such an extent, you will always find it very profitable, taking into consideration the outlay, which consists chiefly of the price of lessons.

The visiting maid is generally expected to understand hair treatment, hair-dressing and manicuring. Add massage, chiropody and facial dermatology, and you have a complete equipment. You will usually find it more profitable to include as many branches as possible, for in that way you can stay longer with each patron, and so avoid the loss of time in going from house to house. As your business increases, many ways of economizing time will present themselves. For instance, one visiting maid spends two entire days each week in a family hotel, attending several ladies regularly. Another spends a day each week in a home where there are four daughters, and she gives a hair treatment and manicure to each of these as well as to the mother.

Our large cities have schools where courses in all of the above subjects are offered. If you cannot reach one of these, you can probably make arrangements with some professional in a smaller town to work with her and learn her trade as an apprentice. Prices of the schools vary; here is a representative list of fees: Hair-dressing, fifteen dollars. Facial massage, fifteen dollars. Body massage, twenty-five dollars. Manicuring, ten dollars. Dermatology, including treatment of the scalp and complexion, fifty dollars. Chiropody, seventy-five dollars. These courses

"ADD MASSAGE, CHIROPODY AND FACIAL DERMATOLOGY, AND YOU HAVE A COMPLETE EQUIPMENT"

range in length of time for a term from two to twelve weeks.

These fees are high and they cover a complete and scientific knowledge of the subjects under consideration. For a practical working knowledge that will be sufficient to start you in business, you can take an abbreviated course at any of the schools. One offers fifteen lessons, covering the practical points of hair-dressing, manicuring and facial massage, for fifteen dollars, or half a dozen lessons in any one of these branches for five dollars. If you have very little money to expend upon lessons it would be best to limit yourself to the study of the hair and scalp, for this is the line of work most commonly in demand. Many women who would consider it extravagant to have their finger - nails or their complexion cared for by a professional are obliged to resort to expert treatment of the hair.

It is against my principles to encourage amateurish and unskilled work of any kind; but to the girl who wants to take up this profession and cannot afford lessons, I say, take it up anyway. Begin on a small scale;

"THE LONG EMERY-BOARD IS NOW USED"

don't pretend to know any more than you do; save from your little earnings to take a five or ten dollar course later on. From time to time you can add to this education. Meanwhile, read up on your subjects in books that are authoritative.

Start out by giving a first-class shampoo and do not offer to do any more, for it is not safe for you to undertake scalp treatment until you have learned to do it properly. But with a little practise, which your friends will permit you to gain upon them, any deft woman can shampoo successfully. The following method is safe for any hair except possibly in the case of a diseased scalp, and you do not intend to handle such a case. First of all, cleanse the hair and scalp before you wash them, which seems a bit paradoxical, but it is the secret of all good shampoos. Part the hair as you work so as to get at the scalp at every point. With a stiff brush or a comb used with a lifting, sideward motion, not to scrape the scalp; remove all the dandruff and dust from the scalp; then brush it out from the hair. Dissolve a saltspoonful of borax in a glass of warm water and wash the scalp with this, rubbing it in with a vigorous motion of the fingers. During this process two handfuls of soapbark should be boiling and steeping in a saucepan of water; strain this and add the strained liquid to a bowl of warm water. Hold the head over this and scrub hair

and scalp thoroughly, rinsing afterward in three waters, to the last of which the strained juice of a lemon has been added. Dry the hair in the sun, beside a radiator or with fans; never with towels.

As you advance with your work you will learn to treat difficult subjects, such as oily hair, dry hair, falling hair, and so on. Scalp massage is generally acknowledged now to be the basis of all scalp treatment, and you should add this to your repertoire as soon as possible.

Hair-dressing has a technique of its own, but there is a natural knack about it and it is doubtful whether everyone can be successful in this art. After you have once grounded yourself in it you will be obliged to take a new lesson from time to time, so as to be well posted on all the new touches, such as the French twist just now in vogue at the time.

New implements for beauty treatments are introduced frequently. Keep yourself familiar with these, for your patrons will want you to be abreast of the times. Inasmuch as the long emery-board is now used upon the nails where the short one used to be, add to your outfit a long board. Scalp-brushes, which look like tooth-brushes, are now used in applying tonics, and your patron will want one of her own.

The average price for a shampoo given at the patron's own home is fifty cents, carfare being additional. A manicure is usually thirty-five cents. Some visiting maids charge fifty cents an hour, whatever kind of work they do during that time.

It is a legitimate part of the business to prepare various cosmetics for sale in connection with the work, provided you prepare good cosmetics. With the experience which will come to you with each new patron you will soon be able to work out your own formulas for hair tonics and cold creams, and the sale of these articles will add materially to your income. You will above all things be most careful not to use any ingredient which can be in the slightest degree harmful.

A parting word—be dainty yourself in dress, person and mannerisms. In this way you will be agreeable to the dainty women who employ you to make them so. And this daintiness need not prove an expensive item, for its foundation is absolute cleanliness and neatness. Choose dark material for your business suit, but freshen it with the spotless aprons you will carry in your handbag, and do not attempt to dress hair or manicure finger-nails until your own are beyond criticism.

"SCALP-BRUSHES WHICH LOOK LIKE TOOTH-BRUSHES"

THE TEMPTATION OF TOMMY

By T. JENKINS HAINS

Illustrations from Drawings
By ELIOT KEEN

H E WAS a little chap not more than four feet high, and his seven summers had left him with a large head and serious face over a somewhat meager body and thin legs. But there was a quick agility and nervous force in his movements that showed him to be a child of no weak constitution. He gazed timidly up at the helmsman of the launch that was taking him aboard the man-of-war, and, although he had never seen a boat before, he asked in a low, quiet, but very positive manner, "Lemme guide her?"

The man at the little steering-wheel looked down. He apparently had not heard aright. The child wanted something and he glanced backward to where the father, an officer of regular service who commanded the nearest vessel, sat and chatted with his superior, the Admiral of the fleet at anchor in the roadstead. But the Admiral's invitation to come aboard the flag-ship and bring the little chap with him had made an impression upon the official mind that was not to be confounded with nursery duties. The boy must look out for himself, and the officer paid no heed to the helmsman's glances.

"I say, lemme guide her," repeated the lad; "lemme make her go—I kin do it if you kin—'taint nothin' holdin' that little wheel," and to prove it he made a quick pass at the spokes, reaching past the helmsman's legs.

At that moment a tug came tearing by at full speed, and the sudden sheer due to the boy's grip caused her captain to port his helm quickly to avoid running the launch down. The wash of the bow wave smashed against the head of the launch and burst into a shower of spray, wetting everyone aboard. The Admiral grew red with anger and spoke harshly to the coxswain, ordering him to report the tugboat for carelessness. He had failed to see the lad's action at his own steering-gear.

The look the father bestowed upon Tommy was not encouraging. Tommy recognized it with grim forebodings, but nothing could happen for some time, as there would be no spanking scene upon the flag-ship. Deep in his heart he was a bit frightened at the sudden lurch and burst of spray. He let go the wheel before even the now angry helmsman could brush him aside. Then he sat and gazed out over the sparkling harbor, enjoying the brisk air and motion as only a lively boy could.

He had determined in less than five minutes to become a helmsman when he grew up. The Admiral's duties were not inviting. It was nothing to sit and talk and give rough orders. The real thing of life was to hold that little wheel and make a launch go where one wanted. He sidled back to the man and looked up.

"Say, mister, lemme take her just once—lemme guide her, will you?" said he again.

"You don't guide boats, son—you guide horses," whispered a blue-jacket sitting near. "You steer boats."

"Lemme steer her, then——"

"Hook her forrads," interrupted the helmsman in a low tone. Then he pulled a bell. The man at the engine threw over a lever and the launch slowed up, coming alongside a huge, high-sided ship. A long stairs reached away to her rail above, and Tommy's father and the Ad-

miral climbed them, leaving the boy to follow in care of the coxswain.

It was a new world above. Tommy left the launch sadly, not before exacting a promise from the coxswain that he would let him guide her the next time.

Upon the broad decks of the man-of-war there were many things to interest and attract the lad, and he gazed in awe at the magnificent master-at-arms in his uniform, and was subdued by the thundering crash of the guns as they sent forth the Admiral's salute. Then he was led away and put in the care of a steward.

During mess-time Tommy sat in the ward-room and was chaffed by all the junior officers of the ship, so that he was afraid to eat, although the salt air had sharpened his appetite. The officers were a lively set of young men, and after they were through with him, his long and enforced silence and good behavior in the cabin of the Admiral was most trying. Hungry and restless, he chafed at the restraint. The steward seemed friendly, and at the first opportunity the boy made his way to the pantry.

Among the many dainties there the condensed milk offered the greatest possibilities. The steward, a discerning fellow, recognized this at once and gave his young friend some of the sweet, white stuff with the end of a spoon, and Tommy sat and licked it greedily. It was a new kind of candy for him, and his boyish taste reveled in it—it was so white, clean and sticky.

"Kin I have some more?" he asked.

"Just one spoonful," said the wise steward; "it'll make you sick if you eat too much."

"Have all those tin cans got condensed milk in them?" asked Tommy, pointing to a row which stood upon a high shelf and held in place by a wooden batten.

"Yes, they're all chock-full—haven't been opened yet," said the steward.

"Does cans of milk cost much?" inquired the youngster.

"Oh, yes—a whole lot," said the man.

"How much?" asked Tommy definitely.

"A whole dollar a dozen," said the steward, becoming bored.

"I mean apiece?" said Tommy.

"Ten cents," said the steward, shortly.

"Ah, that ain't much—I got more'n that in my pocket. Where do you buy 'em?" asked the lad.

"Ashore," jerked the steward.

"I know—but where?" insisted the boy. "Kin you sell 'em?"

"No, no," replied the steward. He had been busy fixing a dish of nuts for the ward-room mess, and he took the dish and started forward with it.

"You stay here until I come back and I'll give you another spoonful," said he as he went out.

Tommy sat quietly waiting for some minutes and eyed the cans upon the shelf. The captain wished something, so the steward did not return immediately. The minutes dragged and the lad's appetite, still unsatisfied and now sharpened again by the taste of the sweet stuff, began to assert itself. He gazed longingly at the open can from which the steward had helped him. It was far above his

452

reach, but being an active, wiry little fellow, he sat studying the distance. No steward appeared. He began to
wonder if he could hide a can of the condensed milk and
take it ashore with him, and at last he climbed upon the
shelves and hoisted himself to the top one, where the little
tins stood. He was much excited and almost lost his hold
when a step sounded outside, but whoever it was passed
on. The cans were very pretty in their paper covers, and
he gazed longingly at them for a few moments. Then he
took one and began to descend. He reached the deck
just as the steward's voice sounded outside the pantry
door. He shoved the can under his little blouse and
waited with red cheeks and expectant eyes.

The steward entered, but was too busy to notice the
lad's manner or the swelling under the blouse.

"Ah, so you waited for me," he said, and he took down
the can of milk and gave Tommy a spoonful.

The boy looked abashed and hung his head.

"I don't want no more," he said sheepishly.

The steward glanced at him sharply, then at the can.
None of the milk had been taken from it during his absence. But he was too busy to pay further attention and
fathom the affair. He put the can back again and Tommy
went forth with his ill-gotten prize. It was some time
before the launch would take him ashore, and the lad
went about in a shame-faced way, his spirits subdued
and a feeling of meanness upon him. The can also occupied his attention, and he felt that everybody was looking
at the swelling in his blouse just above his waistband.
He grinned and blushed when an officer offered to show
him one of the great guns and, slipping away, ran aft.
He would have put the can back again willingly if he could
have done so without being seen, but, with the steward
in the pantry, this was too risky. He would have to carry
the load of crime in his blouse until he went ashore.

Finally the sharp, shrill tones of the bos'n's whistle

rose and fell upon the evening air, and the lau
called away to take the Admiral and his guest
Tommy was haled into her without notice or ce
and took his place forward near the wheel, feel
his father would certainly see the protuberance
clothes should he dare go aft. The officers came
and the launch steamed away toward the shore, no
red and quiet in the rays of the setting sun.

Tommy gazed out over the darkening water
sunset attracted him. The launch was heading
directly into it, and it seemed a nice thing to p
straight for the great fiery globe that was now resti
the edge of the sea. He forgot all about everythin;
the helmsman's promise. Then he edged toward l

"Lemme guide her now," he said.

"I can't," snapped the man. "Ask your pa fir

Tommy looked aft. The two officers were
silently into the sunset. They were not busy, and
vanished.

"Paw, let me guide her, won't you," came the
the lad. He could wait no longer.

"Paw, let me guide her—I kin do it."

The man at the wheel looked askance, but th
smiled and nodded assent. Tommy had already
the wheel-spokes. Then the launch, under th
direction, held her way as before, the man standin
correct any mistakes in the steering.

The boy's mind was in a whirl. He was trembli
excitement. The boat obeyed each impulse of hi
little wheel, and he tried to head her straight at the
sun. The vibrations of the propeller stimulate
and his eyes were bright and his lips were parted w
launch drew near the wharf.

"I'll take her now, sonny," said the helmsmar
do fine—you'll be all right."

"No, no; I'll take her alongside," piped Tom

"I AM SORRY," HE SAID, THEN A BLISSFUL RECOLLECTION BRIGHTENED HIS EYES, AND HE ADDED,
"BUT I DID GUIDE HER ALL RIGHT—DIDN'T I, PAW?"

kin do it." And he struggled to hold on to the wheel as the man took it. Then something happened. The waistband of his blouse burst, and the can of condensed milk rolled to the floor of the launch and landed at the Admiral's feet.

Tommy rushed to seize it, but his father was there before him.

"Where did you get this?" asked the officer.

Tommy looked at the Admiral and hung his head.

"What were you going to do with this?" snapped his father, sharply.

"Eat it, sir," said Tommy, meekly. And as he spoke the Admiral laughed until he turned red in the face.

"Here, coxswain, take this boy back aboard and see that he gives this can to the steward," said the officer.

"Why not let him keep it?" whispered the Admiral, spluttering and getting his breath.

But the father pretended not to hear, and Tommy, with his face red with shame, turned away and whimpered.

On the way back to the ship the lad's mind was active. To face that crowd of officers and hear their fun was more than he could bear. Why had he taken the can? If he could only get it back without meeting all those men. He knew the steward would forgive him, for he was kind. He drew near the coxswain, who held the can, and he looked hard at him through the tears.

"Can't I keep it?" he asked, softly.

"Not by no means, sonny," said the man, kindly but firmly, with a shake of his head.

"Are you going to give it back to the steward—or shall I?" asked the lad.

The other men in the launch were listening, and they broke forth into hoarse laughing.

"I won't make ye climb up all them steps," said the coxswain, winking at the man at the engine. "It's very bad to be caught 'hookin' things. Ye ought to be ashamed."

"I am," said Tommy, penitently; "I—I—I couldn't help it, and he started to whimper again out of pure humiliation.

"Never mind, then, I'll take it up fer ye," said the coxswain, and the men grinned.

"Thank you," said Tommy, and he put his arms around the bearded sailor's neck and hugged him. The coxswain patted him and winked at his comrades, and as the boat drew alongside the ship he sprang up a hanging ladder forward and climbed to the deck.

Tommy didn't see the can of milk, and he thought the coxswain was very active to get to the steward's pantry and back again in so short a time. Then they let him steer the craft back ashore. He was very quiet and sad when his mother met him and took him in hand to put him to bed for punishment.

"Are you sorry you took what didn't belong to you?" she asked, as she led him to his father to say good-night.

He hung his head with the shameful memory.

"I am sorry," he said, then brightened up, "but I did guide the launch all right—didn't I, paw."

HOW ROSSITER SAW THE LADY MOON
By ALIX THORN

"BUT you see, Katie," said four-year-old Rossiter, standing with sturdy legs far apart and speaking slowly and impressively, "you see I never saw the moon rise, and"—this very pathetically—"'p'r'aps I never shall." And nurse Katie answered with a quick look at nurse Mary from the next cottage.

"Sure, Rossiter, you're asleep as soon as your head touches the pillow at half-past six. You couldn't stay awake to see the Lady Moon if you tried."

Rossiter scorning further conversation turned away, dragging behind him a long, leafy branch. Oh, heartless Katie! If only father and mother weren't away visiting Aunt Jane! Why, everybody at the inn was talking about the moon! The big boys and girls were going on moonlight picnics and drives all the time just to see the moon.

However, if fate in the person of Katie was unkind, there was much to interest any small boy this August afternoon—the flocks of crows that flew, cawing, high above his head; the funny, twisty brook that hurried through the orchard, talking to itself as it ran; the sheep that grazed in the field near by. It was a wonderful world, and, disappointment forgotten, off trudged Rossiter to look up a certain lofty evergreen that he had observed growing against the hillside. It seemed practicable to take said evergreen home with him, and keep it till the following Christmas, when, in the glory of lighted tapers and shining tinsel, it would stand in the library, a miracle for all the world to see. But when at last he reached the tree it looked a trifle large to cut down and move. Fortunately, there were many other smaller ones to choose from. Not till a full hour after did Rossiter realize that he had wandered far, and was very ready to start back to the cottage.

Now, what had become of the brook? Where was the great Christmas tree, whose plumy green arms rested against the hillside? Everything looked unfamiliar. A panic seized him, and he called loudly: "Oh, Katie, come Katie!" but no one answered. "I'm losted," he sobbed, "losted like Lucy Grey," Katie reads about."

Up at the cottage, distracted Katie was vainly looking for her charge—in the orchard, by the brook and through the barn. The boys and girls formed searching parties while the shadows grew longer; down the lane a cow-bell jangled loudly. The sunset flooded the mountain ranges, the glowing ball sank from sight, and twilight fell.

As the night shut down, Rossiter, forlorn and hopeless, perched on a stone in the wood-lot, hid frightened eyes in small, grimy hands and cried miserably; cried for a cheerful cottage and a certain little white bed—would he were safely tucked in that bed, hearing Katie's crooning voice in the nursery near by as she soothed baby.

He lifted his head and peered around at the strange outdoors. How big and cold the shadowy mountains seemed, so tall, so far away. Suddenly on the horizon line appeared a wonderful glow, then before his wondering, wide-opened eyes a golden circle peeped above the mountain-tops, ever larger and larger, rounder and rounder, till slowly and majestically the full moon traveled up the sky.

"It's Katie's Lady Moon!" murmured the child in an awe-struck whisper. Brighter it glowed till the dim fields were illuminated, and, behold, fairy-land was all about him.

Sometime later a merry party of returning picnickers came up the road, and seeking a short cut to the inn, hurried through the wood-lot, tired but happy with their long day. Great was their surprise to find the solitary little figure sitting silent, supporting his chin in one small, cold hand, his earnest eyes upraised to the sky, tears dried on the round cheeks. Hearing the voices, he remembered his sad plight, and burst into tears. "I'm losted," he cried, and stretched imploring arms.

"Why, it is Mrs Seymour's little boy," cried a young lady. "We'll take you home, dearie. Pick him up, Jack, and we'll hurry on. They must be awfully frightened about him."

A pale, tearful Katie ran out to meet them and snatched her charge close to her motherly breast. "Was you glad to see me, Katie?" said Rossiter, both arms round her neck.

"That I am, darlin'," answered smiling Katie.

"But, oh, Katie," he cried, "listen, Katie, I did see the moon rise, your *Lady Moon*."

A VACATION EPISODE

A One-Act Farce for Three Actors

By L. O. LENNART

ILLUSTRATED FROM DRAWINGS BY LOUISE HUDSON

CHARACTERS:

MISS HAZEL BENTON (*a college girl who is newly engaged*); MISS MAY FORD (*another college girl*); MR. GEORGE FELDON (*the fiancé of* HAZEL).

SCENE:

Sitting-room in a farm-house. MISS BENTON *and* MISS FORD *discovered peeling apples.*

MAY (*holding up long peel of apple*): Isn't it strange that we should meet here!

HAZEL: Splendid, I think.

MAY: Yes, of course, but queer, anyhow. Think of it—on a farm. Who would ever have thought of meeting you on a farm!

HAZEL: Or you!

MAY: Well, I wouldn't have been here except for that last term. It simply wore me out. I had to go somewhere or die.

HAZEL: Same with me—and a farm is the best place in the world for a rest.

MAY: Well, I'm delighted you decided on this one. I can have somebody civilized to speak to now when I'm tired of conversing with robins and larks.

HAZEL (*in surprise*): Why, do you never see anyone out here?

MAY: Oh, yes, we see farmers.

HAZEL: But——

MAY: And milkmaids.

HAZEL: I don't mean them. I mean—you know what I mean.

MAY: Yes, but we don't see them. We hear a great deal about the coming men, but none of them ever seem to arrive. There is a young man from the city, however, who came here about the middle of July. He's been over here once or twice to see me.

HAZEL (*shyly*): Oh, May! that reminds me that——

MAY: What?

HAZEL (*in apparent embarrassment*): I forgot——

MAY: Forgot what?

HAZEL: To tell you last night that——

MAY (*dropping knife and leaning toward* HAZEL *eagerly*): Oh, Hazel, what is it?

HAZEL: I'm engaged.

MAY: No!

HAZEL: Yes.

MAY: Honest?

HAZEL: Honest.

MAY: Oh, Hazel! Who is he?

HAZEL: The best man in the world!

MAY: Of course, but——

HAZEL: You see, it happened in June. I haven't seen him since.

MAY (*astonished*): Haven't seen him since! Why, mercy! this is the first week in August. What in the world has separated you?

HAZEL: I know it seems strange, but he was called away the first part of June. It seems that his uncle has several farms or something and wanted George—that's his name, you know—George—isn't it sweet? Well, as I was saying, his uncle wanted George to come out and go from farm to farm to oversee the cattle or the corn or the poultry or something, and George had to go. His uncle paid for his education, you know, so of course it was really compulsory. Of course, it's hard on me. I won't see him again until he comes back to the city in the autumn.

MAY: How provoking! But don't you write to each other?

HAZEL: Yes, isn't it provoking? Of course we write, but George hurries from one spot to another so unexpectedly that I never know where he is exactly. I just sent him my new address yesterday when I found out the name of the post-office where our letters arrive. But, then, I haven't been so very lonesome. I've been too busy for that. But just think how he feels.

MAY (*cheerfully*): Oh, don't worry about him. No doubt he's enjoying himself at this very moment.

HAZEL: Enjoying himself!

MAY (with conviction): Without a doubt.

HAZEL (in shocked surprise): May! How can you talk so!

MAY: Out of sight is out of mind, you know.

HAZEL: May Ford!

MAY: Oh, don't look so dreadfully shocked. These men are all alike.

HAZEL: But George wouldn't speak to another girl when I was around.

MAY: Perhaps not. But he might console himself with half a dozen when you're away.

HAZEL (tapping her foot angrily): I don't believe it. Not of my George, anyway.

MAY (soothingly): Now, don't get angry, dear. Perhaps your George is the exception that proves the rule. In such a case I take back all I said. But what did you say his name was?

HAZEL: Feldon—George Feldon.

MAY (laughs): Oh, how funny!

HAZEL (indignantly): Funny!

MAY: I mean what a coincidence. Feldon is the name of the man who is staying at the next farm. He arrived unexpectedly last week, and now, when I come to think of it, he did tell me that he was overseeing affairs for his uncle, who was too busy with other things to attend to farming himself.

HAZEL: George here—at the next farm!

MAY: Yes, if there aren't two Feldons.

HAZEL: Oh, May! What shall I do? (Rises).

MAY: Go on peeling your apples. Mrs. Brown wants them for her pies as soon as possible, you know! She said so when we offered to help.

HAZEL: But George is here. I think I'll put on my white dress——

MAY: But he won't be here until——

HAZEL (interrupting): Do you like my hair arranged low in this way? Don't you think the other style is more becoming to me?

MAY: I——

HAZEL (unheeding): And he has come to stay at the next farm! Isn't it wonderful! (Goes to window.) To think that we should come—May, it is my George. He's coming down the path this very minute. He must have heard that I was here.

MAY: But he doesn't know that you are here—at least not yet.

HAZEL: Then what is he coming here for?

MAY: To see me.

HAZEL: You!

MAY (impatiently): Yes. Didn't I tell you that he had been here before?

HAZEL (haughtily): Oh, I see. He's been enjoying himself, has he?

MAY: Nonsense!

HAZEL: And all this time I've been breaking my heart over him.

MAY: But——

HAZEL (bursting into tears): No, I won't see him, and if you tell him that I'm here I'll never speak to you again as long as I live.

MAY: But he's knocking.

HAZEL: Sh—I'll hide behind the screen.

MAY: But isn't that rather——

HAZEL (interrupting): No—I'll put my fingers in my ears. Remember—don't tell.

(Enter GEORGE FELDON.)

GEORGE: Good morning, Miss May.

MAY: Why, good morning, Mr. Feldon. How you startled me! Won't you sit down?

GEORGE (taking a chair): Thanks, I believe I will. Walking in the sun is rather fatiguing. What are you doing? Peeling apples?

MAY: Yes.

GEORGE: For puddings?

MAY: No—guess again.

GEORGE: Pies?

MAY: Yes; how did you know?

GEORGE (fanning himself with his hat): Well, I imagined puddings and pies were the only things that apples were used for in the country.

MAY: I suppose you have a great many other things made of apples in the city.

GEORGE: Perhaps; but there isn't one of them that can compare with your pies.

MAY: Oh, Mr. Feldon, I'm afraid you are a sad flatterer. (Aside) They are Mrs. Brown's pies, but it is not worth while to undeceive him.

GEORGE: Why, I thought a flatterer was a man who always said pretty things to other girls. You surely would not believe that of me.

MAY: Don't you? Well, never mind if you don't. I always wanted to meet you, anyhow.

GEORGE (much flattered and surprised): Me!

MAY: Yes. Well, not exactly you, but anyone who comes from the city.

GEORGE (stiffly): Indeed!

MAY: Yes, someone of whom I can ask the questions I've been thinking about so earnestly for the last five years at least.

GEORGE: Won't that take rather long?

MAY: Not very. I hardly know where to begin, though. There's so much to ask. Let me see—tell me all about the world.

GEORGE (startled): That's a great deal to tell all at once, and then, besides, it isn't really very interesting.

MAY: Well, then, begin with some part of the world. Begin with the cities.

GEORGE (hesitatingly): The cities—well, the cities are—really, Miss Ford, you see there isn't anything interesting to tell you about the cities. You know, they are all so much alike.

MAY (pouting): I don't see that I can tell much from that. You forget that I'm out here on a farm. You must remember I'm not able to see a city if I stand in the doorway or walk out to the potato-patch. Don't you think that by trying real hard you could tell me what a big city looked like?

GEORGE (wipes forehead): Well, there are a great many houses—houses of all kinds, from little huts to large palaces. Then there are churches and courts of justice and theaters, and—well, other places of amusement. And the people are always rushing about trying to get their lunch or catch a train.

MAY: Train!

GEORGE: Yes, train. Didn't you ever hear about a train—a great iron machine that draws rows of houses on wheels—a machine whose life is fire and whose breath is steam?

MAY: Oh, Mr. Feldon, have you seen it? You must remember we are ten miles back from the depot and do all our travelling in hay wagons. Have you really seen a train?

GEORGE (pompously): Hundreds of times. There are other things, though, more wonderful still — electric machines which make all the streets at night as light as day—other electric machines which send the thought of one person to another even though they are thousands of miles apart.

MAY (in apparent great astonishment): Do they really have such things in the cities?

GEORGE: Yes, and other things, too.

MAY: Oh, tell me some more.

GEORGE (drawing his chair closer to her): Did you ever have your photograph taken?

MAY (wonderingly): Photograph! What in the world is a photograph?

GEORGE: A picture—that is, it's something like a picture. You know the photographer—he's the man who takes the picture—has a little black box called a camera, with a little round hole in one end. The photographer turns this hole toward the person, turns a spring, and an impression of the person is made upon the plate. This, by means of a chemical process, is printed on paper, and you have an exact image of yourself.

MAY (*doubtfully*): Is it true? Are you surely telling me the truth?

GEORGE: The very truth.

MAY: Then I suppose I must believe you. It's very wonderful, of course, very wonderful! But when the boiler bursts, or the fuse burns out, or the wire breaks, or the slide of the camera gets out of order—how sad it must be? (*She laughs outright.*)

GEORGE (*stiffly*): I suppose I owe you an apology. I did not know the extent of your information. I understood from w h a t you have told me that you had lived all your life in the country and knew nothing about the city. That is what I w a s led to believe.

MAY: Oh, I assure you it h a s a l l been very interesting. You're angry now, aren't you? Don't s a y no. Nothing in the world aggravates a woman so m u c h as her inability to make a man angry. It was a pity to tease you, but y o u didn't quite understand m e when I asked you about the world. I d i d n' t m e a n t h o s e things you told me about. Of c o u r s e, I know a b o u t t h e m—I could gain s u c h knowledge f r o m books if nowhere else. I meant the people you m e e t in the world.

GEORGE (*disgustedly*): T h e p e o p l e ! Oh, they're quite commonplace.

MAY (*open-eyed*): Commonplace! Do you mean to say they a r e not different f r o m the farmers who have l i v e d here all their lives?

GEORGE (*with much decision of manner*): Exactly.

MAY : But I heard——

GEORGE (*interrupting*): There are a few who are superior in some ways, but, really, as a general rule, they are all cast in the same mold.

MAY: And you mean to say that you never met anyone whom you considered your equal—never met anyone who inspired you with the wonderful passion of which the poets love to rave?

GEORGE: Well, I confess I did, Miss Ford. I was once inspired with that passion, or thought I was.

MAY: How romantic!

GEORGE: And burned with all the fires of love.

MAY: Correctly quoted!

GEORGE: Until hot weather came.

MAY (*glancing nervously toward screen, which shakes ominously*): Oh! And then what happened?

GEORGE: Then I found that the girl I really cared for was not in the city where I thought she was. I found I was altogether mistaken.

MAY (*in horror*): Mr. Feldon, how shockingly fickle you are. I am ashamed of you! I will not listen.

GEORGE: You'll have to. You asked me you know. I cannot understand what it was, whether the air of the fields went to my brain, or the freshness and purity of the simple country life showed me the true state of my feelings; but o n e thing became clear to me and is clear to me now—t h e girl I love is not here—here in this very place.

M A Y: Mr. Feldon!

G E O R G E: You are not angry with me for telling you, are you, Miss Ford? You have b e e n such a sweet, true friend to me ever since I came, and I must confess to someone. M i s s Ford, will you——

M A Y (*jumping to her feet and upsetting pan of apples*): I'll not listen to another word of such n o n s e n s e.

G E O R G E (*with emphasis*): N o n s e n s e! I w a s never more earnest in all my life. I i n s i s t that you shall hear me. If you will——

M A Y (*interrupting and putting her h a n d s over her ears*): I don't want to hear it.

GEORGE: B u t you must listen.

MAY: If y o u only knew——

G E O R G E (*unheeding*): I insist u p o n your attention, for you must know that the girl I love, and h a v e

" MY DEAR HAZEL, THE NEXT TIME YOU PLAN A SURPRISE FOR ME, CHOOSE SOME OTHER HIDING PLACE THAN ONE NEXT TO A WINDOW "

loved from the first moment I saw her, is at this very moment standing behind that screen.

HAZEL (*upsetting screen and rushing out*): George !

GEORGE: So you wouldn't come out, wouldn't you? Well, we're about even now, young lady.

HAZEL : But how did you know I was there?

GEORGE : My dear Hazel, the next time you plan a surprise for me, choose some other hiding place than one next to a window. As for you, Miss May, I think you and I can cry quits.

MAY (*from doorway*): Hazel, are your bridesmaids going to wear pink?

(*Curtain.*)

6

JUST HOMELY VERSE

WHEN "UNCLE TOM" STRIKES TOWN

By FRANK FARRINGTON

"UNCLE TOM" has come, by thunder!
  Thet's the show thet al'ays draws.
It'll make the people plunder
  Fam'ly savin's banks, because
Everybody's sure o' gettin'
  Money's worth at thet 'ere show.
All the folks around is settin'
  Store on takin' time to go.

Don't you hear the bloodhounds' bayin'
  Soundin' through the village loud?
Don't you hear the band a-playin',
  Marchin' down the street so proud?
"2 Marks 2" on donkeys ridin',
  Little Eva rigged up neat,
Curls her angel face a-hidin',
  Women sayin', "Ain't she sweet."

Uncle Tom with crinkly, wooly
  Wig an' burnt-cork-blacked-up face,
All the children think he's bully
  As they wave their hats an' race
Along beside his movin' cabin—
  Topsy, sittin' on the floor,
"Golly, what a time I'se habin'!"
  Hollers through the open door.

Down the flat a tent's a-rising,
  Flag a-floatin' high above.
People think it's most su'prisin'
  How those hustlin' showmen shove
Things along. Percession grand will
  Purty soon be 'rivin' there,
And inside the tent the band will
  Play each old-time Southern air.

I tell you now, if I do say it,
  I hev' seen some purty fair
Shows—"Old Homestead" as they play it
  In New York, with oxen there
On th' stage, an' city actin';
  But there ain't another show
Beats the real old mind-distractin'
  Play of "Uncle Tom," I know.

HOW SPECKLES STOLE HER NEST

By KATHERINE L. DANIHER

OLD SPECKLES was a knowing hen—she looked so
  very wise
When other hens would cackle over every new-laid prize,
And when each morning they would seek their cozy nests
  of hay,
The wily Speckles strutted off and hid herself away.
So when from twenty busy hens but nineteen eggs were
  shown,
'Twas whispered 'mongst the feathered flock that Speckles
  was the drone.
"The lazy thing!" said Crooked Beak, "she's too stuck up
  to work;
If I were Farmer Stebbins I would see she didn't shirk.
She's proud of her fine pedigree, for she's a Plymouth
  Rock,
And feels above us Leghorns, though I'm sure we're
  better stock."
"Just let them talk," thought Speckles, "for my turn is
  coming soon,
And by and by those saucy hens will sing another tune."
So one fine day she disappeared and soon the news went
  'round
Among the wondering chickens, that she wasn't to be
  found.
In vain did Farmer Stebbins hunt, for, search where'er
  he would,
He finally was forced to think the hen was gone for good.
One morning when the robins woke the echoes all around,
From underneath the doorstep came a cheeping, chirping
  sound,
And suddenly (would you believe a hen could play such
  tricks?)
The missing Speckles strutted forth with fourteen fluffy
  chicks!
While softly clucking to her brood, she proudly marched
  away
To where the envious biddies stood in wonder and dismay.
And Farmer Stebbins now declares of all his flock the best
Were hatched beneath the doorstep when old Speckles
  stole her nest.
Thus often on life's journey do we notice as we go
That those who cackle loudest have the least results to
  show;
While quiet perseverance, caring naught for praise or
  blame,
May, at the final reckoning, put scoffers all to shame.

FOR THE HOME FOLKS

WANTED—MOTHER'S PAY-DAY

By ALICE MAY DOUGLAS

THE mother has never had one, though many a year
    she's toiled,
And the myriad cares of the household her cheeks of the
    rose despoiled;
She has delved from early morning to the setting of the sun,
And received no compensation for the faithful service done.
Oh, never a day there passes but so many things she sees
She longs to buy for the dear ones—some playthings a
    child to please,
Or a necktie new for father, if only she had the pelf;
But mother, with all the wishing, has never a thought of self.
All say she can share their wages, if only she'd think to ask;
Yet to seek her coin like a beggar— she cannot stoop to the
    task!
That mother shall never go needy with emphasis all say,
But oh, if, with all their planning, they'd plan for her own
    pay-day.
For why should she feel her wages must come like a charity,
And she an account must render whatever her spendings be?
On a secret trip to the village she'd like at times to go;
Or to succor some needy neighbor, nor let the home folks
    know.
I wish that the mighty people all over this great broad land
Would demand a lawful payment for work of the mothers'
    hand,
For where the matter of wages to her own home folks is left
She is of her well-earned money more often than not bereft.

WHAT GRANDMOTHER USED TO SAY

By KATHERINE MARCH CHASE

IF BEFORE your door a rooster crows,
    Whether it rains or whether it snows,
Somebody's coming that very day—
That is what grandmother used to say.
"Shad-scale" and "mare-tail" clouds in the sky,
When weather has been a long time dry.
Sure sign of rain the very next day—
That is what grandmother used to say.
If ever the salt you chance to spill,
Just guard your temper with a will;
You're in for a fight ere close of day—
That is what grandmother used to say.
If you, while reposing in your bed,
Should by any chance dream of the dead,
You'll get a letter from far away—
That is what grandmother used to say.
If you drop the dishrag on the floor,

Pull down the blinds and bolt the door;
An untidy person calls that day—
That is what grandmother used to say.
If in the sky, the while the rain falls,
There's blue enough to make overalls,
That's a sign you can soon go out to play—
That is what grandmother used to say.

THE NEW AND THE OLD

By JOSEPHINE E. TOAL

SIS does the baking now for us—
    She's been to cooking-school
And learned the latest fads and fuss,
    So things are made by rule.
With cook-book, scales and measuring-cup
    She makes a great parade,
And all the flour is measured up
    While all the sugar's weighed.
Now, sometimes when she's started in
    She hasn't quite enough
Of raisins, spice or gelatin
    Or some new-patent stuff;
Then I must chase off to the store
    As fast as I can go,
And fetch it very quickly or
    The cake will all be dough.
She has a mixer for the bread,
    A cooker run by steam,
A chafing-dish, a thing to shred,
    A beater that's a "dream."
We have for dinner consommés
    And fricassees and bisques;
For supper, chips and mayonnaise;
    For breakfast, puffs and whisks.
But now and then Sis goes away,
    Or takes a little rest,
Then mother has her baking-day—
    That's when I eat the best.
Ma doesn't cook by recipe,
    She stirs in this and that;
No matter what it's meant to be,
    It always turns out pat.
When mother hasn't eggs or spice,
    Why, something else will do
To make the pudding just as nice
    And just as wholesome, too.
They're on the labor-saving plan,
    They do the work up soon—
Ma's one old battered mixing-pan
    And one old wooden spoon.

Some Original Ideas

By MARY KILSYTH

old-fashioned washstands that were made in the Colonial times to fit into a corner of the bedrooms. The exterior fittings of the washstand were an opaque striped dimity that matched the cover of the bed. The protector fastened against the wall was a finely spotted swiss muslin put up with a narrow heading. The top of the washstand was covered with white oilcloth (the kind used on kitchen tables), and over this a spread of cotton-faced piqué was laid. A standing towel-rack was kept near the washstand to hold fresh linen, and the slop-jar, when not in use, was pushed under the dimity curtain to one side of the understructure of this washstand, which was an empty flour barrel on which two wide, smooth boards were nailed. A variation of this idea may be carried out in a corner of a room by having a three-cornered board fitted into the angle. Sometimes the barrel may be discarded, and, instead, cleats of wood for supporting the board top may be secured to the wall itself.

The hangings for the washstand may be selected to suit the colors in the room, and a thick or thin texture used according to the

A CHAIR SWING

A SENSIBLE WASHSTAND

THE home that must be furnished on a moderate sum of money often has an advantage in general attractability over a house that is fitted up on an expensive scale.

Miss Alcott's "Little Women" illustrates in a not wholly fictitious way the development of ingenuity in the home through the necessities of poverty. Real heroines, under something of the same limitations, are, at the present time, imprinting their originality in many quaint and effective devices for themselves and their families.

Looking back a few years and contrasting the attempts at that time for beautifying the house with those of our own day, there is a decided, noticeable progress. The vital interest that is felt nowadays in this work does not stop at traditions of the past, but seeks to improve existing conditions with better facilities at hand, and the wideness of the field for endeavor is only limited by the number of homes.

In two bedrooms that were lately visited by the writer there were two pleasing suggestions for combining a necessary utility with a decorative appearance.

The idea of building a washstand against the wall was not a novel one, but the way in which it was carried out was unusual. A jog in the wall at the right of the mantel gave ample space for holding the toilet set. Too often the facilities for bathing are inconvenient from being disposed too closely together. This is the chief fault of the

FOR THE HOME

individual taste. Cretonne may take the place of the dimity, and linen at the back against the wall instead of the muslin.

The arrangement of the top of a bureau has a great deal to do with the orderly and restful expression that is desirable in a sleeping-room. If one of the small drawers that are usually found in the upper part of a bureau is reserved for small articles for toilet use, there will be less difficulty in keeping the top of the bureau in tidy fashion. A box for the brush and comb is an addition to the equipment of the bureau and a convenience in dressing. A pretty way to make a box for this position is to take two of the ordinary pasteboard boxes in which shoes are sent home from the shops, cut each box carefully apart and then cover each piece with muslin, silkoline, silk or linen. The pairs that match in size are then overhanded together and returned to the original shape with invisible stitches and the cover fastened at the front with narrow ribbon.

The bureau scarf may be made of hemstitched butcher's linen or of cotton-faced piqué with the edges scalloped and buttonholed with mercerized linen floss,

A BUREAU WITH SEPARATE GLASS

In leaving a door into a chamber open for ventilation it is often desirable to screen a portion of the room from the hall. This may be accomplished by hanging a door-guard over the opening between the hinges. The guard illustrated is made of two strips of heavy brown linen sewed together, with the bottom fringed and knotted and the top ornamented with old Japanese sword-hilts.

A fireplace curtain was lately devised by a home-maker who, after trying to harmonize a discordant combination of bright-blue tiling with a green wall-paper, found her task impossible without effacing one or the other of the decorations. As there was no grate under the mantel, it was a simple matter to hang a green-and-white Japanese cotton material over the objectionable tiles.

The charm of an open fire was never fully realized in one country home until a chair swing was installed near its cheerful glow. The idea of using a piazza chair in this manner was the result of a discussion on having a swinging settle in the room, and the disappointment of finding the spaces of the sitting-room too limited for the larger piece of furniture.

A FIREPLACE CURTAIN

A DOOR-GUARD

A BABY IN CAMP

By HARRIET CARYL COX

"I SHALL have my two weeks August first," Tom remarked one night at supper. "Can you be ready for our vacation then?"

"I guess so," I answered, slowly. At this lack of enthusiasm on my part Tom opened his eyes.

"Why, it won't take two days to get ready for camp," he said in surprise. "Why, do you want more time?"

"Camp," I repeated after him. "What on earth are you talking about?"

"Why, our vacation, surely," he replied. "What else do you suppose? Haven't we been planning for a whole year to go camping again in that blessed old tent?"

"Yes," I said, and I presume there was a touch of exasperation in my voice, "but goodness! Tom, that was before the baby came. You don't suppose we can go camping with a baby, do you?"

"Certainly," he replied, promptly. "Why not?"

"But in a tent!" I expostulated. "Whoever heard of such a thing—and, Tom, he is only five months old."

"I know, but I don't see the difference. Suppose he was seven months."

"Well, I do," I retorted. "You are simply crazy. It was all very well for us last year. I'll admit that we did have a glorious time and that it did us both worlds of good, but we had only ourselves to think of then. With a baby, a little baby, it is impossible." I said this with a final air. Being the baby's mother, I felt that I knew a thing or two about him and his many requirements.

Tom sat and gazed at me silently for several seconds.

"Now, look here, my dear girl," he finally ventured, in a conciliatory tone. "I don't want to suggest anything out of reason, and you know I wouldn't run any risk with that blessed boy, not for all the vacations in the world, but let's just reason this thing out and find out what the objections are and why it is impossible. It seems the simplest thing in the world to me."

"Of course it does," I cried. "You're a man and you don't know half the things it takes to run a baby."

"Well, what, for instance?"

"His food, first of all. You know it has to be cooked and kept cool in glass jars. It isn't as if we were feeding him on a food just prepared with hot water."

"A one-flame kerosene stove," Tom suggested, promptly, seizing a pad and writing it down. "Eighty-five cents, madam; at a Monday morning bargain sale."

I could not help laughing. Anything else than a camp fire had not suggested itself to me.

"Yes," I admitted, grudgingly. "Of course I could cook it in a double boiler over that, but how about keeping the food cool? We'd have no ice-chest, and there mustn't be the slightest possibility of its souring. Just a little sourness, you know, might give him cholera infantum."

"Oh, don't!" he said, holding up his hands. "If we aren't near enough to a place where we can get ice to pack in an old box, I'll invent something. Don't you worry on that score I'll see that baby's food keeps cool, if I have to dig a ten-foot well for it."

"Yes, and spill it all in drawing it up with some one of your wonderful inventions," I retorted, somewhat assured, I must confess, by his confident air.

"What next?" he queried. "The first two, and most important, items have been disposed of."

His prompt dismissal of these two things was characteristic, and I vainly searched through my mind for some absolutely convincing and conclusive argument against the scheme, but meanwhile Tom proceeded with his argument:

"If our boy were a delicate hothouse plant, like some of the white-faced, peaked youngsters around, of course I wouldn't say a word, but you know he's as hearty and well as a baby can be. There isn't a baby on the street—and, let me see, how many are there, twenty-seven?—who is as strong as he, and you know he's an out-of-door baby, and has been from the very first. He stays out of doors now pretty nearly all day in his carriage in the yard; the only difference will be that there it will be all the time, and the air will be purer and sweeter because it will be free from the taint of city smells. And he shall lie on the ground, and it will do him as much good as it does us, even if ants do crawl over him and he gets 'as dirty as a pig.'"

He could not resist this last dig at me, and I forgave him, for the picture he drew was certainly a charming one, and I felt, way down in my heart, that after all he was right.

"And can you get ready?" he repeated, smiling.

"Perhaps," I admitted.

And this is how we did it.

To my great astonishment, Tom did not insist on going to Sebago, as we had the year before. Optimistical, as he was, he admitted that it was just as well to be within easy reach of a good doctor in case of emergency.

We chose a quiet town, accessible by electric cars, wherein was a small lake surrounded by woodsy shores and fertile fields, with scattered here and there an old-fashioned farmhouse. For our tent site we selected the open end of a field which sloped from a high knoll down to the cool depths of a ferny dell and the sandy shores of a crystal-clear little lake. The lake and a spring near by supplied us with water for washing and cooking, but for drinking purposes and for the baby's use we obtained water from the great well of the hundred-and-fifty-year-old farmhouse, with roof sloping down to the always-hospitably-open door. The picture of the old home, soft and gray with age, as it appeared across the well-mown fields, when we approached it in our daily trip for milk and vegetables, I shall never forget.

Our camp equipment consisted of the tent, with a mattress for Tom and me, made, as previously, of hay stuffed into a pair of gray summer blankets sewed together; rubber sheet, pair of summer blankets, oil-stove, gallon can of kerosene, four tin plates, potato knife, kettle, frying-pan, spoons, borax, soap, towels, glass jar of sugar, one of salt, tin can of matches, nails, rope, hammer, hatchet, several cans of condensed soup, package of prepared flour for griddle cakes, oatmeal, rice, and from the farm we obtained potatoes, beans, tomatoes and corn, while Tom occasionally wandered away from camp and returned home with a slice of steak or a piece of mutton for a broth.

In addition to necessaries for our own use, I took for the baby his three nursing-bottles, which, when empty, I kept in a pan of water in which borax was dissolved; a whole box of rubber nipples (in case of accident), safety-pins galore, two small funnels for pouring his food into the bottles, an agate double boiler, a surply of his food, and four glass jars in which to keep it. The bed for his Royal Highness we made of hay, packed tightly into a covering of heavy bleached cotton, and this we laid in the bottom of a large, shallow box which we begged of a village grocer, and which Tom devotedly lugged two miles. The box was so broad the youngster could throw out his arms at will and not hit the sides, and just deep enough so he couldn't roll out, though once he did surprise us by flopping over upon our mattress with a soft little thud.

There was, of course, the mosquito problem, for those little pests would come into the tent at night despite our spraying oil of pennyroyal about and keeping a horrid smudge fire in front of the tent, which disturbed us vastly more than it did the sharp little creatures.

The first morning, despite the canopy of netting which we had hung over our son, his poor little head and face were a sight to behold. It would have troubled a phrenologist as to the true shape of the child's head and his resulting characteristics to have seen those great lumps standing out like the peaks of a mountain range, with little valleys between, and the cruel red blotches on his soft, fair skin were enough to make one weep. Indeed, in the early morning light, when Tom's ejaculation, "Look at that baby," aroused me from a deep sleep, I thought some fearful disaster had befallen the precious little lad; but when he looked at me with his cheerful grin, and seemed disturbed not at all by his newly acquired ornaments, I was quieted into consenting to stay, though my first declaration was that we would pull up stakes that very morning and depart for home.

"If we only had one of those big, round, dome-like covers of netting such as they have to put over food," I said mournfully, looking from the baby to Tom, then back to the poor, disfigured little face once more.

"I've got it!" that husband of mine cried, finally, jumping to his feet. "You don't happen to have any tape in that handy work-bag of yours, do you?" The aforesaid bag having furnished so many surprisingly convenient articles, Tom had a sublime faith in its capacity.

"I don't know," I answered, rummaging in the cretonne bag with its draw-strings. "Why, yes, see here." I held up four balls of cheap, black, cotton tape. They had been there for ages.

He grabbed them eagerly. "Tacks?" he cried.

"Of course!" I replied, rummaging for them. "What are you going to do?"

"You wait," he said, importantly. "Just watch me."

So, like a wise and dutiful wife, I said nothing, but picked up the baby, whom he had unceremoniously dumped into the middle of our mattress, and sat back and watched.

First, he tipped over the box, which was baby's bed, and fitted the netting over it, as if he were simply covering it neatly, and sewed strips of the tape over every seam he made in the netting. Indeed, when it was done, it was a complete box of netting, minus a cover. Then he cut from a willow tree near-by eight slender shoots of even size. Tipping the box back into the proper position, he nailed at each corner one of these shoots, so that he had four uprights for all the world like four old-fashioned bed-posts. To complete the canopy scheme, he tacked the other four shoots across the top, connecting the uprights, and then slipped the covering of netting over it all. The strips of tape he had sewed on exactly followed the line of the framework, and there was as nice a frame of mosquito netting as one could wish.

"Now to fasten it down to the edge of the box, so that 'twill keep down tight, and yet we can get at the boy easily," Tom said, sitting down beside me.

It was my turn now. "You 'tend the baby and I'll fix that," I said; and Tom, with a smile half-doubtful as to the success of my ingenuity, lay back and frolicked with the boy, while from my convenient bag I abstracted a card of "snap fasteners," such as women put to every use under the sun, and sewed the ball parts on a strip of tape six inches apart, which strip I tacked around the top outside edge of the box. Then I sewed the other part of the fasteners to another tape in positions to exactly correspond with the first, and this was sewed to the bottom of the frame of netting. As I finished the work, I glanced at Tom. He was absorbed in exercising the boy, and had evidently forgotten on what I was working, so I brought the canopy down, pressed each fastener onto its mate, and, behold, I had as complete a mosquito-proof bed as one could well devise.

"Look there," I said to Tom, and Tom looked, and then he whistled, and then he turned to the baby: "You have a very smart mama," he said, solemnly.

The next problem was the keeping of the boy's food cool. Tom had sworn he could do it, so I awaited results with interest. About twenty feet away from the tent there was a tangle of bushes under a pine tree, where the sun seldom rested. Here he dug a square hole, one by two feet, and two feet deep. In this cavity he put clean, wet sand from the lake shore, packed it down solidly and then covered it with a layer of green leaves. When I had made my supply of food for the day, put it into the jars and let it cool in the breeze, I would bury the jars as deep as possible in the cool sand, of course keeping them tightly covered. Only the tops were out of the sand, and these I covered with leaves. In this way the food kept perfectly, as well as if I had had the most perfectly equipped ice-chest obtainable. On very hot days, and there were several of them, Tom would wet the whole thing down once or twice, and the evaporation kept things cool. Indeed, I kept our own milk and pail of butter in this improvised ice-chest with perfect results.

So the way was cleared for ease and comfort. With no house to care for, the work of the day became mere play, and long and happy were the hours we three spent together, gathering health and strength from the pure, life-giving air and contact with Mother Earth. Never was there so good a baby. With a thin wool blanket under him to keep away any possible dampness, he would lie for hours looking up at the waving trees and watching birds and friendly squirrels, cooing softly to himself in a strange, sweet little language known only to himself and his fond parents, to whom this gurgling was the sweetest music of the woods.

As the days passed, the baby, already strong, grew stronger. Each night I rubbed his little body till it fairly glowed, and night and morning Tom put him through his exercises in a way that would have alarmed any mother but one who was used to it. First on one hand, then on the other, he would balance the little body, while the boy fairly crowed with delight. But his greatest achievement was making the little fellow stand. With each little hand clasped tightly above his papa's middle finger, at Tom's words, "Come, boy," and a gentle lifting, the baby would straighten his little legs and come up to his feet, standing there in perfect delight and sending forth the greatest string of joyful exclamations. He loved the exercise so that he would stop his worst fit of crying (and he did cry sometimes) if once Tom would give him his fingers to clutch, and cries would become a happy prattle as he stood up, his little mouth wide open and his face beaming with joy.

So strong and straight did his legs become, and so firm his grasp, that before we came away, he would stand by himself, holding fast to a stick—such a tiny little bit of humanity, in the world for only five months, yet instinct with life and joy.

And when our two weeks were over and we returned to town, never was there a prettier sight than he, his little face, arms and hands burned the russet bronze the summer girl so covets. Friends who had predicted dire failure to our plan and a speedy return looked at him in amazement, while the children in our neighborhood designated him as "the baby who went camping." But Tom says, "Pooh, it was only a sensible thing to do. If grown folks can be comfortable in a tent for two weeks, so can a baby. Why not?"

And our own experience leads me to pass it on to other mothers, and to echo his words, "Why not?"

NOVELTIES MADE OF HANDKERCHIEFS

HAVE you ever stopped to think of the number of things that nowadays are made from a handkerchief? Sometimes two or more are necessary to complete an article, but many of the prettiest ideas are carried out using only one.

The latest novelty made from a single handkerchief is a nightingale or baby's cape. (See page 463.) For it is needed a perfectly square twelve-inch hemstitched and embroidered handkerchief, one and one-half yards of wash ribbon and four yards of lace one inch wide. From one of the corners cut to the center of the handkerchief; then, folding it cornerwise so that the cut is directly in front of you, measure off one and one-half inches each side of it on the fold. Now cut the neck about an inch deep in back and one and one-half inches deep in front. Then, by slightly moistening the thumb and first finger and rolling the goods, make as narrow a hem as possible. After this, overhand the lace on the nightingale, putting very little around the neck, and fulling the rest on evenly. Tie the cape in front with the ribbon, and sew a

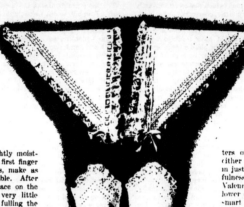

COLLAR AND CUFFS FOR SHIRT-WAIST OR NIGHTGOWN

BAG FOR SOILED HANDKERCHIEFS

small bow an inch more than half-way up each side, for the armholes. If you wish the cape to be plainer, or if it is desired for a larger child, a gentleman's fine linen handkerchief, with a nicely embroidered initial for the left shoulder, is very neat and effective.

A dainty cap, shown in the illustration with the nightingale, is made from a single handkerchief. One that was beautifully fine and sheer and on which the embroidery was very dainty was selected. One side of the handkerchief is folded back to the depth of two inches and the opposite side is then turned back to meet it, the folds being made so that the embroidered edges are right side up. A frill of narrow German Valenciennes lace is ruffled and sewed on the underside of the scallop of the narrow or front fold, and then the handkerchief is lightly folded so that the two double edges of the plain portion meet. The cap is now turned to the wrong side and these edges neatly overhanded together to the depth of four inches from the bottom, the remainder being gathered and drawn up close to form the crown. A box plait three-quarters of an inch wide is made either side of the back and sewed in just far enough to adjust the fulness properly. A piece of the Valenciennes is ruffled under the lower edge of the cap, and two smart little bows made of wash ribbon are sewed to the top and back of the cap, using wash ribbon also for the ties.

The glove and handkerchief cases are made from men's colored handkerchiefs. The case embroidered with the word "Gloves" is made from a single handkerchief, and a square of fine lawn matching the latter in color. The embroidery is done first and the word is either written or stamped in the exact center and then worked with mercerized cotton. The piece of lawn is cut the same size as the handkerchief, and then a quarter of an inch is turned in all around and the square basted and then hemmed to the handkerchief with stitches which do not show on the right side. The finished square is folded into three parts and ribbons sewed on at each end and in the center to tie the sides together. (See illustration.)

The handkerchief-case utilizes two handkerchiefs, together with the necessary lawn for lining. Two pieces of cardboard are cut one-half an inch smaller all around

GLOVE-CASE MADE FROM A COLORED HANDKERCHIEF

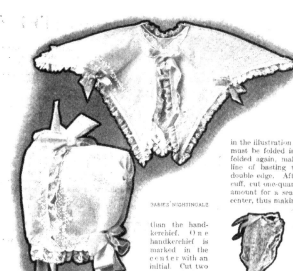

BABIES' NIGHTINGALE

BABIES' CAP

Valenciennes to the edge of the beading and continue it all around under the scalloped edge of the handkerchief. Two rows of beading about three inches long are joined together and threaded with ribbon and sewed to the front edges of the collar pieces, thus joining them. The backs meet in a point and are simply tacked together. Ribbon is threaded through the beading and a small rosette finishes the front ends.

For the cuffs which appear in the illustration just below the collar a handkerchief must be folded in half on the diagonal, and then folded again, making a still smaller triangle. Run a line of basting thread about four inches from the double edge. After ascertaining the correct size for cuff, cut one-quarter inch from this line, allowing that amount for a seam. Cut the big piece through the center, thus making two large and two small pieces for

A DAINTY CORSET-COVER

than the handkerchief. One handkerchief is marked in the center with an initial. Cut two pieces of lawn same size as handkerchiefs. One handkerchief is fastened over each cardboard square and then the lawn linings are basted into place and the edges overhanded together. The two squares are joined together by ribbon ties, the position of which is clearly shown.

The handkerchief corset-cover, while not exactly a novelty, is still so attractive that it seemed desirable to show one. Three handkerchiefs, a piece of insertion, lace to match, beading and ribbon for the neck, waist and armholes, are the required materials. The three handkerchiefs are folded in half, point to point, and cut on this line, and one of these halves is again cut in quarters. These smaller portions form the fronts; their cut edges are held down by French knots and edged with lace. Pattern No. 1080 may be used as a guide for shaping the lower portion of the back and the under-arms. The handkerchiefs are simply joined together with one or two rows of insertion, and then joined to form a straight strip. The shoulder straps are made of the insertion and beading and edged with lace. Narrow beading is sewed flat to the neck edge and the wider is made the correct waist size. Adjust fulness of cover at fronts and back and sew to beading.

The collar-and-cuff set on page 464 are fashioned from embroidered handkerchiefs. For collar the square is cut once across from corner to corner, making two triangular pieces. The cut edges are folded back once to the right side and a piece of beading sewed down to cover the raw edge. Overhand a ruffle of narrow

HANDKERCHIEF OR VEIL CASE TO MATCH GLOVE-CASE

each cuff. The lower edge of each small triangle is stitched to the lower edge of the large piece, care being taken that the small piece when turned back comes right side up. Finish scalloped edges with a ruffle of narrow lace.

The bag shown is made of two embroidered handkerchiefs. The top handkerchief is left in the folds in which it came from the shop; which folds or plaits are basted down and then a circular opening two and a half inches in diameter is cut in the center. The raw edge is turned over once on right side and covered by beading through which ribbon draw-strings are run. When the opening is finished place the two handkerchiefs together, the cut one on top, as in illustration. Then join as pictured with feather-stitching.

CLUNY LACE FOR TABLE DECORATION

By GRACE ALINE LUTHER

N EXTREMELY ornamental and decorative variety of lace-work has just been made possible to needleworkers by the advent of some new heavy linen braids. These braids represent all the leading thread combinations of Cluny, that beautiful real lace which has so long been a favorite because of its large and effective patterns and substantial durability. The French nuns are most expert in producing it, and seem to feel no dread of the endless pins and ever-twisting bobbins used in this pillow lace. To the average American woman, real lace-work, whether point or pillow, stands for a sad tangle of valuable time, overstrained eyes and nerves, so that she will hail with satisfaction these Cluny braids, which will place the accomplishment of this simple and very attractive lace-work within the compass of pleasant needlework.

The characteristic of Cluny lace is a certain heaviness and firmness of braid effects and connecting stitches, which allow, at the same time, a bold openness of design, making the lace essentially useful in household decoration, although, with the present vogue of heavy dress trimmings, it lends itself quite satisfactorily to these ornamentations and accessories. As a border for centerpieces, tea-cloths and doilies, buffet scarfs, curtain and door panels, it is beyond doubt the most ornamental lace, and bids fair to rival Battenberg along lines over which it has previously held undisputed sway. Cluny work has one unfailing advantage over Renaissance or Battenberg lace—when the braid is well basted it is three-quarters done, for, owing to the presence of a small bobbin corresponding to the twisted threads of real lace, very little stitchery is needed beyond the secure fastening of the braid to hold together the different motifs which form the design.

A twenty-four-inch centerpiece is shown at top of the next page, and it seems almost incredible that this gives an example of braid-work practically without lace stitchery. A few Mechlin ribs are all that is required beyond a painstaking basting and fastening of the various braids together. The accompanying cut illustrates the braids which are used in this centerpiece and the three following designs—it shows

five very representative patterns from a list of fifteen or twenty varieties.

As to the method of making, there is very little to explain. All straight Cluny braids have draw-threads, so that the large circles and surrounding waved lines of straight braid are easily shaped to the pattern. The shell braid used as a border is overhanded to the straight braid. One precaution is essential, however, in all Cluny—both in basting and finishing the work must either be done in an embroidery frame or with a piece of oilcloth back of the pattern, so as to prevent all inclination toward drawing or puckering the braids. The oilcloth is preferable, and a small piece only will be necessary when the work undertaken is of large proportions. This piece may be basted on different sections of the design as the work progresses. Between the two parallel rows of braid at the inside and also at the outside of the design a sort of medallion braid is inserted, being alternately caught above and below, which sets it in points—a sort of ornament very characteristic of the bobbin lace.

The use of two needles will be found helpful in inserting this braid, one for each side of the space which is being filled. The braid is fastened with a tight buttonhole or knot stitch between each so-called medallion, and the thread then run along the straight braid across the intervening space to the point where the next buttonhole-stitch is to be taken. The criss-cross of small braid is next applied to the pattern before the small pointed ovals in each scallop are filled. Here again two needles are called into requisition, but two pieces of braid are also used, which are alternately passed from one side to the other, thus forming a sort of basketry work. One of these lengths of braid runs in its series of zigzags in one piece all around the entire center. The other is cut at each of the light sections of the design, as will be discovered on following the lines of braid in the illustration.

Each intersection of the braid must now be caught and the extra short ends inserted, which are required to fill the spaces above the joining of the ovals. The first is done without breaking the thread, by simply taking a fine knot-stitch at each point where the braids cross, the needle then being run along the braid to the next point of intersection. Care must be taken to

CLUNY LACE SCARF-END

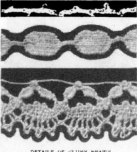

DETAILS OF CLUNY BRAIDS

fasten neatly and securely all ends of braids whether straight or fancy, and this is especially important as regards all short lengths, which, unless well buttonholed to their supporting pieces, will surely pull out in the wear and tear of use and laundry.

The pointed ovals before mentioned are now to be filled. The same medallion braid is also used here—two pieces crossed honiton-wise at the center and continued at each side. The last are all held in place by the Mechlin ribs, which consist simply in this case of two parallel stitches from straight to fancy braid with the thread alternately woven under and over, each forming a solid rib.

The lace may now be pressed, but not removed from the pattern, which must not be done before inserting the linen center. Only the innermost basting is removed for this, and the circular linen set within the encompassing braid, which is then overhanded closely to the linen. Then the lace may be removed from the pattern and the raw edges of the center neatly turned in and fastened on the wrong side.

Two sizes of doilies are made to match this centerpiece, one twelve-inch, the other nine. As the method of procedure in these is the same as above, detailed description is unnecessary, a survey of the illustrations showing where braid or Mechlin rib is employed. In these it will be noticed that the medallion braid is not the same as used before, the connecting narrow portion being longer,

TUMBLER DOILY

PLATE DOILY

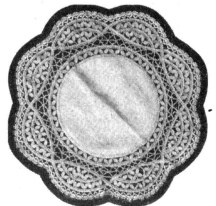

CENTERPIECE OF CLUNY LACE

but the other varieties correspond with the center.

The scarf-end illustrated is suitable for buffet or bureau, and, since it has a repeating border, may be made any length, from three-quarters of a yard to two or more yards. It is always best to begin with the straight-edged braid. Baste and draw this into position and next overhand the shell braid around the edges. This shell-edge is employed to make small flower forms by drawing the top thread above its tiny medallions and also the upper thread of the shell proper. These threads are tied and the braid-ends overhanded together. The small filling braid is zigzagged on as before described, two pieces or one being employed, according to the space, and the large medallion braid is also used. The leaf forms in the corners are easily shaped from the straight braid and held in place with medallion and lacing braid.

The linen center is inserted also in the manner before described. In a word, the problems to be met with in this lace-work are few in number and it is easily within the reach of any needlewoman's skill, as it involves none of the intricacies of pillow lace. The actual stitchery progresses more readily than in any other lace-work, while the final result is decorative and compares most favorably with real bobbin Cluny lace.

A well-made piece of Cluny enhanced by the rich background of a mahogany table, will satisfy both the esthetic and practical demands of the most exacting housewife, since such decoration may be truly called both beautiful and durable.

AN AUGUST OUTING SONG

By HARVEY PEAKE

BEFORE

OH, THIS is the season of outdoor life,
   Of days unrestrained and free,
It's vacation time from the State of Maine
To the Florida Keys and across the plain,
To San Francisco and back again,
   From the lakes to the Mexic Sea!
The seaside resorts are jammed with guests,
   And the beaches with bathers lined,
There are camps on mountain, plain and lake,
At the springs the crowds their thirst do slake
   With draughts of nauseous kind!

   Then pack up the tent and have it sent
      To the point of nearest fun!
   The golfing set and the tennis net,
      And the fishing-rod and gun!
   The light canoe, just built for two
      (We'll row on moonlight nights);
   Put the hammock in, and the mandolin,
      For we're off for a month's delights!

AFTER

It wouldn't have been so very bad
   If it hadn't rained each day!
And leaked with most persistent bent
Through the top of our little canvas tent,
Until all our edibles were blent
   In a most distressing way!
The mosquitoes were having an outing, too,
   And selected this selfsame spot;
But as they hadn't come here to be drowned,
They came inside and flew around,
   And kept things very hot!

   Then hang up the tent with its mildewed scent,
      There's water in every thread!
   The golfing set is likewise wet,
      And the gun with rust is red!
   Our clothes are torn and weather-worn,
      Our bodies are filled with bites,
   With colds distrest; now need we rest
      When back from the month's delights!

THE MOTHERS' ADVISORY CLUB

This is little Elizabeth Brock of Macon, Mo., raised on **Mellin's Food** from birth, and noted everywhere for her sunny disposition and perfect health.

Mellin's Food will make milk agree with your baby, and he will keep perfectly well all Summer long.

You can even travel with your baby, if you want to, and change the milk supply without risk, if you use **Mellin's Food** to prepare the milk.

Send to-day for a free sample of Mellin's Food and try it.

MELLIN'S FOOD CO.,   BOSTON, MASS.

ITEM OF GREATEST GENERAL INTEREST

To Help Some Little Traveler

WHEN I was a little four-year-old I was restless and nervous. When mother often took me on short journeys it was one of her problems to keep me amused, that I might not be a nuisance both to her and the other passengers; so four things always went in the hand-satchel with us — a paper of pins, a bar of yellow soap, a paper of tacks and a little tack-hammer. As soon as I grew troublesome, the paper of pins was produced and I forthwith stood up on the car seat and commenced to ornament the back by sticking in pins in long lines, in rows around the buttons, and in queer-looking figures, which I fondly imagined were "stars." When mother saw I was beginning to tire, she would suggest putting them all back neatly in the paper. This took some time and was very interesting, as mother had made it a matter of pride with me to put each pin through its own four little holes. Then, when the delights of looking around the car or devouring "animal" crackers, a leg at a time, had palled on me, the bar of soap, the tacks and the little hammer were brought forth. That was even more fun than the pins. I generally forsook the hammer entirely to put the tacks in the soap, but enjoyed mightily pulling them out with the little claw end. I can remember mother telling of a tired man with a very tired child, who was on the train once when we started, having come many miles then, and having many more to go after we left. The little girl was restless and nothing he could do would keep her quiet, until mother passed over half of her paper of pins to him, when he exclaimed, with gratitude, "Madam, you are a wonderful woman!"   HELEN CHAPIN

QUESTIONS

How Shall She Keep Them from Spoiling this Baby?

I AM A young mother, twenty-two years old, and my little boy is fifteen months. He has developed lately,

EDITED BY THE READERS OF THE DESIGNER

Beginning with this number, and until further notice, the contribution to this department each month which appears to be of the greatest general interest will be paid for at the rate of two cents a word. For each other contribution published, one dollar will be paid as heretofore. Slips or coupons will not be necessary, but the name and address of the sender must be plainly written on the first page of all contributions. This new arrangement is made in compliance with the latest ruling of the Post-Office Department regarding contests and prize offers.

after being very tractable, quite a temper. Some of my family think it funny to see such a mite strike and kick, and they laugh at his naughty ways. So I'd like to ask two questions: What shall I do to break him of these ways without being cruel to him? and How can I convince the older relatives that, by and by, they'll not like the temper that now seems to them so cunning?   E. K.

Excessive Timidity

WILL some mother suggest a remedy for excessive timidity in my little girl? She is two years old, and still continues to cry all the time a visitor is in the house. Meeting people on the street does not affect her in the least, but as soon as any stranger enters the house she begins to weep bitterly. I have tried letting her "cry it out," as I have been advised to do, but at the end of an hour she was still sobbing hysterically with no signs whatever of stopping.   MRS. B.

ANSWERS

Let the Children Sleep

HAVING taught school for years, I have collected my own statistics among the young folks, and each year canvass the school once or twice. I find the rosy, happy, eager child has always been allowed to sleep. The little, puny, nervous child has been the victim of a conscientious discipline that routs the poor, tired, sleepy baby out of bed because it is seven o'clock, or six, or even, as I once had a child tell me, "I get up at half-past four every morning." By the way, that particular child fell out of the race in the grammar school on account of nervous prostration. My own little girl goes to bed at half-past seven and gets up when she gets ready; that is, when she is wide awake, except, of course, on school mornings, when she is called in time for a simple toilet and her breakfast, but then she goes to bed at half-past six. I think it is wicked to make a child get up before it has had enough sleep. If it must get up moderately early, then let it go to bed correspondingly early.   A.

Turn the Little Feet to Pasture

SURELY, let the small boy be a barefoot laddie. I am the mother of two little ones, and have let them go barefoot during the hot summer months ever since they were old enough to lie on the floor and kick up their little pink heels; and two more robust little ones one never need wish to see. I never knew of their taking cold by going barefoot, but I have known of their taking cold from getting their feet wet when wearing shoes. And oh, what delight to run out after a warm shower and paddle in the water on the soft grass, or even in the soft, warm mud! I write from experience. I was a child not so very many decades ago, and went barefoot, too, and was not a boy either. Let the children live close to nature and you will be well repaid, even if you must take time occasionally to wrap up a stubbed toe.

G. U.

An Adverse Opinion on the Subject

I TRIED letting my little boy go barefoot last summer, and found it a source of much annoyance, as he was continually coming in crying with a cut or a splinter in his foot, and also made a great fuss when called to put his shoes and stockings on. I have decided this summer to allow him to go barefoot only as a great treat on special occasions, such as when he goes to the seashore, or where there is a nice sandy or grassy place to play, and then only during the morning hours. Shoes and stockings must go on for the afternoon.

MRS. O. E. S.

What Mrs. B. Thinks

THE practise of letting little children run barefoot is a very dangerous one. If we could be sure that there were no rusty nails or bits of glass around, it might be all right. Even an ordinary scratch coming in contact with tetanus germs might lead to very serious results. Clothe your little boy's feet in light-weight cotton stockings and roomy, stout-soled shoes (or sandals). He will be just as comfortable and much safer from danger than the "barefoot boy."

MRS. B.

How this Mother Arranges the Little Duties

IN ANSWER to M J., I will tell the plan I follow with my two daughters in regard to their small duties. I find, after trying many plans, that giving each child to do answers much the best. The little tasks one can do as well as the other they perform each week turn about. If they choose to exchange work some days I make no objection, as long as it is well and promptly done. I think it is apt to discourage a child if its work is never done—if it thinks it is liable to be called on at any time to do tasks that it is apt to think—quite truly, too, sometimes—someone else should have done. By all means give a child definite work, and then insist on it being done promptly and satisfactorily.

M. B.

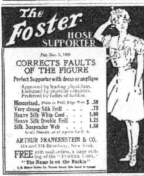
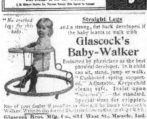

The Mothers' Advisory Club.—Concluded.

A Hammock for Baby

Few mothers seem to know of the comfort and convenience of a hammock instead of a cradle for baby. I put up hammock hooks in several rooms, so baby could always take her naps in the most comfortable one. The hooks are screwed near the door and window casings, and the window curtains hide the hooks at the window. Then I bought a woven hammock, full size, not a "baby hammock," with a pillow at one end, which spreads it. On hot days baby was put in it with nothing under her, for she was very fat. She would have been too warm on a bed, but in the hammock the free circulation of air kept her comfortable. She took long naps, and did not break out with the heat.   W. C. R.

Utilizing the Screen Door

I wonder how many mothers have ever thought of utilizing the screen door as an amusement for the little ones on the warm summer days. Draw in bold outline with chalk a flower, a bird, an animal or any figure which will interest the child, and which will be simple in outline. Then two children provided with a darning-needle, threaded with bright yarn of appropriate color, sit one indoors, the other out, and, weaving back and forth, will be delightfully amused as the picture unfolds before them. The yarn is easily removed, the outline washed off and another picture drawn.   G. G. J.

A Letter of Thanks from One Mother

Let me thank The Designer readers who so kindly replied to my question in these columns about that "selfish little fellow." I wish to especially thank J. H. I have followed her advice and it works to a charm.   C. L. C.

A Difference of Opinion

The January number of The Designer was the first copy of that magazine I had ever seen, and I read with much interest the various departments, among others the "Mothers' Advisory Club." I do not know to what extent it is permissible to comment on any article, but I wish to express myself regarding one paragraph. "Mrs. S. B. H.," in reply to "L. M. L.," tells of having suddenly thrown two dippers of water on her little daughter for screaming and kicking. Do you really think that was a wise and safe way? While it may have been very effectual in curing her of the habit, think of the possible effect of a sudden shock of cold water on the head of a child who, as the mother says, "was very delicate, and had many illnesses until about two years old." My own little son is not as yet old enough to reason with in any way, but I feel quite sure I shall never try that remedy. I much prefer that of P. E. F.—tying the child in a

chair or putting small strips of court-plaster over its mouth, neither of which has any dangerous after-effects.
M: s. R. W.

The Dreaded Dysentery

The little item entitled "Massage for the Baby," with which I heartily concur, leads me to give my preventive for dysentery or diarrhea. Keep a flannel band on the baby from the time it is born until the teeth are all through—summer and winter, night and day. I like the shaped knit bands best, but any soft flannel will do. Have straps over the shoulders to hold it up, and keep it pinned firmly to the napkin to hold it down. Always change the band at night, the same as you do the clothes. (Children should not wear the day clothing at night.) Keep the band clean and dry, and with proper diet baby will seldom be troubled with dysentery. This band keeps the bowels from becoming chilled when the clothes creep up, or when the bed-clothes have been kicked off on a warm night. I believe one of the main causes of dysentery is a cold on the intestines.   Z. H.

Quassia as an Enforcer of Obedience

Several years ago, I suffered an attack of nervous prostration. My little ones were in danger of being utterly spoiled by my utter inability to discipline them. Driven almost to the verge of despair, one day an inspiration came to me. Gathering the children about me I explained that I was going to procure a medicine which I alone could give, and which was to be administered for two things—disobedience and quarreling. I procured from our druggist ten cents' worth of quassia chips, and putting a small quantity in a bottle, added water and a tablespoonful of brandy to keep it from souring. I labeled it "Mother's Medicine for Disobedience and Quarreling. Dose, one teaspoonful." To-day it stands in my medicine-cabinet a reminder of the time when "necessity was the mother of invention." At night the little ones usually had to be frequently reminded it was time to prepare for bed. I had only to speak the magic word "Quassia," and each one obeyed instantly. A few days later during the visit of a neighbor we were annoyed by the running in and out of the little ones. After his departure I called them into my room, and standing them in a row gave each child its first dose. A few moments later I glanced out of my window and saw each one with a cup of water, washing and sputtering at a great rate. When the next caller came, it was only necessary for me to point to the bottle and quietly say, "Quassia." The mere mention of the medicine insured prompt and cheerful obedience, and "the charm" tided us over a period of great danger. The habit of obedience and respect became fixed, and remains until this day.   "Mother Pratt"

FOR LOVELY WOMAN

By JANE ELIOT

TO REDUCE FLESH

A CHARMING writer has said, in a vein of satire, that it is the study of every woman—that is, every pretty woman—to become either a little stouter or a little thinner. Of course, all women will deny this aspersion, but then it is true that the precise medium between corpulence and leanness is hard to attain, and still harder to keep. And when such a condition extends to obesity, on one hand, and emaciation, on the other, what charms can survive the change?

One of the misfortunes of the age is "flesh." A beautiful girl who to-day may have a perfectly molded figure in a few fleeting years may develop into a veritable mountain of flesh. Her movements will become slow and painful, exercise will be next to impossible, and many little actions cannot be performed. She will not be able to button her own shoes or stoop to pick up a pin. She will be unequal to going up or down stairs, to shopping on foot, or to dressing her own hair. Dancing, horseback-riding, calisthenics—these will be out of the question. Sluggishness of body brings sluggishness of mind, and her slowness to follow in conversation and in alertness in repartee will only add to the unfavorable impression her flesh produces.

The opposite condition is almost, if not equally, as deplorable, for who can admire hollow eyes, lankiness, a flat, narrow chest, shrunken shoulders, sharp elbows, skinny arms, shriveled hands and thin ankles? If one attempts padding to hide defects, life in summer becomes unbearable.

If I have pictured with inexorable fidelity, it is not to give an additional sting to those already painfully conscious of their misfortune, but to inspire an earnest determination to escape such a fate, whether it is already upon them or only impending. They may rejoice forever, for there is a remedy. Science and physiology can now prescribe certain diets and lay down certain rules which control so definitely the increase and decrease of flesh that anyone not a victim of actual disease can diminish or add to her weight with absolute certainty, and without fear of unpleasant re-

sults, for one can follow the simple rules given without a moment's hesitation.

One's weight should always be in proportion to the height. Taking as a standard a woman between twenty-five and thirty years:

If her height is 5 feet, she should weigh 110 pounds.

If her height is 5 feet 1 inch, she should weigh 115 pounds.

If her height is 5 feet 2 inches, she should weigh 120 pounds.

If her height is 5 feet 3 inches, she should weigh 125 pounds.

If her height is 5 feet 4 inches, she should weigh 130 pounds.

If her height is 5 feet 5 inches, she should weigh 135 pounds.

Adding five pounds to each additional inch in height. This scale applies only to women, as men should be heavier in proportion to their height.

If this flesh is properly disposed over the body, the limbs and features will present gently waving outlines, frequently dimples, and curves will predominate instead of sharp angles and straight lines. Proportions in persons of the same height will also be found to vary but little, because the proportions are in perfect harmony.

In this paper I will deal only with how to reduce the flesh—the next will be devoted to the thin person. Of course, if one is the victim of disease and it is the cause of fleshiness, or if there is any great change about to take place in her physical life, causing unusual drain upon her system, she should under no circumstances attempt to follow out the rules I give here. Under ordinary circumstances they may be strictly and harmlessly adhered to, and will be found well-nigh infallible.

It is true that certain kinds of food make fat much more rapidly than others. Then it must be remembered that a great part of what we popularly term fat is simply watery fluid in the tissues. When this is very abundant, it is called "bloat." Reduce this watery fluid and confine the diet to such food as is least fat-making, and the problem of controlling flesh is solved. I will speak of diet in detail next month.

(To be continued)

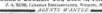

THE KITCHEN KINGDOM

A FEW DESSERTS MADE OF WHIPPED CREAM

BY BEATRICE STURGES

HAVE YOUR cream perfectly sweet and cold. Place in a cold bowl and have beater cold also. Always whip cream before putting in flavoring or sugar. For simple dessert which may be fixed in one large dish or in individual dishes or cups take slices of sponge-cake or lady-fingers one or two days old (fresh ones will not do), place them in bottom of dish and moisten with sherry. Then put on a spoonful of strawberry or raspberry jam. On this heap the whipped cream, flavored faintly with vanilla or almond. Put one or two drops of jam on top of cream, then set away on ice until very cold.

When your fresh raspberries are not as large or as nice as they should be, put them in a bowl and mash thoroughly. Add pulverized sugar and let them sit awhile. Whip cream and sweeten slightly. When nearly stiff, pour in your fruit and beat all up together. When thoroughly mixed, turn into a cold glass dish and put on ice until ready to serve.

Another delicious dessert has cake-crums for one important ingredient. Small sponge-cakes bought at the baker's for a penny apiece, or lady-fingers, are best, as they dry quicker. If the cake does not crum just right, put it in the oven, broken in pieces, and soon it can be crumbled as small as desired. Keep these crums on a dry dish. Then whip cream—not very stiff—flavor it with a liberal quantity of maple sirup. Then pour in the cake-crums. This will make the mixture so stiff that you may not be able to finish the beating with the whipper. In this case use a silver spoon and stir vigorously. When thoroughly mixed, put into separate glass dishes or cups. Put a small bit of tart jelly—crab-apple is good for this—in the bottom of each dish. The sirup and the cake furnish almost all the sweetening needed. Any other flavor may be used, but the maple is delicious and blends with the cream perfectly. Macaroon-crums mixed in the same way with whipped cream make a dainty dessert. In this case, flavor the cream with almond, and do not use much sugar.

Bananas mashed to a paste will mix deliciously with whipped cream. They can be used merely as flavoring if preferred. In this case, line the serving-dish with lady-fingers which have been slightly sprinkled with sherry, and then fill in with the cream mixture.

Pineapple juice is another delicious flavoring to use in whipped cream. This will be found worth trying with the cake-crums. Mix cream and crums exactly as directed for the maple cream, but flavor with pineapple instead, and have slices or bits of pineapple at the bottom of the dish and also on top.

Cake is too rich to serve with desserts such as these. Dainty sugar wafers are preferable.

IN HUCKLEBERRY TIME

BY ELEANOR MARCHANT

Huckleberries are so wholesome and nutritious, and yet are such inexpensive luxuries during the summer months, that the clever housekeeper will doubtless welcome the following novel suggestions and dainty methods for preparing the fruit, the flavor of which is undoubtedly enhanced and rendered more appetizing by a slight degree of cooking:

Frozen Blueberry Shrub.—Heat slowly two quarts of blueberries (without water), squeeze the fruit through a cheese-cloth bag, adding a thinly sliced cucumber, a small cupful of powdered sugar and a teaspoonful of gelatin dissolved in a little hot water; cover closely, allowing it to remain until almost cold, then skim out the cucumber and any seeds, turning at once into a chilled freezer. Turn the crank for about five minutes and then stir in a cupful of thick cream beaten with three tablespoonfuls of sugar and the whipped white of one egg. When frozen sufficiently, repack in a melon-mold, and at serving-time unmold on a layer of sponge-cake resting on a round crystal platter, and garnished with sprigs of fresh crystalized mint.

Cuban Blueberry Pudding.—Crumble together half a pound of macaroons with two slices of stale cake, sprinkle with two tablespoonfuls of grated cocoanut; toss the ingredients lightly with a silver fork until thoroughly blended, and then

The Kitchen Kingdom.—*Continued.*

pour over a cupful of boiling hot cream, sweetened with loaf sugar and flavored with a few drops of lemon-juice. Stir until cold and smooth and then fold in the stiffly beaten whites of two eggs. Butter a pudding mold and fill with alternate layers of fresh berries and the pudding batter, steaming for about an hour and a half. Turn out on a hot platter and serve immediately, accompanied by a foamy lemon sauce.

Blueberry Tea-Cakes.—Use for this one pint of clabbered sour cream, into which is stirred a teaspoonful of baking-soda, adding half a teaspoonful of salt, two tablespoonfuls of molasses, a heaping tablespoonful of melted butter, two tablespoonfuls of brown sugar and a large cupful of graham flour sifted with half a cupful of whole-wheat flour. Mix well, beating with a flat wooden spoon, and then stir in a cupful of blueberries, baking in rather flat cakes in a moderate oven. When cooked, tear lightly apart and butter, sifting over a little powdered cinnamon.

Blueberry Chess Cakes.—Pare and grate one small cocoanut; boil one pound of sugar in two-thirds of a pint of water for fifteen minutes, then stir in the cocoanut and boil ten minutes longer; remove from the fire, and while still warm add half a pint of blueberries, a few drops of lemon-juice and yolks of two eggs. Turn the mixture into small crimped patty-pans that have been lined with rich pie-crust and bake about ten minutes in a quick oven; when cold, garnish each with a star of sweetened whipped cream pressed through a pastry tube.

Blueberry Mint Glace.—Cover a quart of blueberries with cold water and bring slowly to boil, mashing the fruit, as it becomes tender, with a wooden spoon; remove from the fire and strain through a puree sieve, adding a cupful of sugar to every pint of fruit juice and stirring until the sugar is entirely dissolved. Turn into the freezer, and when half frozen pour in a large cupful of meringue flavored with a little lime-juice; freeze hard; line a chilled ornamental mold about two inches in depth with the blueberry glace and fill the center with stiffly beaten sweetened cream, flavored with mint. Adjust the cover securely and bury in ice and rock-salt for at least two hours to chill and ripen. Serve with a chilled wine sauce.

Blueberry Rice Cups.—Boil in slightly salted water for twenty minutes a cupful of washed rice, then add a scant pint of ripe blueberries, a cupful of granulated sugar and a dusting of grated nutmeg, continuing the cooking until the rice is tender. Remove from the fire and when almost cold stir in a cupful of whipped cream beaten with the yolk of one egg and two tablespoonfuls of chopped nut meats. Pour into small cups or timbale molds and place directly on the ice to chill and harden. At serving-time turn out in small sherbet glasses, pouring over each a tablespoonful of the chilled wine sauce as for above recipe.

Balky Lamps

There are thousands and thousands of lamps that don't work, all for the lack of the proper chimney.

Right shape, right length, right size, right glass.

MACBETH'S chimney; my name is on it or it isn't a MACBETH.

My Index explains all these things fully and interestingly; tells how to care for lamps. It's free—let me send it to *you*. Address

MACBETH, Pittsburgh.

The Kitchen Kingdom.—*Concluded.*

COLD COMFORTS FOR HOT DAYS

BY AGNES K. SHEPARD

Peach Layer.—To a pint of milk add a pinch of salt; put in double boiler and scald; beat together one cupful of granulated sugar and two eggs; add to milk; bring to a boil until it is like thin custard—be careful not to burn—set aside to cool. When cold, add half pint of pure cream and the sirup from a pint jar of b andied peaches; put in freezer and freeze. When frozen fairly hard, pack a square or brick mold half-full of the cream, then put a layer of the peaches, from which the sirup has been poured (if whole, cut in halves and remove stones), then fill mold with cream, being careful to fill every bit of space; bind edge of mold with paper and press on cover. Dip a piece of muslin in melted butter or wax; cover joint; pack mold in salt and ice until wanted. This is well worth the trouble.

Currant Frappé.—Bring slowly to boil a pound of granulated sugar and a quart of water—boil seven minutes; skim; pour into freezer and turn carefully until it is like soft snow; then add one small glass of currant jelly and the whites of two eggs beaten together until they are light and foamy; one-quarter box of gelatin which has been thoroughly dissolved and strained; then freeze for ten minutes longer. Fill fruit mold and pack in ice for two hours to ripen. Serve on glass dish garnished with bunches of currants which have been chilled, dipped in white of egg and dusted with powdered sugar.

Venetian Sherbet.—Simmer one pound of sugar and one quart of water together until sugar is dissolved, then boil five minutes; skim and set aside. When cool, add a quart of raspberries mashed and strained through a fine cheese-cloth, the juice of one lemon, juice of one large orange; put in the freezer and turn slowly until frozen moderately hard. Cut small muskmelons in half; remove stringy part and seeds; set on ice to chill. When ready to serve, fill each half of the melon with the sherbet. Place lace-paper doily on plate and serve half melon to a person. For a pink-and-green lunch this is an attractive as well as a delicious dessert.

WHEN PEACHES ARE RIPE

BY E. M. LUCAS

A delicious method of serving peaches is to pare and quarter them, sprinkle well with powdered sugar, place in a glass jar, adjust the rubber and lid and bury in ice and salt for about two hours or longer. At serving time, place in glasses with a tablespoonful of whipped cream on top. These may be served in place of ice-cream at evening parties. The tops may be sprinkled with blanched chopped almonds or with pounded macaroons.

Peaches and Cream Frozen.—Pare and stone a quart of peaches, press through a vegetable press, add half a pint of sugar and turn into the can of the freezer, add the juice of a lemon or half a glass of currant jelly. Turn the crank until the mixture begins to stiffen, then add half a pint of cream and finish freezing. Increase the amount of ingredients if a larger quantity is wanted.

Peach Mousse.—This is a delicious ice, very easily prepared. Pare one dozen very ripe peaches, add half a pint of sugar. Soak one ounce of gelatin in half a cupful of water; place the cup in boiling water and stir until the gelatin is melted; strain into the peach pulp and whip until the mixture begins to thicken, then add very gradually, beating all the time, one pint of whipped cream. When it becomes too stiff to beat, pour into a mold, press on the cover over a piece of thick brown paper, and pack in equal parts of ice and salt. Let stand three or four hours before serving. Frequently the mold is lined with the mixture and the center filled with sliced and sugared peaches; these are covered with more mousse and the whole is frozen.

Peach Sherbet.—Boil one pint of water and half a pint of sugar for twenty minutes; cool, add the juice of one lemon and one pint of peach pulp. Freeze as for ice-cream. This is served in cups as it melts very quickly. A sherbet, that will keep frozen as long as a cream, is made by adding to the hot sirup a teaspoonful of gelatin that has been soaked in enough cold water to cover for ten minutes. When cold, add the peaches, and when the mixture is frozen, add to each gallon of frozen sherbet a meringue made from the stiffly beaten white of one egg and one tablespoonful of powdered sugar.

Peach Sauce.—Pare the fruit and cook to a pulp. To a pint of pulp allow one tablespoonful of butter and one cupful of sugar. Mix a teaspoonful of corn-starch with a tablespoonful of cold water, add to peach pulp, cook five minutes, add teaspoonful of lemon or almond extract and serve hot with batter or bread pudding.

Peach Cake.—Butter a shallow square baking-pan, and put in a layer of quartered peaches. Beat yolks of two eggs until thick, add one cupful of milk. Sift one pint of flour with two level teaspoonfuls of baking-powder and half a teaspoonful of salt; add eggs and milk, and lastly fold in the stiffly beaten whites of eggs. Pour this batter over peaches and cook in a medium oven for three-quarters of an hour. Serve hot or cold, as preferred.

Peaches with Rice.—Cook half a cupful of rice in milk until tender and dry; add half a cupful of sugar and a teaspoonful of lemon extract. Press into cups that have been rinsed in cold water. Unmold and serve with peaches cut small, mixed with a sirup made of one cupful each of sugar and water boiled ten minutes and the juice of one lemon added. Chill sirup before using.

Of all the famous things made by the National Biscuit Company none surpass Social Tea Biscuit in those high qualities which mark superlative excellence.

Temptingly attractive in appearance, delightfully flavored and touched with sweetness, they meet the demands of every occasion.

They improve a poor dessert, make a good one better, and are just the associate for an afternoon cup of tea.

Serve from the beautiful box—identified by the In-er-seal Trade Mark of the National Biscuit Company on each end.

The old-fashioned Graham Crackers of Dr. Graham were a wholesome article of food, but so tasteless and uninviting that it almost required a prescription to get people to eat them.

Since the National Biscuit Company revolutionized the making and baking of Graham Crackers, everybody eats them and loves them for their own intrinsic goodness.

Take a toothsome munch whenever you feel that way. You'll be surprised at the increased physical comfort and ease with which you perform your tasks.

Protected by their moisture proof package they come from the oven to you in all their original freshness and purity—a gift of health.

Ask for the Graham Crackers of the National Biscuit Company with the In-er-seal Trade Mark appearing on each end of the package.

NATIONAL BISCUIT COMPANY

THE TABLE SPREAD FOR THE LUNCHEON

A SEASIDE LUNCHEON

By ELEANOR MARCHANT

HOW often during the summer, when possibly domiciled in a small cottage at the shore, and with but limited facilities for entertaining, does the busy housekeeper receive with dismay the intelligence that some friend is visiting in the neighborhood; for with the memory of past courtesies strongly before her she realizes the necessity as well as the pleasure of entertaining in her honor. Under such circumstances, a seaside luncheon will be found filled with delightful possibilities, combining as it does the elusive charm of novelty in its unique table decorations as well as in the seasonable dainties that comprise the simple yet most appetizing menu.

The invitations should consist of squares of sea-green water-color paper adorned with delicate sprays of dried seaweed, and through which are apparently swimming a number of tiny fish painted in water-colors; and the list of dainties will read as follows:

Mrs. John Darley Dent
Wednesday, August 16th, at
half after one
A Seaside Luncheon
Surfside Cottage, Larchmont

The hostess in selecting her menu should keep two objects in view—first, not to attempt more than she can easily accomplish with the means and assistance at her command; and secondly, that the viands served shall be as distinctively novel in appearance and flavor as thought and ingenuity can devise. The following list of good things is suggested as easily planned and carried out, even with the limited resources of a summer cottage:

Clam Cocktails in Sea-Shells	
Crackers Olives	*Salted Peanuts*
Mussel Broth	*Pulled Bread*
Nautilus Whales	*Saratoga Chips*
Jellyfish Salad	*Starfish Pastics*
Sea-Urchins Cake	*Lemonade*

The clam-cocktails are prepared after the usual formula and served in a deep scalloped shell instead of the customary glass, resting on a bed of shaved ice and garnished with feathery parsley to represent seaweed.

For the mussel broth, fry to a golden brown in a granite saucepan one slice of salt pork cut into dice, adding half a minced onion, one chopped carrot, a bay-leaf, one teaspoonful of beef extract and two cupfuls of cold water; cover closely and place where the ingredients may simmer slowly until tender; then strain through cheese-cloth and when cold remove every particle of fat that

NAUTILUS CUTLET

may have accumulated on top. Just before serving, place in a shallow baking-pan a quart of mussels that have been carefully washed, setting the pan in a hot oven until they have opened, when the mussels should be quickly removed from the shells and added together with the liquor to the prepared stock; allow it to just reach the boiling point. season highly with cayenne and a dash of sherry wine and serve in small cups with a little grated pilot biscuit on the top of each portion.

The individual nautilus are in reality breaded fish cutlets of any preferred variety, and form a most artistic course. Mince the cooked fish in small pieces, sprinkling with salt, paprika and lemon juice, molding the cutlets by the addition of a little white cream sauce, in the shape of tiny boats; allow them to stand overnight on the ice, then egg and crum them, frying them a delicate brown in hot fat; affix to each before serving a sail of white tarlatan, surmounted by a small pennant; placing

STARFISH PASTIES

the miniature crafts on dessert-plates, surrounded by waves of tartar sauce colored a delicate green with a little spinach juice. The whales accompanying this course, are prepared from small round cucumbers, and are extremely grotesque; cut from the top of each a long narrow slice, carefully scooping out the pulp and seeds, standing the hollowed receptacles in boiling water until ready to use, when they may be filled with cooked green peas flavored with a little fresh mint; readjust the piece on top, cutting a wide mouth in one end, using two whole cloves for eyes and fastening in a slit cut in one end a fan-shaped tail of green crêpe paper.

The jellyfish salad may be prepared the day before the luncheon, utilizing as the foundation a clear aspic jelly, molded in alternate layers, with chopped hard-boiled eggs, in shallow cups. These are unmolded at serving-time in large clam-shells that have been lined with crisp heart lettuce leaves, garnishing with

a cream dressing and frillettes of moss parsley. Serve in connection with the salad course starfish pasties, which are easily made from rich pie-crust cut in irregular star shape with a sharp knife; arrange them in a shallow pan, dust with salt and white pepper and sprinkle thickly with grated cheese (the latter giving them a very realistic appearance)

SEA-URCHIN ICE-CREAM

and crisp in a hot oven. Serve the starfish piled on a folded napkin.

The sea-urchins comprising the dessert service are molded, by the assistance of ice-cold butter paddles, from stiffly frozen pistachio cream, following the semblance of the real fish as closely as possible. Use bits of candied cherries for the staring eyes, and cover the bodies with halved pistachio nuts in hedgehog fashion; these may also be prepared the day previous, and if wrapped in paraffin-paper can be packed in a water-tight tin pail, which is buried in ice and rock salt until wanted. At serving-time place each urchin on a round of angel cake, surrounding with a sea foam of sweetened whipped cream.

The luncheon table may be rendered most attractive, by first covering it with the asbestos pad and then with a white linen cloth, over which may be laid a large seine net of the coarse-mesh kind. At each individual cover drape the net slightly, placing under a fold a small candy-box in the shape of a tiny lobster, as shown in the illustration, and directly in the center, resting on a mirror lake, arrange a full-rigged sailboat piled high with confections, concealing the edge of the mirror with a wreath of moss parsley to simulate the seaweed. Name-cards designating where the guests are to be seated may take the form of small golden anchors, cut from drawing-paper and carefully gilded, wound and tied with a gilded cord, with the name and date inscribed, while odd-shaped shells and tiny wooden pails and boats may contain stuffed olives, radishes, salted nuts and salt-water taffy. Use white wax candles for lighting the table.

A SILK PATCHWORK QUILT WHICH IS SELF-LINED

By MAUD KIDDER

ALTHOUGH many people in this day of machine-made articles no longer make patchwork quilts, there are still plenty of women, especially in the country and smaller towns, to whom time is not money, and who cling to the old-time way of using their "pieces," instead of selling them to the ragman, as the city woman usually does.

Surely nothing can be more interesting than to go into a farmhouse way back in the country and hear the family history related, or at least the feminine portion of it, as one looks at a silk patchwork quilt made years ago.

The first silk dress, bits of ribbon from a particularly fetching bonnet, a piece of the wedding-gown and dress relics of numerous other bygone events are all embodied in the silk pieces which form the quilt. Each piece as it is pointed out brings to mind some interesting story, and the owner is generally delighted to find a listener.

The simple but beautiful quilt here shown is made by using pieces of silk about three and a half to four inches square, which are basted onto squares of old and rather firm cotton cloth (old sheets are the best to use).

The blocks of silk and cotton, after being basted together as in the illustration shown at the top of the next page, are first trimmed to make both edges true and then turned over a very narrow seam, and basted neatly, as in the next illustration. The next step folds the

PORTION OF COMPLETED STRIP, WRONG SIDE,
BEFORE FEATHER-STITCHING

block diagonally and overhands it together, making a triangle of the block. This is clearly shown in the last illustration, which is finished and ready to have the basting threads removed. All kinds and styles of silk may be used—flowered, striped, plain or plaid—and there

should be a good variety of blocks, both light and dark, before beginning to put together. The blocks are overhanded together, a light and dark alternately, in a long strip, which may be either the length or the width of the quilt as desired. Another strip is then made and joined to the first one on the bias (or long) sides of the blocks, keeping always a light opposite a dark block.

When four or six strips, the required length, are set together, begin the

PORTION OF COMPLETED STRIP, RIGHT SIDE,
WITH FEATHER-STITCHING

feather-stitching, which is done over all the seams and on both sides of the quilt, and may be executed with red, green or any preferred shade of knitting silk. The feather-stitching should be done rather closely, and will completely cover all sewing, which need not be perfectly done for that reason.

It is easier to feather-stitch these strips in sections than to work on the finished quilt, which will be heavy. Then put these sections together and you have only a few long rows to feather-stitch. The edge is finished with a small cord the color of the silk used in feather-stitching.

If it is not desired to make the quilt solid of these blocks, it is very pretty made in sections of, say, six or eight rows of blocks, and these set together with strips of black silk from four to eight inches wide. This makes a good couch quilt, but is not so pretty for a bed as the solid blocks. When strips of black silk are used between the patchwork blocks it would make the whole more harmonious if black silk were used for the feather-stitching and fine black cord for finishing the edge.

In a room where a single color predominates, it might seem advisable to make the connecting strips of this color whatever it may be, instead of the black silk before mentioned, and in such a case the feather-stitching and cord would, of course, match in color the strips of silk.

SQUARE OF SILK AND LINING COTTON BASTED
TOGETHER

At the end of the rows of strips there will be a V-shaped opening, which must be filled with a block made one-half of dark and one-half of light silk, but so

SQUARE OF SILK AND COTTON WITH
EDGES TURNED

folded that one-quarter of each light and dark will come on each side (note block at end of completed strip. Also note the quarter blocks which come at the pointed ends of the rows).

Care must be taken to keep the contrast between light and dark well marked, and not to have two blocks of same color near each other.

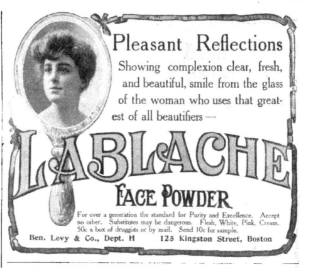

SQUARE FOLDED DIAGONALLY AND SEWED UP

The quilt is thus alike on both sides, with its lining in the middle, and is of fair thickness, thus being quite warm, as well as exceedingly rich and handsome.

To Measure for Standard Patterns

For the Pattern of a Lady's Waist or other Garment requiring a Bust Measure taken.—Pass the tape under the arms and around the fullest part of the body, holding it well up across the back, and drawing it moderately tight.

For the Pattern of a Lady's Skirt or any Garment requiring Waist or Hip Measure.—Take the Waist Measure OVER the Dress, when the Waist and Hip Measures are fairly proportionate. When the Hips are large in proportion to the Waist, take the Hip Measure, passing the Tape easily around the Hips, about six inches below the Waist.

For the Pattern of a Lady's Sleeve.—Measure around the Upper Arm, one inch below the lower part of the arm-pit.

In Ordering Patterns for a Miss or Girl it is usual to order by the Age; but when she is extra large or small for her Age, instead of ordering by Age, order by Bust or Waist Measure, but give the Age also, taking the Measures the same as for Ladies.

For the Pattern of a Hat, Bonnet, Hood, etc.— For Children and Youths it is customary to order by the Age; but when the Head is extra large or small for the Age, instead of ordering by Age, order by Head Measure or Hat Size. For Adults, order by Head Measure or Hat Size. To measure, put the Measure about the Head.

For the Pattern of a Doll, or for Patterns for Garments for a Doll, whether Lady, Gentleman, Girl, Boy or Baby, take the Length of the Doll from the Top of the Head to the Sole of the Foot, measuring PARALLEL with the Doll and NOT along the CONTOUR.

For the Pattern of a Man's or Boy's Coat or Vest.—Measure around the Body, UNDER the Jacket, OVER the Vest usually worn. In ordering for a Boy, give the Age also.

For the Pattern of a Man's or Boy's Overcoat.— Measure around the Breast, OVER the Vest that is usually worn. In ordering for a Boy, give the Age also. Breast Measures for Overcoats should be two inches larger than Breast Measures for other Coats.

For the Pattern of a Man's or Boy's Trousers.— Measure around the Body, OVER the Trousers at the Waist. In ordering for a Boy, give the Age also.

For the Pattern of a Man's or Boy's Shirt —For the size of the Neck, measure the exact size where the Neck-Band encircles it, and allow one inch—thus: if the exact size be 14 inches, select a Pattern marked 15 inches. For the Breast, measure around the Body, OVER the Vest, UNDER the Jacket or Coat, close under the arms. In ordering a Boy's Shirt Pattern, give the Age also.

THE STANDARD FASHION CO.

12-16 Vandam St., New York

HELPS ALONG THE WAY

EDITED BY THE READERS OF THE DESIGNER

Beginning with this number, and until further notice, the contribution to this department each month which appears to be of the greatest general interest will be paid for at the rate of two cents a word. For each other contribution published one dollar will be paid as heretofore. Slips or coupons will not be necessary, but the name and address of the sender must be plainly written on the first page of every contribution sent. This new arrangement is made in compliance with the latest ruling of the Post-office regarding contests and prize offers.

GENERAL INTEREST ITEM

USE ONE FOOT ON THE TREADLE

The sewing-machine with many women is in constant use. How to make sewing on it less irksome is a subject that must appeal to them directly. Many there are who complain of actual physical distress occasioned by sewing upon the machine. To these I would suggest running the treadle with one foot, alternating to the other when a feeling of fatigue is experienced. The idea was suggested to me by a machinist. I acted upon it with gratifying results, finding that the work does not jar the whole body as when both feet are used. The method seems to do away with much of the fatigue, and I can now sew for hours without feeling any weariness.

BESSIE L. RUSSELL

QUESTIONS

HOW SHALL SHE CLEAN THIS HAT?

Can any one of the readers tell me how to clean a white silk hat so it will look like new?   MRS. L. G.

WHAT AILS THIS MAYONNAISE AND JELLY?

Will someone please tell me why sometimes in making mayonnaise dressing it will not thicken? Once in awhile I have this happen. What can one do with a mayonnaise which has curdled? I have tried five years to make jelly. Once in a number of times I succeed. What causes it to become sirup? How can one make jelly of peaches, raspberries, blackberries and strawberries when one cannot get currants for the necessary pectine?   HOLLYWOOD

ANSWER FOR NERVOUS ONE.

In reply to "Nervous One" I will submit this bed-bug remedy that has been tried and found to be a sure cure for the pests: Take moth-balls and break them up into small bits, put into a bottle and dissolve with gasoline. Use a long-nosed oil-can and inject into all cracks and crevices and paint over exposed surfaces when possible, as the mixture will not injure anything but the bugs so it can be used freely.   OLA.

WHEN THE WINDOWS ARE OPEN

A friend of mine has invented a contrivance which is especially serviceable in the flats and apartment-houses of our dirty cities. This is no more nor less than a frame the width of the window and about a foot high, which will fit snugly in the aperture when the window is open. These frames she covered with cheese-cloth—and rejoices in the absolute spotlessness of her sleeping-rooms as well as in their continued state of healthful airiness.   M. J.

TO STRETCH THE CURTAINS

Every woman knows how essential it is to have a stretcher for lace curtains after they have been laundered, but not everyone possesses a stretcher. If you will stretch a quilt on the clothes-line and pin the curtain to it nicely, you will have your curtains looking as fresh after they are dry as if they had been placed in a stretcher.

MRS. W. E.

LITTLE HELPS ALONG THE WAY

Just one little joyful word,
Though by no one it is heard;
Just a pleasant smile and way,
To greet your comrades every day.
Say no evil, think no wrong,
Crowding care out with a song;
Banish fears that court disaster,
Of your own mind be the master.
Loving charity will pay,
By helping others on the way.

LEONORA E. MILLER

THE DESIGNER

TO STRENGTHEN THE EYES

Oculists say that the vast majority of eye troubles are due to weakness of the muscles and not to any defect in the sight itself. In many cases these muscles can be strengthened by care and exercise. When quite young my eyes troubled me, so I went to an oculist and was fitted with glasses. I have had to wear them ever since. Some time ago my two younger children began to complain of their eyes. I had heard of the following treatment helping others, so I tried it on their eyes. In a short time their eyes seemed greatly strengthened. Stand erect, hold the head firm, and look steadily at a coin held before you in your fingers. Gradually move the coin nearer until it is only four inches from the eyes, then move it back again to arm's length, keeping your gaze riveted on it all the time. Then move the coin from one side to the other at arm's length, then up and down in the same way, always keeping the head rigid and making the eyes do all the turning. These exercises will in a short time build up the eye-muscles and enable them to resist ordinary eye-strain, and often do away with the necessity of glasses. MOTHER

(Will the sender of this item kindly let us have her address so check may be sent her.)

RAT-PROOF CHICKEN COOPS

As the poultry-raiser lays her plans and calculates her outlay at this season, she may be relieved of considerable anxiety by this economical means of protecting the young poultry from the ravages of rats, weasels, minks, skunks, and such other "varmints." Set two stakes or small posts just as far apart as the coop is long. Drop a joint of old stovepipe down over each stake. Tin may be used, but if so, be sure that posts are tinned as high as the cleats, and so smoothly that no intruder can ascend them to the coop. Nail cleats on the inside of these stakes about two and one-half feet from the ground. Build your coop of any ordinary materials, place it upon the cleats, and nail securely to both cleats and posts. A twelve-inch board with some cleats nailed upon it will make stairs for this elevated chicken-house. The chickens are quickly and easily taught to go to their quarters if the old hens are tied by one foot to the stakes by means of long rag-strings (do not use cord, as it is too hard), and the little chicks then quietly driven into the coops a few times. In coops like this chickens are safe from any harm. The first year my mother tried this plan she set four small posts in the ground, dropped a joint of old stovepipe over each, and set a wagon-bed, which was not being used that summer, upon wire cables, which were extended from post to post so as to come under the ends of the wagon-bed. Placing one side-board upon the wagon bed to give the required slope, she took an old oilcloth, which had not been considered good enough for continued service on the kitchen-table and, stretched it from the top of the side-board to the opposite side of the wagon-bed, fastening it securely on all sides with carpet-tacks. Thus, without any cost and the use of discarded materials, was made a coop which was a shelter for nearly two hundred chickens until they became so large that the coop would no longer accommodate them, when they were removed to the chicken-house proper. Not a chicken was lost, and this on a farm with stone walls and woods infested by all kinds of chicken-eating animals. S. R. H.

USEFUL TO THE COOK

To dip broth or soup from the kettle when cooking, and the fat is on it, draw the kettle forward to the hot part of the range, making the soup boil furiously. This raises a large bubble in the middle of the pot from which a cupful of soup at a time may be dipped out—the fat all goes to the sides of the pot. E. C. P.

A HANDY BOARD

Many housekeepers I am sure will be interested in a little board I have made expressly for my own use. It is nothing more than the ordinary bread-board secured from the ten-cent store, nicely covered several times with newspaper, and then a covering of canton flannel or a piece of outing flannel neatly whipped along the four edges. When this is finished, make a case, as you would for a pillow, out of cotton and, of course, as large as the board, and put three buttons on closing end, also three buttonholes. When in a hurry to press a seam or tab-collar or shirt-waist, slip your case on the board and press to your heart's content in the dining-room, away from the kitchen heat. The handy board should be a part of every well-regulated household. M. E. C.

TO CLEAN CARPETS

To thoroughly clean a carpet, soak some coarse sawdust in gasoline, sprinkle it over the carpet on the floor, brush it into the carpet, rubbing it well into the soiled parts with the broom; sweep it well off, going over the ground a second time, and you will be surprised to find what a change it will make in your carpets. It will not hurt the most delicate colors and the sawdust will all brush off, taking the dirt with it. By this process it will be found unnecessary to remove the carpets from the floor when cleaning-time comes.
ELIZABETH DEAN

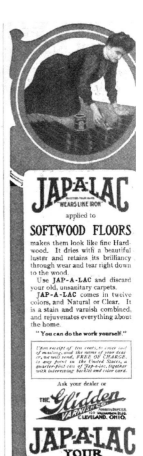

KNOTS AND WHATNOTS

1.—CUBE

```
1 . . . 2

3 . . . 4

   5 . . . 6

7 . . . 8
```

1—2. A common means of conveyance.
3—4. The sound of bells.
5—6. A dressing for food.
7—8. A girl's name.
3—7. A bag for money.
1—5. Spans of horses.
4—8. To plunge into water.
2—6. A brother's daughter.
1—3. To step lightly.
2—4. Fruit of certain kinds of trees.
5—7. Position of a city.
6—8. Leisure.

> Beginning with this number, and until further notice, each month we will pay two cents a word for six letters of not over one hundred words each, addressed to this department, and each containing a complete list of answers to the puzzles of the previous month. Each letter and list must have the name and address of sender plainly written in the upper corner of the first page. This new arrangement is made to comply with the latest ruling of the Post-Office Department regarding contests and prize offers.
> THE EDITOR OF KNOTS AND WHATNOTS,
> 12-16 Vandam Street,
> New York City.

2.—RHYMED TREES

What tree rhymes with a sort of hymn? With a jest? With a wave? With a large game animal? With money? With the grape plant? With the rudder of a ship? With a stormy month? With jolly? What hardwood tree and fruit-tree rhyme with each other.

3.—ELIMINATED VOWELS

The following are all names of well-known songs:
"'Ts th lst rs f smmr."
"Mrchng thrgh Grg."
"Rl Brtnn."
"Hwth."
"nn Lr."
"ld blck J."
"Cmng thrgh th ry."
"ld Grms."

4.—INITIAL CHANGES

We saw the —
Which runs the —
And followed it far up the —

She did her —
To mend the —
And does not like to hear you—

Poor Tomkins —
And paid his —
And then to all his woes gave —

Yes, thanks, I'll —
A piece of —
I always like the things you —

Of course she —
Poor Tom and —
And then she sent them off to —

5.—THE UNNAMED PULLMAN

THE NAME OF THIS PULLMAN CAR, THE NAME OF THE CITY WHERE IT BELONGS AND THE NAME OF THE PORTER STANDING IN THE VESTIBULE ARE ALL "BURIED" OR CONTAINED IN THE NAME OF THE RAILROAD. THE FORMER IS ALSO THE NAME OF AN IMPORTANT ISLAND IN THE MEDITERRANEAN, THE CITY IS AN IMPORTANT ONE IN THE MIDDLE STATES, AND THE NAME OF THE PORTER IS A SHORT WORD OF THREE LETTERS.

e exile —
:d to a —
desert wastes, and rock and —

m threw the —
'er the —
it did not wait to hear it —

or Fred would —
dollar —
id works away with might and —

6.—PI

The following letters spell four ex-
:dingly common surnames of people:
bbehiijmnnnnoooorrsatw

7.—GREEK CROSS

```
        1   2   3
        .   .   .
    .   .   .   .
    .   .   .   .
        4   5   6
```

—4. Buyer.
—5. Endanger.
—6. All-powerful.
The transverse letters form the same
ords.

ANSWERS TO JULY PUZZLES

1. WORD SQUARE.—
```
        H   E   A   R   T
        E   R   R   O   R
        A   R   I   S   E
        R   O   S   E   S
        T   R   E   S   S
```

2. FRACTIONAL PROBLEM.—Miscellaneous.
3. Russia, San Marino.
4. AN ENIGMATICAL LETTER.—Dear Sir: If
understand your bill you have overcharged
:e by ten dollars. This I cannot put down to
aihonesty, for when I settled up before, the
ill was right. I intend to look over all the
ems in future, and herewith give you notice
iat any account overcharged will be returned
npaid. Yours very truly, J. INNIS.
5. BEHEADINGS.—Supper, upper; crow, row;
:ast, east; fold, old; Spain, pain; sword, word;
ock, lock; Fred, red; herring, erring; cape,
pe.
6. THE UNNAMED SHIPS.—Buenos Aires,
:ssie; Marseilles, Marie; Annapolis, Anna or
.nn.
7. ENIGMA.—A diver's suit.
8. DOUBLE DIAGONAL.—
```
        T   E   A   C   H   E   R
        O   R   A   N   G   E   S
        S   T   A   M   M   E   R
        I   N   D   I   C   E   S
        P   E   N   A   N   C   E
        A   D   V   I   S   E   R
        S   P   E   A   K   E   R
```
Diagonal words: Trainer, Reminds.
9. ADDITIONS.—Primate, primrose; capsize,
apable; pigmy, pigtail; humbug, hummock;
iumdrum; margay, margin, marking, marrow,'
narshy, marten, martin.

LIST OF THOSE WHO RECEIVE CHECKS
FOR MAY ANSWERS.

No one got the answer to No. 3 exactly correct, so judgment was passed on the other six
knots.
$2 to Mrs. Fannie L. Higgins, Litchfield, Me.
$1 each to Ruth M. Peters, Upham's Corners,
Mass.; Katherine Haren, St. Louis, Mo.; Mrs.
John E. Holloway, Chesterfield, N. J.; Margaret
C. Boss, Athol, N. S.; and Kate Willis, Brook-
lyn, N. Y.

HONORABLE MENTION: Mrs. E. H. Hall, Mrs.
L. H. Dustin, Chester Dorr, Mrs. E. L. Spooner,
Mrs. Bertha Sackett, Mrs. M. A. Ohlinger,
Charlie Lehmer (After solving all the hard ones
correctly, Charlie, why did you forget to answer
No. 7?), Miss Vesta Ohlinger, Miss Mary Kirby,
E. W. Depue, Jessie Howell Hull and Mrs.
Frances M. Huynes.

Right Now

There never was a better time to find out
the whole truth about Fels-Naptha soap
than right now.

Right now

is the time to try it on your fine sheer lawns, organdies,
dimities, silk shirt-waists and all the light delicate materials of summer wear.

Right now

is the time to prove how perfectly it takes out grass-
stains, blood-stains and grease-spots that nothing else
will move; and how beautifully it cleans, sweetens and
purifies the daintiest goods without scalding or hard
rubbing; and without injury to fabrics.

Right now

is the time to do away with nauseating suds-steam
through the house, the unhealthy heat of a washing fire;
the exhausting wash-board labor and expensive wear-
and-tear on clothes.

Right now

is the time to forsake the out-of-date and laborious ideas of a past
generation; and adopt a sensible comfortable modern wash-day.

Right now

is the time,—if your grocer hasn't Fels-Naptha—to write for a free
sample and follow the easy directions on the wrapper— *Write now.*

Fels-Naptha   Philadelphia

KNITTING

ABBREVIATIONS:—k—Knit plain; sl—Slip a stitch; p—Purl; n—Narrow; b—Bind; o or th o—Thread over; o. n—Over and narrow; k 2 tog—Knit 2 together. Make one—Make a stitch thus: Throw the thread in front of the needle and knit the next stitch in the ordinary manner. (In the next row, or round, this throw-over is used as a stitch.) Or, knit one and purl one out of the same stitch. * Stars or asterisks mean that the details given between them are to be repeated as many times as directed before going on.

BABIES' KNITTED SACK WITH CROCHETED YOKE AND BORDER. — Materials: Two skeins white Saxony, one skein blue Saxony, three steel knitting-needles, No. 12, one bone crochet hook, No. 1, two yards No. 2 blue ribbon.

Body of Sack.—Use steel needles and white wool. Cast on 55 stitches, knit plain. Second row—Plain. Third row—Purl. Fourth row—Plain. Purl and plain until there are 7 ribs of purling on right side. Put in blue wool. Knit first row, purl second and so on for 7 rows, having plain knitting on same side of white purled stripe, making ripple. Make 6 stripes of white, 6 of blue, and on the last row of blue turn and knit 5 stitches from top. Cast on 40 stitches for sleeve, leaving the 50 on the body to be taken up later. With third needle make 9 stripes of white, 9 of blue, for sleeve. Bind off 5 sts from bottom of sleeve, drop 1; bind off 5 more, drop 1. Continue to the top of sleeve. Turn and knit 5 stitches. Knit the 50 on the body and continue for 10 stripes of white. Knit second sleeve same as first and second front same as first; *when binding off, drop every sixth stitch from bottom of sack.*

Yoke.—Use crochet hook and white wool. Make 4 s c stitches in each stripe of sack. Second row—Make s c in every stitch of preceding row, taking up back of stitch same as slipper stitch. Third row — Same, only narrow every fifth stitch by working 2 sts together. Fourth row—S c in each stitch, narrow only in each corner of sleeve and on top. Repeat this row until yoke is 2½ inches deep. Make holes for ribbon by making d c in every third s c of yoke with 2 ch between.

Border.—Use blue wool and make 5 ch; fasten in center of holes made for ribbon; repeat. Second row—5 ch, fasten in center of preceding 5 ch. Make four rows, finish with picot of 3 ch, fasten twice in 5 ch and once between 5 ch. *Sleeve.*—Make 3 s c in each stripe of sleeve. Second row —

Narrow every fifth stitch. Third row—Same as second. Fourth row—S c in each stitch. Make 3 rows and finish with border like rest of sack. With the first finger and thumb work the dropped stitches across body and sleeves to make the openwork.

Glove Case.—Materials: One-half yard of China silk, one-half yard of half-inch ribbon, a spool of No. 30 white cotton, wadding and sachet-powder.

Cast on 111 stitches and knit the following pattern on two steel needles:

First row—Sl 1, k 2, * o, n, k 2 (n, o twice, n) twice, k 3, n, o, k 1; repeat from * five times.

Second row—O, k rest plain, knitting 1, and seaming 1, of loops made by putting thread over twice in previous row. *All even rows are knit the same to the fiftieth.*

Third row—Sl 1, k 3, * o, n, k 3, n, o twice, n, k 4, n, o, k 3; repeat from * five times.

Fifth row—Sl 1, k 4, * o, n, k 9, n, o, k 5; repeat from * five times.

BABIES' KNITTED SACK WITH CROCHETED YOKE AND BORDER

Seventh row—Sl 1, k 5, * o, n, k 7, n, o, k 7; repeat from *.

Ninth row—Sl 1, k 6, * o, n, k 5, n, o, k 9; repeat from *.

Eleventh row—Sl 1, k 7, * o, n, k 3, n, o, k 3, n, o twice, n, k 4; repeat from * five times.

Thirteenth row—Sl 1, k 8, * o, n, k 1, n, o, k 2 (n, o twice, n) twice, k 3; repeat from *.

Fifteenth row—Sl 1, k 9, * o, k 3 together, o, k 5, n, o twice, n, k 6; repeat from *.

Seventeenth row—Sl 1, k 10, o, k 3 together, k 2 (n, o twice, n) twice, k 3, n, * o, k 1, o, n, k 2 (n, o twice, n) twice, k 3, n; repeat from * three times, o, k 1, o, n, k 2 (n, o twice, n) twice, k 4, o, k 1.

Nineteenth row—Sl 1, k 11, * o, n, k 3, n, o twice, n, k 4, n, o, k 3; repeat from * five times.

Twenty-first row—Sl 1, k 12, * o, n, k 9, n, o, k 5; repeat from *.

Twenty-third row — Sl 1, k 2, n, o twice, n, k 7, * o, n, k 7, n, o, k 7; repeat from *.

Twenty-fifth row—Sl 1, k 14, * o, n, 5, n, o. k 9, repeat from *
Twenty-seventh row—Sl 1, k 15, * o, k 3, n, o, k 3, n, o twice, n, k 4; peat from *.
Twenty-ninth row—Sl 1, k 16, * o, n, 1, n, o, k 2 (n, o twice, n) twice, k 3; peat from *.
Thirty-first row—Sl 1, k 2 (n, o twice, twice, k 7, * o, k 3 together, o, k 5, o twice, n, k 6; repeat from *.
Thirty-third row—Sl 1, k 18, o, k 3 gether, k 2 (n, o twice, n) twice, k 3, n, o, k 1, o, n, k 2 (n, o twice, n) vice, k 3; repeat four times from *, 1, o, k 1.
Thirty-fifth row—Sl 1, k 19, * o, k 3, n, o twice, n, k 4, n, o, k 3; repeat om *.
Thirty-seventh row—Sl 1, k 20, * o, k 9, n, o, k 5; re-eat from *.
Thirty - ninth row— l 1, k 2, n, o twice, k 15, * o, n, k 7, o. k 7; repeat from *.
Forty-first row—Sl 1, 22, * o, n, k 5, n, o, 9; repeat from *.
Forty-third row—Sl , k 15, n, o twice, n, 4, * o, n, k 3, n, o, 3, n, o twice, n, k 4; epeat from *.
Forty - fifth row—Sl , k 13 (n, o twice, n) wice, k 3, * o, n, k 1, ι, o, k 2 (n, o twice, ι) twice, k 3; repeat rom *.
Forty-seventh row— Sl 1, k 2 (n, o twice, n) hree times, k 1, n, o wice, n, k 6, * o, k 3 ogether, o, k 5, n, o wice, n, k 6; repeat rom *.
Forty-ninth row—Sl l, k 13 (n, o twice, ι) twice, k 3, n, * o, k 1, o, n, k 2 (n, o twice, n) twice, k 3, n; repeat.
Fiftieth row—K plain, and all even rows following, same, except the sixty - fourth and eightieth.

KNITTED GLOVE CASE

Fifty-first row—Sl 1, k 15, n, o twice, n, k 4, n, * o, k 3, o, n, k 3, n, o twice, n, k 4, n, repeat from *.
Fifty-third row—Sl 1, k 22, n, * o, k 5, o, n, k 9, n; repeat.
Fifty-fifth row—Sl 1, k 2, n, o, twice, n, k 15, n, * o, k 7, o, n, k 7, n; repeat from *. Fifty-seventh row—Sl 1, k 20, n, * o, k 9, o, n, k 5, n; repeat. Fifty-ninth row—Sl 1, k 19, n, * o, k 3, n, o twice, n, k 4, o, n, k 3, n; repeat from *. Sixty-first row—Sl 1, k 18, n, * o, k 2 (n, o twice, n) twice, k 7, n, k 1, n; repeat from *. Sixty-third row— Sl 1, k 2 (n, o twice, n) twice, k 7, n, * o, k 5, n, o twice, n, k 6, o, k 3 together; repeat from *. Sixty-fourth row—N, k rest plain. Sixty-fifth row— Sl 1, k 16, n, o, k 1, o, k 3 (n, o twice, n)

twice, k 3, n, * o, k 1, o, n, k 2 (n, o twice, n) twice, k 3, n; repeat four times from *. Sixty-seventh row—Sl 1, k 15, n, * o, k 3, o, n, k 3, n, o twice, n, k 4, n; repeat from *. Sixty-ninth row—Sl 1, k 14, n, * o, k 5, o, n, k 9, n; repeat. Seventy-first row—Sl 1, k 2, n, o twice, n, k 7, n, * o, k 7, o, n, k 7, n; repeat from*. Seventy-third row—Sl 1, k 12, n, * o, k 9, o, n, k 5, n; repeat. Seventy-fifth row—Sl 1, k 11, n, * o, k 3, n, o twice, n, k 4, o, n, k 3, n; repeat from *. Seventy-seventh row—Sl 1, k 10, n, * o, k 2 (n, o twice, n) twice, k 3, o, n, k 1, n; repeat. Seventy-ninth row—Sl 1, k 9, n, * o, k 5, n, o twice, n, k 6, o, k 3 together; repeat from *. Eightieth row— N, k rest plain. Eighty-first row—Sl 1, k 8, n, o, k 1, o, k 3 (n, o twice, n) twice, k 3, n, * o, k 1, o, n, k 2 (n, o twice, n) twice, k 3, n; repeat from * four times. Eighty - third row—Sl 1, k 7, n, * o, k 3, o, n, k 3, n, o twice. n, k 4, n; repeat from *.
Eighty-fifth row—Sl 1, k 6, n, * o, k 5, o, n, k 9, n; repeat. Eighty-seventh row—Sl 1, k 5. n, * o, k 7, o, n, k 7, n; repeat. Eighty-ninth row—Sl 1, k 4, n, * o, k 9, o, n, k 5, n; repeat from *. Ninety-first row—Sl 1, k 3, n, * o, k 3, n, o twice, n, k 4, o, n, k 3, n; repeat from *. Ninety-third row—Sl 1, knit 2, n, * o, k 2 (n, o twice, n) twice, k 3, o,.n, k 1, n; repeat from *. Ninety-fifth row—Sl 1, k 1, n, * o, k 5, n, o twice, n, k 6, o, k 3 together; repeat from *. Ninety-sixth row—Knit across plain. Repeat the pattern once, thus making two points; then bind off. With a crochet hook make a shell of 5 tr c about every fourth stitch all around the piece. Then 8 tr c in middle of every 5 tr c all around. Then 3 ch, 1 d c between second and third tr c, 3 ch, 1 d c between fourth and fifth tr c, 3 ch, 1 d c between sixth and seventh tr c, 3 ch, 1 d c between shells; repeat all around.
Cut from the China silk two pieces the size and shape of the lace cover, then cut a strip one and one-half inches wide, which fold lengthwise; gather and sew around the outside piece. Cut two pieces of wadding the same size as the silk pieces, and sprinkle sachet-powder generously between them. Baste the two pieces of silk together, with the wadding between them, turn in the edge of the lining to fit the outside, and stitch together. Tack the lace cover in place over the outside, and fold with the two points together. Cut the ribbon in four lengths, and sew two to each side for tying the case together.

FASHION NOTES FOR MEN

By ALINE DE CARDEVA

IT IS doubtful if men's fancies were ever catered to any more than they are at the present moment. Every little whim is elaborated upon to an unprecedented extent. Sisters and wives and cousins are kept busy looking out for new ideas for their men folks, and it is not an unusual thing to see a group of young women in front of a haberdasher's window, holding an animated discussion on the display.

There are certain styles in walking-sticks, certain styles in umbrellas, certain styles in scarf pins and, in fact, there are certain styles in almost every article of wearing apparel the male member lays claim to. And if the smart girl wants her brother or her cousin, or, perhaps, somebody's else cousin to be in the foremost ranks of the procession of fashion, she must help him to get there if he has not the ambition to do so himself. So she spends the afternoon gazing in various windows, and occasionally she ventures into the haber-shop itself for a closer inspection of its wares.

It might be said, with some truth, that when a certain style has been the vogue for several seasons it has become generally recognized and should no longer claim the title "smart"; for then it has lost its exclusiveness. The Prince of Wales walking-stick has held the top notch of fashion for so long that a radical change is long overdue, and is here at last, and now walking-sticks carried by the best dressed men have neither handle nor crook. The top is capped with a piece of silver or the natural wood is finished in cap fashion. Of course, there are crook handles, horn handles and bent handles, just as there always were; but the change mentioned refers to the introduction of the plain switch cane. There are certain styles to be observed in choosing a walking-stick with a fancy handle. For instance, the stick made of piano wood and having a slightly bent end with a silver snake twisted around it is by far the smartest of crooked handles. Then there is the time-honored bamboo, with a ram's-horn handle mounted with silver, which always appears elegant. The shepherd's crook, with carved handle and a silver or gold plate six inches below

the curve, is another conventional shape that will remain in style for many a day to come. Pimento is a popular wood this season and is being made up in both elaborate and plain styles. Very slender canes seem to have had their day. The tendency now runs to club effects rather than to a happy medium. At all events, the very smartest walking-stick to be had, according to the dictates of masculine fashion creators, is the straight pimento of a little over average weight.

As to umbrellas there are new handles and new silks constantly coming upon the market. Just now favor leans toward the club handle—unfinished and unmounted. When an irregular knot of the most irregular sort can be had it is considered ultra swagger and is held for the approval of a patron whose book account means a goodly portion of the annual rental. Furze wood has been voted the popular wood of the year, and is being used extensively in fine umbrellas.

Buck-horn handles come in a variety of shapes, ranging from the original

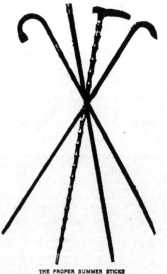

THE PROPER SUMMER STICKS

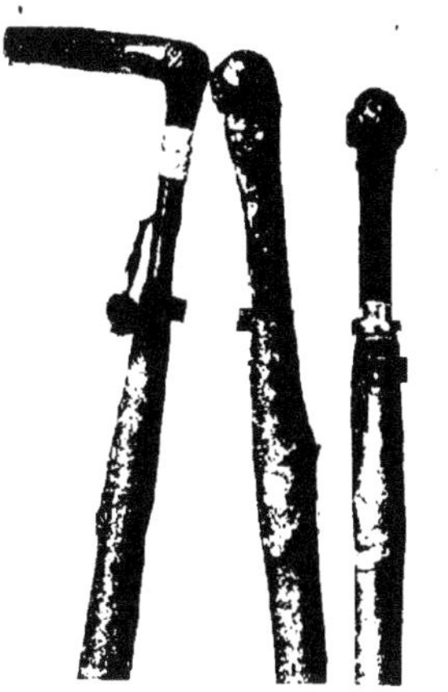

THE ALWAYS USEFUL UMBRELLA

horn to intricately carved designs. Silver mountings are the usual accompaniment to these handles, and small bits of gold, in the shape of nail heads and rivets, are occasionally noticed.

As a matter of fact, there are few really distinct styles in umbrellas outside the regulation club and crook handles and taffeta and gloria coverings. From time to time new materials are brought out and extensively advertised as best to turn rain, but their merit is eventually put in the shade by substantial silks that have been tried and not found wanting.

When there are so many pretty scarf pins that men must like, the question of what might be considered smartest arises. In the first place it must be mentioned that bar pins are being revived with renewed favor. These are not only worn on sporting occasions, but during the day at business. Of course there is but one kind of tie they look well in, and that is the English Ascot or puff tie. Enameled fox heads with shining eyes set in the center of a three-inch bar pin make a striking appearance. Horse heads, dog heads and tiger heads are equally attractive. While amethysts, turquoise and pearls are mounted in the same manner.

In leather goods there are any number of new articles, all of which are useful and attractive. Since week-end visits have become so popular, men are beginning to appreciate the value of getting their belongings together in a hurry, and many of these convenient little leather contrivances are proving indispensable property. The week-end razor-box contains two blades, and is so neatly gotten up that a man can slip it in his coat pocket and forget it is there until he wants to use it. And then there is the week-end roll, which is made of pig-skin and fitted with all the necessary toilet articles one would need in a week's time or longer.

HOW TO TAKE STANDARD MEASURES, ETC.

In ordering Misses', Girls', Children's or Boys' Patterns, be sure to order for the age corresponding with the actual measure.

In taking Bust or Breast Measure, pass the tape under the arms and around the fullest part of the Body, holding it well up across the Back, and drawing it moderately tight; also take Waist, Hip, Arm and Head Measures as described on page 480.

TABLES OF CORRESPONDING MEASURES.

Corresponding Bust, Waist and Hip Measures for **Ladies**:

Bust,	32	34	36	38	40	42	44	46	48	50	inches.
Waist,	20	22	24	26	28	30	32	34	36	38	inches.
Hip,	37	39	41	44	47	50	53	56	59	62	inches.

Corresponding Bust and Arm Measures for Ladies, and Bust and Arm Measures and Ages for **Misses**:

Bust Measure,	29-30	31-32	33-34	35-37	38-40	41-43	44-46	inches.
Arm Measure,	9	10	11	12	13	14	15	inches.
Age,	12 to 13	14 to 15	16 to 17					years.

We strongly advise Purchasers of Skirts, etc., to obtain patterns by **Hip Measure** rather than Waist Measure, both being given on the label. A variation in waist measure is more easily adjusted than a variation in hip measure. **Hip measure for Ladies is taken six inches below the waistline.**

Latest Lengths in Standard Skirt Patterns for Ladies.

Finished Front Lengths from Waist:
Frou-frou Length, 1¼ in. on floor ....43¼ in.
Regulation Round Length, touching floor ....42 in.
Short Round Length, 1 in. above floor ....41 in.
Instep Length, 2 in. above floor ....40 in.
Shorter (Outing) Length, 4 in. above floor ....38 in.

Finished Back Lengths from Waist:
Regulation Round Length, touching floor all around, 2¼ inches longer than the Regulation Front Length ....44½ in.
Short Sweep Length, from 2½ to 3½ ins. longer than Regulation Round ....47 to 48 in.
Medium Sweep Length, 4 to 6 in. longer than Regulation Round ....49½ to 50½ in.
Long Sweep Length, 9 to 10 in. longer than Regulation Round ....53½ to 54½ in.
Short Round Length, 1 in. above floor all around ....42½ in.
Instep Length, 2 in. above floor all around ....41½ in.
Shorter (Outing) Length, 4 in. above floor all around ....39½ in.

Patterns cut in sizes Small, Medium and Large correspond to

Bust Measure,	33	36	41	inches.
Waist Measure,	21	24	29	"

Corresponding Head Measure and Cap or Hat Size.

Head Measure,	20¾	21⅛	21½	21⅞	22¼	22⅝	23	23⅜	23¾	24⅛	24½	in.
Cap or Hat Size.	6½	6⅝	6¾	6⅞	7	7⅛	7¼	7⅜	7½	7⅝	7¾	

Corresponding Age, Bust, Waist, Hip and Arm Measures, and Finished Lengths from Neckline to Floor and in Skirt Effects, for **Children, Girls and Misses.**

Age,	½	1	2	3	4	5	6	7	8	9	10	11	12	13	14	15	16	17	yrs.
Bust,	19	19¾	20½	21¼	22	22¾	23½	24¼	25	26	27	28	29	30	31	32	33	34	in.
Waist,	20	20½	21	21½	22	22½	23	23	23¼	23½	24	24½	24½	25	25	24½	24	24	in.
Hip,	20	20½	21	22	22½	23½	25	26	27	28	29½	30½	32	33	34½	35½	37	38½	in.
Arm Measure,					7	7	7	7	8	8	8	8	9	9	10	10	11	11	in.
Length from Neckline to Floor (Back).	21	24½	27½	30	32½	34½	36½	38½	40½	42½	44½	46½	48½	50½	52¼	54	55½	57	in.
Finished Skirt Front Length From Waist.	11¼	11½	12	12¾	13½	14⅝	15¼	16	16¾	17⅝	19½	21½	23½	26½	29½	32½	35½	38½	in.
Finished Skirt Length from Bottom of Armhole.	14½	15	15⅞	16⅞	18	19½	20¼	21¼	22¼	23⅝	25½	27¾	30	33¼	36½	39¾	43	46½	in.

For **Men's** and **Boys'** Overcoat, Coat and Vest Measures: Take Breast Measure over the vest, not over the coat or jacket.

For **Boys'** Trousers Measures: Measure the waist over the trousers, and for full-length trousers measure the leg from the fork to the heel of the shoe.

For **Men's and Boys'** Shirt Measures: Take the Breast Measure over the vest, and see that one of the Neck Measures specified on the label corresponds with the size of collar worn.

Corresponding Breast and Neck Measures for **Men**.

Breast,	32	34	36	38	40	42	44	46	in.
Neck,	13 13½ 14	13½ 14 14½	14½ 15 15½	15 15½ 16	15½ 16 16½	16 16½ 17	16½ 17 17½	17 17½ 18	in.

Corresponding Age, Breast, Waist and Leg Measures for **Boys**.

Age,	2	3	4	5	6	7	8	9	10	11	12	13	14	15	16	yrs.
Breast,	20½	21¼	22	22¾	23½	24¼	25	26	27	28	29	30	31	32	33	in.
Waist,	20½	21½	22	22½	23	23½	24	24½	25½	26	27	27½	28½	29	30	in.
Leg,	13½	15	16¼	17½	18¾	19¾	21	22¼	23¼	24½	25½	26¾	27¾	29	30	in.

Corresponding Age, Head Measure and Cap or Hat Size.

Age,	½	1	2	3	4	5	6	7	8	9	10	11	12	13	14	15	16	yrs.
Head Measure,	17	18½	18⅞	19¼	19⅝	20	20⅛	20⅜	20¾	20¾	20¾	21⅛	21⅛	21⅛	21⅛	21⅛	21⅛	in.
Cap or Hat Size.	5¼	5¾	5⅞	6	6⅛	6¼	6⅜	6⅜	6½	6½	6½	6⅝	6⅝	6⅝	6¾	6¾	6¾	

ALL SEAMS ALLOWED FOR

Agents for STANDARD PATTERNS will cheerfully exchange any STANDARD PATTERNS if unopened and in good order.

NOTES OF NEW BOOKS

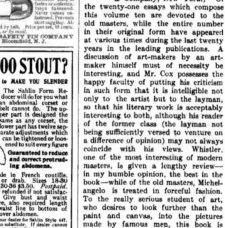

By LILIAN DYNEVOR RICE

"OLD MASTERS AND NEW," by Kenyon Cox. (Fox, Duffield & Company, New York.) Of the twenty-one essays which compose this volume ten are devoted to the old masters, while the entire number in their original form have appeared at various times during the last twenty years in the leading publications. A discussion of art-makers by an art-maker himself must of necessity be interesting, and Mr. Cox possesses the happy faculty of putting his criticism in such form that it is intelligible not only to the artist but to the layman, so that his literary work is acceptably interesting to both, although his reader being sufficiently versed to venture on a difference of opinion) may not always coincide with his views. Whistler, one of the most interesting of modern masters, is given a lengthy review—in my humble opinion, the best in the book—while of the old masters, Michelangelo is treated in forceful fashion. To the really serious student of art, who desires to look further than the paint and canvas, into the pictures made by famous men, this book is recommended.

"THE DARK LANTERN," by Elizabeth Robins. (Macmillan Company, New York.) Any book from this author's pen, coming after such a remarkable one as "The Magnetic North," must necessarily suffer by comparison. But for a writer who created such strong, lovable, virile characters as the *Boy* and the *Colonel*, such a whimsically, wicked half-child, half-woman as *Maudie*, to descend to delineation of the neurotic, unpleasant *Katharine Dereham*, a half-insane brute like *Dr. Garth Vincent*, a libertine like *Prince Anton*, seems lamentable indeed, and when the same writer exchanges the bleak, stern, pure cold of the Klondyke, cruel, though it may be, for the sickly atmosphere of the hospital and sanatorium, then, indeed, it makes the reviewer wonder in amaze what has wrought the transformation. That "The Dark Lantern"—which title, by the way, refers to *Dr. Vincent*—has a morbid interest as a story there is no denying, but it is of the same interest as attaches itself to "The Heavenly Twins" and novels of that ilk, and to stoop to such an audience as books of that class command is altogether too low an aim for the author of "The Magnetic North."

"A KNOT OF BLUE," by William R. Wilson. (Little, Brown & Company, Boston.) Mr. Wilson's former story, "A Rose of Normandy," published two years ago, is now in its fifth edition, and in the reviewer's opinion this, his latest work, is even a better romance. The scene is laid in old Quebec, and the time is shortly after the Great Louis had ceased to reign in France. The "knot of blue" was the bow given by *Aimee de Marsay* to *Raoul de Chatignac* to wear to the war, but before he proves himself worthy of her colors many are the adventures and trials he undergoes, in some of which he acquits himself with credit, while in others, just the reverse—notably in the game of chance with the *Royal Four* in the Maison Sombre. The gratification of personal revenge is the motif of the story, and intrigue, plotting and desperate hate go to its accomplishment. There are many stirring scenes, none more so than the denouncing of *Raoul* as a traitor, and his consignment to prison; or the announcing of his pardon to the *Royal Four*, who having conspired for his ruin, are in the midst of a hilarious banquet in anticipation of the success of their schemes when the most unwelcome news of his release is brought them.

"ON THE FIRING LINE," by Anna Chapin Ray and Hamilton Brock Fuller. (Little, Brown & Company, Boston, Mass.) Miss Ray is the author of that sprightly and pleasant little romance of modern Quebec, "By the Good Sainte Anne," which, by the way, has just been issued in a new and handsome edition, and in this collaboration with Mr. Fuller she scores another success. The scene is laid in South Africa during the time of the Boer War, and the descriptions of life in the English camp are most interesting. No less so is the pretty love story which twines itself around the young Canadian soldier, *Harvard Weldon*, and the

English girl, *Ethel Dent*. It is easy to recognize Miss Ray's hand in the picturing of the captivating women, and it is no less easy to see where the masculine touches of Mr. Fuller give strength to situations where the men predominate. The combination of authors in this case is a most happy one.

"A LITTLE GARDEN CALENDAR," by Albert Bigelow Paine. (Henry Altemus Company, Philadelphia.) "This is the story of a year, and begins on New Year's day. It is the story of a garden—a little garden—and of a little boy and girl who owned the garden, and of the Chief Gardener, who helped them." Now, you know just what this little book is about, and in Mr. Bigelow's own words, but until you read it through you can never realize what a charming book it is, and how wholly fascinating it will prove for the little folks for whom it is written. All children have a born-in love for gardening, even if in their mistaken efforts they occasionally dig up what had better be left planted, and ignore the weeds which were better uprooted, and fortunate, indeed, is the youngster who is permitted a plot of ground of his own to hoe and plant and water, where agricultural errors may be overlooked. But even if the bit of Mother Earth is not obtainable, Mr. Bigelow shows how a most interesting and delightful garden may be instituted in flower-pots, and even peas, beans and corn raised in them. Any healthy-minded child will read the book with pleasure for the story it contains, and all-unconsciously absorb much valuable botanical knowledge, which can be fixed all the better in his young mind if mother or father will supply the earth-filled flower-pots and the necessary seeds.

"DAVID RANSOM'S WATCH," by Mrs. G. R. Alden. (Pansy.) (Lothrop, Lee & Shepard Company, Boston, Mass.) Admirers of "Pansy's" writings, and there are many, will find this latest of her pen-children a pleasant, even story of home interests, which, if it does not rise to great heights, certainly does not go down into the depths, and which does not aggressively inflict a moral on the reader, although the kindly influence good people can scatter around them is made manifest. Miss Hannah Sterns' suitor, Ben Ransom, a cheerful, handsome ne'er-do-well, several years younger than herself, indulges in a little flirtation with Lucy, a silly, pretty young girl, who acts as helper in the *Sterns'* household. Living up to a rigid sense of duty, even though it nearly breaks her heart, and, although the flirtation has gone no further than the stealing of one or two careless kisses, *Hannah* insists that *Ransom* and *Lucy* marry, which union results only in disaster, save for the coming of a little daughter, who lives to be the darling and the blessing of the elder brother, from whom *Ben*

separated in early life, This little maid is quaintly named *Watch*, and the story of her simple and pleasant home life and wooing will be read by young girls with enjoyment, or even by the older folk.

"MISS BILLY," by Edith Keeley Stokely and Marian Kent Hurd. (Lothrop Publishing Company, Boston, Mass.) Here we have another story for girls, and a cheerful, bright one it is, too. *Miss Billy* is a fascinating lassie in her early teens, and she has a manly young brother and a stately elder sister whose dignity far outstrips her years, not to mention a sensible and affectionate father and mother. Being forced by reverses in fortune to move to an uncongenial and most unattractive locality, *Miss Billy* determines to lift her neighbors and her surroundings to her own social status instead of sinking to theirs, and by her buoyancy of spirits and indomitable pluck enlists on her side not only her own family but every small child in the neighborhood, to the wonderful beautifying of that part of the town and the moral betterment of the residents. Determined not to be outdone by his sister, *Theodore*, the manly brother, who is at heart the least bit of a dandy, sets out to earn his own living as tender of a soda-water fountain in the leading drug store of the town, but as all the young ladies he knew in his palmier days come in to be regaled free of cost with the delightful foamy beverage, and as all such refreshment is charged against his salary, he puts his pride in his pocket and secures a much more remunerative if less high-toned engagement driving a team. *Billy*, *Beatrice* (the haughty sister) and *Theodore* are real young folks, full of fun and high endeavor and considerable of the old Adam, as occasional temper gusts evince, and they will be found good, healthy associates for other young folks who will heartily sympathize with their triumphs and defeats and be glad of the good fortune which comes to them before the book closes.

"TOR, A STREET BOY OF JERUSALEM," by Florence Morse Kingsley. (Henry Altemus Company, Philadelphia.) A hungry and ragged little waif is *Tor*, and he makes his entrance on the scene of the story by biting the hand of *Fisherman Peter*, the Apostle, who catches him stealing from a blind beggar. Later when *Tor* himself is blinded by the whip lash of *Pilate's* driver, he has his sight restored by the touch of the Master, and ever afterward follows, an humble little disciple, in the footsteps of the Loved One. He is a very human little boy, however, in spite of the wondrous period in which he lives and awe-inspiring events of which he is an observer, and his history is told in a sincere, simple way that will appeal to the minds of even very young children.

THE DESIGNER for SEPTEMBER

PRICE, TEN CENTS

THE DESIGNER for September will present coats, jackets, waists and toilettes for ladies and young folk. Of special interest to mothers will be an article on "Costumes for Grammar and High School Scholars," while "Points on Dressmaking" will contribute timely directions for lining coats and jackets.

"Domestic Affairs in the Land of the Dragon" will be the subject of Laura B. Starr's "Housekeeping all Over the World" series, and Bertha Hasbrook, "In the Interest of Bread-Winning," advises "Catering" to the girl who loves to cook and to arrange attractive table decorations. Mary Kilsyth will contribute "The Modern Bed," containing important suggestions regarding springs, mattresses and the bed itself. "Taming Squirrels," by Craig S. Thoms, will appeal to lovers of pets, and especially to children. Another good thing for the children will be the tale of "The Purr-Puss and the Spit-Cat," by Caroline Fuller, author of "The Alley Cat's Kitten"; and still a third will be a drill, "The Harvesters," by Charles Edward Harrison.

In "Mothers' Work and Workers" Jane E. Stewart will give an interesting summary of the Mothers' Clubs, illustrated with photographs of the club presidents.

"The Son of Elizabeth," by Celia E. Shute, is a short story conveying a lesson which it would be well for the parent to consider who, in the upbringing of that most sensitive of all plants, the little child, attempts to make theories and rules take the place of all-sheltering affection judiciously mixed with merry nonsense and much romping. That capital continued story, "Miss Ginter of Ginterville," by Nina Welles Tibbot, will come to a conclusion in the September number.

In fancywork will supply "Decorative Uses for Blue-Print Cloth," "Lace Collars," "Crochet" and "Netting."

In this number will begin a most interesting series by Jessie Garwood Fritts: "At the Sign of the Silver Smith," treating of silver and its place in refined homes. "Catchups and Pickles" and "The Savory Tomato" will be given especial attention in "The Kitchen Kingdom." "For Lovely Woman" will continue its efforts in feminine beautifying, and "The Mothers' Advisory Club," "What Women are Doing," "Helps Along the Way," and "Etiquette Hints" will be full of interesting and valuable information.

LILIAN DYNEVOR RICE, Editor.

THE STANDARD FASHION CO.
12-16 Vandam St., New York

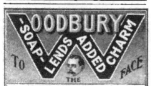

WHAT WOMEN ARE DOING

EDITED BY THE READERS OF THE DESIGNER

Beginning with this number, and until further notice, the contribution to this department each month which appears to be of the greatest general interest will be paid for at the rate of two cents a word. For each other contribution published one dollar will be paid as heretofore. Slips or coupons will not be necessary, but the name and address of the sender must be plainly written on the first page of every contribution. This new arrangement is made in compliance with the latest ruling of the Post-office Department regarding contests and prize offers.

GENERAL INTEREST ITEM

SOUVENIR POSTAL CARDS

One woman of my acquaintance has made a good many dollars from the making of photographic postal cards. If you live near any place of historic interest, of great natural beauty, or of university or cathedral attraction, you have your chance. A very small camera will suffice for your part of the work, the woman of whom I speak having used successfully a tiny camera, taking pictures only two and a quarter by three and a quarter inches. The woman spoken of not only took photographs of general local interest on postals, placing them in stores, where they sold readily, but she took others of children, adults and animals. The postals, bought by the gross from a prominent photo firm, ready prepared for printing, cost a trifle over a cent each, and with the chemicals for development, etc., cost about two cents each to prepare. Losses from various causes brought the cost up to about three cents each postal. They sold at five cents each, the made-to-order ones bringing from fifteen to twenty-five cents each. Another kind of work she does is the making of postals from films or negatives taken by other people. For this work, where the risks of negative making are taken by others, and she just does the printing, her charges are ten cents each for less than four from one film or negative, and for larger quantities at the rate of two for fifteen cents. Any one who likes this work can readily make more than pin-money from this pretty fad. And if one cares to do so, one can add other branches, such as finishing for other amateurs who, for any reason, do not care to do this work.
May Myrtle French

SHE MAKES HANDKERCHIEFS

An intimate friend of mine earns a tidy sum, to help clothe herself, by making handkerchiefs. She procures handkerchief linen or India linen, dainty laces and insertions. Some she merely hemstitches, while others she trims with lace, drawn-work, braid, embroidery, etc. She hunts for odd shapes and dainty patterns. Prices range from fifteen cents, plain hemstitched ones, to point-lace ones for two dollars and fifty cents.
L. M. W.

PICKLING AND PRESERVING BY THE DAY

Being compelled through circumstances to make my home with a son-in-law, and feeling the need of my own money, last spring I sent off several cards to ladies living in the suburbs, where help is very scarce, offering to put up jellies, preserves and pickles as they came in season, at two dollars a day (one dollar and fifty cents if I had assistance). From May until November first I earned one hundred and ten dollars, and had six months rest before me. This may serve as a hint to some other independent, though dependant woman.
Mrs. E. P.

A REAL MILLINERY PARLOR

In a conservative town in Ohio, a young woman I know has made quite a success of a Home Millinery business. In her girlhood days she learned the millinery trade, and when, later in life, she found herself again obliged to earn money, she thought of going on with the business; but the rent of a show room in the town would cost her about five hundred dollars yearly, then she would be obliged to leave her home and her invalid mother, so she conceived the idea of having a millinery parlor at home. She lived about four squares from the center of town, quite out of the business part, but on one of the best streets. After she made up her mind to try her plan, she went to Dayton and spent two weeks in the wholesale house, getting acquainted with the styles. The firm then allowed her a number of pattern hats to sell on commission, and she purchased a small stock of ribbons and other trimmings. She did not take out her furniture and make her home look like a store, but left all her things and added a show-case and some boxes. At her opening she had beautiful palms and flowers her mother had raised, these decorated the rooms beautifully. She had her name neatly printed on a sign with "millinery parlors" beneath. A great many people attended her opening, and although there are six other millinery stores in the town of about four thousand and five hundred inhabitants, she did well from the first. She made a specialty of steaming, cleaning, and using materials that had been used before, and this attracted a great many people. I have known her to have customers come from twelve miles away to have her trim their hats. The "millinery parlors" have been established about six years. A mortgage that was on her property has been lifted, and she has a bank account and a business rating. She usually has the services of one or more girls, who are learning the trade and do not have to be paid. She does her own housekeeping, with the aid of her sister, and has a beautiful, well-furnished home.

N. E. B.

SHE OWNS A STORAGE HOUSE

Indianapolis boasts the only woman in Indiana, perhaps in the United States, who conducts a storage house on a large scale. Leaving business college seven years ago, Miss Y——— accepted a position as bookkeeper for a large storage house. Here she kept her eyes open learning so much of the business that, when a new manager was needed, the position was offered her. So great was her success as a manager, and so well has she mastered the details of the work, that now she conducts successfully a three-story storage house, in the very heart of the business district, not as manager, but as proprietor.

Marie Davis

TURNIP SEED FOR PIN MONEY

One spring, when I was having the vegetable cellar cleaned, I found a box of turnips nicely sprouted. I had them planted in a row along the garden fence. They grew fast, bloomed well, and were finally covered with well-ripened seed pods. These I gathered, shelled, cleaned and sent to the grocer. In July all were sold and the grocer gave me a crisp

Be your own Beauty Doctor

There is but one method of acquiring and retaining a beautiful, clear, delicately tinted complexion in hot, sticky weather, when dust and perspiration make the face greasy and unpleasant to look upon—not to mention how it feels. The pores of the skin must first be rid of all impurities, and the circulation gently stimulated to carry nutrition to all the tiny cells and tissues.

Pompeian Massage Cream

builds up and rounds out the contour of the face and form by cleansing, exercising and feeding the skin, *through* and *through* and strengthening the muscles. It removes all wrinkles, blackheads, roughness and irritation, without encouraging the growth of hair or causing the skin to shine—imparting a glow of health and beauty that only nature at her best can give.

We Send a Free Sample

and our course in massage without charge, if you will send us the name of your dealer (see coupon), and tell us whether or not he sells Pompeian Massage Cream. If he does *not*, did he try to sell you some inferior kind, saying it was "just as good"?

We need you to buy of your dealer whenever possible. Do not accept a substitute for Pompeian under any circumstances. If your dealer does not keep it, send us his name, and we will send a 50c. or $1.00 jar of the cream, postpaid, on receipt of price.

POMPEIAN MFG. CO.
95 Prospect St., Cleveland, O.

CUT THIS OUT AND SEND IT TO US

Pompeian Mfg. Co.
95 Prospect St.
Cleveland, Ohio

Gentlemen:—In consideration of my having filled in blank below, please send, without cost to me, one copy of your book on facial massage and a liberal sample of Pompeian Massage Cream.

Name ....
Address ....
Dealer's Name ....
Address ....
Dealer DOES NOT keep Pompeian Massage Cream.

2 Styles——"Prophylactic" (Rigid Handle) and "P.S." (Prophylactic Special) New Flexible Handle

Sold Only in a Yellow Box—for your protection. Curved handle and face to fit the mouth. Bristles in irregular tufts—cleans between the teeth. Hole in handle and hook to hold it. This means much to cleanly persons—the only ones who like our brush.

The Pro-phy-lac-tic

Adults 35c. Youths 25c. Children's 15c. By mail or at dealers. *Send for our free booklet, "Tooth Truths."* FLORENCE MFG. CO., 83 Pine St., Florence, Mass.

BIG INCOMES $25 to $50 a Week for getting orders for our celebrated Teas, Coffees, Baking-Powder, Spices and Extracts. *For special terms address* THE GREAT AMERICAN TEA CO., Dept. 277 31 and 33 Vesey Street, New York

Agent's Outfit Free! Rim Strainer; fits any pan. Agents make 3 to 5 dollars per day. Large Catalogue new goods free. Richardson Mfg. Co., Dept. 8, Bath, N. Y.

AGENTS WANTED For RUSS BLEACHING BLUE In great demand if once used. Success assured. THE RUSS CO., Box 20, South Bend, Ind.

Standard Patterns

are now sold for

5c, 10c and 15c

What Women are Doing.—*Concluded.*

five-dollar bill, saying : "I wish you had raised ten-dollars' worth instead of five, for my customers were all so glad to have fresh, home-grown seed." I determined to act on this hint, as I remembered there were also several other grocery stores in town, and my effort had cost me so little trouble; so this year I have prepared a much larger crop
                                    B. P. D.

HOW TWO GIRLS SUPPORT THEMSELVES

Two young girls near us were left orphans, with very little money. They had a small and pretty home, but objected to taking boarders. The youngest girl, being very skilful with her needle, began making linen turnovers and sets of collar and cuffs, in drawn-work, hemstitching or embroidery. She soon had all she could do, as her work was especially good. Her elder sister one day was lamenting that she had not the same skill, and remarked: "The only thing in that line in which I excel is making buttonholes." "Well, that's a good specialty," replied a friend. "I'll engage you to make them in my new shirt-waists." Her skill soon became known and she is now able to work very rapidly. Thus the girls support themselves very well without leaving their home.
                                    C. R. M.

A BUSINESS WOMAN'S LUNCH-ROOM

There has recently been opened in the heart of the business section a charming little luncheon-room for the business women of New York. It is called "The Princess Club," and is run by an enterprising Chicago woman, who, having been in the restaurants of that city run in a similar manner, came to the conclusion that such a place would become very popular in New York, where there is such a crying need for a place of that sort in the down-town business districts. This lady, Miss Lewis by name, realized the need for some such place, and tried for several months to win over the business men who employed women in their offices. She succeeded in interesting a great many of them, who quickly appreciated what a boon this would be to the business woman. At last Miss Lewis's plans were realized in the attractive lunch-room she has instituted in Nassau street. For a very low price one can get the very daintiest food. She charges twenty-five cents for a monthly admission ticket or, in lieu, five cents admission each day. The tables are covered with spotless linen, bright silver, and, above all, the dishes are clean and the food healthful and nourishing. As one mounts the two short flights of stairs leading to the room of the club, one is ushered into a charming little rest-room, containing a piano, the latest music, pretty pictures and cozy easy-chairs. The tiny but prettily furnished reading-room is just off the rest-room. There is a bookcase filled with the latest books, the privilege of reading which costs one dollar a year; a magazine-stand filled with magazines; a desk and chair in mission style, the former filled with printed stationery for use of members. Last of all comes an immense room, filled with small tables, at which the dainty, appetizing luncheon is served. There are absolutely no restrictions, and the young women patrons, being naturally refined, are appealed to by the wholesome atmosphere of the place generally.
                                    L. H. S.

PRESERVES PAID HER WAY THROUGH COLLEGE

A young woman of my acquaintance found herself called upon to earn, in some way, the money needed for her college course. As her only talent seemed to be making preserves, she made an abundance of two kinds, which for oddity and deliciousness were unsurpassed. They were muskmelon, or cantaloup preserve, and red watermelon preserve. To make the muskmelon preserve: Peel and seed the melons, which should be ripe but not mushy, slice into small pieces, and to each pound of melon add three-quarters of a pound of granulated sugar, and to each four pounds of melon add the juice of one lemon. Place sliced melon, sugar and lemon in alternate layers in a stone jar and let stand overnight. Next morning drain off all juice and boil it till it drops thick from the spoon, then put in the melon. Boil a few minutes, take out the melon, drop the pieces into a pint-size glass jar; again boil sirup thick and pour over the preserve slowly to fill all crevices with sirup. Seal up at once while hot. The lemon may be omitted, as some prefer the natural flavor of the cantaloup. For the watermelon preserve: Select ripe melons; remove the seeds and rinds; cut the red part only —not a bit of the white—into small slices or dice. Weigh, and use just half as much granulated sugar, and to each six pounds of melon use two lemons—juice and grated yellow rinds only. Put all together on the fire in a granite or porcelain pan. Boil slowly. It will take quite a while, as at first it will all seem to boil to water. Stir often until quite thick, then dip into one-pint glass jars and seal. This preserve seems so odd that it must be seen and tasted to be appreciated. It has a delicate, honey-like flavor and beautiful coloring. The young woman of whom I write made more money than she required for her college course by selling her delicious wares among the well-to-do families of her town.
                                    Mrs. M. F. D.

FLORICULTURE TALKS

Negligee Garments for Summer Comfort

By M. W. PARK

8824—Ladies' Plaited Bolero Dressing-Sack. 6 sizes, 32 to 42 inches bust measure. 5 yards 22 or 3½ yards 36. Price, 15 cents.

FLORAL NOTES

SOOT FERTILIZER—A tea made from wood soot is a good fertilizer for Begonias and also for Pansies. Apply once or twice a week, being careful not to have it too strong. A half-pint of soot to a gallon of water will make a fertilizer of sufficient strength for these plants.

Lavender—The herb known as Lavender may be grown from either seeds or cuttings. It is valuable for its sweet fragrance. The branches, when cut and dried and placed between cotton in the bottom of bureau drawers, give a pleasant odor to bed linen or underwear. Branches of the herb for drying should be cut about the time the plant comes into bloom.

Grass Pink—This pink is known by the name of old-fashioned or clove pink. The plant is perfectly hardy and blooms profusely in early summer. Its perfume is delicately spicy, although its flowers, being small, are not particularly showy.

Forget-me-nots—Myosotis dissitiflora is one of the best Forget-me-nots, and is easily raised from seeds. The flowers are charming in form and color, being of a beautiful blue. They appear early in spring on plants grown outdoors, and continue to open for several weeks. The plants like a cool, moist, shady place, and make a fine carpet for a bed of Narcissus or other hardy spring-blooming bulbs. This is one of the very few plants which have really blue blossoms.

Hoya Carnosa—A Hoya rarely blooms well until it becomes pot-bound. A very small pot will accommodate quite a large plant. It is not best to encourage a too constant and thrifty growth of foliage if you want an abundance of flowers. Dry off the plant till the wood is well ripened, and partially starve it until late in the season if you wish winter blooms. This is one of the very few plants which will often be loaded with lovely flowers, while a thrifty one—that is to say, one with abundant foliage—frequently will not produce a single bloom.

Yucca in Winter—The foliage of the Yucca is evergreen, and a clump of the plants has a pleasing effect upon the lawn in winter. The large tuft of glaucous-green foliage remains as fresh and attractive throughout the cold weather as it does in summer. It is a suitable plant for the cemetery on account of its perennial habit and graceful, creamy, bell-shaped flowers, as well as its power to withstand a drought in summer.

Viola Odorata—This violet is perfectly hardy, and will endure the winter in any well-drained soil. It is readily propagated from seed which is sown in the autumn. The plants like a deep, rich, moist soil and a shady situation. The flowers are very fragrant, come in profusion in spring, and are beautiful in coloring. A bed on the north side of a building usually gives satisfactory results.

Lemon-Scented Verbena—This plant is a favorite with almost everyone on account of the sweet fragrance of its leaves. Any ordinary potting compost suits it.

Pansies — Pansy plants which are started from seeds sown in August or early in September will bloom early in spring, and the plants thus raised will far surpass in vigor those raised from spring-sown seeds, while the flowers themselves will be larger, handsomer and far more numerous.

Malva Crispa—This is a beautiful foliage plant for the lawn in summer. It is an annual, growing to the height of five or six feet from seeds which have been sown in the spring. The leaves are large and round with ruffled or crimped edges. The plants will stand frosts of considerable severity, remaining fresh and green when other plants in the same locality are wilted down by the cold. The chief attraction of this plant is the beauty of its foliage.

8863—Ladies' Japanese Dressing-Sack, 4 sizes, 32 to 44 inches bust measure. 3¾ yards 22 inches wide, or 2⅞ yards 36, or 2¼ yards 44. Price, 15 cents.

9375—Ladies' Dressing-Sack (high or Pompadour neck). 7 sizes, 32 to 44 inches bust measure. 5⅝ yards 22 inches wide, with 4½ yards of lace insertion and 6½ yards of lace edging. Price, 15 cents.

THE OXALIS

The Oxalis is a family of plants comprising hardy and greenhouse species, differing greatly in habit and manner of growth. There is perhaps no flower that affords more pleasure at a small expense than the Oxalis. Persons who have never seen a pot or basket of it in full bloom would be slow to believe that such a mass of foliage and flowers could spring from such an insignificant-looking little bulb. The bulbs of some species are not larger than a pea, and none exceed in size a filbert, which they somewhat resemble. Most of the Ox-

9068—Ladies' and Misses' Kimono Wrapper or Lounging-Robe or Dressing-Sack. 5 sizes, 28 to 44 inches bust measure. Price, 15 cents.

Negligee Garments.—*Continued.*

9130 — Ladies' Dressing-Sack (tucked or gathered in front, with bishop or bell sleeves and with or without the cape collar, with ends meeting or separated, or the turnover or standing collar). 8 sizes, 32 to 46 inches bust measure.   5¼ yards 22 inches wide.   Price, 15 cents.

8782—Ladies' Dressing-Sack.   7 sizes, 32 to 44 inches bust measure.   4¾ yards 22 inches wide, or 4¼ yards 27, or 3½ yards 36.   Price, 15 cents.

9044—Ladies' Box-Plaited Dressing-Sack (with round front yoke and standing or turnover collar; with or without the large collar or the cuffs). 7 sizes, 32 to 44 inches bust measure   5¼ yards 22 inches wide, or 4¾ yards 27, or 4¼ yards 36, with 6½ yards of lace edging and 2½ yards of ribbon.   Price, 15 cents.

9104—Ladies' Matinee or Dressing-Sack (with high or open neck and full or three-quarter length sleeves; with or without the lining). 6 sizes, 32 to 42 inches bust measure.   5¼ yards 22 inches wide, or 4 yards 36, or 3½ yards 44.   Price, 15 cents.

Floriculture.—*Concluded.*

alis have been imported from the Cape of Good Hope and South America, but in some parts of Pennsylvania a native species can be found, and the common yellow variety, known as wood-sorrel, is a weed in many places. The plants are not all bulbous-rooted; some are herbaceous and form quite large plants; others are of a shrubby nature. The foliage varies in size and color, as well as the flowers. Some have moderately large leaves, others quite small, shading in color from a clear green to a bronzy red. The flowers are of different shades of yellow, pink and red, and some of them have considerable fragrance.

If desired for blooming in winter the Oxalis should be planted as early as August or September. They are often planted singly in four-inch pots, but a better show is procured by putting from four to eight bulbs in a five-inch or six-inch pot. The soil most suitable is a mixture of light loam, sand and well-rotted cow manure. The bulbs should be covered about an inch deep, or less, according to size. After planting, moisten the soil and set in the shade until the leaves appear, then give plenty of light and a moderate supply of water. Their season of bloom is usually quite long. Some plants of Oxalis rosea bloom continuously for several months. When the leaves turn yellow, the plant should be watered sparingly for awhile, then dried off altogether and given a season of rest, letting it remain in the dry soil during this period. Repot the plant in fresh soil when the season of rest is over. The bulbs increase rapidly, and in a short time cover the pot with a mass of foliage.

Among the best varieties of this lovely plant are the Boweiana, Floribunda, Versicolor and Buttercup. The leaves of the first named are thick and large, and the rose-colored flowers are borne in clusters of six or eight to a stem. The blossoms of Floribunda are pink and smaller in size than Boweiana, and are borne on short, fleshy stems. Plants of the Floribunda may be set in the garden border in summer, where it will bloom profusely for four or five months.

An interesting fact regarding the Oxalis is that almost all of the species go to sleep at night by closing up their clover-like leaves and dainty flower-cups, but open them wide again fresh and lovely with the earliest gleam of morning light.

Versicolor is considered by many amateur gardeners as the best of all the varieties for hanging-baskets, as it is of drooping habit. The bulbs of this particular variety are exceedingly small, and should be planted half a dozen or more in a five-inch pot. This they will soon fill and cover with their graceful, delicate foliage.

Oxalis are very satisfactory plants for house-culture, requiring very little care, and yielding a generous return for the smallest attention.

There are few plants in the floral kingdom that possess the stateliness and grace of the beautiful Lilies. Such an almost endless variety is in cultivation at the present day that it is, many times, hard for one to decide which is the most beautiful. They are so rich and waxy in texture, varying in color from brilliant red and orange to a beautiful snowy white. Many of them are thickly spotted with darker shades and most delicately tinted.

Lilies are not as difficult or troublesome to cultivate as many persons think them to be, but require beds that are well drained. The soil should be a mixture of loam, sand and thoroughly decayed cow manure. The bulbs should be planted about six inches deep, and a handful of sand put around and under each bulb when planting. A great mistake is often made by planting the bulbs too shallow. If mulched during the hottest summer months they will produce an abundant supply of beautiful flowers. Although almost all lily bulbs are hardy, it is found best to give them some protection during winter. A covering of manure, leaves or straw will answer quite well. They are very suitable plants to grow among shrubs, as the shrubs will aid in protecting them from the cold winds and driving rains, to which most of the Lilies are very sensitive. It is best to plant them where the ground is at least partially shaded, as success with them depends on keeping the bulbs as cool as possible during the intense heat of summer days.

The habit and general character of these plants are so varied they may be used in different ways for decoration. Some are suitable to grow as single specimens, or for rock work, while others are best suited to use in a mixed border. When grown in groups, as they sometimes are, it is very important to have them properly and artistically arranged. This can be done only by one who has a knowledge of their habits and peculiarities. Lilies are usually propagated by division of the bulblets or offsets from the parent bulb. They can also be propagated from seeds, but this is rather a tedious process, as it requires several years for the seedlings to reach the blooming period. Imported bulbs are now sold so cheaply, and the flowers generally prove so much finer, that it really does not seem necessary to waste time raising them from seed.

The best time to reset the bulbs is in the autumn after the foliage has died down. The bulbs will then be ripe. If disturbed while the foliage is yet green, there is danger of losing the bulbs. Also moving them in early spring will sometimes injure the bulbs and cause them to decay. One or more varieties of this lovely class of plants should find a place in the garden of every person who is interested to to any extent in flowers.

ANSWERS TO CORRESPONDENTS

RULES

In order to insure a reply under this heading it is necessary to give a pseudonym under which the querist may be answered. The full name and address of the writer must also be given. This will never, under any circumstances, be published. Questions which are to be answered in The Designer for September must reach the editor not later than July 12th.

No answers to correspondents will be sent by mail unless a two-cent stamp or stamped envelope is received at this office. Address all such letters to the Editorial Department, Standard Fashion Company, 12-16 Vandam St., New York City.

Adela.—You can either dress your three-year-old boy in manly fashion in a suit such as 1151, shown on page 415 of this number of The Designer, making it of white or colored linen, gingham or chambray, or you can select little dresses, such as 1150, on page 414, making these of similar material as suggested for the suit. He can wear a wide-brimmed white or colored straw hat with a ribbon band and streamers, or with a silk pompon at one side, and for foot-covering white, tan or black socks and soft kid shoes or ankle ties. If he is susceptible to cold, it would be better to substitute long, thin wool or cotton stockings for the socks.

Dorthea.—Soak the finger tips in luke-warm water to which has been added the juice of a lemon—two cupfuls of water to one lemon is about the correct proportion—until the skin is soft enough to push away the nails with a bone or ivory instrument made for the purpose. Do not push the skin hard enough to bruise it. A little simple tincture of benzoin dropped in the water each time the hands are washed will aid in whitening them, so too will wearing gloves at night after rubbing the hands with some good toilet cream. Be sure to cut holes in the palms of the gloves for ventilation. Gently pinch the sides of the fingers together to make the nails narrower, and keep the nails themselves trimmed to a pretty, rather long oval. Wear a high-bust, well-fitting corset and do not attempt to reduce the size of your bust. A young woman of eighteen should be fully developed.

M. M. J.—You will find on page 480 full directions for taking measurements before ordering a Standard Pattern. You will observe that it is expressly stated that if the hips are large in proportion to the waist, the hip measure should be taken when ordering a skirt pattern. This is because it is much easier to adapt the larger waist size to the figure than it would be to change the smaller hip size to fit large hips.

Persevering.—The series "In the Interest of Bread-Winning" began in the June number. The back numbers will be sent you on receipt of ten cents for each number desired. Either stamps or silver may be sent, and the postage on the books will be prepaid. Miss Hasbrouck has given so far three very novel and practical suggestions as to occupation, and has many others in contemplation.

H. B. Lewis.—You will find some excellent and new ideas on the subject of home decoration in the article given this month. "The Transformation of a Farm-House," on pages 441 to 443. The idea of covering the walls with denim, then decorating them in frieze or panel fashion with flowers cut from cretonne or chintz seems to be exactly what you want, for neither the denim nor the chintz is expensive, and individual fancy is given full scope in the arrangement of the garlands.

Martha E. V.—The Designer for May contains several pretty designs for lingerie hats of different patterns, while The Designer for July tells just how such hats must be made if a wire foundation be desired. Either of these numbers will be sent to you on the receipt of ten cents in stamps or silver. In The Designer for June are given directions for making a lace hat of Battenberg braid, which head-covering might be classed along with lingerie hats, although, strictly speaking, the embroidered lawn or linen hat is what is meant by the term.

Hostess.—On page 356 of The Designer for July you will find some novel and pleasant ways to entertain your friends if you do not care to have dancing or cards, and do not wish to spend much money on the preparations. For refreshments you can have ice-cold watermelon, the slices cut very thick, all the rind removed, then the red portion cut in little blocks; lemonade colored red with raspberry juice; small cakes with pink icing, and small sandwiches of ham or tongue. This will carry out the red color-scheme, will be tasteful and not expensive.

Estelle K.—We would advise you to write to the general passenger agents of the different railroads for descriptive booklets of the summer resorts on their lines. These books generally contain a list of desirable hotels and boarding places and are a great help in deciding upon a place to spend one's vacation. Be sure to enclose postage when you write.

Alice.—The German spelling of the word harp is harfe, and melody is spelled melodie in the German language.

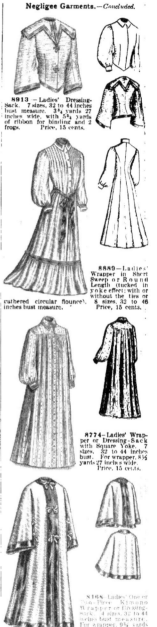

Negligee Garments.—Concluded.

8913 — Ladies' Dressing-Sack. 7 sizes, 32 to 44 inches bust measure. 3¾ yards 27 inches wide, with 5½ yards of ribbon for binding and 2 frogs. Price, 15 cents.

8889—Ladies' Wrapper in Short Length or Round Length (tucked in yoke effect; with or without the ties or belt). 8 sizes, 32 to 46 inches bust measure. Price, 15 cents.

8774—Ladies' Wrapper or Dressing-Sack with Square Yoke. 7 sizes, 32 to 44 inches bust. For wrapper, 8¾ yards 27 inches wide. Price, 15 cents.

8468—Ladies' One or Two-Piece Kimono Wrapper or Dressing-Sack. 4 sizes, 32 to 44 inches bust measure. For wrapper, 9¾ yards 20 inches wide, with 2½ yards of 20-inch silk for bands, and 5½ yards of ribbon to trim. Price, 15 cents.

RUBENS INFANT SHIRT

Answers to Correspondents.
Concluded.

SEA SHORE.—For a bathing-suit we would suggest either dark-blue or black brilliantine. If made by any of the patterns shown in the July DESIGNER, with trimmings of braid or contrasting materials, you will have a decidedly stylish and comfortable suit. Wear an oilskin cap or hat and bathing-slippers.

HIGHBRIDGE.—No, we never advocate the use of peroxide of hydrogen or any other bleach for the hair. It will surely split the ends and eventually ruin it. To keep it light, wash your hair with sulphur soap or a reliable shampoo.

ESTHER B.—A great many men and women inclined to stoutness feel their weight more in the summer months than at any other time of year, therefore we would suggest that you follow a course of diet for a time. Give up all sweetmeats, hot bread, cake and other pastry, drink sparingly of tea and coffee, eat meat only once a day and try and live on fresh vegetables, fruit, fish and chicken. Lime-juice taken at least twice a day will be very good for you; it can be stirred in a little ice-water and taken with or without sugar. You can procure the bottled lime-juice at almost any druggist's.

FRITZ.—It is said that a rose geranium plant growing in a room will rid the apartment of flies. These bothersome insects have a rooted dislike for the odor of the leaves of the plant and will not remain long where it is. You could purchase several of the plants and keep one in the living-room and in each of the bedrooms.

J. D. W.—Do not take a cold plunge bath if it renders you so weak; it probably affects your heart action and will do you more harm than good. The way for you to take a morning bath is to fill the tub a foot deep with warm or tepid water; stand in this while you sponge your entire body with the cold water. It will be well to dissolve a generous handful of sea salt in the basin of cold water before taking the sponge bath. You will find after this kind of bath you will feel vigorous and comfortable.

SUMMER GIRL.—Cold cream applied before retiring will alleviate the burning sensation occasioned by sunburn. To rub the cream on the face very lightly and then apply a little rice powder before one goes out will be found an admirable way to preserve the skin.

MARJORIE'S MOTHER.—Why do you not give your little daughter a set of Louise Alcott's books? These stories never lose their charm, and the life described in "Little Women" and "Little Men" will endear the author to her forever.

COLGATE'S
VIOLET TALC
WITH THE ONLY PERFECT SIFTER

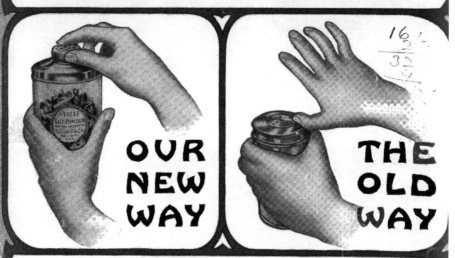

OUR NEW WAY

THE OLD WAY

*We Couldn't Improve the Powder,
so We Improved the Box*

Your Fingers Get the Benefit

The particular woman does not want to use her finger nails for anything that will mar them. The illustration above shows that our new sifter cannot injure soft hands and manicured finger nails as do the old-fashioned boxes. It is as smoothly finished as a piece of Sterling Silver, turns as easily as the stem of your watch, concentrates the fall of the powder on any desired spot, *and, best of all, costs you no more.*

Our powder is a wonderful combination of the best toilet and medicinal qualities. Its uses are manifold, and every one from the head of the house down to the baby needs it in one way or another, especially in warm weather.

COLGATE & CO.
Makers of the Famous Cashmere Bouquet Toilet Soap
ESTABLISHED 1806   NEW YORK

t

nar
and
s a
fall

ies.
eds

Lightning Source UK Ltd.
Milton Keynes UK
UKHW020635090223
416652UK00001B/302